A Comprehensive English Usage

张道真 英语用法

（大众珍藏版 · 第三版）

张道真 著　　　武光军 改编

中国人民大学出版社

· 北京 ·

图书在版编目（CIP）数据

张道真英语用法：大众珍藏版/张道真著；武光
军改编. --3版. --北京：中国人民大学出版社，
2022.4

ISBN 978-7-300-30470-0

I.①张… II.①张… ②武… III.①英语—语法—
自学参考资料 IV.①H314

中国版本图书馆 CIP 数据核字（2022）第 049872 号

张道真英语用法（大众珍藏版·第三版）

张道真 著
武光军 改编
Zhang Daozhen Yingyu Yongfa (Dazhong Zhencangban·Di-san Ban)

出版发行	中国人民大学出版社			
社 址	北京中关村大街 31 号		**邮政编码**	100080
电 话	010-62511242（总编室）		010-62511770（质管部）	
	010-82501766（邮购部）		010-62514148（门市部）	
	010-62515195（发行公司）		010-62515275（盗版举报）	
网 址	http://www.crup.com.cn			
经 销	新华书店			
印 刷	涿州市星河印刷有限公司		**版 次**	2011 年 11 月第 1 版
规 格	148 mm×210 mm 32 开本			2022 年 4 月第 3 版
印 张	20.125 插页 2		**印 次**	2022 年 4 月第 1 次印刷
字 数	615 000		**定 价**	79.00 元

　　张道真先生是我国英语界的泰斗、著名的英语语法学家。张道真先生所编著的《张道真英语用法》以实用为主要特色，选例精当，博采众长，影响久远而广泛，早已成为我国英语语法界的一面旗帜，为我国的英语语法教育做出了不可替代的贡献。

　　正如张道真先生在第一版前言中所说，《张道真英语用法》最大的特点是：将英语语法和英语词汇结合起来："这些年，我深深体会到，语法与词汇的关系紧密相连。语法要用词汇来体现，而词汇又需借助语法来形成句子，两者的关系如同人的骨骼与血肉。"《张道真英语用法》面向大众，深入浅出，成为了我国英语语法和用法学习的一棵常青之树，惠及着一代又一代的学人。

　　随着时代的发展，知识的更新，本书无论在体系上还是在时代性上都需要与时俱进，以充分反映语言的发展，满足当下学习者的需求。基于这种考虑，我们对本书进行了系统修订。修订的原则和主要内容如下：

　　第一，整体上调整了原书的编写框架。《张道真英语用法》原来的编写框架为词典模式，即按照字母顺序从 A–Z 进行内容的排列。这样的编写框架可以方便读者学习，但是不太利于读者构建起整体的语法框架，不太利于读者理清语法和用法的脉络。为此，本次修订从语法的角度整体上进行设计，共分为五个部分：1. 词法；2. 句法；3. 惯用法；4. 语言运用；5. 词汇用法。这样就为读者构建起清晰有效的语法系统，从而理清语法和用法的脉络，有效提高学习效率。

　　第二，随着时代的发展，原书的部分例句已经过时，原来个别例句的中文翻译现在看来存在不当之处，我们对这些问题都进行了全面而恰当的处理。

　　例如：原书中第 570 页，"They had journeyed to Russia on a mission."

的原译文为"他们到俄国去执行一项任务。"，现在一般已不用"俄国"这样的表述，应译为"他们到俄罗斯去执行一项任务。"；原书中第389页，"If I were you, I'd go to night school."的原译文为"我要是你，我会上夜校。"，现在已基本没有"夜校"这样的说法，我们就删除了该例句；原书中第486页，"There are now over a hundred makes of micro-computers for sale."的原译文为"现在市面上卖的微电脑有一百多种。"，"微电脑"这样的说法，现在已基本不用，我们就删除该例句；等等。

第三，对原书全部内容进行了认真通读，改正了个别的拼写错误、标点不当、内容遗漏等，使新版本在编校质量方面更臻完善。

第四，增加微课视频，对知识点进行详细讲解，并配套练习题检验学生掌握情况。

我们希望，这次新修订的《张道真英语用法》能够一如既往，经得住时间的检验，永远是大家的好朋友。

武光军

2022 年 3 月于北京

改编者武光军教授简介

武光军，现为北京航空航天大学外国语学院教授，北京外国语大学中国外语教育研究中心博士，中国联合国教科文组织全国委员会咨询专家，曾任北京第二外国语学院英语学院院长、外国语言文学一级学科负责人，主持国家社科基金项目两项，发表高水平学术论文 30 余篇，出版教材及专著三部，2018 年获评北京市优秀教师。主要研究领域为英语语言文学及翻译学，对英语语法有深入独到的研究。

修订后的《张道真英语用法》（大众珍藏版·第二版），与时俱进，焕然一新，具有以下鲜明的特色：

第一，本书结构宏富，涵盖英语常用词汇、短语和英语常识的各个方面，集英语用法之大成，是一本权威的英语用法工具书；

第二，本书以系统的用法知识为纲，将英语用法和常用词汇、短语和英语常识紧密结合，学习者可得事半功倍之效；

第三，全书旁征博引，用例经典，佳词名句，俯拾皆是；

第四，全书内容简明扼要，条分缕析，适合广大英语学习者学习、收藏和研究。修订过程中，我们先后征求了多位专家学者的意见和建议，他们分别是：著名语言学家、北京外国语大学博士生导师刘润清教授，清华大学外国语学院院长、博士生导师刘世生教授，北京理工大学外国语学院副院长、英语语言学博士李京廉教授，清华大学外国语学院英语系主任、英语语言学博士何宏华教授。其中，何宏华教授审读了全书内容，并提出了十分具体的修订意见。

《张道真英语用法》（大众珍藏版·第二版）是张道真先生一生关于英语用法研究的成果总结，它与我们同时出版的《张道真英语语法》（大众珍藏版·第二版）是姊妹篇，内容互为补充，互为表里，搭配使用。相信两书的出版，一定会惠及千千万万的英语学习者和英语研究者。我们借此机会，特向张道真先生的夫人郑琳女士以及帮助我们出版此书的各位专家、学者和朋友们表示衷心的感谢。

中国人民大学出版社外语分社

2011 年 11 月

　　我开始从事英语教学和英语语法研究并出版第一本英语语法书至今，不觉已四十余年。这些年，我深深体会到，语法与词汇的关系紧密相连。语法要用词汇来体现，而词汇又需借助语法来形成句子，两者的关系如同人的骨骼与血肉。语言是人类文明的载体之一，语言同时又应体现时代的精神。正因为如此，我决定写一部新的姊妹篇式的《英语语法》和《英语用法》。经过两年多的艰苦努力，这两本书终于出版问世，可以供大家参考使用了。

　　这两本书与其他论述英语语法或英语用法的书相比，其最大的特点是：它们都将英语语法和英语词汇结合起来。具体体现是：

　　第一，在讲解过程中把两者紧密结合在一起。例如，在《英语用法》中，不仅讲述了常用词的用法、前后缀的处理、近似词的比较以及表达法的区别等用法知识，而且还提供了大量例句来说明其语法特点。又如，本书在讲解助动词和情态动词时，也几乎讲到了所有这类词的用法；在讲解各个词类（名词、代词、形容词、副词、介词、连词等）时，对常用的有关词汇都作了简明扼要的论述。第二，对动词句型做了重点讲解，不仅讲述了各种句型结构，而且每种结构都列举了大量例句来说明其特点，甚至列举了用于这类结构的所有常用词。之所以对动词句型做这样的重点处理，是因为它是语言的核心和脊柱。掌握了动词句型，可以说就掌握了语言的基础和关键。第三，这两本书中提供了数倍于其他语法书的例句。表面上看，似乎不成比例，但这些例句是在大量资料中精心挑选出来的，是反映现代英语语法、用法的典型例句。通过学习、分析和掌握这些典型例句，读者可以大大提高学习、掌握英语语法和词汇的速度与效率，进而更深入地学习和掌握英语。第四，全书以语法为纲，把词汇知识条理化。英语语法复杂多变，英语单词成千上万，在学习时如果只是一知半解或只知其一，不知其二，那就很难对其融会贯通和运用自如。这两本书互为补充、彼此参见并以系统的语法知识为纲，把零散的词汇环环连接，融为一体。它们好比是一个网络，把语法与词汇交织在一起，使读者触类旁通、举一反三。

最近二三十年来，国外优秀的语法书和有关字典源源不断地涌现出来。但这些书大部分都是针对英美读者撰写的，与我们中国人学习英语的实际需要尚有一定的距离。要缩短或消除这个距离，就只能靠我们中国的语言工作者，因为他们最了解中国人学习英语的特点和需要。今天我们所看到的这两部全新版的《英语语法》和《英语用法》就是为适应这一需要而编写的。在编写过程中，我力求有的放矢，紧密结合中国人学英语所经常遇到的问题进行讲解。书中的例句浅显、地道、实用，充分体现现代英语的特点。此外，上述两书还通过译文，对英语和汉语语法中的共性与不同进行了讲解和比较。

这两本书适合于各种英语水平的人使用。英语水平高的人，可以借助它来整理和检验自己的语言知识，加强自身的语言应用能力。水平一般的读者，最好能对本书反复研读，让英语规律和体现这些规律的元素在头脑中扎根，并在此基础上进行大量的阅读和练习，从而在语言实践中印证、增强和掌握这些知识。

我四十多年前开始研究英语语法，最近 20 年来仍继续研究英语语法和词汇，并撰写了多部书籍。然而，将英语语法和词汇结合起来一同论述，并以姊妹篇的形式同时出版，这还是第一次。相信这两部着眼于新世纪、立足于新观念的全新版《英语语法》和《英语用法》，定会使各位读者受益无穷。

张道真

2002 年 4 月于北京

目　录
CONTENTS

扫描上方二维码，
浏览视频资源

一、词法
思维导图

名词

动词

形容词

副词

连词

连接副词

数词

助动词

情态动词

反身代词

介词

冠词

限定词

词法

两种拼法的词

相同发音的词

两种读音的词

缩略词

1. 名词

❀ 可数名词与不可数名词：

可数名词指那些可以分为个体的东西，因此可有复数形式，也可加不定冠词：

They went for a walk in the garden. 他们到花园里散步去了。

They often went for walks in the gardens or parks. 他们常常在花园或公园里散步。

不可数名词所指东西不能分作个体，因此没有复数形式，不能加不定冠词：

She is fond of music. 她喜欢音乐。

He is full of vitality. 他充满活力。

英语中有许多名词是不可数的，在汉语中却似乎是可数的，如：

advice	baggage	equipment	furniture	homework
information	knowledge	luggage	machinery	money
music	news	traffic		

一条消息 an item of news　　　　一件家具 a piece of furniture

一项忠告 a piece of advice　　　　一件衣裳 an article of clothing

这类词作主语时，后面要跟单数动词：

There was not much traffic on the roads yesterday. 昨天公路上车不太多。

No news is good news. 没有消息就是好消息。（谚语）

有些不可数名词以 -s 结尾，特别是一些学科名词：

acoustics	aerobics	aerodynamics	aeronautics
athletics	classics	economics	electronics
ethics	genetics	gymnastics	linguistics
logistics	mathematics	mechanics	obstetrics
physics	politics	statistics	thermodynamics

有些疾病名称也以 -s 结尾：

diabetes	measles	mumps
rabies	rickets	shingles

这类词作主语时，动词要用单数形式：

Mathematics is a subject studied in nearly every school. 数学是几乎每个学校都学的科目。

Measles is in most cases a harmless illness. 麻疹在多数情况下都是无害的病。

但在一定情况下也可跟复数动词：

Politics have never interested me. 政治活动我从来不感兴趣。

The acoustics of the new concert hall are excellent. 新音乐厅的音响效果好极了。

有些名词表示由两部分构成的东西，都作复数形式，如：

glasses	jeans	knickers	pants
pyjamas	shorts	tights	trousers
binoculars	pincers	pliers	scales
scissors	shears	tweezers	

这种名词常可以用 a pair of（一副，一条）修饰：

Have you got a pair of scissors? 你有一把剪刀吗？

He bought two pairs of shorts. 他买了两条短裤。

也可不用修饰语：

He watched the horse-race through (a pair of) binoculars. 他用望远镜看赛马。

He was wearing striped pyjamas. 他穿了一套带条纹的睡衣。

❀ 个体名词及集体名词：

可数名词中多数是个体名词，也有一些是集体名词。最常见的集体名词有：

army	audience	committee	company	crew
enemy	family	flock	gang	government
group	herd	navy	press	public
staff	team			

在用这类名词作主语时，后面动词有时用复数形式：

A flock of wild geese were flying over head. 一群雁正从头上飞过。

The crew are paid to do all the work on the ship. 船员被雇来干船上的各种工作。

有时用单数形式：

The Edison Telephone Company was presently swallowed up by the Bell Telephone Company. 爱迪生电话公司最近被贝尔电话公司吞并了。

Our navy is made up of all warships. 我们的海军由所有战舰组成。

但在很多情况下，须根据意思来决定后面的动词用单数还是用复数：

family
{
My family is very large. 我家人很多。（作为整体看待）
His family are waiting for him. 他家里人在等他。（指成员）
}

enemy
{
The enemy has suffered severe losses. 敌人遭受严重损失。
The enemy are in flight. 敌军正在逃遁。
}

committee
{
The Committee of Public Safety is to deal with the matter.
公共安全委员会将处理这事。
The committee are of the opinion that the time is inopportune.
委员们认为时机不合适。
}

government
{
My Government is interested in the situation there.
我国政府对那里的局势很关注。
The Government have recently increased taxation.
政府最近加税了。
}

public
{
The British public is interested in sports.
英国公众对体育感兴趣。
The public are (is) requested not to litter in the park.
要求公众在公园不要乱扔东西。
}

audience
{
It was late, but the audience was increasing.
已经很晚，但观众还在增加。
The audience were (was) excited by the show.
这场演出使观众很兴奋。
}

team
{
The team is the best in the league.
这个队是联盟中最强的队。
The team are driving to the game in their own cars.
队员们都乘坐自己的车到球赛场地。
}

staff
> The staff was very efficient.
> 工作班子效率很高。
> The school's teaching staff are (is) excellent.
> 学校的教学人员都很好。

❀ 具体名词和抽象名词：

具体名词指看得见摸得着的东西。其中大多数都是可数名词：

There the most common fruits are pears, apples, peaches, persimmons and grapes. 最常见的水果有梨、苹果、桃、柿子和葡萄。

表示物质的名词一般是不可数的，有时可用于复数形式，表示不同种类的或几份的：

Copper and silver are both metals. 铜和银都是金属。

Two beers, please. 请给我两杯啤酒。

有时复数形式表示数量之多：

Four miles to the east of them lay the blue waters of Lake Michigan. 在他们以东 4 英里是密执安湖蔚蓝的湖水。

We have all heard of the sands of the seashore. 我们都听说过海岸边的大片沙滩。

有时在单数名词前可加不定冠词，表示"一种""一阵"等：

Magnolias have a wonderful perfume. 木兰花有一种奇妙的香味。

A fine rain began to fall. 开始下起了一阵小雨。

抽象名词表示抽象概念，一般是不可数的，但在个别情况下却可以加不定冠词：

He had a warm affection for his mother. 他对妈妈有一种温馨的感情。

What a joy to have you with us. 有你和我们在一起是多么高兴的事。

有时还可用于复数形式：

Friendship multiplies joys and divides griefs. 友谊能增加欢乐，分担（减少）悲痛。

The hotel has all modern comforts. 这家酒店有各种舒适的设备。

❀ 修饰名词的介词短语：

名词，特别是抽象名词后常可跟一个介词短语，完成其意思。有些跟一个由 to 引起的短语：

He failed to make any contribution to the cause. 他没能对这个事业做出

什么贡献。

His <u>devotion to his work</u> was an example. 他对工作的献身精神堪称模范。

常见的这类名词有：

access	addiction	adherence	allegiance	allergy
allusion	alternative	answer	antidote	approach
aversion	contribution	damage	devotion	disloyalty
exception	fidelity	immunity	introduction	preface
prelude	recourse	reference	relevance	reply
resistance	return	solution	threat	witness

有些跟一个由 for 引起的短语：

My <u>love for you</u> is deeper than the sea. 我对你的爱比海还深。

Their <u>desire for expansion</u> had increased. 他们扩张的野心越来越大。

这类名词常见的有：

admiration	appetite	aptitude	bid	craving
credit	cure	demand	desire	disdain
dislike	disregard	hunger	love	need
provision	quest	recipe	regard	remedy
respect	responsibility	room	substitute	sympathy
synonym	taste	thirst		

还有些名词跟 on 或 upon 引起的短语，如：

assault	attack	ban	comment	concentration
constraint	crack-down	curb	dependence	effect
embargo	hold	insistence	reflection	reliance
restriction	tax			

有些名词跟 with 引起的短语，如：

affinity	collision	collusion	connection
correspondence	dealing	dissatisfaction	encounter
familiarity	identification	intimacy	intersection
link	quarrel	relationship	
sympathy			

还有一些其他情况，如：

reaction against	safeguard against	insurance against
departure from	escape from	quotation from
authority over	control over	controversy over

❀ 名词作定语及构成合成名词：

名词作定语是极其普通的现象，这和汉语是一致的，如：

paper flower 纸花	orange juice 橘汁
power plant 发电厂	fire brigade 消防队
press conference 记者招待会	news broadcast 新闻广播
seat belt 安全带	identity card 身份证
cotton goods 棉织品	inquiry office 问询处

有时两个名词在一起可构成合成词：

toothbrush 牙刷	airport 机场
bathroom 浴室	lampshade 灯罩
seaside 海边	bookmark 书签

有些写成一个词，有些用连字符连接起来，有些不带连字符。这种合成词和用名词作定语的结构界限是很不清楚的。一般说来，合成词在字典中常单列成一个词条，以 fire 一词为例，它构成的合成词都列在后面，如：

fire alarm 火警	firearm 枪支
fire brigade 消防队	fire department 消防处
fire engine 消防车	fire extinguisher 灭火器

名词的复数形式

❀ 英语中大多数名词都以加 -s 或 -es 的方法构成复数形式。加的方式归纳如下：

名词类别	加　法	读　法
一般名词	加 -s cat → cats dog → dogs	读作 /s/ 或 /z/ /kæts/ /dɒgz/
以 se、ze、ce、ge 结尾的词	加 -s rose → roses size → sizes price → prices bridge → bridges	读作 /ɪz/ /ˈrəʊzɪz/ /ˈsaɪzɪz/ /ˈpraɪsɪz/ /ˈbrɪdʒɪz/

名词类别	加　法	读　法
以 ch、sh、ss、s、x 结尾的词	加 -es match → matches wish → wishes glass → glasses bus → buses tax → taxes	读作 /ɪz/ /ˈmetʃɪz/ /ˈwɪʃɪz/ /ˈɡlɑːsɪz/ /ˈbʌsɪz/ /ˈtæksɪz/
以"辅音 +y"结尾的词	变 y 为 i 再加 -es city → cities	读作 /z/ /ˈsɪtɪz/
以"元音 +y"结尾的词	y 不变，加 -s boy → boys	读作 /z/ /bɔɪz/

以 th 结尾的词，如前面为长元音，加 -s 后，读 /ðz/：

mouth /maʊθ/ → mouths /maʊðz/

path /pɑːθ/ → paths /pɑːðz/

另外 house 读作 /haʊs/，加 -s 后读作 /ˈhaʊzɪz/。

❀ 有许多名词单复数形式相同，如：

a deer　　　　ten deer

许多表示动物或鱼类的名词有这种现象：

bison	cod	deer	fish	gold fish
grouse	halibut	moose	mullet	reindeer
salmon	sheep	shellfish	swine	trout

还有许多单复数同形的词，如：

aircraft	crossroads	dice	gallows	grapefruit
hovercraft	insignia	means	mews	offspring
series	spacecraft	species	steelworks	

表示某国人的英语单词也是单复数同形的，如 Chinese, Japanese, Swiss：

Her boyfriend is a Swiss from Geneva. 她的男朋友是一个来自日内瓦的瑞士人。

The Swiss have been neutral for centuries. 瑞士人几世纪以来都保持中立。

❀ 以 f 和 fe 结尾的词，变为复数时多变 f 及 fe 为 ves：

calf—calves　　　　elf—elves　　　　　　half—halves

knife—knives   housewife—housewives   leaf—leaves
life—lives   loaf—loaves   sheaf—sheaves
shelf—shelves   thief—thieves   wife—wives
wolf—wolves

但也有一些以 f 结尾的词可以直接加 -s，如 roofs, cliffs, dwarfs, handkerchiefs, chiefs, proofs, beliefs, gulfs。个别词可有两种加法，如：scarf—scarfs 或 scarves, hoof—hoofs 或 hooves。

❀ 以 o 结尾的名词，多数可直接加 -s，如：

bamboos	cuckoos	embryos	Filipinos	folios
kangaroos	kilos	memos	photos	pianos
radios	solos	studios	tobaccos	zoos

有一部分这类词需加 -es，如：

dominoes	echoes	embargoes	heroes	negroes
potatoes	tomatoes	torpedoes	vetoes

下面的名词在 o 后加 -s 或 -es 都可以：

archipelago(e)s	cargo(e)s	fresco(e)s	halo(e)s
mango(e)s	manifesto(e)s	memento(e)s	salvo(e)s

❀ 还有一些名词有不规则的复数形式。

最常见的有：

child—children   foot—feet   man—men
woman—women   tooth—teeth   goose—geese
mouse—mice   ox—oxen   louse—lice

有些词随着它们也有不规则的复数形式：

fisherman—fishermen   policewoman—policewomen
grandchild—grandchildren

还有一些名词是从其他语言借用的，特别是拉丁词，可以有它们自己的复数形式，它们很多是技术性或文气的词：

nucleus—nuclei   radius—radii   stimulus—stimuli
aquarium—aquaria   memorandum—memoranda   sanatorium—sanatoria
larva—larvae   vertebra—vertebrae   formula—formulae
analysis—analyses   crisis—crises   hypothesis—hypotheses

basis—bases   criterion—criteria

有少数名词有两种复数形式：

appendix—appendices 或 appendixes

index—indices 或 indexes

另外，下面的名词都是外来词（由法语借来），单复数形式相同，作单数时末尾的 s 不发音，而作复数时应读作 /z/：

bourgeois	**corps**	**précis**
chassis	**patois**	**rendezvous**

复合名词大多数只是通过在末尾加 **-s** 或 **-es** 的办法构成复数：

railways   fruit-salads   bathing suits

shortcomings   drawbacks   go-betweens

但有些合成词，通常只将里面的主体词变为复数：

looker(s)-on   runner(s)-up

son(s)-in-law   editor(s)-in-chief

hanger(s)-on   bird(s) of prey

集体名词：

集体名词是指那些由个体组成的集体的名称。常见的集体名词有：

community	team	navy	jury	council
audience	press	media	opposition	enemy
cast	aristocracy	proletariat	nobility	

集体名词作主语时，后面谓语是用单数形式还是复数形式，要根据意思决定。如果表达的是一个整体，则用单数形式；如果表达的是它的成员，则用复数形式。如：

The audience has already expressed its approval. 观众已表示同意。

The audience are requested to be in their seats by 7:25. 请观众 7:25 前坐好。

The Committee of Public Safety is to deal with the matter. 公安委员会将处理此事。

The committee quarrel as to who should be the chairman. 委员们争吵谁应任主席。

但在某些情况下，作单数或复数看待都可以：

The <u>enemy</u> is (are) retreating. 敌人正在撤退。

The <u>audience</u> was (were) very excited by the show. 观众对此次演出感到非常兴奋。

2. 动词

动词有许多种类，主要有下面这些。

❀ 规则动词与不规则动词：

这主要从词形上考虑，凡是加 -ed 方式构成过去式及过去分词的为规则动词，以其他方式构成过去式及过去分词者为不规则动词：

规则动词	不规则动词
wash (washed, washed)	go (went, gone)
live (lived, lived)	do (did, done)
study (studied, studied)	come (came, come)

英语中大部分动词都是规则动词。不规则动词只有一百多个，但它们大多是些常用动词，是比较活跃的。因此要学好英语，最好把这些不规则动词的三种形式（如 **do did done, go went gone, bring brought brought, buy bought bought**）都一一背熟。这是掌握各种时态、语态的第一步。同时还要知道 **-s, -ing, -ed** 等词尾的加法。这里把几种词尾的加法归纳如下（所用动词都是规则动词）：

动词种类	动词举例	-s 加法 / 例词	-ing 加法 / 例词	-ed 加法 / 例词
一般动词	work	works	working	worked
以 sh ch ss x z o 结尾的词	wash reach pass mix buzz echo	加 -es washes reaches passes mixes buzzes echoes	washing reaching passing mixing buzzing echoing	washed reached passed mixed buzzed echoed
以 e 结尾的词	live	lives	去掉 e 再加 -ing living	只加 -d lived
以"辅音＋y"结尾的词	cry	变 y 为 i, 加 -es cries	直接加 -ing crying	变 y 为 i, 加 -ed cried

动词种类	动词举例	-s 加法 / 例词	-ing 加法 / 例词	-ed 加法 / 例词
以"单元音+辅音"结尾的单音节词	plan beg	plans begs	末尾辅音字母双写再加词尾 planning begging	 planned begged
以 ie 结尾的词	lie	lies	变 ie 为 y 再加 -ing lying	只加 -d lied
以 ic 结尾的词	picnic	picnics	加 -k 后再加词尾 picnicking	 picnicked

▲ 下面以 e 结尾的动词，在加 -ing 时，不必去 e，而直接加上去：
　hoe—hoeing　　　dye—dyeing　　　tiptoe—tiptoeing
　eye—eyeing　　　age—ag(e)ing

▲ 以"单元音+辅音结尾"的重读音节，加 -ing 和 -ed 时，末尾的辅音字母也要双写：
　prefer—preferring—preferred　　　permit—permitting—permitted

▲ 在英式英语中，像 travel, quarrel 这种以 l 结尾的词，加词尾时，l 也要双写：
　travel—travelling—travelled　　　quarrel—quarrelling—quarrelled
　但美式英语中，l 却不双写。

▲ 在英式英语中，有时在美式英语中，下列词加词尾时，末尾字母也双写，
　尽管这个音节不重读：
　program—programming—programmed
　kidnap—kidnapping—kidnapped
　worship—worshipping—worshipped
　hiccup—hiccupping—hiccupped
　handicap 加 -ed/-ing 时也将 p 双写：handicapped/handicapping

❀ 及物动词与不及物动词：

（1）及物动词都跟有宾语，宾语有下面几类：

1）名词：

Show your passport, please! 请出示护照！

2）代词：

She didn't say anything about it. 她对此什么也没说。

3）动名词（短语）：

I enjoyed talking to you. 我和你谈话很高兴。

4）不定式（短语）：

Hope <u>to see you again</u>. 希望再次见到你。

I'll show you <u>what to do</u>. 我将告诉你该怎么办。

5）复合结构：

I'm glad to see <u>you (doing) so well</u>. 看你（干得）这样好我很高兴。

6）从句：

I hear <u>(that) she's going to have a baby</u>. 我听说她要生孩子了。

Tell me <u>what you have in mind</u>. 谈谈你的想法。

7）数词：

"How many do you need?" "We need <u>two</u>." "你们需要多少？""我们需要两个。"

8）名词化的形容词等：

You can't expect me to do <u>the impossible</u>. 你不能指望我做不可能的事。

（2）不及物动词不能跟宾语。 这类动词后面有时也跟一定的结构，如跟某种介词，例如：

amount to	apologize for	believe in	belong to
consist of	depend on	hint at	hope for
insist on	lead to	listen to	object to
pay for	qualify for	refer to	relate to
rely on	resort to	speak to	sympathize with
talk to	wait for		

（3） 多数动词都可以既作及物动词，又作不及物动词，例如：

作及物动词	作不及物动词
The farmer <u>grows</u> crops.	Crops <u>grow</u> well.
Bill <u>runs</u> a hotel.	The dog <u>ran</u> after the cat.
A maid <u>opened</u> the door.	The door <u>opened</u> slowly.
He <u>stopped</u> the car promptly.	The car suddenly <u>stopped</u>.
She <u>speaks</u> two languages.	Who are you <u>speaking</u> to?

✿ **双宾动词是及物动词（double-transitive verb）：**

有些动词可以跟两个宾语，一个直接宾语，一个间接宾语。直接宾语通常指受益（影响）的人，间接宾语多指某样东西，例如：

He gave **his daughter** *a camera*. 他给了他女儿一部相机。

Could you send **me** *the check* right away? 你可否立即把支票寄给我?

She showed **us** *her new car.* 她让我们看了她的新车。

在上面句子中，直接宾语（黑体）在前，间接宾语（斜体）在后。

一般说来，直接宾语如果比较短（例如代词或带冠词或物主代词的名词），都放在间接宾语前面；如果直接宾语比较长或是表示强调，则可放到间接宾语后面，但前面常加介词 to：

直接宾语在前	直接宾语在后（前面加介词 to）
Show me your passport.	He showed his passport to the policeman.
He sent his wife a gift.	He sent some flowers to his girlfriend.
They awarded her a prize.	They awarded a prize to the French painter.
Can you lend us your bike?	We lent our car to a friend of ours.

还有些动词，在把直接宾语放到后面时，不加介词 to，而加介词 for：

直接宾语在前	直接宾语在后（加介词 for）
Mother bought her a necklace.	Mother bought a necklace for her youngest daughter.
That will save us a lot of trouble.	That will save a lot of time for us.
Then she read him the letter.	Then she read a letter for him.
Sing us a song.	Sing a song for us, please.

常用的这类动词有：

book	build	buy	cook	cut
design	fetch	find	fix	get
make	mix	order	pick	play
pour	prepare	save	set	sing
spare	win			

有些双宾动词的直接宾语通常只能放在前面，例如：

It cost me £500.

I envy you your good luck.

We can't promise you anything now. Allow us two hours to get things ready.

常见的这类动词有：

allow	ask	bet	cause	charge
cost	deny	draw	envy	forgive
grudge	promise	refuse		

❀ 系动词（link verb）：

英语中有些动词常和表语一起构成谓语，例如：

It's getting dark. 天黑起来了。

The situation is quite encouraging. 形势相当令人鼓舞。

这类动词称为系动词，常用的系动词有：

appear	be	become	come	fall
feel	get	go	grow	keep
look	prove	remain	seem	smell
sound	stay	taste	turn	

❀ 合成动词（compound verb）

合成动词由两个词构成，中间常有连字符，例如：

Such vaccine can be mass-produced cheaply. 这种疫苗可以便宜地大批生产。

The old man chain-smoked the Panda brand. 这位老人不停地抽熊猫牌的烟。

不规则动词

不规则动词是学英语的人必须掌握的，特别是那些常用的词。好的字典和语法书后面都有不规则动词表，应充分加以利用。为了帮助大家掌握常用的不规则动词，这里特指出几点：

❀ 过去式与过去分词同形的词：

现在式	过去式	过去分词
bend	bent	bent
bind	bound	bound
bleed	bled	bled
bring	brought	brought
build	built	built
catch	caught	caught
deal	dealt /delt/	dealt /delt/
dig	dug	dug
dream	dreamt /dremt/, dreamed	dreamt /dremt/, dreamed

feed	fed	fed
feel	felt	felt
fight	fought	fought
find	found	found

❀ 现在式、过去式和过去分词互不相同或不全相同的词：

forgive	forgave	forgiven
freeze	froze	frozen
give	gave	given
go	went	gone（表"到过某地"时用 been）
grow	grew	grown
hide	hid	hidden
know	knew	known
lie	lay	lain
ride	rode	ridden
ring	rang	rung
rise	rose	risen
run	ran	run
see	saw	seen
shake	shook	shaken
show	showed	shown
sing	sang	sung
speak	spoke	spoken
spin	span, spun	spun
steal	stole	stolen
swim	swam	swum
take	took	taken
tear	tore	torn
throw	threw	thrown
wake	woke	woken
write	wrote	written

❀ 现在式、过去式及过去分词完全相同的词：

bet	bet	bet（亦可作 betted, betted）
cost	cost	cost
cut	cut	cut
hit	hit	hit
hurt	hurt	hurt
let	let	let
put	put	put
set	set	set
shut	shut	shut
split	split	split

❀ 一些易混淆的动词：

fall	fell	fallen
feel	felt	felt
find	found	found（发现）
found	founded	founded（建立）
fly	flew	flown（飞）
flow	flowed	flowed（流）
lay	laid	laid（放）
lie	lay	lain（躺）
strike	struck	struck（打，敲击）
stroke	stroked	stroked（抚摸）
wind	wound /waʊnd/	wound /waʊnd/（蜿蜒）
wound /wuːnd/	wounded	wounded（使受伤）

❀ 有些动词有两个过去分词形式，一个规则、一个不规则，这里前面的形式较常用：

现在式	过去式	过去分词
mow	mowed	mowed, mown
prove	proved	proved, proven
sew	sewed	sewn, sewed
sow	sowed	sown, sowed
swell	swelled	swollen, swelled

❀ 还有些动词，过去式和过去分词都各有两个形式：

现在式	过去式	过去分词
bid	bid, bade	bid, bidden
burn	burned, burnt	burned, burnt
dwell	dwelled, dwelt	dwelled, dwelt
kneel	kneeled, knelt	kneeled, knelt
leap	leaped, leapt /lept/	leaped, leapt /lept/
wet	wetted, wet	wetted, wet

❀ 注意美式英语和英式英语的差别：

△ burn, dream, lean, learn, smell, spell, spill, spoil 在美式英语中都作为规则动词，在英式英语中作不规则动词时较多，也有作规则动词的。

△ wake 在美式英语中可作规则动词。

△ spit 在美式英语中的过去式和过去分词有 spit, spat 两种形式：

The soldier spat at his enemy. 那个士兵冲着敌人吐口水。

David spit his gum into an ash can. 戴维把口香糖吐到垃圾桶里。

△ quit 和 wet 在英式英语中为规则动词，而在美式英语中为不规则动词：

quit quit quit　　　wet wet wet

△ fit 在美式英语中通常也作不规则动词：fit　fit　fit

△ dive 在英式英语中为规则动词，而在美式英语中有时作不规则动词：

dive　　　dived 或 dove /dəuv/　　　dived

△在美式英语中 get 的过去分词为 got 或 gotten。

3. 形容词

❀ 形容词的种类：

形容词大体上可以分为下面这些种类：

种　类	例　句
特点形容词 qualitative adjective	She told us a sad story. 她给我们讲了一个凄伤的故事。 A small red car drove up. 一辆红色的小车开了过来。

种 类	例 句
类别形容词 classifying adjective	She'll apply for financial help. 她将申请经济补助。 They supply us with our daily necessities. 他们向我们供应日用必需品。
强调形容词 emphasizing adjective	He was a complete idiot. 他是一个十足的白痴。 He was a total failure. 他完全失败。 That's absolute nonsense. 这完全是胡说八道。
状态形容词 adjective indicating state	He was still awake. 他还醒着。 We're quite worried. 我们非常发愁。

此外还可按结构分为 -ing 形容词、-ed 形容词及复合形容词，后面将分别进行讨论。

❀ 形容词的句法作用：

作定语 作表语 作宾语补足语 作状语	She is a conscientious worker. 她是一个工作很负责的人。 Her eyes are blue. 她的眼睛是蓝色的。 We must get everything ready. 我们必须把一切准备好。 Much disappointed he went home. 他很失望，于是就回家了。

有时可用作同位语（a）或独立成分（b）：

a. People, old and young, rushed over to help. 老老少少都赶过来帮忙。

b. Strange to say, she soon recovered. 说也奇怪，她不久就痊愈了。

❀ 专作表语（补语）的形容词：

某些形容词，通常仅用作表语（补语），特别是一些由 a- 开始的词：

She was still alive. 她还活着。

He was all alone. 他孤孤单单一个人。

下面的形容词通常仅用作表语（补语），和系动词一道构成谓语：

afraid	asleep	glad	sorry
alive	awake	ill	sure
alone	content	ready	well

❀ 形容词的位置：

作定语时，形容词一般都放在所修饰词的前面，若有几个形容词，其顺序大致如下：

(article)	color	origin	material	purpose	noun
	red	Spanish	leather	riding	boots

西班牙红皮马靴

a	brown	German	beer		mug

一只棕色的德国啤酒杯

a	Venetian	glass	flower		vase

一只威尼斯的玻璃花瓶

表示大小、高度、长度等的形容词多放在前头：

a big modern brick house 一座现代化的大砖房

a tall ancient oak tree 一棵高大的古橡树

在多数情况下这和汉语是一致的。

❀ 放在名词后面的形容词：

有少数形容词有时可放在所修饰名词的后面：

Is there a doctor available? 能请到医生吗?

We'll have to consult the other countries concerned. 我们得和其他有关国家磋商。

He was the only Englishman present. 他是唯一在场的英国人。

Japan proper excludes the outlying islands. 日本本土不包含四周的岛屿。

有些形容词和它修饰的名词已构成固定的短语：

secretary general 秘书长   Poet Laureate 桂冠诗人

Attorney General（美）司法部长   President Elect 当选总统

court martial 军事法庭

如果形容词本身有修饰语，也常可放在所修饰名词的后面：

This will be a warning to people eager for a quick cure. 这对急于取得快速疗效的人是一个警告。

He is one of those people likely to veto the proposal. 他是可能对此提案提出否决的人之一。

另外，**something, somebody, somewhere** 这类词的修饰语也可放在它们后面：

Have you read anything interesting recently? 你近来看了什么有意思的文章了吗?

Let's go somewhere quiet. 咱们到一个安静的地方去。

❀ 名词化的形容词：

有些形容词已名词化，可以和 the 连用，代表一类人：

The numbers of the unemployed are still increasing. 失业人数还在增加。

The state must care for the poor. 国家必须关心穷人。

另外，一些表示国家的形容词也可用作名词：

The industrious Dutch are admired by their neighbors. 勤劳的荷兰人受到邻国的崇敬。

The Irish in America retain sentimental links with Ireland. 美国的爱尔兰人仍然和爱尔兰保持感情上的联系。

此外，还有一些表示抽象概念的形容词也可以这样用：

She's interested in the supernatural. 她对超自然的东西很感兴趣。

They ventured into the unknown. 他们冒险进入未知世界。

在不少短语中形容词起名词的作用：

He left for good. 他不回来了。　　He enjoyed it to the full. 他尽情享受。

in common 有共同之处　　in public 在公众场合

on the sly 偷偷地　　　　on the loose 逍遥法外

-ed 形容词

-ed adjectives 主要表示以 **-ed** 结尾的形容词，也包含一些不以 **-ed** 结尾的过去分词，为了方便，都称作 **-ed adjectives**。

这类形容词多数由及物动词的过去分词变成，因此有被动意思，可作表语，也可作定语：

The little girl was a little frightened. 那小姑娘有点儿害怕。（作表语）

The frightened horse began to run. 受了惊吓的马开始跑了起来。（作定语）

What are you so excited about? 什么事你这样激动？（作表语）

The excited children were opening their Christmas presents. 激动的孩子们正在打开他们的圣诞节礼物。（作定语）

这类形容词很多，常见的有：

amused	astonished	broken	closed
completed	complicated	confused	covered
crowded	decided	delighted	deserted
devoted	disappointed	discouraged	distinguished
dressed	excited	finished	frightened
illustrated	injured	interested	known
lined	lost	married	offended
pleased	puzzled	qualified	reserved
satisfied	surprised	surrounded	tired
unexpected	unknown	unmarried	unqualified
worried	wounded		

有些这类形容词并无被动意思，而有完成的意思，例如：

My father is a retired general (= a general who has retired). 我父亲是一位退休将军。

The escaped convict (= convict who had escaped) has been captured. 逃犯已被抓获。

下面这些都属于这一类：

accumulated	dated	escaped	faded
fallen	retired	swollen	wilted

还有一些这类形容词，意思和有关动词的意思有些差异，例如：

She is attached to the place. 她很喜欢这个地方。

（比较：They attached a label to my luggage. 他们在我的行李上贴了一个标签。）

He is spending a year in advanced studies. 他用了一年时间从事高级研究。

（比较：They soon advanced to the outskirts of the city. 他们很快推进到城郊。）

这类形容词有：

advanced	attached	determined	disposed	disturbed
guarded	marked	mixed	noted	

另外还有一些这类形容词是由名词 +ed 构成的，例如：

She is a <u>gifted</u> pianist. 她是个有禀赋的钢琴家。

She had a purple <u>flowered</u> headscarf. 她有一条紫色印花头巾。

下面的形容词都属于这一类：

armored	barbed	bearded	detailed	flowered
freckled	gifted	gloved	pointed	principled
salaried	skilled	spotted	striped	urbaned
veiled	walled	winged		

此外，还有少数这类形容词，既不和相关动词，又不和相关名词有意思上的联系，甚至没有相关的动词或名词，例如：

The team made a <u>concerted</u> effort to win the game. 队员们同心协力来打赢这场球。

His <u>beloved</u> wife had died. 他心爱的妻子去世了。

下面这些形容词都属这一类：

antiquated（陈旧的）	ashamed（羞愧的）
assorted（什锦的）	beloved（心爱的）
concerted（同心协力的）	deceased（死去的）
indebted（负债的）	sophisticated（尖端的）

4. 副词

❀ 副词的作用：

副词主要用来修饰动词：

A plane flew <u>overhead</u>. 一架飞机从头顶飞过。

有时还可修饰形容词、另一副词或整个句子：

She dances <u>extremely</u> well. 她舞跳得极好。

除了作状语，副词还可常常用作：

（1）表语：

I'll be <u>down</u> in a minute. 我一会儿就下（楼）来。

The moon is <u>up</u>. 月亮已经升起。

（2）定语：

The buildings <u>around</u> were badly damaged. 附近的楼房都被严重破坏。

（3）作宾语补语（共同构成复合宾语）：

He did not want them <u>around</u>. 他不想让他们待在他身边。

❀ 副词的种类：

副词主要可分为下面这些种类：

（1）方式副词（adverb of manner）：

He described his own view <u>accurately</u>. 他准确地描述了自己的看法。

许多以 -ly 构成的副词都属于这一类，还有一些不以 -ly 结尾的这类副词：

direct	fast	hard	loud	quick	right
slow	solo	straight	tight	well	wrong

（2）方面副词（adverb showing aspect）：

有些副词表示在哪一方面存在某种情况，称为方面副词：

It's <u>politically</u> short-sighted not to do so. 不这样做，在政治上是短视的。

She was far beneath him <u>socially</u>. 她比他的社会地位要低得多。

常见的这类副词有下面这些：

biologically	commercially	economically
emotionally	financially	geographically
intellectually	logically	morally
politically	psychologically	racially
scientifically	socially	statistically
technically		

（3）时间副词（adverb of time）：

Is there anything on <u>tonight</u>? 今晚有什么活动吗？

Hope to see you <u>soon</u>. 希望不久和你再见。

有不少副词属于这一类，如：

when	recently	lately	presently	now
later	immediately	yesterday	tomorrow	tonight

在美国表示一周里的每一天都可用作副词：

I don't have to work <u>Friday</u>. 星期五我不必工作。

有时还可用其他一些名词作副词：

<u>Mornings</u> I usually go for a walk by the river. 早晨，我通常在河边散步。

（4）频率副词（adverb of frequency）：

英语中频率副词不少，说明"经常的程度"。它们表示的频率可以用下表表示：

频繁程度	频率副词	举　例
100%	always	He is always like that. 他总是那样。
	usually	I usually get up at six. 我通常六点起床。
	often	He is often late. 他常常迟到。
	frequently	They were frequently in debt. 他们常常负债。
	normally	I normally go to bed early. 我通常睡得早。
	sometimes	Sometimes we are quite busy. 有时我们相当忙。
	occasionally	She came only occasionally. 她只是偶尔到这里来。
	seldom, rarely	Barking dogs seldom bite. 爱叫的狗很少咬人。（谚语） He rarely left his room. 他很少离开他的房间。
	hardly ever	It hardly ever snows here. 这儿几乎从不下雪。
	almost never	They almost never quarrelled. 他们几乎从不吵架。
0%	never	Truth never grows old. 真理永远不会过时。（谚语）

除了上面这些最常用的频率副词，还有一些其他相近的副词：

We don't see much of each other. 我们不常见面。

They meet regularly on Friday. 他们经常星期五见面。

（5）程度副词（adverb of degree）：

程度副词表示一个情况的程度：

We love him dearly. 我们深深地爱着他。

I enjoyed the show immensely. 这次演出，我非常欣赏。

常见的这类副词有：

very	much	quite	rather	little
slightly	fully	pretty	greatly	deeply
strongly	badly	well	heavily	considerably
soundly	hard	intensely	remarkably	immensely
radically	drastically	significantly	notably	

还有些副词与这类副词意思相近：

They are utterly disappointed. 他们极为失望。

You are perfectly correct. 你完全正确。

（6）强调副词（emphasizing adverb）：

有些副词对谓语加以强调，称为强调副词，例如：

We've just finished the preparations. 我们刚完成准备工作。

I certainly wish you victory. 我确实希望你们取得胜利。

常见的这类副词有：

absolutely	certainly	just	positively
quite	really	simply	surely

（7）句子性副词（sentence adverb）：

有些副词修饰整个句子，说明说话人对这句话的态度，该副词常以逗号和句子的其他部分分开：

Surprisingly, no one was hurt. 令人惊异的是没人受伤。

Luckily, she was in when I called. 幸好，我去时她在家。

常见的这类副词有：

curiously	fortunately	happily	luckily	naturally
oddly	sadly	strangely	surprisingly	unfortunately

还有些副词也修饰整个句子：

Apparently they had a row. 显然，他们吵架了。

Obviously this can't be finished in a single day. 显然，这不可能在一天内完成。

❀ 副词的位置：

表示方式和时间的副词多数都放在谓语或宾语的后面：

I'll send her over immediately. 我立即派她过来。

Don't speak so loud. 讲话不要如此大声。

方式副词有时也可放在谓语前面：

He gladly accepted the invitation. 他愉快地接受了邀请。

I carefully wrapped the gift in pretty paper. 我仔细地用漂亮纸把礼物包上。

当谓语包含情态动词或助动词时，方式副词也可放在这类动词和主要动词之间：

She had carefully measured out the right quantity of medicine. 她已仔细量出了适量的药。

They could easily get another girl to do the typing. 他们可以很容易地找到另一位姑娘来打字。

频率副词通常放在谓语前面（a），系动词 be 的后面（b），或情态动词或助动词和主要动词之间（c）：

a. He often does this. 他常常这样做。

   She seldom writes to us. 她很少给我们写信。

   They occasionally come to see us. 他们偶尔来看我们。

b. She is always like that. 她总是那样。

   He was rarely late. 他很少迟到。

c. Lost time is never found again. 失去的时间再也找不回来。（谚语）

   They have hardly ever quarrelled. 他们几乎从未吵过架。

sometimes 有时还可放在句首或句末，甚至放在动词后面：

Sometimes we're busy and sometimes we're not. 我们有时很忙，有时不忙。

Every man is a fool sometimes, and none at all time. 人会一时犯傻，但不会老是犯傻。（谚语）

never 放在句首时，后面句子要倒装：

Never will we bow the knee to hegemonism. 我们永远不会向霸权主义屈膝。

句子副词常可放在句首，或插在句子中间：

Strangely, I've never seen that program. 说也奇怪，我从未看过这个节目。

She was not, however, aware of the circumstances. 但她对情况并不清楚。

I thought, perhaps, you were expecting someone. 我想你或许是在等人。

5. 连词

连词有两类：

✿ 并列连词——连接并列的分句：

The tongue is not steel yet it cuts. 舌头不是钢做的，却能伤人。

Do you want a bath at once, or shall I have mine first? 你马上洗澡还是我先洗？

He had no friends, nor did he make any. 他没有朋友，也没有交朋友。

并列连词还可连接其他并列的成分：

The house was never clean nor tidy. 这个房子从不干净，也不整齐。

It is strange yet true. 这很奇怪，却是真实的。

❀ 从属连词——引起各种从句：

When he got up he felt dizzy. 他站起来时感到头晕。

They are generous although they are poor. 他们虽然贫穷，却很大方。

6. 连接副词

有些状语，包括副词或短语，可起连接的作用，把一个句子或从句和另一个句子或从句连接起来，例如：

Bicycling is good exercise; moreover, it doesn't pollute the air. 骑自行车是很好的运动，而且它不会污染空气。

The rain was heavy—consequently the land was flooded. 雨很大，因此土地被淹了。

这些都可称为连接状语，和连词的作用差不多。大体上有下面几类：

❀ 一种这类状语提供更多情况，可译为"还""也""此外""而且"等：

also	as well	at the same time	besides
furthermore	moreover	on top of that	too

I am not looking for a job. Furthermore, I am not going to look for a job. 我现在没有找工作，而且我也不打算找工作。

Her intentions were good. Besides, it was pleasant to be with her. 她的意图是好的，而且和她在一起也很愉快。

❀ 另一类这种状语表示另一同样的事情。可译为"同样地""也"等：

again	by the same token	equally
in the same way	likewise	similarly

She must be more reasonable, but by the same token you must try to understand her point of view. 她应当更讲道理，但同样地你也应设法了解她的观点。

My brother was taught to read by my mother, and similarly, so was I. 我哥哥是我母亲教会阅读的，同样地我也是（她教会的）。

❀ 另一类这种状语表示"尽管"等，如：

all the same	alternatively	by contrast
conversely	even so	however
instead	nevertheless	none the less
on the contrary	on the other hand	rather
still	then again	though

He's charming; <u>nevertheless</u>, I don't quite trust him. 他很有魅力，尽管如此我不完全信任他。

She is naughty; <u>all the same</u> we have to laugh at her tricks. 她很调皮，尽管如此，她的花招仍然引得我们发笑。

❀ 还有一类状语表示"因此"等，如：

| accordingly | as a result | consequently | hence |
| so | thereby | therefore | thus |

He studied hard, <u>thus</u> he got high marks. 他很用功，因此得分很高。

He was too sick to stay. <u>Accordingly</u>, we sent him home. 他病得厉害，不能再待，因此我们把他送回家了。

❀ 此外，还有一些时间状语，表示"后来""最后""之后"等，如：

afterwards	at last	at once	before long
eventually	ever since	finally	immediately
instantly	last	later	later on
next	presently	since	soon
soon after	subsequently	suddenly	then
within minutes	within the hour		

We parted, and we haven't met <u>since</u>. 我们分手了，此后再也没有见面。

He escaped from prison but was <u>subsequently</u> recaptured. 他从监牢里逃出，但后来又被抓获了。

❀ 另有一些状语表示"以前"或"同时"，如：

at the same time	beforehand	earlier	first
in the meantime	meanwhile	previously	simultaneously
throughout			

I'll call you when he comes. <u>In the meantime</u> I'll give you something to do. 他来时我将叫你，在这段时间我将给你点儿事做。

I know he is untruthful, but <u>at the same time</u>, I must admit he is a good worker. 我知道他不说真话，但同时我得承认他工作不错。

7. 数词

基数词（cardinal numbers）：

英语的主要基数词如下：

1 one	13 thirteen	70 seventy
2 two	14 fourteen	80 eighty
3 three	15 fifteen	90 ninety
4 four	16 sixteen	100 a hundred
5 five	17 seventeen	1,000 a thousand
6 six	18 eighteen	10,000 ten thousand
7 seven	19 nineteen	100,000 a hundred thousand
8 eight	20 twenty	1,000,000 a million
9 nine	30 thirty	10,000,000 10 million
10 ten	40 forty	100,000,000 a hundred million
11 eleven	50 fifty	1,000,000,000 a billion
12 twelve	60 sixty	

所有其他数字都可由它们构成：

两位数：17　seventeen　　29　twenty-nine　　84　eighty-four

三位数：150　a hundred and fifty

365　three hundred and sixty-five

500　five hundred

703　seven hundred and three

852　eight hundred and fifty-two

999　nine hundred and ninety-nine

（在美式英语中 and 通常省掉：one hundred fifty dollars）

四位数以上：最好自后向前，每三位数加一逗号，第一逗号前为 thousand，第二逗号前为 million，第三逗号前为 billion：

5, 670	five thousand six hundred and seventy
46, 000	forty-six thousand
920, 000	nine hundred and twenty thousand
8, 005, 450	eight million, five thousand, four hundred and fifty
38, 000, 000	thirty-eight million
300, 000, 000	three hundred million
12, 000, 000, 000	twelve billion

当基数词和复数名词连用时，后面动词一般也用复数形式：

Twenty people were injured in the accident. 在事故中，有 20 个人受了伤。

Over a hundred people were invited to the party. 一百多人被邀参加了晚会。

但在谈钱、时间、距离、重量等时，作为整体看待，后面的动词也可用单数形式：

A thousand pounds is a lot of money. 1 000 英镑是很多钱。

Twenty years is a long time. 二十年是很长的时间。

❀ 序数词（ordinal numbers）：

序数词绝大多数都由相应的基数词加 -th 构成，如：

11th eleventh   24th twenty-fourth   100th hundredth

但有几个序数词比较特殊：

第一 **1st, first**   第二 **2nd, second**   第三 **3rd, third**

第 23 **23rd, twenty-third**   第 31 **31st, thirty-first**

第 72 **72nd, seventy-second**

有几个序数词在拼法上与基数词略有出入：

第五 **5th, fifth**   第八 **8th, eighth** /eɪtθ/

第 12 **12th, twelfth**

以下这类基数词要变 y 为 i，再加 -eth：

第 20 **20th, twentieth**   第 40 **40th, fortieth**

这类数词多用作定语：

Our room is on the 23rd floor of this building. 我们房间在这座大楼的 23 层。

We held a party to celebrate the 100th anniversary of the founding of the university.

我们举行了一个晚会，庆祝大学建校一百周年。

也可用作表语、宾语等：

Jane is the <u>second</u> of our four daughters. 简是我们四个女儿中的老二。

You will be the <u>fifth</u> to speak. 你将是第五位发言。

在谈编了号的东西，我们可以用基数词表示顺序：

the first part → part one

the tenth chapter → chapter ten

如果数字较长，序数词总避免使用，而且读法也常常简化：

第 204 号房间　Room 204 ['ruːm 'tuː 'əu'fɔː]

第 572 页　page 572 ['peɪdʒ 'faɪv 'sevən 'tuː]

第 6 号　车厢 Carriage No. 6

❀ 分数（fractions）：

多数分数都由基数词和序数词合成，基数词代表分子，序数词代表分母：

$\dfrac{2}{3}$　two-thirds　　$\dfrac{7}{9}$　seven-ninths　　$\dfrac{5}{12}$　five-twelfths

$2\dfrac{3}{5}$　two and three-fifths　　$47\dfrac{7}{8}$　forty-seven and seven-eighths

除分子为 1 的情况（如 $\dfrac{1}{9}$ 读作 one ninth）外，其他情况中的序数词一概用复数。但有几个特殊情况：

$\dfrac{1}{2}$　a half　　$\dfrac{1}{4}$　a quarter　　$\dfrac{3}{4}$　three-quarters

复数分数词中间多有一个连字符：

More than two-thirds of the globe's surface is water. 地球表面的三分之二是水。

分数在句中主要用作：

主语：

Over <u>nine-tenths</u> of China's inhabitants belong to the Han ethnicity. 中国人口的十分之九以上都是汉族。

宾语或介词宾语：

They used <u>one fifth</u> of the money for capital construction. 他们用五分之一的资金进行基本建设。

They account for <u>one sixth</u> of the population. 他们占人口的六分之一。

定语:

It's only <u>one twentieth</u> the thickness of a human hair. 它只有人头发丝的二十分之一细。

The mass of an electron is <u>1/1850</u> that of a hydrogen atom. 电子的质量只是氢原子质量的 1/1850。

状语:

China is <u>one sixth</u> larger than the United States. 中国比美国大六分之一。

This substance reacts <u>one tenth</u> as fast as the other one. 这种物质的反应速度是另一物质的十分之一。

在以分数词作主语时,后面的动词可用复数形式或单数形式,根据意思决定:

Two-fifths of the dwellings have more than six people per room. 五分之二的住宅每间房住 6 个人以上。

Two-fifths of the land is now under cultivation. 有五分之二的土地变成了耕地。

❀ 小数(**decimals**):

小数基本上用基数词读,只是在整数和小数之间的 "." 读作 **point**(英国人有时把零读作 **nought**):

3. 6   three point six

0. 4   zero (或 nought) point four

0. 05   zero point zero five 或 (nought) point nought five

14. 397   fourteen point three nine seven

小数作定语时较多:

There has been an increase of <u>20.5</u> percent. 增长了 20. 5%。

The library contains over <u>1.5</u> million books. 图书馆藏书为 150 万册。

△分数在很多情况下可以用百分数表示:

Unemployment has increased <u>1.5 percent</u>. 失业率上升了 1. 5%。

interest at <u>10%</u> per annum 年利率为 10%

0 在美式英语和英式英语中都可读作 zero，在英式英语中有时读作 nought。但温度中的零度在两国都读作 zero（后面的 degree 用复数）：

Zero degrees Celsius is thirty-two degrees Fahrenheit. 摄氏零度等于华氏 32 度。在号码中 0 常读作 /əʊ/，可拼作 oh：

My account number is four two three oh six. 我的账户号码是 42306。

307-4922（three oh seven, four nine double two）

（在美国也可说 three zero seven, four nine two two）

在比赛分数中，0 在英国称作 nil，在美国称作 zero 或 nothing。

The score at half time is: Scotland three, England nil. 半场的比分是：苏格兰三分，英格兰零分。

在网球赛中，0 分也可用 love 表示：Forty-love, Andrews to serve. 40 比零，安德鲁斯发球。

8. 助动词

auxiliary verb 指"助动词"，主要用来构成时态、语态、否定及疑问结构。现将英语中的助动词列表如下：

助动词	在句中作用	例子
be	构成时态、构成被动语态	I'm not feeling well. 我感到不大舒服。 We've been looking for you. 我们一直在找你。 She was born in Boston. 她是在波士顿出生的。 He has been given an award. 他获奖了。
do	构成疑问句、构成否定句、用于强调	Do you know French? 你懂法语吗？ She didn't show up. 她没出席。 Do have one more. 务请再吃一个。
have	构成完成时态	Where have you been? 你到哪里去了？ He had already gone home. 他已回家了。 She's been waiting for you. 她一直在等你。
will shall	构成将来时态	Will you be in tonight? 你今晚在家吗？ Shall I help you? 要不要我帮你的忙？
would should	构成过去将来时态	He said he would come. 他说他会来。 I asked if we should go. 我问我们是否要去。

助动词一般没有特殊意思。另有一些情态动词，也称情态助动词。

它们一般都有一些意思，如 can 表示"可以""能够"，may 表示"可能""可以"。

9. 情态动词

情态动词是助动词的一部分，也可称为情态助动词（modal auxiliaries）。它们和动词不定式（多不带 to）构成谓语，表示一定的意思，如"必须""可能""能够"等。可用来提出请求、建议等，有时使语言显得更得体、更客气。

情态动词有下面这些：

can	could	may	might	must	ought
shall	should	will	would	(need)	(dare)

其中 shall, should, will, would 有时单作助动词，构成时态等。need, dare 只在一定情况下用作情态动词（它们将另行讨论）。

❀ 情态动词的共同特点是：

它们在第三人称后不加 -s；

构成疑问句和否定句不需用别的助动词；

除了 ought 外，所有情态动词都和不带 to 的不定式构成谓语；后面有时可跟完成形式、进行式或被动式。

❀ 基本意义如下：

必须，需要：

Must we bring our passports with us? 我们必须带护照吗？

Need I apply for a visa to that country? 到那个国家需要签证吗？

能力，可能性：

She can speak six languages. 她能讲六国语言。

I couldn't persuade him to change his mind. 我没法劝他改变主意。

可能，或许：

She might have difficulty in getting a job. 她找工作可能有困难。

I could lend you a little money. 我可以借给你一些钱。

应当，应该：

He ought to take care of it. 他应该负责此事。

Should we give them help? 我们应当帮助他们吗？

肯定会（不会）：

We <u>shall</u> stand behind you. 我们肯定会支持你。

I knew they <u>wouldn't</u> let us down. 我知道他们不会令我们失望的。

❀ 后面动词的各种形式：

完成形式：

He <u>may</u> have forgotten about the whole thing. 他可能忘了整件事了。

We <u>ought</u> to have notified them beforehand. 我们本该事前通知他们的。

进行形式：

She <u>may</u> still be working in the office. 她可能还在办公室工作。

You <u>shouldn't</u> be idling your time away. You <u>should</u> be doing some work. 你不应这样把时间混掉，你应当干点儿工作。

完成进行形式：

You <u>must</u> have been thinking of something else. 你一定是在想别的事。

You <u>needn't</u> have been staying up so late. 你无须待到这么晚还不睡的。

被动形式：

Reference books <u>may</u> not be taken out of the room. 参考书不可带出室外。

This factor <u>ought</u> to be taken into consideration. 这个因素应当考虑进去。

10. 反身代词

反身代词也可称为自身代词（Self pronoun），都由物主代词或人称代词加 self 构成：

myself	yourself	himself/herself/itself
ourselves	yourselves	themselves

oneself 也是反身代词。

❀ 这类代词用作宾语时最多：

I don't mean to praise <u>myself</u>; I have my faults. 我无意赞扬我自己，我有我的缺点。

I don't know how to express <u>myself</u>. 我不知道该怎样表达我的意思。

常用在某些固定的词组中：

I hope you'll both <u>enjoy yourselves</u>. 希望你们两人都玩得高兴。

He said nothing but helped <u>himself</u> to some more strawberries. 他没说什么，只又吃了一些草莓。

此外还有：

absent oneself	avail oneself of	behave oneself
distinguish oneself	excuse oneself	hide oneself
pledge oneself	pride oneself on	

❀ 自身代词还可用作介词宾语：

She looked at herself in the mirror. 她看了看镜子里的自己。

You ought to be ashamed of yourself. 你应当感到羞愧。

可与介词构成状语、定语等：

They discussed the matter among themselves. 他们在一起讨论了这件事。

He was quite pleased with himself. 他很扬扬自得。

❀ 常可用作同位语：

The novel itself has glaring faults. 那本小说本身有严重的缺点。

He was himself inclined to agree with them. 他自己倾向于同意他们的意见。

可用来表示强调，甚至有状语的性质，因此可以放到句子后部去：

I prefer to do the work myself. 我宁愿自己干这项工作。

She must decide that herself. 她得自己来决定。

❀ 有时可用作主语（多和另一主语并列，有时和 as 及 than 连用）：

I hope Miss Green and yourself are keeping well. 希望格林小姐和你身体健康。

My wife and myself were invited to the party. 我妻子和我都被邀参加这次晚会。

❀ 有时用作表语：

That poor boy was myself. 那个可怜的男孩就是我自己。

❀ 可构成一些短语：

among themselves 他们相互间

They were busy arguing among themselves. 他们忙着相互争论。

They were always quarrelling among themselves. 他们老是相互争吵。

between ourselves 咱们私下说说（不可向别人说）

Between ourselves, I think Mr. Holmes has not quite got over his illness yet. 咱们私下说说，我认为霍姆斯先生的病还没完全好。

All this is—er—you know—between ourselves. 这一切，嗯，你知道，

我们只是私下说说。

by oneself 一个人，自己

You'll have to go by yourself. 你得自己一个人去。

I study by myself for an hour. 我自己学习了一个钟头。

for oneself 为自己

He has a right to decide for himself. 他有权为自己做出决定。

He made no complaint for himself. 他没为自己抱怨什么。

in oneself 就其本身来说，本人

He is not bad in himself, but he's so weak-minded. 他本人并不坏，只是他是那样优柔寡断。

They were good men in themselves, but they had to make a living too. 他们本身都是好人，但他们也得谋生。

not be oneself 身体不适

I haven't been myself for weeks. 好几个星期，我身体都不舒服。

I'm not feeling myself. 我身体感到不适。

to oneself 供自己用

She had a room to herself. 她自己有单独的一个房间。

I want a little time to myself. 我想有些自己的时间。

11. 介词

介词（preposition）是一种虚词，不能独立在句子中担任成分，但可以引起短语，在句中担任成分，如作表语、定语、状语等：

They are in trouble. 他们出麻烦了。（作表语）

A friend in need is a friend indeed. 患难中的朋友是真朋友。（作定语）

介词数量不多，却是英语中最活跃的词，大部分句子都离不开它。很多短语或习惯表达都由它构成。翻开一页书你不难找到大量介词。因此掌握介词的用法是学好英语的关键。

❀ 介词有三大类：

简单介词（simple preposition）：

about	across	after	against	along
among	around	at	before	behind

below	beneath	beside	besides	between
beyond	but	by	down	during
except	for	from	in	like
of	off	on	opposite	over
near	past	round	since	through
till	to	towards	under	until
up	with	per	via	underneath

合成介词（compound preposition）：

alongside	inside	into	onto	outside
throughout	upon	within	without	

短语介词（phrasal preposition）：

according to	along with	apart from
as for	as to	because of
by means of	due to	in between
in front of	in spite of	instead of
in accordance with	next to	on account of
on behalf of	on board	up to
owing to	with regard to	prior to
together with		

短语介词和带介词的短语中间的界限不是很清楚。许多短语，如 in addition to, as a result of, in line with, in view of, for the sake of 等，说是短语介词也未尝不可。大体上说来，在意思和作用上接近一个介词的，就可当作短语介词，如：

in front of 接近 before　　　　　in spite of 接近 despite

in addition to 接近 besides　　　apart from 接近 besides

❀ 介词可和许多动词构成短语，甚至构成短语动词，如：

accuse... of	agree with	agree on (about)
agree to	apologize to... for	arrive at (in)
ask for	believe in	belong to (in)
care for	congratulate... on	crash into
depend on	die of	divide into

dream off	enter into	get in (to)
get on (off)	insist on	laugh at (about)
listen to	look at	look after
look for	operate on	pay for
prevent from	remind... of	run into
search for	shout at	smile at
speak to	suffer from	take part (in)
talk to (with)	think of (about)	throw at (to)
translate into	trip over	write to (about)

❀ 介词可以和许多形容词连用：

afraid of	angry with (about)	anxious about
anxious for	blue with (cold)	clever at
dependent on	different from	disappointed with
disappointed at (about)	dressed in	frightened of
good at	ill with	impressed by (with)
independent of	interested in	kind to
(be) lacking in	(be) made of (from)	near (to)
nice to	pleased with	polite to
proud of	responsible for	rude to
shocked at (by)	sorry about	sorry for
surprised at (by)	typical of	wrong with

❀ 介词还可以跟在许多名词后面，如：

attempt at	attention to	break with (from)
capacity for (of)	concern for	confidence in
difficulty with	discussion about	example of
hope of (for)	hunger for	increase in
interest in	lack of	loyalty to
marriage to	proof of	reason for
responsibility for	satisfaction with	thirst for
thought of	time for	tour of

也可和名词构成许多短语，如：

above all (things)	at a distance	at a loss
at all events	at first	at least
at length	at most	at the end (of)
by car (plane, etc.)	by chance	by the way
for example	for instance	for the sake of
in advance	in all	in any case
in fact	in public	in secret
in the end	in time	in turn
in vain	of course	of one's own accord
on duty	on fire	on purpose
on sale	on the contrary	on the sly
on the whole	out of date	out of order
out of patience	out of practice	out of touch
out of the question	to one's mind	to one's surprise
to some extent	to the point	with child
with regard to	without doubt	

❀ 在有些情况下，介词可处于句末，它的宾语放前面。最常见的是由疑问词引导的句子（疑问词就是介词的宾语）：

Where does the parcel come <u>from</u>? 这个包裹是哪里寄来的？

Which book are you most interested <u>in</u>? 哪本书你最感兴趣？

有些定语从句也有这类情况（关系代词是介词的宾语）：

This is the film (which) she told me <u>about</u>. 这就是她跟我谈起的那部电影。

That's something (which) I feel quite proud <u>of</u>. 那是我感到自豪的一件事。

还有一些短语动词的被动结构也如此：

They are well taken care <u>of</u> in the nurseries. 他们在幼儿园得到很好的照顾。

He hated being looked down <u>upon</u>. 他讨厌被人看不起。

另外还有一些作定语的不定式情况也如此：

She had no one to talk <u>to</u>. 她没有人可以交谈。

He had a lot of things to take care <u>of</u>. 他有很多事情要管。

She is not easy to get along <u>with</u>. 她不太好相处。

✿ 有时有些介词可以省略，特别是一些作表语的介词短语。例如在下面句子中的 of 有时省略：

They are (of) the same height. 他们身高一样。

His nose is (of) a funny shape. 他的鼻子形状很滑稽。

又如某些作定语的不定式，后面的介词有时也省略：

She has no money to buy food (with). 她没有钱买食物。

I had only an hour to do it (in). 我只有一小时时间来做这事。

另外 way 前的介词 in 有时也省略：

The work must be finished (in) one way or another. 这项工作必须以某种方式完成。

Do it (in) your own way. 按你自己的方式做。

不过要注意，在没有把握时还是不省略为好。

12. 冠词

冠词的基本用法：

冠词在英语中是一个重要问题，在使用每一个名词时都要考虑是否要加冠词，以及加哪个冠词。冠词分定冠词（the definite article）和不定冠词（the indefinite article）两种。the 为定冠词，a 和 an 为不定冠词。总的说来，定冠词表示一个（些）特定的东西，有时可译为"这""那"，例如：

Do you see the house over there? 你看到那边那栋房子了吗？

Show me the books you bought. 把你买的那些书拿给我看看。

但在很多情况下却不必译出"这""那"，例如：

Read the text, please. 请读课文。

Write it on the blackboard. 把它写在黑板上。

在指一个（些）特定的人或东西时，称为特指。上面句子中的名词都指一个（些）特定的人或东西，都是特指，因此前面要加定冠词 the。与之相对，并不指某一（些）特定人或东西时称为泛指。一个名词，若是泛指，就不能加定冠词，而是加不定冠词或不加冠词。可数名词单数前可加不定冠词 a 或 an，不可数名词和可数名词复数前都不加冠词。现把冠词的主要用法概述如下：

	特指（加定冠词）	泛指（不加定冠词）
可数名词单数	Look at the picture. 瞧这张画。 Who is the little girl? 这小女孩是谁？	She painted a picture. 她画了一张画。 I saw a girl in the picture. 在画里我看到一个女孩。
可数名词复数	Where did you put the pictures? 你把画放在哪里了？ Where are the girls? 姑娘们在哪儿？	I bought some pictures. 我买了几张画。 Some girls came over. 几个姑娘走了过来。
不可数名词	Drink the milk. 把奶喝掉。 The soup is delicious. 这汤味道很好。	Do you like milk? 你爱喝牛奶吗？ I'll have tomato soup. 我要西红柿汤。

some 可说是 a/an 的复数形式。

了解了冠词的基本用法还不够，还要了解各类名词的特殊情况。

❀ 专有名词前的冠词用法：

专有名词（如人名、地名）前一般不加冠词：

Tom comes from Britain. 汤姆是英国人。

Japan is in East Asia. 日本在东亚。

Canada is in North America. 加拿大在北美。

但有一些特殊情况：

（1）在江河、海洋、山脉、群岛、沙漠名称前要加 the：

the Yellow River（黄河）　　　　the Rhine（莱茵河）

the Pacific（太平洋）　　　　the South China Sea（南海）

the Himalayas（喜马拉雅山脉）　the West Indies（西印度群岛）

the Sahara（撒哈拉大沙漠）　　the Suez Canal（苏伊士运河）

（2）多数的饭店、电影院、博物馆、美术馆等建筑的名称前加 the：

the Hilton Hotel（希尔顿饭店）

the Odeon Cinema（奥迪温电影院）

the British Museum（大英博物馆）

the Tate Gallery（泰德美术馆）

the Palace Theatre（皇宫剧院）

the UN Security Council（联合国安理会）

the White House（白宫）

（3）某些国名前要加 the：

the People's Republic of China（中华人民共和国）

the United Kingdom（联合王国）　　the United States（美国）

the Netherlands（荷兰）　　　　　　the Philippines（菲律宾）

（4）街名、路名、湖名及某些建筑、组织名称前一般不加冠词：

New Street（新街）　　　　　　　Willow Road（杨柳路）

Lake Michigan（密执安湖）　　　　Oxford University（牛津大学）

Victoria Station（维多利亚火车站）　Birmingham Airport（伯明翰飞机场）

Times Square（时代广场）　　　　　Hyde Park（海德公园）

Salisburg Cathedral（索斯伯利大教堂）

Manchester City Council（曼彻斯特市政会）

（5）报纸名称前多加 the，而杂志名称前多不加 the：

The Times（《泰晤士报》）

The Washington Post（《华盛顿邮报》）

The Observer（《观察家报》）

New Scientist（《新科学家》杂志）

US News and World Report（《美国新闻及世界报道》）

Reader's Digest（《读者文摘》）

（6）在月份、周日及节日名称前一般不加冠词：

He was born in May. 他五月出生。

I'll be back on Saturday. 我星期六回来。

National Day (Labour Day) isn't far off. 不久就是国庆节（劳动节）。

How do you celebrate New Year's Day (Christmas)？你们怎样庆祝新年（圣诞节)?

❀ 普通名词前的冠词用法：

（1）一些独一无二的东西名称前要加 the：

The earth goes round the sun. 地球绕着太阳转。

He looked up at the stars in the sky. 他望着天上的星星。

We must do more to protect the environment. 我们要为保护环境做更多工作。

Our world is only a small part of the universe. 我们的世界只是宇宙的一小部分。

What is the highest mountain in the world? 哪座山是世界上最高的山？

The air was full of butterflies. 空中尽是蝴蝶。

（2）彼此都知道何所指的名词前要加 the，否则不加：

特指（知其何所指）	泛指（不指特别的人或物）
You must go and see the doctor. 你要去看医生。 Please pass me the salt. 请把盐递给我。 Where are the children? 孩子们在哪里？ Did you lock the car? 你把车锁了吗？	She is a good doctor. 她是一位好医生。 We need to take salt. 我们需要摄入盐分。 I like to play with children. 我喜欢和孩子们玩。 We're going to hire a car. 我们准备去租一辆车。

（3）一些大家都熟悉的东西的名称前常加 the：

Don't stand in the rain. 不要站在雨里。

The wind is still blowing. 风还在刮。

在有形容词修饰时，有时也可加不定冠词：

A light rain began to fall. 开始下起一阵小雨。

A gentle wind was blowing over the lake. 湖上刮着一阵微风。

但 weather 和 sunshine 前不能加不定冠词。

（4）抽象名词前一般不加冠词，但有些抽象名词可以具体化，也可以加冠词：

一般抽象名词（不加冠词）	具体化后可加不定冠词
He loves beauty. 他爱美。	Your daughter is a beauty. 你的女儿是个美人。
Knowledge is power. 知识就是力量。	She has a good knowledge of English. 她对英语了解很深。
He did it out of kindness. 他这样做是出于好心。	A forced kindness deserves no thanks. 勉强做的好事不值得感谢。
He soon lost favour. 不久他失宠了。	I want to ask a favour of you. 我想请你帮一个忙。

如果一个抽象名词用于特指，也可加定冠词：

The president has the power to veto bills. 总统有权否决法案。

I'll never forget the kindness you've shown me. 我永远不会忘记你对我们的好。

（5）有些个体名词也可抽象化，这时也可不加冠词。试比较下面句子：

用作个体名词（需加冠词）	抽象化后可不加冠词
We rented a room.	There is still room for improvement.
我们租了一个房间。	还有改进余地。
They had their wedding in a church.	Do you go to church every Sunday?
他们在一座教堂结婚。	你每个星期天都去做礼拜吗？

在特指时前面也可加 the：

The room you reserved is on the 9th floor. 你订的房间在九楼。

That's the church I told you about. 这就是我跟你谈到的那座教堂。

（6）物质名词通常不加冠词，但在一定条件下也可加冠词：

物质名词通常不加冠词	有时也可加冠词
I don't drink coffee very often.	Bring me a coffee.
我不常喝咖啡。	给我一杯咖啡。
She never drinks brandy.	I'll have a brandy.
她从来不喝白兰地酒。	我要一杯白兰地。

（7）某些名词前通常可加 the：

1）某些可数名词单数加 the 可表示一类：

The giraffe is the tallest of animals. 长颈鹿是最高的动物。

The dollar is the currency of the United States. 美元是美国货币。

2）某些表示某国人的名词前可加 the，表示这个国家的人：

The French are famous for their food. 法国人因法国菜而出名。

The Chinese invented printing. 中国人发明了印刷术。

其他还有：the Spanish（西班牙人），the Dutch（荷兰人），the Irish（爱尔兰人），the Welsh（威尔士人），the Swiss（瑞士人），the Japanese（日本人）

3）某些形容词前可加 the 表示一类人：

The homeless need more help from the government. 无家可归的人需要政府给予更多帮助。

Among the blind the one-eyed man is king. 山中无老虎，猴子称大王。（谚语）

4）有形容词最高级修饰的名词前一般要加 the：

The best mirror is an old friend. 老朋友是最好的镜子。（谚语）

The greatest talkers are always the least doers. 说得最多的人往往干得最少。（谚语）

但有时可以加 a 来表示"非常"：

He is a most remarkable man. 他是一个非常出色的人。

5）序数词前一般要加 the：

We celebrated the 50th anniversary of the founding of the Republic. 我们庆祝了共和国成立 50 周年。

有时可加 a，表示"再次""又一个"：

She thanked him a second time. 她再次向他道谢。

Then a third man rose to speak. 接着又一个人起来发言。

在编了号的东西前不加冠词：

Turn to page 30. 翻到第 30 页。

I'll take Room 405. 我要第 405 号房间。

（8）有些名词通常不加冠词：

1）三顿饭的名称前一般不加冠词：

When do you have breakfast? 你什么时候吃早饭？

After lunch he had a nap. 午饭后他睡了一会儿午觉。

有时前面也可加不定冠词：

I only want a small supper. 晚饭我只想吃一点东西。

We had quite a good dinner. 我们吃了一顿好饭。

2）星期、月份和日期前一般不加冠词：

We have no classes on Thursday afternoon. 我们星期四下午没课。

The book is due on May 21st. 书 5 月 21 日到期。

有时前面也可加不定冠词：

This happened on a Friday. 这是在一个礼拜五发生的。

We're having a very wet April. 现在是一个雨水很多的四月。

3）可数名词复数前，若系泛指，多不加冠词，如是特指则需加 the：

泛　指	特　指
She has blue eyes.	In the eyes of my mother I'm only a child.
她眼睛是蓝色的。	在我妈看来，我还是一个孩子。
They are good films.	How did you like the films?
它们是好电影。	这些电影你觉得怎样？

4）在一些含有两个并列名词的词组中，名词前常不加冠词：

day after day 日复一日	arm in arm 手挽手地
step by step 一步一步地	inch by inch 一寸一寸地
with knife and fork 用刀叉	on land and sea 在水上和陆地
from top to bottom 从上到下	shoulder to shoulder 肩并肩地
side by side 并排	from beginning to end 从头至尾

在许多情况下，是否加冠词只是一个用法问题，很难有合逻辑的解释，试比较下面短语：

加定冠词	不加冠词
listen to the radio 听广播	watch TV (television) 看电视
play the piano (guitar) 弹钢琴（吉他）	play basketball (chess) 打篮球（下棋）
catch the train 赶火车	go by train (bus) 坐火车（汽车）去
play the fool 干傻事，胡闹	play truant 逃学
have the flu 患流感	get appendicitis 得了盲肠炎
in the morning (evening) 早（晚）上	by day/at night 白天 / 夜晚

特别是一些短语，加不加冠词以及加哪个冠词，只是一个用法问题，很难讲道理，这就得作为整体来记，试比较下面这些短语：

名词前加 the	名词前加 a (n)	名词前不加冠词
at the end of one's tether 黔驴技穷	come to a bad end 没有好结局	make ends meet 使收支相抵
in the end 最后	come to an end 结束	no end of 无尽的
read between the lines 看出字里行间的意思	drop someone a line 给某人写几行	in line with 使符合
come to the point 谈到正题	stretch a point 放宽一点	in point of fact 实际上
go out of the way 特意……	in a way 从一方面说	by way of 借道
have the last word 最后说了算	in a word 总之	by word of mouth 口头上（传送）
at the expense of 靠损害……	at a disadvantage 处于不利地位	be sick at heart 打心里厌恶
in the long run 从长远说	in a sense 从一个意义上说	in love with 爱上（某人）
on the contrary 相反……	on a diet 吃特定饮食	on foot 步行（去）

13. 限定词

限定词指一些用在名词前面限定其意义的词。它们和形容词不同，它们不起描绘作用，一般也没有比较级和最高级。限定词有两类，一类可称为特指限定词（specific determiners），一类可称为泛指限定词（general determiners）。

❀ 特指限定词说明它后面的名词指一些特定的人或东西。这类限定词有：

定冠词——the：

The judge divorced the couple.（这位）法官判决这对夫妇离婚。

指示代词——this, that, these, those：

Who is this (that) girl? 这（那）个姑娘是谁？

Who painted these (those) pictures? 这（那）些画是谁画的？

物主代词——my, your, his, her, its, our, their：

That's my (his, her, their, our) philosophy. 这是我（他，她，他们，我们）的哲学。

What's its name? 它叫什么名字？

❀ 泛指限定词说明后面的名词指某类人或东西中的一（几）个或一部分，它们主要是：

不定冠词——a(n)：

A gentleman is asking to see you. 一位先生要求见你。

He gave me an apple. 他给了我一个苹果。

一些表示数量的词和不定代词：

a few	a little	all	another	any	both	each	either
enough	every	few	fewer	less	little	many	more
most	much	neither	no		other	several	some

I bought a few (both) pictures. 我买了几张画（两张画我都买了）。

Do you want any (more, a little) coffee? 你要不要（再来一点儿，一点儿）咖啡？

一些限定词也可用作代词：

There is one (enough) for each of us. 我们每人都有一个（足够的）。

Have you got one (any)? 你有吗？

14. 两种拼法的词

有些词有两种拼法，现把常用的这类词列出如下：

> acknowledgement—acknowledgment（承认）
>
> adviser—advisor（顾问）
>
> ambiance—ambience（环境，气氛）
>
> annex—annexe（附加部分）
>
> artifact—artefact（人工制品）
>
> bylaw—byelaw（地方法规）
>
> carcass—carcase（尸体，残骸）
>
> caster—castor（脚轮，调味瓶）
>
> caviar—caviare（鱼子酱）
>
> chaperone—chaperon（未婚少女的年长陪伴人）
>
> chilli—chili（甜椒，辣椒）
>
> cipher—cypher（密码，暗号）
>
> conjurer—conjuror（魔术师）
>
> connection—connexion（联系，连接）
>
> curtsy—curtsey（女子屈膝礼）
>
> dexterous—dextrous（灵巧的，熟练的）
>
> dispatch—despatch（发送，派遣）
>
> douse—dowse（浸泡，浇洒）
>
> dyke—dike（堤坝）
>
> gram—gramme（克）
>
> grandad—granddad（爷爷）
>
> granny—grannie（奶奶）
>
> guerrilla—guerilla（游击队）
>
> gypsy—gipsy（吉普赛人）
>
> hiccup—hiccough（打嗝儿）
>
> hippie—hippy（嬉皮士）
>
> hooray—hurrah—hurray（欢呼声）
>
> icon—ikon（雕像，圣像，偶像）
>
> impostor—imposter（冒名顶替者，江湖骗子）

inflection—inflexion（抑扬的声调）

jibe—gibe（嘲讽，嘲笑）

judgement—judgment（判断）

kilogram—kilogramme（千克，公斤）

likeable—likable（讨人喜欢的）

liquorice—licorice（甘草）

mackintosh—macintosh（雨衣）

mantelpiece—chimneypiece（壁炉台）

milligram—milligramme（毫克）

movable—moveable（可移动的，活动的）

Muslim—Moslem（穆斯林）

nosy—nosey（爱打听的，好管闲事的）

OK—okay（好，没事）

phoney—phony（假的，伪造的）

sheikh—sheik（阿拉伯酋长）

siphon—syphon（虹吸管）

swap—swop（交换）

veranda—verandah（阳台，门廊）

还有少数词有两种拼法，如：

球拍：racket 或 racquet

监狱：jail 或 gaol（但美式英语中只用 jail 一种拼法）

四轮运货马车：wagon 或 waggon（但美式英语中只用 wagon 一种拼法）

个别词有三种不同拼法：

hello—hallo—hullo（招呼语）

yoghurt—yoghourt—yogurt（酸奶）

另有很多动词，可以 -ize 或 -ise 结尾，如：

realize—realise　　　　　　civilize—civilise

但在美式英语中用 -ize 时较多。同样地由这类词构成的名词也有两种拼法，如：

organization—organisation　　　mechanization—mechanisation

15. 相同发音的词

英语中有许多词音同而拼法不同，现择要列出如下：

altar—alter /ˈɔːltə/

bass—base /beɪs/

bear—bare /beə/

berry—bury /ˈberi/

blew—blue /bluː/

boar—bore /bɔː/

born—borne /bɔːn/

bough—bow /baʊ/

bread—bred /bred/

break—brake /breɪk/

bridal—bridle /ˈbraɪdl/

caught—court /kɔːt/

cell—sell /sel/

cereal—serial /ˈsɪərɪəl/

chord—cord /kɔːd/

complement—compliment /ˈkɒmplɪmənt/

coarse—course /kɔːs/

core—corps /kɔː/

council—counsel /ˈkaʊnsl/

creak—creek /kriːk/

cue—queue /kjuː/

curb—kerb /kɜːb/

currant—current /ˈkʌrənt/

cymbal—symbol /ˈsɪmbl/

dear—deer /dɪə/

dew—due /djuː/

die—dye /daɪ/

draught—draft /drɑːft/

earn—urn /ɜːn/

fare—fair /feə/

feat—feet /fiːt/

fir—fur /fɜː/

flaw—floor /flɔː/

flea—flee /fliː/

flour—flower /ˈflaʊə/

fort—fought /fɔːt/

foul—fowl /faʊl/

gorilla—guerrilla /gəˈrɪlə/

grate—great /greɪt/

hair—hare /heə/

hangar—hanger /ˈhæŋə(r)/

heal—heel /hiːl/

heard—herd /hɜːd/

here—hear /hɪə/

heroin—heroine /ˈherəʊɪn/

hoarse—horse /hɔːs/

hole—whole /həʊl/

key—quay /kiː/

knead—need /niːd/

knew—new /njuː/

knight—night /naɪt/

knot—not /nɒt/

know—no /nəʊ/

lain—lane /leɪn/

leak—leek /liːk/

lessen—lesson /ˈlesn/

loan—lone /ləʊn/

made—maid /meɪd/

mail—male /meɪl/	main—mane /meɪn/
maize—maze /meɪz/	medal—meddle /'medl/
minor—miner /'maɪnə/	moan—mown /məʊn/
morning—mourning /'mɔːnɪŋ/	naval—navel /'neɪvl/
none—nun /nʌn/	one—won /wʌn/
packed—pact /pækt/	pain—pane /peɪn/
peace—piece /piːs/	peal—peel /piːl/
pedal—peddle /'pedl/	peer—pier /pɪə/
place—plaice /pleɪs/	plain—plane /pleɪn/
poll—pole /pəʊl/	pore—pour /pɔː/
pray—prey /preɪ/	principal—principle /'prɪnsəpl/
profit—prophet /'prɒfɪt/	raise—raze /reɪz/
rap—wrap /ræp/	raw—roar /rɔː/
retch—wretch /retʃ/	ring—wring /rɪŋ/
road—rode /rəʊd/	role—roll /rəʊl/
root—route /ruːt/	sail—sale /seɪl/
sauce—source /sɔːs/	scene—seen /siːn/
sea—see /siː/	seam—seem /siːm/
shear—sheer /ʃɪə/	sole—soul /səʊl/
some—sum /sʌm/	son—sun /sʌn/
stair—stare /steə/	stake—steak /steɪk/
stalk—stork /stɔːk/	stationary—stationery /'steɪʃənəri/
steel—steal /stiːl/	storey—story /'stɔːri/
tail—tale /teɪl/	tear—tier /tɪə/
there—their /ðeə/	threw—through /θruː/
throne—thrown /θrəʊn/	toe—tow /təʊ/
too—two /tuː/	vain—vein /veɪn/
wail—whale /weɪl/	waist—waste /weɪst/
wait—weight /weɪt/	war—wore /wɔː/
warn—worn /wɔːn/	way—weigh /weɪ/
week—weak /wiːk/	whether—weather /'weðə/
witch—which /wɪtʃ/	whine—wine /waɪn/

另外，read 的现在式和 reed 同音，过去式与 red 同音；lead（铅）与 lead 的过去式 led 同音。还有不少三个词同音的情况，如：

awe—oar—ore /ɔː/	buy—by—bye /baɪ/
cent—sent—scent /sent/	cite—site—sight /saɪt/
flew—flu—flue /fluː/	meat—meet—mete /miːt/
pair—pare—pear /peə/	peak—peek—pique /piːk/
rain—reign—rein /reɪn/	rite—right—write /raɪt/
saw—soar—sore /sɔː/	so—sew—sow /səʊ/
ware—wear—where /weə/	

16. 两种读音的词

有不少英语单词可有两种读法，这有几种主要情况。

❀ 同形异义词：

有不少词，形式相同，意义不同，有时读音也不同，现举例如下：

bow	/baʊ/	v.	He bowed and left the room. 他鞠了一躬，离开了房间。
	/bəʊ/	n.	They hunted with bows and arrows. 他们用弓箭打猎。
lead	/liːd/	v.	A path leads up the hill. 一条小路通向山上。
	/led/	n.	Lead is a heavy metal. 铅是一种很重的金属。
live	/lɪv/	v.	Where does he live? 他住哪儿？
	/laɪv/	adj.	We saw a live rattlesnake. 我们看见一条活的响尾蛇。
minute	/ˈmɪnɪt/	n.	Just a minute. 请等一会儿。
	/maɪˈnjuːt/	adj.	The area affected is minute. 受影响的地区很小。
row	/rəʊ/	n.	They were standing in a row. 他们站成一排。
	/raʊ/	n.	He had a row with his wife. 他和妻子吵了一架。
sow	/səʊ/	v.	We sowed our vegetable seeds yesterday. 昨天我们种下了菜籽。
	/saʊ/	n.	He bought a sow in the market. 他在市场上买了一头母猪。
tear	/teə/	v.	Why did you tear the letter into pieces? 你为什

么把信撕碎?

| | /tɪə/ | *n.* | He laughed till the tears came. 他笑得眼泪都流出来了。 |

| wind | /waɪnd/ | *v.* | The stream winds through the valley. 溪流蜿蜒流过河谷。 |

| | /wɪnd/ | *n.* | A gentle wind was blowing. 吹来一阵和风。 |

| wound | /wuːnd/ | *v.* | He was wounded in the leg. 他腿部受了伤。 |

| | /waʊnd/ | *v.* | She wound a blanket round the child. 她给孩子裹上一床毯子。 |

❀ 有些词词类转换后重音也跟着改变，如：

| contest | /'kɒntest/ | *n.* | Did you enter the contest? 你参加比赛了吗? |

| | /kən'test/ | *v.* | They contested every inch of the ground. 他们争夺每一寸土地。 |

| contract | /'kɒntrækt/ | *n.* | We made a contract with them. 我们和他们订了一份契约。 |

| | /kən'trækt/ | *v.* | They contracted to build that bridge. 他们订了合同修那座桥。 |

| record | /'rekɔːd/ | *n.* | Play some records of dance music, please. 请放些跳舞的音乐唱片。 |

| | /rɪ'kɔːd/ | *v.* | The programme was recorded. 节目录下来了。 |

| suspect | /'sʌspekt/ | *n.* | Several suspects were arrested. 有几名嫌疑犯被捕。 |

| | /sə'spekt/ | *v.* | I suspected that he had been in jail. 我怀疑他蹲过监狱。 |

这类词很多，下面是一些常见的这种词：

abstract	accent	ally	combine	conduct
conflict	conscript	construct	contest	contrast
convert	convict	defect	desert	dictate
discount	escort	export	extract	frequent
import	increase	insult	intrigue	object
perfect	permit	present	produce	progress
project	prospect	protest	rebel	record
recount	refund	reject	reprint	subject
survey	suspect	torment	transfer	transport

另外有些词用作不同词类时，读音有少许变化，例如：

advocate	/'ædvəkeɪt/	v.	He advocated a change of policy. 他主张改变政策
	/'ædvəkɪ(ə)t/	n.	He was an advocate of free trade. 他提倡自由贸易。
associate	/ə'səʊʃɪeɪt/	v.	I didn't want to associate with it. 我不愿和它发生联系。
	/ə'səʊʃɪət/	n.	They are business associates. 他们是商业上的伙伴。
duplicate	/'dju:plɪkeɪt/	v.	Please duplicate this letter. 请把这信复印一份。
	/'dju:plɪkɪ(ə)t/	n.	Keep a duplicate of the letter. 保留这封信的复印件。
separate	/'sepəreɪt/	v.	She soon separated from him. 她不久和他分手了。
	/'sepərɪ(ə)t/	adj.	The children sleep in separate beds. 孩子们分床睡。

下面这些词都有这个现象：

advocate	appropriate	approximate	articulate	associate
consummate	degenerate	delegate	deliberate	designate
duplicate	elaborate	estimate	graduate	initiate
intimate	moderate	separate	subordinate	

❀ 此外，有一些以 -se 结尾的词，在作动词时读 /z/，作名词或形容词时读 /s/，如：

	作名词或形容词		作动词
house	/haʊs/	(n.)	/haʊz/
use	/ju:s/	(n.)	/ju:z/
abuse	/ə'bju:s/	(n.)	/ə'bju:z/
excuse	/ɪk'skju:s/	(n.)	/ɪk'skju:z/
misuse	/'mɪsju:s/	(n.)	/'mɪsju:z/
refuse	/'refju:s/	(n.)	/rɪ'fju:z/
close	/kləʊs/	(adj.)	/kləʊz/
diffuse	/dɪ'fju:s/	(adj.)	/dɪ'fju:z/

17. 缩略词

在英语中有许多词可以缩短成一个或几个字母，称为缩略词。缩略词有下面几类：

❀ 保留第一个字母的缩略词（用第一个字母代表整个词）：

p. = page（p.239 第 239 页；30 pp.30 页）

C = Celsius（Heat the oven to 180℃. 把炉灶加热至摄氏 180 度。）

p = pence（They cost 5 p. 它们价钱为五便士。）

❀ 保留前几个字母的缩略词（用前几个字母代表整个词）：

Vol. = volume（Vol. Ⅲ 第三卷）

Prof. = professor（Prof. Richard Evans 理查德·埃文斯教授）

Co. = company（Jones & Co. 琼斯公司）

❀ 省去几个字母的缩略词：

dept. =department（Dept. of Physics 物理系）

km =kilometer（60 km an hour 每小时 60 千米）

mg =milligram（300 mg of calcium 300 毫克的钙）

❀ 由词首构成的缩略词（即由两个或几个词的第一个字母构成的词）：

CD = compact disc（激光唱盘）

USA = United States of America（美国）

VIP = very important person（贵宾）

以上均按字母读音。有些这类词拼在一起读音，像一个词一样，如：

UNESCO 读作 /juˈneskəʊ/（联合国教科文组织）

NATO 读作 /ˈneɪtəʊ/（北大西洋公约组织）

laser 读作 /ˈleɪzə/（激光）

这类词称作 **acronyms**（首字母缩略词），前面都不加冠词。

二、句法
思维导图

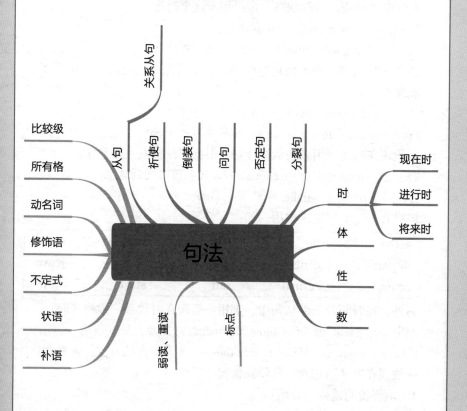

关系从句

从句

比较级

所有格

动名词

修饰语

不定式

状语

补语

析使句

倒装句

问句

否定句

分裂句

句法

时 — 现在时 / 进行时 / 将来时

体

性

数

弱读、重读

标点

1. 时

（1）现在时

现在时态有两个，一是一般现在时，一是现在进行时。

❀ 一般现在时：

一般现在时主要表示一些经常、反复甚至一直发生的事：

The sun rises in the east. 太阳从东边升起。

The Yellow River flows into the Yellow Sea. 黄河流入黄海。

有许多动词表示一种状态，常可用于这个时态：

She loves classical music. 她喜欢古典音乐。

I want to have something to drink. 我想喝点什么。

还有一些动词，表示极短暂的动作，不宜用于进行时，也可用于一般现在时：

Now I declare the meeting open. 现在，我宣布开会。

I promise never to smoke again. 我答应再也不抽烟了。

一般现在时还可用来表示按计划、根据安排要发生的动作：

The delegation arrives here tomorrow. 代表团明天到这里。

Is there a film on tonight? 今晚有电影吗？

但只有少量动词能这样用，如：

arrive	be	begin	close	come
depart	dine	end	go	leave
open	return	sail	start	stop

另外，在时间及条件从句中，都用一般现在时代替一般将来时：

After you finish the letter show it to me. 信写完后，给我看看。

I'll come to see you if you're free tonight. 如果你今晚有空，我来看你。

一般现在时还可用在一些特殊情况中：

1）电影说明或剧情介绍：

In *Death on the Nile*, Linet Ridgeway is the young and beautiful heiress to an immense fortune, but she has a lot of enemies. 在《尼罗河惨案》中，林奈·里奇韦是一大笔财产的年轻漂亮的继承人，但她有很多敌人。

2）新闻标题或小说章节题目：

Bank Robbery: Robbers take $100,000. 银行劫案：匪徒抢走 100 000 美元。

3）动作解说，特别是电视解说词：

Watch me. I switch on the current and stand back. 瞧着我，我通上电流，往后站。

Hunt takes the ball forward quickly. Palmer comes across, tries to intercept him. 亨特快速向前带球，帕尔默跑了过来设法截住他。

4）舞台动作和图片解说：

He sits down, shivers a little. Clock outside strikes twelve. 他坐了下来，略微有些颤抖。外面的钟敲了 12 点。（舞台说明）

The Queen arrives for the Opening of Parliament. 女王出席国会开幕式。（图片说明）

5）戏剧性描绘（主要用在小说或报道文字中，突然由过去时转为现在时，使情节显得历历在目）：

They threatened to shoot, but the marchers could not be stopped. The unarmed workers press on and on... 他们威胁着要开枪，但却没法挡住游行的人，手无寸铁的工人继续向前行进。

6）某些特殊句型：

Here comes the bus. 公共汽车来了。

There goes the bell. 铃响了。

❀ 现在进行时主要表示现在正在进行的动作：

Why is the little girl crying? 那个小女孩为什么在哭？

What are you worrying about? 你为什么事发愁？

前面第一框列出的表示状态和感觉的动词，有时意义转变表示动作也可用于进行时：

表示状态	表示动作
We have a nice home.	We are having supper.
I don't see anything.	He's seeing a friend off.
You look beautiful.	What are you looking for?
I don't mind.	I'm minding the baby.
This shows you're right.	He is showing a friend around.
I think it's a good idea.	What are you thinking of?

有个别动词，两种时态都可以用，没有太大差别，例如：

How do you feel about it? 你对此有何感觉？

How are you feeling today? 你今天感觉如何？（用这种时态显得比较亲切）

有时可用现在进行时表示常常发生的动作，来表示某种情绪：

He is always thinking of his work. 他老是想到他的工作。（赞扬）

She is always complaining about something. 她老发牢骚。（厌烦）

He is constantly leaving his things about. 他老是把东西乱扔。（不满）

The girl is doing fine work in school. 这姑娘学习很不错。（赞美）

如改为一般现在时则只是说明事实，不带任何情绪。

动词 be 一般不用于进行时态，但有时用于进行时态表示一时的表现：

You're not being modest. 你这样说不太谦虚。

He's being silly. 他（这样做）是在发傻。

现在进行时也可表示最近按计划或安排要进行的动作（这时多有一个表示未来时间的状语）：

I'm seeing my doctor today. 我今天去看我的医生。

Who's interpreting for you? 谁将替你当翻译？

能这样用的也只有少量动词，如：

arrive	come	dine	do	go
have	leave	lunch	play	return
see	sleep	start	stay	work

但 be going to 这个结构则可经常用来表示将来情况，或表示"准备（打算）做某事"：

He's going to buy her a coat. 他打算给她买一件大衣。

I'm not going to touch a thing tonight. 今晚，我不打算吃任何东西。

或表示"即将发生"或"预计要发生的事"。

There is going to be a thunderstorm. 要有雷暴了。

在时间或条件从句中也可用这种时态表示将来的动作：

Don't mention this when you're talking to him. 你和他谈话时，不要提及此事。

Come and see us if you're passing through this city. 如果你从这个城市经过，请来看我们。

（2）进行时

进行时态表示正在进行的动作，例如：

They're putting up more buildings. 他们正在盖更多楼房。

She'll be coming over for a short stay. 她将要来小住一段时间。

用于这种时态的动词可称为动态动词（dynamic verbs）。另有不少动词表示一种状态，通常不能用于进行时态，称为静态动词（static verbs）。下面这些动词一般不宜用于进行时态：

admire	adore	appear	astonish	be
believe	belong to	concern	consist of	contain
deserve	desire	despise	detest	dislike
envy	exist	fit	forget	hate
have（有）	hear	imagine	impress	include
interest	involve	keep	know	lack
last	like	look like	love	matter
mean	owe	own	please	possess
prefer	reach	realize	recognize	remember
resemble	satisfy	see	seem	sound
stop	suppose	surprise	survive	suspect
understand	want	wish		

但在一定情况下，其中某些动词也可用于进行时态，例如：

be（用于进行时态时表示一个暂时的表现或特点）：

I'm not being hard on anybody! I'm being sensible. 我这样做不是对谁苛刻，我只是理智行事。

Am I being extravagant? 我这样是不是太浪费？

have（用来表示一个动作时，也可用于进行时态）：

They're having supper now. 他们现在在吃晚饭。

We were having a discussion. 我们在讨论一件事。

see（表示"去找某人""接见"等时，也可用于进行时态）：

I'm seeing my dentist this afternoon. 今天下午我去看牙。

Madame is ill and is not seeing anybody today. 夫人有病，今天任何人都不见。

hear（表示"审问""听取"时也可用于进行时态）：

Which judge is hearing the case? 哪位法官审这个案子？

My brother was hearing me practise my part in the play. 我哥哥这时在听我练习剧中的台词。

有许多动词有多种意思，在表示一种意思时不能用进行时态，而在表示另一种意思时却又可以。

试比较下面的句子：

{ This food tastes good. 这菜好吃。
The cook is tasting the soup. 厨师在尝汤。

{ He weighs 150 pounds. 他体重 150 磅。
The grocer was weighing the biscuits on his scales. 杂货商在用称称饼干。

{ Roses smell sweet. 玫瑰很香。
She was smelling the flowers. 她在嗅花。

（3）将来时

表示未来动作或情况有许多方法：

❀ 用一般将来时（各个人称后都可用 **will**，英式英语和美式英语中都如此，口语中多用 **'ll** 这一形式）：

I (We) will give you a definite answer tomorrow. 我（们）明天给你明确的答复。

Where will (shall) I see you? 我在哪里和你碰头？

❀ 用将来进行时（这在口语中用得很多，尤指安排要做的事）：

I must go; the students will be waiting for me. 我得走了，学生们要等我的。

Will you be taking your leave in Qingdao? 你会在青岛休假吗？

❀ 用将来完成时及将来完成进行时（指将来某时前应已发生的事）：

He'll have calmed down in the morning. 明天早上他就会已平静下来。

I'll have been teaching for thirty years this winter. 到今年冬天，我就已任教三十年了。

❀ 用 **be going to** 结构（表示准备要做的事或预期要发生的情况）：

When are you going to get your hair cut? 你准备什么时候去理发？

We are going to call her this evening. 我们打算今晚给她打电话。

❀ 用现在进行时（表示按已定计划要做的事）：

We're going to Beijing this autumn. 我们今年秋天到北京去。

I'm seeing my aunt on Saturday. 礼拜六我去看我姑姑。

❀ 用一般现在时（表示根据日程表或时刻表要做或要发生的事）：

The autumn term starts on September 1st. 秋季学期 9 月 1 号开学。

用在条件从句及某些其他从句中：

I'll join you tomorrow if I have time. 如果有时间，我明天来参加你们的活动。

We'll have the outing tomorrow unless it rains. 我们明天去郊游，除非下雨。

❀ 用 be + 不定式结构（表示按计划、安排要发生的事，还可能有其他意思）：

How am I to pay this debt? 我怎么能偿还这个债？

❀ 用情态动词构成的谓语（也可表示将来情况）：

How can I get in touch with her? 我怎么能和她取得联系？

You should get everything ready tomorrow. 你必须明天把一切准备好。

❀ 一些其他结构：

The plan is bound to succeed. 这个计划一定会成功。

They are scheduled to arrive at 9:30. 他们定于九点半到达。

2. 体

aspect 是一个语法名词，可译作"体"。英语中主要有三种体，一种是完成体（**perfective aspect**），下面句子的画线部分都是完成体：

We got to the station after the train had left. 我们抵达车站时，火车已经开了。

If we had got there a little earlier, we'd have caught the train. 如果我们早点儿到那儿，就赶上火车了。

I am (was) sorry to have missed the lecture. 我很遗憾误了这堂课。

She regrets (regretted) having abandoned the plan. 她懊悔放弃了这个计划。

一种是进行体（**progressive aspect**），下面句子中的画线部分都属于进行体：

I was reading a novel yesterday. 昨晚我在看一本小说。

She may be waiting for us. 她可能在等我们。

还有一种完成进行体（perfect progressive aspect），下面句子中的画线部分就是完成进行体：

The fire <u>had been burning</u> all night. 火着了一夜。

You <u>should have been looking</u> after the baby. 你这段时间是应当照看孩子的。

时间和体交织在一起，就构成各种时态，与上面三种体相对的是简单体：

时间 ＼ 体	简单体	进行体	完成体	完成进行体
现在	简单现在时	现在进行时	现在完成时	现在完成进行时
过去	简单过去时	过去进行时	过去完成时	过去完成进行时
将来	简单将来时	将来进行时	将来完成时	将来完成进行时
过去将来	简单过去将来时	过去将来进行时	过去将来完成时	过去将来完成进行时

3. 性

英语不像其他欧洲语言，名词一般没有阴阳性之分。只有少数名词分阴阳性，如：

阳性名词	阴性名词
god 神	goddess 女神
emperor 皇帝	empress 女皇（皇后）
king 国王	queen 女王（王后）
prince 王子	princess 公主
actor 男演员	actress 女演员
duke 公爵	duchess 公爵夫人
count 伯爵	countess 女伯爵，伯爵夫人
master 男主人	mistress 女主人
host 男主人（对客人而言）	hostess 女主人
landlord 男房东（地主）	landlady 女房东（地主）
heir 继承人	heiress 女继承人
poet 诗人	poetess 女诗人
headmaster 男中学校长	headmistress 女中学校长
chairman（男）主席	chairwoman 女主席

priest 教士   priestess 女教士

manager 经理   manageress 女经理

hero 英雄   heroine 女英雄

bridegroom 新郎   bride 新娘

lad 少年   lass 少女

wizard 巫师   witch 女巫

fiancé 未婚夫   fiancée 未婚妻

policeman 男警察   policewoman 女警察

waiter（饭店）服务员   waitress（饭店）女服务员

steward（轮船、飞机）服务员   stewardess（轮船、飞机）女服务员

shepherd 牧羊人   shepherdess 牧羊女

widower 鳏夫   widow 寡妇

nephew 侄儿   niece 侄女

lion 狮子   lioness 母狮

tiger 老虎   tigress 母老虎

其中 poetess 不常用，现在 poet 也可指女诗人，steward 和 stewardess 现在都以 flight attendant 代替。

4. 数

可数名词和不可数名词的区分在英语中是一个重要问题，因为它牵涉到名词的单复数形式和是否要加冠词及加哪个冠词。这对中国学生来说尤其困难，因为许多我们看来似乎可数的名词在英语中却是不可数的，例如：

一条消息   不能直译，而需说 a piece (an item) of news

一件家具   需说 a piece of furniture

一张纸   需说 a sheet (piece) of paper

一件衣服   需说 an article of clothing

一片面包   需说 a slice of bread

一根草   需说 a blade of grass

一件行李   需说 a piece of luggage

一件工作   需说 a piece of work

因此在学英语时，不能凭汉语概念去推，而要一个词一个词去研究，看哪个名词是可数的，哪个名词是不可数的。另外，许多英语名词有不同的意思，用于一个意思时是不可数的，用在另一个意思时却是可数的，现举例说明如下：

作可数名词	作不可数名词
Is there a church in your town?	What time does church begin?
你们城里有教堂吗？	礼拜什么时候开始？
She teaches in a high school.	No school today!
她在一所中学教书。	今天不上课！
It's a teachers' college.	Are you at college?
这是一所师范学院。	你在上大学吗？
I'll get you a glass of water.	Glass breaks easily.
我去给你倒杯水来。	玻璃很容易破碎。
He went out to buy a paper.	I need some typing paper.
他出去买一张报纸。	我需要一些打字纸。
Did you have a good time?	I just have no time for it.
你玩得好吗？	我就是没有时间做这事。
Here is a difficulty for us to get over.	We had no difficulty in finding the place.
我们要克服一个困难。	我们找到这地方没有困难。
It is a hard work to understand.	I can't find work in this town.
这是一本难懂的作品。	在这座城市，我找不到工作。

有不少抽象名词通常是不可数的，但有时表示具体的东西则成为可数名词：

抽象名词（通常不可数）	指具体东西时成为可数名词
He had no real sense for beauty.	Your daughter is quite a beauty.
他没有真正的美感。	你的女儿是个大美人。
These thoughts gave him great pleasure.	It is a great pleasure to work with you.
这些想法使他很高兴。	和你在一起工作是很愉快的事。
I wish you joy.	My children are a great joy for me.
祝你快乐。	我的孩子是我最大的乐趣。
Thank you for your kindness.	A forced kindness deserves no thanks.
谢谢你的好心。	勉强的善行不值得感谢。（谚语）

有些抽象名词可转为可数名词，表示一类：

抽象名词（不可数）	表示一类（可数）
Art lies in concealing art.	Translation is an art.
艺术妙在隐藏艺术。（谚语）	翻译是一种艺术。
Chinese culture is widely known in Europe.	Ancient Egypt had an advanced culture.
中国文化在欧洲众所周知。	古埃及有先进的文化。
Is war necessary?	It's not a popular war.
战争是必要的吗？	这是一场不得人心的战争。
He thanked her with genuine affection.	He had a warm affection for his mother.
他怀着真情感谢了她。	他对母亲有一种温馨的感情。

反过来，有些个体名词可以抽象化，用作不可数名词：

个体名词（可数）	抽象化后成为不可数名词
It's a charming room.	Is there room for me in the car?
这是一间迷人的房间。	车里还有我坐的地方吗？
Is it a single bed or a double bed?	Time for bed!
这是一张单人床还是双人床？	该睡觉了！
We saw a vast sea before us.	He was buried at sea.
我们看到面前是辽阔的大海。	他葬身大海。
It was a general hospital.	Grandma has already left hospital.
这是一家综合医院。	奶奶已经出院了。

另外物质名词是不可数的，但在一定情况下也可用作可数名词：

物质名词（通常不可数）	用作可数名词
Would you care for some soup?	They supply various soups.
你要不要喝点汤？	他们提供各式各样的汤。
Could I have some coffee?	Could I have two coffees?
我可否要点咖啡？	我可否来两杯咖啡？
She made a pot of tea.	It was a wonderful tea.
她泡了一壶茶。	这是一种非常好的茶。
Let's have ice cream for dessert.	I want six ice creams.
咱们吃冰淇淋作甜点。	我要六份冰淇淋。

表示风、雨等的名词，通常是不可数的，但一定情况下也可用作可

数名词：

作不可数名词	作可数名词
The wind blew down the trees. 风把树刮倒了。	A gentle wind was blowing over the lake. 湖上吹过一阵清风。
We had too much rain this summer. 今年夏天雨水太多。	A fine rain began to fall. 开始下起一阵小雨。
There was a rainbow in the sky. 天上有一道彩虹。	Pink clouds floated in a pale sky. 粉红色的云朵飘浮在淡色的天空中。
Snow falls in winter. 冬天下雪。	A heavy snow was falling. 天下着大雪。

有些意思相近的名词，有些是可数的，有些却是不可数的：

可数名词（加冠词 a 或 an）	不可数名词（不加冠词）
I wished him a pleasant journey. 我祝他旅途愉快。	He is fond of travel. 他喜欢旅行。
He wanted a job, any sort of a job. 他需要工作，什么工作都行。	I cannot find work in this town. 在这座城市我找不到工作。
It is a true act of friendship. 这是一次真正友好的行动。	All action is based on judgment. 一切行动都是以判断力为基础的。
He earns a salary of £8,000 per annum. 他年薪 8 000 镑。	No work, no pay. 不劳无获。

另外，习惯用法起很大作用。许多可数名词在短语中就不带冠词了，如 on account of, in place of, see eye to eye 等。这时就要把短语作为整体来记，不要再管可数、不可数的问题。另外有些特殊现象可以细心观察，例如有些可数名词在有 little、much 等词修饰时，就成了不可数名词：

There is little difference between the two words. 这两个词没有什么差别。

（比较：There are many differences between the two languages. ）

There wasn't any change in him. 他没有什么变化。

（比较：I hope there will be a change in the weather. ）

又如许多名词都是用于复数形式的：

She brought the box of groceries in. 她把那箱日用杂货搬了进来。

All the proceeds go to the orphanage. 全部收入都给了孤儿院。

On the outshirts they passed a steel mill. 在郊区他们经过一座钢铁厂。
要真正解决这个问题，就得勤于查一部较好的字典，不肯定时就查一查，慢慢就可掌握这方面的规律了。

5. 比较级

形容词的比较级和最高级分别表示"更……"和"最……"：
She is happier than usual today. 她今天比平时更高兴。
I am the happiest man on earth. 我是世界上最快活的人。
这种比较级和最高级有两种构成法：加词尾 -er 和 -est。
单音节的词都这样构成。构成时注意：

情况	加法	例词
一般情况	直接加 -er, -est	taller, tallest; quicker, quickest
以一个辅音字母结尾	将该字母双写再加 -er, -est	bigger, biggest; fatter, fattest
以辅音 + 不发音的 e 结尾	只加 -r 和 -st	wider, widest; later, latest

双音节词中，以 y 结尾的词，也这样构成比较级和最高级，但要先变 y 为 i 再加词尾：

easy → easier, easiest　　　　　　　busy → busier, busiest

另外，有少数其他双音节词也可这样构成比较级和最高级。

narrow → narrower, narrowest　　　simple → simpler, simplest

clever → cleverer, cleverest　　　　quiet → quieter, quietest

前面加 more 和 most：
三音节和更多音节的词都可以这种方式构成比较级和最高级：

beautiful	more beautiful	most beautiful
intelligent	more intelligent	most intelligent
interesting	more interesting	most interesting

下面这些双音节词，用前两种方法都可以：

common	handsome	narrow	polite	simple
cruel	likely	obscure	remote	stupid
gentle	mature	pleasant	shallow	subtle

如：

gentle
{ gentler   gentlest
  more gentle   most gentle }

polite
{ politer   politest
  more polite   most polite }

以 un 开头和以 y 结尾的三音节词（如 unhappy, unlucky），用上述两种方法构成比较级或最高级都可以。

另外，有少数形容词有不规则的比较级和最高级：

good	better	best
bad	worse	worst
little	less	least
many, much	more	most
far	farther, further	farthest, furthest
old	older, elder	oldest, eldest

well 和 ill 分别有不规则的比较级 better 和 worse。

在使用比较级时常有 than 引起的结构说明和什么相比：

He has no more sense <u>than</u> a kid. 他还不及一个孩子有头脑。

The weather was worse <u>than</u> we had expected. 天气比我们预想的坏。

She is now happier <u>than</u> she has ever been. 她现在比过去任何时候都更快活。

It is easier <u>than</u> I thought. 这比我想的容易。

than 后若为人称代词，口语中用宾格时较多，在正式文体中也可用主格：

He has more time <u>than</u> me (I). 他的时间比我多。

They are wiser <u>than</u> us (we). 他们比我们聪明。

有时也可不跟 than 引起的结构：

The sea was now <u>calmer</u>. 海平静了。

比较级还可用在某些特别结构中：

It's <u>more or less</u> circular. 它大体上呈圆形。

<u>The more</u> difficult the questions are, <u>the less</u> likely I'll be able to answer them. 题目越难，我越答不出。

在使用最高级时，前面多加定冠词，后面多有一个短语或从句说明比较的范围：

That's the best film I have ever seen. 这是我看过的最好的电影。

It was the highest mountain in this region. 这是这个地区最高的山。

在用作表语时常可不带定冠词：

Beef is nicest slightly underdone. 牛肉稍稍有点不熟最好。

Housing conditions are worst among the black people. 黑人居住条件最差。

如有所有格之类的修饰语，**the** 就不要用：

She's the school's most popular teacher. 她是学校最受欢迎的老师。

He's my youngest (eldest) brother. 他是我最小的弟弟（大哥）。

在最高级前有时可有一个序数词修饰：

It's the second largest city in China. 它是中国第二大城市。

It's perhaps the country's fifth biggest oilfield. 它可能是我国的第五大油田。

6. 所有格

名词所有格由名词加"'s"构成，表示"（某人）的"：

her sister-in-law's mother 她嫂子的母亲

the editor-in-chief's office 总编辑室

以 s 结尾的复数名词后只需加 "'" 来构成所有格：

the teachers' reading-room 教师阅览室

在以 s 结尾的专有名词后，加 "'s" 较多，也可只加 "'"，但都读 /ɪz/：

Dickens's novels 狄更斯的小说　　Tess's family 特斯的家

Socrates' ideas 苏格拉底的思想　　Marx' views 马克思的看法

❀ "'s" 主要加在表示人或高级动物的名词后：

Have you read *The Hunter's Diary*? 你读过《猎人日记》吗？

Gulliver's Travels is a very interesting book.《格列佛游记》是一本非常有趣的书。

除此之外还可加在：

1）表示时间的名词后：

It's about half an hour's drive from here. 乘车去约半小时可到。

They wanted three weeks' notice before I left. 他们要求我，离职要在

三周前通知他们。

2）表示由人组成的集体名词后：

Is that your government's policy? 这是你们政府的政策吗？

What's the majority's view? 多数人的意见怎样？

3）表示国家、城市等的名词后：

We visited some of the city's scenic spots. 我们参观了这座城市的一些风景区。

About two-thirds of the earth's surface is covered with water. 地球表面约有三分之二被水覆盖。

4）某些机构的名称后：

Tell us a little about the school's history. 给我们谈谈校史吧。

We stayed at the station's waiting-room until evening. 我们在车站候车室一直待到晚上。

现在，名词所有格的使用范围越来越广，除了上面提的几种情况外，还有不少名词可以这样用，如：

the treaty's ratification 条约的批准 science's role 科学的作用

the word's function 这个词的作用 the novel's plot 小说的情节

不过使用这种结构要谨慎。在口语中用 **of** 引起的短语表示所有关系还是比较多的，如：

the future of television 电视的未来

in the name of freedom 以自由的名义

7. 动名词

"动词的 -ing 形式"指动词（原形）加词尾 -ing，其中包括动名词及现在分词。-ing 形式中作用和名词相当的称为动名词（gerunds），其他的称为现在分词（present participles）。由于现在分词这个名字不够理想（"现在"两字易引起误会），有些语法学家认为可以把两者并在一起，统称"-ing 形式"。但在实际运用上，把两者加以区分是有好处的，因此多数语法学家都把它们分开处理。这里我们也分开处理。

❀ 动名词的用法

动名词主要起名词的作用，因此它可以在句中：

（1）作主语

<u>Collecting</u> stamps is a hobby of mine. 集邮是我的一个爱好。

<u>Talking</u> mends no holes. 空谈无济于事。（谚语）

有时可用先行词 **it** 作主语，而把作主语的动名词放到后面去：

Is it any good <u>explaining all this</u>? 解释这些有用吗？

It's nice <u>being with you</u>. 和你在一起很好。

有时在 **there is** 后可用动名词作主语：

She's made up her mind; <u>there's no arguing with her</u>. 她已打定主意，用不着再和她辩论。

He's bad-tempered; <u>there's no denying it,</u> but he's also a genius. 他脾气不好，这是无可否认的，但他也是一位天才。

（2）作宾语

Would you mind <u>filling out this form</u>? 你可否把这张表填一下？

He avoided <u>giving us a definite answer</u>. 他回避给我们作肯定的答复。

有很多动词或动词短语能用动名词作宾语，常见的如：

admit	appreciate	avoid	consider	delay
deny	detest	dislike	endure	enjoy
escape	excuse	fancy	feel like	finish
forgive	give up	(can't) help	imagine	involve
keep (on)	leave off	mention	mind	miss
postpone	practise	put off	resent	resist
risk	stop	(can't) stand	suggest	understand

还有不少动词后面可跟动名词也可跟不定式作宾语，例如：

Do you like <u>playing (to play)</u> chess? 你喜欢下棋吗？

I propose <u>making (to make)</u> a change in the plan. 我建议把计划作些调整。

这类动词常见的有：

(can't) afford	attempt	(can't) bear	begin	continue
deserve	dislike	fear	forget	hate
intend	like	love	need	neglect
prefer	propose	regret	remember	start
try	want			

这两种结构有时意思差别不大，有时却有些差别，例如：

{ I remember telling you about her. 我记得曾跟你谈过她的事。
{ Remember to meet me tonight. 记得晚上和我会面。

{ I shall never forget seeing her for the first time. 我永远不会忘记第一次和她见面的情景。
{ I forgot to ask him about it. 我忘了问他这件事。

{ This wants washing. 这需要洗。
{ I want to have a wash. 我想去洗一洗。

{ She tried writing out her views. 她试着把她的看法写出来。
{ I'll try to improve. 我将尽力改进。

作介词的宾语：

动名词作介词宾语的时候特别多，例如：

She was very fond of speaking French. 她很喜欢讲法语。

I don't feel like going to the movie. 我不想去看电影。

有很多动词短语后面可跟这样的宾语，常见的如：

accuse of 指控	aim at 目标是
approve of 赞成	be afraid of 害怕
be capable of 能够	be engaged in 正从事
be fond of 喜欢	be good at 善于
be interested in 对……有兴趣	be keen on 迫切想
be opposed to 反对	be proud of 对……感到骄傲
be responsible for 对……负责	be sick of 讨厌
be suitable for 对……合适	be tired of 对……厌倦
be used to 对……习惯	charge... with 控以……罪名
depend on 依靠	devote to 献身于
dream of 梦想	excuse... for 原谅（某事）
feel ashamed of 感到羞愧	feel like 想做某事
get accustomed to 习惯于	not hear of 不允许
insist on 坚持	keep... from 使……不
look forward to 盼望	object to 反对
persist in 坚持（做下去）	prevent... from 阻止（做某事）

refrain from 忍住（不做某事）　　set about 着手（做某事）

spend... in 花在（某事上）　　stop... from 阻止（做某事）

succeed in 成功（做好某事）　　suspect... of 怀疑

take part in 参加（做某事）　　thank... for 谢谢（做某事）

think of 想（做某事）

另外，很多介词都可和动名词构成短语作状语等：

On reaching the city, he called up Lester. 一抵达那座城市，他就给莱斯特打了电话。

He looked surprised at seeing us. 他看到我们时显得很吃惊。

Without waiting for any reply, he left the room. 他不等回答就走出房去。

下面介词都可以这样用：

about	after	against	at	before	besides
by	for	from	in	into	on
since	to	upon	without		

此外介词还可和动名词构成短语修饰名词：

I need something for killing flies. 我需要一种灭蝇的药。

He couldn't conceal his surprise at seeing her there. 他无法掩饰看到她在那里时的惊讶情绪。

下面名词都可以有这样的修饰语：

apology (for)	art (of)	astonishment (at)	chance (of)
excuse (for)	habit (of)	honour (of)	hope (of)
idea (of)	importance (of)	intention (of)	means (of)
necessity (of)	objection (to)	opportunity (of)	plan (for)
possibility (of)	process (of)	reason (for)	right (of)
skill (in)	surprise (at)	way (of)	

（3）作定语或构成合成名词

动名词也常常用作名词的修饰语，也可构成合成词，如：

singing competition 歌咏比赛　　swimming pool 游泳池

dining-car 餐车　　sleeping-pills 安眠药片

opening speech 开幕词　　milling-machine 铣床

close-planting 密植　　deep-ploughing 深耕

△现在分词也可作名词修饰语，两者的差别是现在分词往往表示所修饰名词的动作，而动名词则不然。试比较下面的词组：

带现在分词的词组	带动名词的词组
a waiting train 等候着的火车	a waiting room 候车室
a sleeping child 睡觉的孩子	a sleeping pill 安眠药片
working people 劳动人民	working conditions 劳动条件
a flying saucer 飞碟	a flying suit 飞行衣

分词常可改成定语从句，如：a waiting train 可改为 a train that is waiting，而 a waiting room 只能改成 a room for waiting。

（4）作表语

Her job is operating a bulldozer. 她的工作是开推土机。

The real problem is getting to know the needs of the customers. 真正的问题是了解消费者的需要。

△有时动名词前面有一个代词（宾格）、物主代词、名词或名词所有格，表示它是谁的动作：

I don't mind you (her) going with us. 我不介意你（她）和我们一道去。

Mary's grumbling annoyed him. 玛丽的嘟嘟囔囔使他很烦。

有时还有完成形式或被动形式：

I apologize for not having kept my promise. 我没遵守诺言，向你表示歉意。

They insisted on being treated as equals. 他们坚持对他们要平等相待。

❀ 现在分词的用法

现在分词起其他许多作用：

（1）构成进行时态或进行式：

所有进行时态均由助动词"be + 现在分词"构成：

Her heart was beating violently. 她的心猛烈地跳着。

I'll be here. I'll be helping you. 我将待在这里，帮助你们。

一些其他进行式也由它构成：

It's nice to be sitting here with you. 现在和你坐在一起很好。

You must be joking. 你准是在开玩笑。

（2）用作表语（或称补语）：

The food smells inviting. 这菜香味怡人。

The matter is pressing. 这件事很紧急。

能这样用的分词很多，不少都已变成了形容词，常见的有：

alarming	amazing	amusing	annoying
appalling	astonishing	bewildering	boring
challenging	charming	confusing	convincing
depressing	disappointing	discouraging	disgusting
distressing	disturbing	embarrassing	enchanting
encouraging	exciting	frightening	humiliating
inspiring	interesting	inviting	misleading
obliging	pleasing	pressing	promising
refreshing	rewarding	shocking	surprising
terrifying	thrilling	touching	tiring

（3）用作定语：

It's a booming town. 这是一座迅速繁荣起来的城市。

Food will not get cheaper under existing conditions. 在现在情况下，食品不会便宜下来。

除了上面列出的现在分词外，还有不少分词可以这样用，如：

bleeding	booming	declining	decreasing	developing
diminishing	dwindling	dying	existing	following
growing	increasing	leading	living	loving
missing	moving	prevailing	recurring	reigning
remaining	resounding	retreating	rising	ruling
running	smiling	surrounding	telling	threatening
travelling	trying			

在用现在分词作定语时，它在意思上接近一个定语从句，如：

developing countries ＝ countries that are developing

a growing city ＝ a city that is growing

在更多情况下，作定语的分词（短语）都放在所修饰词的后面，意思上和从句差不多：

There is a gentleman asking (=who is asking) to see you. 有一位先生要求见你。

Anyone following (=who follows) this advice could find himself in trouble. 照这个建议做的人可能会遇到麻烦。

有时还可构成合成词作定语：

a fine-looking building 一座漂亮的楼房

oil-bearing crops 油料作物

far-reaching effects 深远的影响

（4）用作状语（现在分词多表示主语的动作）：

The manager approached us smiling. 经理笑着向我们走来。

Glancing at the clock, I saw it was midnight. 我望了望钟表，看见已经是午夜了。

Not knowing what to do, I went home. 我不知道怎么办好，就回家了。

有时这类状语可由 when 和 while 引起：

Be careful when crossing the street. 过街时要当心。

Don't mention this while talking to him. 和他谈话时，不要提及此事。

现在分词如果不表示主语的动作，它前面可以有一个名词表示它是谁的动作（可称为它逻辑上的主语）：

We explored the caves, Peter acting as guide. 由彼得做向导，我们探察了那些洞穴。(Peter acted as guide)

The shower being over, we continued to march. 阵雨过后，我们继续前进。(When the shower was over)

Weather permitting (If the weather permits), we'll have an outing tomorrow. 如果天气允许，我们明天将出去郊游。

这种结构可称作独立结构（absolute construction）。

现在分词作状语时，它表示的动作通常和主语表示的动作同时或几乎同时发生。如果它表示的动作发生较早，要用现在分词的完成形式：

Having slept (As I had slept) for twelve hours, I felt marvellous. 由于我睡了 12 个钟头的觉，我感到舒服极了。

Ash, having forgotten (When he had forgotten) his fear, had become bored and restless. 阿什在忘掉他的恐惧之后，变得无聊和不安起来。

（5）构成复合宾语：

现在分词可以在一些动词后和一名词或代词构成复合宾语：

My clumsy mistake set everybody laughing. 我笨拙的错误使大家都笑了起来。

She caught me smoking a cigarette. 她撞见我抽烟。

有相当多动词后面可跟这种宾语，常见的如：

feel	find	get	have	hear	keep
leave	notice	see	set	start	watch

其中有些（如 see, hear, feel, notice, watch 等），既可跟现在分词构成的复合宾语，也可跟不带 to 的不定式构成的复合宾语，两者的差别是现在分词表示正在进行的动作，而不定式表示完成的动作：

I saw a girl watering the flowers. (She was watering the flowers.) 我看见一个女孩儿在浇花。

I saw the man sit down. (He sat down.) 我看见那个人坐了下来。

有时两者之间没有什么差别：

Did you notice him leave (leaving) the house? 你听见他离开这座房子了吗？

I saw the train coming (come) into the station. 我看见火车开进站来。

有几个现在分词可起连词作用：

Supposing he does not come, what shall we do? 要是他不来怎么办？

You may go out providing you do your homework first. 如果你先把作业做好，你可以出去。

还有些现在分词可用作介词：

There was nothing in the street excepting two dogs. 除了两条狗，街上什么都没有。

Everybody here has the influenza including myself. 包括我在内所有人都患上了流感。

这类分词有：

according to	barring	concerning	considering
depending on	excepting	excluding	following
including	owing to	regarding	

8. 修饰语

修饰语指修饰名词的单词、短语和从句，特别是放在名词后面的那些，主要由以下成分充当：

❀ 形容词及它引起的短语：

I'll do everything <u>possible</u> to help you. 我将尽我所能来帮助你。

He invented a machine <u>capable</u> of sending off signals. 他发明了一种能发送信号的机器。

❀ 副词：

I could see the river <u>far down below</u>. 我可以看见下方远处的河流。

The clouds <u>above</u> began to get thicker. 上面的乌云越来越浓。

❀ 介词短语：

He painted a girl <u>with a pigtail</u>. 他画了一个梳辫子的姑娘。

He seemed to be a man <u>without a care</u>. 他似乎是一个无忧无虑的人。

❀ 不定式短语：

The enemy failed in their attempt <u>to land on the island</u>. 敌人在岛上登陆的企图失败了。

Perhaps in years <u>to come</u> we shall meet again. 或许，在未来的岁月中我们还会相见。

❀ 分词短语：

We lived in a room <u>facing the south</u>. 我们住在一间朝南的房子里。

These were the chief problems <u>confronting us</u>. 这些是我们面临的主要问题。

❀ 定语从句：

You can take any room <u>you like</u>. 你愿住哪间房就住哪间房。

There are some people here <u>(who) I should like you to meet</u>. 这儿有几个人我想让你见见。

9. 不定式

不定式是动词的一种形式，多数前面都带 **to**，例如：

I'm so glad <u>to see</u> you. 我很高兴见到你。

这种动词非常有用，在句子中可作各种成分：

作宾语：

He offered to help us. 他主动提出帮助我们。

Mary begged to go with us. 玛丽恳求和我们一道去。

在很多动词后都可以跟这样的宾语，常见的有：

afford	agree	aim	arrange	ask
attempt	beg	begin	care	choose
consent	continue	dare	decide	demand
desire	determine	endeavour	expect	fail
forget	hate	help	hope	intend
learn	like	love	manage	mean
neglect	offer	plan	prefer	prepare
pretend	promise	refuse	remember	start
trouble	try	undertake	volunteer	vote
wait	want	wish		

有些动词后的宾语由一个连接代（副）词引起的不定式短语构成：

They taught me how to repair farm tools. 他们教我怎样修理农具。

We must decide whether to go or to stay. 我们得决定去还是留。

构成复合宾语（多由名词或代词 + 不定式构成）：

They encouraged me to try again. 他们鼓励我再试一下。

He wants you to call him back at 11. 他要你 11 点钟给他回电话。

有些动词（如 feel, have, hear, let, make, notice, see, watch 等）后的复合结构中不定式不带 to：

What made you think like that? 什么使你这样想？

Don't forget to have him call me tonight. 别忘了让他今晚给我打电话。

甚至在 look at 和 listen to 之后也如此：

Look at the boy run. 瞧这个男孩儿跑。

He sat listening to him climb the stairs. 他坐着听他爬上楼来。

但这类句子变为被动结构时，不定式的 to 不能省略：

They were made to work day and night. 他们被迫日夜干活。

She was often heard to sing this song. 人们常常听到她唱这首歌。

作状语，可表示目的、结果、原因等：

They ran over to welcome the delegates. 他们跑过去欢迎代表们。（目的）

What have I said to make you so angry? 我说了什么话使你这样生气？
（结果）

We jumped with joy to hear the news. 听了这消息我们高兴得跳了起来。
（原因）

在某些作表语的形容词后也可用不定式作状语：

She was surprised to find him there. 她发现他在那儿很吃惊。

We are eager to take part in the work. 我们急于参加这项工作。

另外，不定式还可用作状语，修饰整个句子：

To be frank, we don't trust him. 坦率地说，我们不信任他。

To tell you the truth, I don't like the idea. 说老实话，我不喜欢这个想法。

作定语：

I have a lot of things to do tonight. 今晚，我有很多事要做。

There is nothing to be worried about. 没有什么值得发愁的。

I don't have many chances to talk to him. 我没有多少机会和他讲话。

There is no need to worry. 没有必要发愁。

作主语：

To err is human, to forgive is divine. 犯错误是人之常情，能宽恕则难能可贵。（谚语）

To know something about English is one thing; to know English is quite another. 懂点儿英语是一回事，掌握英语完全是另一回事。

但把不定式放在句首的情况是很少的，在多数情况下都在句首用一个先行词 it 作主语，而把不定式表示的真正主语放到后面，这样可使句子显得更平稳：

It's better to be on the safe side. 稳重行事还是比较好一点儿。

It takes 30 hours to get there by train. 坐火车到那里要 30 个小时。

在许多形容词（如 **all right, difficult, easy, foolish, good, hard, nice, possible, proper, right, unwise, wise, wrong** 等）后面可用这种不定式作主语的结构，特别是它后面有时有一个 of 引起的短语：

(It's) Awfully good of you to come and meet us. (=You're awfully good to...) 非常感谢你来接我们。

It's unwise of them to turn down the proposal. (=They are unwise to...) 他们拒绝这个建议是不明智的。

作表语（补语）：

Her only wish was to <u>do something for him</u>. 她唯一的愿望是为他做一些事。

Your job is to <u>type the memo</u>. 你的任务是把备忘录打出来。

不定式前面有时可加一个用 **for** 引起的短语，表示这是谁的动作：

His idea is <u>for us</u> to travel in separate cars. 他的意思是我们分乘不同的汽车。

It's not easy <u>for a foreigner</u> to learn Chinese. 外国人学汉语是不容易的。

另外，不定式还可有进行形式、完成形式和被动形式，也有否定式：

It's nice <u>to be sitting</u> here with you. 现在和你一起坐在这里很好。

You were silly <u>not to have locked</u> your car. 你没锁车，太傻了。

 在情态动词后的动词原形是不带 to 的不定式，它们将在情态动词有关各节中讨论。

10. 状语

状语主要修饰动词，说明动作发生的时间、地点、方式及背景等。它主要由下面这些表示：

❀ 副词：

We'll have to act <u>quickly</u>. 我们得赶快行动。

She's doing <u>well</u> in school. 她在学校学习很好。

❀ 介词短语：

She's working <u>in a computer company</u>. 她在一家电脑公司工作。

He traveled <u>around the world</u> for a few years. 他在世界各地旅游了几年。

❀ 词组：

I didn't see her <u>this morning</u>. 今天早上我没有看到她。

We went there <u>once a year</u>. 我们一年去那里一次。

❀ 现在分词（短语）：

The girls are busy <u>packing</u>. 姑娘们在忙着收拾东西。

The boy came <u>running</u> into the room. 那男孩跑着来到屋里。

❀ 过去分词（短语）：

She entered, <u>accompanied by her daughter</u>. 她由女儿陪同走进屋来。

<u>Disappointed</u> he returned to his hometown. 他很失望，就回老家了。

❀ 不定式（短语）：

Her sister came over <u>to help</u>. 她妹妹过来帮忙。

<u>To save</u> the child, he laid down his life. 为了救那个孩子，他献出了自己的生命

❀ 形容词：

He returned home, <u>weary and exhausted</u>. 他回到家时，疲惫不堪。

She ran over, <u>eager to help</u>. 她跑了过来，很想帮忙。

❀ 名词：

He was <u>way</u> behind others. 他远比别人落后。

A tube of toothpaste can last me <u>months</u>. 一管牙膏够我用好几个月。

❀ 从句：

Make hay <u>while the sun shines</u>. 趁热打铁。（谚语）

Stay <u>where you are</u>. 站在原地。

11. 补语

complement 指 "补语"，可以是主语的补语（也可称为表语），用在系动词后，与它构成合成谓语。有很多东西可以作主语的补语，如形容词：

His advice proved <u>sound</u>. 他的劝告证明是对的。

The temperature has stayed <u>hot</u> this week. 这星期气温一直很高。

能跟这种补语的系动词有：

appear	feel	keep	remain	stay
be	get	look	seem	taste
become	go	pass	smell	turn
come	grow	prove	sound	

名词：

You'll make <u>a good husband</u>. 你会是一个好丈夫。

It sounds <u>a good idea</u>. 这听起来是个好主意。

We can remain <u>friends</u>. 我们可以继续做朋友。

能跟这种补语的系动词有：

be	constitute	look	remain	sound
become	feel	make	represent	turn
comprise	form	prove	seem	

代词：

Is this one <u>yours</u>? 这一个是你的吗？

It's <u>nothing to be ashamed of</u>. 这没有什么可耻之处。

介词短语：

Who is <u>on duty</u>? 今天谁值班？

This is <u>against the law</u>. 这是违法的。

副词：

Are you <u>through</u> with the work? 你干完了吗？

I'll be <u>round</u> in a little while. 我一会儿就来。

从句：

That's <u>where we differ</u>. 这是我们的分歧所在。

My idea is <u>that we still have a long way to go</u>. 我的意见是，我们还有很多路要走。

❀ 在多数情况下我们都用系动词 **be** 和主语补语构成谓语。有少数其他动词后面有时也可跟一个补语，例如：

He was born <u>an orphan</u>. 他生下来就成了孤儿。

She lay <u>awake</u> the whole night. 她整夜躺着没睡着。

❀ 另外，在某些动词后，宾语也可有补语。宾语的补语主要是：

形容词：

Do you think it <u>necessary</u>? 你认为这有必要吗？

Facts have proved these worries <u>groundless</u>. 事实证明，这些忧虑是没有根据的。

名词：

They made her <u>head of the delegation</u>. 他们让她当了代表团团长。

Don't be so formal. Call me <u>Jim</u>. 不要这样正式，叫我吉姆好了。

They appointed him <u>ambassador to the UN</u>. 他们任命他为驻联合国大使。

现在分词：

I saw him <u>working</u> in the garden. 我看见他在花园里干活。

Did you notice her <u>leaving</u> the house? 你看到她离开这屋子了吗？

过去分词：

I hate to see any bird <u>killed</u>. 我不愿意看到鸟被打死。

I have heard him <u>criticized</u> many times. 我曾多次听到他受到批评。

不带 to 的不定式：

It's so quiet that you could hear a pin <u>drop</u>. 是那样安静，针掉到地下都听得见。

I saw her face <u>go</u> pale. 我看到她的脸变得苍白。

介词短语：

I'm glad to find you <u>in good health</u>. 我很高兴看到你身体健康。

We could hear the children <u>at play</u> outside. 我们可以听见孩子们在外面玩耍。

副词：

I'm glad to find you <u>in</u>. 我很高兴看到你在家。

He was pleased to see her <u>back</u>. 看见她回来了，他很高兴。

12. 从句

clause 是一个包含主语和谓语的结构。

❀ 简单句（simple sentence）只包含一个这样的主谓结构：

What are you looking for? 你在找什么？

We took a taxi home. 我们坐出租车回家了。

❀ 并列句（compound sentence）包含两个或更多这种结构（称为分句），由并列连词连接：

I went and she went also. 我去了，她也去了。

I would have written before but I have been ill. 本该早给你写信的，但我病了。

You can come now or you can meet us there later. 你可以现在来，也可以稍晚和我们在那里碰头。

❀ 复合句（complex sentence）包含一个这样的主谓结构充当一个句子成分，称为从句（subordinate clause），与它相对，句子的主要部分（即它的主语和谓语）称为主句（main clause）。根据在句中的不同作用，从句又分为主语从句、宾语从句、表语从句、定语从句、状语从句等。

13. 关系从句

关系从句也称定语从句（attributive clause），由于是关系代词或关系副词引导的，因此也称为关系从句。

关系代词有 who, whom, whose, which, that 五个词。关系副词有 where, when, why 三个词。它们都可引导从句做定语，在从句中这些关系代词或副词也担任一定成分，如作主语、宾语、状语等（画线部分为关系从句）：

The girl who spoke is my best friend. 发言的姑娘是我最好的朋友。（从句修饰 girl，在从句中 who 作主语，代表 girl。）

The girl to whom I spoke is my cousin. 我和她讲话的那个姑娘是我的表妹。（从句修饰 girl, whom 在从句中作介词 to 的宾语。）

A mental patient is one whose mind is diseased. 精神病人是大脑有病的人。（从句修饰 one, whose 在从句中修饰 mind。）

She was not in the train which (that) arrived just now. 她不在刚到的那列车上。（从句修饰 train，在从句中 which 或 that 作主语。）

This is the town where I was born. 这就是我出生的城市。（从句修饰 town, where 作状语，修饰 was born。）

At the time when I saw him, he was quite well. 我见到他时，他身体相当好。（从句修饰 time，在从句中 when 作副词，修饰 saw。）

These are the reasons why we do it. 这就是我们这样做的原因。（从句修饰 reasons，在从句中 why 是副词，修饰 do。）

这类句子可说是由两个句子合成的：

He has got a girlfriend. She works in a hospital.

可合并成：He has got a girlfriend who works in a hospital.

Here is an article. It might interest you.

可合并成：Here is an article which might interest you.

❀ 在关系代词中 who 代表人，在作宾语时用 whom 这个形式，whose 代表一个物主代词：

He is a good physician who cures himself. 能给自己治病的是好医生。（谚语）

Then I telephoned the doctor whom Charles recommended. 然后，我给

查尔斯推荐的医生打了电话。

I have never met a girl <u>whose</u> intellect could match hers. 我从未遇到过一个姑娘，智力可与她相比。

which 代表物或动物：

He lives in the house <u>which</u> (that) is opposite ours. 他住在我们家对面的房子里。

The dog <u>which</u> was lost has been found. 丢失的狗找到了。

That is a factor <u>which</u> we mustn't neglect. 这是我们不能忽视的一个因素。

that 可以代表人也可代表物：

He <u>that</u> would eat the fruit must climb the tree. 想吃果子的就得爬树。（谚语）

She is the girl <u>that</u> you saw in school. 她就是你在学校见到的那个姑娘。

在代表人时，用 who 比用 that 的时候多。在代表物时，用 that 比用 which 时更多。在用作宾语时，whom，that，which 都常常省略：

This is the man (whom/that) I gave it to. 这就是我把东西交给他的那个人。

I have just met a lady (whom/that) I saw last week. 我刚才见到了我上星期见到的那个小姐。

但在紧跟一个介词时不能省略：

This is the boy <u>to whom</u> I gave the money. (但可说 This is the boy I gave the money to.)

This is a subject <u>about which</u> we might argue for a long while. (但可说 This is a subject we might argue for a long while about.)

关系副词 **where** 引导地点状语从句，意思接近 **in (at) which**：

Do you know a shop <u>where</u> I can find sandals? 你知不知道我能买凉鞋的商店？

We are in a position <u>where</u> we may lose a large sum of money. 我们在此处境下可能会损失一大笔钱。

关系副词 **when** 引导表示时间的定语从句，意思接近 **at which time**：

There are moments <u>when</u> I forget all about it. 有时候，我完全忘了这件事。

There came a day <u>when</u> the rain fell in torrents. 有一天，下着滂沱大雨。

关系副词 **why** 引导表示原因的定语从句（有时 **why** 可以省略）：

That's no reason why you should leave. 这不是你该离去的理由。

That's one of the reasons (why) I asked you to come. 这是我要你来的原因之一。

❀ 定语从句有两种，一种是限定性定语从句（**restrictive attributive clause**），一种是非限定性定语从句（**non-restrictive attributive clause**）。限定性定语从句限制所修饰词的意思，使之表示特定的人或东西，如果把它去掉，意思就不清楚，甚至没有意义：

Paris is a city I've always wanted to visit. 巴黎是我一直想访问的一座城市。（如只说 Paris is a city，就没有什么意思。）

People who take physical exercise live longer. 从事体育锻炼的人活得长些。（如只说 People live longer，就没有意义。）

由此可看出限定性定语从句在句中占重要地位。在日常口语中，大部分定语从句都属于这类：

Is that the seat you reserved for me? 这是你留给我的座位吗？

Show me the coat you bought. 把你买的大衣给我瞧瞧。

前面所给例句也都属于这一类。

非限定性定语从句多用在书面语中，如果去掉，句子还可以成立，使用它只是为了多提供一点情况。在多数情况下都用一个逗号把它和句子的其他部分分开，在译为汉语时多译成两个并列句：

That afternoon there was a search for Sophia, whom no one had seen since lunch. 那天下午大家都在找索菲娅，午饭后谁都没见过她。

Chopin, whose works are world-famous, composed some of this music in this room. 肖邦的作品是世界驰名的，有些音乐就是在这间屋子里谱写的。

They went to the Royal Theatre, where they saw Ibsen's *Peer Gynt*. 他们去了皇家剧院，在那里他们看了易卜生的《皮尔·金特》。

关系代词 that 不能用在非限定性定语从句中。why 后也不跟这种从句。

❀ 在非限定性定语从句中，**which** 起很大作用，可以说大部分这类从句都是由它引导的。它引导的从句一般修饰一个名词：

The current, which is very rapid, makes the river dangerous. 水流湍急，这条河很危险。

My new car, which I paid several thousand pounds for, is not running well. 我的新车花了我好几千英镑，却不太好开。

有时和介词一起用：

This morning some port wine came, for which I have to thank you. 今天早上送来了一些波尔图葡萄酒，为此我得向你道谢。

There are two (bottles) left, one of which is almost finished and the other of which is not quite. 只剩两瓶，一瓶快喝完了，另一瓶没完全喝完。

which 有时在从句中起定语的作用：

He spoke in Greek, which language I could only follow with difficulty. 他讲的是希腊语，这种语言我只能勉强听懂。

Tom spent four years in college, during which time he learned French. 汤姆在大学度过了四年，在此期间他学了法语。

这类从句有时还代表前面整个句子或句子的一部分：

This I did at nine o'clock, after which I sat reading the paper. 我九点钟干这个，之后我就坐着看报。

She may be late, in which case we ought to wait for her. 她可能晚到，那样我们就要等等她。

❀ 在不少情况下关系代词可以省略。在限定性定语从句中，如果关系代词在从句中作宾语，则常常可以省略掉：

The people (who/that) you were talking to are Swedes. 你和他们谈话的是瑞典人。

Have you anything (which/that) you want to leave with us? 你有什么东西要留在我们这儿吗？

在某些表示时间、地点、方式的词后，关系代词或副词在口语中有时省略：

I'll never forget the day (that) we met. 我永远不会忘记我们见面的日子。

The reason (that) I bought red roses is that Jane likes them. 我买红玫瑰的原因是简喜欢它们。

14. 祈使句

祈使句中的动词都用动词原形（即不带 to 的不定式），可以表示命令、请求、叮嘱、邀请、劝告等：

<u>Fasten</u> your seat belt. 系好安全带。

<u>Be</u> sure to get here before nine. 务必九点以前到。

否定形式多用 don't 开始，也可用 never 引起：

<u>Don't</u> trouble to come over yourself. 你不必费神亲自来了。

<u>Don't</u> worry. I'll soon be all right. 别担心，我很快就会好的。

主语通常不表示出来，但为了表示话是对谁说的，也可表示出来或加称呼语：

<u>Parents with children</u> go to the front. 带孩子的家长到前头去。

<u>Mary</u>, come here—<u>everybody</u> else stay where you are. 玛丽到这里来，其他人都留在原地。

有时前面加 you 只是为了强调，或表示"不高兴""厌烦"等情绪：

<u>You</u> do it right away. 你给我马上就去做。

<u>You</u> take your hands off me! 把你的手给我拿开！

为了强调，前面也可以加 do：

<u>Do</u> be quiet! 务必安静！

<u>Do</u> forgive me—I didn't mean to be rude. 务请原谅，我无心对你粗鲁无礼。

有时加一个 please 使语气显得客气一些：

<u>Please</u> do not lean out of the window. 请不要把身子探向窗外。

Come in, <u>please</u>. 请进。

有时后面可加一个简短问句：

Give me a hand, <u>will you</u>? 帮我一个忙，好吗？

Don't tell anybody, <u>will you</u>? 不要告诉任何人，好吗？

这类句子有时可起条件句的作用：

<u>Go straight</u> on and you'll see a church. 径直往前走，你会看到一座教堂。

<u>Stir</u>, and you are a dead man. 动一下，就要你的命。

此外，let 也可引起祈使句：

<u>Let</u> me see. Do I need to go shopping today? 让我想想，今天要不要出去买东西？

<u>Let's</u> put the matter to the vote. 咱们对这件事进行表决。

否定结构多在 let's 后加 not 构成，也可在前面加 don't：

<u>Let's</u> <u>not</u> say anything about it. 这事咱们谁也别说。

<u>Don't</u> let the baby fall. 别让宝宝掉下来了。

15. 倒装句

一个句子如果主语在前谓语在后，就是自然语序。反之，如果主语在后谓语或谓语的一部分提前，则称倒装语序，这种句子称为倒装句。下面是倒装句的主要情况：

疑问句多数为倒装句：

Are you free tonight? 你今晚有空儿吗？

How are things going? 情况怎么样？

但若主语是疑问词，或由疑问词修饰，则句子用自然语序：

Who is standing there? 谁站在那儿？

How many people are going with you? 多少人和你一道去？

由 **there** 和 **here** 引起的句子多用倒装语序：

Where bees are, there is honey. 有蜂就有蜜。（谚语）

There were many things to be done. 有很多事要做。

Here comes a bus! 来了一辆公共汽车！

如果主语为人称代词，则可用自然语序：

Here he comes. 瞧他来了。

There she is. 她就在那儿。

由 **so** 引起的表示"也如此"的句子，通常要用倒装语序：

"We must leave now." "So must we." "我们得走了。" "我们也得走了。"

If Julia can do it, so can I. 如果朱丽娅干得了，我也干得了。

由 **neither**、**nor** 引起的句子也如此：

If you won't go, neither shall I. 如果你不去，我也不去。

"I won't do such a thing." "Nor will I." "我不会这样做。" "我也不会。"

省略了 **if** 的虚拟条件句，语序也要倒装（用 **had, were, should** 开头）：

Had I been informed earlier, I could have done something. 如果早一点儿通知我，我还可能做一点儿什么。

Were she here, she would support the proposal. 如果她在这里，她会支持这项建议。

Should anyone call, tell him to wait for me here. 万一有人找我，让他在这里等我。

某些让步从句中也可能用倒装语序：

Come what may, we'll always stand by you. 不管发生什么情况，我们

都会站在你一边。

Try as I would, I could not persuade him to give up the idea. 尽管我努力这样做，我却没能劝说他放弃这个想法。

以 never, little, often, (not) only, not until, hardly, scarcely 等引起的句子常用倒装语序：

Never shall we bow down to our enemies. 我们绝不会向敌人弯腰屈膝。

Little does he care whether we live or die. 他才不会在乎我们的死活。

Often did we warn them not to do so. 我们曾多次警告他们不要这样做。

Only then could the work be seriously begun. 只有到那时，这项工作才能认真地开始。

Not only did he speak more correctly, but he spoke more easily. 他不仅说得更正确，而且讲得更不费劲了。

Hardly had he arrived when she started complaining. 他刚到，她就开始发起牢骚来。

Under no circumstances must we relax our vigilance. 在任何情况下，我们都不应放松警惕。

Little did he realise the danger he faced. 他几乎没意识到他面对的危险。

当一个句子没有宾语，而主语又比较长时，常可把状语连同谓语放到主语前头：

Before them lay miles of undulating moorland. 他们前面是一片高低起伏的荒原。

From the distance came occasional shots. 从远处传来零星的枪声。

Through the window came in wafts of intoxicating fragrance. 从窗口吹入一阵阵醉人的清香。

Directly in front of them stood a great castle. 正对着他们矗立着一座巍峨的城堡。

有时可以把表语和系动词 be 提到主语前面：

Near the southern end of the village was a large pear orchard. 靠近村子南头，有一座很大的梨园。

Hidden underground is a wealth of gold, silver, copper and zinc. 地下埋藏了大量的金、银、铜、锌。

在描写一个情景时，有时为了使景象更生动，可以把 out, in, up,

down, away 之类状语放在主语前面，同时把主语和谓语的位置倒换：

Up went the arrow into the air. 飕的一声箭射上了天空。

Following the roar, out rushed a tiger from among the bushes. 一声吼叫，呼地从林子里冲出一只老虎。

在某些句型中需用倒装语序：

Long live peace! 和平万岁！

May our friendship last forever! 祝我们的友谊万古长青。

另外，在引语后，主语常可放到动词后面：

"Where do you live?" asked May.（May asked 也可以，或说 she asked。）

"Listen!" whispered my mother.（或 she whispered。）

△如果主语为人称代词，则仍放在动词前面。

16. 问句

问句主要有四类：

❀ 一般疑问句（**general question**），也可称为"是非问句"（**Yes/No Question**），一般用 **Yes** 或 **No** 回答：

"Are you interested in going?" "Yes." "你有兴趣去吗?" "有。"

"Do you know that lady?" "No." "你认识那位女士吗?" "不认识。"

这种问句都用助动词、情态动词或动词 be 开头，读升调。

❀ 特殊疑问句（**special question**），也被称作 **Wh-** 问句，因为它们都是用疑问词开始的：

What's happened to your sister? 你妹妹怎么啦？

How are you going to do it? 你准备怎样办？

这种问句都以疑问词开头，后面结构基本上和一般疑问句相同，通常用降调。主语由疑问词表示或修饰时，句子用自然语序：

Who told you that? 这是谁告诉你的？（Who 作句子主语）

How many people are coming to join us? 多少人来参加我们的活动？（How many 修饰主语）

❀ 选择问句（**alternative question**），由两部分组成，由 **or** 连接，问哪部分属实：

Are you from the South or from the North? 你是南方人还是北方人？

Does she study or work there? 她在那里学习还是工作？

or 前的部分通常用升调，后面部分用降调。句子结构和一般疑问句差不多。

❀ 反意问句（disjunctive question），先提出一个情况或看法，问是否属实。前面是一个陈述句，后面加一个简短问句，称为 Question tag。一般前面用降调，后面用升调，简短问句和陈述句的动词形式要一致（用同一时态或同一情态动词），陈述句为肯定句时，简短问句用否定结构：

You've got my E-mail, haven't you? 你接到了我的电子邮件了，对吧？

They can do the work by themselves, can't they? 这工作他们自己就能干，对吧？

如果前面是否定句，则简短问句需用肯定结构，在回答这种问题时要小心，答案为否定句时，前面要用 No，若是肯定回答则用 Yes，这和汉语是不一样的：

"She wasn't here at that time, was she?" "No, she wasn't." "那时她不在这儿，对吧。" "对，那时她不在这里。"

"You aren't interested in sports, are you?" "But yes. I like sports very much." "你对运动没兴趣，对吧？" "不，我很喜欢运动。"

带 never, hardly, seldom 的句子也算否定句：

You've never been in Hong Kong, have you? 你从没去过香港，对吧？

You seldom play tennis, do you? 你很少打网球，对吧？

在你对你说的话十分肯定时，后面的简短问句也可以用降调：

Shanghai is the biggest city in China, isn't it? (↘)？上海是中国的第一大城市，对吧？

It's a beautiful day, isn't it (↘)？今天天气好极了，是吧？

这种简短问句也可加在祈使句后：

Give me a hand, will you? 帮我一下好吗？

Let's take a taxi, shall we? 我们坐出租车去，好吗？

在个别情况下，特别是在表示感兴趣、惊讶、关怀及其他反应时，有时简短问句和前面句子可以同为肯定句结构：

So you're getting married, are you? How nice! 你要结婚了，是吗？真不错！

She wants to win the championship, does she? 她想拿冠军，是吧？

有时提出揣想、征求对方意见时也可以这样用：

You're mother's at home, is she? 你妈在家，对吧？

You can eat eel, can you? 你能吃鳝鱼，对吧？

还有一些其他类型的问句：

❀ 陈述问句（declarative question）——有时一个陈述句通过使用升调，可以变成问句：

You're working in the same department? 你们在同一部门工作？

This is your office? 这是你的办公室？

You think we shouldn't do that? 你认为我们不应当这样做？

❀ 回应问句（echo question）——别人说一句话时，可接着提一个问句：

"I'm getting married." "You're getting married?" "我要结婚了。" "你要结婚了吗？"

"The boss wants to see you." "What for?" "老板要见你。" "为什么？"

❀ 否定问句（negative question）——常表示惊讶或责难，有时译为"难道……"：

Can't you speak Mandarin? 你（难道）不能讲普通话？

Didn't you say you'd phone me? 你不是说了要给我打电话的吗？

也有时表示一种赞叹，常用降调，可译为惊叹句：

Isn't it a marvellous film? 这电影真精彩！

Hasn't he grown! 他长得真高了！

有时可提出建议、邀请、看法等：

Don't you think we should try again? 你不觉得我们该再试试？

It's a fine book, don't you agree? 这是一本好书，你同意吧？

在回答这种问题时要注意，如果是肯定回答，要用 Yes，否则用 No：

"Don't you want to go with us?" "Yes, I do." "难道你不想和我们一道去？" "不，我想去。"

"Aren't you from the same city?" "No, we aren't." "你们难道不是来自同一座城市？" "是的，我们不是来自同一座城市。"

❀ 修辞性问句（rhetorical question）——这种问句并不要求人回答：

Is that a reason for despair? 这难道是灰心丧气的理由？

Why don't you take a taxi? 你何不坐出租车去？

17. 否定句

一般句子的否定结构的构成方式可概述如下：

借助助动词 do：

She doesn't know English. 她不懂英语。

Don't be late for supper. 吃晚饭别晚了。

在情态动词、助动词或系动词后加 not：

We won't be able to come tonight. 我们今晚来不了了。

She hasn't got well yet. 她还未痊愈。

在不定式、现在分词及动名词前加 not：

She hesitated, not knowing what to say. 她犹豫了一下，不知说什么好。

They criticized him for not giving others help. 他们批评他不帮助别人。

在句子的其他成分前加 not：

Not a soul was to be seen. 一个人也看不见。

It was a declaration of rights, not a guarantee of rights. 它是权利宣言，却不是权利的保证。

The most important aspect of a sentence is its meaning, not its form. 一个句子最重要的（方面）是它的意义，而不是它的形式。

用 not 代表一个否定结构的从句：

Drop that gun! If not, you'll be sorry. 放下枪，否则你会后悔。

I am to get a royalty but not until it gets into its second thousand. 我会得到版税，但要等出到第二个一千册时才会有。

❀ 有些带宾语从句的句子，特别是动词为 think, believe, suppose, imagine 等时，我们通常把主要谓语变为否定结构，而不是把从句的谓语变为否定结构，尽管否定的意思是在从句上（这从句子的译文可以看出）：

I don't believe she will like the idea. 我相信她不会赞成这个想法。

I don't suppose you've been here before. 我想你从前没来过这里。

但在 hope 后可以跟否定结构的从句：

I hope he won't be away long. 我希望他不会离开太久。

另外某些宾语从句可以带否定结构，特别是表示惊讶时：

Oh, I thought you weren't coming. 哦，我还以为你不来了哩。

So it's you! I thought you'd never be here again. 啊，是你！我以为你再也不会来了哩。

在 **appear, seem, expect, happen** 等跟不定式的句子，也有类似情况，在日常口语中常可把前面动词变为否定结构，如把不定式变为否定式则显得过于正规：

Jim doesn't seem to like you. 吉姆似乎不太喜欢你。

（Jim seems not to like you. 比较文雅）

I don't expect her to turn up at the meeting. 我估计她不会来开会。

❀ 否定疑问句有几种用法：

表示惊讶或不快（常可译为"难道"）：

Didn't you go and see your mother yesterday? 你难道昨天没去看你母亲？（我以为你会的。）

Hasn't he got up? It's ten o'clock.（难道）他还没起床？已经 10 点了。

表示赞叹（常可译为惊叹句，句子用降调）：

Isn't the baby cute? 这宝宝真可爱！

Isn't a lovely day? 今天天气真好！

表示责难：

Can't you walk a little faster? 你不能走快点儿吗？

Didn't I tell you to come early? 我不是让你早点儿来的吗？

较客气地提出请求、邀请、看法等：

Why don't you come and spend the weekend with us? 你何不来和我们共度周末？

Wouldn't it be better to play some classic music? 放点儿古典音乐是不是更好？

18. 分裂句

有时为了强调可以把句子中的一部分提前，而把其他部分变为一种定语从句，如：

（例句译文省略）

Nancy saw a snake in the garden.

可改为 { Nancy was the girl who saw a snake in the garden.
The girl who saw a snake in the garden was Nancy.

也可改为 { A snake was what Nancy saw in the garden.
What Nancy saw in the garden was a snake.

也可改为 { The garden was (the place) where Nancy saw the snake.
(The place) Where Nancy saw the snake was the garden.

又如 John went to town to see his grandma on Sunday.

可改为 { Sunday was (the day) when John went to town to see his grandma.
(The day) When John went to town to see his grandma was Sunday.

也可对动词加以强调，甚至对整个句子加以强调：

The girl cried for help.

可改为 What the girl did was (to) cry for help.

A young boy drove the car away.

可改为 What happened was (that) a young boy drove the car away.

还有一种强调的办法，就是使用 **it**，如：

It was Helen who found the key on her bed yesterday.

这种强调句也可使用否定结构：

It wasn't my brother who found the key... It was Helen who...

如果强调的主语为人称代词，则有两种改法：

It is I who am to blame. （正式说法）

It's me that's to blame. （口语说法）

如想避免过于正规或过于口语化，则可以说 **I'm the person (the one) who's to blame.**

也可用下面的结构：

It wasn't until yesterday that I received the letter.

It was only when I read your letter that I realized what was happening.

19. 弱读、重读

有一些词有弱式与强式两种读法，例如：

What are you looking at /æt/? 你在瞧什么？

I'm looking at /ət/ you. 我在瞧你。

有这种情况的词多为介词、代词、连词、冠词和助动词。这类词通常不重读，这时都读作弱式。弱式读法读 /ə/ 时最多，有时元音消失，

少数词读 /ɪ/。强式读法按拼写形式读，例如：（例句译文省略）

> she was /wəz/ alone.
> It was /wəz/ snowing.
> "Were you there?" "Yes, I was /wɒz/."（句末多重读）

> I must /məs/ say goodbye to you now.
> You really must /mʌst/ go with us.（表示强调）

> Where have /əv/ they gone?
> You should have /əv/ told us.
> What shall we have /hæv/ for dessert?（have 在这里不是助动词）

否定结构多重读：

can't /kɑːnt, 美 kænt/   mustn't /ˈmʌsnt/   wasn't /ˈwɒznt/

下面是一些有弱式或强式两种读法的词：

拼写形式	弱式读法	强式读法
a	/ə/	/eɪ/
am	/(ə)m/	/æm/
an	/ən/	/æn/
and	/(ə)n(d)/	/ænd/
are	/ə(r)/	/ɑː(r)/
as	/əz/	/æz/
at	/ət/	/æt/
be	/bɪ/	/biː/
been	/bɪn/	/biːn/
but	/bət/	/bʌt/
can	/k(ə)n/	/kæn/
could	/kəd/	/kʊd/
do	/d(ə)/	/duː/
does	/dəz/	/dʌz/
for	/fə(r)/	/fɔː(r)/
from	/frəm/	/frɒm/
had	/(h)əd/	/hæd/
has	/(h)əz/	/hæz/
have	/(h)əv/	/hæv/

he	/(h)i/	/hi:/
her	/(h)ə(r)/	/hɜː(r)/
him	/(h)ɪm/	/hɪm/
his	/(h)ɪz/	/hɪz/
is	/z, s/	/ɪz/
must	/m(ə)s(t)/	/mʌst/
not	/nt /	/nɒt/
of	/əv/	/ɒv/
our	/ɑː(r)/	/aʊə(r)/
saint	/s(ə)nt/（英）	/seɪnt/
shall	/ʃ(ə)l/	/ʃæl/
she	/ʃi/	/ʃi:/
should	/ʃ(ə)d/	/ʃʊd/
sir	/sə(r)/	/sɜː(r)/
some	/s(ə)m/	/sʌm/
than	/ð(ə)n/	/ðæn/（少用）
that（连词）	/ð(ə)t/	/ðæt/（少用）
the	/ðə, ði/	/ði:/
them	/ð(ə)m/	/ðem/
there	/ðə(r)/	/ðeə(r)/
to	/tə/	/tu:/
us	/əs/	/ʌs/
was	/w(ə)z/	/wɒz/
we	/wi/	/wi:/
were	/wə(r)/	/wɜː(r)/
who	/hʊ/	/hu:/
would	/wəd, əd/	/wʊd/
will	/(ə)l/	/wɪl/
you	/jʊ/	/ju:/
your	/jə(r)/	/jɔː(r)/

20. 标点

英语的标点符号有以下几种（大部分和汉语是差不多的）。

❀ 句号（**full stop**）——放在陈述句或祈使句末尾：

It's raining again. 又下雨了。

Let's go. 走吧。

❀ 问号（**question mark**）——用在问句后：

Did you have a good trip? 你一路都好吗？

How is your mother? 你母亲怎样？

Is Lily with child? 莉莉怀孩子了？

有些句子形式上是问句，而实际上是祈使句，也可以不加问号：

Would you please put your name down. 请把名字写下来。

❀ 叹号（**exclamation mark**）——放在感叹句末尾：

What nonsense! 真是胡说八道！

How wonderful! 真精彩！

还可用在表示强烈情绪的祈使句中：

Put down your gun! 把枪放下！

Down on your knees! 跪下！

还可用在带 ah、oh 等感叹词的句子或其他带有强烈感情的句子中：

Oh, dear me! 啊，我的天哪！

They have no right to be here! They must leave at once. 他们无权留在这里！他们必须马上离开。

❀ 逗号（**comma**）——可用在许多地方表示停顿：

（1）放在呼语后：

Come in, Mr. Patterson. 请进，派特森先生。

Sit around me, children. 孩子们，围着我坐。

（2）用来列举事物（最后名词前多用 and）：

She plans to visit Egypt, India, Thailand and some other Asian countries. 她打算访问埃及、印度、泰国和其他一些亚洲国家。

She bought a hat, a scarf, a skirt and a pair of shoes. 她买了一顶帽子、一条头巾、一条裙子和一双鞋。

（3）用在一系列形容词之间：

She was a tall, slender, golden-haired and nice-looking girl. 她是一个高高个子、苗条身材、金色头发的漂亮姑娘。

It was an expensive, ill-planned and wasteful project. 这是一项昂贵的、计划不周的、浪费严重的工程。

（4）把一些并列的成分分开：

He got up, washed, dressed and then had his breakfast. 他起床，洗脸，穿衣服，然后吃早饭。

She was fond of skating, boating and swimming. 她喜欢溜冰、划船和游泳。

（5）用来把插入成分和句子其他部分分开：

She was not, however, aware of the circumstances. 但是她并不知道这个情况。

This is, I believe, all the news concerning the society. 我相信这就是关于协会的所有消息。

（6）把同位语及非限定性定语从句和句子的其他部分分开：

This is Mr. Wood, director of our hospital. 这是我们医院院长伍德先生。

He'll stop in Tokyo, where his sister is studying. 他将在东京停留，他的妹妹在那里念书。

（7）把状语从句或其他一些状语（如用分词表示的状语）和句子的其他部分分开：

This medicine, taken in time, can be very effective. 这种药如果及时吃，会很有效。

Shaking all over, she didn't say a word. 她浑身颤抖，一句话也没说。

（8）用在其他需要停顿的地方：

Whether or not he will come, I have no idea. 他究竟来不来我不知道。

This can be, and should be, corrected. 这可以而且应该纠正。

（9）用在日期、地址及书信中：

March 5th, 1999

2045 Broadway, New York, NY 10024

Dear Nancy,

All the best, David

❀ 分号（semicolon）——用来连接两个意思上紧密相连的并列句：

The sun was already low in the sky; it would soon be dark. 太阳已经很低了，很快就要天黑了。

He knew everything about me; I knew nothing about him. 他对我的情况很清楚，而我却对他一无所知。

It is a fine idea; let's hope that it is going to work. 这是一个好主意，但愿它能行得通。

有时连接两个含有逗号的分句：

She was determined to succeed whatever the cost; she would achieve her aim, whoever might suffer on the way. 不管付出什么代价，她都决心要成功；不管谁为此受到损害，她也要达到目的。

❀ 冒号（colon）——主要用在列举的东西前面：

There are in English two articles: the definite article and the indefinite article. 在英语中有两种冠词：定冠词和不定冠词。

These garments should be made of natural material: cotton, silk, wool or leather. 这种衣服应该用自然材料做成，如棉布、绸缎、毛料或皮革。

还可用来引起引语：

Kenneth Morgan writes: "The truth was..." 摩根写道："事实是……"

Shakespeare said: "Neither a borrower nor a lender be." 莎士比亚说："既不要找人借钱，也不要借钱给人。"

也可用在附加的解释性分句前面：

You can't count on him to help: he is such a busy man. 你不能指望他帮忙，他是这样一位大忙人。

❀ 破折号（dash）——主要用来列举一些事物，把插入语和解释性话语和句子的其他部分分开：

My mother—who rarely gets angry—really lost her temper. 我很少生气的母亲真的发脾气了。

We had a great time in Greece—the kids really loved it. 我们在希腊玩得很好，孩子们确实很喜欢那儿。

破折号后有时加上一个后想起的东西：

Let Tess help her—if she wants help. 让特丝去帮助她——如果她需要帮助的话。

That's wonderful—really it is. 那太好了——的确。

❀ 引号（quotation mark）和汉语引号的用法差不多，主要用在引语前后：

Longfellow wrote, "Life is real! Life is earnest!" 朗费罗写道："生活是真实的！生活是严肃的！"

Do you know the origin of the saying "A little learning is a dangerous thing"? 你知道"一知半解很危险"的出处吗？

也可用来加在书名、剧名等的两头：

His next play was *Macbeth*. 他的下一部剧是《麦克白》。

I borrowed Dickens' novel *A Tale of Two Cities*. 我借了狄更斯的小说《双城记》。

有时放在一个词或词组前后，让人注意它的特别意义：

Thousands were imprisoned in the name of "national security." 数以千计的人被以"国家安全"的名义投入狱中。

单引号（' '）和双引号（" "）没有什么差别。在美国双引号用得多一些，在英国单引号用得多一些。

❀ 括号（brackets）——多用在解释性或补充性短语等前后：

I ordered two coffees and an ice-cream (for her). 我叫了两杯咖啡和一份冰激凌（是给她的）。

Mount Robson (12,972 feet) is the highest mountain in the Canadian Rockies. 罗布逊峰（12 972 英尺高）是加拿大段洛基山脉的最高峰。

还可用在数字及注脚前后：

Our objectives are (1) to increase output, (2) to improve quality and (3) to maximize profits. 我们的目标是：（1）提高产量，（2）改善质量和（3）获取最大利润。

This is a feature of Shakespeare's later works (see Chapter Eight). 这是莎士比亚晚期作品的一个特点。（可参阅第八章）

❀ 撇号（apostrophe " ' "）——主要用于下面情况：

（1）构成名词所有格：

my cousin's daughter   the country's capital

（2）用在紧缩形式中（表示某字母省略）：

I'm from Harbin./We'd like to stay./You mustn't forget it./Yes, ma'am.

（3）构成字母等的复数形式：

How many 5's have you got? 你们有几个五分？

Roll your r's. 发 r 时要卷舌。

during the 1990's 20 世纪 90 年代

❀ 连字符（**hyphen**）主要用来构成合成词：

good-natured   sister-in-law

还可构成 **21** 至 **99** 的数词：

twenty-three   thirty-1st

在转行时也需用它（一个词的一部分需转入下行，前一部分后要加连字符）。

扫描上方二维码，
浏览视频资源

三、惯用法
思维导图

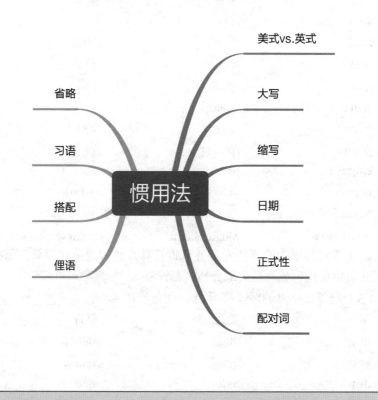

美式vs.英式

省略

习语

搭配

俚语

惯用法

大写

缩写

日期

正式性

配对词

1. 美式 vs. 英式

美式英语和英式英语的差别主要有四方面：

❀ 语音：

这是最明显的。归纳起来主要有下面八点：

（1）r 的读音：

在美式英语中词尾及音节末的 r 是读出来的，而在英式英语中一般不读出：

	美音	英音
sir	/sɜːr/	/sɜː/
bird	/bɜːrd/	/bɜːd/
first	/fɜːrst/	/fɜːst/
girl	/gɜːrl/	/gɜːl/
world	/wɜːrld/	/wɜːld/
occur	/əˈkɜːr/	/əˈkɜː/
prefer	/prɪˈfɜːr/	/prɪˈfɜː/
thirteen	/θɜːrˈtiːn/	/θɜːˈtiːn/
thirsty	/ˈθɜːrsti/	/ˈθɜːsti/
Saturday	/ˈsætərdeɪ/	/ˈsætədeɪ/
university	/juːnɪˈvɜːrsɪti/	/juːnɪˈvɜːsɪti/

（2）美式英语中的某些元音音节带有鼻音，特别是在西部，而在英式英语中这种鼻音在大部分地区都没有。

（3）美音 o 字母的短音接近 /ɑ/，而英音读 /ɒ/ 音：

	美音	英音
dog	/dɑg/	/dɒg/
god	/gɑd/	/gɒd/
dot	/dɑt/	/dɒt/
stop	/stɑp/	/stɒp/
forgot	/fəˈgɑt/	/fəˈgɒt/
geography	/dʒɪˈɑgrəfi/	/dʒɪˈɒgrəfi/

（4）字母 a 在不少词中，英音读 /ɑː/ 音，而美音读 /æ/ 音：

	美音	英音
class	/klæs/	/klɑːs/

glass	/glæs/	/glɑːs/
past	/pæst/	/pɑːst/
bathroom	/ˈbæθrʊm/	/ˈbɑːθrʊm/
after	/ˈæftə/	/ɑːftə/
faster	/ˈfæstə/	/ˈfɑːstə/

（5）字母 u 的长音，英音多读作 /juː/，而美音多读作 /uː/：

	美音	英音
news	/nuːz/	/njuːz/
duty	/ˈduːti/	/ˈdjuːti/
tune	/tuːn/	/tjuːn/
neutral	/ˈnuːtrəl/	/ˈnjuːtrəl/
renew	/rɪˈnuː/	/rɪˈnjuː/
illuminate	/ɪˈluːmɪneɪt/	/ɪˈljuːmɪneɪt/
enthusiastic	/ɪnˌθuːzɪˈæstɪk/	/ɪnˌθjuːzɪˈæstɪk/
résumé	/ˈrezʊmeɪ/	/ˈrezjʊmeɪ/

（6）以 -ary、-ery 或 -ory 结尾的词，英美的读音有时不同，美音常多一个音节：

	美音	英音
secretary	/ˈsekrəteri/	/ˈsekrətri/
imaginary	/ɪˈmædʒɪneri/	/ɪˈmædʒɪnəri/
preliminary	/prɪˈlɪmɪneri/	/prɪˈlɪmɪnri/
stationery	/ˈsteɪʃəneri/	/ˈsteɪʃənri/
inventory	/ˈɪnvəntɔːri/	/ˈɪnvəntri/
dignitary	/ˈdɪgnɪteri/	/ˈdɪgnɪtri/
signatory	/ˈsɪgnətɔːri/	/ˈsɪgnətri/

（7）以不重读的 -ile 收尾的词，英音多读作 /aɪl/，而美音读作 /əl/：

	美音	英音
missile	/ˈmɪsəl/	/ˈmɪsaɪl/
fertile	/ˈfɜːtəl/	/ˈfɜːtaɪl/
reptile	/ˈreptəl/	/ˈreptaɪl/
projectile	/prəˈdʒektəl/	/prəˈdʒektaɪl/

（8）一些从法语中借用的词，英美的读音也有所不同，美音多重读

最后音节（和法语一致），而英音则不然：

	美音	英音
ballet	/bæ'leɪ/	/'bæleɪ/
paté	/pæ'teɪ/	/'pæteɪ/
fiancé	/ˌfɪɑ:n'seɪ/	/fɪ'ɑ:nseɪ/
garage	/gə'rɑ:ʒ/	/'gærɑ:ʒ/
buffei	/bʊ'feɪ/	/'bʊfeɪ/
café	/kæ'feɪ/	/'kæfeɪ/

还有一些细微的差别，如字母 o 的长音，英音读 /əʊ/，美音读 /oʊ/，但不明显；又如 thorough 这个词，美音读 /θʌrəʊ/，英音读 /θʌrə/。这些在较好较新的字典中都会标出，这里就不多谈了。

✿ 词汇：

在这方面英式英语和美式英语是有些差别的，即各有一些自己专用的词：

美式英语	英式英语	
airplane	aeroplane	（飞机）
anyplace, anywhere	anywhere	（任何地方）
apartment	flat, apartment	（单元房）
area code	dialing code	（电话区号）
attorney, lawyer	barrister, solicitor	（律师）
busy	engaged	（占线）
cab, taxi	taxi	（出租车）
call collect	reverse the charges	（收话人付费）
can	tin	（罐头）
candy	sweets	（糖果）
check, bill	bill	（餐馆账单）
coin-purse	purse	（钱包）
cookie, cracker	biscuit	（饼干）
corn	sweet corn, maize	（玉米）
crib	cot	（小儿床）
crazy	mad	（发疯）
cuffs	turn-ups	（裤脚翻边）

diaper	nappy	（尿布）
doctor's office	doctor's surgery	（诊所）
dumb, stupid	stupid	（愚蠢）
elevator	lift	（电梯）
eraser	rubber, eraser	（橡皮）
fall, autumn	autumn	（秋天）
faucet, tap	tap	（水龙头）
first floor	ground floor	（底层）
second floor, etc.	first floor, etc.	（二楼等）
flashlight	torch	（手电筒）
flat (tire)	flat tyre, puncture	（车胎瘪气）
freeway	expressway, motor way	（高速公路）
French fries	chips	（炸薯条）
garbage, trash	rubbish	（垃圾）
garbage can, trash can	dustbin, rubbish bin	（垃圾桶）
gas, gasoline	petrol	（汽油）
gear shift	gear lever	（变速杆，换挡杆）
highway	main road	（城市间的公路）
hood	bonnet	（发动机上方的车盖）
intersection	crossroads	（十字路口）
mad	angry	（生气）
mail	post	（邮件）
mean	nasty	（卑鄙，恶劣）
movie, film	film	（电影）
one-way (ticket)	single (ticket)	（单程票）
pants, trousers	trousers	（裤子）
pavement	road surface	（路面）
pitcher	jug	（带柄水罐）
pocket-book, purse, handbag	handbag	（女用手提包）
railroad	railway	（铁路）
raise	rise	（提薪，加工资）

rest room	public toilet	（公用洗手间）
round trip	return ticket	（来回票）
schedule, timetable	timetable	（时刻表）
sidewalk	pavement	（人行道）
sneakers	trainers (=sports shoes)	（运动鞋）
spigot, faucet	tap	（户外水龙头）
stand in line	queue	（排队）
stingy	mean	（小气，吝啬）
store, shop	shop	（商店）
subway	underground	（地下铁道）
truck	lorry	（卡车）
trunk	boot	（车后存物箱）
vacation	holiday(s)	（较长假期）
windshield	windscreen	（汽车的风挡）
zee	zed	（字母"z"的读音）
zipper	zip	（拉链）

尽管如此，两国大部分的词是共同的。

另外有些带冠词及副词的短语也有少量差别：

美式英语	英式英语
different from (than)	different from (to)
do something over (again)	do something again
live on... street	live in... street
Monday through (to) Friday	Monday to Friday
twenty-five after two	twenty-five past two
(a)quarter of one	a quarter to one

此外还有一些美式英语中用的短语，例如：

announce against 宣布反对

Many show business people have <u>announced against</u> the Republican candidate. 许多演艺界人士宣布反对共和党候选人。

announce for 公开表示支持

The union <u>announced for</u> the Democratic candidate. 这家工会公开表示支持民主党候选人。

ante up 交（费）

Each person is being asked to <u>ante up</u> $12 to cover expenses. 每个人要交 12 美元用来支付开支。

bail out 避开

My advice to you is to <u>bail out</u> now before there's trouble. 我劝你趁问题没出来之前及早避开。

bang away at 盘问

The detectives <u>banged away at</u> him for hours. 侦探们盘问了他好几个小时。

apples and oranges 完全不同

You can't compare inner city schools and schools in the suburbs—they're <u>apples and oranges</u>. 你不能把市内学校和郊区学校相比，它们完全不同。

on somebody's ass 紧紧跟着

There's a Mercedes <u>on my ass</u> and it's making me nervous. 有一辆奔驰车紧跟着我，使我很紧张。

这往往是使美式英语的口语不好懂的因素之一，但正式语言中这种专门的美式短语相对用得比较少。

❀ 拼写：

美式英语中一些词的拼法和英式英语略有不同，最明显的是：

（1）许多英式英语中以 **-our** 结尾的词，在美式英语中都拼作 **-or**：

美式英语	英式英语	美式英语	英式英语
color	colour	honor	honour
labor	labour	neighbor	neighbour
behavior	behaviour	harbor	harbour
savior	saviour	splendor	splendour

（2）许多英式英语中以 **-re** 结尾的词，在美式英语中都拼作 **-er**：

美式英语	英式英语	美式英语	英式英语
center	centre	theater	theatre
meter	metre	liter	litre
millimeter	millimetre	centiliter	centilitre
caliber	calibre	amphitheater	amphitheatre

（3）以 **-el** 结尾的词，在美式英语中可直接加词尾，而在英式英语中需要将 1 双写再加词尾：

美式英语	英式英语	美式英语	英式英语
marveled	marvelled	marvelous	marvellous
traveled	travelled	traveler	traveller
labeled	labelled	labeling	labelling
canceled	cancelled	canceling	cancelling

（4）美式英语中很多动词以 **-ize** 结尾，而在英式英语中可以 **-ize** 结尾，也可以 **-ise** 结尾：

美式英语	英式英语
realize	realize/realise
civilize	civilize/civilise
materialize	materialize/materialise
mechanize	mechanize/mechanise
capitalize	capitalize/capitalise
但：paralyze	paralyse
analyze	analyse

（5）其他还有一些词在英式英语和美式英语中拼法不同：

美式英语	英式英语
defense	defence
license	licence
practice, practise	practise（*v.*）
aluminum /ə'lu:mɪnəm/	aluminium /ˌælu'mɪnɪəm/
catalog(ue)	catalogue
check	cheque（支票）
jewelry	jewellery
pajamas /pə'dʒɑ:məz/	pyjamas /pɪ'dʒɑ:məz/
program	programme
tire	tyre（车胎）
whiskey	(Scotch) whisky, (Irish) whiskey

❀ 语法：

相对来说美式英语和英式英语的差别是比较小的，值得注意的有下面几点：

（1）have 的否定式及疑问式：

美式英语	英式英语
I don't have any money.	{ I don't have any money. { I haven't any money.
she doesn't have any children.	{ She doesn't have any children. { She hasn't any children.
Do you have any children?	{ Do you have any children? { Have you any children?
Does he have any brothers?	{ Does he have any brothers? { Has he any brothers?

过去英国人用 Have you...? I haven't... 这类形式的较多，现在用 Do you have... 和 I don't have... 这类形式的人更多了，但前一种形式还有人用。目前很多人都用 have got 代替 have：

Have you got any sisters? I haven't got any sisters.

（2）在某些从句中的动词形式：

<u>美式英语</u>

It's important that he be told.

I asked that I be allowed to see her.

<u>英式英语</u>

It's important that he should be told.

I asked that I should be allowed to see her.

这种差别现在越来越不明显了，两种形式（即原形与 should be 结构）在英美两国语言中都很常见。

（3）现在完成时在英式英语和美式英语中的用法基本上是一致的，但在美式英语中常有用一般过去时代替现在完成时的情况：

美式英语	英式英语
He's just gone home.	He's just gone home.
He just went home.	
Lucy just called.	Lucy has just called.
I lost (I've lost) the keys.	I've lost the keys.

Did you eat
Have you eaten } already?   Have you eaten already?

I didn't call Judy yet.
I haven't called Judy yet.   I haven't called Judy yet.

（4）个别动词在美式英语和英式英语中有不同拼法：

Her shoes <u>fit</u> badly.

Her shoes <u>fitted</u> badly.

I've never really <u>gotten</u> to know her.

I've never really <u>got</u> to know her.

He <u>wet</u> his handkerchief.

He <u>wetted</u> his handkerchief.

He <u>quit</u> the room angrily.

He <u>quitted</u> the room angrily.

另外有许多动词在美式英语中为规则动词，而在英式英语中为不规则动词：

	美式英语		英式英语	
burn	burned	burned	burnt	burnt
dream	dreamed	dreamed	dreamt	dreamt /dremt/
lean	leaned	leaned	leant	leant /lent/
learn	learned	learned	learnt	learnt
smell	smelled	smelled	smelt	smelt
spell	spelled	spelled	spelt	spelt
spill	spilled	spilled	spilt	spilt
spoil	spoiled	spoiled	spoilt	spoilt

这些词以 t 结尾的形式在英国比较多，但也有不少人用带 -ed 的形式。另外 ate 和 shone 在美式英语中分别读作 /eɪt/ 和 /ʃoʊn/，而在英式英语则读作 /et/ 和 /ʃɒn/。

（5）有个别用法有些小的差异：

美式英语

The committee <u>meets</u> tomorrow.

Hello, is <u>this</u> Susan?

It looks <u>like</u> it's going to rain.

He looks at me <u>real strange</u>.（或 really strangely）

One should get to know <u>one's</u> neighbours.

英式英语

The committee <u>meet</u> (meets) tomorrow.

Hello, is <u>that</u> Susan?

It looks <u>as if</u> (like) it's going to rain.

He looked at me <u>really strangely</u>.

One should get to know neighbors.

美式英语与英式英语虽然有这些差异，但相同的部分还是主要的，并不影响交流。特别是随着电影、电视及广播影响的增加，两者的差异可能会越来越小。

2. 大写

在英语中下面这类词的第一个字母要大写：

❀ 人名（连同称号、头衔）：

Mozart	Miss Green	Lady Dory
Sir Walter Scott	Nancy	Mr. Snow
Lord Byron	Reverend P. Brown	

❀ 地名（里面的冠词或短的介词不大写）：

Brazil	Paris	the British Isles
Stratford-on-Avon	The Thames	the Grand Canyon
the Suez Canal		

❀ 书名、电影名、歌名等（里面的冠词和短的介词不大写）：

David Copperfield	*Three Men in a Boat*
Gone with the Wind	*Auld Lang Syne*
A Dictionary of American Idioms	

❀ 月份、星期、节日名：

April	Saturday	New Year's Day
Christmas	May Day	the Moon Festival
St. Valentine's Day	Halloween	

❀ 由专有名词派生的形容词：

Polish   British   Siberian   Californian

Victorian   Martian   Elizabethan   Shakespearean

❀ 品牌名，某人的作品：

The cheapest detergents are Surf and Tide. 最便宜的洗涤剂是 Surf 牌和 Tide 牌的。

He bought a second-hand Chevrolet. 他买了一辆旧的雪佛莱汽车。

In those days you could buy a Picasso for £300. 那时，你用三百英镑就可买一张毕加索的画。

此外，I 要大写，句子开头的第一个字母也大写：

"What's that?" she asked. "那是什么？"她问道。

表示季节、方位等的名称通常不大写：

In spring the weather gets warm. 春天天气转暖。

Italy is in the south of Europe. 意大利在欧洲南部。

但在一定情况下也可以大写，例如：

talks on nuclear disarmament between East and West 东西方间的核裁军谈判

In the United States, the South means the states south of Pennsylvania and the Ohio River. 在美国，南方指宾州及俄亥俄以南各州。

president, prime minister 这类词，有人大写，有人不大写：

The President addressed the nation. 总统对全国发表演说。

She saw the president get off the plane. 她看到总统走下飞机。

3. 缩写

在一些情况下，人称代词和助动词，或是助动词或情态动词与 **not** 可以缩短成一个词，称为紧缩形式，例如：

She's waiting for us.

He won't be here tonight.

在口语中，这种紧缩形式是经常用的，写下来就成为下面这个样子。在口语化的文字材料（如书信）中，人们也时常这样写。英语中的紧缩形式可归纳如下：

紧缩形式	读音	意义
I'm	/aɪm/	I am
I've	/aɪv/	I have
I'll	/aɪl/	I will
I'd	/aɪd/	I had/I would
you're	/jɔː(r)/	you are
you've	/juːv/	you have
you'll	/juːl/	you will
you'd	/juːd/	you had/you would
he's	/hiːz/	he is/he has
he'll	/hiːl, hɪl/	he will
he'd	/hiːd/	he had/he would
she's	/ʃiːz/	she is/she has
she'll	/ʃiːl, ʃɪl/	she will
she'd	/ʃiːd/	she had/she would
it's	/ɪts/	it is/it has
we're	/wɪə(r)/	we are
we've	/wiːv/	we have
we'll	/wiːl, wɪl/	we will
we'd	/wiːd/	we had/we would
they're	/ðeə(r)/	they are
they've	/ðeɪv/	they have
they'll	/ðeɪl, ðel/	they will
they'd	/ðeɪd/	they had/they would
there's	/ðəz/	there is/there has
there'll	/ðəl/	there will
there'd	/ðəd/	there had/there would
aren't	/ɑːnt/	are not
can't	/kɑːnt/ /kænt/	can not
couldn't	/ˈkʊdnt/	could not
daren't	/deənt/	dare not
didn't	/ˈdɪdnt/	did not

doesn't	/ˈdʌznt/	does not
don't	/dəʊnt/	do not
hadn't	/ˈhædnt/	had not
hasn't	/ˈhæznt/	has not
haven't	/ˈhævnt/	have not
isn't	/ˈɪznt/	is not
mightn't	/ˈmaɪtnt/	might not
mustn't	/ˈmʌsnt/	must not
needn't	/ˈniːdnt/	need not
oughtn't	/ˈɔːtnt/	ought not
shan't	/ʃɑːnt/	shall not
shouldn't	/ˈʃʊdnt/	should not
usedn't	/ˈjuːsnt/	used not
wasn't	/ˈwɒznt/	was not
weren't	/wɜːnt/	were not
won't	/wəʊnt/	will not
wouldn't	/ˈwʊdnt/	would not

1. 不要把 it's 和 its（物主代词）相混。
2. am not 在简短问句中紧缩为 aren't。
   I'm late, aren't I?
3. can't 在英式英语中读作 /kɑːnt/，在美式英语中读作 /kænt/。
4. daren't, shan't, usedn't 在美式英语中不常用。
5. may not 一般不紧缩成一个词。mayn't 是很少用的。
6. let's 是 let us 的紧缩形式。
7. 在不规范的英语中，有人用 ain't 代表 am not, are not, is not, have not,
   has not：
   I ain't going to do it.
   我不会这样做。

4. 日期

对日期的表示法英国和美国是有差别的。

在英国通常的写法是　　　　日子／月份／年份：

25 May 1999　　　　　　　　14 June 1905

有时日子后面加上 **st**、**nd**、**rd** 或 **th**，年份前有人加逗号，但不加者更多，不过在句子中还是应加逗号：

31st April（，）1988　　　　　2nd July 1997

23rd March 1973

但：She was born on 4 August, 1977.

有时完全以数字表示：

29/7/1998（1998 年 7 月 29 日）或 29-7-1998; 29. 7. 1998

在美国，多先写月份，再写日期，年份前加逗号：

May 25, 1999　　　　　　　　June 14, 1905

全用数字表示时，也按这个顺序：

7/29/1998（1998 年 7 月 29 日）或 7-29-1998; 7. 29. 1998

因此全用数字表示日期时英国人和美国人有时会有不同理解，例如 **5/6/1999** 美国人会认为是 **1999 年 5 月 6 日**，而英国人会认为是 **1999 年 6 月 5 日**。

较长的月份常常缩短：

Jan.　　Feb.　　Mar.　　Apr.　　Aug.　　Sept.　　Oct.

Nov.　　Dec.

现将日期和年份的读法表示如下：

25 May 1999 = May the twenty-fifth，nineteen ninety-nine

或 the twenty-fifth of May，nineteen ninety-nine

May 25 1999（美式），读作 May（the）twenty-fifth，nineteen ninety-nine

1100 = eleven hundred

1905 = nineteen and five 或 nineteen O /əu/ five

2000 = two thousand

2004 = two thousand and four

问日期时可说：What's the date (today)?

5. 正式性

语言有正式与非正式之分。一般说来，书面语是比较正式的，尤其是写文章、报告、商业书信、公文通知等文体时，选词都要注意。

日常口语、给朋友或家人写信，则比较随意，语言是非正式的。懂得区分正式与非正式语言，说话和写作可以比较得体。

这两种语言可以通过语法结构表现出来，这里举一些例子加以说明：

	正式语言	非正式语言
紧缩形式多用于非正式语体	They have left already. It is not necessary. We will not have time for it.	They've left already. It isn't necessary. We won't have time for it.
介词的位置不同	For whom is the present? In which century did he live? By whom was the book written?	Who's the present for? Which century did he live in? Who was the book written by?
关系代词的用法不尽相同	This is a subject about which we might argue for a long while. The girl to whom I spoke is my cousin.	This is a subject we might argue for a long while about. The girl I spoke to is my cousin.
有些不定代词在正式语体中作单数，在非正式语体中可作复数	None of the cures really works. Neither of us likes him. If any of them gets hungry, they can have some biscuits.	None of the cures really work. Neither of us like him. If any of them get hungry, they can have some biscuits.
有些代词的用法不同	Whom did they send there? "Who said that?" "He did." Tom and I are going to do it.	Who did they send there? "Who said that?" "(It was) him." Tom and me are going to do it.
省略句多用于非正式语体中	Have you had your breakfast? Be careful what you say. There is nobody at home.	Had your breakfast? Careful what you say. Nobody at home.

另外词汇的选择也有些差别，有些词主要用于非正式场合，另外一些词则可用于正式场合或中性场合（介于两者之间的场合），例如：

正式场合	中性场合	非正式场合
repair	mend	fix
commence	begin/start	begin/start
in order	all right	OK
Thank you	Thank you	Thanks
I beg your pardon?	Pardon?/Sorry?	What?

6. 配对词

英语中有不少短语是由两个配对的词构成的。最常见的由两个名词加 and 构成，如：

bits and pieces 零七八碎   board and lodging 食宿
body and soul 全身心地   bread and butter 生计
cup and saucer 一副杯盘   flesh and blood 亲骨肉
heart and soul 全心全意   (move) heaven and earth 竭尽全力
kith and kin 亲友   knife and fork 刀叉
law and order 法律与秩序   nearest and dearest 最亲密的人
pros and cons 利弊   sex and violence 色情与暴力
ups and downs 起伏变化   women and children 妇孺

也有些短语由两个形容词加 and 构成：

alive and well 活蹦乱跳   black and white 白纸黑字
born and bred 出生长大   drunk and disorderly 酗酒闹事
ready and waiting 一切准备好   safe and sound 安然无恙

也有些短语由两个副词加 and 构成：

back and forth 来回地   backwards and forwards 来回地
far and near 到处，从各处   far and wide 到处，到各地
first and foremost 首先，最重要的 here and now 现在马上（就干）
hither and thither 这儿那儿，到处 in and out 进进出出
really and truly 的的确确地   to and fro 来回地
up and down 来回地，上下地   well and truly 确实地

7. 省略

为了省事和避免不必要的重复，常常有些词可以省略，特别是在日常口语中。最常见的情况有下面这些：

（例句译文省略）

❀ 回答中的省略：

在回答别人的问题时，常常可省略一些词（至于省略了哪些词，从

问句中就可看出）：

"What's your favourite colour?" "Light green." （如说 My favourite colour is light green. 就太啰唆了。）

"How are you getting along with your work?" "Pretty well."

"How are you feeling today?" "Much better."

在回答一般疑问句时可以更活一些：

"Have you spoken to him?" "Not yet."

"Would you like to come?" "Sure."

"Is she coming?" "Definitely."

"Do you think so?" "Absolutely."

"Do you mind if I sit here?" "Certainly not."

❀ 问句中的省略：

在接着别人的话提出问句时常可有一部分词省略：

"She stays with her aunt." "Does she?"

"They are starting up a music club." "Are they?"

"I've checked all the rooms." "Have you?"

在向别人提出问题时有时也省略一些词：

"Seen Diana recently?" "Anybody against it?"

❀ 陈述句中的省略：

在回应别人的话语时，有些词常可省略：

"I think Mary should be told." "She has been."

"I'm not joking." "Neither am I."

"I think we're right." "I'm sure we are."

"You're to stay here tonight!" "But l can't, and I mustn't."

有时在日常口语中，如不造成误会，单独的句子中也有些词可以省略：

(Be) Careful what you say.

(It) Won't work, you know.

(I) Hope to hear from you soon.

"(I wish you a) Happy New Year." "The same to you."

❀ 感叹句中的省略：

感叹句中常常可以省略一些词：

Nothing doing!

Stupid!

Nonsense!

Damn it all!

❀ 并列句中的省略：

并列句中，尤其是第二分句，常可省略一些词以避免重复：

He majors in physics and I in chemical engineering.

She never said she was homesick, but she was.

❀ 复合句中的省略：

复合句中的从句，在不少情况下，会有一些词省略，特别是 **as** 和 **than** 引起的从句：

The situation there was not so bad as had been painted. 那里的情况没有描绘的那样糟。

We will, as always, stand on your side. 我们要一如既往地站在你们一边。

另有不少状语从句可有一些词省略（常常省略的是主语和动词 **be**）：

Fill in the application as (it is) instructed. 按照要求填好表格。

This viewpoint, however understandable (it is) is wrong. 这种观点不管多么可以理解，都是错误的。

Phone me if (it is) necessary. 必要时给我打电话。

As (it is) scheduled they met on January 20. 他们按照计划在 1 月 20 日碰头。

❀ 不定式短语中的省略：

在一定情况下，不定式短语中可有一部分词省略：

"Are you coming to visit us this summer?" "We hope to (do so)." "今年夏天你们来看我们吗？" "我们希望这样。"

I don't smoke now, but I used to (smoke). 现在我不抽烟，但我过去是抽的。

❀ 冠词和名词省略的情况：

在新闻标题、提纲、剧本提示、书名中冠词有时省略：

(A) WOMAN WALKS ON (the) MOON

(The) Algerian crisis led to (the) downfall of (the) French Government Vassilisa

(Open door quickly; to Alyosha): You here again. (Exit into the garden.)

History of China before the Qing Dynasty

在一些句子中，两个并列的名词前的冠词有时省略：

The birth took place this morning, and both (the) mother and (the) child are doing well. 孩子是今早生的，母子都平安。

When host and guest appeared, they received a standing ovation. 宾主步入大厅时，大家都起立鼓掌。

在口语中一些有名的专有名词有时会省略一个名词：

He's staying at the Hilton (= the Hilton Hotel).

We're going to see the play at the Mermaid (= the Mermaid Theatre).

8. 习语

习惯用语（idioms）：

英语中有大量习惯用语，它们由两个或更多单词构成，却有特别的意思，在很多情况下，它们的意思很难从构成它们的单词推想出，而必须作为整体来理解、记忆。例如 put across 是一个习惯用语，这两个单词连初学的人都认识，但连在一起意思就不容易弄清楚了。只有把它放在句子中，意思才会清楚，例如：

He knew how to put his ideas across. 他知道怎样讲清楚他的想法。

She put that song across better than anyone else. 这首歌曲她比其他任何人都演唱得好。

这类习惯用语成千上万，给学习者造成很大困难。但它们又非常重要，只有掌握了它们，才算掌握了地道的英语。地道的英语可以译成 idiomatic English。idiomatic 就是从 idiom 这个词派生出来的。从这里也可看出，学好 idioms 是学好英语的关键。

（1）动词短语（phrasal verbs）：

大量的习惯用语是由动词构成的。其中动词短语是最重要的一部分。通常它由动词 + 介词（或副词）构成。以 come 一词为例，它可构成：

come about 发生

come across sb./sth. 碰到

come along 出现

come apart 散开

come around 恢复知觉

come by 得到

come down 下跌

come down on 斥责

come down with 患上（某种疾病）

come for 来接（某人），来取（某物）

come forward 站出来

come from 来自

come home to 明白过来

come in 上台（执政），上市

come in (first) 得（第一名）

come in for 受到（批评、谴责等）

come into being 开始存在，建立

come into blossom 开花

come into conflict 发生冲突

come into effect 开始生效

come into fashion 开始时兴

come into power 开始执政

come near 差一点儿就

come of 由……造成

come off 脱落，举行，成功

come on 进行，生长

come on (upon) 碰上

come out 出版，开花，罢工

come out against 宣布反对

come out for 表示支持

come out with 提出，说出

come round 恢复知觉，转而同意

come through 经历（危险等）

come to 总共有，苏醒过来

come to a conclusion 得出结论

come to a halt 停下来

come to an end 结束

come to blows 打了起来

come to fruition 实现，结果

come to grief 出事，失败

come to grips with 设法解决

come to life 活跃起来

come to light 被发现

come to nothing 没有结果

come to one's senses 头脑清醒过来

come to one's attention 受到（某人）注意

come to one's assistance 援助某人

come to the point 谈正题（帮助等）

come up 走过来，发生

come up against 遭到（困难等）

come up to 达到（标准等）

come up with 提出

除了常用动词（如 bring, look, go, put, take 等）构成大量动词短语外，大部分动词都能构成一些动词短语。这是学英语时必须攻下的一个堡垒。

（2）动词短语以外的习惯用语：

除了动词短语外，英语中还有大量其他习惯用语，例如：

1）动词构成的其他短语：

除了动词短语外，还有不少由动词构成的其他短语，例如：

curry favour with 拍（某人）马屁

fish in troubled waters 浑水摸鱼

hide one's light under a bushel 韬光养晦

hit the nail on the head 击中要害

iron out differences 消除分歧

join forces with 和……联手

kill two birds with one stone 一箭双雕

know where the shoes pinches 知道症结所在

2）形容词构成的短语，以 **good** 为例，就可构成许多短语：

as good as 和……一样，可说是

have a good time 玩得很好

have a good mind to 很想

hold good 仍然有效

give... a good scolding 好好说了一顿

be all to the good 有利

make good (the loss) 赔偿（损失）

for good 长期地，永远地

3）名词构成的短语，如：

the apple of one's eye 掌上明珠	a bag of bones 骨瘦如柴
a bed of roses 万事顺利	birds of a feather 一丘之貉
a bolt from the blue 晴天霹雳	castles in the air 空中楼阁
a fish out of water 如鱼离水	the pros and cons 利弊

4）介词引起的短语，以 **at** 为例，就可构成许多短语：

at a distance 在一定距离	at a loss 不知所措
at all events 不管怎样	at any rate 不管怎样
at first 最初，开始时	at last 最后
at least (most) 至少（多）	at leisure 从容地
at length 详细地	at once 立即
at one stroke (a blow) 一下子	at present 目前
at random 随意地，胡乱地	at sea 茫然，不知所措
at the outset 从一开头	at times 有时候

5）其他短语：

all along 一直地	all but 几乎
all in all 总的说来	once and for all 一劳永逸地
and so on (forth) 等等	one and all 所有的人
What of it? 那有什么关系？	know what's what 懂行

9. 搭配

搭配（collocations）：在英语中搭配也是一个重要问题，一个名词有什么形容词能和它一起用、一个动词能用什么名词作它的宾语，

这都是搭配问题。英语的搭配中就有习惯用法问题，以 **gorgeous** 为例，可以说：

a gorgeous dress 华丽的衣裳

gorgeous scenery 美丽的风景

a gorgeous room 豪华的房间

a gorgeous sunset 艳丽的落霞

a peacock's gorgeous tail 孔雀美丽的尾羽

gorgeous girls 漂亮的姑娘们

a gorgeous cake 可口的蛋糕

a gorgeous dinner 盛宴

gorgeous weather 美好的天气

a gorgeous time 愉快的时光

又如 **brilliant** 这个词，可有下面的搭配：

brilliant sunlight 明亮的阳光

brilliant light 耀眼的灯光

brilliant colours 鲜艳的颜色

brilliant jewels 闪闪发光的首饰

a brilliant blouse 颜色鲜艳的衬衫

brilliant plumage 艳丽的羽毛

a brilliant future 光明的前途

brilliant victories 辉煌的胜利

brilliant thoughts 光辉的思想

a brilliant man 聪慧的人

a brilliant idea 聪明的想法

a brilliant mind 杰出的头脑

a brilliant pianist 有才华的钢琴家

a brilliant scientist 卓越的科学家

a brilliant speaker 出色的演说人

brilliant research 出色的研究工作

a brilliant success 辉煌的成就

a brilliant novel 精彩的小说

这对一个中国人是特别困难的，因为汉语也有自己的搭配，如果按我们的习惯去安排英语的搭配，往往出现不地道的说法。这种搭配常常是不合逻辑的，例如我们可以说 a golden opportunity（千载难逢的机会），而把 opportunity 换成它的同义词 chance 却不行。可以说 change one's mind a lot 和 Thank you very much，把 a lot 和 very much 互换却不行。学英语是一个艰辛的过程，主要的困难就在这里。

✿ 不同场合的语言：

在不同场合怎样讲话才得体也是一个困难问题。如第一次见面得说 "How do you do?" 熟人见面则说 "How are you?" 开始讲话可说 "(I'm) So glad to see you." 临别时可说 "It's been a pleasure talking to you." 请人吃饭时，可以说 "May I help you to some fish?" 或 "Would you care for a cup of coffee?" 给餐馆打电话订座，可以说 "Could I reserve a table for three for eight o'clock?"（这比 "Could you keep me a table for three persons for eight o'clock?" 更自然。）又如在旅行社你可以问 "Is it a direct flight or do I have to change?"（这比说 "Does the plane go straight there or do I have to get another one?" 自然。）如果你生活在说英语的国家，只要留意和看一些会话的书这些是可以学会的。

综上所述，除了学语法、掌握基本词汇，学各种习惯用语和用法（包括搭配）是至关重要的。要解决这个问题需要长时间的观察和积累，借助好的辞书，并在电影、小说等活的材料中学。做一个有心人，可以加快学习的进程。

10. 俚语

俚语是一部分相熟的人之间口头上的用语，有其独特的意思，只有他们能听懂，例如：

See you down at the boozer (=pub). 咱们在小酒店见。

He's a real prat (=fool). 他是一个真正的傻瓜。

这种俚语也是不稳定的，不久也可能过时，因此不宜学用。学生用了老师也会改过来，文章中用了编辑也会改过来。因此书中这种用语是少见的，除非是小说作者故意要表现某种人物的特点而使用它。真遇到这种情况有俚语词典可以查阅。

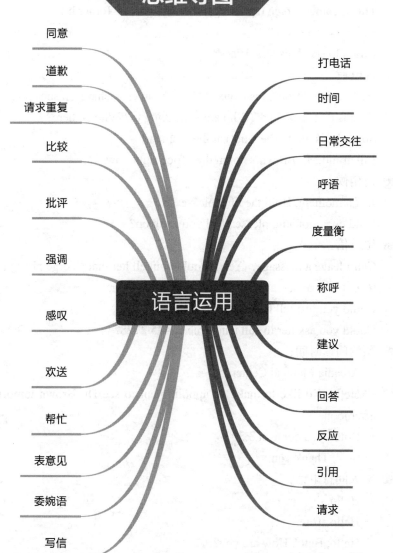

同意

道歉

请求重复

比较

批评

强调

感叹

欢送

帮忙

表意见

委婉语

写信

语言运用

打电话

时间

日常交往

呼语

度量衡

称呼

建议

回答

反应

引用

请求

1. 打电话

下面是打电话时的一些常用说法：

（例句译文省略）

❀ 给人打电话：

Hello. Could (Can) I speak to Mr. Wilson?

This is James Green (speaking). (It's Margarette Terner here.)

Hello. Is that Carol?

I want to speak to Mrs. Black.

❀ 接电话：

Hello. Richardson's residence. (This is) James Richardson speaking.

Who is that speaking? (Who am I speaking to?/Who is there?）

Sorry, he is not in (he's out) at the moment.

I'm afraid Mr. Brown's not in the office right now.

❀ 请稍候：

Just a moment. Hold the line. please.

Hold on a moment. please. Will you hang on?

❀ 留口信：

Can I leave a message? (Yes.) Would you tell her that George phoned?

(Can I take a message?) I'll call (ring) again later.

Could you just tell her that Ruth called?

Could you ask her to call (ring) me at 435 2728?

❀ 预约门诊时间：

—Arcadia Medical Center.

—Hello. I'd like to make an appointment to see Dr. Brown tomorrow afternoon.

—Could you come at 3:30?

—Sure. Thank you.

❀ 熟人间打电话：

—Hello.

—Hello, Tom.

—Hello, Betty. How are you?

—Just so-so. And you?

—Not so good, I'm afraid.

*　　*　　*

—I'm afraid I can't talk to you now.

—OK. I'll phone after lunch.

—OK. Goodbye.

—Goodbye.

❀ 问问题

Could I have extension three three four five?

I'd like to make a collect call to (626)3184495.

Is this the railway station (the Personnel Office)?

Could you speak louder? It's a bad line (connection).

2. 时间

时间表示的方法很多，现简述如下：

❀ 某个时刻的表示法：

（1）整钟点用 o'clock 表示（o'clock 有时可省略）：

Try to get there at <u>five o'clock</u>.

You must be back by <u>nine (o'clock)</u>.

整钟点之间的时间用 past 或 to 表示（美国用 after 或 of 表示）：

	英国说法	美国说法
（30 分钟以内用 past）		
4 点半	half past four	half after four
5 点 20 分	twenty past five	twenty after five
12 点 5 分	five past twelve	five after twelve
（30 分以后用 to）		
六点三刻	(a) quarter to seven	(a) quarter of seven
9 点 40 分	twenty to ten	twenty of ten
10 点 55 分	five to eleven	five of eleven

（2）完全用数字表示（上午用 a.m. 表示，下午用 p.m. 表示）：

05:00	5 a.m.	12:20	twelve twenty
21:00	9 p.m.	02:45	two forty-five (a.m.)

| 12:00 | noon | 11:30 | eleven thirty (a.m.) |
| 00:00 | midnight | 19:50 | seven fifty (p. m.) |

为了表示准确，也可加上 minutes：

It was twenty minutes past five.

She arrived at five minutes to eleven.

在口语中钟点数常可省略：

"What time is it?" "It's twenty minutes (quarter) past."

9:05 可读作 "nine oh five" 或 "nine five"。

为了表示出是上午还是下午，通常都加上 a.m. 或 p.m.：

The shops will be opened at 10 a.m.

They will arrive in Hong Kong at 9:30 p.m.

可以和钟点连用的介词除 at 外还有 by, after, before, until, till, since：

Be sure to finish everything before ten tonight. 一定要在今晚 10 点前把一切都完成。

She worked until ten. 她一直工作到 10 点。

She hadn't slept a wink since two o'clock. 两点以后，她一会儿都没睡着。

表示大约的时刻，可在前面加 about 或 around (at 有时可省略)：

We got the airport (at) about nine. 我们 9 点前后到达机场。

The fire started (at) around midnight. 火是午夜前后着起来的。

❀ 某段时间表示法：

一天主要有 morning, afternoon, evening, night 这几段时间，前面一般用介词 in, 如有词修饰时用 on, night 常和 at 连用，有时和 by 连用：

In those nights I only had my daughter with me. 在那些夜晚，只有我女儿和我在一起。

Nothing could be going on there so late at night. 这么夜深，不会有什么事。

They sleep by day and hunt by night. 它们白天睡觉，夜间猎食。

有时可和 this, that, tomorrow 等连用，这时不再加介词：

Are you free this evening? 你今晚有空吗？

She stayed with us until the following afternoon. 她和我们待在一起直到第二天下午才走。

日期前通常用 on, 有时用 at:

They said she would arrive on the following Sunday. 他们说她将在下星期天到达。

A reception was held on New Year's Day (Eve). 元旦（除夕）开了一个招待会。

We shall be with you at Easter (Christmas). 我们将在复活（圣诞）节来。

❀ 某些短暂时间的表示法:

有些短暂时间，如 dawn, daybreak, sunrise, dusk, nightfall, sunset, twilight，常和 at 一起用:

At dawn we rose and knocked at the gate of the city. 天亮时，我们起来敲城门。

Someone knocked on our door at midnight. 午夜时，有人敲我们的门。

The doctor was awakened at dead of night. 在深更半夜时，医生被叫醒了。

We started at sunrise. 我们在日出时出发了。

At dusk the lights of the city come on. 黄昏时分，城里的灯都亮了。

She often sits in the garden at twilight. 在黄昏时分，她常在花园里坐坐。

❀ 一些时间副词（状语）:

下列副词或状语可和完成时态或一般过去时连用:

in the past	just	lately	previously	recently

Lately I've taken to making my own clothes. / A sad accident happened there lately.

A few days previously Shelley had written to him. / Previously she had very little time to work.

下列副词（状语）通常和过去时一道用:

at one time	earlier	earlier on	formerly
once	originally	sometime	then

Once dinosaurs walked these plains. 恐龙一度在这些平原上活动。

She was formerly head of a large department store. 她过去是一家大百货公司的头头。

下列副词常可和将来时态连用：

afterwards	at once	before long	eventually
immediately	in a minute	in a moment	in future
in the future	later	later on	one day
one of these days	shortly	someday	sometime
soon	sooner or later	within minutes	within the hour

Can we talk about it <u>later on</u>? 我们可否晚些时候谈这事？

No one knows what will happen <u>in the future</u>. 没人知道将来会发生什么情况。

下列副词多指现在情况（和过去及将来对比），多和现在时态一起用：

at the moment	at present	currently
just now	now	nowadays
presently	right now	these days

<u>At present</u> we are living in Boston. 现在我们住在波士顿。

<u>Nowadays</u> children are much healthier. 现今孩子们比较健康了。

3. 日常交往

日常交往有一些固定的说法，现择要概述如下：

（部分例句译文省略）

❀ 介绍人：

通常都用下面这类话介绍未见过的人：

Tom, do you know Nancy? Nancy, this is my friend Tom.

Betty, I don't think you've met Diana.

I don't think you two know each other, do you?

This is my cousin (classmate) Paul.

Can (May) I introduce Bill Patterson? （这是较正式的说法）

在介绍之后，彼此可以说 "How do you do?"（正式）"Hello." 或 "Hi."（随便说法）。美国人常说 "How are you?"

❀ 打招呼：

较正式的说法是：Good morning (afternoon/evening).

较随便的说法是：Hello(Hi).（非常随便）

在离开时较正式的说法是：Good morning (afternoon/evening/night).

说 Goodbye 比较不正式。说 Bye 比较随便。

孩子们之间说 Byebye 时较多。"See you." 和 "See you later (tomorrow, etc.)." 都是比较随便的说法。

还可说 "Cheerio(cheers)."（这是英国较随便的说法），"Take care." 或 "It is nice to meet you."

Goodnight 只用于告别。

❀ 问候：

见面常常需说一些问候的话：

How are you? How are things? How's it going?

美国有时说：How (are) you doing?

正式的回答是：Very well, thank you. And you?/ Fine, thank you.

较随便的回答是：Fine (Great), thanks./ Not too bad./ OK./ So-so./ All right./ (It) Could be worse.

❀ 特别祝愿语：

在节日等场合说的祝愿话为：

Happy New Year (Easter)!

Merry Christmas!

Happy birthday!

Many happy returns.

❀ 道歉：

表示歉意主要说 "Excuse me."（事前）或 "Sorry."（事后）：

Excuse me. Could I get past? 对不起，我能过去吗？

Excuse me, could you tell me the way to the station? 对不起打扰一下，去车站怎么走？

Oh, sorry, did I step on your foot? 啊，对不起，我踩你的脚了吧。

"I beg your pardon." 是比较正式的道歉语：

I beg your pardon. I didn't realise this was your seat. 请原谅，我不知道这是你的座位。

❀ 请人重复他的话：

在别人的话没听清或没听懂时，可以说"Sorry?/ What?/（I beg your) Pardon?"美国人多说"Pardon me?"

"Is Nina in?" "Sorry?" "I said, 'Is Nina in?'"

"I'll be back Saturday." "What?" "I'll be back Saturday."

"May I speak to Mr. Green?" "Pardon (I beg your pardon)?" "May I speak to Mr. Green?"

❀ 谈旅行等：

在别人出去旅行时可以说：

Have a good trip.（旅途愉快。）

英国人多说"**Have a good journey.**" "**Safe journey home.**"（一路平安。）在旅行回来之后，在接人时可以说：

Did you have a good journey (trip/flight)?

How was the journey (trip/flight)?

在别人参加某项活动时，可以说：

Have a good time!

Enjoy yourself.（美国有时只说 Enjoy!）

在别人参加考试或困难活动时可说"Good luck!"

在别人回来时，可说"Welcome back."

在别人出去度假时，可说"**Have a good holiday**（美：vacation）/ **Have a good time.**"

回来时可以说"**Did you have a good holiday?**"

❀ 吃饭等：

在吃饭过程中客人总说一些赞美的话，例如：

This is very nice.

The soup is delicious.

Your wife is a marvellous cook.

饭后可以说：

It was a marvellous meal.

That was lovely (delicious); thank you very much.

祝酒时可说：

Cheers!（干杯！）Your health.（祝你健康。）

Here is to Lily!（为莉莉干杯！）

Here's to the happy couple!（为这对幸福的夫妻干杯！）

Here's to the new job!（为新工作干杯！）

❀ 邀请或提出请求：

在邀请别人时一般可以这样开始：

Would you like to...?

Could you come to...?

回答时可以说：

Thank you very much. That would be very nice.

Sorry. I'm afraid I'm not free.

参加之后也要说句感谢的话，例如：

Thank you very much. That was a wonderful evening.

提出请求时可以说：

Could you lend me a pen?

May I use your telephone?

Might I have a look at your pictures?

回答时可以说 certainly, sure, of course 等。

❀ 在书信中的客气话：

在书信中常需说些客气话，例如：

Give my best wishes (regards/greetings/love) to...

Remember me to your...

Say hello to... for me.

也可说：

My wife sends her best wishes (regards) to you all.

如果表示慰问，可以说：

I was very (terribly/extremely) sorry to hear that...

Please accept my deepest sympathy.

❀ 表示感谢：

表示感谢时可说：

Thank you very much./Thank you./Thanks (a lot).

回答可以是：

Not at all./Don't mention it./You're welcome.

That's OK.（比较随便的说法）/That's quite all right.

也还有些其他表示感谢的说法：

I greatly appreciate your kindness (what you've done for me).

I'm frightfully (much) obliged to you.

I'm obliged to you for all you've done for me.

4. 呼语

和人讲话时，有时需使用呼语，表示这话是对谁说的。

❀ 在句子中的位置与汉语不同，在多数情况下，呼语都放在句子末尾：

Come over here, Jane. 简，到这边来。

Let me help you, Tom. 我来帮你的忙，汤姆。

如果想引起对方注意，也可把呼语放在句子前面：

Louisa, how long have you been here? 路易莎，你在这里有多久了？

Mrs. Smith, come this way, please. 史密斯夫人，请到这边来。

有时也可插在句子中间：

I must warn you, John, that if you do that again you'll be punished. 约翰，我必须警告你，如果你再这样做会受到处分。

Don't you think, Helen, it would be better to go by plane? 海伦，你不觉得坐飞机去更好吗？

❀ 呼语的形式：包括专有名词、名词（指人的以及加上头衔的）：

John/Smith, doctor, nurse, dad, mom, children, Prof. Sinclair

Mr., Mrs., Miss, Ms. 这类头衔不宜单独用作呼语，要和名字一起用：

Don't worry, Miss Patterson. 佩特森小姐，不要着急。

I'll take you there, Ms. Green. 格林女士，我带你去。

但 **doctor, nurse** 可以这样用：

Is it anything serious, doctor? 这个病严重吗，医生？

Come quickly, nurse. 护士，快来。

有个别头衔可用作呼语，但需放在句末：

Are you free this afternoon, Professor? 你下午有空吗，教授？

Goodbye, Captain. 再见，上尉。

对家人亲戚的称呼也可用作呼语：

Is this your car, Uncle? 这是你的车吗，叔叔？

Good morning, Auntie Ruth. 早上好，鲁思阿姨。

对一大伙人可称 Ladies and gentlemen（这是较正式的称呼），everybody（这是较随便的称呼）：

<u>Ladies and gentlemen</u>, welcome to our city. 女士们，先生们，欢迎你们访问我们的城市。

Keep quiet, <u>everybody</u>. 请大家安静。

对孩子们也可这样称呼：

<u>Girls</u>, I have some good news for you. 姑娘们，我有好消息告诉你们。

对顾客可用 sir 和 madam（多缩短成 ma'am）相称：

Do you want anything to drink, <u>sir</u>? 你想喝点什么吗，先生？

5. 度量衡

度量衡方面的问题是比较复杂的，这里作些扼要的讨论：

❀ 公制（metric system）与英制（imperial system）：

	公制（缩写形式）	英制（缩写形式）
长度 /（尺寸）	milimetre 毫米（mm） centimetre 公分（cm） metre 米（m） kilometre 千米，公里（km）	inch 英寸 foot 英尺 yard 码（yd） mile 英里（m）
面积	hectare 公顷（ha） （等于 2.47 英亩，15 市亩） are /ɑː/ 公亩（合 100 平方米）	acre 英亩（a） （合 6.07 市亩） square mile 平方英里（sq mile） （合 640 英亩）
容积（体积）	millilitre 毫升（ml） centilitre 厘升（cl） （合 10 毫升） litre 公升（l） （合 100 厘升，1 000 毫升）	fluid ounce 液量盎司（floz） pint 品脱（pt） quart 夸脱（q）（合 2 品脱） gallon 加仑（gal）（合 8 品脱）
重量	milligram 毫克（mg） gram 克（g） kilogram 千克，公斤（kg） tonne 公吨（t） （合 1 000 公斤）	ounce 盎司，英两（oz） pound 磅（lb）（合 16 盎司） stone 英石（st）（合 14 磅） hundredweight 英担（cwt） （合 8 英石） ton 吨（t）（合 20 英担，1 016.04 公斤）

这两种制度同时存在。在英国各行各业用公制的较多，但在某些行业中也有用英制的，如谈身高、体重，餐馆、酒店用英制也不少。在美国在日常生活中用英制的较多，但像 stone, hundredweight 这种词则用得很少。另外，kilo 常用来代替 kilogram, metric ton 可用来代替 tonne。

❀ 谈尺寸：

在谈尺寸时常可用"数字 + 度量单位 + 形容词"表示，例如：

The building is 200 feet high. 那座楼有 200 英尺高。

He was about six feet tall. 他有 6 英尺高。

有时 foot 可以和复数一起用，例如：

The spear was about six foot long. 矛约 6 英尺长。

如说"……英尺……英寸"，inches 可以省略：

It's two foot six long. 它的长度是 2 英尺 6 英寸。

若 foot 用复数形式，则 inches 不能省：

He is six feet six inches tall. 他 6 英尺 6 英寸高。

谈身高时可加 tall, 也可把它省略：

She was six feet tall. 她身高 6 英尺。

He was six feet six. 他身高 6 英尺 6 英寸。

谈宽度时可用 across 表示：

The stream is 8 feet across. 小溪有 8 英尺宽。

The river is half a mile across. 河有半英里宽。

另外，下面短语也可用来谈尺寸：

in breadth	in depth	in height
in length	in thickness	in width

The classroom is 30 feet in length and 15 feet in breadth. 那个教室长 30 英尺，宽 15 英尺。

The statue is eleven feet in height. 那个雕像高 11 英尺。

❀ 谈面积：

谈面积时常可用 square 这个词：

Its European territory covered about 2,000,000 square miles. 它欧洲的领土约有 200 万平方英里。

144 square inches equals to 1 square foot. 144 平方英寸等于 1 平方英尺。

They are said to be as little as 300 sq. cm. 据说，他们可以小到 300 平方厘米。

如果要更准确，可加上 **in area**：

These hot spots are often hundreds of square miles in area. 这些热点，面积常常达到千百平方英里。

The island is only 0.4 square kilometres in area. 这座岛面积仅 0.4 平方公里。

square 还可用来表示"见方"：

Each family has only one room eight or ten feet square. 每家人只有一间 8 平方英尺或 10 平方英尺的房间。

This piece of wood is two metres square. 这块木头为两平方米（即每边两米）。

比较大的面积可用 **hectare** 或 **acre** 表示：

In 1975 there were 220 million hectares under cultivation. 1975 年时，有 2.2 亿公顷的耕地。

His land covers twenty acres. 他有 20 英亩土地。

如果谈圆形面积，可有两个办法，一是 **in circumference**（周边有多长），一是 **in diameter**（直径有多长）：

The earth is almost 25,000 miles in circumference. 地球周长几乎有 25 000 英里。

The four main vessels were 2.3 mm in diameter. 四根主血管直径为 2.3 毫米。

也可用 **radius**（半径）表示：

It had a radius of fifteen kilometres. 它的半径为 15 公里。

表示长、宽、高可以用 **by** 或"×"号：

The island measures about 25 miles by 12 miles. 这个岛约 25 英里长、12 英里宽。

The box measures approximately 26 inches long × 25 inches wide × 16 inches deep. 这个箱子约 26 英寸长、25 英寸宽、16 英寸高。

Each section is $2 \times 2 \times 1$ metres in size. 每一块体积为 $2 \times 2 \times 1$ 米。

❀ 谈体积（容积）：

体积通常以 cubic 表示：

The container has a volume of 24 <u>cubic</u> metres. 这个容器容积为 24 立方米。

Its brain was close to 500 <u>cubic</u> centimeters (49 cubic inches). 它的脑子接近 500 立方公分（49 立方英寸）。

液体和气体的体积可以 litre 和 gallon 等表示：

This bottle holds two <u>litres</u>. 这个瓶子装两公升。

Nearly 5 <u>litres</u> of blood are pumped by the heart every minute. 心脏每分钟要压出 5 公升的血。

Wine production is expected to reach 4.1 billion <u>gallons</u> this year. 酒的产量今年可望达到 41 亿加仑。

A <u>gallon</u> of petrol costs £1. 25. 1 加仑汽油价钱是 1.25 英镑。

The amount of air being expelled is about 1,000 to 1,500 <u>mls</u>. 呼出的气约为 1 000 至 1 500 毫升。

牛乳、啤酒的量多用 pint、quart 或 gallon 表示，在英国 pint 本身有时就用来指牛乳或啤酒：

Two <u>pints</u> today, please. 今天我要两品脱的奶。

They stopped at the pub for a <u>pint</u>. 他们到酒店喝了一品脱的啤酒。

❀ 谈距离：

谈距离时，多用"数词 + 距离单位 +from、away from 或 away"这样的模式：

Our office is about eight kilometres <u>away from</u> my home. 我们的办公室离我家约 8 公里。

The sun is 92 million miles <u>away</u>. 太阳离这里有 9 200 万英里。

距离还可以用到那里需要的时间表示：

They lived only <u>five hours away</u> from our town. 他们的住处离我们的城市只 5 个钟头的路。

It's <u>an hour and a half from</u> London. 它离伦敦只有 1 个半钟头。

为了更确切，可以把交通方式说出来：

It's less than <u>eight hours' drive from</u> here. 开车到那里不到 8 个钟头。

It's about <u>five minutes' walk from</u> the bus stop. 从公共汽车站走到那里只要 5 分钟。

问距离时可用 **how far**：

<u>How far</u> is it to Oxford? 这里离牛津多远？

"<u>How far</u> is it (from here)?" "Two hundred and fifty kilometres from here." "它（离这儿）有多远？" "有 250 公里远。"

❀ 谈重量：

谈重量时常可用 **weigh** 这个词：

He <u>weighs</u> 150 pounds. 他体重为 150 磅。

也可用 **in weight** 或 **weight**：

It's smaller in size but greater <u>in weight</u>. 它体积小，但分量重些。

Her <u>weight</u> has been steady at fifty kilos for the last ten years. 十年以来她的体重都稳定在 50 公斤。

问分量多大时可以说：

How much (What) does the box weigh? 箱子有多重？

How heavy is it? 它有多重？

❀ 谈温度：

谈温度一般用 **centigrade(C)**，**Fahrenheit(F)**，度数用 **degree** 或 "。" 表示：

Today's temperature is 30℃ (a degree above zero). 今天气温是摄氏 30 度（零上 1 度）。

The temperature was probably 50℉. 气温可能是华氏 50 度。

有时 "摄氏" "华氏" 可以不说出来：

The room had a temperature of 20°. 室温是 20 度。（不可能是华氏）

Roger has a temperature of 103°. 罗杰的热度有 103 度。（不可能是摄氏）

零下温度可用 **below zero**（或 **freezing**）表示：

The temperature is fifteen degrees <u>below zero</u> at night. 夜间气温为零下 15 度。

It's amazingly cold: it must be twenty degrees <u>below freezing</u>. 天冷得出奇：一定有零下 20 度了。

❀ 谈速度等：

谈速度时多用 "数字 ＋ 距离名称 ＋per（a 或 an）＋ 时间长度" 表示：

My speed in shorthand is 120 words per minute. 我速记的速度是每分钟 120 个字。

a velocity of 160 km/sec 1 秒钟 160 公里的速度

这个公式还可用来谈其他东西（如价钱、频度、比例等）：

In Indonesia there are 18, 100 people per doctor. 在印度尼西亚，18 100
人才有一名医生。

The average cereal consumption per head per year in the U.S.A is 900 kg.
美国每年每人的平均谷物消费量为 900 公斤。

6. 称呼

谈到某人时，有四种称呼法：

（1）家人、朋友和孩子可以名字（**first name**）相称：

Bill will come round this afternoon. 比尔下午要来。

对某些人可以连名带姓一起称呼：

At that time Lyndon Johnson was U. S. President. 那时林登·约翰逊是
美国总统。

Have you read anything by James Joyce? 你看过詹姆斯·乔伊斯的作
品吗?

（2）如表示尊敬，可以用"头衔 + 姓"相称：

This is Mr. Pound. 这位是庞德先生。

Professor Patterson is asking for you on the phone. 帕特森教授请你接
电话。

常见的头衔有：

Ambassador	Archbishop	Bishop	Councillor
Doctor	Father（神父）	Governor	Inspector
Judge	Justice	Miss	Mr.
Mrs.	Ms.	President	Professor
Superintend			

此外，军衔（如 **Captain, Sergeant, General** 等）、皇室头衔（如
King, Queen, Prince, Princess 等）等都可以这样用：

Have you seen the film *General Gordon*? 你看过《戈登将军》这部电
影吗?

Lord Perry is now chancellor of the University. 佩里勋爵现在任该大学

的校长。

Princess Diana 戴安娜王妃　　　　Sir Geoffrey 杰弗里爵士

（3）有时只用姓称呼，这主要是谈大家都知道的人物，如政治人物、运动员、作家等：

The women's 5,000 metres was won by Jones. 女子 5 000 米赛跑，琼斯胜出了。

How do you like Shaw's plays? 你觉得萧伯纳的戏剧如何？

对雇员或在士兵、学生、队员之间也可以这样称呼：

Ask Browning to come to my office. 让布朗宁到我办公室来。

Bruce and Gray can team up. 布鲁斯和格雷可以组成一组。

❀ 对人说话有两种称呼法：

（1）对亲属、朋友和孩子，都以名字相称：

Is this your car, Bill? 比尔，这是你的车吗？

Where is your Dad, Alice? 你爸爸在哪儿，艾丽斯？

（2）比较客气、正式的称呼是"头衔 + 姓"：

How are you, Mr. Johnson? 你好，约翰逊先生！

Here is your ticket, Miss Green. 你的机票，格林小姐。

这些头衔很少单独用，但当要称呼对方而不知姓名时，可用 **sir** 或 **madam**：

Excuse me, sir. How do I get to the station? 打扰，先生，我怎样去车站？

Thank you, madam. 谢谢你，夫人（小姐）。

Doctor 可用来称呼医生：

When shall I come back, doctor? 我什么时候再来，医生？

7. 建议

日常口语中有许多方式提出建议，现举例说明如下：

❀ **could** 常可客气地提出建议：

Could we take the 9:30 train? 我们可否坐 9 点半的火车？

Could we discuss the two problems separately? 这两个问题我们可否分开讨论？

❀ **may (might) as well** 也可提出建议：

We may as well stay here for another day. 我们不妨在这里再待一天。

You might as well talk it over with the manager. 你不妨好好与经理谈谈。

❀ **It might be a good idea…：**

It might be a good idea to hire a boat. 租一条船可能是个好主意。

It might be a good idea to go separately. 分开走可能是一个好办法。

❀ **might 常可用在建议中：**

You might stay with us. 你可以住我们这儿。

You might consider moving to a smaller house. 你可以考虑搬进一个较小的房子。

❀ **shall we 也是一个常用语：**

Shall we inform the police about it? 这事咱们要不要报告警察？

Shall we try somewhere else? 咱们要不要到别处试试？

❀ **had better 也可客气地提出建议：**

We'd better consult a specialist. 我们最好找一位专家咨询一下。

We'd better not bring this up now. 我们最好现在暂不提此事。

❀ **let's… 是提出建议很方便的形式：**

Let's meet again tomorrow morning, shall we? 咱们明天上午再碰一次头好吗？

Let's not talk about the question for the time being. 咱们暂时别谈此事。

❀ **why don't you… 也可用来提出建议：**

Why don't you ask your uncle for advice? 你何不找你叔叔出主意？

Why don't you (Why not) go by subway? 何不坐地铁去？

❀ **suggest 更可用来提出建议：**

I suggest setting up a committee to take care of this. 我建议成立一个委员会来负责此事。

I suggest we send her to hospital right away. 我建议马上送她进医院。

❀ **还可用 I thought (wonder) 引起从句提出建议：**

I thought we might plant some trees round the area. 我考虑我们可以在这一带种些树。

I wonder whether (if) we could have a little talk after the meeting. 我在想，是否会后我们能稍稍谈一谈。

其他还有很多提出建议的方式，如利用 **ought to, should, I suppose** 等：

I think we should organize a trip to this place. 我想，我们应当组织一

次郊游到这个地方。

Oughtn't we to report this to the police? 我们应不应当把这件事报告警察?

在回答这类建议时，可根据情况作简短的回答：（例句译文省略）

"Shall we take a walk?" "Why not."

"What about (meeting) Thursday?" "Fine."

还可说 **"That's a good idea." "That's all right." "We'd better not do it."**

帮人出主意也有许多方式，例如：

❀ **直接出主意：**

I strongly advise you to keep away from these people. 我极力劝你别和这些人来往。

My advice is to quit the job right away. 我的意见是马上离职。

❀ **婉转地出主意：**

I should adopt a different approach. 我会采取另一种做法。

If I were you, I would stay. 我要是你，我就会留下。

I wouldn't leave so soon. 我不会这样快离开。

You might talk this over with your mother. 你可以和你妈妈好好谈一次。

You might as well let her decide. 你不妨让她自己决定。

❀ **比较坦率或向下属提出意见：**

You'd better write everything down. 你最好把什么都写下来。

I think you should reconsider your decision. 我认为你应重新考虑你的决定。

Perhaps you can come again tomorrow. 或许你可以明天再来。

❀ **严厉地提出意见：**

Make sure that all the lights are off before you go to bed. 睡觉前一定要关灯。

Drop the gun, or I'll kill you. 把枪放下，否则我就打死你。

Be sure to send out all the invitations today. 一定要在今天把请帖都发出去。

8. 回答

在回答别人问题时，若是一般疑问句，多用 **Yes** 或 **No** 回答，后面有时加点解释：

"Did you enjoy the meal?" "Yes. It was very good." "饭吃得好吗？" "好，饭很不错。"

"Has she gone home?" "No. She went to the cinema with Ruth." "她回家了吗？" "没有，她和鲁思看电影去了。"

"Are the books difficult?" "Yes, they are, for me at least." "这些书难吗？" "难，至少对我如此。"

有时可以更灵活些：

"Did she like it?" "Oh, very much, she said it was marvellous." "她喜欢吗？" "啊，非常喜欢，说是精彩极了。"

"Did he talk to you?" "A little. Not much." "他和你谈话了吗？" "谈了一点儿，没多谈。"

❀ 在回答一般疑问句时有时用 **not** 或 **so** 构成的简单回答：

"Will it rain today?" "I hope not." "今天会下雨吗？" "希望别下。"

"Can you come to our party?" "I'm afraid not." "你能来参加晚会吗？" "恐怕不行。"

"Are you short of hands?" "Not at the moment." "你们缺人吗？" "目前不缺。"

"Will Nancy go with us?" "I should think so." "南希和我们一起去吗？" "我想会的。"

"Are they doing all right now?" "I suppose so." "现在他们进展顺利吗？" "我想是顺利的。"

如果回答不肯定，可以避免做肯定的回答：

"Did they succeed?" "Sorry, I don't know." "他们成功了吗？" "对不起，我不知道。"

"Do you think they'll agree?" "I'm not sure." "你想他们会同意吗？" "我说不准。"

在回答否定问句时，要注意使 **yes**、**no** 和自己的答语一致：

"Didn't you see my letter?" "No (I didn't)." "你没看到我的信吗？" "对，没看到。"

"Haven't you got your passport with you?" "Oh, yes. I had it in my suitcase." "你难道没带着护照？" "哦，不，在我的手提箱里。"

❀ 在回答特殊疑问句时，常可作简短回答，用一个词或几个词，避免重复全句：（例句译文省略）

"How old is Harry?" "Thirteen. I think."

"How far is the place?" "About an hour's drive."

"Where are you going?" "To town."

"When are you coming back?" "Tomorrow."

但有时需要用一个整句回答：

"What are you going to do tonight?" "I might go to a concert."

"Why can't you go with us?" "Because I have a lot of things to do."

❀ 在回答选择问句时，只需选择一个正确的答案：

"Do you want traveller's cheques or currency?" "Traveller's cheques, please."

"Is Mary going home now or a little later?" "She may stay here for another week."

在回答不十分明确时，可用 "well...":

"Are you coming or not?" "Well, let me think it over."

在回答反意问句时，用 yes 或是 no，要和自己的答案一致（不要受汉语影响）：

"You have no objection, do you?" "No, I don't." "你不反对，是吧?" "是的，我不反对。"

"You don't like classical music, do you?" "But yes, I like it very much." "你不喜欢古典音乐，对吧?" "不，我非常喜欢。"

9. 反应

对别人讲的话和看到的情况可以有种种反应。最常见的反应是惊叹，如：

Oh, how nice! 啊，真不错！

How kind you are! 你真好！

What nonsense you talk! 你说什么瞎话！

也可用否定问句回应：

Isn't that a good idea? 这想法真好！

Isn't that terrible? 真糟糕！

Isn't that interesting? 真有意思！

大体说来，对别人的话可有下列几种反应：

（1）吃惊或感兴趣：

"It's only five minutes' drive from our house." "Really?" "那地方开车五分钟就到。""真的吗？"

Good Heavens! It'll get into the papers. 我的天啦！这会登到报上去的。

Lord, what a beautiful day. 天啦，今天天气真好。

"I haven't seen her for over ten years." "Good God." "我有十几年没见到她了。""天哪。"

My God, what are you doing there? 我的老天爷，你在那里干什么？

有时可用简短问句做出反应：

"He gets free meals." "Does he?" "他吃饭不要钱。""真的吗？"

"They're starting up a new business." "Are they?" "他们要开一个新店。""是吗？"

还有其他一些反应表达法：

Well, that's interesting. 啊，这很有意思。

How strange! 多么奇特！

Why, what a surprise! 嗨，真令人惊讶！

Fancy seeing you here! 想不到在这里见到你！

（2）感到高兴：

"I've booked the tickets." "Oh, that's great." "我已买好机票。""啊，这太好了。"

That's wonderful. 这太好了。

"We can reserve some seats for you." "Great." "我们可以给你们订座。""那太好了。"

"I'll stay here for a couple of days." "How marvellous." "我将在这里待一两天。""太好了。"

"We'll spend three days in Rome." "How lovely!" "我们将在罗马待三天。""真不错！"

（3）感到宽慰：

"He's out of danger now." "That's a relief." "他已脱离危险。" "这使人宽慰。"

"The children have all come back." "Thank goodness." "孩子们都回来了。" "谢天谢地。"

"None of them got injured." "Thank heavens for it." "他们谁也没受伤。" "真感谢老天爷。"

（4）感到不快：

Bother! I've missed the train. 糟糕！我误了火车了。

Damn! I left the keys at home. 倒霉！我把钥匙丢家里了。

I just missed the last train. Damn! 我没赶上末班车，糟糕！

Hell, what do you want me to do anyway? 妈的，你到底要我干什么？

"It's broken." "Oh, hell!" "破了。" "糟糕！"

What a nuisance! I've forgotten my ticket. 真糟糕！我忘了带车票了。

（5）感到失望或遗憾：

"They're going to demolish it." "That's a shame. It's a nice place." "他们将拆毁这房子。" "真遗憾。这地方还挺好的。"

"They're leaving tomorrow." "What a pity!" "他们明天就走了。" "真遗憾。"

"Jennie has had an accident." "Oh no! What happened?" "珍妮出了车祸。" "糟糕，情况怎样？"

（6）表示同情：

"Soon it was pouring with rain." "Oh dear." "不久下起倾盆大雨。" "糟糕。"

"My wife is ill." "How awful! Has she seen the doctor?" "我妻子病了。" "糟糕！她去医院了吗？"

"My husband has just been sacked." "That's terrible." "我丈夫刚被解雇了。" "这太糟糕了。"

10. 引用

（例句译文省略）

❀ 引用别人的话有两种方式，一是用直接引语（**direct speech**）：

He said, "Goodbye," and left.

"May I see the manager?" she asked.

另一种是用间接引语（**indirect speech**）：

He said goodbye and left.

She asked whether she could see the manager.

直接引用别人的话时，只需引用原话并在所说的话前后加上引号就行了。转述别人的话时就有许多要注意的地方，如时态：

She said, "Henry is busy." → She said (that) Henry was busy.

代词的变化：

She asked, "May I go now?" → She asked if she might go now.

副词的变化：

He said, "I'll be back tonight." → He said he'd be back that night.

❀ 由于英语语法有时态一致（**the sequence of tenses**）的规定，引用语应和引用词在时态上一致（如引用词为 **said**，引用语中谓语时态应与之一致）：

<u>原话</u>

I don't know English.

I'm single.

I can't swim.

I'm waiting for a friend.

John phoned just now.

Have you ever been to Shanghai?

How long have you been waiting?

Will you be free tonight?

Where will you be staying?

He was born in 1980.

<u>引语</u>

He said he didn't know English.

He told me he was single.

She said she couldn't swim.

She said she was waiting for a friend.

He said John (had) phoned just now.

He asked if I had ever been to Shanghai.

He asked how long I <u>had been waiting</u>.

She asked whether I'<u>d be</u> free that night.

She asked where <u>we'd be staying</u>.

He said he was born in 1980.

（这时时态不必变）

有<u>些</u>情态动词要变，如 **can** 变为 **could**，**may** 变为 **might**。但 **must, might, could, ought, should, would** 可以不变：

原话

Maria <u>may know</u> her address.

We <u>must hurry</u> up.

They <u>might be</u> in the garden.

<u>Could</u> you give me some help?

You <u>ought</u> to do it well.

You <u>should work</u> harder.

<u>Would</u> you <u>come</u> nearer?

引语

He said Maria <u>might know</u> her address.

He said we <u>must hurry</u> up.

He said they <u>might be</u> in the garden.

He asked whether I <u>could give</u> him some help.

He said we <u>ought to do</u> it well.

He said I <u>should work</u> harder.

She asked if I <u>could go</u> nearer.

✿ 由于说话的角度不同，在改为间接引语时，人称代词及物主代词也需作调整：

原话

I know <u>your</u> sister.

I will help <u>you</u>.

<u>We</u> certainly will support <u>you</u>.

I'm grateful for what <u>you</u>'ve done.

引语

He said <u>he</u> knew <u>my</u> sister.

She promised that <u>she</u> would help <u>me</u>.

He said <u>they</u> certainly would support <u>us</u>.

She said <u>she</u> was grateful for what <u>I</u>'d done.

有时状语也需作调整：

原话

We've lived <u>here</u> for ten years.

I might see her <u>this evening</u>.

We're leaving <u>tomorrow</u>.

I may go there <u>next spring</u>.

引语

He said they had lived <u>there</u> for ten years.

He said he might see her <u>that evening</u>.

He said they were leaving <u>the following day</u>.

He said he might go <u>the following spring</u>.

❀ 引用词除了 **say, ask** 外还可以有许多别的词：

原话

You are wanted on the phone.

That's a good idea.

Where have they gone?

Are you interested in going?

How many students are absent?

引语

She <u>told</u> me that I was wanted on the phone.

He <u>agreed</u> that was a good idea.

She <u>wondered</u> where they had gone.

They <u>wanted to know</u> if I was interested in going.

She <u>wanted to find out</u> how many students were absent.

在问句变为间接引语时，要用自然语序（即和陈述句相同的语序，见上例）。

❀ 祈使句改为间接引语时常可用一个不定式表示：

原话

Come in!

Don't park your car here.

Put down your gun!

Answer my questions, Tom.

引语

She asked me to go in.

The policeman told me not to park my car there.

They ordered him to put down his gun.

She told Tom to answer her questions.

感叹句一般不宜改为间接引语，直接引语更生动一些：

"You monster!" she shouted.

"Great Heavens!" cried Betty.

11. 请求

提出请求方式很多。

❀ 用问句形式（多用情态动词开始）：

May I have a look at your passport? 我可否看一下你的护照？

Would you tell her that I called? 你可否告诉她我打过电话来？

Do you think you could spare me a few minutes? 你能给我几分钟时间吗？

Would you mind waiting a moment? 你可否等一会儿？

Would you kindly wake me up at six? 劳驾六点钟叫醒我。

❀ 用陈述句形式：

A packet of biscuits, please. 请给我一包饼干。

An orange juice will do. 一杯橘汁就行了。

I think I'll have a chicken soup. 我想我要一份鸡汤。

I'd be grateful if you could take me home. 如果你送我回家，我会很感激。

I'd appreciate it if you could drop in tonight. 你今晚来一趟我会很感激。

I suppose you could stay here for another day. 我想你可以再待一天。

I wonder if you'd do me a favour. 不知你可否帮我一个忙。

You are kindly requested not to smoke. 对不起请不要吸烟。

❀ 用祈使句形式：

Have another bun. 再吃一块面包。

Please help me carry this box. 请帮帮我抬一下这个箱子。

Be sure to get back before six. 务请在 6 点以前回来。

12. 同意

表示同意的方法很多，最普通的是用 **yes**：

"We'd better leave earlier." "<u>Yes</u>, I agree." "我们最好早点动身。""是的，我同意。"

"It's a nice restaurant." "<u>Yes</u>, you are right." "这家餐馆不错。""是的，你说得对。"

"That's a wonderful film." "<u>Yes</u>, isn't it?" "这部片子很精彩。""可不是吗？"

"I was rather careless." "<u>Yes</u>, you were." "我有些粗心大意。""是这样。"

但对方若说的是否定句，则不能用 **yes**，而要用 **no**：

"She's not easy to get along with." "<u>No</u>." "她不好相处。""是的。"

"It isn't going to rain, is it?" "<u>No</u>, it isn't." "不会下雨，是吧？""是的，不会下。"

"You won't tell him?" "<u>No</u>, I won't." "你不会告诉他吧？""不会。"

此外还有许多表示同意的办法：

"Then we'll have more leisure." "That's true." "那样我们空闲的时间就多一点。""是这样的。"

"Smoking is bad for your health." "I agree with you." "抽烟对健康不利。""我同意你的意见。"

"Children shouldn't see such films." "You're absolutely right." "孩子们不应当看这种电影。""你说得完全对。"

"That ballet dancer was superb." "Absolutely." "那位芭蕾舞演员棒极了。""确实的。"

"We need a rest." "Exactly. Let's have a break." "我们需要休息一下。""正是，咱们休息一会儿吧。"

"Will you help me?" "Certainly (I will)." "你能帮助我吗？""没问题。"

另外还有许多表示同意的话，如：

You're perfectly right. 你说得完全对。

That's for sure. 这是肯定无疑的。

I couldn't agree more. 我完全同意。

13. 道歉

表示道歉的方式很多，常见的说法现分述如下：

❀ 正式道歉的话：

I apologize for not coming to the party. 我没来参加晚会，向你道歉。

Please accept my sincere apologies. 请接受我诚挚的歉意。

I must offer my apology for not coming to your party. 我没来参加你的晚会，必须向你道歉。

Please accept my apologies for this unfortunate incident. 发生了这件不幸的事，请接受我的道歉。

❀ 普通表示歉意的话：

Sorry, did I step on your toe? 对不起，踩你的脚了吗？

(I'm) Sorry to bother you. 对不起，麻烦你了。

I'm sorry to have disturbed you. 对不起，打扰你了。

I'm awfully sorry that this occurred. 发生了这事，我非常抱歉。

I'm terribly sorry to give you all this trouble. 我非常抱歉给你带来这么多麻烦。

Forgive me interrupting you. 请原谅我打断你的话。

You must forgive my inexperience. 你要原谅我没有经验。

I regret that I shall not be able to come. 很遗憾我不能来。

在回答这类道歉的话时可以说 **"It's all right." "It doesn't matter." "Forget it." "Don't worry about it." "That's okay."** 等。

14. 请求重复

当人家说了话，自己没听清楚，要请人重复时，有许多说法，一些是比较正规的说法：

"What about tomorrow at five?" "Sorry, what did you say?" "明天下午五点怎么样？" "对不起，你说什么？"

"Where shall we meet?" "Would you repeat that? I didn't quite catch it." "我们在哪儿碰头？" "你能否再说一遍，我没听清楚。"

有时也可说，**"Beg your pardon?"** 但这比较正式，且有点过时。

"Did he agree?" "Beg your pardon?" "Did he agree?" "他同意吗？" "请

再说一遍。""他同意了吗？"

"Did they like the idea?" "I beg your pardon?" "I said if they liked the idea?" "他们赞成这个想法吗""请再说一遍。""我说他们赞成这个想法吗？"

但还有许多比较随便的说法，例如：

"Have you seen my dictionary?" "Sorry?" "Have you seen my dictionary?" "你看见我的字典了吗？" "对不起，没听清楚。" "你看到我的字典了吗？"

在美式英语中，一般都说 "**Excuse me?**" 或 "**Pardon me?**"

"I guess you see him sometimes." "Excuse me?" "I thought you saw him sometimes." "我猜你有时见到他。" "请再说一遍。" "我想你有时见到他。"

还有一些更随便的方式请人重复他们的话：

"Do you want some tea?" "What?" "Do you want some tea?" "你要不要喝点茶？" "什么？" "你要不要喝点茶？"

"Will you be in tonight?" "Eh?" "I said will you be in tonight?" "你今晚在家吗？" "什么？" "我说你今晚在家吗？"

有时用 **again** 表示"请再说一次"：

What's his name again? 请再说一次他叫什么名字。

15. 比较

compare 表示"比较"：

I am now <u>comparing</u> the two versions. 我正在比较两个版本。

在表示"和……相比较"时，多用介词 **with**，有时用 **to**：

Let's <u>compare</u> the copy <u>with</u> the original. 咱们把复制品和原画比较一下。

He began <u>comparing</u> himself <u>with</u> the other students. 他开始把自己和其他学生比一比。

有时和 **can** 连用，表示"能和……相比"：

He cannot <u>compare</u> with Shakespeare. 他不能和莎士比亚相比。

Walking can't <u>compare</u> with flying. 走路没法和飞行相比。

也可用于"把……比作"，这时多用介词 **to**：

Shakespeare <u>compared</u> the world <u>to</u> a stage. 莎士比亚把世界比作舞台。

He <u>compared</u> the heart <u>to</u> a pump. 他把心脏比作水泵。

有时可用过去分词引起状语，表示"和……比起来"，这时可用介词 **with** 或 **to**：

The severest toil was child's play <u>compared with</u> this. 和这相比，最苦的活也不过是儿戏。

<u>Compared to</u> many women, she was indeed very fortunate. 和许多女人相比，她的确是非常幸运的。

16. 批评

批评人有各种方式。对比较熟的人可以进行直率的批评，还可用语气表示批评的严峻程度：

That's not right. You shouldn't act like that. 这是不对的，你不应该这样做。

Why did you lie to me? 你为什么对我撒谎？

Why are you so careless? 你为什么这样粗心大意？

You shouldn't talk back to your mother. 你不应当和你妈妈顶嘴。

一般来说，批评要注意分寸，应学会婉转地进行批评，例如：

You could have talked me beforehand. 你事前告诉我一声就好了。

You could have been more careful. 你还可以更小心一点儿的。

17. 强调

在日常口语中我们常常对某个词或词组加以强调，这可能是表示赞扬、谴责等情绪，例如：

You <u>do</u> look nice today! 你今天确实很漂亮！

You are <u>so</u> stupid! 你真愚蠢！

也可能为了对比：

"Why weren't you at the party?" "I <u>was</u> at the party." "你为什么没参加晚会？""我参加了。"

I don't play football now, but I <u>did</u> play a lot when I was younger. 我现在不踢足球，但我年轻时踢的可不少。

强调有三个主要方法：

❀ 语调：

我们可以通过重读的办法对某个词加以强调。同样一句话，我们可以重读不同的词（下面的黑体词就是强调部分）：

Nancy visited us yesterday. 南希昨天来看望我们了。(Not someone else.)

Nancy **visited** us yesterday. (She didn't do anything else.)

Nancy visited **us** yesterday. (She didn't visit others.)

Nancy visited us **yesterday**. (Not today.)

通常我们可以重读助动词或情态动词或动词 **be** 来对句子加以强调：

She has done her best. 她已尽了力了。

I am trying to help them. 我正设法帮助他们。

You must keep this in mind. 你要牢牢记住这一点。

It was a tremendous success. 这的确很成功。

在没有这类动词时，我们可以在动词前加 **do** 来强调：

I do hope you'll come. 我的确希望你来。

She does like this city. 她的确很喜欢这座城市。

Please! Do be quiet a moment. 求你！务必安静一会儿。

❀ 词汇：

有时可用一些词汇来表示某种强调：

Thank you so much. 真是非常感谢。

It was such a lovely day. 天气是那么好。

You are just the person we need. 你正是我们需要的人。

I really think you did right. 我真地认为你做对了。

What ever are you doing there? 你在那儿到底在干什么？

What on earth do you mean? 你到底是什么意思？

Goodness, you gave me a start! 我的天，你吓我一跳！

I don't care a damn what he does. 我才不在乎他干什么。

It's a miracle that you returned at all. 你竟然回来了，真是奇迹。

有些副词，如 **sure, certainly, definitely, absolutely** 等，都可起强调作用：

You are definitely wrong. 你肯定是错的。

He sure is tall. 他的确很高。

She's <u>absolutely</u> right. 她绝对正确。

You <u>certainly</u> are lazy. 你的确很懒。

❀ 句子结构：

有时通过改变句子结构来对某部分加以强调。一个常用的办法是将强调的部分提前：

People like that I Just don't understand. 这种人我就是不懂。

Strange people they are! 他们是些怪人！

Fool that I was! 我真傻！

A marvellous show they gave! 他们的表演真精彩！

How he escaped capture, nobody knows. 他怎么逃脱了抓捕，谁也不知道。

还有一个办法是用 it 来改变句子结构：

Was it you that broke the window? 是你打破窗子的吗？（对主语加以强调）

It was the President that Jean shot yesterday. 杰恩昨天枪杀的是总统。（强调宾语）

It was Monday night that all this happened. 这一切是星期一夜里发生的。（强调状语）

It was not until I saw Mary that I felt happy. 直到见到玛丽我才高兴起来。

还可用 what 来改变结构：

What you need is a good rest. 你需要的是好好休息。

What I want to say is this. 我想说的是这一点。

另外，以 as、though 引起的状语从句，可以把表语提前：

Young as he was, he knew what was going on. 他虽然很小，却知道在发生什么事。

Tired though she was, she went on working. 尽管她累，她还是继续干活。

18. 感叹

感叹句常见的有下面几类：

❀ 由 **how** 引起的感叹句：

<u>How</u> well you look! 你气色真好！

How kind you are! 你心肠真好!

Strawberries! How nice! 草莓! 多好呀!

❀ 由 **what** 引起的感叹句（若后面为可数名词单数要加 **a**）：

What a good heart you have! 你的心肠真好!

What beautiful weather (lovely flowers)! 多好的天气（美的花）!

❀ 带 **so** 和 **such** 的句子：

You gave me such a fright! 你吓了我一跳!

You can have no idea what a girl she is. Such character! Such sense! 你不知道这姑娘多好。那样好的性格! 那样有头脑!

❀ 某些否定问句：

Isn't it a marvellous film! 这电影真精彩!

Aren't these pictures lovely! 这些画多好看呀!

❀ 很多句子和短语甚至单词可以通过语气成为感叹句：

So you are here at last! 你到底还是来了!

Look out! Mind your head! 小心! 当心脑袋!

Get out! You scoundrels! 滚开! 你们这些恶棍!

Amazing! Wonderful! 真令人惊异! 太精彩了!

19. 欢送

见到人首先要打招呼。

通常用 **hello**、**hi** 这类词（在美国 **hi** 用得更多一些）：

Hello, Michael, how are you today? 喂，迈克，今天好?

"Hi," said Nancy, "come in." 南希说："嗨，请进。"

还有一些其他较随意的招呼语，例如：

Well, old chap, sit down and make yourself comfortable. 嗨，老伙计，请坐，不要拘束。

Well, well, it is nice to see you again. 嗯，再次见到你很高兴。

比较正式的招呼语为 **good morning** 等：

Good afternoon. Could I speak to Mr. Brown, please? 下午好，可否请布朗先生接电话?

good day 在英国已经不太通用，但在美国还有人用。

在节日时可以致节日的问候，如"Merry (Happy) Christmas.""Happy New Year.""Happy Easter." 回答时可重复这个问候语，也可说"And Happy Christmas to you too.""The same to you!" 或"And you!" 当别人向你说"Happy Birthday to you." 或"Many happy returns." 你可以说"Thank you."

美国人在告别时有时说"Have a nice day."（比如在商店、餐馆可以对顾客说）：

"Have a nice day.""Thank you.""祝好运。""谢谢。"

英国人有时说 cheers 或 cheerio：

"See you tonight then, cheers." I said and put down the receiver. "那么今晚见，再见。"说完我挂上话筒。

The sooner the better! Cheerio! 越快越好！再见！

在和不太熟的人告别时，还可加上一些客套话：

It was nice meeting you. Hope you have a good trip back. 见到你很高兴，祝你旅途愉快。

I look forward to seeing you in Shanghai. Goodbye. 盼望在上海再和你相见，再见。

20. 帮忙

在日常生活中主动提出给别人帮忙是很必要的。对不同人有不同提出的方式。

对顾客常可说：

Can I help you? 我能帮你什么忙吗？

What can I do for you? 我能为你做什么？

一个比较客气的说法是"Would you like...":

Would you like something to drink? 你想喝点儿什么吗？

They've got good ice-cream here. Would you like to try some? 这里的冰淇淋不错，你想尝吗？

还可用 can I, shall I 等客气地提出帮助：

Shall I help to fill in this form for you? 要不要我帮你填这个表格？

Let me help you carry the bag to your room. 我来帮助你把行李搬到你房里去。

和比较熟的人还可更直接地提出建议：

I'll show you to your room. 我来带你到你房间去。

在接受别人的帮助时，可以各种方式做出回应：（例句译文省略）

"Shall I get a copy for you?" "Yes, please."

"Shall I show you round the house?" "Oh, yes, please. That would be lovely."

在不接受帮助时，可以说 **"No, thank you."** 或 **"No, thanks."**：

"Would you have another cup of tea?" "No, thank you."

"Do you want more bread?" "No, thanks." "I'll get you a blanket." "Please don't bother."

21. 表意见

He may be in bed now. 他可能已经睡了。（猜测）

She might not like the idea. 她可能不赞成这个想法。（估计）

You must be cautious. 你必须谨慎从事。（劝告）

We should leave earlier. 我们应早点儿动身。（建议）

还有一些可以利用各种状语使句子带有主观色彩：

有许多副词给句子加上说话人的看法，例如：

<u>Surprisingly</u>, none of us were injured. 说也奇怪，我们谁也没受伤。

<u>Naturally</u> she's attached to the place. 她自然很喜欢这个地方。

这类副词常见的有：

absurdly	astonishingly	coincidentally	curiously
fortunately	happily	interestingly	ironically
luckily	miraculously	mysteriously	naturally
oddly	of course	sadly	strangely
surprisingly	unexpectedly	unfortunately	unhappily

少数副词可以和 **enough** 一道用：

He lives next door, but <u>strangely</u> enough I rarely see him. 他住在隔壁，但说也奇怪，我很少见到他。

<u>Curiously</u> enough he had never seen the little girl. 说也奇怪，他从未见过那个小姑娘。

有些状语对句子进行解释，例如：

As a rule we get home about six o'clock. 一般说来，我们 6 点左右到家。

On average we receive five letters a day. 我们平均一天收到五封信。

这类状语常见的有：

all in all	altogether	as a rule	at a rough estimate
basically	by and large	essentially	for the most part
fundamentally	generally	in essence	in general
on average	on the whole	overall	ultimately

另外有些状语对一句话作些说明，表示只在某种程度上如此，例如：

The work is more or less finished. 这项工作大体上完成了。

To some extent that was my own fault. 在某种程度，这得怪我自己。

常见的这类状语如：

almost	in a way	in effect	more or less
practically	so to speak	to some extent	virtually

有些状语表示肯定的程度，可依次列出如下：

possibly	Possibly we'll meet again soon. 我们可能不久还会见面。
perhaps, maybe	Perhaps (Maybe) they will help us. 或许他们会帮助我们。
hopefully	Hopefully we'll win. 但愿我们能赢。
probably	He is probably about 40. 他或许 40 岁左右。
presumably	Presumably he was going for a swim. 估计他是去游泳。
almost certainly	Almost certainly they will fail. 几乎可以肯定，他们会失败。
certainly	Certainly I will see you into the train. 我肯定会送你上车。
no doubt, doubtless	It was doubtless (no doubt) his own fault. 肯定得怪他自己。
definitely	I'll definitely be home before six 我肯定在 6 点以前回来。

此外，还有不少副词或状语使句子带上主观色彩，例如：

<u>Obviously</u> I can't do all this by myself. 显然，这件事我不能一个人干。

<u>Honestly</u> I don't mind. 真的，我不在意。

<u>Frankly</u> I don't like the idea. 坦白地说，我不赞成这个想法。

22. 委婉语

euphemism /ˈjuːfɪmɪzəm/ 指委婉的说法。一些不雅的词常可用另一词代替。例如：

pass away（去逝）表示 die（死）；

comfort women（慰安妇）代替 women in army brothels（军妓）；

re-education camps（再教育营）代替 political prisons（政治监狱）；

bottom（臀部）代替 arse（屁股）；

bathroom, restroom 等代替 toilet（厕所）

23. 写信

❀ 写信格式：

正规书信一般把自己的地址写在右上角。一般先写门牌号、街名、（公寓号）；第二行写地名，小地名在前，大地名在后，最后写区号；接着可写自己的电话号码。在地址下面可写日期。美国多先写月份，再写日期，再写年份。英国则日期在前，月份在后。

680 Lombard Street. #3 San Francisco, CA 94133

Tel. (415）397-2776

July 4，1999（英式：**4 July 1999**）

在正规书信或商业书信中，常把收信人的称号、地址写在左上角。熟人间通信则不必如此。开始的地方可以与日期平或稍低一点儿。

一般书信都用 Dear... 开头。熟人可直呼其名，如 Dear Helen, Dear Jim。较正式的则需写出头衔，如 Dear Ms. Patterson, Dear Professor Jones。如不知对方姓名，可写 Dear Sir(s)，Dear Sir or Madam, Dear Madam。

带头衔时则不要写名字而只写姓，不要写 Dr. Charles Smith，而只写 Dr. Smith。在 Dear... 后，较熟的人可加逗号（，），在商业书信中加冒号（：），在英国有时什么也不加。

　　书信正文在 Dear... 下面的一行开始，或空一行再开始。第一行要缩行。结尾时，正式的信多写 Yours sincerely（或 Sincerely yours）。那种以 Dear Sirs, Dear Madame 开头的信，多写 Yours faithfully。对较熟的人或家里人，则可写 Yours、See you 或 Love（男人间一般不用 Love 结尾）。在较正式书信中，在 Yours sincerely 前还可加上一句祝愿的话，如 With best wishes 或 With kind regards。不认识的人则不必如此写。在美国有时还可在信末写 Yours truly。

　　最后则是签上自己的名字，如是手写的信，签上名字就完了，如是打字的信，签字后还在下面用正体字打出来。和家人或好友写信可以只签名字不加姓。在正式信函中姓和名字都签上。

❀ 正式信函举例：

Jackson School of Business
The Glenn Building
Jackson, Mississippi 39208
Tel. (001）555-4800
July 2nd, 1999

Circulation Manager
Business World
312 Herald Drive
Detroit, MI 48230

Dear Sir or Madam,

I should like to have 30 reprints of the article "How to Read a Profit and Loss Statement," which appeared in the March 17 issue of *Business World*. I plan to distribute this article to the students in my accounting class. Could you take the trouble to make them and send them to me in a couple of weeks? I will gladly pay for the cost of the reprints and postage.

Very truly yours,
Bolanche Jmhoff
(Mrs.) Bolanche Jmhoff
Accounting Instructor

❀ 非正式信函举例：

Madison

September 20

Dear Mom and Dad,

I miss all of you. I hope everything is fine at home.

Let me tell you about my first few days. I arrived in Madison two weeks ago. I'm staying at the student dormitory. Students here usually wear very casual clothing. Some students do not take school very seriously. Some of them even talk in the library.

It is autumn. The leaves on the trees are changing colour. Right now some students are playing football outside. Tim asked me to join them. But I have to study. My teachers have given us a lot of homework.

Love

Miguel

❀ 明信片短信举例：

Dear Alice,

In the picture you see the Golden Gate Bridge in San Francisco. It's one of the longest bridges in the world. We can take a bus across it. We can also walk across.

I'm staying with my aunt. And I'm going to school in Richmond. It takes about half an hour to get to school by bus.

I love San Francisco. This weekend I'm going to see a play at the Opera House.

How are you? Please write. Take care.

Pamela

❀ 信封写法：

Circulation Manager
Business World
312 Herald Drive
Detroit, MI 48230

Miss Pamela Cooper
c/o Mrs. G. Patterson
2019 23rd Ave.
Richmond, S. F. CA 94125
U. S. A

 c/o 是 care of 的缩写，表示"由……转交"。

扫描上方二维码，
浏览视频资源

五、词汇用法
A

1 -able

-able 是一个很有用的词尾，可构成许多词，表示"可以……的""值得……的"（带有被动意思），常见的带有这种词尾的词有：

adorable 可爱的

(in)advisable（不）宜于做的

(in)applicable（不）适用的

(un)approachable（不）易接近的

(in)believable（不）可信的

(in)calculable 可以（无法）估计的

(in)conceivable 可以（无法）想象的

(in)curable 可以（无法）治疗

debatable 可以争论的

despicable 可鄙的

eatable 能吃的

(in)escapable 可以（无可）逃避的

(in)estimable 可以（无法）估计的

(in)evitable 可以（无法）避免的

(in)excusable 可以（无法）原谅的

(in)explicable 可以（无法）解释的

laughable 可笑的

lovable 可爱的

(in)measurable 可以（无法）衡量的

(im)movable 可以（无法）搬动的

(un)navigable 可以（不能）航行的

notable 值得注意的

noticeable 引人注意的

(in)numerable 可数的（无数的）

(in)passable 可以（无法）过得去的

(im)payable（不）可以支付的

(im)penetrable 可以（无法）穿透的

(im)practicable 可以（无法）行得通的

(un)reasonable（不）合理的

reconcilable 可以调和的

(ir)refutable 可以（无法）驳斥的

(un)reliable 靠得（不）住的

(un)reparable 可以（无法）补救的

respectable 令人尊敬的

(in)surmountable 可以（无法）克服的

(in)tolerable 可以（无法）忍受的

unforgetable 无法忘怀的

(in)variable（不）可变的

(in)vulnerable（不）易受伤害的

washable 可以洗涤的

还有一些带 **-able** 词尾的词有其他意思：

comfortable 舒适

knowledgeable 懂得很多的

sizable 相当大的

suitable 合适的

preferable（两者中）更好的

agreeable 宜人的，（可以）同意的

remarkable 可观的

其中有些可变 **e** 为 **y**，成为副词：

comfortably 舒适地   remarkably 相当可观地

agreeably 宜人地　　　　　　preferably 最好是

2　above—over

above 表示"在……上方"：

We flew <u>above</u> the clouds. 我们在云层上方飞行。

The moon was now <u>above</u> the trees. 这时月亮在树的上方。

✿ **over** 也可表示这种意思，有时两者可以换用：

We saw a helicopter <u>above (over)</u> the house. 我们看见房子上方有一架直升飞机。

A lamp was hanging <u>over (above)</u> the table. 电灯悬挂在桌子上方。

但 **over** 可表示"在……上面"：

Spread a cloth <u>over</u> the table. 在桌上铺一块桌布。

She wore a shawl <u>over</u> her shoulders. 她肩上披着一块披巾。

这时不能用 **above**。

两者都可用于引申意义，表示"超过""……多"：

It weighs <u>above (over)</u> ten tons. 它的重量超过 10 吨。

Its population is <u>over (above)</u> two million. 它的人口有两百多万。

但表示温度、高度时多用 **above**：

The temperature is ten degrees <u>above</u> zero. 气温是零上 10 度。

The summit of Qomolangma is <u>above</u> 8,000 meters above sea level. 珠穆朗玛峰海拔 8 000 多米。

而表示速度、年龄时 **over** 用得更多：

At the time he was driving at <u>over</u> 100 mph. 这时他的车速为每小时一百多英里。

You have to be <u>over</u> 18 to see this film. 你得超过 18 岁才能看这部电影。

3　accuse—charge

accuse somebody of something 表示"指责或指控某人干某事"：

She <u>accused</u> him of having broken his word. 她指责他违背了诺言。

The police accused him of murder. 警察指控他犯了谋杀罪。

❀ charge 也有类似意思，表示正式控告时，用 charge somebody with something 时更多一些：

They charged him with theft. 他们控告他盗窃。

He was charged by the police with breaking the law. 警察控告他违法。

4 across—over—through

across 表示：

穿过，跨过（从一边到另一边）：

He hurried across the bridge. 他匆匆穿过桥。

She went across the street to buy a paper. 她过街去买一份报。

❀ over 有时也可用于类似意义：

See if you can jump over (across) the stream. 看你能否跳过那条小溪。

在（河、街等的）另一边：

The woods are across the river. 树林在河对面。

The bus stop is just across the road. 公共汽车站就在马路对面。

over 也可用于类似意思：

His village is just over (across) the border. 他的村子就在边界对面。

❀ 在表示"穿越（过）"时常可用 through：

We walked through the woods. 我们穿过树林。

They drove through several towns. 他们驱车穿越了几座城镇。

若想到的是平面，也可用 across：

We walked across the ice. 我们从冰上走了过去。

They drove across the desert. 他们驱车从沙漠上驰过。

若表示"越过（较高的东西）"，用 over 较好：

The children are climbing over the wall. 孩子们在爬墙。

若只表示"在一个平面上（活动）"，而不是到另一边，用 over 也较好：

We often walk over the fields. 我们常常在田野中散步。

5 admission—admittance

❀ **admission** 表示"允许进入"（这个词日常用得比较多）：

Admission by ticket only. 凭票入场。

Admission to the school is by examination only. 只有通过考试方能入学。

❀ **admittance** 也有类似意思，但用得较少，只用于少数场合：

NO admittance except on business. 非公莫入。

6 adopted—adoptive

adopted 通常指"领养的"：

She was very kind to the adopted child. 她待收养的孩子很好。

❀ **adoptive** 则指"收养……（的人）"：

She is the child's adoptive mother. 她是孩子的养母。

7 advance—advancement

advance 作名词时可表示"进展""发展"：

Science has made great advances in the last fifty years. 最近50年，科学有了很大的进展。

Without heavy industry there can be no economic advance. 没有重工业，就没有经济的发展。

❀ **advancement** 则表示"促进"：

The aim of a university should be the advancement of learning. 大学的目标应当是促进学术的发展。

The Royal Society for the Advancement of Science 皇家科学促进会

8 Adverb or Adjective

有不少形容词和副词同形，现列举一些常见的这类词：

clean   I clean forgot it. 我完全忘了。（副词）

         You must keep it clean. 你要把它保持干净。（形容词）

dead	She was dead tired. 她累极了。（副词）
	She has been dead now for a year. 她至今已去世了一年了。（形容词）
direct	The train goes there direct. 火车直接开到那里。（副词）
	This is the most direct road. 这是一条最直的路。（形容词）
easy	Easier said than done. 说来容易做来难。（副词）
	That's easy. 这很容易。（形容词）
fair	He always plays fair. 他一贯做事公正。（副词）
	That's a fair comment. 这是公允的评论。（形容词）
fast	Don't drive so fast. 不要开这么快。（副词）
	My watch is fast. 我的表快了。（形容词）
fine	He's doing fine in school. 他在学校学习不错。（副词）
	We had a fine time. 我们玩得很好。（形容词）
flat	Lie down flat and breathe deeply. 平躺，深呼吸。（副词）
	The floor is quite flat. 地板很平。（形容词）
free	The books are given away free. 这些书免费发放。（副词）
	The refreshments are free. 茶点免费。（形容词）
hard	They tried hard to succeed. 他们努力争取成功。（副词）
	Only hard work gives good result. 只有勤奋刻苦才能取得好成绩。（形容词）
high	The eagle flies high. 老鹰展翅高飞。（副词）
	A high building, a low foundation. 高楼要有深地基。（谚语）（形容词）
just	It's just what you need. 这正是你要的。（副词）
	He had just cause for anger. 他理所应当生气。（形容词）
late	You've come too late. 你来得太晚了。（副词）
	You're three minutes late. 你晚了三分钟。（形容词）
loud	Speak louder. 讲大声点。（副词）
	He's a loud voice. 他声音很大。（形容词）
low	We bought low and sold high. 我们低价买高价卖。（副词）
	The moon was low in the sky. 月亮低低地悬在天上。（形容词）
most	Of these sports, I like rowing most. 在这些运动中，我最喜欢

划船。（副词）

The busiest men have the <u>most</u> leisure. 最忙的人空闲最多。（谚语）（形容词）

pretty	Her sister is still <u>pretty</u> sick. 她的姐姐仍然病得相当厉害。（副词）
	What a <u>pretty</u> garden! 多漂亮的花园！（形容词）
quick	I'll be round as <u>quick</u> as I can. 我将尽快赶来。（副词）
	Be <u>quick</u>! 赶快！（形容词）
real	He was <u>real</u> sorry. 他的确很难过。（副词，美国用法）
	This is a <u>real</u> diamond. 这是一颗真正的钻石。（形容词）
right	You did <u>right</u>. 你做得对。（副词）
	You are <u>right</u>. 你是对的。（形容词）
sharp	Come at one o'clock <u>sharp</u>. 一点钟准时来。（副词）
	Bill is a <u>sharp</u> boy. 比尔是一个机灵的孩子。（形容词）
short	The driver stopped the car <u>short</u>. 司机猛地把车停住。（副词）
	He gave a <u>short</u> speech. 他做了一个简短的讲话。（形容词）
slow	Drive <u>slow</u> through the village. 经过村子时，开慢一点。（副词）
	This is a <u>slow</u> train. 这是一列慢车。（形容词）
sound	He sleeps <u>sound</u> every night. 他每晚都睡得很熟。（副词）
	A night's <u>sound</u> sleep made me feel much better. 睡了一夜好觉使我感觉好多了。（形容词）
straight	Go <u>straight</u> on for two miles. 径直往前走两英里。（副词）
	The streets were <u>straight</u>. 街道很直。（形容词）
sure	<u>Sure</u> I'll help you. 我肯定会帮助你。（副词）
	I am <u>sure</u> smoking hurts you. 我肯定抽烟对你有害。（形容词）
tight	Shut the door <u>tight</u>. 把门关紧。（副词）
	These shoes are too <u>tight</u> for me. 这双鞋我穿太小。（形容词）
well	You behave <u>well</u>. 你表现很好。（副词）
	All is <u>well</u> with us. 我们一切都很顺利。（形容词）
wide	Open your mouth <u>wide</u>. 把口张开。（副词）
	The river is a mile <u>wide</u>. 这条河有一英里宽。（形容词）
wrong	You guessed <u>wrong</u>. 你猜错了。（副词）
	Cheating is always <u>wrong</u>. 骗人总是错的。（形容词）

9 afflict—inflict

这两个词都是动词，但意思不同。

❀ **afflict** /ə'flɪkt/ 表示 "使痛苦""折磨"：

He was afflicted by rheumatism. 他受风湿病之苦。

Famine and war still afflicted the country. 饥荒和战争还在折磨这个国家。

❀ **inflict** /ɪn'flɪkt/ 表示 "对……造成（灾难、损失等）"：

The hurricane inflicted severe damage on the island. 飓风对海岛造成严重损害。

Only cruel people like to inflict pain. 只有冷酷无情的人喜欢给人施加痛苦。

10 after—afterward(s)

after 可用作：

作介词，后面跟名词、代词或动名词：

I never saw him after that. 在那之后，我再也没见到过他。

She felt much better after taking the medicine. 吃完药后，她感觉好多了。

作连词，引起状语从句：

After we had finished the work we had a little rest. 干完活后，我们休息了一会儿。

You'll feel better after you take the pills. 吃完药丸后，你会感到好一些。

作副词：

A moment after there was a knock at his door. 过了一会儿，有人敲他的门。

We had dinner and went home after. 我们吃完晚饭，之后就回家了。

❀ **afterwards**（美作 **afterward**）为副词，表示 "在这之后""后来" 等：

Afterward they had lunch in the garden. 在这之后，他们在花园里吃了午饭。

He sobered up afterward. 后来，他清醒过来了。

11 ago—before

ago 表示"（多少时间）以前"，多用在状语中：

This happened a long time <u>ago</u>. 这是好久以前发生的事。

She was here a moment <u>ago</u>. 她前一会儿还在这里的。

有时可用在表语中：

How long <u>ago</u> was it? 这是多久前的事了？

That was over twenty years <u>ago</u>. 这是 20 多年前的事了。

在表示过去某时以前时，需用 **before**：

She told me her husband had died four years <u>before</u>. 她告诉我，她丈夫已于四年前去世了。

（比较：My husband died four years <u>ago</u>.）

12 all right—alright

all right 是非常有用的短语，可表示：

行，好吧（多用于问句或回答）：

Is that <u>all right</u> for you? 对你这样行吗？

<u>All right</u>, you can have the room. 好吧，你可住这个房间。

身体好了，情况不错：

I am <u>all right</u> now. 我现在没事了。

Everything will be <u>all right</u>. Don't worry. 一切都会好的，别发愁。

顺利地，不错：

Did you catch the train <u>all right</u>? 你顺利赶上火车了吗？

I hope they've arrived <u>all right</u>. 我希望他们已顺利到达。

❀ 有些人把 **all right** 写作 **alright**：

The answers are <u>alright</u>. 这些回答不错。

They seem to be doing <u>alright</u>. 他们似乎干得不错。

但许多人认为这不标准，应当写作 **all right**。

13 allow—permit—let

这三个词都表示"允许"：

❀ **allow 和 permit 是同义词，常常可以换用：**

They don't allow (permit) students to smoke in the classroom. 他们不允许学生在教室抽烟。

Her father would not permit (allow) her to eat sweets. 她父亲不允许她吃糖果。

这两个词也可用于被动结构：

The children are not allowed (permitted) to play on the grass. 孩子们不可以在草地上玩耍。

We are not permitted (allowed) to talk in class. 我们不可以在课堂上互相交谈。

这两个词也可用动名词作宾语：

We don't allow (permit) smoking on this plane. 在这架飞机上，我们不可以抽烟。

这种句子也可变为被动结构：

Smoking is not allowed (permitted) on this plane. 这架飞机上不允许抽烟。

但 **it** 作主语时，只有 **permit** 可用于被动结构：

It is not permitted to smoke on this plane. 不允许在这架飞机上抽烟。

这时不能用 **allow**。

❀ **let** 的意思虽然接近上面两个词，但一般只能用在 **let somebody do something** 这个结构中（不能用于被动结构）：

Let me carry the bag for you. 让我来帮你提行李。

They won't let me go in. 他们不让我进去。

let 还可和许多副词或介词连用：

Better let in some fresh air. 最好放些新鲜空气进来。

Mother wouldn't let us out in this weather. 这样的天气妈妈不让我们出去。

14 allow—allow of

allow 表示"允许"，而 **allow of** 表示"容许……"：

The crowd parted to allow her through. 人群向两边闪开让她通过。

She didn't allow her emotions to get the better of her. 她没有让情绪打败自己。

You allow of no exceptions? 你不容许有例外情况?

The problem allows of only one solution. 这问题只能有一个解决办法。

The situation allows of no delay. 形势不容许耽误。

15 almost—nearly

almost 和 nearly 意思很相近，多译为"几乎"：

I have almost finished the book. 这本书我几乎已经看完了。

The river was almost frozen. 河水几乎已经结冰。

可修饰形容词、副词等：

The streets were almost empty. 街上几乎空无一人。

We see each other almost every day. 我们几乎天天见面。

nearly 可译为"几乎""差不多"：

It is nearly midnight. 现在几乎已经是午夜了。

The job is nearly finished. 这项工作几乎已经完成了。

在不少情况下两者几乎可以换用：

The girl nearly (almost) fainted. 这姑娘差点（几乎）晕倒了。

They have almost (nearly) run out of food. 他们的食品几乎（差不多）已经吃完了。

但也有一些差别。例如 almost 可以和 no, nothing, never 这类否定词连用：

Almost no one believed her. 几乎没有人相信她的话。

这时却不宜用 nearly，但 not nearly 可表示"远远不（够）"：

There are not nearly enough people to do the job. 干这工作，人手远远不够。

We don't do nearly enough to help. 我们远没给予足够的帮助。

16 also—too—as well

also 和 too 的意思差不多，都表示"也"，also 多放在主要动词前面（a）或系动词 be 后面（b），有时也可放在其他位置：

a. They also agreed with me. 他们也同意我的意见。

Mary has also gone to town. 玛丽也进城了。

b. I was also there. 我也在那里。

　　She was also a teacher. 她也是一位教师。

有时也可放在整个谓语前面（a），有时也可放在句末甚至句首（b）：

a. I also am writing a short story. 我也在写一篇短篇小说。

　　This room also was bathed in sunshine. 这间房也沐浴在阳光中。

b. Her son had gone also. 她儿子也去了。

　　Also, Peter had taken that course. 彼得也选过那个课。

too 多数放在句末（a），偶尔也可插在句子中间（b）：

a. I can dance and sing too. 我也能唱歌跳舞。

　　My sister likes swimming, and I do, too. 我妹妹爱游泳，我也爱游泳。

b. We, too, are going away. 我们也将离开。

　　He realized that she too was exhausted. 他意识到，她也筋疲力尽。

❀ **as well** 也可表示这个意思，多放在句子后面：

It's been a grief to him as well. 这也令他很伤心。

They do military training as well. 他们也进行军事训练。

这三个表达方法，前两种比较普遍，**as well** 在美国用得比较少。但注意在否定句中这三个都不能用，而需用 **either**：

Helen isn't here today. Nancy isn't here either. 海伦今天不在这里，南希今天也不在。

You can't cook Chinese food and I can't either. 你不会做中国菜，我也不会做中国菜。

---

⑰ alternate—alternately—alternative—alternatively

alternate 可作动词，读作 /ˈɔːltəneɪt/，表示"交替"：

Day alternates with night. 昼夜交替。

Work alternates with sleep. 工作和睡眠互相交替。

alternate 也可作形容词，读作 /ɔːltɜːnɪ(ə)t/，表示"交替的"（a）和"每隔……"（b）：

a. French and English are alternate courses. 法语和英语是交替开设的课程。

　　It was a week of alternate rain and sunshine. 这是晴雨交替的一个礼拜。

b. He comes on <u>alternate</u> days. 他隔天来一次。

Meetings are held on <u>alternate</u> Thursdays. 会议礼拜四开，隔周开一次。

❀ **alternately** 是其副词形式，表示"交替地""轮换着"：

We work our shifts <u>alternately</u>. 我们轮换着上班。

The little girl <u>alternately</u> sulked and made scenes. 这小姑娘一会儿生闷气，一会儿和人吵架。

❀ **alternative** 作为形容词，表示"另一种""可供选择的"：

There was no <u>alternative</u> route open to her. 她面前没有另一条路。

They are <u>alternative</u> ways of expressing the same idea. 它们是表达同样意思的其他方式。

<u>alternative</u> questions 选择问句

它也可用作名词，表示"可作的选择""替代的东西"：

What <u>alternatives</u> are there? 还有什么可供选择的？

We must leave her. There was no other <u>alternative</u>. 我们必须离开她，没有别的办法。

❀ **alternatively** 是相关的副词，意思是"作为替代"，可译为"要不""或者"：

A fine of £10 or <u>alternatively</u> six weeks' imprisonment. 罚款 10 镑，要不就监禁六个星期。

<u>Alternatively</u>, you can use household bleach. 或者，你可以使用家用漂白粉。

18 **although—though**

although 和 **though** 意思基本相同，表示"虽然""尽管"，可引起一个让步从句，放在主句前面（a）或是放主句后面（b）：

a. <u>Although</u> it was barely four o'clock, the lights were already on. 尽管才刚四点钟，但灯已经亮了。

<u>Though</u> we are poor, we are still happy. 我们虽然穷，但仍然很快活。

b. They are generous <u>although</u> they are poor. 虽然穷，但他们却很大方。

The speech is good, <u>though</u> it could be better. 报告很好，尽管还可以更好。

在正式语言中用 **although** 时较多。在省略句中，一般用 **though**：

An ass is an ass though laden with gold. 尽管驮着金子，驴还是驴。（谚语）

The girl, though plain, had a good kind face. 这姑娘虽然不漂亮，却有一张端庄善良的脸。

另外它还可用于 **as though**、**even though** 这种词组中：

My father acted as though nothing had happened. 我父亲表现得似乎什么也没发生似的。

Even though it's hard work, I enjoy it. 尽管活很累，我却爱干。

此外 **though** 还可用作副词，表示"但""不过"等：

You can count on him, though. 不过你可以依靠他。

For our village, though, it wasn't a bad year. 对我们村子来说，这倒不是一个坏年景。

⑲ altogether—all together

altogether 是副词，表示：

完全：

I don't altogether agree with him. 我不完全同意他的意见。

The thing is not altogether impossible. 这事不是完全不可能的。

总共：

There are altogether 100 families involved. 总共牵涉到 100 家人。

总的说来：

Altogether, the children have done very well. 总的说来，孩子们干得很好。

❀ **all together** 意思完全不同，表示"大家在一起"：

It has been so long since we were all together. 我们好久没有在一起团聚了。

⑳ amateur—amateurish

amateur 来自法语，读作 /ˈæmətə, ˈæməˌtɜː/，作名词时表示"业余演员（运动员）"：

Our actors were amateurs. 我们的演员都是业余的。

作形容词时，表示"业余的"：

Acting with an <u>amateur</u> theatrical group can be fun. 和业余剧团在一起演戏可能很有意思。

❀ **amateurish** /ˈæmətərɪʃ, ˈæmə͵tɜːrɪʃ/ 是另一形容词，表示"蹩脚的"：

I'm afraid the golf I play is very <u>amateurish</u>. 恐怕我的高尔夫球打得很蹩脚。

21   amiable—amicable

这两个词拼法很相近，但意思却不同。

❀ **amiable** 表示"和蔼可亲""亲切友好"：

She was sweet and <u>amiable</u>. 她很可爱，很和蔼可亲。

Our neighbours are <u>amiable</u> people. 我们的邻居很亲切。

❀ 而 **amicable** 表示"和睦友好""友善的"：

We came to an <u>amicable</u> agreement. 我们达成了友好的协议。

The two nations settled their quarrel in an <u>amicable</u> way. 两国友善地解决了它们的纠纷。

22   among—amongst

among 表示"在……中间"（主要指三个或更多人或物之间）：

She prefers to live <u>among</u> working people. 她更愿意生活在劳动人民中间。

Divide the money <u>among</u> the six of you. 这笔钱你们六个人分。

也可表示"是……中间的一个"：

Shelley is <u>among</u> the world's greatest poets. 雪莱是世界上最伟大的诗人之一。

Paris is <u>among</u> the largest cities in the world. 巴黎是世界上最大的城市之一。

amongst 和 **among** 的意思相同：

The food was divided <u>amongst</u> the poor. 食物都分给了穷人。

❀ **among** 用的时候比较多一些。

23 another—other

❀ another 可用作形容词，表示：

另一个：

He could get another girl to do the job. 他可以另外找一个女孩干这份工作。

It happened in another country. 这事发生在另一个国家。

再来一个，又一个（=one more）：

In another year she goes to school. 再过一年她就上学了。

He opened another shop last year. 去年他又开了一家店。

（和某数词连用）还，再，又：

Where shall we be in another ten years. 再过 10 年我们会在哪里？

She remained in London for another four days. 她在伦敦又待了四天。

也可用作代词，表示"另一个"：

Saying is one thing and doing another. 说是一回事，做是另一回事。（谚语）

I don't like this one, show me another. 我不喜欢这一件，另拿一件给我看。

❀ 在表示"另一些"时，要用 other，也可译作"别的""其他的"：

Have you any other books on the subject? 你还有这方面的其他书吗？

They also try to fool other people. 他们也企图欺骗别人。

它也可作代词，表示"别人""另外那个（些）"：

She thinks only of others' good. 她只想别人的好处。

One is a boy, the other is a girl. 一个是男孩，另外那个是女孩。

24 anti-

anti- 是一个前缀，表示"反对""对抗"等：

I was no anti-imperialist when I left home. 我离家时，还根本不是一个反帝国主义分子。

He became strongly anti-Austrian in his sentiments. 他变得具有强烈的反奥地利情绪。

I soon became anti-British. 不久，我就变得反对英国了。

常见的带有这个前缀的词有：

anti-apartheid 反种族隔离的   antibacterial 抗细菌的

antibiotic 抗菌的，抗菌素   antibody 抗体

anticlockwise 逆时钟方向的   antidote 解毒药

anti-colonial 反殖民主义的   anticorrosive 防腐蚀的，防腐剂

anti-fascist 反法西斯的   anti-feudal 反封建的

antifreeze 抗凝剂，防冻剂   antifriction 抗摩擦的

antigas 防毒气的   antimagnetic 防磁的

antimissile 反导弹的   antiphlogistic 消炎的，消炎药

anti-seismic 抗地震的   antiaircraft 防空的

antitank 反坦克的   anti-social 不爱社交的

25 anticipate—expect

anticipate 主要表示：

预见，预期，预料：

Could you have <u>anticipated</u> this situation? 你能预见到这种情况吗？

We <u>anticipated</u> where they would try to cross. 我们预料到他们将在哪里渡河。

抢先做某事，提前准备：

We <u>anticipated</u> their visit by buying plenty of food. 我们为他们的来访提前准备，买了大量食品。

He tries to <u>anticipate</u> all my needs. 他设法提前准备以满足我的需要。

第一种用法不要和 **expect** 相混，后者主要表示"期待、预料、指望"（得到某东西或发生某情况）：

He <u>expected</u> no gratitude, no recognition for this. 他并不期待感谢和承认。

I had not <u>expected</u> such an amount of praise. 我没料到有这么多赞扬。

26 anyone—anybody

anyone 和 **anybody** 意思相同，表示：

某人（用于疑问句、否定句及条件从句，常可译作"什么人""谁"等）：

I hope this will not worry <u>anyone</u>. 我希望这不会令人担心。

If <u>anybody</u> is interested, please tell me. 谁要是有兴趣，请告诉我。

任何人：

<u>Anybody</u> will tell you where the bus stop is. 谁（任何人）都可以告诉你公共汽车站在哪里。

<u>Anyone</u> who is over sixteen is allowed in. 任何超过 16 岁的人都可以进去。

27 any time—anytime

any time 表示"任何时候"：

You can come <u>any time</u>. 你可以随时来。

They can leave at <u>any time</u>. 他们什么时候走都行。

any time 也可引起一个从句（通常不用 that）：

<u>Any time</u> you need me, let me know. 不管什么时候你需要我，都可以通知我。

❀ **anytime 可以用作副词，表示"任何时候"：**

The college admits students <u>anytime</u> during the year. 这所大学一年中随时都可以招生。

He can leave <u>anytime</u> he wants. 他想走随时就可以走。

28 anyway—any way

anyway 是副词，表示"不管怎样""反正"：

<u>Anyway</u> this will give us a bit of time. 不管怎样，这能给我们一点时间。

That wasn't my fault, <u>anyway</u>. 反正这不是我的错。

❀ **any way 是两个词，表示"（以）任何方式"：**

He never threatened her in <u>any way</u>. 他从未以任何方式威胁她。

If I can help you in <u>any way</u>, you have only to speak to me. 如果我能以任何方式帮助你，你只需对我说一声。

29 anywhere—anyplace

anywhere 为副词，可以表示：

某个地方（用于疑问句、否定句及条件从句，代替 **somewhere**，常可译为"哪儿""什么地方"）：

He never dared to ask her to go <u>anywhere</u> with him. 他从未敢请她和他一起到哪儿去。

If you think of going <u>anywhere</u>, let me know. 如果你想到哪里，可以通知我。

任何地方：

You can't get it <u>anywhere</u> else. 你在任何别的地方都找不到它。

Just drive me around, <u>anywhere</u>. 就开车带我出去逛逛，到哪儿都行。

美国人常用 **anyplace** 表示同样意思：

We're afraid to go <u>anyplace</u> alone. 我们害怕单独去任何地方。

Airports were more closely watched than <u>anyplace</u> else. 飞机场比任何其他地方看守得更严密。

30 Apostrophe

apostrophe /əˈpɒstrəfi/ 指"'"（撇号），可有下面用法：

❀ 表示有字母省略：

o'er=over	can't=cannot	it's=it is
thro'=through	ma'am=madam	don't=do not
shan't=shall not	couldn't=could not	I'm=I am

❀ 用来构成名词所有格：

Shakespeare's plays	an hour's walk
a dollar's worth	my sister-in-law's mother
a doctor's degree	St Paul's（圣保罗大教堂）
a day's journey	an hour's time
two weeks' wages	

❀ 用来构成字母等的复数形式：

How many 1's are there in travelling? Travelling 这个词中有几个 1?

He makes his 8's like 3's. 他的 8 写得像 3。

31 appendix—appendixes—appendices

appendix 有两个复数形式，一个是 appendixes，一个是 appendices。在表示"盲肠"时，复数多用 appendixes 表示。在表示"附录"时，用 appendices 的较多。

32 approve—approve of

approve 表示"批准""同意"：

Congress <u>approved</u> the budget. 国会批准了这项预算。

The minister <u>approved</u> the building plans. 部长同意了这些建设计划。

❀ approve of 表示"赞同""赞成"：

Her mother did not <u>approve of</u> this match. 她母亲不赞成这桩婚事。

I don't <u>approve of</u> his moral character. 我不苟同他的品德。

33 Arab—Arabian—Arabic

Arab 用作名词时表示"阿拉伯人"：

The <u>Arabs</u> had thirteen votes. 阿拉伯人有 13 票。

用作形容词时表示"阿拉伯（人）的"，例如：

<u>Arab</u> states are to meet again in December. 阿拉伯国家将于 12 月再次开会。

The United <u>Arab</u> Emirates 阿拉伯联合酋长国

The <u>Arab</u> world 阿拉伯世界

❀ Arabic 用作名词时表示"阿拉伯语"：

Do you know <u>Arabic</u>? 你懂阿拉伯语吗？

用作形容词时表示"阿拉伯语（人）的"：

<u>Arabic</u> literature 阿拉伯文学

<u>Arabic</u> numerals 阿拉伯数字

<u>Arabic</u> architecture 阿拉伯式的建筑

❀ Arabian 是形容词，但只限于一些固定名称（特别是与地名 Arabia 有关的名称）中：

The <u>Arabian</u> Peninsula 阿拉伯半岛

the Arabian Sea 阿拉伯海

The Arabian Nights 天方夜谭

阿拉伯人居住的地区称为 Arabia：

The land of the Arabs is called Arabia. 阿拉伯人居住的地区称为 Arabia。

Saudi Arabia 沙特阿拉伯

34 around—round

在用作介词和副词时，这两个词意相同，在美式英语中 around 用得比较多，现把两者的主要意思归纳如下：

❀ 作介词：

在周围，环绕：

The sun shines all around her. 她四周阳光灿烂。

She drew her cloak round (around) her. 她用披风紧紧把自己裹住。

在……附近，在某范围内：

They travelled around Europe. 他们在欧洲四处旅行。

Think of what's happening round the world. 想想在世界上正发生的情况。

❀ 作副词：

向四周，周长：

He looked around but could see nobody. 他向四周望望，却没看见什么人。

It's a tree five feet round. 这是一棵周长五英尺的树。

在……一带（附近）：

I'll see if he's around. 我去看他是否在附近。

He wanted to have a look round. 他想在这一带看看。

大约：

He owns around 200 acres. 他约有 200 英亩土地。

He paid round £20 for it. 为此，他付了约 20 英镑。

构成某些短语动词：

The new academic year comes round in autumn. 新学年在秋天到来。

Irving got <u>round</u> the problem in a novel way. 欧文以一种新的办法解决了这个问题。

从这里可以看出这两个词的用法是大致一致的。关于这两词的详细用法可参阅一本好的字典。

35 rouse—arouse

这两个词的意思比较接近。

❀ rouse 主要表示"唤醒""惊醒"：

The noise <u>roused</u> me. 这响声把我惊醒了。

I was <u>roused</u> by the telephone bell. 我给电话铃吵醒了。

也可表示"激起，引起（某种情绪）"：

This <u>roused</u> their anger. 这激起了他们的愤怒。

His conduct <u>roused</u> their suspicion. 他的行为引起了他们的怀疑。

❀ arouse 主要表示"引起……"：

Their sufferings <u>aroused</u> our pity. 他们受的苦引起我们的怜悯。

His suspicions were again <u>aroused</u>. 他的疑心被再次引起。

但也可表示"叫醒""惊醒""唤醒"等：

I was suddenly <u>aroused</u> by a slight noise. 我突然被一个轻微的响声惊醒。

He wanted to <u>arouse</u> them to fight for their own emancipation. 他想唤醒他们为自己的解放而斗争。

36 arrive—reach

arrive 为不及物动词，表示"到达"，常和介词 at 或 in 连用。表示"到达（某地方）"时多用 arrive at：

Soon they <u>arrived</u> at the station. 不久，他们就抵达车站了。

He <u>arrived</u> at Shelley Hot Springs on Sunday night. 星期天夜里他来到雪莱温泉。

表示"到达（某城市或国家）"时多用 arrive in：

We <u>arrived</u> in London in the morning. 早上我们抵达伦敦。

When did you <u>arrive in</u> Europe? 你什么时候抵达欧洲的？

有时 **arrive** 可单独使用，或和一介词或副词连用：

When did you <u>arrive</u>? 你什么时候到的？

Smith <u>arrived</u> at 4 o'clock. 史密斯是四点钟到的。

I <u>arrived</u> here yesterday. 我是昨天到达此地的。

We <u>arrived</u> home towards evening. 快天黑时，我们到家了。

arrive at 也可用于引申意义，表示"做出（决定）"等：

What decision did you <u>arrive at</u>? 你们做出了什么决定？

I wish he would <u>arrive at</u> some conclusion. 我希望他能得出某种结论。

❀ reach 也表示"到达"，但它是及物动词，可以直接跟宾语：

They <u>reached</u> the village in the afternoon. 下午他们抵达了那个村子。

When did you <u>reach</u> Los Angeles? 你什么时候抵达洛杉矶的？

它也可用于引申意义：

Finally they <u>reached</u> an agreement. 最后，他们达成了一项协议。

They were unable to <u>reach</u> a decision. 他们没法做出决定。

37 artist—artiste

artist 指美术家、艺术家、演员：

The picture was painted by a famous <u>artist</u>. 这张画是一位著名画家画的。

She is an operatic <u>artist</u>. 她是一位歌剧演员。

❀ artiste 指舞蹈及歌唱演员：

Some very famous <u>artistes</u> are appearing this summer at the festival. 一些著名舞蹈及歌唱演员将在今夏的艺术节上献演。

a Parisian cabaret <u>artiste</u> 一位在巴黎歌舞厅表演的演员

38 as

as 一般用作连词，可以引起：

时间状语从句，表示"当……时"：

<u>As</u> he slept he dreamed a dream. 他睡觉时，做了一个梦。

We get wiser as we get old. 随着年龄的增长，我们也变得聪明些了。

while 和 **when** 也可引起时间状语从句。

原因状语从句，表示"因为""由于"：

As all the seats were full he stood up. 由于所有座位都有人了，他站了起来。

As you make your bed, so you must lie on it. 你这是自作自受。

since、**because** 和 **for** 也有类似意思，关于它们的差别，后面再谈。

方式状语从句，表示"依照""按照""如""像"：

When in Rome do as the Romans do. 入乡随俗。（谚语）

As you know, I'm not much at letter-writing. 正如你知道的，我不善于写信。

△有时可引起分词：

As scheduled they met on January 20. 按照计划，他们在 1 月 20 日碰了头。

It usually happens as described above. 通常会像上面描述的那样发生。

比较状语从句，表示"像……一样地"：

You know as much about that as I do. 这一点你知道的和我一样多。

I haven't done as much as I should have liked. 我没有做得像我希望的那么多。

让步状语从句，表示"尽管""虽说"（这时句子有一部分倒装）：

Intelligent as she was, she had not much insight. 尽管她聪明，却不太有洞察力。

Poor as he was, he was honest. 他虽说穷却很诚实。

此外它还可和一个名词连用，表示"作（为）""看成"等，这时它的作用接近介词：

He has taken up photography as a hobby. 他把摄影作为一种业余爱好。

Perhaps I can act as spokesman. 或许，我可以充当发言人。

有时还可和形容词、分词等连用：

The idea struck him as novel. 这个想法，他感到很新鲜。

They agreed to regard the chapter as closed. 他们同意这事到此结束。

39 as... as

as... as 表示"像……一样":

She is <u>as</u> tall <u>as</u> her elder sister. 她像她姐姐一样高。

He speaks French <u>as</u> well <u>as</u> a Frenchman. 他的法语讲得像法国人一样好。

They aren't <u>as</u> clever <u>as</u> they appear to be. 他们并不像他们看起来那样聪明。

在这种结构中还可用一些状语:

You're not <u>half</u> <u>as</u> clever <u>as</u> you think you are. 你并不如你想象的一半聪明。

She went out with a man <u>twice</u> <u>as</u> old <u>as</u> her. 她和一个年龄比她大一倍的男子外出了。

It cost <u>three times</u> <u>as</u> much <u>as</u> I had expected. 它花的钱比我预期的多两倍。

Water is <u>eight hundred times</u> <u>as</u> dense <u>as</u> air. 水的密度是空气密度的800 倍。

在英语中有大量带这种结构的短语,常见的如:

as black as coal 像煤一样黑

as blind as a bat 像蝙蝠一样瞎撞

as brave as a lion 像狮子一样勇敢

as bright as day 亮得如同白昼

as busy as a bee 像蜜蜂一样忙碌

as cheerful as a lark 像百灵鸟那样欢快

as cold as ice 像冰一样冷

as cunning as a fox 像狐狸一样狡猾

as easy as ABC 易如反掌

as fair as a rose 像玫瑰一样美

as fat as a pig 胖得像猪

as fierce as a tiger 凶猛得像老虎

as gentle as a lamb 驯服得像只羊羔

as graceful as a swan 像天鹅一样优美

as grasping as a miser 爱钱爱得像守财奴

as greedy as a wolf 贪婪得像只狼

as heavy as lead 像铅一样沉重

as hot as pepper 像辣椒一样辣

as light as a feather 像羽毛一样轻

as loud as thunder 像打雷一样响

as obstinate as a mule 像骡子一样倔犟

as patient as an ox 像牛一样有耐心

as proud as a peacock 像孔雀一样高傲

as quick as lightning 像闪电一样快

as red as a cherry 像樱桃一样红

as sharp as a needle 像针一样尖

as sour as vinegar 像醋一样酸

as steady as a rock 稳若岩石

as strong as a horse 像马一样健壮

as stupid as donkey 像驴一样笨

as sweet as honey 像蜜一样甜

as swift as wind 像风一样快

as tame as a cat 像猫一样柔顺

as timid as a hare 像野兔一样胆怯

as tough as leather 像皮革一样硬

as ugly as a toad 像蛤蟆一样丑

as vain as a peacock 像孔雀一样虚荣

as white as snow 像雪一样白

40 as if—as though

as if 和 **as though** 意思基本上相同，可引起从句，表示"就仿佛""就像……"：

I rememberd the whole thing <u>as if</u> it happened yesterday. 我记得整个情况，就仿佛是昨天发生的一样。

We felt <u>as though</u> we had witnessed the whole thing. 我们感到仿佛目

击了整个这件事似的。

当从句和主句的主语一致，从句谓语中又包含 be 时，则 as if 引起的从句中的主语和 be 可以省略：

The boy started, <u>as if</u> awakened from some dream. 这男孩猛地一惊，就仿佛从梦中惊醒似的。

She glanced about <u>as if</u> in search of something. 她向四周望了望，仿佛在找什么似的。

在它们引起的从句中，谓语要用虚拟语气：

He looked at me <u>as if</u> I <u>were</u> mad. 他瞧着我，仿佛我疯了似的。

She remembered it all <u>as if</u> it <u>were</u> yesterday. 她全都记得，就像是昨天发生似的。

不过在口语中，在这种情况下用 was 的时候更多。

在 **look as if (though)** 后，也可用陈述语气，表示可能真是某种情况：

She looks <u>as if</u> she is rich. 她看起来像是有钱的样子。（可能真如此）

You look <u>as though</u> you know each other. 你们看起来像是互相认识。

as to 有两个主要用法：

引起短语，表示"至于"：

<u>As to</u> the journey, we must decide about that later. 至于这趟旅行，我们以后再作决定。

<u>As to</u> that, I haven't decided yet. 至于那一点，我还没决定。

引起从句等，表示"关于"（常可不译出）：

I have not yet decided <u>as to</u> what papers it had better be sent to. 我还没决定把它寄给哪些报纸最好。

She had no idea <u>as to</u> what she ought to do. 她不知道该怎么办。

41 as well as

as well as 常可连接两个并列的成分，可译为"和""也""还"等：

It is a political <u>as well as</u> an economic question. 这是一个政治问题也是一个经济问题。

Women, <u>as well as</u> men, have a right to work. 女人，和男人一样，也

有工作权利。

有时后面可跟动名词，有时可译为"（不仅）而且""除了……还"：

Smoking is dangerous, as well as making you smell bad. 吸烟不仅有危险，而且还让你有难闻的味道。

As well as breaking his leg, he broke his arm. 除了腿，他还折断了一条胳膊。

注意下面两句话的差别：

She sings as well as playing the piano. 她（又）能唱歌，又能弹钢琴。

She sings as well as she plays the piano. 她唱歌唱得和弹钢琴弹得一样好。

42 assure—ensure—insure

❀ assure 表示"向（某人）保证""肯定地说"：

I assure you that this medicine cannot harm you. 我向你保证这药对你没有害处。

They assured the passengers that there was no danger. 他们向乘客保证，没有危险。

也可用于 assure of 这个短语中：

I assure you of my full support for your plan. 我向你保证，全力支持你的计划。

They assured us of his ability to work. 他们向我们保证，他有能力工作。

❀ ensure 表示"保证（有）""使一定得到"：

This medicine will ensure you a good night's sleep. 这个药可以确保你睡一夜好觉。

His reputation was enough to ensure that he was always welcome. 他的名望足以保证他随时会受到欢迎。

One more touchdown will ensure (insure) victory. 再进一球可确保获胜。

❀ insure 表示"给……保险"：

She insured her car against theft. 她给车买了防盗险。

He insured the house for $40,000. 他给房子买了 40 000 美元的保险。

在美式英语中，insure 也可表示"确保"：

I shall try to <u>insure</u> that your stay is a pleasant one. 我将设法确保你待得很愉快。

43 at

at 是一个非常活跃的词，可表示：

在（某处或某场合）：

He was not <u>at</u> his office. 他不在他办公室里。

I live <u>at</u> 403, Brook Street. 我住在布鲁克街第 403 号。

They had left their luggage <u>at</u> the station. 他们把行李留在车站了。

在（某个时刻，某时期）：

<u>At</u> daybreak we started on our journey. 天亮时，我们开始了我们的行程。

We shall be with you <u>at</u> Easter. 我们将在复活节与你们相聚。

向，对（表示方向、目标等）：

We must "shoot the arrow <u>at</u> the target." 我们必须"有的放矢"。

I don't know what you're driving <u>at</u>. 我不知道你这话是什么意思。

为了，对于（表示引起某种情绪的原因）：

He looked surprised <u>at</u> seeing us. 看到我们，他显得很惊讶。

<u>At</u> this news they were highly indignant. 听了这消息，他们非常愤怒。

We all rejoiced <u>at</u> the news of your success. 听到你成功的消息，我们都很高兴。

在……情况下（表示一个动作的起因）：

He was writing <u>at</u> the request of Mr. Liu. 他是应刘先生的请求写信的。

<u>At</u> the mere thought of it my heart began to beat fiercely. 只要想到这儿，我的心就开始猛烈地跳动。

在某方面：

He is an expert <u>at</u> repairing clocks. 他是修钟专家。

She was working hard <u>at</u> two new songs. 她在用心写两首新歌。

引起短语作表语，表示状态或动作：

The country was <u>at</u> peace then; now it is <u>at</u> war. 这国家那时和平相处，

而现在则兵戎相见。

引起短语作状语，表示价格、数量和速度等：

The train was going <u>at</u> its full speed. 火车正全速前进。

Please come <u>at</u> your earliest convenience. 请在方便的情况下尽早来。

44 at—in—on

这三个介词都可用来表示地点。

大致说来，一个地点在脑中是一个点时，多用 **at**，现列出一些 at 引起的地点状语，如：

at the club	at the door
at the desk	at the gate
at a party	at a meeting
at a concert	at a lecture
at the match	at a place
at the bus stop	at the station
at school	at university
at college	at someone's wedding

如果想到的是一个空间，多用 **in**，如：

in the room	in the office
in the park	in the woods
in the garden	in the box
in Tokyo	in France
in the world	in the universe
in the East	in the car
in the lift	in one's mind
in one's heart	in one's bag
in a company	in the city
in the sky	in the rain

在美国也可说 **in school**   **in college**   **in the air**

如果想到的是一个平面或是一条线，则多用 **on**：

on the table	on the wall

on the ceiling	on page 20
on a farm	on the lake
on the sea	on the tree
on the river	on the third floor
on earth	on the moon
on one's way	on the journey
on the train	on flight 410

引起短语表示时间时，如果想到的是某一点时间，用 **at** 时较多，如：

at 5 o'clock	at an early hour
at dawn	at midnight
at noon	at daybreak
at dark	at lunch time
at present	at the moment
at this time	at the weekend
at half past two	at 3:00
at the beginning	at the end of the year

表示节日和阶段的名词前也可用 **at**：

| at Easter | at Christmas |
| at this stage | at that period |

在表示较长的一段时间时，多用 **in**：

in the morning	in the afternoon
in the evening	in the night
in July	in 1996
in one's youth	in the 1970s
in the past	in the future
in all these years	in this century
in spring	in this decade
in the past few years	in the daytime

在表示"……之后"时，也可用 **in**：

in an hour	in a day or two
in twenty minutes	in sixty days
in time	in no time

in a fortnight   in a few years

在表示某一天时多用 **on**：

on Monday   on the 23rd

on Christmas Day   on New Year's Day

morning 等词若有定语修饰时，前面也需用 **on**：

on Tuesday morning   on Friday evening

on an autumn night   on New Year's Eve

在有 **this, last, one** 等词修饰时，这些名词前一般不再加介词，如：

one day   this morning

that evening   last Tuesday

next Sunday   every afternoon

all day   any time

有时也有些习惯用法问题，如：

by day   at night

over the weekend（美国人的说法） over the years

45 at first—first—firstly

at first 表示"开始时""起初"：

At first he was a little shy, but now he acts more natural. 开始时他有些腼腆，但现在他表现得很自然了。

There was a little trouble at first, but things were soon quiet. 起初有点小麻烦，后来情况就平静了。

❁ **first** 也可作状语，表示：

初次、第一次：

Where did you first meet? 你们第一次是在哪儿见面的？

We first went there last year. 我们第一次到那里是去年。

先、首先：

First think and then speak. 先想后说。（谚语）

You must finish your work first. 你要先完成你的工作。

❁ **firstly** 也是副词，用来列举理由等，可译为"首先"或"第一"：

Firstly, she did not intend to marry at all; secondly, she meant to go on with her studies. 首先，她根本不想结婚；其次，她打算继续学习。

Vitamin C has many roles to play in weight control. <u>Firstly</u>, it is needed for hormone production. 维生素 C 对控制体重有很多作用。第一，产生荷尔蒙需要它。

但有些人不爱用这个词，而愿用 **first** 代替：

First (ly), let me deal with the most important difficulty. 首先，让我谈谈最突出的困难。

46 at last—last—lastly

at last 表示"（等候较长时间）最后终于"：

<u>At last</u> I understand the situation. 最后，我终于理解了这一形势。

I'm happy to meet you <u>at last</u>. 我很高兴，终于碰到了你。

如果不强调经过长时间等待，则用 **finally** 更好一点：

She <u>finally</u> gained control of herself. 最后，她控制住了自己。

Thus the question was <u>finally</u> settled. 就这样，这问题最后解决了。

❀ **last** 也可用作副词，表示：

最后：

He laughs best that laughs <u>last</u>. 谁笑在最后，谁笑得最好。（谚语）

<u>Last</u>, I would like to summarize the points of my argument. 最后我要总结一下我的论点。

上次：

He saw her <u>last</u> in Paris. 他上次是在巴黎和她见面的。

❀ **lastly** 主要用于列举理由等，表示"最后（一点）"：

<u>Lastly</u>, let me mention the great support I've had from my wife. 最后，我要提一提我妻子给我的巨大支持。

47 at present—presently

at present 表示"现在""此刻"：

<u>At present</u> we are living in Richmond. 现在，我们住在里士满。

She's all right <u>at present</u>. 此刻，她没事。

❀ **presently** 表示"不久""过一会儿"：

Presently Alice appeared. 不久，艾丽斯出现了。

But presently he grew calmer. 但过一会儿，他平静了一些。

在美国可用来表示"现在"，在英国也有一些人这样用：

He is living presently in New York. 他现在住在纽约。

We are presently reading Shakespeare's tragedies. 我们现在在看莎翁的悲剧。

在这样用时不宜把它放在句首或句尾（但 **at present** 可以）。

48　athletics—athletic—athlete

athletics 表示"运动"（尤指田径运动）

As the modern Olympics grew in status, so too did athletics. 随着现代奥林匹克运动会的地位愈来愈高，田径运动也如此。

He has retired from active athletics. 他已退休，不再从事田径运动。

❀ **athletic** 为形容词，表示"（爱）运动的""健壮的"：

Being athletic, Tom found the climb quite easy. 由于身体健壮，汤姆觉得爬山很容易。

athletic activities 体育活动

❀ **athlete** 表示"运动员"：

British athletes won five gold medals in the Olympics. 英国运动员在奥运会上获得五枚金牌。

Ball-players, runners, boxers, swimmers, etc. are athletes. 球员、赛跑者、拳击手、游泳者等都是运动员。

49　attempt—try

attempt 可作动词，表示"企图""试图"（做某事），可以：

跟不定式：

Shelley attempted to get in touch with them. 雪莱试图和他们取得联系。

She attempted to get up, but she couldn't. 她试图爬起来，却没能爬起来。

跟名词和代词：

She is attempting a difficult task. 她是在试图做一件困难的工作。

He attempted the most impossible and brought it off. 他试图做一件最不可能的事，却成功了。

✱ try 也可表示类似的意思，表示"试图、设法（做某事）"，主要跟不定式：

Mary tried to cheer me up. 玛丽试图让我高兴起来。

I'll try to be more careful next time. 下次，我要设法更小心一些。

在口语中有时和 and 连用（=try to...）：

Try and see if you can do it. 设法看看你是否能做到。

We started to try and help them. 我们设法帮助他们。

在日常口语中用 try 时较多，用 attempt 显得有点文气。这两个词也都可用作名词。attempt 可译为"企图""试图""尝试"：

They are beginning a new attempt to solve the problem. 他们正作解决问题的新尝试。

They made no attempt at escaping. 他们没有企图逃跑。

try 主要表示"试一试"：

We've already had a try at it. 我们已经试过。

After a few tries they gave up. 试过几次之后，他们就放弃了。

try 多用在口语中，在书面语中通常用 attempt。

50 attendant—assistant

attendant 通常指"服务员"，如加油站、停车场、衣帽间的服务员：

The room attendant speaks a little English. 客房服务员会讲一点英语。

She stopped the car and told the attendant to fill it up. 她把车停下，让服务员把油加满。

a car-park attendant 停车场服务员

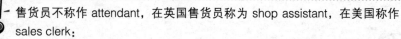

售货员不称作 attendant，在英国售货员称为 shop assistant，在美国称作 sales clerk：

"This record is entirely sold out," said the shop assistant. 售货员说，"这种唱片已全部卖光。"

He is a sales clerk at a music store. 他是一家音乐商店的售货员。

51 attorney—solicitor—lawyer—barrister

lawyer 是 "律师" 最经常的说法：

The lawyer asked the court for an adjournment of the case. 律师请求休庭。

The court appointed a lawyer for the accused. 法庭指定一位律师为被告辩护。

❀ 在英国，在高等法院为原告或被告出庭的律师称为 barrister，为客户提供法律咨询，准备法律文件，并在较低法院出庭的称为 solicitor。在美国代表客户处理法律事务并出庭辩护的称为 attorney。

The defendant was represented by his attorney. 被告由律师代表出庭。

52 aural—oral

aural 的读音为 /ˈɔːrəl/ 或 /ˈɑʊrəl/，表示 "听力的"：

In the aural test the student listens to spoken language. 在听力测验中，学生听口述的材料。

We have used both written and aural material. 我们使用了书面和听力材料。

❀ oral 读作 /ˈɔːrəl/，表示 "口头的"：

In an oral exam, you don't write the answers; you say them. 在口试中，你不必写出答案，而是说出答案。

An oral agreement was not enough. 口头协议是不够的。

oral 还可表示 "口服的" "口腔的"：

It's an oral vaccine. 这是一种口服疫苗。

oral surgery 口腔外科手术

53 avail

avail 可用作动词，表示 "有用" "起作用"：

All his efforts did not avail. 他的一切努力都没有用。

Talk will not avail without work. 不实干空谈不起作用。

avail oneself of 可表示 "利用（机会等）"：

He quickly <u>availed himself of</u> the opportunity. 他很快抓住了这个机会。

You should <u>avail yourself of</u> the books in the library. 你应用好图书馆的藏书。

avail 也可用作名词，主要用于下面短语：

of no avail（作表语）没有用：

All his efforts were <u>of no avail</u>. 他的努力都没有用。

Crying is <u>of no avail</u> now. 哭现在没用。

to no avail（多作状语）没用：

Every effort was made, but <u>to no avail</u>. 做了一切努力，但没有用。

They tried hard to save him, but <u>to no avail</u>. 他们努力挽救他，但没有用。

这个词比较文气，口语中用得比较少。

与它同根的形容词 **available**，在日常倒用得很多，表示"可以找到""可供使用"等：

Is there a doctor <u>available</u>? 能找到医生吗？

This dress is <u>available</u> in all sizes. 这种连衣裙有多种尺寸。

The telephone is now <u>available</u>. 电话现在可以用了。

54 **avenge—revenge**

这两个词都表示"报仇"。

❀ **revenge** 多指"为自己报仇（复）"：

He <u>revenged</u> himself on his enemies. 他向敌人报了仇。

I will <u>revenge</u> that insult. 我要为那次侮辱报复。

也可指"为……报仇"：

Hamlet <u>revenged</u> his dead father. 哈姆雷特为死去的父亲报了仇。

He <u>revenged</u> the murder of his sister. 他向杀害他妹妹的人报了仇。

❀ **avenge** 多指为别人报仇：

Hamlet undertook to <u>avenge</u> the murder of his father. 哈姆雷特着手为父亲的被谋害报仇。

I wanted to <u>avenge</u> Mary and punish Jim. 我想为玛丽报仇，惩罚吉姆。

也可用于 **avenge oneself on**，表示"对……进行报仇（复）"：

He <u>avenged himself on</u> the enemy. 他向敌人报了仇。

She avenged herself on the murderer of her father. 她向谋杀她父亲的人报了仇。

55　await—wait

await 为及物动词，表示"等候"：

I await your decision. 我等候你的决定。

We were all awaiting his answers. 我们都在等他们的回答。

这个词比较文气一些，日常口语中多用 **wait for** 代替它：

They waited for her arrival. 他们等候她的到来。

Time and tide wait for no man. 岁月不等人。（谚语）

wait for 后面有时跟复合结构：

We are waiting for the rain to stop. 我们在等雨停。

She waited for him to come to her. 她等着他来找她。

wait 后还可以跟不定式：

I'm waiting to use the computer. 我在等着使用电脑。

We'll wait to hear what he thinks. 我们将等着，听他的想法。

wait 后也可不跟什么特别结构：

Wait here, don't go away. 在这儿等着，不要走开。

Shall I have to wait long? 我需要等很久吗？

56　awake—wake—awaken—waken

这四个词都是动词，在英式英语中 **awake** 和 **wake** 是不规则动词，而在美式英语中却是规则动词：

(a)wake　　　　　(a)woke　　　　　(a)woken
英式英语（美国也有人用这种形式）

(a)wake　　　　　(a)waked　　　　　(a)waked
美式英语

而 **waken** 和 **awaken** 在美英式英语中都是规则动词：

❀ 在这四个动词中 **wake** 用得最多，表示"醒（来）"或"唤（惊）醒"（常和 **up** 连用）：

Has she woken so early before? 她过去醒过这么早吗？

I'm awfully sorry to <u>wake</u> you <u>up</u>. 非常抱歉，把你闹醒了。

❀ **waken** 是比较文气的说法：

I <u>wakened</u> early. 我醒得很早。

<u>Waken</u> me about 7, please. 请在约七点钟叫我。

❀ **awake** 和 **awaken** 也可表示同样的意思：

I have not <u>awakened</u> so late in years. 多少年，我都没醒过这么晚了。

A knocking on the door <u>awakened</u> her. 敲门声惊醒了她。

但这也是比较文气的说法。这两个词用于引申意义时较多：

I slowly <u>awoke</u> to the danger that threatened me. 我慢慢地认识到了威胁着我的危险。

That <u>awakened</u> their enthusiasm for this subject. 这激起了他对这个话题的热情。

另外，**awake** 还可用作形容词作表语，表示"醒着"：

Is he asleep or <u>awake</u>? 他睡着了还是醒着？

I could hardly keep myself <u>awake</u>. 我很难不让自己睡着。

> awake 不能用 very 修饰，而要说 wide awake, fully awake：
>
> He was <u>wide awake</u> when he reached the village. 他抵达村子时，已完全醒了。
>
> She rose, still not quite <u>fully awake</u>. 她起身时，还没完全醒过来。

57 award—reward

这两个词形相近，意思却不同。

❀ **award** 表示"奖金""奖品"：

The Academy <u>Awards</u> are given out once a year. 科学院奖金每年颁发一次。

The Olympic winner received a gold medal as an <u>award</u>. 奥林匹克优胜者获得一枚金质奖章作为奖品。

❀ **reward** 表示"报酬""酬谢（金）"：

He received no <u>reward</u> for his services. 他的服务没得到酬谢。

<u>Rewards</u> are given for the capture of these criminals. 抓住这些罪犯，将发奖金。

58 awful—awfully

awful 是形容词，有两个意思，一是"可怕"：

He died an awful death. 他死得很惨。

It was an awful war. 这是一场可怕的战争。

但在日常口语中，它表示"糟糕"的时候更多：

It was an awful film. 这是一部很糟糕的片子。

Your grammar is awful. 你的语法很糟。

有时也可用作副词，表示"非常"之类的意思：

10 years sounds like an awful long time. 10 年听起来是非常长的时间。

I've got an awful lot of work to do. 我有大量工作要做。

❀ **awfully** 是副词，表示"非常""极为"，修饰形容词：

It's awfully cold outside. 外边冷极了。

The village looks awfully pretty. 那村子看起来漂亮极了。

59 awhile—a while

awhile 是副词，表示"一小段时间"：

I may have to stay there awhile. 我可能得在那里待一小段时间。

He worked awhile as a pharmacist. 他有一段时间当药剂师。

❀ **a while** 表示"一段时间""一会儿"：

After a while the train stopped. 过了一会儿，火车停了下来。

I've thought about it a long while. 这事我想了很长时间了。

60 backward—backwards

backward 为形容词，表示：

向后的：

She gave the house a sad <u>backward</u> glance. 她向后对这栋房子凄伤地望了一眼。

She took a <u>backward</u> step. 她往后退了一步。

落后的：

He's a little <u>backward</u> in his studies. 他学习有点落后。

They seemed to be <u>backward</u> in the technique. 他们似乎在技术上很落后。

✤ **backwards** 为副词，在美国也可用 **backward** 作副词，表示"向后""倒着"：

He took two steps <u>backwards</u>. 他向后走了两步。

The hummingbird can fly <u>backwards</u>. 蜂鸟可以倒着飞。

backwards and forwards 表示"来回地"：

We strolled <u>backwards and forwards</u> on the lawns. 我们在草坪上来回遛。

The train goes <u>backwards and forwards</u> between the two towns. 这列火车在两座城市间来回开。

61 bad—badly

bad 为形容词，表示：

坏，不好，（食品）坏了：

What <u>bad</u> weather we're having！天气真糟糕！

The fruit has all gone <u>bad</u>. 水果都坏了。

不舒服，（身体某部分）不好，有毛病：

He has a bad back so we have a hard bed. 他背不好，因此我们用了一张硬床。

My eyes have been rather bad of late. 近来我的眼睛不大好。

严重，厉害：

I've got a bad headache. 我头疼得厉害。

Is the pain very bad? 痛得厉害吗?

bad 的比较级为 **worse**, 表示：

更坏，更糟：

The weather was worse than I had expected. 天气比我预料的坏（糟）。

We couldn't have had worse news. 消息不能再坏了。

更严重，更厉害：

At least, he's no worse. 至少他的情况没恶化。

The storm grew worse and worse. 暴风雨越来越厉害了。

bad 的最高级为 **worst**, 表示 "最坏的" "最糟的" "最严重的"：

She is the worst singer I know. 她是我知道的最糟的歌手。

This is the worst cold I ever had. 这是我患过的最严重的感冒。

❀ **badly** 为副词，表示：

坏，不好：

He has behaved very badly to you. 他待你很不好。

This garment is badly knitted. 这件衣服织得很糟。

严重，厉害：

He was bleeding badly. 他血流得很厉害。

The building was badly damaged. 大楼严重损坏。

迫切地：

I am badly in need of your advice. 我迫切需要你出主意。

He wanted very badly to smoke. 他迫切想抽烟。

badly 的比较级也是 **worse**，表示 "更差" "更糟" "更厉害"：

You're playing worse than ever. 你弹得比过去任何时候都差。

He behaved even worse than usual. 他表现得比平常还差。

badly 的最高级也是 **worst**，表示 "最坏地" "最严重地"：

This child acts worst when there is company about. 有客人时，这孩子表现得最糟。

Of all the people they suffered (the) worst. 在所有人中，他们受苦最多。

在表示"更迫切""最迫切"时，多用 more 和 most 构成比较级和最高级：

She wanted him more badly than ever. 她现在比过去更迫切地需要他。

This is the area that most badly needs our support. 这是最迫切需要我们支持的地区。

62　baggage—luggage

在英国 **baggage** 或 **luggage** 都指行李，但用 **luggage** 的人更多一些：

They had left their luggage at the station. 他们把行李存在车站了。

在美国都把行李称为 **baggage**：

A porter carried our baggage to the train. 一个搬运工把我们的行李搬到了火车上。

这两个词都是不可数名词，若要表示"一件行李"，可说 a piece of luggage（baggage）：

How many pieces of baggage have you got? 你有几件行李？

63　banknote—note—bill

banknote 指纸币或钞票：

Some of the banknotes were terribly dirty. 有些钞票脏得要命。

❀ 在英国通常用 **note** 表示"钞票"：

I paid for the tickets with a ten-shilling note. 我用一张 10 先令的钞票付了车票钱。

She sent him four five-pound notes. 她寄给了他四张五英镑的钞票。

❀ 在美国通常都用 **bill** 表示这个意思：

He handed me a ten-dollar bill. 他递给我一张 10 美元的钞票。

She took out a five-dollar bill. 她拿出一张五美元的钞票。

64　bare—barely

bare 是形容词，表示"光秃的""空无一物的"：

The top of the hill was bare. 山顶光秃秃的。

He lived in a bare house. 他住在一栋空无一物的房子里。

❀ **barely** 是副词，表示"仅仅能（只有）""勉强能"：

We had barely enough time to catch the train. 我们的时间勉强够赶上火车。

He was so weak that he could barely stand up. 他是那样虚弱，仅仅能站起身来。

有时用在下面这类句子中，表示"刚刚……就"：

He had barely arrived when he had to leave again. 他刚一到，就又要走了。

I had barely said my name before he led me to the operating room. 我刚刚说出我的名字他就把我带到手术室去了。

65 bass—base

这两个词读音相同，都读作 /beɪs/，但意思不同。

❀ **bass** 表示"男低音（歌手）"：

The opera star is a fine bass. 那位歌剧明星是一位优秀的男低音。

也可作形容词，表示"低音的"：

a bass saxophone (guitar) 低音萨克斯管（吉他）

❀ **base** 表示"基础""基地"

It serves the economic base. 它为经济基础服务。

Shelley thus laid the base for his future thinking. 就这样，雪莱打下了未来思想的基础。

The weary troops marched back to the base. 疲惫的士兵行军回到了基地。

由 **base** 派生出三个词 **basis**、**basic** 和 **basically**。**basis** 为名词，表示"基础""根据"：

These committees have a mass basis. 这些委员会有群众基础。

The rumor has no basis. 这种谣言毫无根据。

basic 为形容词，表示"基本的"：

They lacked the basic necessities of life. 他们缺乏基本的生活必需品。

the basic skills of reading, writing and communicating 读、写及交流的基本技巧

basically 为副词，表示"基本上"：

They believe that men are basically good. 他们相信，人本质上是好的。

These labour leaders are basically social-democrats. 这些工会领袖基本上是社会民主党人。

66 bath—bathe

bath 读作 /bɑ:θ/，在英国表示：

洗澡：

I shall have a hot bath and go to bed. 我去洗个热水澡，然后上床睡觉。

The football team are having baths. 足球队员在洗澡。

美国人多说 take a bath：

He takes a cold bath every morning. 他每天早晨洗个凉水澡。

澡盆、浴室：

Clean out the bath when you've done. 洗完了，把澡盆洗干净。

It has two bedrooms, a kitchen and a bath. 它有两间卧室、一间厨房和一间浴室。

在美国多用 **bathtub** 或 **tub** 表示"澡盆"：

I spent hours in the warmth of the bathtub. 我在澡盆的热水里泡了几个钟头。

He was sitting in the tub. 他坐在澡盆里。

在美国 **bathroom** 除表示"浴室"外，还可表示"公共厕所"：

Is there a bathroom in this restaurant? 这家餐馆有厕所吗？

bath 在英国也可用作动词，表示"（给……）洗澡"：

Mother had to bath the baby. 母亲得给宝宝洗澡。

She bathed in cold water winter and summer. 不论寒暑她都用凉水洗澡。

在美国不这样说，而说 **take a bath** 或用 **bathe** /beɪð/ 这个词：

Then I took a bath. 然后，我洗了一个澡。

After that I returned to my apartment to bathe and change. 在那之后，我回到家里洗澡换衣服。

They used the water to bathe the babies. 他们用这些水给婴儿洗澡。

在英国 bathe 表示"游泳"或"在水里浸泡"：

I like to bathe in the sea. 我喜欢在海里游泳。

但这种用法已经有些老式，现在多说 go swimming 或 go for a swim：

She's going for a swim. 她现在去游泳。

美国人有时说 take a swim：

I went down to the beach and took a swim. 我到海边去游了游泳。

在表示"洗涤（伤口）"时，在英国和美国都用 bathe 这个词：

First bathe the wound with hot water. 先用热水洗涤伤口。

The doctor told him to bathe his eyes twice a day. 医生让他每天洗两次眼睛。

"洗日光浴"，应用 sunbathe /ˈsʌnbeɪð/ 表示（而不能说 sunbath）。

67 be (as an auxiliary verb)

be 可用作助动词，用来构成：

进行时态或进行形式：

How long have you been studying the problem? 这问题你研究多久了？

You're supposed to be working. 你现在应当在工作。

被动语态或被动形式：

The road is being repaired. 路正在修。

You might be asked to speak at the meeting. 可能请你在会上发言。

68 be (as a link verb)

作系动词时，后面可跟各种成分和结构：

跟形容词：

Be quiet! 安静点！

跟名词：

It's a hard nut to crack. 这是一个棘手的问题。

代词或数词：

She was only five then. 那时她才五岁。

He is twenty-seven now. 他现在 27 岁了。

副词：

I'll be round in a little while. 我一会儿过来。

I haven't been out much recently. 我最近没太出门。

介词短语：

She is in excellent health. 她很健康。

I'm a bit under the weather. 我有点不大舒服。

动名词：

Her job is taking care of the baby. 她的任务是看宝宝。

Talking to you is talking to the wall. 和你谈是对牛弹琴。

不定式：

My plan was to go from Wuhan to Nanjing by boat. 我的计划是从武汉坐船到南京。

Your job is to clean the kitchen. 你的任务是打扫厨房。

分词：

The situation is quite encouraging. 形势很令人鼓舞。

The table is covered with dust. 桌上尽是尘土。

从句：

My idea is that you shouldn't have left the country. 我的意见是你不应该离开那个国家。

Now the question is where we can get the raw material. 现在的问题是在哪里能找到原料。

69 beach—shore—coast

beach 指海滩：

They walked for a while along the beach. 他们沿海滩走了一会儿。

❀ **shore** 指海岸：

We found many shells on the sea-shore. 我们在海岸上找到许多贝壳。

Let's go on shore. 咱们到海岸上去。

❀ **coast** 指海岸（线）：

There are numerous islands off the coast. 海岸边有许多岛屿。

70 bear—endure—stand

这三个词都表示"忍受"。

❀ bear 多指忍受疼痛、麻烦等：

I can't <u>bear</u> this weather. 我受不了这种天气。

We must face the trouble and <u>bear</u> it. 我们必须面对并忍受麻烦。

bear 后面还可跟不定式、动名词等：

She can't <u>bear</u> to be laughed at. 她受不了被人嘲笑。

She can't <u>bear</u> me to be unhappy. 她不忍心看我这样不高兴。

❀ endure 多表示忍受困难、痛苦等：

He <u>endured</u> (bore) the pain as long as he could. 他尽量久地忍住疼痛。

You must be ready to <u>endure</u> hardships. 你必须准备忍受艰难困苦。

❀ stand 也可表示"忍受"：

He could not <u>stand</u> the strain. 他受不了这种紧张。

I can't <u>stand</u> (bear, endure) the new manager. 我受不了那位新经理。

这三个词是同义词，在很多情况下可以换用，bear 和 stand 较常用，endure 意思更强一点。

71 beautiful

表示"漂亮""好看"的词很多，下面这些词都不同程度地表示了这一个意思：

beautiful	pretty	handsome	good-looking
attractive	gorgeous	stunning	lovely

beautiful 和 **pretty** 通常都用来描绘女人和小孩。**beautiful** 可译为"美（的）""漂亮"，**pretty** 可译为"俊俏""漂亮"：

He saw a <u>beautiful</u> young girl with golden hair. 他看到一位美丽的金发姑娘。

She was so astonishingly <u>pretty</u>. 她漂亮得让人惊讶。

这两个词也可用来形容其他东西，如 beautiful scenery, beautiful night, beautiful room, beautiful flowers, beautiful clothes, pretty place, pretty clothes, a pretty garden, a pretty house 等。用来形容

男人的时候比较少。

attractive, good-looking 使用比较广泛，男人、女人都可以修饰：

She had grown into an <u>attractive</u> girl. 她长成一位漂亮的姑娘了。

She was a <u>good-looking</u> woman of over thirty. 她是位 30 多岁的漂亮女人。

handsome 一般用来修饰男人，可译为"漂亮""俊美"：

He is not <u>handsome</u>, but is very pleasant looking. 他并不英俊，但招人喜爱。

也可用来形容体态俊美、端庄稳重有风韵的女人：

Madeline was a <u>handsome</u> young woman. 玛德琳是一位俊俏有风韵的女人。

Would you describe that woman as <u>handsome</u> or beautiful? 你觉得应当把那女人形容为"俊俏"还是"美丽"？

gorgeous 可表示"华丽""漂亮"：

She was a <u>gorgeous</u> blonde. 她是一个漂亮的金发女郎。

The peacock spread its <u>gorgeous</u> tail. 孔雀展开了它华丽的羽毛。

stunning 也可表示"漂亮"：

You look <u>stunning</u> today. 你今天看上去很漂亮。

lovely 可表示"漂亮""可爱""美好"：

She regarded Helen as simply <u>lovely</u>. 她认为海伦就是很漂亮。

She is endowed with a <u>lovely</u> character. 她天生具有可爱的性格。

72 **because—as—since—for**

这四个词的意思有些接近，都可译为"因为"，但它们中间也有一些差异：

❀ **because** 一般指出直接的原因，在回答 **why** 引起的问句时都会用它：

Why didn't you go to the concert? —Because I had a bad headache.
为什么你没去听音乐会？ ——因为我头疼得厉害。

He distrusted me <u>because</u> I was new. 他不信任我，是因为我是新来的。

because 引导的从句，通常放在主句后面，但为了强调也可放在前面：

Because I worked fast, I finished early. 因为我干得快，所以我完成得早。

❀ **as** 和 **since** 引导的原因从句常可放在前面：

As all the seats were full I stood up. 因为所有座位都有人，我就站了起来。

Since we've no money, we can't buy it. 因为我们没有钱，我们没法买它。

有时也可放在后面：

We didn't know what to do as we are not his parents. 我们不知怎么办好，因为我们不是他的父母。

He could not answer the question, since he had not made up his mind. 他不能回答这个问题，因为他还没拿定主意。

❀ **for** 用在书面语中的时候较多，引起的分句对前面的话进行解释，常用逗号把它和前面的分句分开：

He shook his head, for he thought differently. 他摇了摇头，因为他有不同想法。

The days were short, for it was now December. 白天很短，因为这时已经是 12 月。

这种用法已经有些老式。

另外 **because of** 也表示原因，但后面总是跟名词（或代词）：

She won't come out because of asthma. 由于气喘，她不想出来。

Because of this we decided to leave early. 由于这个，我们决定早些动身。

73 become—get—grow—come—go—turn—run—fall

become 是一个系动词，表示"变成"，后面可以跟：

名词：

Naturally he became chairman of the commission. 自然，他成了委员会主任。

His dream has now become a reality. 他的梦想现在成了事实。

形容词：

She became very fond of her. 她变得非常喜欢她了。

Gradually he became silent. 慢慢地，他变得沉默起来。

跟过去分词：

The room soon became crowded. 房间很快变得拥挤起来。

Jamie was becoming annoyed with me. 杰米变得对我不高兴起来。

除 become 外，还有一些词有类似意思，它们都在一定范围内表示这种变化：

❀ **get**（在口语中用得很多，常有较活译法）：

She got quite impatient. 她变得很不耐烦起来。

I hope you won't get overtired. 我希望你不要太累。

❀ **grow**（在书面语中用得比较多，常表示逐渐的变化）：

Truth never grows old. 真理永远不会过时。（谚语）

The fox may grow grey, but never good. 狐狸会变老，却不会变好。（谚语）

❀ **come**（只限用于少数形容词或过去分词前，表示一个渐变的过程）：

Wrong never comes right. 错的永远不会变成对的。（谚语）

Your shoelaces have come undone. 你的鞋带散了。

❀ **go**（可表示颜色的变化或状态的变化，只和某些词搭配）：

She went pale at the news. 听了这消息，她脸色变得苍白。

Fish soon goes bad in hot weather. 大热天鱼很容易坏。

❀ **turn**（多用来表示颜色的变化，有时也可表示状态或身份的变化）：

His hair turned grey in a few weeks. 在几个星期中，他头发就变灰白了。

The milk will soon turn sour. 牛奶很快就会变酸。

❀ **run**（只限于和少数形容词搭配）：

The river was beginning to run dry. 这条河开始干涸。

My blood ran cold. 我的血都凉了。

❀ **fall**（只和某些词搭配）：

At the President's entry everyone fell silent. 总统进来时，大家都安静下来。

I fell prey to evil dreams. 我受到噩梦的折磨。

74 begin—start—commence

begin 和 **start** 都可以表示"开始"。可以表示：

（某事）开始：

When does the play begin? 戏什么时候开始？

School begins at eight o'clock. 八点钟开始上课。

开始（做某事）：

We'd better begin work immediately. 我们最好马上开始工作。

We at once began making preparations. 我们立即开始做准备工作。

在这个意义上两者的用法是差不多的，在较正式场合，用 **begin** 或许更好一些。

start 还有一些意思，是不能用 **begin** 代替的，如：

动身，出发：

We must start early. 我们要早动身。

At last the bus started. 最后客车出发了。

发动：

We couldn't start the car. 我们发动不了汽车啦。

They start wars when they want something. 他们想得到什么时，就发动战争。

开办：

We'll be able to start a shop. 我们可以开一家商店。

He intended to start business on the following day. 他打算第二天就开始做生意。

start 还有许多其他意思，如：

start a fire 生火	start proceedings 起诉
start an infant 怀孕	start a watch 上表

✿ **commence** 也可表示"开始"这个意思：

We commence a sentence with a capital letter. 我们用大写字母放一个句子开头。

He commenced studying law. 他开始学法律。

在日常口语中，**begin** 和 **start** 用得较多，**commence** 主要用于书面语中，但在美国，特别是在西部和南部，也有一些人用它。

75 believe—believe in

believe 在多数情况下，都用作及物动词，表示"相信"，可跟三种结构：

跟名词或代词：

She could scarcely believe her eyes. 她简直不能相信自己的眼睛。

I just can't believe a single word you say. 你说的话，我一句都不能相信。

You can ask my mother if you don't believe me. 你如果不相信我，可以问我母亲。

跟从句：

I believe it is going to flower this year. 我相信它今年会开花。

She believed the fault lay with him. 她相信，这是他的错。

跟带不定式（或形容词）的复合结构：

They believed him to be innocent. 他们相信，他是无辜的。

I believe it to have been a mistake. 我相信，这是一个错误。

believe in 是一个短语，表示：

信仰，相信：

Marxism believes in the primacy of matter. 马克思主义者相信物质是第一性的。

I don't believe in the theory. 我不相信这个理论。

信赖，对……有信心：

You can believe in him; he'll never let you down. 你可以信赖他，他绝不会令你失望。

If you believe in yourself you can succeed. 如果你对自己有信心，就能成功。

相信有：

Only 29 percent of the population believe in a personal God. 只有 29% 的人相信有人模样的上帝。

主张，认为，是好的：

He believes in plenty of fresh air and exercise. 他认为大量新鲜空气和运动是好的。

I've always believed in being broad-minded. 我一向主张宽宏大量。

☞ believe 不能用于进行时态。

76 below—under—underneath—beneath

这四个词意思相近，也有一些差别。

❀ **below** 可用作介词，也可用作副词。

作介词时表示：

在……以下：

The Dead Sea is <u>below</u> sea level. 死海在海平面以下。

Water was found about three feet <u>below</u> the surface. 在地面约三英尺以下找到了水。

在下面，在……下方：

Miners work <u>below</u> the surface of the earth. 矿工在地表下面干活。

Sign your name <u>below</u> mine on this document. 在这个文件上我的名字下面签上你的名字。

（用于引申意义）比……差，价钱较低：

He can't be much <u>below</u> (under) sixty. 他 60 岁不会差多少。

He was <u>below</u> Mary in intelligence. 他的智力比玛丽的差。

below 也可用作副词，表示：

（作定语）下面的，下方的：

Write your name in the space <u>below</u>. 把你的名字写在下面空白处。

I could see the river far down <u>below</u>. 我可以看到下方远处的河流。

（作状语）在下面，在下方：

Please affix your signature <u>below</u>. 请在下方签字。

A detailed description is given <u>below</u>. 下面有详细的描述。

（作表语）在下面：

The grocery was <u>below</u>. 杂货店在下面。

<u>Below</u> is an example of a typical business letter. 下面是一封典型商业信函的例子。

❀ **under** 主要用作介词，表示：

在……下面：

Push the stool under the table. 把凳子推到桌子下面去。

She sat very still under the trees. 她在树下静静地坐着。

在这个意义上它和 **below** 意思相近，**under** 表示"在……正下方"，而 **below** 可以指近处下面，也可指远处的下方。

（用于引申意义）在……管辖下，受……照顾：

Each province was placed under a military governor. 每个省由一位军人省长管辖。

He has been under the doctor for some weeks. 几个礼拜以来，他一直受医生的照顾。

不到（某个数量、年龄等）：

You can do the job in under an hour. 这工作你不到一个钟头就能干完。

He earns under £20 a week. 他一星期赚的钱不到 20 英镑。

（引起短语作表语）在……的过程中，正在经受：

The matter is under consideration. 这件事正在考虑之中。

I am under the doctor's treatment. 我正接受医生的治疗。

（引起短语作状语）根据（协议、法律等）：

Under this agreement, he is permitted to return to his own country. 根据这个协议他获准回到自己的国家。

I raise the objection under Article 5 of the Constitution. 根据宪法第五款，我提出了反对意见。

（引起短语作状语）列在……项下：

In this book, you'll find "tiger" under "cats." 在这本书里，你会发现"老虎"列在"猫科"动物项下。

You will find these two books listed under "Biography." 你会发现这两本书列在"传记"项下。

under 只在以下情况用作副词：

This book is for children six years and under. 这本书是给六岁及以下儿童看的。

The cost will be £2 or under. 成本将为两英镑或两英镑以下。

❀ **underneath** 可用作介词或副词。作介词时表示"在……下面"：

A cat was sleeping underneath the table. 一只猫在桌子下面睡觉。

Have you looked underneath the bed? 你在床底下找了没有？

作副词时表示：

下面，里面：

The ice remained, but there was no water underneath. 冰还在，但下面却没有水。

She wore a fur coat with nothing underneath. 她穿一件皮大衣，里面什么也没有。

在内心里：

He may seem ambitious but he is a modest man underneath. 他也许显得野心勃勃，但内心里是一个谦逊的人。

But he wasn't hard, underneath he was kind. 但他并不厉害，内心里他是很善良的。

这个词比较文气，在日常口语中用 under 和 below 时更多。

❀ beneath 也可指 "在……下面（方）"：

There is a large cellar beneath (below, under) the kitchen. 厨房下面有一个大地窖。

The daffodils were growing beneath the trees. 水仙花长在树下。

但这个词也较文气，用于上述意思时较少，但有时用于引申意义及短语中：

What he said is beneath contempt. 他说的话不值一理。

He will do nothing beneath his dignity. 他不会做不合身份的事。

77 beside—besides

beside 是介词，表示 "在……旁边"：

The church is beside the river. 教堂在江边。

Helen reserved a seat for me, beside her own. 海伦给我也订了一个座位，就在她旁边。

❀ besides 也可作介词，但意思不同，表示 "除了……"：

Besides you, no one is qualified. 除了你，没有人合格。

There are in China over fifty minorities besides the Han ethnicity. 在中国，除了汉族还有 50 多个少数民族。

另外，besides 还用作副词，表示 "除此之外" "而且"：

Besides, she's a wonderfully dutiful girl. 除此之外，她还是一个极其负责的姑娘。

I don't like those shoes; besides, they're too expensive. 我不喜欢那双鞋，而且价钱也太贵。

78 besides—except—apart from

这三个词有时容易混。

❀ besides 表示"除了……（还有）"（有"加"的作用）：

Besides knowing some French, she was fluent in Italian. 除了懂些法语，她的意大利语也很流利。

Besides the violin, he plays the piano and the flute. 除了拉提琴，他还能弹钢琴和吹笛子。

❀ except 也是介词，表示"除了……（都）"（有"减"的作用）：

I like all musical instruments except the violin. 除了提琴，我什么乐器都喜欢。

We go there every day except Sunday. 除了星期天，我们每天都去。

❀ apart from 则兼具两者的意思：

除了……还，除……之外：

Apart from the violin, he plays the piano and the flute. 除了拉提琴，他还能弹钢琴和吹笛子。

Apart from the cost, it will take a lot of time. 除了花钱，它还需投入许多时间。

除了……（都）：

I like all musical instruments apart from the violin. 除了提琴，我什么乐器都喜欢。

Apart from that, all goes well. 除了这一点，一切都很顺利。

在否定结构后，这三个词都可以用，意思差不多，但用 apart from 时更多：

He has nothing besides (except, apart from) his salary. 除了薪水，他别无所有。

Apart from them, I had no one to talk to. 除了他们，我没有别人可以交谈。

79 between—among

这两个词的根本差别是 between 指两者之间，而 among 指一些东西或人之中：

Between the two trees is a space of ten feet. 两棵树之间有 10 英尺的空地。

His house is hidden among the trees. 他的房子隐藏在树木之间。

此外 between 还有许多其他用法，如：

指时间：

Come between nine and ten o'clock. 在九、十点之间来。

指数量：

He is a man between fifty and sixty. 他是一个五六十岁的男子。

指关系：

I don't want any ill-feeling between us. 我不希望我们之间有任何恶感。

指差别：

Is there much difference between British and American law? 英国法律和美国法律之间差别大吗？

有时说明几方面间的两两相互关系：

It has increased the contradiction between Germany, Italy and France. 这增加了德国、意大利和法国之间的矛盾。

Switzerland lies between France, Italy, Austria and Germany. 瑞士位于法、意、奥、德之间。

而 among 可用来表示"是……中间的一个"：

I was among the first to arrive. 我是首批到达的人之一。

Shelley is among the world's greatest poets. 雪莱是世界上最伟大的诗人之一。

又可和人称代词连用，表示"共同""一起"：

Among them, they collected over a hundred pounds. 他们共同筹集了一百多英镑。

The three men had $30 among them (selves). 这三个人一共有 30 美元。

在三个或更多人之间分配或合用时，among 和 between 都可以用：

The children divided the money among (between) them. 孩子们在他们

之间把钱分了。

I shared the food <u>between</u> (<u>among</u>) all my friends. 我把食物和所有朋友一起共享。

80 big—large—great

这三个词都有"大"的意思，却有一些差别。

❀ **large** 多用来修饰具体的东西：

I want a <u>large</u> box; this is too small. 我要一个大盒子，这个太小。

Which country is <u>larger</u>, America or Canada? 美国和加拿大哪个国家大些?

只偶尔用来修饰抽象东西：

He was given a <u>large</u> allowance. 他得到一大笔津贴。

但常可和某些量词连用：

He made a <u>large</u> amount of money. 他赚了大量的钱。

She buys things in <u>large</u> quantities. 她大量买东西。

❀ **big** 既可以修饰具体东西：

There was a bed and a <u>big</u> wardrobe. 有一张床和一个大衣橱。

She works in a <u>big</u> hospital. 她在一家大医院工作。

也可修饰抽象的东西：

He said the office expenses were too <u>big</u>. 他说办公室的开销太大。

The <u>biggest</u> problem at the moment is unemployment. 目前最大的问题是失业。

这个词在日常口语中用得比较多。

❀ **great** 主要用来修饰抽象的东西：

It was a <u>great</u> loss to us. 这对我们是巨大的损失。

Your work has shown a <u>great</u> improvement. 你的工作有很大改进。

有时有较活的译法：

He was a young man with <u>great</u> talent. 他是一个非常有才华的青年。

It demonstrated their <u>great</u> love for him. 这表明了他们对他的热爱。

有时也可修饰具体的东西（比 **large** 更带感情色彩）：

Little strokes fell <u>great</u> oaks. 一点点地砍也可伐倒大橡树。（谚语）

Small leaks will sink a great ship. 小漏洞能使大船沉没。（谚语）

此外，**great** 还有下面的意思：

伟大的，重要的：

He is a great scholar. 他是一位伟大的学者。

It is one of the great books of the 19th century. 这是 19 世纪伟大的作品之一。

（口）妙，好极了：

Then a great idea came to him. 这时他想到一个很妙的主意。

This concerto is great! 这首协奏曲好极了！

十足的（可译作"大"），极能……的：

He was a great talker. 他是个极能吹的人。

He's a great music lover. 他是个热爱音乐的人。

用于 a great deal (many) 表示好多：

We learnt a great deal from them. 我们从他们那儿学到很多东西。

He lost a great quantity of blood. 他失了大量的血。

81　boot—trunk

汽车上的存物柜在英国称为 **boot**：

Is the boot open? 存物柜是开着的吗？

在美国则称为 **trunk**：

They put the suitcases in the trunk. 他们把箱子放在存物柜里。

82　border—boundary—frontier

border 指"边界"：

We were near the border between France and Germany. 我们靠近法、德两国的边界。

The criminal escaped over the border. 犯人越过边界逃跑了。

❀ **boundary** 可表示"边界（线）"：

Boundaries may be changed by treaties. 边界线可根据条约改划。

The river is the boundary between the two countries. 这条河是两国的边界线。

也可指较小地区的边界：

This wall marks the boundary of the school grounds. 这条墙标出了学校校园的边界。

That river forms the boundary between the two counties. 那条河是这两个县之间的边界。

但指一个国家的边界（地区）时，不能用 boundary，而需用 borders：

the borders of Switzerland 瑞士的边界地区

❀ frontier 也可表示"边界"：

Lille is close to the frontier between France and Belgium. 里尔靠近法国和比利时的边界。

Troops established a road block on the frontier. 士兵在边界上设了路障。

在美国 the frontiers 指早年未开发的地区：

Areas near the frontiers in America were rough and lawless in the old days. 在早期，美国未开发地区很粗野少礼、无法无天。

frontier 也可表示"（科学等）新开拓的领域"：

The forntiers of medical knowledge are being pushed farther onward as time goes on. 随着时间的推移，医学知识新开拓领域不断向前推进。

83 born—borne

这两个词都是 bear 的过去分词，都读作 /bɔːn/。

❀ 在表示"出生"时，都说 be born：

No one is born wise. 没有人生下来就有智慧。（谚语）

All men are born equal. 人生而平等。

❀ 若后面跟有 by 引起的短语，则用 borne 这个形式：

He was borne by Eve. 他是夏娃生的。

若用于主动语态，也用 borne 这个形式：

She had borne many children. 她生了许多孩子。

用于其他意义时，过去分词都用 borne 这个形式：

The cost will be borne by our company. 费用将由我们公司承担。

His story was borne out by later information. 他讲的情况都被后来的情报证明了。

84 borrow—lend—loan

borrow 表示"向人借""借来"：

May I borrow your bag? 我能否借一下你的口袋？

He was often sent out to borrow. 他常常被派出去借钱。

❀ **lend** 表示"借给"：

Could you lend me some money? 你能否借给我一点钱？

He offered to lend me some books. 他主动提出借给我几本书。

❀ 在美国 **loan** 也可表示"借（钱）给"：

Can you loan me a hundred dollars? 你可否借给我一百美金？

The bank loaned him £5, 000 to start a business. 银行贷给他 5 000 英镑来开一家店。

在英国 **loan** 可以表示"借出（一些珍贵的东西）"：

He loaned his collection of pictures to the public gallery. 他把他的一批藏画借给了公共美术馆。

但要借用搬不动的东西时，这三个词都不能用，可以说：

Could we have the use of your office? 我们能借用一下你们的办公室吗？

I'd like to use your phone. 我想借用一下你的电话。

85 both

both 可作代词也可作形容词（有人称为限定词）。作代词时，它表示"两者（人）"，在句中可担任许多成分：

作主语：

Both should make concessions. 双方都要做让步。

Both of them are from Lisbon. 两人都来自里斯本。

作宾语或构成复合宾语：

I wish both of you well. 希望你们两人都好。

作同位语：

They both love dancing. 他们两人都喜欢跳舞。（作主语同位语）

They invited us both to the party. 他们邀请了我们两人参加晚会。（作

宾语同位语）

Mary sends you <u>both</u> her love. 玛丽向你们两人问好。（作间接宾语的同位语）

在作同位语时，它可有不同位置：

They <u>both</u> laughed. 两人都笑了。（放在动词前面）

They were <u>both</u> college students. 两人都是大学生。（放在动词 be 后面）

They have <u>both</u> fallen asleep. 两人都睡着了。（放在助动词后面）

They will <u>both</u> be sent abroad. 两人都将派往国外。（放在第一个助动词后面）

They can <u>both</u> swim. 他们两人都会游泳。（放在情态动词后面）

作形容词（或称限定词）时，它都用作定语，表示"两人（者）都"：

<u>Both</u> these questions are easy to answer. 这两个问题都容易回答。

She clasped Helen's hand in <u>both</u> hers. 她用双手握住海伦的手。

both 不能用在否定句中。在表示"两人都不……"时要用 neither 或 either：
<u>Neither</u> of his parents was there. 他的父母都不在那里。
I didn't see <u>either</u> of them. 他们两人我都没见到。

86 both ... and ...

both ... and 是一种连词，可以用来连接：

两个名词（可译为"和"）：

<u>Both</u> she <u>and</u> Sophia were pleased with the girl. 她和索菲娅都喜欢这个姑娘。

You've given <u>both</u> your uncle <u>and</u> myself a lot of trouble. 你给你姑父和我找了很多麻烦。

两个形容词（可译为"既……又"）：

Sophia was <u>both</u> glad <u>and</u> sorry to see her. 索菲娅看到她既高兴又难过。

The food was <u>both</u> bad <u>and</u> insufficient. 那些吃的既糟糕又不够。

两个介词短语（可译为"既……也"）：

She was ashamed, <u>both</u> for herself <u>and</u> for Diana. 她感到羞愧，既为自己也为戴安娜。

I did all this both for you and for myself. 我做这一切是为了你，也为我自己。

两个动词（可译为"既……也"）：

He both speaks and writes Spanish. 他既会说西班牙语，也会写西班牙语。

Tonight they will both sing and dance. 今晚，他们将又唱歌又跳舞。

87 brand—make

brand 和 make 都可表示"牌子"，但有差别。

❀ 一些日常用品的牌子多用 brand 表示：

They sell three brands of tea. 他们出售三种牌子的茶叶。

What is your favourite brand of soap? 你最喜欢什么牌子的香皂？

❀ make 多指汽车、机器等的牌子：

What make of car did you buy? 你买的什么牌子的汽车？

What make of television is yours? 你的电视机是什么牌子的？

88 breast—bosom

breast 可以指"胸脯"：

He struck his breast. 他捶打自己的胸脯。

He had a white handkerchief in the breast pocket of his jacket. 他上衣胸前口袋里有一条白手绢。

breast(s) 也可指妇女的乳房：

A baby sucks milk from his mother's breast. 婴儿吮吸母奶。

women with small breasts 小乳房的妇女

❀ bosom /ˈbuzəm/ 指"前胸"：

She has a well developed bosom. 她有丰满的前胸。

这是比较文气的词。bust 可指妇女的胸围（实指乳房）：

She has a very large bust. 她胸围很大。

Good posture also helps your bust look bigger. 姿势对也可使你的乳房显得大一些。

89 breathe—breath

breathe /briːð/ 是动词，表示"呼吸"：

He was breathing hard. 她呼吸很困难。

It's healthy to breathe deeply. 深呼吸对身体有好处。

❀ **breath** /breθ/ 是名词，表示"呼吸"或"呼吸的气"：

The patient's breath grew stronger. 病人的呼吸比较有力了。

He was now short of breath. 他现在气短。

也可指"吸一口气"：

He took a deep breath and jumped into the water. 他深深吸了一口气跳入水中。

90 bring—take—fetch

bring 表示"拿来""送来""带来"等（与 come 的方向一致）：

He will bring us the tickets tomorrow. 他明天给我们送票来。

He has brought his luggage with him. 他把行李带来了。

❀ **take** 则表示"带去""送去""拿走"等（与 go 的方向一致）：

I'm going to take you somewhere else. 我将带你到一个别的地方去。

I took my things to the hotel last night. 我昨晚把我的东西送到旅馆里去了。

❀ **fetch** 一般指去某处把某物（人）拿（接）来：

I asked him to fetch me an evening paper. 我让他去给我拿一份晚报来。

Fetch me the flute from my drawer. 把我抽屉里的笛子取来。

91 Britain—British—England

Britain（不列颠）或 **Great Britain** 包括英格兰、苏格兰和威尔士。**The United Kingdom**（联合王国）包括英格兰、苏格兰、威尔士和北爱尔兰。**The British Isles**（不列颠群岛）指不列颠、爱尔兰及沿岸的所有小岛。

❀ 联合王国的公民为 **British**（英国人）：

The British drink a great deal of tea. 英国人茶喝得很多。

The British are a freedom-loving race. 英国人是热爱自由的民族。

British 也可用作形容词：

I'm German, but my wife is British. 我是德国人，我妻子是英国人。

The British people live in Britain. 英国人住在不列颠。

有些人更愿称自己为 English（英格兰人），Scottish（苏格兰人），Welsh（威尔士人）或 Northern Irish（北爱尔兰人）。

❀ England（英格兰）只是英国的一部分，苏格兰人和威尔士人不喜欢别人把他们称作 English。在报纸上，英国人有时被称为 Briton：

The youth, a 17-year-old Briton, was searched and arrested. 这个青年是个 17 岁的英国人，受到搜查并被逮捕。

92 broad—wide

broad 和 wide 都可表示"宽"。

❀ wide 用得稍多一些，特别是在口语中：

They came to a wide river. 他们来到一条宽阔的河边。

The street is very wide. 这条街很宽。

❀ broad 也可这样用：

The broad boulevard had four traffic lanes. 宽阔的林荫道有四行车道。

在谈到某些物件时，多用 wide 修饰，而不用 broad：

He saw a wide bed in the room. 在房里他看到一张很宽的床。

The car is too wide for the garage. 汽车太宽，进不了车房。

在谈到身体某些部位时，用 broad 时较多：

Their backs (shoulders, chests, bosoms) are broad. 他们的背（肩、胸、胸脯）很宽。

另外，broad 常可用于引申意义：

He has a broad outlook. 他的视野很广阔。

Our minister has broad views. 我们的部长有广阔的视野。

93 bus—coach

bus 指一般的公共汽车：

Then they took a bus into the town. 于是他们搭公共汽车进城。

❀ **coach** 在英国指较舒适的长途公共汽车：

The coach leaves Cardiff at 2:30. 长途汽车两点半离开卡迪夫。

在美国长途公共汽车仍称作 **bus**：

Soon a silvery grey hound bus appeared. 不久一辆银灰色灰狗巴士出现了。

坐公共汽车去某地，可用 **by bus (coach)** 表示：

Shall we walk or go by bus? 我们走着去还是坐公共汽车去？

We went by coach. 我们是坐公共汽车去的。

上下公共汽车可用 **get on, get off** 表示：

Let's get on the bus. 咱们现在上车。

I'll get off (the bus) at the next stop. 我下一站下（车）。

94 **but**

but，通常读作 /bət/，强调时读作 /bʌt/。可用作连词或介词。

用作连词时主要表示"但是""可是""而""却"等，可连接：两个并列分句：

Honey is sweet, but the bee stings. 蜂蜜好吃，但蜜蜂螫人。（谚语）

She pretended to be angry, but she was not. 她假装生气，却并未生气。

两个并列成分：

Slow but sure. 慢而稳。

They see the trees but not the forest. 他们见树而不见林。

有时可开始一个句子：

I always thought that. But then I'm probably wrong. 我一贯是那样想的，不过或许我是想错了。

but 用作介词时，主要有两种用法：

用在某些否定语后，表示"只……"：

He eats nothing but hamburgers. 他只吃汉堡包。

No one but me saw her. 只有我看见她。

用在其他情况下，表示"除了（去）……"：

Who but a fool would do such a thing? 除了傻瓜谁会干这样的事？

He seldom talked about anything <u>but</u> painting. 除了绘画，他很少谈任何东西。

还可用在 but for 中，表示"要不是……"（句子谓语多用虚拟语气）：

<u>But for</u> the storm, we should have arrived earlier. 要不是碰上暴雨，我们是会早些到的。

<u>But for</u> my lifebelt, I should have drowned. 要不是有救生圈，我都淹死了。

此外还可用在 next (last) but one 中，表示"隔壁再过去""倒数第……"等：

He lives in the <u>next</u> house <u>but one</u>. 他住在隔壁再过去一家。

He was the <u>last but one</u> to arrive. 他是倒数第二个到的。

95 by

by 主要用作介词，表示：

在……旁边，从……旁边：

They went for a picnic <u>by</u> the Black Sea. 他们到黑海边野餐。

He passed <u>by</u> the park. 他从公园旁经过。

（用在被动结构后）由，被，用：

He was brought up <u>by</u> his aunt. 他是由他姑姑带大的。

He was killed <u>by</u> a grenade. 他是被手榴弹炸死的。

（说明手段、方式等）通过，用：

We want to settle this <u>by</u> direct negotiation with them. 我们想通过和他们直接谈判解决这个问题。

We have to express our thought <u>by</u> action. 我们要用行动表达我们的思想。

（和动名词连用）手段、方式：

<u>By</u> helping them we are helping to save ourselves. 靠帮助他们来帮助拯救自己。

There is nothing to gain <u>by</u> waiting. 等待没有什么好处。

（和 train, bus, plane 等连用）交通工具和方式：

We'll go home <u>by</u> subway. 我们将坐地铁回家。

I returned to town <u>by</u> the midnight express train. 我坐午夜快车回到城里。

增减程度等：

Their wages have gone up (down) <u>by</u> 10 percent. 他们工资提高（降低）了 10%。

We lost the match <u>by</u> one goal. 我们以一球之差输了这场比赛。

到某时（即到某时，已发生某情况）：

<u>By</u> then he was more than fifty years of age. 到那时他已 50 多岁。

<u>By</u> 1980 the number had grown to 1.2 billion. 到 1980 年时，人口已增至 12 亿。

96　cabin—cabinet

cabin 指轮船上的小房间：

a passenger cabin 客舱　　　　　　cabin passengers 房舱旅客

也可指飞机上的座舱：

the First Class cabin 头等机舱

❀ **cabinet** 指存放药品、文件等的柜子：

a medicine cabinet 药品柜　　　　a china cabinet 瓷器陈列柜

a filing cabinet 公文柜　　　　　a kitchen cabinet 碗柜

也可指"内阁"或"内部会议"：

The Prime Minister invited each member of the cabinet to state his views.
首相邀请每位内阁成员陈述自己的看法。

We'll decide that question in cabinet. 这个问题将在内阁会议中决定。

97　café—cafeteria

café /ˈkæfeɪ/ 是可以买饮料和便餐的小吃店，在英国这类店里是不卖酒的。

❀ **cafeteria** /ˌkæfɪ'tɪərɪə/ 指自助餐厅。

98　called—named

called 和 **named** 都可表示某人叫什么名字。

❀ 在日常口语中多用 called：

What is this thing called? 这东西叫什么？

He was reading a book called *The Way of All Flesh*. 他在看一本书，书名是《众生之道》。

❀ named 在日常口语中用得不多，多用在书面语中：

Did you ever hear of a painter <u>named</u> Raphael? 你听没听说过一个名叫拉斐尔的画家？

Anna had a boyfriend <u>named</u> James. 安娜有个男朋友名叫詹姆斯。

99 **can—could—be able to**

can 和 could 都是情态动词，都和动词原形构成谓语。can 的否定式为 cannot（不能分开写），在口语中多用 can't 这个形式，在英国读作 /kɑːnt/，在美国读作 /kænt/。could 的否定式为 could not，常可紧缩为 couldn't，读作 /ˈkʊdnt/。

在表示"能够""有能力做某事"时，can、could 和 be able to 意思是差不多的。can 说明现在情况：

Can you translate this sentence into English? 你能把这个句子译为英语吗？

（也可说：Are you able to translate this sentence into English?）

could 可用作 can 的过去式，说明过去的情况：

She <u>couldn't</u> understand his state of mind. 她不能理解他的心态。

（也可说：She wasn't able to understand his state of mind.）

但 **be able to** 可以更明确地表示时间关系（可用于多种时态）：

<u>Will</u> you <u>be able</u> to join us? 你能参加我们的活动吗？

We won't <u>be able</u> to catch that train. 我们赶不上那班火车。

She said she <u>wouldn't be able</u> to go with us. 她说她无法和我们一起去。

I haven't <u>been able</u> to do that up till now. 到现在为止，我还没能这样做。

She said she <u>hadn't been able</u> to get in touch with them. 她说她还未能和他们联系上。

be able to 还可和 **may, might, should** 等情态动词一起用：

I <u>may be able</u> to get a ticket for you. 我可能能给你弄到一张票。

She <u>might be able</u> to help us. 她有可能帮我们的忙。

You <u>should be able</u> to understand this. 你应当能理解这一点。

She <u>wouldn't be able</u> to accomplish all this alone. 她独自一人是不可能完成这一切的。

be able to 还可用在非谓语形式中：

He felt bad for not <u>being able</u> to lend a hand. 他因不能帮忙而感到遗憾。

She watched all this happen, not <u>being able</u> to do anything. 她眼看着这一切发生，却毫无办法。

在上面这些情况下，**can** 和 **could** 都是没法用的。

除了表示"能够"，**can**、**could** 还有一些其他用法，是不能用 **be able to** 代替的。这些用法主要是表示：

可能性（可译为"可以""可能"）：

I'm like that—you <u>can't</u> alter me. 我就是这样，你不可能改变我。

It was so dark that we <u>could</u> see nothing. 天是那样黑，我们什么也看不见。

允许（可译为"可以""能"）：

I asked if I <u>could</u> use her phone. 我问可否用她的电话。

I knew I <u>couldn't</u> stay here. 我知道我不能待在那儿。

请求（可译为"可否"，用 **could** 显得更委婉）：

<u>Could</u> you lend me some money? 你可否借我点儿钱？（比 Can you... 更客气点儿）

<u>Could</u> I borrow your thermos? 我可否借用一下你的暖瓶？（比 Can I... 稍客气点儿）

有时会：

Children <u>can</u> be very tiring. 孩子有时很令人头疼。

不相信或惊异（多用于否定句或疑问句）：

He <u>can't</u> be more than thirty. 他不可能超过 30 岁。

How <u>can</u> you be so conceited? 你怎么能这样高傲？

后面的动词可用完成或进行形式：

They <u>can't</u> have gone out because the light's on. 他们不可能出去了，因为灯还亮着。

They <u>couldn't</u> be still waiting for us. 他们不可能还在等我们。

could 还有一些特殊用法：

用于虚拟条件句：

You <u>could</u> get a better job if you spoke a foreign language. 如果你能讲外语，你可以找到好一点儿的工作。（但你不能）

We could have caught the train if we had left a little earlier. 要是我们动身稍早一点儿，我们就能赶上火车了。

用于温和的批评：

You could ask me before you use my phone. 你打电话之前，可以问我一声。

You could have helped me—why did you just sit and watch? 你本可帮助我的，为什么只坐在一旁瞧着？

"could＋不定式的完成形式"可用来谈过去的事，表示：

那时（不）可能：

I do not see how I could have done otherwise. 我看不出那时我还能有别的做法。

I couldn't have won, so I didn't go in for the race. 我不可能获胜，因此我没参赛。

本来可以（但没那样做）：

I could have lent you the money. Why didn't you ask me? 我本来是可以借钱给你的。你为什么没向我借？

I could have gone with you, because I was there at that time. 我本来可以和你一起去的，因为那时我也在那里。

差点儿做了某事（但还没有这样做）：

I was so angy I could have killed him. 我是那样生气，差点把他杀了。

She felt miserable. She could have cried. 她感到很痛苦，她差点儿哭了。

（谁）会能够：

Who could have supposed you were going to do such a thing? 谁会想到你会做出这样的事！

Nobody could have foreseen such a calamity. 没人想到会出这样的祸事。

100 **can't help**

can't help 可用在几种结构中：

can't help (it) 控制不住，没有办法：

"I couldn't help it. It was an impulse. 我控制不住，这是一种冲动。

can't help doing something 禁不住做某事，不由得不做某事：

She couldn't help smiling. 她禁不住笑了起来。

We cannot help being impressed by their zeal. 我们不由得不被他们的热情所感动。

can't help somebody doing something 不能使某人不做某事

We couldn't help them seeing us. 我们无法让他们不看到我们。

She could not help the tears of rage rolling down her face. 她止不住她愤怒的眼泪顺着面颊流下来。

can't help but 不由得不……（这个结构美国用得较多）：

You can't help but respect them. 你不由得不尊敬他们。

I can't help but wonder what I should do next. 我不由得不想知道下一步该怎么办。

101 careful—careless—carefree

这三个词都是由 care 派生出来的。

❀ careful 表示"小心的""当心的""细心的"：

Be more careful with your work. 你的工作要再细心一些。

Be careful not to break anything. 当心别打破什么了。

❀ careless 表示"粗心的""不小心的"：

One careless step may cost a life. 一步不小心，可能会丧命。

A careless mistake cost the company millions of pounds. 一个粗心的错误使公司蒙受数百万镑的损失。

❀ carefree 表示"无忧无虑的"：

With the exams over, we felt happy and carefree at last. 考试一过去，我们终于高高兴兴，无忧无虑了。

102 carriage—car—truck

在英国 carriage 多指火车的一节车厢：

I'll be sitting in the third carriage from the front of the train. 我将坐在

从前往后第三号车厢里。

The first-class carriage is in front. 头等车厢在前头。

❀ 在美国用 car 表示：

The railway bought 200 new cars. 铁路购置了 200 个新车厢。

但在英国某些特殊用途的车辆仍称作 car：

dining car (restaurant car)　　　　　餐车　sleeping car 卧铺车

❀ 在英式英语中敞篷货车称作 truck 或 wagon：

A long truck loaded with bricks. 一辆长长的载砖货车。

The engine is pulling a train made up of coal wagons. 火车头牵引着一列运煤敞篷车。

在美国，（敞篷）货车称为 boxcar。

103　carry—take

carry 主要表示把人或物送到某处，可有种种译法：

The wounded man was carried away. 受伤的人被抬走了。

A taxi carried me to the station. 一辆出租车把我送到车站。

此外，它还可用于引申意义：

Can you carry all these figures in your head? 你脑子里能记住这么多数字吗？

He carried the news to everyone in the village. 他把消息传递给村子里每个人。

She was afraid of carrying the infection to her child. 她担心把病传染给孩子。

The newspapers all carried the story on the front page. 报纸都在头版刊登了这个报道。

The shop carries a variety of clothes. 这家店出售各种服装。

❀ **take** 相对比较简单，主要表示"送住某处"（可译为"送""带"等）：

It's your turn to take the children to school. 今天轮到你送孩子们上学。

The taxi took me back to Boston. 出租车把我送回波士顿。

104 cause—reason

cause 可以作名词和动词。作名词时，表示"原因""起因"：

The cause of the fire was a cigarette end. 火灾的起因是一个烟头。

No one could guess the cause. 没人能猜出这件事的起因。

偶尔也可译作"理由"：

You have no cause for complaint. 你没有抱怨的理由。

cause 还可用作动词，表示"引起""造成"：

He declined, fearing to cause her inconvenience. 他婉言谢绝，怕给她造成不便。

His action caused much excitement. 他的行为引起很大轰动。

有时跟—复合宾语，表示"使……"：

What caused him to change his mind? 什么使他改变了主意？

Heating a copper bar will cause it to expand. 对铜棒加热会使它膨胀。

❀ **reason** 主要表示"理由"：

You have no reason to disbelieve him. 你没有理由不相信他。

He refused to disclose the reason why he did it. 他不肯透露他这样做的理由。

但有时也可以表示"原因"：

The reason for my lateness is that I missed my bus. 我迟到的原因是我误了车。

For some reason he was neither surprised nor frightened. 由于某种原因，他既不吃惊也不害怕。

105 cement—concrete

cement 表示"水泥"：

He's outside mixing cement. 他在外面搅拌水泥。

❀ **concrete** 指"混凝土"：

Cement, sand and water are mixed to make concrete. 水泥、沙子和水搅拌成混凝土。

The walk was paved with concrete. 人行道是用混凝土铺的。

钢筋水泥可由 **reinforced concrete** 表示。

106 certain—sure

certain 和 sure 是同义词，都表示"肯定（无疑）"，两者几乎都用在同样结构中：用作表语（跟从句）：

I was certain (sure) he had seen me. 我肯定他看见我了。

I am not sure (certain) whether he will come. 我不能肯定他是否要来。

和 of 或 about 连用：

I am quite certain (sure) of that. 这一点我完全肯定。

We are not sure (certain) about his ability to do this. 我们不能肯定他有能力做此事。

跟不定式：

You are certain (sure) to be happy with them. 和他们在一起，你一定会很愉快。

不跟特别结构（用 sure 时多以人为主语，用 certain 时多以 thing、it 等作主语）：

Nothing is yet certain. 一切都还没有确定。

How can you be sure? 你怎么能确定？

Is it quite certain? 这是否已很确定？

用于 for certain (sure)，表示"肯定地"：

I cannot say for certain (sure) when he will arrive. 我不能肯定地讲他什么时候会到。

We leave tomorrow for sure (certain) . 我们明天一定动身。

用于 make sure (certain) 表示"弄肯定"：

Please make sure (certain) that the house is properly locked. 请务必把房子锁好。

Always make certain (sure) of your facts. 在任何情况下，都要把事实弄准确。

sure 有时可用作定语：

Dark clouds are a sure sign of rain. 乌云是肯定要下雨的征兆。

There is only one sure way to succeed. 只有一个有把握取得成功的办法。

certain 只偶尔用作定语：

There's no certain cure for this disease. 这种病没有有把握的治疗方法。

Capture means <u>certain</u> death. 被停必死无疑。

在日常口语中 **sure** 用得更多一些，特别是在下面这类句子中：

<u>Be sure</u> to write to me as soon as you get there. 到了，千万给我来信。

We must go cautiously, slowly, <u>to be sure</u> ! 我们肯定必须谨慎缓慢地前行。

但在下面这种句子中都用 **certain**：

It is <u>certain</u> they will win the election. 肯定无疑，他们选举会获胜。

It is <u>certain</u> that he did not apply for the job. 他肯定没申请这份工作。

107 chairman—chairwoman—chairperson—chair

主席一般用 chairman 表示：

Glyn Ford is the <u>chairman</u> of the commission. 格林·福特是委员会主席。

❀ 如果是女人，得称 chairwoman：

Margaret Downes is the <u>chairwoman</u> of the institute. 玛格丽特·唐斯是那个研究所的所长。

❀ chairperson 指男人、女人都可以：

This is Rose Williams, <u>chairperson</u> of the Consultative Committee. 这是咨询委员会主席罗斯·威廉斯。

❀ 也可把主席称作 chair：

The speaker rose to address the <u>chair</u>. 发言人起身向主席讲话。

108 cheers—cheerio

英国人和美国人敬酒时都常说 "Cheers!"

To Mr. Jackson, Britain's special Ambassador to all the world! <u>Cheers</u>! 向英国全世界的特别大使杰克逊先生祝酒！干杯！

<u>Cheers</u>, Helen, drink up. 干杯，海伦，请喝完。

有些英国人用 "Cheers!" 表示 "谢谢" 或 "再见"：

That's just what I want. <u>Cheers</u> ! 这正是我需要的，谢谢！

See you tonight, then. <u>Cheers</u> ! 今晚见，再见！

❀ 在英国还有一个 "再见" 的表示法，就是说 Cheerio（这比 cheers

用得更多一点儿):

The sooner the better! Cheerio! 越快越好！再见！

109 chef—chief

chef /ʃef/ 指餐馆或饭店的主厨：

She passed on the recipe to the <u>chef</u>. 她把烹调说明递给主厨。

❀ chief 是一个单位的头头（负责人）：

The <u>chief</u> of the Italian delegation addressed the UN. 意大利代表团团长在联合国大会上发了言。

This is the <u>chief</u> of the engineering section. 这位是工程科的科长。

110 chemist—chemist's—drugstore—pharmacy

chemist 一般表示"化学家"：

He was a very clever <u>chemist</u>. 他是一位聪明的化学家。

在英国 chemist 也指药剂师：

They had to be <u>chemists</u>. 他们必须是药剂师。

❀ chemist's 或 chemist 在英国也可指药房（除药品外，里面还卖化妆品和一些家用物品，如牙膏、牙刷等）：

She bought a bottle of vitamin tablets at the <u>chemist's</u>. 她在药房买了一瓶维生素片。

She bought the perfume at the <u>chemist</u> in St. James' Arcade. 这种香水她是在圣詹姆斯商场里的一家药房买的。

❀ 在美国药房都称 drugstore，里面除药品外也卖化妆品，甚至还卖食品。

❀ 在美国还把它称为 pharmacy：

an all-night <u>pharmacy</u> 一家通宵营业的药房

111 cheque—check

在英国 cheque 指支票：

He received a <u>cheque</u> from Mr. James for fifty pounds. 他收到詹姆斯先

生寄给他的一张 50 英镑的支票。

❀ 在美国支票称为 check：

He wrote his mother a check. 他给他母亲开了一张支票。

在美国 check 还可表示餐馆里的账单：

I'll ask the waiter for my check. 我要向服务员要账单。

而在英国餐馆账单称为 bill：

He signed to the waiter to bring the bill. 他做手势让服务员拿账单来。

112 chicken—hen—chick

chicken 指鸡或鸡肉：

Don't count your chickens before they are hatched. 鸡还没孵出就先别数。（谚语）

Do you like fried chicken? 你喜欢吃炸鸡（肉）吗？

❀ 母鸡称为 hen：

The hen has laid an egg. 母鸡下了一个蛋。

❀ chick 指小鸡：

The chicks have to stay in the nest. 小鸡得待在鸡窝里。

113 childish—childlike

childish 表示"幼稚""孩子气的"：

Her childish remark embarrassed everyone. 她幼稚的话使大家都很尴尬。

Don't be childish. 不要孩子气了。

❀ childlike 表示"像孩子的""稚真的"：

He felt an almost childlike wonder at the beauty of the forest. 他对森林的美感到一种孩子般的惊讶。

Tears came to his eyes as he remembered her childlike look. 他想到她稚真的模样时，眼中充满了泪水。

114 China—Chinese

China 指中国，正式名称为中华人民共和国：

China's population is by far the largest of any country. 中国是全世界人口最多的国家。

❀ Chinese 指"中国人"或"汉语"：

The Chinese were the first people to make porcelain. 中国人最早制作瓷器。

Chinese is taught in many Japanese schools today. 今天很多日本学校都教汉语。

Chinese 还可作形容词，表示"中国的"：

The tradition of Chinese art is more than 3,000 years old. 中国的美术有三千多年的传统。

旧的形式 Chinaman 现在已不通用，而且招人反感。

115 choose—pick—select

choose 表示"选择"，它的过去式为 chose，过去分词为 chosen：

Of two evils choose the less. 两害相权，取其轻者。（谚语）

She chose her words with care. 她选词很细心。

❀ pick 可表示"挑选"：

We picked the coolest room among those available. 在现有的房间中，我们挑选了最凉快的一间。

❀ select 也可表示"挑选""选择"：

Please select a few nice apples for my mother. 请给我母亲挑几个好苹果。

He selected an appropriate birthday card for his mother. 他给他母亲挑了一张合适的生日卡。

这三个词是同义词，select 比较正式，在日常口语中 choose 和 pick 用得比较多。

另外，choose 后面可跟不定式，表示"愿意""宁愿"：

He did not choose to help me. 他不愿帮助我。

As a youth he chose to be a cartoonist. 他年轻时立志做一个漫画家。

116 surname—Christian name—first name

❀ surname 指姓，亦称 family name：

Bill Smith's <u>surname</u> is Smith. 比尔·史密斯姓史密斯。

What's your <u>family name</u>? 你姓什么？

❀ 名字则由 **Christian name** 或 **first name** 表示。在英国多说 **Christian name**，在美国一般说 **first name**，在英国非基督徒也说 **first name**：

My surname is Smith, my <u>first (Christian) name</u> is John. 我姓史密斯，我的名字叫约翰。

在正式表格中，通常要你填写你的 **surname** 以及你的 **first name** 或 **forename**。**forename** 这个词只在书面语中使用。在美国，名字有时用 **given name** 表示。

117 city—town

❀ city 通常指较大的、较重要的城市：

London, Paris and New York are all large cities. 伦敦、巴黎、纽约都是大城市。

❀ town 可以指城市或市镇：

Manchester is a dirty and smoky <u>town</u>. 曼彻斯特是一座肮脏、多烟的城市。

I arrived that evening at my native <u>town</u>. 那天晚上，我来到我的故乡（出生的城市）。

也可指市中心区（和郊区相对）：

I've been down <u>town</u> all morning. 整个早上我都在城里（市中心区）。

118 class—form—grade

class 指学校里的一个班（级）：

Are you in the first-year <u>class</u> or the second-year <u>class</u>? 你是一年级还是二年级？

If <u>classes</u> were smaller, children would learn more. 如果班小，孩子还可多学到一些东西。

❀ 在许多英国学校和美国一些私立学校，也用 **form** 这个词表示班级（年级）：

Fred is now in the fifth <u>form</u>. 弗雷德现在念五年级。

Children who have just started school go into the first <u>form</u>; the oldest children are in the 6th <u>form</u>. 刚上学的孩子进入一年级，年龄最大的孩子在六年级。

❀ 在美国多用 **grade** 表示 "年级"：

An elementary school in America has eight <u>grades</u>. 美国小学有八个年级。

The play was presented by the third <u>grade</u>. 这个剧是三年级学生演的。

119 classic—classical

classic 作为名词表示 "古典作品"：

Dickens' *A Tale of Two Cities* is a literary classic. 狄更斯的《双城记》是一部古典文学作品。

Shakespeare's plays were all <u>classics</u>. 莎士比亚的戏剧都是古典作品。

复数形式有时指古希腊罗马文学：

He read classics at Oxford. 他在牛津（大学）念古希腊罗马文学。

形容词 **classic** 有两个意思：

古典的，典范的：

Anthony Trollope was a <u>classic</u> Victorian novelist. 特罗洛普是维多利亚时期的古典小说家。

Theyer wrote a <u>classic</u> biography of Beethoven. 瑟耶写了一部典范的贝多芬传。

典型的：

This statement was a <u>classic</u> illustration of British politeness. 这项声明是英国人彬彬有礼的典型例证。

a <u>classic</u> case of typhoid 伤寒症的典型病例

❀ 还有一个形容词 **classical**，表示：

古典的：

She likes <u>classical</u> literature. 她喜欢古典文学。

Bach and Beethoven wrote <u>classical</u> music. 巴赫和贝多芬谱写古典音乐。

有关古希腊罗马的：

The Parthenon is a <u>classical</u> building. 帕特农神庙是古希腊的建筑。

Latin is a <u>classical</u> language. 拉丁语是古罗马的语言。

传统的：

<u>Classical</u> scientific ideas about lights were changed by Einstein. 关于光的传统科学观念被爱因斯坦改变了。

<u>classical</u> physics, as opposed to quantum physics 与量子物理学相对的传统物理学

120 clergyman—minister—priest

clergyman 指神职人员，英国教会的牧师也叫 clergyman。

❀ minister 一般指新教的牧师：

The <u>minister</u>'s voice was solemn. 牧师的声音很庄严。

❀ priest 指天主教的神甫、司铎等：

The <u>priest</u> who take the services at that church is the Rev. P. Brown. 在那个教堂主持礼拜的是布朗神甫。

121 cloakroom—checkroom

在英国 cloakroom 指衣帽间，在美国有时称为 checkroom。在英式英语中 cloakroom 也可用作厕所的委婉的说法。在美式英语中，checkroom 也可指火车站行李临时存放处。

122 close—shut

close /kləʊz/ 和 shut 是同义词，都表示"关上"：

He <u>closed</u> the door softly behind him. 他轻轻把门关上。

She sighed and <u>shut</u> her eyes for a minute. 她叹了一口气，把眼睛闭上了一会儿。

两者都可用于被动结构：

The post office is <u>closed</u> (<u>shut</u>) on Saturday afternoon. 邮局星期六下午关门。

The windows are <u>closed</u> (<u>shut</u>) . 窗子都关上了。

也可作不及物动词，表示"关（不）上"：

The window <u>shuts</u> easily. 窗子很容易就关上了。

Many libraries <u>close</u> on Saturdays. 许多图书馆星期六不开门。

closed 可用作定语：

We discussed all this behind <u>closed</u> doors. 这一切我们都是私下谈论的。

而 **shut** 却很少这样用。

close 还可用于更多意思，例如：

They decided to <u>close</u> the border. 他们决定封闭边境。

The firm decided to <u>close</u> its London branch. 这家公司决定把伦敦分公司关掉。

The exhibition is <u>closed</u> to the public on Sunday. 展览会星期天不对外开放。

The airport is <u>closed</u> for the time being. 机场暂时关闭。

Then he <u>closed</u> the interview. 然后，他结束了面谈。

We always <u>close</u> business at 7 p.m. 我们总是在下午7点停业。

This meeting is <u>closed</u>. 现在闭会。

在这些句子中都不能使用 **shut**。

123 clothes—clothing—cloth

clothes /kləʊðz/ 指衣服：

Mother bought us some new <u>clothes</u>. 妈妈给我们买了一些新衣服。

这个词前不能加 a，表示"一件衣服"。可说 a garment、a piece of clothing 或 an article of clothing。在日常谈话中人们多谈具体的衣服，如 a dress、a coat、a jacket 等。但 clothes 前面可加 many、few 这样的词：

He had to buy a good many clothes. 他得买很多衣服。

I took her a few spare clothes out of the wardrobe. 我从衣柜里给她拿出几件不用的衣服。

❀ **clothing** 是衣服的统称：

There is nothing but <u>clothing</u> in this cupboard. 这个柜子里只有衣服。

I changed my <u>clothing</u> and drank some brandy. 我换了衣服，喝一点白兰地。

❀ **cloth** 指"布"：

His suits were made of expensive <u>cloth</u>. 他的衣服是用昂贵的料子做的。

How much <u>cloth</u> does it take to make a blouse for her? 给她做一件女装衬衫要多少布料？

cloth 可用作可数名词，表示"抹布""桌布"等：

Have you any <u>cloths</u> for polishing the furniture? 你有擦家具的抹布吗？

Pass the <u>cloth</u>, please. I want to clean the windows. 请递给我一块抹布，我要擦窗子。

124 collaborate—cooperate

这两个词意思很相近，都可译作"合作"。

❀ **collaborate** 表示"合作（从事某项文化活动）"：

Two authors <u>collaborated</u> on this novel. 两位作家合力写这本小说。

John <u>collaborated</u> with his father in writing the book. 约翰和他父亲合作写这本书。

还可表示"通敌"：

Anyone who <u>collaborates</u> should be shot. 通敌的人都应枪毙。

Few people <u>collaborated</u> with the occupying army. 很少人和占领军合作。

❀ **cooperate**（或拼作 co-operate）表示一般的"合作"：

The three clubs <u>cooperated</u> in planning a party. 三个俱乐部合作筹办一个晚会。

They would not <u>co-operate</u> with him. 他们不愿和他合作。

cooperate 有时含有帮忙的意思：

The editors agreed to <u>co-operate</u>. 编辑们同意帮忙。

They are willing to <u>cooperate</u> in the training of medical personnel. 他们愿意在培训医疗人员方面帮忙。

125 college—university—institute—school

college 一般指大学（用于抽象意义，作不可数名词）：

We were in <u>college</u> together. 我们一块儿上大学。

还可用作定语：

The <u>college</u> buildings are very beautiful. 这所大学校舍很漂亮。

这个词可表示"学院"或综合大学的一个学院（这时为可数名词）：

I go to the Teachers' <u>College</u>. 我上师范学院。

Ted entered the State University as a freshman in the <u>College</u> of Arts and Sciences. 特德进入州立大学，成为文理学院的一年级学生。

❀ **university** 指综合性大学：

He studied at Edinburgh <u>University</u> (the <u>University</u> of Edinburgh). 他上爱丁堡大学。

也可指"上大学"（这时作不可数名词）：

He'll have four years at <u>university</u> after he leaves school. 他中学毕业后要上四年大学。

❀ **institute** 也可表示学院或研究所：

the Massachusettes <u>Institute</u> of Technology 麻省理工学院

The university plans to establish an <u>institute</u> for Chinese studies. 大学准备建立一所汉学研究所。

❀ **school** 一般指学校，可指小学、中学或专科学校：

an elementary <u>school</u>（美）小学

a primary <u>school</u>（英）小学

a high <u>school</u> 中学

a commercial <u>school</u> 商业学校

a technical high <u>school</u> 技术高中

an art <u>school</u> 美术学校

也可指某些大学的院系：

The London Hospital is a medical <u>school</u> of London University. 伦敦医

院是伦敦大学的医学院。

the School of Engineering 工程学院

a graduate school 研究生院

the School of Veterinary Medicine at the University of Pennsylvania 宾州大学兽医学院

126 comment—commentary

❀ **comment** 可表示"评语""评论""意见"：

The teacher wrote his comments in the margin of the composition. 老师在作文边上写了他的评语。

No comment! 无可奉告！

❀ **commentary** 多表示一连串的解说词：

He accompanied his slides with a commentary. 他一边放幻灯片，一边进行解说。

He kept up a running commentary on the match. 他连续不断地对球赛进行的解说。

有时也可表示评论：

Students were asked to write a commentary on one of Shakespeare's plays. 老师要求学生对莎士比亚的一个剧写出评论。

127 complement—compliment

这两个词读音相同，用作动词时都读作 /ˈkɒmplɪment/，用作名词时都读作 /ˈkɒmplɪmənt/，但意思不同。

❀ **complement** 作动词时表示"起补足作用"：

The wine complements the food perfectly. 酒和菜相辅相成。

A good dessert complemented the dinner. 甜点是一顿饭很好的补充。

作名词时则表示"补足物""补充"：

Wine is the complement to a good dinner. 酒是一顿盛餐的补充。

Travel can be an excellent complement to one's education. 旅行对一个人的教育是很好的补充。

❀ **compliment** 作动词表示"称赞""赞扬"：

Her guests <u>complimented</u> her on her cooking. 她的客人称赞她的菜做得好。

They <u>complimented</u> him on his success (courage). 他们赞扬他的成就（勇气）。

作名词表示"恭维赞扬的话""尊敬的表示"：

<u>Compliments</u> turned her head. 恭维赞扬的话使她昏了头。

She recieved many <u>compliments</u> on her cooking. 她听到很多赞扬她菜的话。

复数形式常可表示"致意""问候"：

Give my <u>compliments</u> to your wife. 请向你妻子致意。

Give him my <u>compliments</u>. 请向他问候。

128 comprehensible—comprehensive

这两个词词形相近，意思却不相同。

❀ **comprehensible** 表示"可以理解的"：

The book is only <u>comprehensible</u> to specialists. 这本书只有专家能懂。

We should try to make the material <u>comprehensible</u>. 我们应设法使这些材料易懂。

❀ **comprehensive** 表示"综合的""全面的"：

We'll have a <u>comprehensive</u> review at the end of the term. 在期末，我们要进行一次全面复习。

The book is a <u>comprehensive</u> study of that war. 这本书是对那次战争的综合研究。

129 comprehension—understanding

comprehension 表示"理解（力）"（不可数）：

The problem is beyond my <u>comprehension</u>. 这问题超出我的理解能力。

The teacher had no <u>comprehension</u> of the boy's problems at home. 老师不理解这男孩儿在家里的问题。

❀ **understanding** 也可表示"理解（力）"（意思和 comprehension 差不多）:

Have you any <u>understanding</u> of this problem? 你理解这个问题吗？

My <u>understanding</u> of the word does not agree with yours. 我对这个词的理解和你不一致。

有时表示"了解"（这时不宜用 comprehension 代替，有时可加 an）:

I doubt whether he had any real <u>understanding</u> of Shakespeare. 我怀疑他是否真正了解莎士比亚。

Few people have an <u>understanding</u> of international law. 很少人懂得国际法。

此外还可表示"谅解"（作可数名词，但只用于单数形式）:

They had a secret <u>understanding</u> with that firm. 他们和那家公司有秘密谅解。

The two men at last reached an <u>understanding</u>. 两人最后达成谅解（协议）。

130 comprise—consist—constitute—compose—make up

comprise 有两个意思：

包括，包含（由……构成）:

The United Kingdom <u>comprises</u> England, Wales, Scotland and Northern Ireland. 联合王国包括英格兰、威尔士、苏格兰和北爱尔兰。

These two books <u>comprised</u> all of his published poetry. 这两本书包含了他已发表的所有诗篇。

构成，占:

Women <u>comprise</u> 51 percent of the population of the nation. 妇女占这个国家人口的51%。

They <u>comprise</u> the overwhelming majority of the white people. 他们构成了白人的绝大多数。

❀ **consist** 和 of 连用，表示"包含，由……构成"（即上面的第一种意义）:

Carbon dioxide (CO_2) <u>consists of</u> carbon and oxygen. 二氧化碳包含碳和氧。

They <u>consist of</u> 1,700 or more tribes. 他们由 1 700 个或更多部族构成。

❀ **constitute** 表示 "构成" (即上面的第二重意义):

Seven days <u>constitute</u> a week. 7 天构成 1 周。

This <u>constitutes</u> a direct threat to them. 这构成对他们的直接威胁。

❀ **compose** 也表示 "构成",但主要用于 **be composed of** 这个句型:

Twelve men <u>compose</u> a jury. 12 个人构(组)成 1 个陪审团。

The instrument <u>was composed of</u> about two thousand parts. 这个仪器由两千个左右部件构成。

❀ **make up** 也可表示同样意思,也主要用于 **be made up of** 这个句型:

Women now <u>make up</u> two-fifths of the British labour force. 妇女构成英国劳动力的 2/5。

All substances <u>are made up of</u> molecules. 一切物质都由分子构成。

131 concerned with—about

concerned 可用作表语,用在下面两种结构中:

be concerned about (for) 关心:

We <u>are</u> all <u>concerned about (for)</u> her safety. 我们都很关心她的安全。

She <u>was</u> much <u>concerned over</u> the plight of the refugees. 她很关心难民的状况。

be concerned with 和 ……有关的:

I <u>am</u> not <u>concerned with</u> that matter any longer. 我不再和这事有关。

This chapter <u>is concerned with</u> space flight. 这一章是有关太空飞行的。

concerned 还可单独作定语,放在名词后面,表示 "有关的":

The man <u>concerned</u> was her husband. 有关的人是她的丈夫。

We shall have to consult the other countries <u>concerned</u>. 我们得和其他有关国家磋商。

它常和 **all, everyone, everybody** 这类词一起用:

He urged <u>all concerned</u> to take an active part in the movement. 他敦促一切有关人士积极参与这个运动。

This was good news to <u>everyone concerned</u>. 这对所有有关的人都是好消息。

132 concert—concerto

这两个词只有一个字母之差，意思却不同。

❀ concert /ˈkɒnsət/ 表示"音乐会"：

Come into town with me and hear a concert. 和我进城去听一场音乐会。

❀ concerto 读作 /kənˈtʃeətʊ/ 或 /kənˈtʃɜːtʊ/，表示"协奏曲"：

There's Beethoven's Violin Concerto. 这里有贝多芬的小提琴协奏曲。

133 confident—confidant

这两个词只差一个字母，意思却完全不同。

❀ confident 是形容词，读作 /ˈkɒnfɪdənt/，表示"有信心的""自信的的"：

She was confident that she would find work. 她有信心她能找到工作。

We were confident of victory. 我们有胜利的信心。

还可用作定语：

He noticed her confident smile. 他注意到她自信的微笑。

Her boyfriend was a young and confident lawyer. 她的男朋友是一个年轻的、自信的律师。

❀ confidant 是名词，读作 /ˈkɒnfɪdænt, -ˈdænt/，表示"能说知心话的人"：

He was a close confidant of the president. 他是总统的知心好友。

如果是女性，要用 confidante 表示：

You are his closest friend and confidante. 你是他最亲近的朋友和能说知心话的人。

134 conscious—consciousness—conscience—conscientious

conscious 为形容词，主要表示：

知道的，意识到的：

He was conscious of his shortcomings. 他知道自己的缺点。

He was conscious that he was being watched. 他意识到他受到监视。

有知觉的，处于清醒状态的：

Is the patient conscious? 病人有知觉吗？

The old man was <u>conscious</u> to the last. 老人直到最后都处于清醒状态。

自觉的，有意识的：

His rudeness was <u>conscious</u>, not accidental. 他的粗鲁无礼是有意识的，不是偶然的。

Man is a <u>conscious</u> being. 人是有意识的动物。

❀ **consciousness** 是它的名词形式，表示"知觉""意识"：

Then he lost his <u>consciousness</u>. 这时他失去知觉。

She hasn't recovered (regained) her <u>consciousness</u>. 她尚未恢复知觉。

❀ **conscience** 是名词，表示"良心"：

A quiet <u>conscience</u> sleeps in thunder. 良心平安，打雷也睡得香。(谚语)

It's against your <u>conscience</u>. 这是违背你的良心的。

I got nothing to hide. My <u>conscience</u> is clear. 我没有什么可隐瞒，我的良心是清白的。

❀ **conscientious** /ˌkɒnʃɪˈenʃəs/ 是形容词，表示"认真的""负责的"：

She is a very industrious and <u>conscientious</u> girl. 她是一个非常勤劳、认真的姑娘。

I like a boy to be <u>conscientious</u> in his work. 我喜欢一个小伙子工作认真。

135 consecutive—continual—continuous

三个词意思相近。

❀ **consecutive** 表示"连续的"：

You can do these sessions on <u>consecutive</u> days if you like. 你如果愿意，可以连续几天地干。

It was his second <u>consecutive</u> win. 这是他连续第二次获胜。

❀ **continual** 表示"经久不息的""连续不断的"(只能用作定语)：

There was <u>continual</u> applause. 掌声经久不息。

The <u>continual</u> strain aged her. 不停的劳累使她老了。

❀ **continuous** 表示"持续不断的"(可作定语，也可作表语)：

The brain needs a <u>continuous</u> supply of blood. 大脑需要不断的血液供应。

The bombardment was <u>continuous</u> from Monday until Friday. 连续的炮轰从星期一持续到星期五。

136 **content**

content 用作名词时读作 /ˈkɒntent/，可表示：

里面的东西（用复数形式）：

Empty out the <u>contents</u> of your purse. 把你钱包里的东西倒出来。

Show me the <u>contents</u> of your suitcase. 把箱子里的东西给我看看。

内容，目录（用复数形式）：

He knew the <u>contents</u> of the report. 他知道报告的内容。

She didn't know the <u>contents</u> of the will. 她不知道遗嘱的内容。

（作品等的）内容（作不可数名词）：

To Marx form and <u>content</u> were inextricably connected. 对马克思来说，形式与内容是密不可分的。

I like the style of the book, but I don't like the <u>content</u>. 我喜欢这本书的文体，但不喜欢它的内容。

含量（不可数）：

Its carbon <u>content</u> is 4%. 它的碳含量是百分之四。

This will increase the sugar <u>content</u> of the grapes. 这会增加葡萄的含糖量。

❀ **content** 还可是另外一个词，读作 /kənˈtent/。它可以用作：

形容词，表示"满意的""满足的"：

You should be <u>content</u> with what you have. 你应满足于现有的东西。

I shall be well <u>content</u> to do so. 我会非常高兴这样做。

动词，表示"使满足"：

Simple praise is enough to <u>content</u> him. 简单的赞扬就足以使他满意。

You will have to <u>content</u> yourself with what you have. 你得让自己满足于现有的东西。

名词，表示"满足的状态"：

Now she began to live in peace and <u>content</u>. 现在她开始生活在平静与满足之中。

We can swim in the river to our heart's <u>content</u>. 在河里，我们可以尽情游泳。

❀ **contented** 还可用作形容词，表示"感到满足的""满意的"：

Everybody feels <u>contented</u>. 每个人都感到很满足。

He seems quite <u>contented</u> with his life. 他似乎对自己的生活很满意。

137 **contrary—opposite**

contrary 可作名词，表示"相反的东西"：

Cruelty is the <u>contrary</u> of kindness. 残酷是和善良相反的。

They say he is guilty, but I believe the <u>contrary</u>. 他们说他有罪，但我相信不是这样。

多用于 **on the contrary**，表示"相反"：

You weren't boring me. <u>On the contrary</u>, you're interesting me frightfully. 你并不使我厌烦，相反，你使我感到极有意思。

"He's no use at all." "<u>On the contrary</u>, I have found him a great deal of use." "他一点儿没用。""相反，我发现他很有用。"

❀ 在谈到相反的东西时，我们也可用 **opposite**：

You are nice; he is just the <u>opposite</u>. 你很好；他恰恰相反。

"High" is the <u>opposite</u> (contrary) of "low." "高"是与"低"相反的词。

138 **convince—convinced**

convince 是动词，表示"使相信""说服"。后面除跟间接宾语外：

有时跟从句：

He <u>convinced</u> me that Howard was innocent. 他使我相信霍华德是无辜的。

She <u>convinced</u> herself that it was so. 她说服自己，情况是这样的。

有的跟 **of** 引起的短语：

I <u>convinced</u> him of my innocence. 我让他相信我是无辜的。

不跟特别结构：

Compulsion will never result in <u>convincing</u> her. 强迫绝不能使她信服。

美国人常可用它表示"说服（做某事）"：

We convinced Anne to go by train rather than by plane. 我们说服安妮要坐火车去而不是坐飞机去。

有些英国人也这样用，但一般人却认为这是错误的，应用 persuade 代替它：

Who persuaded you to join the club? 谁劝说你参加这个俱乐部的？

The salesman persuaded us to buy his product. 推销员劝说我们购买他的产品。

❀ convinced 是过去分词，表示"坚信的""相信的"：

I'm convinced that what you said is right. 我坚信你说的话是对的。

convinced 不宜用 very 或 extremely 修饰，但可用 fully、totally、absolutely 或 firmly 修饰：

They were firmly convinced that they were the rightful owner of the lands. 他们坚决相信他们是土地的合法主人。

He is totally convinced of the truth of the report. 他完全相信这份报告的真实性。

I'm absolutely convinced that you were right. 我绝对相信你是对的。

He was, however, not a hundred percent convinced. 但他还不是百分之百相信。

139 cook—cooker

cook 可以作名词，也可作动词。

作名词时，表示"厨师"或"做饭的人"：

My brother is a cook in a hotel. 我哥哥在一家饭店当厨师。

作动词时，表示"做（饭）"：

She cooked her meals on a gas ring. 她在煤气炉上做饭。

有时可有别的译法：

She cooked meat in wine instead of water. 她用酒而不是水煮肉。

We cooked the pie in the oven. 她在烤箱里烤馅饼。

除了这个词我们还可用别的词表示"做（饭）"：

I must return home to prepare dinner. 我得回家做晚饭。

Marie is getting the breakfast. 玛丽在做早饭。

美国人还用 fix 表示这个意思：

She's fixing supper right now. 这会儿她在做晚饭。

至于具体的烹调，还有许多词可用：

We roast meat and potatoes. 我们烤肉，烤土豆。

She baked bread and cake in an oven. 她在烤箱里烘烤面包和蛋糕。

Boil the potatoes (eggs) for twenty minutes. 把土豆（鸡蛋）煮 20 分钟。

Toast a few slices of bread for me, please. 请给我烤几片面包。

She is steaming fish for supper. 作为晚饭，她在做清蒸鱼。

He stewed the mutton (chicken). 他炖羊肉（鸡）。

The breast can be cut into portions for grilling. 鸡胸脯可以切成块烤着吃。（美国人用 broil 代替 grill）

casserole, braise 也表示"炖"，**barbecue** 表示"（在户外）烧烤"。**poached eggs** 指"水煮荷包蛋"。**fried fish** 表示"煎鱼"，**deep-fried chicken** 指"炸鸡"，**smoked ham** 指"熏火腿"，但烤鸭（牛肉）应说 roast duck (beef)，这时 roast 后不能加 ed。

❀ **cooker**

cooker 指炉头，即上面可以做菜的煤气炉或电炉：

The food was warming in a saucepan on the cooker. 菜在炉子上的平底锅中热着。

美国称作 **stove**：

Put the saucepan on the stove. 把平底锅放在炉头上。

pressure cooker 指"压力锅"

140 **corps—corpse**

这两个词词形相近，但读音不同，意思也完全不同。

❀ **corps** 读作 /kɔː/，表示一个团体（尤指为某一任务组成的团体）：

I just joined the Army Air Corps. 我刚参加陆军航空兵团。

The Peace Corps（美）和平队

a diplomatic corps 外交使团

❀ **corpse** /kɔːps/ 指"死尸"：

Three hours later the <u>corpse</u> was still beside the river. 三小时后尸体还在江边。

141 council—counsel

这两个词词形相像，读音相同，都读作 /ˈkaʊnsəl/，但意思却不同。

❀ **council** 指某些组织（如政委会、理事会等）：

The city <u>council</u> met to discuss the new proposal. 市会议开会讨论新提案。

the U.N. Security <u>Council</u> 联合国安全理事会

State <u>Council</u>（中国）国务院

组织成员有时称 **councillor**：

A member of a council is called a <u>councillor</u>. 理事会的成员称为理事。

❀ **counsel** 可用作名词或动词。

用作名词时表示"劝告""意见""商议"：

Seek an architect's <u>counsel</u> before building the house. 建房前先征求建筑师的意见。

They refused to listen to the old man's <u>counsel</u>. 他们不听老人的劝告。

有时指"辩护律师"：

A <u>counsel</u> is a lawyer who helps people in a court of law. counsel 可指在法庭上帮助人的律师。

作动词时它表示"给……出主意""劝告"：

He <u>counselled</u> her daughter on how to behave at the ball. 他给女儿出主意，在舞会上应当怎样做。

The teacher <u>counselled</u> the boy to study harder. 老师劝告这个男孩儿更用功一些。

counsellor，美作 **counselor**，表示"咨询人（员）"：

She was a marriage guidance <u>counsellor</u>. 她是一位婚姻指导咨询师。

Each student has a <u>counselor</u> to guide him in his choices of classes. 每个学生都有一位咨询员，指导他如何选课。

在美国它也可指"律师"：

The counselor for the defence asked that the case be dismissed. 辩护律师要求法庭休庭。

142 credible—credulous—creditable

credible 表示 "可信的"：

They considered him a credible witness. 他们认为他是一个可信的证人。

His statements are hardly credible. 他的话简直难以相信。

❀ **credulous** 表示 "轻信的" "易受骗的"：

Anne is so credulous that she'll believe anything you tell her. 安是那样容易相信别人，你说什么她都相信。

Some men love to cheat credulous women. 有些男子爱骗易受骗的女人。

❀ **creditable** 表示 "值得赞许的" "成功的"：

His efforts this term have been most creditable. 他这学期的努力值得赞许。

She gave a very creditable performance as Lady Windermere. 她扮演温德弥尔夫人很成功。

143 crib—cot—camp bed

婴儿床在英国称为 cot，在美国称为 crib，而 cot 在美国指行军床（帆布床），在英国这种床称为 camp bed。

144 criterion—criteria

criterion /kraɪˈtɪərɪən/ 表示 "标准"：

What is the major criterion for judging a symphony? 什么是判断交响曲的主要标准？

它的复数形式为 **criteria** /kraɪˈtɪərɪə/：

There are several criteria of a good school. 好学校有几个标准。

145 critic—criticize—criticism—critical—critique

critic 指"评论家"或"批评者"：

He was a musical critic of standing. 他是一个有地位的音乐评论家。

He has been an outspoken critic of the government. 他是一位敢说话的政府批评者。

❀ criticize 表示"批评""提意见"：

He's been criticized in that book. 他在那本书里受到批评。

Would you like to read and criticize my new book? 你愿不愿意看看我这本新书并提出意见？

❀ criticism 表示"批评"或"评论"：

I always think criticism is helpful. 我一向认为批评有好处。

I am reading all the chief criticism of the play. 我正在对这个剧本的所有评论。

❀ critical 表示"批判的""评论性的""挑剔的"：

After Flaubert, critical realism could progress no further. 在福楼拜之后，批判现实主义就再也没取得进展。

His critical essays are sometimes profound. 他的评论文章有时很深刻。

Don't be so critical of everyone else. 不要对别人都那样挑剔。

critical 还可表示"严重的""重要的"：

The patient's condition is now critical. 病人的情况现在很严重。

This was a critical time in his life. 这是他一生中的重要时刻。

❀ critique /krɪˈtiːk/ 表示"批判""评论（文）"：

Marx's critique of Hegel 马克思对黑格尔的批判

The students were required to write a critique of a Hemingway novel. 要求学生写一篇评论一本海明威小说的文章。

critique 是一个文气的词，日常多用 review 表示"评论"，如 a book review（书评）。

146 cry—weep—sob

cry 可以作动词，表示"哭"：

The little girl began to cry. 小姑娘开始哭了起来。

What's the boy crying about? 那个男孩哭什么？

cry 还可表示"叫""喊"：

"Oh, what a beautiful picture," she cried. "多美的画呀！"她叫道。

"Help! Help!" he cried. "救命！救命！"他喊道。

cry 也可用作名词，表示"一阵哭"或"喊叫"：

Yes, have a good cry, Mummy, it'll do you good. 妈，好好哭一场，这对你有好处。

We heard a cry for help. 我们听见有人呼救。

❀ **weep** 也表示"哭"，但指"伤心地哭"或"哀泣"：

She wept when she heard the terrible news. 听到这可怕的消息，她伤心地哭了起来。

Madame Foucault wept quietly. 芙苛夫人静静地哭泣着。

但这词比较文气，主要用在故事小说中。

❀ **sob** 表示"抽泣""哽咽地哭"：

I found a little girl sobbing in the street. 我看到一个小女孩儿在街上哽咽地哭泣。

The child hysterically sobbed. 那孩子歇斯底里地抽泣。

147 cupboard—wardrobe

cupboard 指一般的柜子，如碗柜、食品柜等。**wardrobe** 指较高的衣橱。在美国嵌在墙内的橱柜称为 **closet**（壁橱）。

148 curb—kerb

这两个词读音相同，都读作 /kɜːb/。

❀ **curb** 可以用作动词，表示"限制"、"制止"和"控制"：

They adopted measures to curb the spread of the virus. 他们采取措施来控制病毒的蔓延。

They tried to curb the powers of the Home Secretary. 他们设法限制内政部长的权力。

也可用作名词，表示同样的意思：

He called for much stricter curbs on immigration. 他呼吁更严格地限制

移民。

We are trying to keep a curb on their activities. 我们正设法制止他们的活动。

在美式英语中，curb 也指人行道边：

He pulled up at the curb. 他把车开到人行道边。

❀ 在英国，人行道边称作 kerb：

The taxi pulled into the kerb. 出租车开到人行道边上。

D

149 data—datum

data 是 **datum** 的复数形式，表示"数据""资料"：

He copied the relevant <u>data</u> out of the encyclopedia. 他从百科全书中抄出有关资料。

They have to process a large amount of <u>data</u>. 他们得处理大量数据。

可构成合成词：**data bank (database)** 数据库。

这个词用作主语时，后面跟单数或复数动词都可以：

Very little data is available. 可用的资料很少。

The data are (is) all ready for examination (still being analysed). 资料已全准备好，可供检查（还在分析）。

150 Days—Months—Seasons—Years

表示一个星期中的某一天：

周几多和 **on** 连用，前面不加冠词：

I'll came round to see you <u>on Sunday</u>. 我星期天来看你。

We always go to the cinema <u>on Friday</u>. 我们总是星期五看电影。

还可和 **last, next** 等词连用，不加冠词：

He came to see me <u>last Saturday</u>. 他上星期六来看我了。

<u>Next Thursday</u> the workshop would end. 下星期四培训班将结束。

有时前面可加不定冠词或冠词（多表示对比）：

She was born on a Tuesday in May. 他是五月的一个星期二生的。

He died on the Saturday and was buried on the Sunday. 他礼拜六去世的，礼拜天葬的。

星期一到星期五称为 **weekdays**：

The museum is open 9:00 to 6:00 on <u>weekdays</u>. 博物馆平时从早上九

点开到下午六点。

星期六和星期天称为周末（weekend）（注意前面的介词）：

He has gone away <u>for the weekend</u>. 他出去度周末去了。

（美）What are you doing <u>on the weekend</u>? 你周末准备干什么？

一个星期中的某一天在美国可用作状语（前面不加介词）：

<u>Monday</u> I'll take you to visit my grandma. 星期一，我带你去看奶奶。

She works <u>Mondays</u>. 她星期一工作。

He works (on) <u>weekends</u>. 他周末工作。

❀ **月份：**

月份名称前一般用介词 in，不加冠词：

School starts <u>in September</u>. 学校 9 月开学。

They are going to Europe <u>in April</u>. 他们 4 月到欧洲去。

月份名称前可加 early, late, mid 等词：

We planned to visit the city in <u>late June</u> or <u>early July</u>. 我们打算在 6 月底或 7 月初去访问这座城市。

She ought to finish the work by <u>mid August</u>. 她应在 8 月中旬以前完成这项工作。

They are expected to come here <u>towards the end (middle) of December</u>. 估计他们会在 12 月底（中）以前来。

❀ **季节：**

季节名称前多不加冠词，前面可用介词 in：

Leaves fall in <u>autumn</u>. 树叶秋天凋零。

In <u>spring</u> the weather gets warmer. 春天天气变暖。

<u>Spring</u> was at hand. 春天就要到了。

有时前面也可加定冠词：

Flowers come out in the <u>spring</u>. 花在春季开放。

They usually gave a party in the <u>fall</u>. 他们通常在秋天举行一个晚会。

❀ **年份：**

年份通常由数字表示，多数分为两部分说：

1990 读作 nineteen ninety   1746 读作 seventeen forty-six

1400 读作 fourteen hundred   但 2000 读作 the year two thousand

2005 读作 two thousand and five

如有必要，年份前可加 **AD**（公元后），**BC**（公元前）：

The Chinese were printing by movable type in <u>AD</u> 1050. 中国人在公元后 1050 年已用活字版印刷。

The Great Pyramid dates from around 2600 <u>BC</u>. 大金字塔约在公元前 2600 年建造。

如谈到"……＋年代"，可用加 **s** 的办法表示：

In the <u>1940s</u> she was studying in Paris. 20 世纪 40 年代，她在巴黎求学。
（读作 nineteen forties）

This happened in the <u>seventies</u>. 这发生在 70 年代。

151 deadly—deathly—lethal—fatal

deadly 可表示"致命的"：

Cancer is a <u>deadly</u> disease. 癌症是一种致命的疾病。

Arsenic is a <u>deadly</u> poison. 砒霜是一种致命的毒药。

❀ **deathly** 表示"死一般的"：

The injured man was <u>deathly</u> pale. 那个受伤的人的脸色像死人一般苍白。

The roar of explosion was followed by a <u>deathly</u> silence. 一阵爆炸声之后是死一般的沉寂。

❀ **lethal** 表示"致命的""致死的"：

He took a <u>lethal</u> dose of sleeping pills. 他吃了不少安眠药，足以致命。

<u>lethal</u> chamber 毒气行刑室　　　　<u>lethal</u> weapons 致命武器

❀ **fatal** 也有"致命的"的意思：

We knew she had a <u>fatal</u> illness. 我们知道她患了致命的病。

One of them received <u>fatal</u> injuries. 其中一个人受了致命的伤。

但它还可表示"极其危险的""不幸的"等：

He took the <u>fatal</u> decision to marry Martha. 他做了危险的决定，要和马莎结婚。

The event was <u>fatal</u> to my hopes. 这次事件粉碎了我的希望。

152 deceitful—deceptive

这两个词都是形容词，且都由 deceit 派生，但意思不全相同。

❀ **deceitful** 主要修饰人，表示"（爱）骗人的"：

No one can trust a deceitful person. 没人会信任一个爱骗人的人。

This shows she's deceitful. 这说明她是骗人的。

❀ **deceptive** 表示"骗人的""有欺骗性的"：

This is sheer deceptive talk. 这完全是欺人之谈。

Appearances are often deceptive. 外貌常常有欺骗性。

153 delay—cancel—postpone

delay 主要表示"耽搁""延误"：

Heavy traffic delayed us. 路上车太多，把我们耽搁了。

The train has been delayed for two hours. 火车延误了两小时。

也可表示"推迟"或"拖延"：

They decided to delay the meeting. 他们决定把会议推迟。

I have delayed so long in answering your letter. 我迟迟没给你回信。

❀ **cancel** 表示"把（原定的活动等）取消"：

They cancelled the meeting. 他们把会议取消了。

He cancelled his order for the books. 他取消了这些书的订单。

❀ **postpone** 表示"延期""推迟"：

We have postponed the concert until Friday. 我们把音乐会延期到星期五了。

The game has been postponed for a week. 球赛推迟了一星期。

put off 表示同样的意思：

They decided to put the meeting off until after Christmas. 他们把会议推迟到圣诞节后。

The picnic has been put off because of the rain. 野餐会由于下雨延期了。

154 delighted—delightful

delighted 表示"高兴的"，以人为主语，后面可以：

跟不定式：

We were all <u>delighted</u> to receive your letter. 接到你的信，我们都很高兴。

<u>Delighted</u> to hear you say that. 听你这样说，我很高兴。

跟介词 **with** 或 **at**：

He is <u>delighted with</u> my second article. 他对我第二篇文章感到很高兴。

I was <u>delighted</u> at the news. 听了这消息，我很高兴。

跟从句或不跟什么：

I was <u>delighted</u> that you were successful. 我很高兴，你成功了。

But in secret she was <u>delighted</u>. 但她暗中感到高兴。

❀ **delightful** 表示"怡人的""令人高兴的""愉快的"：

It was a <u>delightful</u> concert. 这是一场令人高兴的音乐会。

We spent a <u>delightful</u> weekend together. 我们在一起度过了一个愉快的周末。

 在 delighted 前不宜用 very，extremely 这类修饰语，但可用 absolutely：
We were <u>absolutely</u> delighted with the girl. 我们极为喜欢这姑娘。

155 deny—refuse—reject—decline

deny 有两个主要意思：

否认（可跟名词、代词、动名词或从句）：

Atheists <u>deny</u> the existence of God. 无神论者否认上帝的存在。

I've never <u>denied</u> it. 对此，我从未否认过。

拒绝给予（后跟双宾语）：

They <u>denied</u> the prisoner all freedom. 他们拒不给予犯人任何自由。

I <u>denied</u> him what he asked. 我拒不答应他的要求。

后一种意思还有一些其他的表示方法：

❀ **refuse**（多跟不定式），表示"不肯""拒不"：

Martin <u>refused</u> to discuss the matter. 马丁不肯讨论此事。

He refused to comply with his father's wishes. 他拒不顺从他父亲的意愿。

还可表示"拒不接受"（后面跟名词或不跟什么）：

He refused their bribe. 他拒不接受他们的贿赂。

If you ask politely, he can't refuse. 如果你客气地提出要求，他不会拒绝。

❀ reject 表示"拒不接受""不采纳"：

They rejected the union demand. 他们拒绝了工会的要求。

He tried to join the army but was rejected. 他想参军，但未被接受。

❀ decline 表示"婉言谢绝"（可跟不定式、名词等）：

She declined their invitation. 她婉言谢绝了他们的邀请。

He wanted me to try some. I declined. 他要我尝一点儿，我婉言谢绝了。

156 dependent—dependant

这两个词都由 depend 派生而来。

❀ dependent 是形容词，表示"依靠的"：

I'll never be dependent on anyone again. 我再也不会依靠任何人。

Good health is largely dependent on the proper nourishment. 身体健康在很大程度上要依靠适当的营养。

❀ dependant 为名词，指"靠……养活的人""家属"：

A man's wife and children are his dependants. 一个人的妻子、儿女是靠这个人养活的。

There are 2,500 U.S. military personnel with 6,000 dependants stationed at the base. 有 2 500 个美国军事人员及 6 000 家属驻扎在这个基地。

157 desert—dessert

这两个词拼法差不多，意思却完全不同。

❀ desert 可用作名词，读作 /ˈdezət/，表示"沙漠"：

The camel is man's best friend in the desert. 骆驼是沙漠中人类最好的朋友。

the Sahara Desert 撒哈拉大沙漠

还可作动词，读作 /dɪ'zɜːt/，表示"遗弃""抛弃""开小差"：

He felt guilty at deserting his wife. 他遗弃了妻子，感到内疚。

The soldier deserted from the army. 这士兵从军中开了小差。

它的过去分词表示"静无一人"：

The station was deserted. 车站静无一人。

❀ dessert /dɪ'zɜːt/ 为名词，表示"餐后甜食"：

What would you like for dessert? 你甜点吃什么？

Let's have ice cream for dessert. 咱们甜食吃冰激凌。

158 detail—details—detailed

detail 在英国读作 /'diːteɪl/，在美国读作 /dɪ'teɪl/。detail 多指"细节"，可用作单数，也可用作复数形式：

Everything in her story is correct down to the smallest detail. 她讲的情况，每个细节都是准确的。

I can still remember every single detail of that night. 那天晚上，每个细节我都还记得。

❀ details 多指"详细情况"：

Philip will give him details of the accident. 菲利普将给他谈这次事故的详细情况。

He can probably tell us all the details we want. 他或许能告诉我们想知道的详细情况。

❀ detailed 为形容词，表示"详细的""仔细的"：

He gave me a detailed account of this work. 他跟我谈了他工作的详细情况。

The detective made a detailed examination of the room. 侦探仔细检查了那个房间。

159 device—devise

device /dɪ'vaɪs/ 是名词，表示一种装置：

The television receiver is an electronic device. 电视接受器是一种电子装置。

a device for catching flies 捕蝇装置　　a nuclear device 核装置

❀ **devise** /dɪ'vaɪz/ 是动词，表示"想出""设计出"：

He devised an instrument to measure light waves. 他设计出了一种测量光波的仪器。

They devised a way of escaping from the prison. 他们想出了一个从监狱中逃出的办法。

160　devote—devoted—devotee—devout

devote /dɪ'vəʊt/ 为动词，表示"献身""把……用在"：

He has devoted his whole life to benefiting mankind. 他把自己的一生献给了为人类造福了。

Every spare moment was devoted to study. 每一点儿空余时间都用在学习上了。

❀ **devoted** 为形容词，表示"忠实的"：

She had a devoted husband. 她有一个忠实的丈夫。

The death of his devoted friend made him sad. 他忠实的朋友去世了，令他很伤心。

❀ **devotee** /ˌdevə'tiː/ 指"献身……的人""热爱……的人"：

devotees of that movement 献身于那个运动的人

a devotee of classical music 热爱古典音乐的人

❀ **devout** /dɪ'vaʊt/ 为形容词，表示"虔诚的""真心的"：

My father is a devout man. 我父亲是个虔诚的人。

She is a devout admirer of French painting. 她是法国绘画真心的崇拜者。

161　differ—different—difference

differ 是动词，表示"（和……）不同"：

Tom differs from his brother in many ways. 汤姆和他的哥哥在很多方

面不同。

The two sisters <u>differ</u> in their interests. 两姐妹在兴趣上各不相同。

有时表示"有分歧""有不同意见":

We must agree to <u>differ</u>. 我们应允许有不同意见。

On one point I <u>differ</u> from (with) you. 在一点上，我和你有分歧。

❀ **形容词形式为 different，表示"不同的":**

Their views are quite <u>different</u>. 他们的看法很不相同。

Now the place looks quite <u>different</u>. 现在这地方看起来完全不同了。

"和……不同"一般都用 different from 表示:

She is <u>different from</u> her sister. 她和她姐姐不同。

Our house is <u>different from</u> your house in several ways. 我们的房子和你们的房子在数个方面不同。

英国有些人说 different to（有些人不很赞成，口语中可这样用，书面语中以避免为宜):

She is so <u>different to</u> Rebecca. 她和丽贝卡是那样不同。

Their system is <u>different to</u> ours. 他们的制度和我们的制度不同。

美国人有时说 different than（英国人则不以为然，在英国最好避免这样用):

Mary is <u>different than</u> Jane (is). 玛丽和简不同。

The English style of football is so <u>different than</u> ours. 英式足球和我们的足球很不同。

"和……没有什么不同"可用 not very (much) different from 或 no different from 表示:

Their rules are <u>not very</u> (much) <u>different from</u> ours. 他们的规则和我们的规则没有多少不同。

Her view is <u>no different from</u> yours. 她的看法和你的看法没有不同。

但不能说 not different from。

❀ **difference 是名词形式，表示"差别""不同之处":**

There are many <u>differences</u> between the two languages. 这两种语言有很多不同之处。

I can't see any <u>difference</u> between them. 我看不出它们之间有什么差别。

make no (little, etc.) difference 表示"没有……影响"：

This <u>made no difference</u> to him. 这对他没有什么影响。

It doesn't <u>make any (much, the least) difference</u> to me what you do. 你怎么做对我没有任何（多少、毫无）影响。

162 directly—direct

directly 有下面几个主要用法：

作副词，表示"直接地"：

I shall write to him <u>directly</u>. 我将直接给他写信。

They have their cash <u>directly</u> from the local government. 他们的现金是直接从地方政府领来的。

在表示这个意思时也可以用 direct（作副词）：

You should have written <u>direct</u> to the president. 你本应直接给校长写信的。

Our money comes <u>direct</u> from the government. 我们的钱是直接从政府领来的。

作副词，表示"径直地"：

She drove <u>directly</u> to school. 她径直开车去了学校。

They made <u>directly</u> for the Palace Hotel. 他们径直去了皇宫酒店。

这时也可用 direct 代替它：

We went <u>direct</u> to the station. 我们直接去了车站。

I'll take a taxi <u>direct</u> to the hotel. 我将坐出租车直接去旅馆。

但如果表示飞机、火车等一路不停到某地，应用 direct（不用 directly）：

You can't go to Manchester <u>direct</u>. You have to change trains at Birmingham. 你不能直达曼彻斯特，你得在伯明翰换车。

作副词，表示"一会儿""马上""不久"（这种用法有点儿老式，用 **right away**、**soon** 等时更多一些）：

Father will be home <u>directly</u>. 父亲马上就到家。

<u>Directly</u> on arriving, he issued orders for the man's arrest. 到达后不久，

他就立即下令逮捕这个人。

这时不能用 direct 代替它。

作连词，表示"一……就"（这是英国用法，美国人不这样用）：

Directly the teacher came in everyone was quiet. 老师一进来，大家都安静了。

You will hear everything <u>directly</u> you come. 你一来就会听到所有情况了。

163 dis-

dis- 是一个非常有用的前缀（词头），可构成大量反义词：

disable 使成残废	disagree 不同意
disappear 消失	disappoint 使失望
disapprove 不赞成	disarm 解除武装
disbelieve 不相信	disclaim 否认
disclose 透露	disconnect 使分开，使脱离
discourage 使泄气	discover 发现
discredit 败坏名誉	disembark 下车（船）
dishonour 败坏声誉	disentangle 使摆脱
disfigure 使变丑	

加在动词或名词等前面，构成动词；常见的如：

disinfect 消毒	dislike 不喜欢，讨厌
dislocate（使骨骼）错位	dislodge 使离开原处
dismember 肢解	dismount 下（马）
disobey 不服从	disown 不承认（关系）
displace 取代	displease 使不高兴
dispossess 剥夺（财产等）	disprove 证明是假的
disqualify 使失去资格	disregard 不理会
dissuade 劝别做某事	

加在形容词等前面，构成形容词，如：

disabled 残废的	disadvantaged 处于不利地位的
disadvantageous 对……不利的	disagreeable 令人不快的
disappointed 失望的	disapproving 不赞同的
disconnected 脱离开的	discourteous 不客气的
diseased 有病的	disenchanted 失望的
disgraceful 不体面的，可耻的	disheartened 沮丧，灰心的
dishonest 不诚实的	disinterested 没有私心的
disloyal 不忠诚的	disobedient 不驯服的
disorderly 杂乱，混乱的	displeased 不高兴的
disrespectful 不尊敬的	dissatisfied 不满足的
distasteful 不合口味的	

❀ 加在名词等前面，构成名词，如：

disadvantage 不利之处	disagreement 分歧
disappearance 消失	disappointment 失望
disapproval 不赞成	disarmament 裁军
disbelief 不相信	discomfort 不舒适
discontent 不满	discount 打折扣
discouragement 泄气	discovery 发现
disequilibrium 不稳定	disgrace 羞辱
disharmony 不和睦	dishonesty 不老实
disinfectant 消毒剂	disorder 混乱
displeasure 不高兴	disquiet 不安
disrepair 年久失修	disrespect 不尊敬
distaste 不悦，讨厌	disunity 不团结

164 disc—disk

在英式英语中 disc 指扁平的圆盘

a revolving metal <u>disc</u> 旋转的金属圆盘：

也可指（激光）唱盘，光盘：

This <u>disc</u> includes the piano sonata in C minor. 这张唱片包括了 C 小钢琴调奏鸣曲。

❀ 在美式英语中这个词拼作 **disk**，表示"圆盘""圆牌"等：

The name of the dead dog's owner was on a <u>disk</u> on its collar. 这只死狗的主人的名字写在狗颈圈的圆牌上。

在英国和美国 disk 都指储存信息（在电脑中使用）的圆盘或光盘：

The image data may be stored on <u>disk</u>. 图像资料可以储存在光盘中。

The <u>disk</u> is then slotted in a desktop PC. 然后，把软盘插入案头的个人电脑中。

compact disc（缩写为 CD）指激光唱片、光盘及电脑资料盘：

The new album is available on cassette or <u>compact disc</u>. 新的音乐选辑将以卡带或激光唱片形式发行。

165 disinterested—uninterested

disinterested 表示"没有私心的"：

He is impartial and <u>disinterested</u>. 他不偏不倚，没有私心。

A judge must be <u>disinterested</u> in the cases he tries. 法官审案不能有私心。

❀ "对……没兴趣"要用 **uninterested** 表示：

I am <u>uninterested</u> in politics. 我对政治没兴趣。

I told him the news but he seemed <u>uninterested</u>. 我告诉他这个消息，但他似乎没兴趣。

166 dispose of—get rid of—remove

dispose of 表示"处理掉"（如扔掉、卖掉等）：

<u>Dispose of</u> these old newspapers. 把这些旧报纸处理掉。

He <u>disposed of</u> his old car. 他把那辆旧车处理了。

还可表示"解决掉"：

He <u>disposed of</u> all the difficulties. 他把所有困难都解决了。

They quickly <u>disposed of</u> the matter. 他们快速把这件事处理掉。

❀ **get rid of** 也可表示"处理掉"：

I'll have to get rid of this worn-out carpet. 我得处理掉这张破旧的地毯。

但它有更多的意思，可表示"摆脱掉""除掉"等：

It's difficult to get rid of insects. 除虫不容易。

There was a lot of rubbish to be got rid of. 有大量垃圾需要扔掉。

❀ **remove** 表示"拿走""除掉""清除"等：

How could I remove the grease stains from my clothes? 我怎样能除掉衣服上的油渍？

He removed all the evidence of his crime. 他消灭了他的一切罪证。

167 distinct—distinctive—distinguished—distinction

distinct 为形容词，表示"清楚的""清晰的""明显的"：

Your pronunciation should be quite distinct. 你的发音应当很清晰。

There's a distinct improvement in her typing. 她打字有明显的改进。

还可表示"不同的"：

Gold is distinct from iron. 金和铁是不同的。

The twins had distinct personalities. 这对双胞胎有不同的个性。

❀ **distinctive** 也是形容词，表示"特别的""突出的"：

She has a distinctive way of speaking. 她讲话方式很特别。

This bird has several distinctive features. 这种鸟有几个突出的特点。

❀ **distinguished** 也是形容词，表示"著名的""杰出的""突出的"：

He is the most distinguished chemist in the country. 他是该国最著名的化学家。

He has had a distinguished career in the diplomatic service. 他在外交界创出了一番突出的业绩。

❀ **distinction** 为名词，表示"区别""区分"：

What is the distinction between ducks and geese? 鸭子与鹅有什么区别？

Can you make (draw) a distinction between these two ideas? 你能区分这两个概念吗？

还可表示"杰出""突出"：

Hardy was a writer of distinction. 哈代是一位杰出的作家。

He served with distinction in the army. 他在军中服役，表现突出。

168 disused—unused—misused

disused 表示"已经不再用了"：

It was stored in a disused garage. 它存放在一个不再使用的车库中。

❀ unused 表示"未用过的""无人使用的"：

a pile of unused fuel 一堆尚未用过的燃料

a row of unused offices 一排无人使用的办公室

❀ misused 表示"错误使用"：

Be sure that these drugs are not misused. 千万注意这些药不得误用。

She misused so many words that we all laughed. 她用错了那么多词，我们都笑了。

169 dive—plunge

dive 是动词，表示"跳水"：

He dived from the bridge and rescued the drowning child. 他从桥上跳下水去，救起了快淹死的孩子。

Most swimming pools have diving boards. 多数的游泳池都有跳水板。

也可表示"往下跳""俯冲"，还可表示"潜水"：

The parachutists dived from the plane. 跳伞员从飞机上跳了下来。

The men dived for pearls. 这些人潜水寻找珍珠。

dive 的过去式为 dived，但在美式英语中常用 dove /dəʊv/ 这个形式：

I dove in after her. 我跟着她跳进水里。

❀ "跳进水里"还可用 plunge（in）表示：

He plunged into the water to save the child. 他跳进水里去救小孩。

He ran to the edge of the lake and plunged in. 他跑到湖边，跳进水里。

170 do

do 是英语中最常用的动词之一。它可以：

用作助动词来构成一般现在时及一般过去时，用在疑问句、否定句及倒装句中：

Where do you live? 你住哪里？

They didn't believe him. 他们不相信他。

I didn't go and neither did she. 我没去，她也没去。

还可用来表示强调或表示刚提到的动作以避免重复：

I do hope you'll stay for supper. 我的确希望你留下吃晚饭。

He does speak well! 他的确讲得好！

"Do you smoke?" "Yes, I do." "你抽烟吗？" "抽。"

用作及物动词，表示"做（某事）"，可以跟名词、代词或动名词：

We did our homework together. 我们一起做的作业。

What does your husband do? 你先生是干什么的？

I did some reading last night. 我昨晚看了点儿书。

有很多动名词可以这样用，如：

cooking	shopping	studying	thinking
talking	knitting	typing	telephoning
washing	sightseeing		

用作及物动词，和不同名词连用，表示不同动作：

Martin has done an excellent article. 马丁写了一篇精彩的文章。

She did some pretty sketches. 她画了几幅漂亮的素描。

它可跟的名词很多，常见的如：

do the room（打扫房间）	do the dishes（洗盘子）
do the windows（擦窗子）	do one's teeth（刷牙）
do one's hair（梳头）	do the vegetable（煮蔬菜）
do the fish（煎鱼）	do the beef（炖牛肉）
do the flowers（插花）	do science（学科学课）
do sums（算算术）	do military service（服兵役）

do a concert（听音乐会）　　do Spain（游览西班牙）

do ten years（关了 10 年）　　do one's guests（招待客人）

do Hamlet（扮演哈姆雷特）

用作不及物动词，表示多种不同的意思：

When in Rome, do as the Romans do. 入乡随俗。（谚语）

Always do to others as you would be done by. 待人如待己。（谚语）

She is doing well in school. 她在学校学习情况良好。

He did very well in the examination. 他考得很好。

Roses do well in clay soil. 玫瑰在黏土地里长得很好。

That will do. 这行（够）了。

That won't do. It's too risky. 那不行，太冒险。

This hotel won't do. 这家旅馆不行。

do 还可用于许多短语，例如：

That will do them no harm. 这对他们没有坏处。

Would you do me a (little) favour? 你能帮我一个（小）忙吗?

I did my best to help them. 我尽了最大努力帮助他们。

You've done your duty. 你已尽了你的责任。

I felt I had done wrong. 我感到我做错了。

171 **doubt—doubtless—doubtful**

doubt 可作动词，也可作名词。作动词时它表示"怀疑"，后面可以跟：
名词或代词：

I doubt the truth of their report. 我怀疑他们报告的真实性。

They doubt his honesty. 他们怀疑他不老实。

从句：

Nobody doubts what he says. 没人怀疑他说的话。

He doubted that the new equipment was really necessary. 他怀疑是否真
的需要新设备。

作名词时也表示"怀疑"，多作不可数名词：

This increased her doubt. 这增加了她的怀疑。

There is not much doubt about his guilt. 对他的罪行没有多少怀疑。

在 there is (have) no doubt 后常可跟 that 引起的从句：

There was no doubt that he was a fine scholar. 毫无疑问，他是一位优秀的学者。

I have no doubt that we shall be able to do something for you. 我不怀疑我们能为你帮忙。

在肯定句中 doubt 后面可跟 whether 引起的从句：

There is some doubt (as to) whether she will come on time. 她是否准时来，有点儿让人怀疑。

有时也可作可数名词：

A sudden doubt came to her mind. 她脑中突然产生了一点怀疑。

She had her doubts whether he would come. 她有点儿疑虑他是否会来。

no doubt 和 without (a) doubt 都可用作状语，表示"毫无疑问"：

Mrs. Warren, no doubt, has her merits. 华伦夫人毫无疑问有她的优点。

Without (a) doubt you have been working very hard. 毫无疑问，你工作一向努力。

❀ **doubtless 也表示同样的意思：**

It was doubtless his own fault. 毫无疑问，这是他自己的错。

Doubtless he would have inside news. 毫无疑问，他会有内幕消息。

❀ **doubtful 则表示"怀疑的""值得怀疑的"：**

She was doubtful of his good intentions. 她对他的良好愿望有点儿怀疑。

The results of the experiment are doubtful. 实验结果值得怀疑。

172 downwards—downward

downwards 在英式英语中为副词，表示"向下"：

Nina glanced downwards. 尼娜往下望了一眼。

He lay on the floor face downwards. 他脸朝下躺在地板上。

❀ **在美式英语中通常用 downward 这个形式作副词：**

The blood from the wound spread downward. 伤口的血往下流淌。

She sat by the window, looking downward. 她坐在窗口往下望。

在英式英语和美式英语中都可用 downward 作形容词，表示"向下的"：

Share prices continued their <u>downward</u> trend. 股市价格继续下跌。

a <u>downward</u> movement of the head 头向下的动作

173 draught—draft

draught 和 draft 在英式英语中都读作 /drɑːft/。在英式英语中 draught 主要有两重意思：

过堂风，一股风：

You may catch (a) cold if you sit in a <u>draught</u>. 如果坐在过堂风里，你可能会感冒。

Turn the electric fan on and make a <u>draught</u>. 把电扇打开，来一股风。

美式英语用 draft /dræft/ 表示：

She felt a <u>draft</u> on her shoulders. 她肩上感觉一股凉风。

Close the window and stop that <u>draft</u>. 把窗子关上，把过堂风止住。

（复）西洋跳棋（美作 checkers ）：

He beat me at <u>draughts</u>. 他和我下西洋跳棋下赢了。

draft 在英式英语中和美式英语中都可用作名词，表示：

草稿，草图：

He had written out a first <u>draft</u>. 他写出了一个初稿。

She is now revising the <u>draft</u> of her essay. 她正在修改文章的草稿。

汇票：

He sent a <u>draft</u> for £100 to his cousin in Ireland. 他给他爱尔兰的表弟寄出了一张 100 英镑的汇票。

在美式英语中还可以表示"征兵"：

When he was 18, he had to register for the <u>draft</u>. 他 18 岁时得登记准备应征入伍。

a <u>draft</u> card 征兵证

draft 还可用作动词，表示"草拟""画草图"：

He <u>drafted</u> out his letter of resignation. 他草拟了他的辞职信。

He <u>drafted</u> the model of the atomic engine. 他画出了原子发动机模型图。

或表示"调派"：

Extra staff were <u>drafted</u> from Paris to Rome. 额外的人员由巴黎派到了罗马。

Extra police officers had to be <u>drafted</u> in. 还得调来更多的警官。

在美式英语中它还可表示"征（兵）"：

He was <u>drafted</u> by the army and served for 4 years. 他应征入伍，服役了四年。

He was <u>drafted</u> into the US Army. 他应征参加了美军。

174 **dress—wear**

dress 可作动词，也可作名词。作动词时它表示：

穿衣服（*vi.*）：

I'll be ready in a moment. I'm <u>dressing</u>. 我一会儿就好，我在穿衣服。

They chatted gaily while they <u>dressed</u>. 他们一面穿衣服，一面高兴地聊着。

给……穿上衣服（*vt.*）：

Please <u>dress</u> the baby. 请给宝宝把衣服穿好。

The child is still too young to <u>dress</u> itself. 孩子太小，不能自己穿衣服。

穿着打扮（*vi.*）：

She <u>dressed</u> well (badly). 她穿着打扮很好（差）。

She always <u>dresses</u> in black. 她老是穿黑色的衣服。

打扮（自己）（*vt.*）：

He is <u>dressed</u> in his uniform. 他穿着制服。

She was <u>dressed</u> in white like a nurse. 她穿着白色衣服，像个护士。

作名词时，它表示：

穿着，打扮（不可数）：

He doesn't care much about <u>dress</u>. 他对衣着打扮不太讲究。

Boys think less about <u>dress</u> than girls do. 男孩子比女孩子想打扮想的少。

服装，衣服（总称，不可数）：

They like to wear their colourful national <u>dress</u>. 他们喜欢穿鲜艳的民

族服装。

The <u>dress</u> of the natives is quite unique. 土著人的衣服很独特。

连衣裙（可数）：

Only women and girls normally wear <u>dresses</u>. 通常只有妇女和姑娘们穿连衣裙。

❀ **wear** 也可表示服装，但不可数，常构成合成词：

Children's <u>wear</u> is down at the other end. 儿童服装在那一头。

Do you sell men's <u>wear</u> here? 这里卖不卖男装？

casualwear 便服	sportswear 运动服
leisurewear 休闲服	evening wear 晚间衣服
holiday wear 假日服装	underwear 内衣

175 due to—owing to

due to 可用作表语，表示"由于"：

The delay was <u>due to</u> heavy traffic. 延误是由于车太多造成的。

His death was <u>due to</u> negligence. 他的死亡是由于玩忽职守造成的。

也可用作状语：

Later he was released <u>due to</u> poor health. 后来，他由于身体很差被释放了。

<u>Due (Owing) to</u> the storm, many people arrived late. 由于那场暴雨，很多人迟到了。

❀ **owing to** 也可用作状语，表示同样的意思：

She is now not active in the movement <u>owing to</u> ill health. 由于身体欠佳，她现在在这场运动中已不太活跃。

<u>Owing to</u> rain, the garden party will not take place. 由于下雨，游园会将无法举行。

但 **owing to** 不能用作表语。

176 during—in

during 是一个介词，常用来表示"在（某段时间）"：

Only two trains left during (in) the morning. 早上只有两班火车开出。

The sun gives us light during the day. 白天里，太阳给我们光明。

这时它和 in 的意思是差不多的，在很多情况下可以换用：

We'll be on holiday during (in) August. 我们八月休假。

I woke up during (in) the night. 我夜间醒了。

在用 during 时我们常强调这个动作持续或反复发生：

He swims every day during the summer. 夏天，他天天游泳。

During the time she still remained silent. 在这段时间，她仍然保持沉默。

另外，during 还可表示"在（某活动）期间"：

Not a word did they exchange during the meal. 在吃饭时，他们之间一句话也没说。

She called you twice during your absence. 你不在期间她来过两次电话。

在这种情况下 in 是不能用的。

177 each—every

each 和 every 都可用作定语，都可译为"每一个"，但意思不太相同。

❀ every 表示"每个……都""人人都"，意思接近 all：

Every cook praises his own broth. 每个厨子都说自己做的汤好。（谚语）

（比较：All cooks praise their own broth.）

Every dog has its day. 人人都有出头日。（谚语）

❀ 而 each 谈"每一个（的情况）"（可说是分开来的情况）：

Each person in turn went in to see the doctor. 每个人轮流进去看病。

He carried a suitcase in each hand. 他每只手提着一只箱子。

在个别情况下两者都可以用：

You look more beautiful each (every) time I see you.

我每次见到你，你都看上去更漂亮了。

注意，every 只能用作定语，而 each 可以用作代词，在句中作：

主语：

Each must do his best. 每人都要尽力。

Two boys entered. Each was carrying a suitcase. 进来两个小伙子，每人提着一只箱子。

宾语或介词宾语：

They checked each of the instruments. 他们检查了每一台仪器。

同位语：

They each had a bedroom. 他们每人有一间卧室。

I fine you each five dollars. 我罚你们每人五美金。

each 还可用作副词，用在句末：

They cost eight pounds each. 它们每个售价八英镑。

I bought the children two ice-cream each. 我给孩子们每人买了两个冰激凌。

each 作代词时后面常可跟一个 **of** 引起的短语：

Each of these phrases has a different meaning. 这些短语各有不同的意思。

A chrysanthemum was presented to each of the ladies. 每位女士都获赠一朵菊花。

of 后也可跟人称代词：

Each of them came at a different time. 他们每人都是不同时间来的。

Each of us sees the world differently. 我们每个人对世界都有不同的看法。

> 以 "each..." 为主语时，后面的代词可用单数，也可用复数：
>
> Each girl wore what she liked best. 每个姑娘都穿她最喜欢的衣服。（较正规的说法）
>
> Each student wore what they liked best.（较随便的说法）
>
> Each of them explained it in his (her, their) own way. 每人对它都有各自的解释。

178 each other—one another

each other 和 **one another** 为相互代词，可表示两人或更多人之间的相互关系，在句中可以：

用作宾语：

We have known each other since we were children. 我们从小就认识。

The members of this family loved each other. 这个家庭的成员互相爱护。

用作介词的宾语：

The three women looked at each other. 这三个女人相互望着。

They were very pleased with one another. 他们相互很喜欢。

和 "'" 一起用：

I hope that you all enjoy each other's company. 我希望你们在一起过得愉快。

They'll sit for hours looking into each other's (one another's) eyes. 他们有时对坐几小时，望着彼此的眼睛。

each other 和 one another 意思相同，one another 稍微文气一点，许多人不爱用它，在谈到两人间相互关系时，仍有人更愿意用 each other，在谈到更多人的情况时，更愿用 one another，虽然这种区分通常已不复存在。

179 east—eastern—easterly—eastward(s)

east 可作名词、形容词或副词。用作名词时表示"东方""东边""东部"：

Our house faces the east. 我们的房子朝东。

Japan is in the east of Asia. 日本在亚洲东部。

大写时可指东方国家或东方地区：

More Americans visit Europe than the East. 访问欧洲的美国人比访问东方国家的美国人多。

the Far East 远东　　　　　　　the Middle East 中东

也可用作形容词，表示"东"：

There is a strong east wind. 有一股强劲的东风。

New York is on the east coast. 纽约在东海岸。

可用于地名：East Africa 东非 East Timor 东帝汶 the East End 伦敦东区

还可用作副词，表示"朝（向）东"：

The Danube flows east into the Black Sea. 多瑙河向东流入黑海。

Is the Atlantic Ocean east or west of the United States? 大西洋在美国以东还是以西？

❀ **eastern** 也是形容词，表示"东……"：

Eastern Europe has cold winters. 东欧冬季严寒。

They traveled in the eastern part of the country. 他们在这个国家的东部旅行。

the Eastern Mediterranean 东地中海　the Eastern Hemisphere 东半球

❀ **easterly** 也是形容词，表示"向东的""由东边吹来的"：

The yacht was continuing in an easterly direction. 游艇继续向东航行。

There was an icy easterly wind blowing off the sea. 有一股由东边海上吹来的凛冽的寒风。

❀ eastward(s) 为副词，表示"向东地"（在美式英语中多用 eastward 这个形式）：

Darius fled away eastwards. 达赖厄斯向东边逃跑了。

The march continued, always eastwards. 不断向东进军。

eastward 有时用作形容词：

an eastward movement 向东的运动

180 economics—economy—economic—economical

economics 是名词，表示"经济学"：

This is one of the basic principles of socialist economics. 这是社会主义经济学的基本原理之一。

Vince is also studying economics. 文斯也学经济（学）。

What does economics deal with? 经济学是讲什么的？

可以用作定语：

She didn't show up for an economics class. 经济学课上她没来。

He teaches at the university's economics department. 他在这个大学的经济系教书。

economics 还可表示"经济情况（效益）"：

The economics of national growth are of the greatest importance to all modern governments. 国民经济增长的情况对所有现代政府至关重要。

the economics of the timber trade 木材工业的效益

❀ economy 也是名词，表示"经济"：

The nation's economy is growing rapidly. 国家的经济迅速增长。

These strikes were damaging the country's economy. 这些罢工损害这个国家的经济。

也可表示"节约"（复数形式表示节约措施）：

He has no need to practice economy. 他没有必要实行节约。

It might be necessary to make a few economies. 可能有必要采取一些节约措施。

❀ economic 是形容词，表示"经济上的"：

We need a rational <u>economic</u> system. 我们需要一个合理的经济制度。

We bought a small car for <u>economic</u> reasons. 出于经济上的原因，我们买了一辆小车。

❀ **economical** 也是形容词，表示"节约的"：

One must be <u>economical</u> of one's time. 我们必须节约时间。

He was industrious and <u>economical</u>. 他勤劳而又节俭。

181 educational—educative

educational 有两重意思：

与教育有关的，教育的：

The <u>educational</u> methods of the West were also introduced. 也引进了西方的教育方法。

<u>educational</u> work　教育工作　　　an <u>educational</u> magazine　教育杂志

有教育意义（作用）的：

It'll be <u>educational</u> for him to do that. 他这样做是有教育意义的。

He found the experience <u>educational</u>. 他发现这段经历有教育作用。

❀ **educative** /ˈedjʊkətɪv/ 只表示"有教育作用的"：

All books, television and movies ought to be <u>educative</u>. 所有书籍、电视、电影都应有教育作用。

182 -ee—-eer

-ee 这可加在某些动词后面，表示"被……的人"，如：

addressee（收件人）　　　　　appointee（被任命的人）

assignee（被指定的人）　　　　conferee（被授予人）

detainee（被拘留者）　　　　　divorcee（离了婚的人）

employee（雇员）　　　　　　internee（被拘禁者）

interviewee（受访人）　　　　nominee（被提名人）

payee（受款人）　　　　　　　referee（裁判）

trainee（受训者）　　　　　　trustee（理事）

vendee（买主）

-ee 也可加在名词、形容词或动词后，表示"有某类情况的人"，如：

refugee（难民） burgee（驳船船员）

patentee（有专利权者） absentee（缺席者）

escapee（逃走者） devotee（献身者）

❀ **-eer** 也可用来构成名词，主要表示从事某活动的人，如：

engineer（工程师） mountaineer（登山队员）

auctioneer（拍卖人） buccaneer（海盗）

mutineer（叛变者） privateer（抢劫敌舰者）

profiteer（投机商） pamphleteer（出版小册子的人）

183 effective—efficient

这两个词都是形容词，但意思不同。

❀ **effective** 表示"有效的""生效的"：

My headache is much better. Those tablets really are effective. 我的头疼好多了，那些药片的确很有效。

The new interest rate becomes effective next month. 新利息下月生效。

❀ **efficient** 表示"效率高的"，可指人：

He needs an efficient secretary. 他需要一个高效的秘书。

A good manager is both competent and efficient. 一个好的经理既要有能力又要效率高。

也可指机器等：

The diesel engine is highly efficient. 这台柴油机效率很高。

Our efficient new machines are much cheaper to run. 我们的新机器效率高，用起来便宜得多。

184 either

either 为不定代词，可表示"两者中的一个"：

You may take either of the roads. 两条路你走哪一条都行。

I don't agree with either of you. 你们两人的意见，我都不同意。

有时不跟 **of** 引起的短语：

Either is acceptable.（两者中）任何一个都可以。

"Which one do you want?" "I don't want either." "你要哪一个？" "哪一个我都不要。"

either 作主语时，一般跟单数动词：

Either of the plans is equally dangerous. 两个计划都同样危险。

但在口语中也有人用复数动词：

Are either of you taking lessons? 你们两人都在上课了？

另外，**either** 还可用作定语（这时有人称为限定词）：

Either proposal will have my support. 两个提案我都支持。

He could write with either hand. 他两只手都能写字。

此外还可表示"两边""两头"：

On either side of the river lie corn fields. 河的两岸都是玉米地。

There was an armchair at either end of the long table. 在长桌子的两头，各有一把扶手椅。

either 还可用作副词，表示"也（不）"，仅用于否定句：

I'm not likely to change either. 我改变的可能性也不大。

As for me, I shall not return there either. 至于我，我也不会回那里。

185 **either... or...**

either... or... 是一种连词，连接两个成分表示两者中的一个，可译为"或是……或是""既不……又不""不是……就是"等。它可连接：

两个并列的主语（动词和最近的主语一致）：

Either your mother or your father may come with you. 你母亲或是你父亲会陪你去。

Either Tim or his brothers have to shovel the snow. 或是蒂姆或是他的兄弟们，得去铲雪。

两个并列的宾语或介词宾语：

I don't speak either French or German. 我既不会讲法语，又不会讲德语。

You'll be interviewed by either Mr. Nelson or Miss Green. 你将由纳尔逊先生或格林女士接见。

两个并列的谓语或表语：

You can <u>either</u> come with me now <u>or</u> walk home. 你要么现在和我一道去，要么自己走回家。

The books were <u>either</u> books on travel <u>or</u> detective novels. 这些书不是游记就是侦探小说。

两个并列的状语或定语：

She will be back <u>either</u> today <u>or</u> tomorrow. 她不是今天就是明天回来。

You can take <u>either</u> the blue <u>or</u> the green one. 你可拿蓝色的或是绿色的那个。

两个并列的分句：

<u>Either</u> you must improve your work <u>or</u> I shall dismiss you. 要么你改进工作，要么我把你辞退。

<u>Either</u> you leave this house <u>or</u> I'll call the police. 要么你离开这屋子，要么我去叫警察。

有时也可在三样东西中选一样：

If you want ice-cream you can have <u>either</u> coffee, lemon <u>or</u> vanilla. 如果你要买冰激凌，你可以要咖啡味的、柠檬味的或是香草味的。

186 electric—electrical

electric 指由电操纵的，使用电的：

an <u>electric</u> fan 电扇　　　　an <u>electric</u> bell 电铃

an <u>electric</u> stove 电炉　　　　an <u>electric</u> iron 电熨斗

a hydro-<u>electric</u> station 水电站

❀ **electrical** 指与电有关的：

<u>electrical</u> engineering 电机工程　an <u>electrical</u> engineer 电机工程师

an <u>electrical</u> apparatus 电气装置　<u>electrical</u> energy 电能

187 else

else 为副词，表示"其他""别的"，通常放在下面这类词后面：

something, nothing 这类代词：

He has nothing <u>else</u> to do today. 他今天没有别的事要干。

Everything else depended upon that. 其他一切都靠那个决定。

someone, somebody 这类代词：

She must have learnt it from someone else. 她一定是从别人那里了解到的。

Everybody else but me has gone to the party. 除了我，别人全都参加那个晚会去了。

somewhere 这类副词：

I'm going to take you somewhere else. 我准备带你到别的地方去。

You can't get it anywhere else. 你在任何别的地方都买不到它。

who, what 等疑问词：

Who else is there in the house? 屋子里还有谁？

Where else did you go? 你还去过别的什么地方？

其他代词：

He taught us to put the interests of the people before all else. 他教导我们把人民的利益放在最重要的位置。

There was little else he could do. 他再没有别的什么可做了。

We don't know much else about his life. 对他生平别的方面，我们知道的很少。

else 还可用在所有格中：

Your words carry more weight than anybody else's. 你的话比任何别人的话都更有分量。

You're wearing someone else's coat. 你穿着别人的大衣。

else 还可构成合成词 **elsewhere**，表示"别处"：

The hotel is full. We must look for rooms elsewhere. 这家旅馆已经客满，我们得到别处找房间。

or else 是一个短语，表示"否则"：

Let's go, or else we'll miss the train. 咱们走吧，否则就赶不上火车了。

Dress warmly, or else you'll catch cold. 穿暖和点，否则你会感冒的。

也可表示"要不就是"：

He must be joking, or else he's mad. 他一定在开玩笑，要不就是疯了。

The book must be here, or else you've lost it. 这书一定在这儿，要不就是你弄丢了。

188 emigrate—immigrate—migrate

emigrate 表示"移民（到国外）"：

Albert Einstein emigrated from Germany to the United States. 爱因斯坦从德国移民到美国。

The ship was full of emigrants leaving Liverpool to emigrate to Australia. 这艘船满载移民，由利物浦移居到澳洲。

emigration 是它的名词形式，表示"移居""迁往国外"：

The population of Ireland has decreased because of emigration. 由于很多人迁往国外，爱尔兰的人口下降了。

They passed new laws on emigration. 他们通过了关于移民海外的法律。

emigrant 是另一名词形式，表示"移居海外的人"：

Thousands of emigrants boarded these ships for the New World. 成千上万的移民搭上这些船前往新世界。

❀ immigrate 为动词，表示"移居（到某国）"：

Many Italians immigrated to the United States. 许多意大利人移民到了美国。

They were encouraged to immigrate to Australia. 他们受鼓励，移民到澳洲。

移民到某个国家的人称为 immigrant：

European immigrants in Australia 澳洲的欧洲移民

A ship carrying over 200 illegal immigrants arrived there yesterday. 一艘载有两百多非法移民的船昨天抵达那里。

名词形式为 immigration，表示"移民"：

There was immigration to America from all the countries of Europe. 从欧洲各国都有人移居美国。

the immigration law 移民法　　　the immigration office 移民局

❀ migrate 表示"迁移（到其他地区）"，可以指人，也可指动物：

People often migrate to another town (or country) to find work. 人们常常迁移到另一座城市（或另一个国家）找寻工作。

Many birds migrate south every winter. 许多鸟每个冬天都迁往南方。

名词形式为 **migration**，表示"迁徙"：

Wars always cause great <u>migrations</u> of people. 战争常常造成民众大迁徙。

He studies the <u>migration</u> of birds. 他研究鸟类的迁徙。

migrant 为形容词，表示"流动的""迁徙的"：

<u>Migrant</u> workers move from country to country in search of work. 流动工人从一国迁到另一国找寻工作。

These <u>migrant</u> birds return every spring. 这些候鸟每年春天飞回来。

migrant 也可作名词，表示"流动工人"或"候鸟（或迁移的动物）"：

Hundreds of <u>migrants</u> are looking for a place to live. 数以百计的流动工人在找地方住。

<u>migrants</u> in the ocean 海洋中的迁徙生物

189 **-en—en-**

-en 是一个有用的后缀（词尾），可以：

加在形容词后构成动词，表示"（使）变……"：

blacken	brighten	broaden	darken	deaden
deepen	fasten	fatten	flatten	freshen
harden	lessen	liken	lighten	loosen
madden	moisten	quicken	redden	ripen
roughen	sharpen	shorten	sicken	stiffen
straighten	strengthen	sweeten	thicken	tighten
weaken	widen	worsen		

加在名词后构成形容词（表示"由……制成"）：

earthen	golden	leaden	silken	wooden	wool(l)en

❀ **en-** 是前缀（词头），可以：

加在形容词前构成动词（表示"使变得"）：

enable	enfeeble	enlarge	enrich	ensure

加在名词前构成动词（表示各种不同意思）：

enact	encamp	encase	encircle	encourage
endanger	enforce	enjoy	enlist	enrage
enrapture	enroll	enslave	enthrone	entitle

190 end—finish

end 可用作动词。作不及物动词时表示：

结束：

The war ended in 1975. 这场战争于 1975 年结束。

When the concert ended I made my way out of the hall. 音乐会结束时我走出大厅。

结尾，结果，结局：

All is well that ends well. 结果好一切都好。（谚语）

The book ended in tragedy. 这本书以悲剧结局。

作及物动词时表示"结束"：

The chairman ended the meeting at ten o'clock. 主席在 10 点结束了会议。

He ended this letter with good wishes to the family. 他以对全家的良好祝愿结束了这封信。

还可以构成短语：

end in 以……告终：

The match ended in a draw. 球赛打成了平局。

The scheme ended in failure. 这一阴谋以失败告终。

end up 最后结局如何：

How does the story end up? 这故事如何结局？

If you drive your car like that, you'll end up in hospital. 如果你这样开车，最后会进医院。

❀ **finish** 也可表示"结束"，和 **end** 的用法很相近，有时可和 **end** 换用：

The performance finished (ended) at eleven o'clock. 表演 11 点结束。

She wants to finish any connection with you. 她想结束和你的任何

联系。

但在表示"完成"这个意思时，不能和 **end** 换用。例如下面句子就如此：

When I've finished the book we'll go out. 我把书看完后，我们就出去。

He who commences many things finishes but few. 开头干许多件事常完成不了几件。（谚语）

191 envious—enviable

envious 表示"忌妒的""羡慕的"：

He tried not to be envious. 他设法不忌妒别人。

She looked at it with envious eyes. 她以羡慕的目光望着它。

后面常常跟一个 **of** 引起的短语：

She was envious of Jennie's good fortune. 她羡慕珍妮的好运气。

She would always be envious of her sister's beauty. 她经常忌妒她妹妹的美。

❀ **enviable** 表示"值得羡慕的"：

He has everything he wants; he's an enviable young man. 他要什么有什么，他是一个令人羡慕的青年。

Susan has an enviable school record. 苏珊的学业成绩是令人羡慕的。

有时可译作"可喜的"等：

He faced his enemies with enviable courage. 他以可喜的勇气面对敌人。

She is able to speak the language with enviable fluency. 她能相当流利地讲这种语言。

192 equipment—instrument—apparatus

equipment 是"设备""装备"的总称，为不可数名词：

They carried most of their equipment on their backs. 他们把大部分装备都背在背上。

We're out to standardize equipment in factories. 我们将使工厂的设备

标准化。

若表示"一件设备"，可用 **a piece of** 表示：

This is a very useful piece of equipment. 这是一件非常有用的设备。

He carried a number of pieces of equipment with him. 他带有许多件设备。

❀ **instrument** 和 **apparatus** 都是可数名词，表示"一件仪器（装置）"：

All surgical instruments must be sterilized before use. 所有外科用具使用前都要消毒。

This apparatus can purify a thousand gallons of water a minute. 这种装置一分钟可净化一千加仑的水。

193 especially—specially

especially 可以表示"特别地"，可以修饰：

形容词：

We need to be especially careful. 我们需要特别小心。

We are especially busy today. 我们今天特别忙。

动词：

Kate especially seems happy. 凯特显得特别高兴。

"Do you like chocolate?" "Not especially." "你喜欢巧克力吗？""不是特别喜欢。"

它还可以表示"特别是"，可以：

和同位语连用：

I like all the children, Lester especially. 我喜欢所有的孩子，特别是莱斯特。

She liked it very much—especially the last part. 她非常喜欢它，特别是最后一部分。

和状语连用：

Noise is unpleasant, especially when you're trying to sleep. 噪声是很讨厌的，特别是当你想睡觉的时候。

The blacks played an important role, especially in Brazil. 黑人起了重要作用，特别是在巴西。

❀ **specially** 意思有相似之处，它表示：

特别（地）：

I don't feel specially inclined to talk to him. 我不是特别想和他谈。

There the beer was specially good. 那里的啤酒特别好。

在这里用 **especially** 也可以。

特意地，专门地：

He has come specially to see you. 他是特意来看你的。

I made a chocolate cake specially for you. 我专门为你做了一块巧克力蛋糕。

在这里则不宜用 **especially**。

194 -ess

-ess 为后缀（词尾），加在名词后构成表示女性或雌性动物的名词：

actress	baroness	countess	duchess	empress
goddess	heiress	hostess	lioness	marchioness
mistress	poetess	priestess	princess	prophetess
seamstress	shepherdess	stewardess	tigress	waitress

195 even

even 为副词，表示"即使""甚至"，可放在各种不同位置：

放在主语前面：

Even a child can understand the book. 即使小孩也能看懂这本书。

Even my mother could not help smiling. 甚至我妈妈也忍不住笑了起来。

放在动词前面：

She even helped me to clean the rooms. 她甚至帮助我打扫房间。

He speaks lots of languages. He even speaks Esperanto. 他能讲许多语言，他甚至能讲世界语。

放在助动词和动词 **be** 后面：

This morning he had not even come to see them off. 这天早上他甚至没

来给他们送行。

He's rude to everybody. He's even rude to the police. 他对谁都粗鲁无礼，甚至对警察也如此。

放在状语前面：

Even at night he seldom relaxed. 甚至晚上他也很少休息。

There are spots even on the sun. 甚至在太阳上也有黑斑。（谚语）

放在其他词前面：

He was afraid to take even a drink of water. 他连喝口水都害怕。

He eats anything—even raw fish. 他什么都吃，甚至吃生鱼。

和 not 连用：

He can't even write his own name. 他甚至连自己的名字都不会写。

She didn't even offer me a cup of tea. 她连一杯茶都没让我喝。

和形容词或副词的比较级连用：

It was cold yesterday, but it's even colder today. 昨天很冷，今天甚至更冷。

You can read even better if you try harder. 如果再努力一点，你还可以念得更好。

用于 even so，表示"尽管如此"：

He seems nice. Even so, I don't really trust him. 他似乎不错。尽管如此，我也不真的信任他。

The fire was out, but even so, the smell of smoke was strong. 火已经扑灭，尽管如此，烟味仍然很浓。

用于 even if，表示"即使"：

They'll stand by you even if you don't succeed. 即使你们不成功，他们也会支持你们。

I hope I can come back, even if it's only for a few weeks. 我希望我能回来，即使只待几个礼拜。

用于 even though，表示"尽管"，和 although 的意思差不多：

He is an honest man, I must say, even though I have opposed him. 尽管我反对过他，我还得说他是一个诚实的人。

She was always afraid of men, even though she had lots of boyfriends. 尽管她有很多男朋友，她总是害怕男人。

196 ever

ever 是一个副词，常和动词连用，可以：

谈过去的动作（意思接近"曾经"，但有较灵活译法）：

Has she <u>ever</u> talked to you about such matters? 她曾和你谈到这类事吗？

No one in this village has <u>ever</u> heard of you. 这个村子里没有人听说过你。

谈将来的动作，起强调作用：

She doesn't want <u>ever</u> to speak of it. 她不想再谈及此事。

If you <u>ever</u> see George, give him my kind regards. 如果你万一见到乔治，代我向他问好。

谈现在的习惯性动作：

She is scarcely <u>ever</u> at home. 她现在很少在家。

Do you <u>ever</u> go to pop concerts? 你有时去听流行音乐会吗？

和 **than** 及 **as** 连用：

Her eyes became more limpid <u>than ever</u>. 她的眼睛比过去更加清澈了。

She was as interested in music <u>as ever</u>. 她对音乐还是像过去那样有兴趣。

ever 还有"永远""老是"的意思（接近 **always** ）：

The material world goes on for <u>ever</u>. 物质世界将永远存在下去。

You will find me <u>ever</u> at your service. 你会发现我永远听你使唤。

在一些合成词或说法中仍保有这个意思：

<u>ever</u>green trees 常青树

his <u>ever</u>-loving wife 永远爱他的妻子

<u>ever</u>-victorious general 常胜将军

<u>ever</u>-increasing population 日益增长的人口

还可用于 **ever since, ever after, ever so, ever such**，起强调作用：

We have been good friends <u>ever since</u>. 从那以后，我们就是好朋友了。

They lived happily <u>ever after</u>. 从那之后，他们就过着幸福的生活了。

Thank you <u>ever so much</u>. 非常非常感谢。

She is <u>ever such</u> a nice girl. 她是那样好的一位姑娘。

此外还可以和疑问代（副）词一道用，也起强调的作用：

What <u>ever</u> put that idea into your head? 什么使你产生这个想法的？

Who <u>ever</u> can be calling at this time of night? 谁这么三更半夜来找我们？

ever 常可和疑问词写成一个词：

<u>Wherever</u> did you get this? 这你是在哪儿买的？

<u>Whoever</u> heard of such a thing? 谁听说过这样的事？

197 every

every 为形容词，也称为限定词。主要有两个意思：

每一个：

<u>Every</u> man working there knew me. 每一个在那里工作的人都认识我。

<u>Every</u> teashop he came to was crammed. 他去的每一家茶馆都挤满了人。

一切，种种：

You have <u>every</u> reason to fear him. 你有种种理由惧怕他。

She made <u>every</u> attempt to help us. 她做了一切努力来帮助我们。

还可与许多词连用，表示不同的意思：

every other 每隔一个：

We have English lessons <u>every other</u> day. 我们每隔一天上一次英语课。

Write on <u>every other</u> line. 隔行写。

every two (three, etc.) 每两（三……）个……：

The American people elect a president <u>every four</u> years. 美国人四年选一次总统。

There are buses to the station <u>every ten</u> minutes. 每 10 分钟有一辆公共汽车进站。

every third (fourth, etc.) 每三（四……）个：

There <u>every third</u> man was down with plague. 那里每三个人就有一个染上瘟疫。

I go there <u>every fourth</u> day. 我隔三天去一次。

every now and then (again) 每隔一些时候，不时：

Every now and then a plane would take off. 隔一会儿就有一架飞机起飞。

He only comes up to London every now and again. 他只是隔一些时候才来伦敦一次。

every day (hour, etc.) 日益（越来越）：

Hogg became every day more conservative. 霍格变得日益保守。

He looked more like his father every hour. 他长得越来越像他爸爸。

every day (night, etc.) 每天（每天晚上等）：

Every night he spoke on the streets. 每天晚上，他都在街头讲演。

Every afternoon he called to ask after her. 每天下午，他都来向她问好。

198 everyday—every day

everyday 是形容词，表示"日常的""天天发生的"：

Then she changed into her everyday clothes. 这时她换上了日常的衣服。

It is a common everyday expression. 这是一个普通的日常用语。

❀ every day 则用作状语，表示"每天"：

She came to see us every day. 她每天都来看我们。

Party membership is growing every day. 党员人数日益增加。

199 everyone—everybody

这两个词意思相同，都表示"人人""大家"：

Everybody has some weak spots. 人人都有弱点。

I stayed at work when everyone else had gone home. 别人都回家了，我还留下干活。

注意 everyone 和 every one 的区别，后者多跟有一个 of 引起的短语：

Go to bed, every one of you! 你们大家都睡觉去。

在反义疑问句中，有时可用 they 代表 everybody：

Everybody has arrived, haven't they? 大家都到了，是吧？

另外，注意下面情况：

Has everybody got his or her ticket? 大家都拿到车票了吗？（较正规说法）

Has everybody got their tickets?（较随便的说法）

When everybody had finished eating, the waiters took away their plates. 大家都吃完时，服务员收走了他们的盘子。（这时只能用 their）

200 exam—examination

exam 和 examination 都表示"考试"，用得最多的是 exam，examination 比较正规，主要在书面语中使用：

I was told the exam was difficult. 据说考试很难。

He did very well in the examinations. 他考得很好。

"参加考试"有下面几种说法：

Many children want to take these exams. 许多孩子想参加这些考试。

After the third term we'll be sitting the exam. 第三学期后，我们将参加考试。

I can't sit for the examination because I'm ill. 因为我生病，没能参加考试。

"考试通过（及格）"多用 pass 表示：

Larry passed university exams at sixteen. 拉里 16 岁时就通过大学考试。

没通过则用 fail 表示：

He failed the written paper (oral part). 他笔（口）试没通过。

She has failed her exam again. 她考试又没及格。

201 except—except for

except 和 except for 都表示"除了"。在 all, every, no, everything, anybody, nowhere 这类词后面，两者可以换用，后面跟名词或代词（作宾格）：

I looked everywhere except there. 除了那里，我到处都找了。

None of them spoke English except (for) Tom. 除了汤姆，他们谁也不会讲英语。

Anything, except (for) water, is likely to block a sink. 除了水，任何东

西都可能把洗涤槽堵住。

在其他情况下，只能用 except for（可译为"除了……外"）：

I've cleaned the house except for the bathroom. 除了浴室外，我把房子都打扫了。

Your composition is good except for a few spelling mistakes. 你的作文很好，只是有几个拼法错误。

except for 有时还可表示"若不是……"：

Except for you, I should be dead by now. 若不是有你，我现在都死了。

She would leave her husband except for the children. 要不是为了孩子，她都离开她丈夫了。

但 except 后可以跟更多结构：

跟介词短语：

He rarely went anywhere except to his office. 他除了去办公室，很少去任何地方。

He cannot spare any time except on Sunday. 除了星期天，他没有空闲时间。

跟带 to 的不定式：

It had no effect except to make him angry. 这除了让他生气，没有别的作用。

The windows were never opened except to air the room for a few minutes. 除了要透几分钟的空气，窗子是从来不开的。

跟不带 to 的不定式（注意句子中的谓语为 do）：

They did nothing except work. 除了干活，他们什么也不做。

He will do anything except cook. 他什么都愿做，就是不愿做饭。

跟从句：

This suit fits me well except that the trousers are too long. 除了裤子太长，这套衣服我穿很合适。

He never came except when he was in trouble. 除非遇到麻烦时，他从不到这里来。

202 excepting—excepted—exception

except 还可用作动词，表示"把……除外"：

You will all be punished, I can except no one. 你们都要受到处罚，谁也不能除外。

The A students were excepted from taking the exam. 得 A 的学生免试。

❀ 常可用 excepting 引起短语，表示"除了"和"（不）例外"：

They were all saved excepting the captain. 除了船长，他们都获救了。

He answered all the questions excepting the last one. 除了最后一道题，所有题目都回答了。

All the boys were late, not excepting Jim. 所有孩子都迟到了，吉姆也不例外。

❀ 有时也可在名（代）词后面用 excepted，表示"除了"和"（不）例外"：

John excepted, everyone was tired. 除了约翰，大家都累了。

Everyone helped, John not excepted. 大家都帮忙，约翰也不例外。

❀ 名词形式为 exception，表示"例外情况"：

There is an exception to every rule. 每条规定都有例外情况。

Most children like sweets, but there are some exceptions. 多数孩子都喜欢吃糖果，但也有例外情况。

可用于 with the exception of，表示"除了"：

I invited everybody with the exception of James. 我邀请了所有的人，除了詹姆斯。

Everyone was tired with the exception of John. 除了约翰，大家都累了。

还可用于 without exception，表示"毫无例外"：

You must answer all the questions without exception. 你必须毫无例外回答所有问题。

All the vehicles are without exception old and rusty. 所有车辆毫无例外，都很旧，锈迹斑斑。

也可用于 be no exception，表示"也不例外"：

The law applies to all European countries; Britain is no exception. 这条规律适用于所有欧洲国家，英国也不例外。

Marketing is applied to everything these days, and books are no exception. 现今什么都要推销，书籍也不例外。

203 exhausted—exhausting—exhaustive

exhausted 表示 "疲惫的" (多用作表语):

She looked exhausted. 她看起来很疲惫。

I'm completely exhausted. 我筋疲力尽了。

有时用作状语:

He returned home, weary and exhausted. 他疲惫不堪地回到家里。

Utterly exhausted, he fell into a deep sleep. 他筋疲力尽, 陷入沉睡之中。

❀ **exhausting** 表示 "使人疲惫的" (作表语或定语):

A day like this must be exhausting to you. 这样干一天一定使你疲惫不堪。

We had a long and exhausting meeting this morning. 今天早上, 我们开了一个漫长、累人的会。

❀ **exhaustive** 表示 "深入彻底的":

The student did exhaustive research before writing the paper. 这学生在写论文前做了深入彻底的研究。

After exhaustive discussion they agreed to the undertaking. 经过深入细致的讨论, 他们同意承办这项事业。

204 expect—hope—wait

expect 是动词, 表示 "期待" "指望" "预料", 后面可以跟各种结构。

跟名词或代词:

He expected no gratitude, no recognition for this. 对此, 他不期待得到感谢和承认。

You can't expect perfection. 你不能指望十全十美。

有时表示 "等":

I'll expect you for supper. 我将等你吃晚饭。

I'm expecting a telegram. 我在等一封电报。

它和 **wait** 有不同之处, **wait** 表示 "等待" "等候":

I waited for you for an hour. 我等你等了一个钟头。

Don't wait for me. 不要等我。

而 **expect** 实际上表示"期待"（在日常口语中说"等"比较随便）：

Come and join us. We'll be <u>expecting</u> you. 来和我们一道去，我们会等你的。

也和 **hope** 不同，试比较下面句子：

We're <u>expecting</u> rain soon. 我们预料不久就会下雨。

We're <u>hoping for</u> rain. 我们盼望下雨。

跟不定式：

I didn't <u>expect</u> to find you here. 我没料到在这里碰到你。

How can you <u>expect</u> to make progress if you don't work hard? 如果你不下功夫，怎么能指望进步？

wait 和 **hope** 后也可跟不定式，但意思不同：

I'm <u>waiting</u> to see the doctor. 我在等着看病。

I <u>hope</u> to see you soon. 希望不久能见到你。

跟复合结构：

You can't <u>expect</u> me to approve of it. 你不能指望我赞同此事。

I didn't <u>expect</u> you back so soon. 我没料到你这么早回来。

hope for 和 **wait for** 后也跟这种结构，但意思不同：

We're <u>hoping for</u> you to come up with some new ideas. 我们希望你能提出一些新想法。

I'm still <u>waiting for</u> you to pay back my money. 我还在等你还我的钱。

跟从句：

We <u>expected</u> that you would stay for a few days. 我们预计你会待几天的。

He never <u>expected</u> that those plans would come about. 他从未料到那些计划会实现。

hope 后也可跟从句，但意思不同：

I hope <u>she'll come and join</u> us. 我希望她会来参加我们的活动。

另外，**expect a baby** 表示"怀孕"：

Juliana is <u>expecting a baby</u>. 朱莉安娜怀孕了。

expect 有时还可表示"想""揣想"（一般和 **I** 连用）：

I <u>expect</u> you're right. 我（揣）想你是对的。

I <u>expect</u> I might as well be going. 我想我该走了。

205 **factory—mill—plant—works**

factory 是一般工厂的通称：

They started the <u>factory</u> in 1989. 这家工厂他们是 1989 年开办的。

a clothing <u>factory</u> 成衣厂   a soap <u>factory</u> 肥皂厂

a textile <u>factory</u> 纺织厂   a glass <u>factory</u> 玻璃工厂

an auto (mobile) <u>factory</u> 汽车工厂

an armament <u>factory</u> 兵工厂

❀ **mill** 也指工厂，多指棉纺厂、钢厂、造纸厂等加工原料的工厂：

Paper is made in a paper <u>mill</u>. 纸是在造纸厂造的。

A cotton <u>mill</u> makes thread from cotton. 棉纺厂把棉花纺成线。

a textile <u>mill</u> 棉纺厂   a steel <u>mill</u> 钢厂

a lumber <u>mill</u> 木材加工厂   a saw <u>mill</u> 锯木厂

a woollen <u>mill</u> 毛纺厂   a silk-reeling <u>mill</u> 丝厂

❀ **plant** 多指重工业工厂：

They have just built a new chemical <u>plant</u>. 他们刚刚修建了一座化工厂。

an aircraft <u>plant</u> 飞机工厂   a power <u>plant</u> 发电厂

a steel <u>plant</u> 炼钢厂   an auto <u>plant</u> 汽车工厂

nuclear <u>plant</u> 核电厂   the Boeing <u>Plant</u> 波音飞机工厂

❀ **works** 可指各类工厂：

The steel <u>works</u> is closed for the holidays. 钢厂因放假关门了。

glass <u>works</u> 玻璃工厂   water <u>works</u> 自来水厂

iron <u>works</u> 炼铁厂   cement <u>works</u> 水泥厂

gas <u>works</u> 煤气厂   brick <u>works</u> 砖厂

206 fair—carnival

fair 有几种意思：

展销会，交易会：

the Frankfort Book Fair 法兰克福书展

a trade fair 交易会

the Guangzhou Commodities Fair 广州商品交易会

农业展销会（农产品及农业设备在此展销，并举行各种牲畜、产品竞赛，还有大型娱乐机器供人们乘坐。）

户外游乐场（有各种设备可供乘坐，可以玩各种游戏并获奖）在美国称为 carnival。

❀ carnival 还有一个意思，就是指狂欢节（活动），包括在街上跳舞、饮酒、游行：

Carnival in Rio 里约热内卢的狂欢节

Each summer the town holds a carnival. 每年夏天，这座城市都举行一次狂欢节。

在香港许多人把它称作嘉年华会。

207 fairly—quite—rather—pretty

这四个词都表示程度，可用在形容词或副词前面。

❀ fairly 表示"相当地"：

It was a fairly large house of red brick. 那是一座相当大的红色砖房。

They are getting along fairly well. 他们相处得相当好。

但它的意思不是很强。如果你讲"She is fairly clever."，这人听到未必很高兴。

❀ quite 也可译作"相当"（但意思比 fairly 稍强一点）：

This is a quite comfortable house. 这是一栋相当舒适的房子。

He speaks Russian quite well. 他的俄语讲得相当好。

quite 还可修饰名词：

There were quite a lot of people at the party. 晚会上有相当多的人。

I have quite a number of books to give you. 我有相当多的书要给你。

有时表示"相当不错（好）的"：

That was quite a party. 这是一个相当成功的晚会。

That's quite a story. 这是一个相当不错的故事。

❀ **rather** 也可译成"相当"（但意思比 **quite** 更强一些）：

I have been rather unwell this week. 这星期我身体相当不好。

She was thin and rather tall. 她很瘦，个子相当高。

它还可用来修饰动词或名词：

It rather surprised me. 它使我相当吃惊。

I was rather pleased when I won the prize. 我获奖后相当高兴。

❀ **pretty** 也表示"相当"，在口语中用得比较多：

Her sister is still pretty sick. 她姐姐的病仍然相当重。

I suppose you can speak French pretty well by now. 我想你现在法语已说得相当好了。

pretty soon 表示"不久"，**pretty well** 表示"快要"：

Pretty soon the lilacs would be in bloom. 不久，丁香就要开花了。

I've pretty well finished. 我快完（成）了。

208 **false—falsehood—falseness—falsity—falsify**

后四个词都是 false 派生出的。

❀ **false** 表示"（虚）伪的"：

It produces a false impression. 它造成一个虚假的印象。

The information might be false. 这项情报可能是虚假的。

false diamond 假钻石	a false friend 假朋友
false modesty 假谦虚	a false passport 假护照
false teeth 假牙	a false alarm 虚惊

❀ **falsehood** 表示"谎言""假话"：

The prisoner told a number of falsehoods. 犯人讲了许多谎言。

Truth, if exaggerated, may become falsehood. 真理说过了头会成为假话。

❀ **falseness** 表示"虚假（性）""不可靠"：

The falseness of the declaration was obvious. 这一宣言显然是虚假的。

This is enough to prove the <u>falseness</u> of such a conception. 这足以证明这种设想是不可靠的。

❀ **falsity** 表示"假"：

He is not troubled by the truth or <u>falsity</u> of the author's account. 对于作者说法的真假，他并不在意。

There's no way we can tell the truth or <u>falsity</u> of a story. 没有办法判断一个故事是真是假。

❀ **falsify** 为动词，表示"窜改""伪造"：

He <u>falsified</u> the accounts. 他窜改账目。

This book <u>falsified</u> the events of the Civil War. 这本书窜改内战的史实。

209 familiar—familiar to—familiar with

familiar 表示"熟悉的"：

I could hear Mary playing a <u>familiar</u> tune. 我可以听见玛丽在弹奏一支熟悉的曲子。

Smog is a <u>familiar</u> occurence in that city. 那座城市经常发生雾霾。

❀ **familiar to** 表示"（对某人）很熟悉"：

These folk tunes are <u>familiar to</u> the local people. 这些民间曲子当地人是很熟悉的。

French is as <u>familiar to</u> him as English. 他对法语就像英语一样熟悉。

❀ **familiar with** 表示"对（某事物）很熟悉"：

She has become <u>familiar with</u> the house. 她对这房子已变得很熟悉。

I am of course <u>familiar with</u> his works. 我当然对他的作品很熟悉。

210 famous—well—known—notorious—infamous

这四个词都是形容词，可用来修饰人。

❀ **famous** 表示"著名的""出名的"：

He is <u>famous</u> for his fine acting. 他因其优秀演技而出名。

The town is <u>famous</u> for its hot springs. 这座城市因其温泉而出名。

❀ **well-known** 的意思也差不多，也表示"出名的""著名的"：

Mother Teresa is <u>well-known</u> for her work with the poor. 特里萨修女因其在穷人中间的工作而出名。

It's a <u>well-known</u> fact that smoking can cause lung cancel. 抽烟能导致肺癌是众所周知的事实。

这两个词中，**famous** 意思更强一些，出名的地区更广一些，知道的人更多一些。用在动词后时，连字符可以去掉：

The building became very <u>well-known</u>. 这座大楼变得很出名了。

✿ notorious 表示"臭名昭著的""声名狼藉的"：

Captain Kidd was a <u>notorious</u> pirate. 基德船长是臭名昭著的海盗。

The guest was really a <u>notorious</u> jewel thief. 这个客人实际上是一个声名狼藉的偷窃珠宝的惯犯。

✿ infamous /ˈɪnfəməs/ 表示"臭名昭著的""无耻的"：

Blue Beard was an <u>infamous</u> character. 蓝胡子是一个臭名昭著的人物。

I was shocked by her <u>infamous</u> behaviour. 她的无耻行径使我吃惊。

211 far

far 可用作形容词，也可用作副词。

用作形容词时表示"远的"：

It's very cold in the <u>Far</u> North. 远北地区十分寒冷。

<u>Far</u> from eye, far from heart. 眼不见，心不烦。（谚语）

the <u>Far</u> East 远东

主要用在疑问句和否定句中：

How <u>far</u> is it from your office to the bank? 从你办公室到银行有多远？

The youth hostel is not <u>far</u> from here. 青年旅舍离这儿不远。

在肯定句中，多用 **a long way**（比 **far**... 自然）：

The station is <u>a long way</u> from here. 车站离这里很远。

far 和 **a long way** 都可和副词 **away** 连用：

The lightning was <u>far away</u>. 打闪的地方很远。

He is <u>far away</u> in Australia. 他远在澳大利亚。

The village is quite <u>a long way</u> away. 那个村子很远。

在现代英语中很少用 **far** 修饰名词，而用 **distant** 和 **far-away** 修饰。

I'd like to travel to distant lands. 我愿到远方旅行。

This is no longer a distant dream. 这已不再是遥远的梦。

They could hear the far-away sound of a waterfall. 他们可以听到远处的瀑布声。

far 也可用作副词。在表示"远"时，多用于疑问及否定句：

How far did you go? 你们走了多远？

We didn't go far. 我们没走远。

在肯定句中多用 **a long way** 代替它：

"Did you walk far?" "Yes, we walked a long way." "你们走得远吗？" "是的，走得很远。"

但 **far** 还有很多用法：

和一副词或一介词短语连用（仍表示"远"的意思）：

Her departure was not far off. 她离开的日子已经不远了。

They live not far behind the hill. 他们住在山那边不远的地方。

He's far past forty. 他已 40 好几了。

说明程度：

How far can he be trusted? 对他能信任到什么程度？

How far was he responsible for what had happened? 对发生的情况他有多少责任？

I didn't know science had got that far. 我不知道科学已发展到这种程度。

和比较级连用，说明程度：

He did far better than I had expected. 他比我预期的干得好得多。

You have far more imagination than I have. 你的想象力比我强得多。

There were far more people out than last Sunday. 这天出来的人远比上星期天多。

和 **too** 连用，表示"太……"：

He was at the station far too early. 他到车站到得太早了。

The lights were far too brilliant. 灯光过于明亮。

The room was small and contained far too much furniture. 房间很小，而家具实在太多。

还可用于许多短语：

Your conduct, as far as I can see, is absolutely unjustifiable. 照我看，你的行为是完全没有道理的。

As far as he was concerned, things were going well. 就他来说，事情是很顺利的。

That is by far the best choice. 这是最好的选择。

Your work is far from (being) satisfactory. 你的工作远不能令人满意。

So far she had been a great success. 到目前为止，她是很成功的。

She doesn't have any sisters so far as I know. 据我所知，她并没有姐妹。

212 farther—further—farthest—furthest

farther 和 further 是 far 的比较级。

farther 表示"更远"：

Manchester is farther from London than Oxford is. 曼彻斯特离伦敦比牛津远。

The bar is at the farther end of the room. 酒吧在这个房间更远的那一头。

further 也可表示"更远"：

On the further side of the hill there is a cottage. 在小山更远的那边，有一座农舍。

She sees no further than her nose. 她鼠目寸光。

但它有更多的意思：

更多的：

He gave no further thought to it. 他不再想它。

I will give you further details later. 我以后再给你谈更多的细节。

另外的，别的：

There being no further business, the meeting was closed. 由于没有别的事要谈，会议闭幕了。

They made further valuable suggestions. 他们提了另外一些宝贵的建议。

进一步的，另行：

They made further arrangements. 他们做了进一步的安排。

The office will be closed until further notice. 这办事处在另行通知前暂

时关闭。

（作副词）进一步：

She did not argue <u>further</u> about it. 她没对此做进一步的争辩。

We'll enquire <u>further</u> into this question. 对这个问题我们将做进一步的调查。

（作副词）再，更多：

The situation there deteriorated <u>further</u>. 那里的局势进一步恶化。

She refused to talk <u>further</u> that evening. 那天晚上，她拒绝再谈。

❀ **farthest** 为 far 的最高级，表示"最远的"：

Which of these cities are the <u>farthest (furthest)</u> from us? 这些城市中哪个离我们最远？

Jane sat <u>farthest</u> from the hostess. 简坐得离女主人最远。

furthest 也表示同样的意思：

The <u>furthest</u> tree is three miles away. 最远的树离这儿三英里。

They have travelled <u>furthest</u> to take part in the Festival. 他们走了最远的路程来参加这个艺术节。

213 fast—quick—rapid—swift

这四个词都有"快"的意思，在日常口语中后两个词用得比较少。

❀ **fast** 日常用得最多，可作形容词，也可作副词：

My watch is <u>fast</u>. 我的表快了。

a <u>fast</u> train 快车　　　　　　<u>fast</u> food 快餐

Don't drive so <u>fast</u>. 车不要开得这么快。

It was a wonderful city, and growing very <u>fast</u>. 这是一座吸引人的城市，发展很快。

❀ **quick** 也用得很多，表示"赶快的""迅速的"，多作形容词：

He was <u>quick</u> to notice his mistake. 他迅速发现了他的错误。

He is a <u>quick</u> (fast) worker. 他是干活很快的人。

也可用作副词：

I'll be round as <u>quick</u> as I can. 我将尽快来。

The train will get you there <u>quicker</u> than the bus. 坐火车去那里比坐公

共汽车更快。

quickly 也是副词，也表示"快"：

His heart began to beat quickly. 他的心脏开始跳得快起来。

Good of you to come so quickly. 你这么快来太好了。

❀ **rapid** 表示"快速的""迅速的"：

Easy stories are the best material to teach rapid reading. 浅易故事是教快速阅读的最好材料。

This type of drill should be given at a rapid tempo. 做这种练习要快速进行。

相应的副词为 **rapidly**，表示"迅速地"：

Rabbits multiply rapidly. 兔子繁殖很迅速。

After sunset, the sky darkened rapidly. 太阳落山之后，天迅速暗了下来。

❀ **swift** 也表示"快的""迅速的"：

You'll need a swift horse to take you there. 你需要一匹快马把你送到那里。

He gave them a swift reply. 他迅速给了他们回答。

相应的副词为 **swiftly**，也表示"快""迅速"：

He came in swiftly. 他迅速走了进来。

And then things happened very swiftly. 之后情况一个个迅速发生。

214 fat

表示"胖"的词很多。有些是中性词（即没有贬义的词），如：

big	broad	bulky	chunky	corpulent	fleshy
heavy	plump	stocky	stout	thick-set	

stout 表示"壮实的""发福的"，**plump** 表示"丰满的"，**heavy** 表示"胖的"，**stocky** 表示"矮胖的"：

She became stout as she grew old. 她年纪大了就发福起来。

She's not grossly fat, but she's plump. 她不算很胖，但很丰满。

The boy was so heavy that he needed extra-large shirts. 这小伙子是那

样胖，他需要买特大号的衬衫。

She was a <u>big</u> woman with a dark complexion. 她是个肤色较黑的大个子女人。

His friend was a <u>stocky</u>, bald man in his late forties. 他的朋友是一个矮胖、秃顶、接近 50 岁的男子。

He was a <u>corpulent</u> and short-tempered little man. 他是个胖胖的、脾气暴躁的小个子男人。

a short <u>thick-set</u> man 一个矮胖的男人

有些甚至带有欣赏的意味，如：

beefy	buxom	chubby	cuddly	portly
solid	tubby	well-built		

其中 **well-built** 表示"身材魁梧的"，**buxom** 表示"胖乎乎的"，**chubby**（多形容儿童）表示"圆滚滚的"，**portly** 表示"胖胖的"：

His friends were all solid, <u>well-built</u> people. 他的朋友都是身体结实、身材魁梧的人。

He liked the <u>buxom</u> ladies in Ruben's paintings. 他喜欢鲁宾画中胖乎乎的女人。

She had grown into a <u>chubby</u> attractive child. 她已长成一个圆圆胖胖、招人喜爱的孩子。

Sitting there was a <u>portly</u> gentleman in his late fifties. 坐在那里的是一位胖胖的接近 60 岁的男士。

也有些词是不太客气、人们不爱听的，如：

dumpy	fat	flabby	gross	obese
overweight	podgy	pudgy	squat	

How <u>fat</u> Giles is getting! 贾尔斯长得真胖！

She's getting old and <u>flabby</u>. 她年纪大了，胖起来了。

<u>Obese</u> people tend to have higher blood pressure than lean people. 胖人比瘦人更容易患高血压。

She was a little woman, and would probably, one day, be a <u>dumpy</u> one. 她现在是个小个子女人，可能有一天会成为矮胖的女人。

obese 和 **overweight** 可用在技术性文章中：

Really <u>obese</u> children tend to grow up into <u>obese</u> men or women. 真正胖的孩子容易长成胖男人和胖女人。

<u>Overweight</u> people run a slightly higher risk of cancer than people of average weight. 胖人比正常体重的人患癌症的风险要稍高一点。

215 **female—feminine—effeminate**

female 表示"女的""雌性的"：

Mares and cows are <u>female</u> animals. 母马和母牛都是雌性动物。

The hunter caught a <u>female</u> monkey. 猎人捕获了一只母猴。

female 也可用作名词，多指雌性动物：

The litter produced two males and seven <u>females</u>. 一窝产下两只公的、七只母的。

The male fertilizes the <u>female's</u> eggs. 雄性动物使雌性动物的卵子受精。

也可指"妇女""女人"：

<u>Females</u> constitute a slight majority of the population. 妇女约占人口的一半稍多一点儿。

Hay fever affects males more than <u>females</u>. 患枯草热的男人比女人多。

❀ **feminine** 指"（像）女性的"：

Gentleness was long considered a <u>feminine</u> trait. 温柔长期以来被认为是女人的特点。

<u>feminine</u> interests（hobbies/pursuits）女人的兴趣（爱好 / 追求）

❀ **effeminate** 只用来修饰男人，表示"女人气的"：

They find European men slightly <u>effeminate</u>. 他们发现欧洲的男人略带一点儿女人气。

这个词最好不用，因为许多人对它有反感。

216 **few—a few**

few, a few 都可用来修饰可数名词，但意思不一样。

❀ **few** 表示"很少"（接近否定）：

He has <u>few</u> friend (= He has hardly any friends). 他朋友很少（几乎没有朋友）。

<u>Few</u> words are best. 少说话最好。（谚语）

❀ **a few** 则有肯定的意思，表示"有几个"：

I've still got a <u>few</u> things to pack. 我还有几样东西要装进去。

Yes, I do know a <u>few</u> words of French. 是的，我的确认识几个法语单词。

△ **quite a few** 或 **a good few** 表示"好多""相当多"：

<u>Quite a few</u> people went to the game. 相当多人去观看了球赛。

The basket had <u>quite a few</u> rotten apples in it. 篮子里有好些烂苹果。

△在 **past (next) few** 中仍有肯定意义，表示"过去（将来）几"：

Ignore this letter if you have paid in the <u>past few</u> days. 如果再过去几天你已付款，这信可不予理会。

Can you come and look after him for the <u>next few</u> days? 在以后几天，你能否来照顾他？

△ **few, a few** 还可作代词，也有同样区别：

用于否定意义

<u>Few</u> of my acquaintances like Sheila. 我认识的人中很少有人喜欢希拉。

I have very <u>few</u> left. 我剩下很少了。

<u>Few</u> of them are any good. 它们没有几个有用。

用于肯定意义

Only a <u>few</u> of the children can read. 只有几个孩子能阅读。

I met a <u>few</u> of my friends there. 在那里我碰到了几个朋友。

I'd like a <u>few</u> of the red ones. 我想要几个红的。

217 **film—picture—movie**

film 指"电影""影片"：

Have you seen the <u>film</u> *Titanic*? 电影《泰坦尼克号》你看过吗？

They were shooting a <u>film</u> in the mountains. 他们在山里拍一部影片。

❀ 在英国有时称作 picture：

Let's go and see a good <u>picture</u>. 咱们去看一部好电影吧。

The chief <u>picture</u> was *Her Dearest Enemy*. 主片是《她最亲爱的敌人》。

❀ 在美国常常称作 movie：

Let's see a light <u>movie</u> for a change. 咱们去看一部轻松的电影换换口味吧。

That <u>movie</u> is now being shown on TV. 这部影片正在电视上播放。

△去看电影在英国用 go to the cinema (the pictures) 表示，在美国则说 go to the movies：

Everyone has <u>gone to the cinema</u>. 大家都去看电影去了。

I'm going to the pictures tonight. 我今晚要去看电影。

△电影院在英国称为 cinema，在美国称为 movie theater 或 movie house。

218 finally—at last—eventually—in the end—at the end

这些词都表示"最后"，但有一些细微的差别。

❀ finally 用得比较广泛，可用于一般意义：

She <u>finally</u> gained control of herself. 她最后控制住了自己。

What decision did you <u>finally</u> arrive at? 你们最后作出了什么决定？

有时也可表示经过长时间等待：

Steve has <u>finally</u> found a job. 史蒂夫最后找到了一份工作。

<u>Finally</u> in 1863 an insurrection broke out. 最后，在 1863 年爆发了武装起义。

❀ at last 表示等待、不耐烦的情绪更强一些（暗示经过一个长的过程）：

<u>At last</u> he knew the meaning of life. 最后他了解了生命的意义。

He felt himself <u>at last</u> absolutely free. 他感到自己最后完全自由了。

❀ eventually 也表示经过一些曲折，"最后"：

It was a long journey, but we <u>eventually</u> arrived. 这是一趟长途旅行，但我们最后还是到了。

<u>Eventually</u> we all must die. 最后，我们都会离开人世。

❀ **in the end** 也表示经过各种曲折、碰到各种问题，"最后……"：

In the end, however, she had reaped her reward. 但最后她还是得到了报答。

At first he opposed the marriage, but in the end he gave his consent. 开始他反对这桩婚姻，但最后他同意了。

❀ **at the end** 只表示"在末尾"：

A declarative sentence usually has a full stop at the end. 陈述句句末常有一个句号。

He wished to be paid at the beginning of the week and not at the end. 他希望一星期开始时发工资，而不是在周末。

219 first—firstly

first 表示"第一个"，可作定语：

The first place I visited was Hyde Park. 我参观的第一个地方是海德公园。

The first thing to do was to have a meal. 第一件该做的事是吃饭。

还可用作副词，表示：

初次，开始时：

We first went there last year. 去年，我们第一次到那里。

When we first lived here, there were no buses. 我们开始在这里住时，没有公共汽车。

先，首先：

First think and then speak. 先想后说。（谚语）

First, he read all the advertisements in the newspaper. 首先，他看了报上所有的广告。

❀ 副词 **firstly** 也可表示"首先""第一"：

Firstly (First), let me deal with the most important difficulty. 首先，让我来处理最大的困难。

Firstly, she did not intend to marry at all; secondly, she meant to go on with her studies. 首先，她根本不想结婚，其次她打算继续上学。

有些人不爱用这个词，而愿用 **first** 代替：

There are three reasons against it: First... 有三个反对理由：首先……

要加以强调时可说 **first of all**（这里不能用 **firstly**）：

First of all, you must be frank. 首先你必须坦白。

First of all, let me say how glad I am to be here. 首先，我说我到这里很高兴。

如果要把开始的情况和后来的情况加以对比，可用 **at first** 这个短语：

At first he was a little shy, but now he acts more natural. 开始时他有些腼腆，但现在他表现得比较自然了。

There was a little trouble at first but things were soon quiet. 开始有些麻烦，但很快形势就平静下来。

220 fit—suit

fit 表示"合身"（指大小合适）：

The coat doesn't fit me. 这件大衣我穿不合身。

This dress fitted her perfectly. 这件连衣裙她穿非常合身。

它的过去式通常为 **fitted**，但美国人有些用 **fit** 这个形式：

The pants fit him well when he bought them. 这条裤子他买的时候很合身。

英国人在口语中也有用这一形式的：

Two years ago these pants fit me perfectly. 两年前，这条裤子我穿完全合身。

suit 的意思与它略有不同，除了大小还指色彩、式样等方面合适：

Casual clothes really don't suit her. 便装的确对她不合适。

A green dress won't suit me. 绿色连衣裙我穿不合适。

suit 还可指其他方面合适：

The arrangement suits them both. 这样的安排对两人都合适。

Would Saturday night suit you? 星期六晚上对你方便吗？

221 flat—apartment—condominium

在英国，单元房（公寓）称为 **flat**：

He rented a flat in central London. 他在伦敦市中心租了一套公寓。

在美国多称为 apartment：

The Smiths live in the apartment above ours. 史密斯一家住在我们楼上的一套公寓里。

住宅楼称为 apartment building (house)：

Several apartment buildings were destroyed. 几座住宅楼被摧毁了。

这类楼房或住房如为住户私人拥有，也可称为 condominium /ˌkɒndəˈmɪnɪəm/，在口语中简称为 condo /ˈkɒndəʊ/：

He urged me to buy a condominium. 他敦促我买了一套住房。

在英国，住宅楼称为 a block of flats：

The building was pulled down to make way for a block of flats. 这座楼被拆掉了，腾出地来盖一座住宅楼。

222 floor—ground

floor 主要指"地板""室内地面"：

The floor of the room is made of hardwood. 房间地板是硬木做的。

The hall has a tiled floor. 大厅里是瓷砖地板。

floor space 表示（房间的）面积：

Now we have houses with a total floor space of 27,000 square metres. 现在我们房子的总面积为 2.7 万平方米。

floor 也可指楼层：

My flat is on the top floor. 我的公寓在顶层。

Her room was on the ground floor. 她的房间在一层。

在英国 the ground floor 指一层，the first floor 指第二层。在美国一层称为 the first floor，第二层称为 the second floor。

✿ 地面通常称 the ground：

He was lying on the ground. 他躺在地上。

The ground all round was very wet and marshy. 四周的土地潮湿、多沼泽。

但海底可称为 ocean floor 或 sea floor：

They have found oil under the ocean floor. 他们在海底找到了石油。

Aquanauts go to the floor of the sea. 海洋研究人员到海底去探查。

223 folk—folks

folk 表示"人们"，美国人多加 -s，英国则多不加：

Different folks like different things. 不同的人喜欢不同的东西。

They were all decent folk. 他们都是正派人。

在美国 folks 常用来表示"家里人（尤其是父母）"：

I'm going home to see my folks tomorrow. 我明天回家去看父母。

有时用来称呼一群人：

Well, folks, shall we go out this afternoon? 伙计们，咱们下午要不要出去？

folk 还可用作定语，表示"民间的"：

folk music 民间音乐   folk songs 民歌

a fork singer 民歌手   folk art 民间艺术

folk dance 民间舞蹈   folk tales 民间传说

224 following—as follows

following 表示"第二个""下一个"（用作定语）：

She stayed with us until the following afternoon. 她在我们这儿一直住到第二天下午。

A rebellion broke out the following year. 第二年发生了叛乱。

也可表示"下面的""下述的"（也用作定语）：

He did it for the following reasons. 他这样做是为了下述原因。

The Labour Office published the following statistics. 劳动局公布了下面的统计数字。

还可以引起一个状语，表示"在……之后"（"紧接……之后"）：

Following the speech, there will be a few minutes for questions. 报告之后，有几分钟提问题的时间。

He died June 6 in Los Angeles following a heart attack. 由于心脏病发作，在 6 月 6 日他于洛杉矶逝世。

❀ "如下"多由 as follows 表示（多用作表语）：

His arguments are as follows. 他的论点如下。

He received a note which ran as follows. 他收到一封短信，内容如下。

225 football—soccer

football 在英国指足球，而在美国指"橄榄球"。在美国，足球称为 soccer /ˈsɒkə/。在英国，橄榄球称为 American football（美式足球）。
在英国，足球赛称为 football match：

Do you want to come to the <u>football match</u>? 你想来看足球赛吗？

在美国，橄榄球赛称为 football game：

Our school won the <u>football game</u>. 我们学校赢了橄榄球赛。

226 for

for 是一个非常活跃的介词，它有很多意思，可以表示：

为了（为了某人，为了某一目的等）：

He would do anything <u>for</u> her. 为了她他可以做任何事情。

He had an operation <u>for</u> a heart disease. 他因心脏病动了一次手术。

因为，由于（常有较灵活的译法）：

France is famous <u>for</u> its wines. 法国因葡萄酒出名。

I'm much obliged to you <u>for</u> telling me. 你告诉了我，我非常感激。

对于：

I've always had a passion <u>for</u> music. 我一向对音乐很热爱。

He expresses sympathy <u>for</u> the common people. 他表现了对普通百姓的同情。

给予（某人），供……用的（常有较灵活的译法，有时译作"的"）：

He didn't have much time <u>for</u> diversion. 他没有多少娱乐的时间。

就……来说：

He was tall <u>for</u> his age. 以他的年龄来说，他的个子是很高的。

<u>For</u> so young a man he had read widely. 作为这样年轻的人，他书读得是够多的。

以……价钱（代价）：

He is willing to work <u>for</u> nothing. 他愿意义务地工作。

作为（意思接近 as）：

I'll keep it <u>for</u> a souvenir. 我将把它留作纪念。

What did you have for lunch? 你午饭吃什么？

前往（某地）：

I bought a ticket for Milan. 我买了一张去米兰的车票。

The ship was for Liverpool. 这艘船是开往利物浦的。

表示时间长度：

For a short time he was an ambassador to France. 有一段不长的时间，他是驻法大使。

He lived at Danvers Street for two months. 他在丹弗斯街住了两个月。

表示距离：

For miles and miles you see nothing but trees. 数英里内，你看到的只是树。

That afternoon we walked for twenty miles. 那天下午，我们走了 20 英里路。

（引起短语作表语）赞成，主张：

Robert was for cutting down the cost of production. 罗伯特主张降低生产成本。

The organization was for an independent Ireland. 这个组织主张爱尔兰独立。

引起短语表示不定式逻辑上的主语：

It would be best for you to write to him. 最好是你给他写信。

The simplest thing is for him to resign at once. 最简单的办法是他立即辞职。

△ **for** 还可用作连词，表示"因为"：

The days were short, for it was now December. 白天很短，因为现在已经是 12 月。

He shook his head, for he thought differently. 他摇了摇头，因为他有不同想法。

这种用法主要出现在书面语中，一般都有逗号把它和前面的分句分开，对前面情况进行解释。

227 **forever—for ever**

forever 有两个意思，一是表示"永远地"：

I hope we'll remain friends <u>forever</u>. 我希望我们永远做朋友。

The lovers promised to be faithful <u>forever</u>. 那对情侣许诺永远相爱。

在这样用时，**for** 和 **ever** 也可以分开写：

She said she would stay here <u>for ever</u>. 她说她将永远留在这里。

That was a point which she had <u>for ever</u> decided. 那是她已永远决定了的一点。

另一个意思是"老是"：

He was <u>forever</u> singing his own praises. 他老是自我赞美。

She was <u>forever</u> complaining about her job. 她老是抱怨自己的工作。

这样用时，只有 **forever** 一种写法（不能分开写）。

228 former—late—latter

former 表示"前……"（现已离职）或"从前的"：

<u>former</u> President Nixon 前总统尼克松

It was the <u>former</u> capital of Turkey. 它是土耳其过去的首都。

late 指"已故的"：

She was an admirer of the <u>late</u> president. 她是已故总统的一位崇拜者。

her <u>late</u> husband 她已故的丈夫

former 还有一个意思"前者"：

Both the pink and blue dresses are pretty, but I like the <u>former</u> better. 那件粉红连衣裙和蓝色连衣裙都很漂亮，但我更喜欢粉红连衣裙。

与之相对，**latter** 表示"后者"：

John and James are brothers. The former is a teacher; the <u>latter</u> is an engineer. 约翰和詹姆斯是两兄弟，前者是教师，后者是工程师。

229 fortune—luck

fortune 表示"命运"或"运气"：

<u>Fortune</u> favours the brave. 命运（之神）偏爱勇敢的人。（谚语）

Let's leave it to <u>fortune</u> where we spend our vacation. 在哪里度假，让运气来决定。

good fortune 表示 "好运气"：

I've heard of your good fortune. 我听说了你的好运。

By good fortune he was not hurt. 他运气好，没受伤。

❀ **luck** 也表示 "运气"：

I'll go and try my luck. 我去碰碰运气。

We have so much bad luck. 我们遇到了很多倒霉的事。

也可表示 "好运气"：

I wish you luck! 祝你好运！

I had the luck to find him at home. 我运气不错，他正好在家。

△这两个词意思相近，**fortune** 一般指较大的事，**luck** 大小事都可指，也可用于 **bad luck**, **awful luck**。

230 **forward—forwards**

forward 可用作副词、形容词和动词。作副词时表示 "向前"：

He came forward and shook me by the hand. 他走上前，握了握我的手。

Sophia hastened forward. 索菲娅匆忙向前走。

可用于 **look forward to**，表示 "盼望"，跟名词或动名词：

I began to look forward to the ball (day). 我开始盼望那个舞会（日子）。

She was looking forward to being a scientist. 她盼望成为一个科学家。

还可用于 **put (bring) forward**，表示 "提出"：

They had put forward a plan for improving the rate of production. 他们提出了一个提高生产率的计划。

He brought forward several new ideas. 他提出了几个新想法。

forward 作形容词时表示 "向前的"：

Drag hinders the forward motion of the aircraft. 空气阻力妨碍飞机向前的运动。

forward 作动词时表示 "转寄"：

They forwarded his mail to his new address. 他们把他的邮件转寄到他的新地址。

❀ **forwards** 也是副词，也是 "向前" 的意思，主要用于 **backwards and forwards**，表示 "来回地"：

He walked <u>backwards and forwards</u> on the lawns. 他在草坪上来回走。

The train goes <u>backwards and forwards</u> between the two towns. 这列火车在两座城市间来回开。

231 free—freely

free 是形容词，表示"自由的"：

He felt himself at last <u>free</u>. 他最后感到自己自由了。

<u>free</u> enterprise 自由经营　　　<u>free</u> trade 自由贸易

<u>free</u> market 自由市场　　　<u>free</u> verse 自由诗体

还可表示"免费的"：

The refreshments are <u>free</u>. 点心是免费招待的。

You need not pay—it is <u>free</u>. 你不必付钱，这是免费的。

也可表示"没事的，有空儿的""没人占的"：

Are you <u>free</u> this evening? 你今晚有空儿吗？

Is this seat <u>free</u>? 这个座位有人占吗？

free 也用作副词，表示"免费地"：

The books are given away <u>free</u>. 这些书是免费赠送的。

He was admitted <u>free</u>. 他免费入场。

❀ **freely** 也是副词，表示"自由地"：

You may speak <u>freely</u>; say what you like. 你可以自由讲话，想说什么就说什么。

232 from

from 最重要的意思是"从""由"。

可以指地点：

The sounds came <u>from</u> the kitchen. 声音由厨房里传来。

She was <u>from</u> Yorkshire. 她从约克郡来。

后面可以跟副词、介词短语，甚至从句：

Then I heard them calling me <u>from</u> below. 这时我听见他们从下面叫我。

The car stopped short only a few inches <u>from</u> where I stood. 汽车在离我站的地方仅几英寸处突然停住。

也可指时间：

Lunch is <u>from</u> eleven a.m. to two p.m.. 从上午11点到下午2点是午饭时间。

<u>From</u> the second half of July his health began to deteriorate. 从7月中起，他的健康开始恶化。

也可表示其他关系：

She received a great deal of praise <u>from</u> Sophia. 她受到索菲娅的大力赞扬。

Great oaks <u>from</u> little acorns grow. 巨大的橡树由小小的橡子长成。（谚语）

还可表示一些其他意思，如：离……（多远）：

The town is sixty miles <u>from</u> London. 这个城镇离伦敦有60英里。

Far <u>from</u> eye, far <u>from</u> heart. 眼不见，心不烦。（谚语）

由于，因为（可有较灵活的译法）：

Famine came and tens of thousands perished <u>from</u> starvation. 灾荒来了，成千上万的人饿死。

She shivered <u>from</u> cold. 她冷得发抖。

阻止……做某事：

He dissuaded me <u>from</u> doing it. 他劝我别做。

I want to save you <u>from</u> making a mistake. 我想帮助你避免犯错误。

从……判断，根据：

<u>From</u> the evidence, he must be guilty. 从证据判断，他一定是有罪的。

<u>From</u> his appearance, you wouldn't think he was old. 从他的外表看，你不会想到他很老。

和……不同（有区别）：

He's different <u>from</u> his brother in character. 他和他哥哥性格不同。

They could not distinguish one <u>from</u> the other. 他们没法把两者区分开。

还可构成许多短语，如：

from beginning to end 从头到尾

from start to finish 自始至终

from morning till night 从早到晚

from time to time 不时地

from door to door 挨门挨户地

from top to bottom 彻头彻尾

from head to foot 从头到脚，浑身

from hand to mouth 勉强糊口

from bad to worse 每况愈下

from now on 从现在起

from that time onwards 从那时起

from... point of view 据……看

from the bottom of one's heart 衷心地

from the first (beginning) 从开头起

apart from 除了

far from 远不是

233 -ful

-ful 词尾可加在名词后构成形容词（表示"充满"或"有某特点"），常见的如：

awful	beautiful	careful	cheerful	colourful
delightful	doubtful	eventful	fearful	forceful
fruitful	harmful	helpful	hopeful	lawful
merciful	painful	peaceful	playful	powerful
remorseful	resourceful	respectful	restful	shameful
sinful	waterful	tearful	wonderful	thankful
thoughtful	truthful			

还可加在名词后，构成另一词，表示某个数量，如：

armful	bagful	basketful	boxful	busful
cupful	glassful	handful	mouthful	pocketful
roomful	shelfful			

234 fun—funny

fun 主要指"有趣的人或事"，为不可数名词：

Tom's good fun; we all enjoy being with him. 汤姆很有意思，我们都喜欢和他在一起。

Picnics are fun. 野餐很有意思。

It's no fun standing out here. 在这儿外边站着，真没意思。

也可指"玩得高兴""兴致"：

What fun we had! 我们玩得真高兴！

Have fun! 好好玩儿！

He didn't want to spoil her fun. 他不想扫她的兴。

He's only learning French for fun. 他学法语只是为了好玩。

❀ 形容词 **funny** 的意思则不同，它表示：滑稽的：

What a funny story! 多么滑稽的故事！

He's a very funny man! 他是一个非常滑稽的人！

奇怪的：

His behaviour was rather funny. 他的行为相当奇怪。

He's a funny sort of person; I don't understand him at all. 他是一个奇怪的人，我完全看不懂他。

不舒服的：

My head had begun to ache and my stomach felt funny. 我的头开始疼，胃感到不舒服。

I feel a little funny today. 我今天感到有点儿不舒服。

G

235 gas—petrol

gas 在英国指煤气：

Turn off the gas. 把煤气关上。

Light the gas! 把煤气点上！

而在美国，**gas** 可指汽油：

I'm sorry I'm late. I had to stop for gas. 对不起我晚了，我得停车加油。

a gas station 加油站

在英国汽油称为 **petrol**：

We can fill (the car) up with petrol at the petrol station. 我们可以在加油站加油。

236 get

get 是英语中最活跃的动词之一，有许多意思和用法，主要表示：

得到，收到等（在很多情况下有较灵活的译法）：

She got such nice marks in school. 她在学校得到了非常高的分数。

I got your card from the hospital. 我收到了你从医院寄来的明信片。

有时可跟一个间接宾语：

I'll get you something to eat. 我去给你弄点儿东西吃。

I'll go and get you a chair. 我去给你搬把椅子来。

到某处（表示位置的变换，和副词或介词连用，有许多灵活的译法）：

Where did you get on? 你在哪儿上车的？

A taxi came along and I got in. 一辆出租车开过来了，我坐了上去。

使……到某处（使别的人或东西改变位置或处境，也跟副词或介词，常有灵活译法）：

Get out your fiddle, Paul. 保罗，把你的提琴拿出来。

They finally got him out of difficulty. 他们最后使他摆脱了困境。

变得（作系动词，表示状态的改变，有各种不同的译法）：

Yes, it's getting chilly. 是的，天凉起来了。

I hope you won't get over-tired. 我希望你不要过累。

（用于完成形式）有（有时有较灵活译法）：

Have you got a timetable? 你有时间表吗？

I haven't got a thermometer. 我没有体温表。

（用于 **have got** + 不定式结构）不得不，必须：

The child's got to have an operation. 孩子必须动手术。

Sophia has got to be compensated. 索菲娅必须得到补偿。

其他一些意思（主要用在口语中）：

Don't answer the telephone. I'll get it. 不要去接电话，我来接。

I don't get it; why did he do that? 我不懂他为什么这样做？

I don't get you; what do you mean? 我不明白，你是什么意思？

It really gets me when he says those stupid things. 他说那些傻话真让我生气。

I tried to get you, but your phone was engaged. 我想法给你打电话，但你的电话占线。

还可用于许多词组，如：

get about 走动，旅行

get across 让听懂，讲清楚

get ahead 取得进展

get ahead of 走在……前面

get along 进行，相处

get anywhere (nowhere) 有（没有）结果

get around 传开，绕过（困难）

get at 拿到，弄清楚

get away 走开，跑掉

get away with 逃脱（惩罚），带着……逃跑

get back 回来，找回来

get back at 报复

get by 通过

get down 下来，击落，写下来

get down to 开始认真干（某事）

get hold of 找到，拿到

get in 进，收（庄稼）

get in touch with 和……联系

get into 进入某种状态，陷入处境

get into the habit of 养成……的习惯

get off 下车，起飞，动身

get round 传开，绕过（困难）

get round to 找到时间做某事

get the better of 占上风

get through 做完（某事），通过

get to 开始（做某事）

get to work 开始干起来

get together 欢聚，碰头

get up 起床，举办（某活动）

get wind 听到风声

237 give

give 也是一个常用动词，也很有用。它主要有下面用法：

表示"给"（多跟两个宾语）：

I gave him her telephone number. 我把她的电话号码给了他。

You can give me some advice. 你可以帮我出点儿主意。

常有较灵活译法：

Can you give me more information? 你能给我提供更多情况吗？

This invitation gave him particular joy. 这个邀请使他特别高兴。

You will forgive me if I have given you pain. 如果我让你难受了，请原谅我。

I will give you my opinion if you like. 如果你愿意，我可以谈谈我的意见。

This tooth is giving me pain. 这颗牙很疼。

（跟一个宾语）表示"发出""作出""举办"等（常有较灵活译法）：

I never <u>gave</u> any such invitation. 我从不发出这样的邀请。

They <u>gave</u> a banquet in honour of the delegation. 他们举行宴会欢迎代表团。

They will <u>give</u> their decision today. 他们今天将作出决定。

Only hard work <u>gives</u> good results. 只有勤奋，才能取得好成绩。

和一个名词连用，表示一个动作：

She <u>gave</u> a loud <u>laugh</u>. 她大笑了一声。

She <u>gave</u> a satisfied <u>smile</u>. 她露出了满意的微笑。

有不少名词可以这样用，特别是那些和动词同形的名词，常见的如：

account	blow	clean	consent	cry
dry	glance	jump	knock	laugh
lecture	look	nod	notice	polish
pull	punch	push	ring	shock
shout	sigh	sketch	smile	squeeze
start	support	tap	wash	welcome

用过去分词作定语，表示"约定的""规定的"：

At the <u>given</u> time she arrived. 在约定的时间，她来了。

They were to meet at a <u>given</u> time and place. 他们将在约定的时间和地点会晤。

用过去分词引起状语，表示"在有……的情况下""如果"：

<u>Given</u> good health, I hope to finish the work this year. 如果身体情况好，我希望在今年完成这项工作。

<u>Given</u> the opportunity he might become an outstanding cartoonist. 如果有机会，他有可能成为一个杰出的漫画家。

还可以构成许多短语：

be given to 喜欢，常爱做（某事）

give and take 互相让步，交换意见

give anything (to do something) 花任何代价

give away 送人，散发，泄露，暴露

give back 还给，恢复（健康）

give credit for 应归功于

give forth 发出（香味等）

give in 交进来，妥协，投降

give in to 迁就，向……让步

give off 散发出（气味）

give on（to）俯瞰，对着

give one to understand 让人认为，向……说明

give one's due 说（某人的）公道话

give one's life (best) to 把一生（最好的一切）献给

give one's regards 向……问好

give oneself airs 摆架子

give oneself up 自首

give out 散发，颁发，宣布

give over to 移交给

give rise to 引起

give the benefit of doubt （在证明有罪前）相信无罪

give thought 考虑

give up 放弃，交出，投降，认输

give way 顺从，让步，垮塌

238 glad—pleased—cheerful—happy

glad 一般用作表语，表示"高兴的"，后面可以跟：

不定式：

Everybody was <u>glad</u> to see him back. 看到他回来，大家都很高兴。

I should be <u>glad</u> to talk to him. 我很高兴和他谈谈。

从句：

I'm so <u>glad</u> I found you in. 我很高兴，你在家。

She was <u>glad</u> that she had controlled herself. 她很高兴，她控制住了自己。

of 或 **about** 引起的短语：

I should be very <u>glad</u> of your help. 得到你的帮助，我会很高兴。

I'm glad about your new job. 我为你的新工作感到高兴。

❀ **pleased** 的意思和 **glad** 差不多，也表示"高兴的"，后面可以：

跟不定式：

Helen was pleased to see him. 海伦很高兴见到他。

I'm quite pleased to be leaving the country. 要离开这个国家了，我很高兴。

跟从句：

I'm very pleased you've decided to come. 你决定来，我很高兴。

He was pleased that Jennie should have this fine chance. 他很高兴珍妮能有这样好的机会。

跟 **at, about** 等介词引起的短语：

I'm pleased at your success. 你成功了，我很高兴。

What's she looking so pleased about? 什么事使她显得这样高兴？

不跟特别结构：

I always feel pleased when I've finished a piece of work. 完成一件作品时，我总是感到很高兴。

Isabel sounded very pleased. 伊莎贝尔听起来很高兴。

❀ **cheerful** 有两个意思：

高兴的，充满喜悦情绪的：

She is quite cheerful and talkative. 她很高兴，话很多。

She wore a cheerful expression. 她脸上带着喜悦的表情。

使人高兴的：

Yellow is a cheerful colour. 黄色是一个使人高兴的颜色。

You could never be unhappy in such a cheerful house. 在这怡人的房子里，你绝不可能不高兴。

❀ **happy** 有几个意思：

愉快的，高兴的，快乐的（可作表语，也可作定语）：

I am happy; I just heard I passed my physics exam. 我很高兴，我刚才听说我的物理考试通过了。

The story has a happy ending. 这个故事有一个愉快的结局。

幸福的：

She will be happy in future. 她将来会很幸福的。

Their marriage has been a <u>happy</u> one. 他们的婚姻是幸福的。

理想的，巧妙的，恰当的：

This seems to be a <u>happy</u> solution. 这似乎是一个理想的解决办法。

A <u>happy</u> thought struck her. 她想到一个很妙的想法。

239 go

go 是最重要的动词之一，它有许多意思及用法。

它最基本的意思是"去""走"（可以和许多副词和介词连用）：

We'd better <u>go</u> in. 我们最好进去。

Then he <u>went</u> back to his seat. 然后，他回到了他的座位上。

它可和现在分词连用，表示"去干某事"：

We often <u>go</u> skating together. 我们常常一道去溜冰。

They <u>went</u> swimming every day. 他们过去每天去游泳。

可以和 **go** 这样用的动词很多，常见的如：

cycling	drinking	fishing	hiking	hunting
rambling	shooting	shopping	skating	surfing
swimming	walking	window-shopping		

还可表示从事某行业，如 **go farming, go teaching, go nursing, go bricklaying, go soldiering**。有时还可表示从事不好的活动：

You shouldn't <u>go</u> boasting about your achievements. 你不应当夸耀你的成就。

Don't <u>go</u> looking for trouble, Maria. 不要去找麻烦了，玛丽亚。

它可以用于许多引申意义（各有不同译法）：

The pain has <u>gone</u>. 不疼了。

My chance has <u>gone</u> from me. 我的机会丧失了。

Spring has <u>gone</u> and summer is here. 春天过去，夏天来了。

We must <u>go</u> through the formal channels. 我们必须通过正式渠道。

Does this road <u>go</u> to the city? 这条路通往城里吗？

Is the machine <u>going</u> properly now? 现在机器运转正常吗？

Most of my money <u>goes</u> in rent. 我大部分的钱都用在房租上了。

The old laws must go. 这些老法律应当废除。

Some papers have gone from my desk. 我写字台上一些文件不见了。

These shoes won't go on. 这双鞋穿不上了。

表示"进行""进展"（可有许多不同译法）：

The meeting went badly. 会开得不好。

When his work wasn't going right, he was restless. 工作不顺利时，他心情很不安。

The banquet went well. 宴会办得很好。

Negotiations were going slowly, and not well. 谈判进展缓慢，也不顺利。

用作系动词，表示"变得"（可有各种不同译法）：

Your hair has gone quite white! 你的头发全白了！

She went pale at the news. 听到这个消息，她的脸色变得苍白。

When I mentioned it to him, he went red. 我对他提及此事时，他脸红了。

Has the firm gone broke? 公司破产了吗？

用在 be going to 这种结构中，表示准备做某事或预计要发生的事：

He's going to buy her some shoes. 他准备给她买双鞋。

I'm not going to argue with you tonight. 我今晚不打算和你争辩。

用过去分词作表语，表示"离开""走了"：

He went away and was gone quite a little while. 他走开了，好一段时间没回来。

How long do you think you'll be gone? 你预计你会离开多久？

可用来指东西，表示"丢失了""用完了"等：

His job was gone. 他的工作丢了。

The supplies are all gone. 补给都用完了。

Just a pain in my chest. It's gone now. 只是胸口有点儿疼，现在不疼了。

用来表示其他许多意思：

The bell has gone. 铃已经响了。

Soon the whistle went. 一会儿哨声响了。

The bulb has gone. 灯泡坏了。

His eyesight is going. 他的视力越来越差了。

My voice has gone because of my cold. 因为感冒，我嗓子哑了。

How does that song go? 那首歌是怎么唱的？

We must go cautiously. 我们必须谨慎行事。

The engine went beautifully. 发动机运转得很好。

What he says goes. 他说了算。

还可构成许多短语，如：

go about 做（某事）

go after 追求，设法得到

go against 违反，对……不利

go ahead 进行，开始（讲话）

go all out 全力以赴

go along 和……一道（干），同意

go and do something 去干某事

go around 流行，传开

go astray 误置

go at 着手（做某事），攻击

go back on 不遵守（诺言），背弃

go beyond 超出，超越

go by 根据……判断，过去

go down 下降，下落

go down on one's knee 跪下，屈膝

go Dutch 各付各的钱

go easy 省着用，慢慢（做某事）

go far 起很大作用，有出息

go fifty-fifty 平均分摊

go for 去（做某事），去找（某人）

go forward 取得进展

go from bad to worse 每况愈下

go halves 平分

go in for 从事（某活动），参加（某项比赛）

go into 调查，了解，讨论

go off 爆炸，发生（情况）

go on 发生，进行，继续

go on for 快到（某时间）

go on with 暂时用一用

go out 熄灭，过时，罢工

go out of the way to 特意做某事

go over 研究，审阅，复习，查看

go round 绕着走，到某处

go slow 不要干太累，怠工

go through 审阅，讨论，看一遍

go through with 进行到底

go to 费（工夫），花（钱）

go to bed（sleep）上床睡觉（睡着）

go together 协调，相配

go under 沉没，陷入困境

go up 上涨，上升

go up in flames 在火中烧掉

go upon 以……为依据

go with 相配，和……交朋友

go without 不吃（东西），没有

go without saying 不用说

240 good

good 为形容词，主要的意思是"好的"（有时有较灵活的译法）：

She was renowned for her <u>good</u> deeds. 她因她的善行而出名。

This watch keeps <u>good</u> time. 这个表走得很准。

还可表示"有效的""能用的"：

The check is <u>good</u> for 90 days. 这张支票 90 天内都有效。

These tires are <u>good</u> for another 10,000 miles. 这些车胎还能走 1 万英里。

还可表示"好好的""足足的"：

Take a good look at it. 好好看一看。

The woman sat down and had a good cry. 那女人坐下，好好哭了一顿。

Her parents gave her a good scolding. 她的父母好好说了她一顿。

It needs a good wash. 它需要好好洗一下。

He played a good hour. 他玩了足足一个钟头。

He ate a good half of the duck. 他把鸭子吃了一大半。

241 gotten

在美式口语中，人们常用 gotten 作为 get 的过去分词，如：

He had gone to work and gotten quite a lot done. 他去上班了，干了不少的工作。

He had gotten some tear gas in his eyes. 他眼睛里沾上了催泪瓦斯。

He must have gotten up at dawn. 他一定天一亮就起来了。

She had gotten married and given birth to a child. 她结了婚，生了一个孩子。

在书面语和正式语言中人们仍用 got 作现在分词。

在 have got（表示"有"）和 have got to（表示"必须"）两个短语中都不能用 gotten 代替 got。

242 Groups of People, Animals or Things

一群人可有多种说法，如：

a group of students 一群学生

a bunch of children 一伙孩子

a company of actors 一批演员

an army of volunteer 一大批志愿者

a band of robbers 一伙强盗

a team of experts 一队专家

a gang of criminals 一伙罪犯

a crowd of lookers-on 一群旁观者

a throng of shoppers 一大批买东西的人

a troop of visitors 一大批参观的人

a swarm of fans 一大批球迷

a party of tourists 一伙旅游者

a clutch of reporters 一群记者

a knot of people 一伙人

一群动物的说法更多，如：

an army of ants 一大群蚂蚁

a swarm of bees 一群蜜蜂

a flight (nock) of birds 一群飞鸟

a herd of cattle (deer) 一群牛（鹿）

a litter of cubs 一窝幼兽

a pride of lions 一群狮子

a flock of sheep (goats) 一群绵羊（山羊）

a pack of wolves 一群狼

a colony (swarm) of insects 一群昆虫

a school of dolphins 一群海豚

a shoal of fish 一大群鱼

a gaggle of geese 一群鹅

a troop of monkeys 一大群猴子

a litter of puppies (kittens) 一窝小狗（猫）

a herd of elephants 一群象

a pack of hounds 一群猎犬

某些物品也有类似说法，如：

a bunch of flowers 一束花

a cluster of grapes 一串葡萄

a bunch of bananas 一把香蕉

a bunch of keys 一串钥匙

a row of houses (chairs) 一排房子（椅子）

a stack of newspaper 一大沓报纸

a roll of banknotes 一卷钞票

a hail of bullets 一阵子弹

a deck of cards 一副纸牌

a sheaf of lilies 一束百合花

a bundle of books 一捆书

a batch of letters 一批信件

a clump of trees 树丛

a pile of magazines 一叠杂志

a squadron of fighter planes 一中队战斗机

a fleet of ships 一队轮船

a spate of protests 一阵抗议

a flood of letters 大批信件

a shower of criticism 一阵批评

a heap of sand 一堆沙子

a set of stamps 一套邮票

a crop of mistakes 大量错误

a host of difficulties (problems) 大量困难（问题）

a collection of short stories 短篇小说集

H

243 habit—custom

habit 表示"习惯"：

You need to form the <u>habit</u> of reading carefully. 你需要养成仔细阅读的习惯。

He has a <u>habit</u> of humming while he works. 他有工作时哼歌曲的习惯。

这个词还可用于某些短语：

He has <u>got into the habit</u> of looking after her. 他已养成了照顾她的习惯。

Don't let the children <u>fall into bad habits</u>. 不要让孩子们染上坏习惯。

❀ **custom** 也可指"习惯"：

It is my <u>custom</u> to go to France for my holiday. 到法国度假是我的习惯。

He arrived early to dust the shop, as was his <u>custom</u>. 他到商店很早，先打扫尘土，这是他的习惯。

但更多表示"习俗"：

The celebration of Christmas is a <u>custom</u>. 庆祝圣诞节是一种习俗。

Social <u>customs</u> vary greatly from country to country. 社会习俗各国差别很大。

244 half—half of

half 可作形容词，也可作名词，表示"半个的"或"一半的"。作形容词时它用在名词（及其修饰语）的前面：

You've only heard <u>half</u> the story. 你只听了半个故事。

<u>Half</u> the apples are bad. 一半的苹果都是坏的。

The dog eats <u>half</u> a pound of meat every day. 狗每天吃半磅肉。

half 作名词时，多和 of 连用，也表示"一半的"或"半……"：

Half of the land is cultivated. 一半的土地都是耕地。

I believe only half of what he said. 他说的话，我只相信一半。

在名词前，**half** 和 **half of** 都可以用，意思差不多：

She spends half (of) her time travelling. 她一半的时间都用于旅行。

Half (of) my friends are workers. 我一半的朋友是工人。

half 常可和表数量的词一起用：

It's only half a mile to the park. 到公园只有半英里路。

I want half a dozen. 我要半打。

这里 **half** 后不能插入 of。

在人称代词前，要用 **half of** 这个结构：

Half of them are there already. 他们一半人都已到那里。

Half of us are on the night shift. 我们一半的人都值夜班。

这里的 **of** 不能去掉。

另外 **half** 还可单独使用（后面不跟什么）：

The money was divided into two halves. 钱分成了两半。

I didn't like the second half of the film. 我不喜欢那部电影的后半部分。

"一个半月" 用 **a month and a half** 表示较好，用 **one and a half months** 也可以：

The round trip was two dollars and a half. 来回票是两块半美金。

I've been waiting an hour and a half（或 one and a half hours）. 我等了一个半钟头。

245 happy—sad

有许多形容词表示 "快乐的""凄伤的" 等。下面按快乐的程度排出一些常用的这类形容词，每个举一个例句：

❀ ecstatic（狂喜的）

The couple was ecstatic at the birth of a son. 这对夫妻生了个儿子，喜出望外。

❀ elated（非常高兴的）

She was elated at the news. 听到这个消息，她非常高兴。

❀ euphoric（高兴之极的）

The mood was almost euphoric. 高兴的情绪几乎是到了极点。

❀ **joyful**（欢快的，可喜的）

Christmas is a joyful day. 圣诞节是一个欢快的日子。

❀ **radiant**（喜气洋溢的）

She was radiant with joy. 她容光焕发、喜气洋溢。

❀ **jubilant**（非常喜悦的）

They were in a jubilant mood. 他们都非常喜悦。

❀ **happy**（高兴的，快乐的）

We are very happy to see you. 见到你，我们非常高兴。

❀ **cheerful**（高兴的，充满喜悦的）

She is quite cheerful and talkative. 她很高兴，话很多。

❀ **jolly**（高兴的，喜悦的）

Everybody was in a very relaxed and jolly mood. 大家的心情都很轻松喜悦。

❀ **light-hearted**（心情轻松的）

She felt light-hearted and optimistic. 她心情轻松，情绪乐观。

❀ **contented**（高兴的，满足的）

Everybody feels contented. 大家都感到满足。

❀ **fulfilled**（完全满足的）

He doesn't feel fulfilled in his present job. 对于目前的工作，他不太满足。

❀ **dissatisfied**（不满足的）

She was dissatisfied with the results. 她对结果感到不满。

❀ **discontented**（不满的）

He's discontented with his wages. 他对工资感到不满。

❀ **moody**（闷闷不乐的）

I keep away from him when he's moody. 他闷闷不乐时，我就躲开他。

❀ **sad**（凄伤的，难过的）

He's still very sad about his sister's death. 对他妹妹的死，他仍然感到很凄伤。

❀ **unhappy**（不高兴的，不愉快的）

Why are you so unhappy? 你为什么这样不高兴?

❀ **depressed**（低沉的，抑郁的）

How depressed she looks! 她显得那样低沉！

❀ **gloomy**（忧郁的，低沉的）

He is a gloomy man; he never looks cheerful. 他是一个忧郁的人，从来不露出高兴的样子。

❀ **glum**（忧伤的，忧郁的）

Don't look so glum. 不要显得这样忧郁。

❀ **dejected**（泄气的，低沉的）

Repeated failure had left them feeling very dejected. 一再的失败使他们感到很泄气。

❀ **despondent**（沮丧的，失望的）

She's despondent about losing her bracelet. 她的手镯丢了，她很沮丧。

❀ **dispirited**（泄气的）

I left eventually feeling utterly dispirited. 最后，我极为泄气地离开了。

❀ **miserable**（痛苦的，悲惨的）

The girl felt so miserable that she wanted to cry. 这个姑娘感到非常痛苦，简直想哭。

❀ **wretched**（可怜的，难过的）

The wretched people are starving. 那些可怜的人在挨饿。

246 hard—hardly—scarcely—no sooner

hard 可用作形容词，也可用作副词。作形容词时表示：

坚硬的：

The ice is as hard as rock. 冰像岩石一样坚硬。

Teak is a hard kind of wood. 柚木是一种很坚硬的木料。

I like hard chairs. 我喜欢硬木椅子。

困难的，艰难的：

It is hard to please all. 要让人人都高兴是困难的。（谚语）

Times are hard. 这是一个艰难的时代。

作副词时它主要表示"努力地""使劲地"：

They tried hard to succeed. 他们努力争取成功。

She was studying <u>hard</u> at the university. 她在大学努力学习。

❀ **hardly** 也是副词，但意思完全不同，它表示"简直不"：

I could <u>hardly</u> speak for tears. 我流着眼泪，几乎说不出话来。

We <u>hardly</u> had time to eat breakfast. 我们几乎没有时间吃早饭。

还可用在下面两种结构中：

hardly ever 几乎从未，很少（接近 **almost never**）：

It <u>hardly ever</u> snows in Florida. 佛罗里达几乎从不下雪。

He <u>hardly ever</u> goes to bed before midnight. 他很少在午夜前睡觉。

hardly... when 刚……就：

<u>Hardly</u> had he arrived <u>when</u> she started complaining. 他刚到，她就抱怨起来。

The local police had <u>hardly</u> finished their examination <u>when</u> the CIA arrived. 当地警察刚检查完，中央情报局的人就到了。

❀ **scarcely... when** 也有相同的用法（表示"刚……就"）：

I had <u>scarcely</u> (hardly) closed my eyes <u>when</u> the phone rang. 我刚合眼，电话铃就响了。

She was <u>scarcely</u> (hardly) inside the house <u>before</u> the kids started screaming. 她刚一进屋孩子们就开始尖叫起来。

<u>Scarcely</u> (hardly) had he gone out <u>when</u> it began to rain. 他刚出门，就下起雨来。

❀ 还有 **no sooner... than** 也表示同样的意思：

I had <u>no sooner</u> closed the door <u>than</u> somebody knocked. 我刚把门关上，就有人敲门。

We <u>no sooner</u> sat down in the train <u>than</u> I felt sick. 我刚在火车上坐下，就感到恶心（晕车）。

△在比较正式或文气的文体中，这三种结构都可用倒装语序：

<u>Hardly</u> had he uttered the words <u>when</u> he began laughing. 他刚说完这些话，就大笑起来。

<u>Scarcely</u> was he out of sight <u>when</u> they came. 他刚走得看不见了，他们就来了。

<u>No sooner</u> had she agreed to marry him <u>than</u> she started to have terrible doubts. 她刚同意嫁给他，她就开始有可怕的疑虑。

247 have

have 是最常用的动词之一，有许多重要的用法：

用作助动词，构成各种完成形式：

I <u>had</u> not seen him for at least ten days. 我至少有十天没见到他了。

<u>Having</u> lived there for two years, he knew the place quite well. 他在那里住过两年，对这地方很熟悉。

表示"有"：

She had never before <u>had</u> that feeling. 她过去从来没有过那种感觉。

常有较灵活的译法：

I <u>have</u> a very bad memory. 我记性很不好。

We've <u>had</u> a lot of rain lately. 近来雨水很多。

He had <u>had</u> a very happy boyhood. 他童年很幸福。

You <u>have</u> a bad temper. 你脾气不好。

在这样用时现在多借助 do(es) 构成疑问式和否定式（英美都如此）：

<u>Does</u> she <u>have</u> blue eyes? 她是蓝眼睛吗？

I <u>don't</u> <u>have</u> any relatives here. 在这儿我没有什么亲戚。

 过去英国人曾用下面办法构成疑问及否定式，现在很少人这样做了：

<u>Have</u> you any views? 你有什么看法吗？

I <u>had</u> not a farthing in my pocket. 我口袋里一文钱都没有。

现在常用 **have got** 表示这个意思：

She's <u>got</u> a new car. 她有一辆新车。

I've <u>got</u> two sisters. 我有两个妹妹。

<u>Have</u> you got a fax machine? 你有传真机吗？

和许多名词连用，表示动作：

I'll go home and <u>have a read</u>. 我要回家看看书。

I had <u>a win</u> in a competition. 我比赛获胜了。

有许多名词可以和 **have** 连用，特别是一些与动词同形的名词，常见的如：

bath	bathe	chat	dance	dislike
dispute	dream	drink	fear	fight
go	interview	laugh	lie (down)	look
love	quarrel	read	respect	rest
ride	run	shave	shower	sleep
smoke	swim	talk	think	try
walk	wash	wish	win	

还有一些其他名词可以和 **have** 连用，表示一个动作，如：

Come in. We're having a scene. 请进，我们在吵架。

She has a music lesson at ten o'clock. 她 10 点钟有一堂音乐课。

和许多名词连用，表示各种不同意思：

He had his meals in the hotel dining room. 他在宾馆餐厅吃了饭。

Then have some coffee. 那么，喝点儿咖啡。

Everybody here has the influenza. 这儿人人都患流感。

Do you often have colds? 你常常感冒吗?

What a life they had! 他们过着什么样的生活啊！

She has had a brilliant success. 她取得了辉煌的胜利。

We have had a small accident. 我们出了一个小事故。

（跟复合结构）表示"让……做某事（发生某事）"：

I'm going to have her live with us soon. 不久，我将让她和我们一起住。

He won't have us criticize his works. 他不让我们批评他的作品。

也可以跟由分词构成的复合宾语：

She's having her eyes tested. 她正在（请人）验光。

She had had the passport visaed for Spain. 她已请人在护照上盖了去西班牙的签证章。

（跟复合结构）让某人到某处，使……处于某位置（有各种不同译法）：

I'm having some friends over for bridge tomorrow. 我明天准备请几位朋友过来打桥牌。

I'm having a tooth out tomorrow. 明天，我要拔一颗牙。

（用于 **have+** 不定式结构）表示"不得不""必须""需要"：

I had to walk very fast to overtake her. 我得走很快才能赶上她。

I'd <u>have to</u> get my father's consent. 我得征求我父亲的同意。

have got+ 不定式表示同样的意思：

When have you <u>got to</u> be back? 你什么时候必须回来？

<u>I've got to</u> get up early tomorrow. 我明天得早起。

还可构成许多短语：

had better (best) 最好

have a care 当心

have a fit 发火，生气（难过）

have a go 试一试

have a say 有发言权

have a good (bad) time 过得（不）好

have a word with 和……讲几句话

have... about one 身边带有

have an access to 可以去（使用）

have an affair with 和……有不正当关系

have an eye (ear) for 善于鉴赏

have an impact on 对……有影响

have back 归还

have compassion (pity) on 同情（可怜）

have confidence (faith) in 对……有信心

have control of (over) 能控制

have designs on 对……有不良意图

have in 请到家里来

have... in mind 想到

have it 声称，硬说

have it out 谈清楚

have no business 无权

have on 穿着，有某项活动

have... on one's mind 有心事

have one's hands full 有大量事要办

have one's own way 按自己的意思办事

have out 拔掉，割掉

have something against 对……有（反对）意见

have to do with 和……有关

have... to oneself 完全由自己使用

248 headmaster—principal

在英国，中学校长称为 headmaster（男）或 headmistress（女）。
在美国，私立中学的校长也有这样称呼的，但多数中学校长都称为
principal。

在英国和美国，大学校长有时也称作 principal：

the Principal of Edinburgh University 爱丁堡大学校长

在美国，大学校长多称作 president：

The President will deliver our commencement address. 校长将作毕业
典礼的演说。

249 help—cannot help—assist

help 表示"帮助"，后面可以：

跟名词或代词：

He read Shakespeare, to help his English. 他看莎士比亚的剧来协助他
学英语。

I helped them as far as I could. 我尽力帮助他们。

跟不定式（带 to 或不带 to）：

By helping them we are helping to save ourselves. 帮助他们也就是帮
助拯救自己。

All this has helped raise farm yields. 这一切帮扶提高了农业产量。

跟带不定式的复合结构（带 to 或不带 to）：

Seeing him would help her to get better. 看到他会帮助她身体好转。

I'll help you solve it. 我会帮助你解决这个问题。

△一般说来美国人不加 to 时较多，现在英国也多如此，加 to 显得
有些正规、文气。

不跟宾语：

Every little helps. 集腋成裘。（谚语）

Crying won't help. 哭没有用。

if one can help it 如果能不做某事（就不做）：

I wouldn't do it if I can help it. 如果我能不做这件事，我不会去做。

It won't occur again if I can help it. 如果能避免，这件事就不会再发生。

△另外，还可用于下面短语中（意思仍然是"帮助"）：

help sb. in sth. 在某方面帮助某人：

She offered to help Rose in the housekeeping. 她主动提出帮罗丝管家。

help oneself (one) to sth. 给自己（帮某人）夹菜（拿烟等）：

Help yourself to a beer. 喝杯啤酒。

May I help you to some more meat? 我给你再夹点儿肉好吗？

Have a cigarette. Help yourself. 抽支烟，自己拿吧。

help out 帮助（克服困难）：

Tom helps out in the store after school. 放学后，汤姆在店里帮忙。

Jane is helping out mother by minding the baby. 简照看宝宝来帮助妈妈。

help with 帮助做某事：

Jim will help with the concert. 吉姆将帮助组织这次音乐会。

She often helps her with the chores. 她常常帮她做家务事。

❀ **cannot help** 可用于下面短语中（在这里 help 的基本意思是"避免"）：

can't help (it) 是没有办法的事，没法控制：

We can't help it that things went badly. 情况不佳，我们也没有办法。

"Why are you crying?" "I just can't help it." "你为什么哭？" "我就是控制不住。"

can't help doing sth. 禁不住做某事：

She couldn't help smiling. 她禁不住笑了起来。

She couldn't help envying Diana. 她不由得不羡慕戴安娜。

can't help sb. doing sth. 不能让某人不做某事：

I can't help him saying that. 我没法不让他这样说。

She could not help her tears rolling down her face. 她没法让眼泪不顺着脸往下流。

can't help but 不由得不：

You can't help but respect them. 你不由得不尊敬他们。

When a friend gave him a ticket to the game, he couldn't help but go. 一个朋友给了他一张看球赛的票，他不由得不去。

❀ **assist** 也表示"帮助"，但是比较文气的说法：

John had come to Wales to assist his father. 约翰来到威尔士来帮助他的父亲。

She employed a woman to assist her with the housework. 她请了一个女工来帮助干家务。

250 high—tall—highly

high 和 **tall** 都表示高，但用法不同。

❀ **tall** 多指人、树、建筑物，也可指山：

The redwoods are very tall trees. 红杉是很高的树。

A tall mountain loomed over the valley. 一座高山耸立在山谷旁。

❀ **high** 也可指人、树或建筑物，山高用 **high** 表示时更多：

You're five feet nine inches high. 你5英尺9英寸高。

A high building, a low foundation. 高楼地基要深。（谚语）

在指离地的高度时多用 **high**，如：

The clouds are very high today. 今天的云层很高。

a large room with a high ceiling 天花板很高的一个大房间

high 还可用于许多引申意义：

The train was going at a high speed. 火车正高速前进。

The cost of living is dreadfully high. 生活费用高得吓人。

He holds a high position in the government. 他在政府担任要职。

❀ **highly** 是副词，表示"高度地""高地"：

It was highly confidential. 这是高度机密的。

The industry of France was not yet highly developed. 那时法国的工业尚未高度发达。

251 high school

在美国，中学称 high school，初中称为 junior high (school)。

英国中学有些也称 high school，如：Leyton Stone High School for Girls（莱东斯顿女子中学）。但多数称为 secondary school。

252 hire—rent—let

租用通常用 hire 或 rent 表示，英国用 hire 时较多，美国用 rent 时较多：

He hired a car in London. 他在伦敦租了一辆车。

We hired a boat and went fishing. 我们租了一条船去钓鱼。

租房都用 rent 表示：

We rented a small house in Newtown. 我们在新城租了一栋小房子。

I'd like to rent one of your rooms. 我想租一间你的房。

rent 也可表示"出租""租给"：

She had a room to rent. 她有一间房出租。

I'll rent it to you at two hundred dollars a month. 我可以把它租给你，每月租金 200 美元。

"出租"也可以用 let 表示：

I asked her if she had any rooms to let. 我问她是否有房间出租。

My aunt lets the top floor of her house to an old friend. 我姑姑把她房子的顶层租给了一位老朋友。

这三个词都可加 out，表示"出租"：

The company hires out cars. 这家公司出租汽车。

They let out cars by the day. 他们按天出租汽车。

253 historic—historical

historic 表示"有历史意义的"：

Waterloo is a historic battlefield. 滑铁卢是个有历史意义的战场。

Japan and China signed a historic peace and friendship treaty. 日本同中国签订了有历史意义的和平友好条约。

❀ historical 表示"历史的"：

The book is based on <u>historical</u> events. 这本书是根据历史事件写的。

There is a good <u>historical</u> film at the cinema about Julius Caesar. 电影院正放映一部关于恺撒的历史片。

△有时 **history** 也可用作定语：

a <u>history</u> book 一本历史书

a <u>history</u> lesson 历史课

254 **holiday—holidays—vacation**

在英式英语中 holiday 或 holidays 指一段假期：

She went to France for a <u>holiday</u>. 她到法国去度假。

She had been to Florence for the Christmas <u>holidays</u>. 她到佛罗伦萨过圣诞假期。

也可指个人休假：

He thought that you needed a <u>holiday</u>. 他认为你应当去休假。

Where are you going for your <u>holidays</u>? 你准备到哪儿休假?

on holiday 表示"在休假"：

Mr. Green is <u>on holiday</u> at present. 格林先生此刻正在休假。

They went <u>on holiday</u> last week. 他们上星期去休假了。

在美国，**holiday** 通常指假日或节日：

Next Wednesday is a <u>holiday</u>. 下星期三是假日。

Christmas is a <u>holiday</u> for everybody. 圣诞节对大家都是一个节日。

在英国，公共假日称作 **bank holiday**。

❀ 在美国较长的假期（包括寒暑假）都用 vacation 表示：

No one goes to the school during the <u>vacation</u>. 假期时，没人到学校去。

All employees are entitled to three weeks of <u>vacation</u> each year. 所有员工每年都有权休三星期的假。

on vacation 表示"度假"：

He is <u>on vacation</u>. 他在度假。

She has gone to Italy <u>on vacation</u>. 她到意大利度假去了。

英国大学的假期也可称为 **vacation**：

I've a lot of reading to do over the vacation. 假期我有很多书要看。

255 homely—plain

homely 在美国常表示"难看的"：

The mother is beautiful, but the daughter is homely. 母亲很漂亮，而女儿却很难看。

The older sister was rather homely. 那位姐姐相当难看。

在英国，**homely** 表示"随和的"：

Even though he is extremely famous, he hasn't forgotten his homely manners. 尽管他极为出名，他仍然没忘记他随和的态度。

❀ 在英国"难看的"用 **plain** 表示：

The girl had a good figure but a plain face. 这姑娘身材不错，但脸却难看。

256 homework—housework

homework 指（学生的）作业：

Have you done your homework? 你的作业做了吗?

❀ **housework** 指"家务活"：

I'm very fond of housework. 我很喜欢（做）家务。

257 honorary—honourable

这三个词都由 honour 派生出来，但意义不同。

❀ **honorary** 表示"荣誉"（作为荣誉给予的）：

He had received the offer of an honorary degree. 他收到通知，要颁给他一个荣誉学位。

He's the Honorary Chairman. 他是荣誉主席。

❀ **honourable** 或 **honorable** 表示"可敬的""值得尊敬的"：

He is descended from an honorable family. 他是一个令人尊敬的家庭的后裔。

He is an honourable fellow. 他是一个可敬的人。

还可表示"光明正大的":

My intentions are honorable. 我的用心是光明正大的。

We must have an honourable peace. 我们必须获得"体面的和平"。

258 horrific—horrifying—horrid—horrible—horrendous

这些词都可表示"恐怖的""可怕的":

The film showed the most horrific murder scenes. 电影里出现了极为恐怖的谋杀场面。

Don't let the children see such horrifying scenes. 不要让孩子们看到这样恐怖的景象。

❀ horrid 还可表示"糟糕的""可恶的":

We had to live in a horrid little flat. 我们不得不住在一套糟糕的小房子里。

What a horrid man! 一个多么可恶的人!

❀ horrible 也可表示这类意思:

The weather is horrible today. 今天天气糟糕极了。

A horrible odour filled the place. 这地方充满难闻的味道。

❀ horrendous 也可表示"骇人听闻的":

The violence used was horrendous. 所使用的暴力是骇人听闻的。

The cost can be horrendous. 价钱可高得吓人。

259 however

这个词有几种用法:

作连接副词,表示"但是""不过":

She was not, however, aware of the circumstances. 但她对这些情况并不了解。

Some of the food crops failed. However, the cotton did quite well. 有些粮食作物歉收,但棉花长得很好。

He said that it was so; he was mistaken, however. 他说情况是这样的,不过他错了。

作连接副词，表示"不管……怎样（如何）"：

They will never succeed, <u>however</u> much they try. 不管他们怎样努力，他们也绝不会成功。

<u>However</u> cold it is, she always goes swimming. 不管天多冷，她总是去游泳。

作疑问副词，作为 **how** 的强调形式（表示惊讶、不解等）：

<u>However</u> did you know that? 你怎么知道这件事的？

<u>However</u> did you make such a mistake? 你怎么会犯这样的错误？

△有些人认为这是不对的，认为 **how** 和 **ever** 应分开写，但一些名家和字典都连着写。

260 human—humane—humanity—humanitarian—humanitarianism

human /ˈhjuːmən/ 为形容词，表示：

人的：

It's beyond <u>human</u> power. 它超乎人力范围。

It's <u>human</u> nature that parents should be frightfully fond of their children. 父母爱子女是人的天性。

合乎人情的，善良有同情心的：

To err is <u>human</u>. 犯错人皆难免。（谚语）

The old woman was very <u>human</u> after all. 那位老妇人毕竟是善良、有同情心的。

human being 指"人类"：

No <u>human being</u> would be capable of such cruelty. 没有人能做出这样残酷的事。

I'm a human being. I can stand on my own feet. 我是人，我可以自立。

human 还可用作名词，表示"人"：

Wolves will not usually attack <u>humans</u>. 狼一般不会袭击人。

❀ humane /hjuːˈmeɪn/ 是另一个形容词，表示"人道的""仁慈的"：

A <u>humane</u> person would not hurt any creature. 一个人道的人不会伤害任何动物。

He was a man of <u>humane</u> character. 他是一个天性善良的人。

❀ **humanity** 为名词，有三重意思：人类，人的总称：

I'd like to do something fine for <u>humanity</u>. 我愿为人类做些有益的事。

He was a radical dedicated to the service of <u>humanity</u>. 他是一个献身为人类服务的激进分子。

人道，仁慈：

It is an act of <u>humanity</u> to help the oppressed. 帮助受压迫的人是人道的行为。

They treated the prisoners with <u>humanity</u>. 他们对待战俘很仁慈。

人性，人的特点：

Our <u>humanity</u> unites us. 人性把我们联系在一起。

History teaches us about <u>humanity</u>. 历史教给我们人的特点。

△ **the humanities** 指"人文学科"（包括文学、艺术、历史、哲学等）。

❀ **humanitarian** 为形容词，表示"人道主义的"：

Many of Galsworthy's plays are <u>humanitarian</u>. 高尔斯华绥的许多剧都是人道主义的。

the <u>humanitarian</u> goals of social reformers 社会改革家的人道主义目标

这个词也可用作名词，表示"人道主义者"：

Shelley depicts him as an advanced <u>humanitarian</u>. 雪莱把他描绘成一个先进的人道主义者。

❀ **humanitarianism** 表示"人道主义"：

Heal the wounded, rescue the dying, practise revolutionary <u>humanitarianism</u>. 救死扶伤，实行革命的人道主义。

△ **inhuman** 是 **human** 的反义词，表示"不人道的""残酷的"：

The <u>inhuman</u> treatment of mental patients shocked the public. 对精神病人的不人道的做法使公众震惊。

The general was <u>inhuman</u> in his treatment of prisoners. 这个将军对待战俘很残酷。

261 -ible

-ible 是一个后缀（词尾），多加在动词或名词后，构成形容词，常见的如：

accessible 可接近的，易得到的

admissible 可进入的，可容许的

audible 可听见的

collapsible 可以折叠的

comprehensible 可以理解的

contemptible 可鄙的

controvertible 可争辩的

credible 可信的

discernible 看得清的，可认出的

edible 可供食用的

eligible 有资格当选的

feasible 可行的，行得通的

flexible 有弹性的，灵活的

forcible 强迫的，暴力的

gullible 易上当的，易受骗的

horrible 可怕的，糟糕的

incorruptible 不受腐蚀的

incredible 难以置信的

indefensible 无法防御的，站不住脚的

indelible 难以磨灭的，擦不掉的

indestructible 破坏不了的，毁灭不掉的

indigestible 难消化的，难懂的

inflexible 坚定不移的，不容变更的
intangible 无形的，难以捉摸的
intelligible 明白易懂的，清晰的
irresistible 不可抗拒的，有诱惑力的
legible（字迹）清楚的，清晰的
negligible 无关紧要的，微不足道的
ostensible 表面上的，诡称的
permissible 容许的，可准许的
plausible 貌似有理的，貌似可信的
reprehensible 应受斥责的
responsible（应）负责任的，责任重大的
reversible 可逆转的，可翻转的
sensible 明智的，合理的
tangible 可触摸的，有形的
terrible 糟糕的
visible 看得见的

262 -ic—-ical

许多形容词以 -ic 结尾，如：

academic 学术的
athletic 运动（员）的
domestic 家务的，国内的
emphatic 强调的
fantastic 荒诞的，奇异的
linguistic 语言（学）的
majestic 雄伟的，庄严的
pathetic 引人怜悯的
photographic 摄影的
syntactic 句法的
tragic 悲剧（性）的

artistic 艺术的
catholic 天主教的
dramatic 戏剧（性）的
energetic 精力充沛的
idiotic 白痴的，十分愚蠢的
magnetic 有磁性的
neurotic 神经质的
phonetic 语音（学）的
semantic 语义（学）的
systematic 系统的

也有不少形容词以 -ical 结尾，如：

biological 生物学的	chemical 化学的
critical 批判的，爱挑剔的	cynical 玩世不恭的
grammatical 语法上的	ideological 思想意识上的
logical 逻辑上的	mathematical 数学上的
mechanical 机械的	medical 医学上的，医疗的
metaphysical 玄学的	morphological 形态学上的
musical 音乐的	physical 身体上的
radical 激进的	surgical 外科的
tactical 战术的	topical 主题的，时事的

有些形容词有两个形式，一个以 -ic 结尾，一个以 -ical 结尾，意思上没有太大差别，如：

algebraic(al) 代数的	arithmetic(al) 算术的
egoistic(al) 利己主义的	fanatic(al) 狂热的
geographic(al) 地理的	geometric(al) 几何的
ironic(al) 冷嘲的，挖苦的	logistic(al) 逻辑的，后勤的
mystic(al) 神秘主义的	
problematic(al) 成问题的，疑难的	
rhythmic(al) 有节奏的	syntactic(al) 句法的
strategic(al) 战略上的	technologic(al) 工艺的

❀ 也有些形容词有这两种形式，但意思上有所差别：

　　　　以 -ic 结尾

classic 典型的，古典的

（ Vosne Romanée is a classic French wine. Vosne Romanée 是典型的法国酒。）

comic 喜剧的

（ comic opera 喜歌剧）

economic 经济的

（ economic problems 经济问题）

electric 电的

（an electric shock 电击）

historic 有历史意义的

（a historic date 一个有历史意义的日子）

<u>以 -ical 结尾</u>

classical 古典的，有关古希腊罗马的

(She's studying classical languages. 她在学习古希腊罗马的语言。)

comical 滑稽的

（a comical expression 滑稽的表情）

economical 节约的

（an economical housekeeper 节约的管家）

electrical 使用电的，电气的

（electrical appliances 电器）

historical 历史的

（a historical novel 历史小说）

 不管是以 -ic 还是 -ical 结尾的形容词，改副词时，都以 -ically 结尾：
geographically 在地理上地　　strategically 在战略上地
但有一个例外，public 的副词形式为 publicly。

263 -ic——ics

有许多名词以 -ic 结尾，有些指人，如：

comic 喜剧演员	critic 批评家
cynic 玩世不恭的人	fanatic 狂热者
mystic 神秘主义者	sceptic 怀疑主义者

也可以指事物：

arithmetic 算术	comic 连环漫画
logic 逻辑学	magic 魔术
music 音乐	tactic 战术

也有许多名词以 -ics 结尾：

acoustics 音响效果，声学	acrobatics 杂技
aerobatics 特技飞行	aerobics 有氧健身法
aerodynamics 空气动力学	aeromechanics 空气力学
*aeronautics 航空学	aerophysics 大气物理学
aesthetics 美学	athletics 体育运动
basics 基本原理	*classics 古典文学
economics 经济学	electronics 电子学
*ethics 伦理学	genetics 遗传学
graphics 制图学	gymnastics 体操（运动）
heroics 夸大其词	histrionics 装腔作势
*hysterics 歇斯底里发作	italics 斜体
linguistics 语言学	*mathematics 数学
obstetrics 产科学	*physics 物理学
specifics 详情，细节	*statistics 统计学，统计资料
thermodynamics 热力学	*tropics 热带地区

其中大部分的相关形容词以 -ic 结尾，少数（如带 * 号的词）相关的形容词以 -ical 结尾。

264 i.e.

i.e. 是拉丁文 id est 的缩写，意思是 "那就是说（=that is to say）"：

It's all the same to me (i.e. either choice suits me.) 这对我都一样（也就是说，两种选择对我都合适）。

This house is not to his taste, i.e. he does not like it. 这座房子不合他的口味，也就是说，他不喜欢。

265 if

if 引起的从句称为条件从句（conditional clauses），整个句子称为条件句（conditional sentences）。

条件句可分两类，一类称为真实条件句（sentences of real condition）。这类句子表示一个可能存在的情况。如谈现在或将来情况，从句中的谓语要用现在时态：

I must leave if that is the case. 如果情况如此，我必须走了。

If you are not free this evening, I'll come some other day. 如果你今晚没空，我就改天再来。

从句中也可能包含别的时态：

I hope you will forgive me if I have given you pain. 如果我让你痛苦了，希望你原谅我。

If it was raining, we usually stayed indoors. 如果天下雨，我们通常都待在室内。

有时条件从句表示纯粹假设的情况，这种句子称虚拟条件句（sentences of unreal condition）。这类条件句中的谓语要用特殊的形式。

如果谈的是过去的情况，条件从句的谓语形式相当于过去完成时，主句中的谓语由"would have + 过去分词"构成：

If I had thought of it, I would have talked to mother. 如果我想到了，我都会跟妈妈讲了。（但我没想到。）

If she had been more cautious, she wouldn't have made that mistake. 如果她细心点儿，她不会犯这个错误。（但不够细心，因而犯了错误。）

在主句谓语中，有时可由 could 或 might 构成：

If we had left a little earlier, we could have caught the train. 如果我们早点儿动身，我们就可能赶上火车了。（但我们动身晚了一点儿。）

I might have forgotten the whole thing if Mary hadn't reminded me. 要不是玛丽提醒我，我可能把整个这件事都忘了。（辛亏她提醒了我。）

有时也可能是谈现在或将来纯粹假设、存在的可能性不大的情况。这时从句中的谓语形式一般相当于一般过去时，主句中的谓语由"would（might 或 could）+ 动词原形"构成。

If you had your choice, where would you go? 如果你自己能选择，你会去哪里呢？（当然你不能自己选择。）

If you knew the circumstances you would (might) forgive me. 如果你了解情况，你是（可能）会原谅我的。（可惜你不了解。）

从句中的谓语如果是 be，多用 were 这个形式，不管是什么人称：

If there were anything to tell, I would tell you. 如果有什么事，我会告

诉你的。（不过目前没什么事。）

You wouldn't be anywhere if it were not for Ruth. 若不是有鲁思，你不会有任何成就。（幸亏有她。）

但在日常口语中，在第一、第三人称单数后，用 **was** 的时候也不少：

If John was (were) here, he would know. 如果约翰在这里，他是会知道的。

There would be endless rows if I was at home. 如果我在家，会有吵不完的架。

虚拟条件句中这类特殊的动词形式多数语法学家都称为虚拟语气（**the subjunctive mood**）。由于存在着一些争议，有些词典避免用这个名称。这类句子有时可用来使语气显得客气一些：

It would be nice if you helped me a bit with the housework. 如果你能帮我做点儿家务活就好了。

Would it be all right if I came round about seven tomorrow? 明天七点左右我来合适吗？

另外 **if** 还可引起宾语从句，表示"是否"：

I asked them if they had any rooms to lent. 我问他们是否有房子出租。

I wonder if I can get some advice from you. 我想知道你能否给我出点儿主意。

还可引起某些短语，如：

as if 仿佛，就像（后面从句中的谓语多用虚拟语气）：

He ordered me about as if I were his wife. 他对我发号施令，就仿佛我是他妻子似的。

He behaves as if he owned the place. 他表现得就像他是这里的主人。

even if 即使：

We'll go even if it rains. 即使下雨，我们也去。

He'll come even if he's ill. 他即使生病也会来。

if need be 如果必要的话：

He would work all day, and all night, too, if need be. 如果必要，他可以整天甚至整夜工作。

if only 但愿，……就好了：

If only she had had more courage! 她再勇敢一些就好了。

If only he didn't drive so fast. 但愿他车没开得那么快。

if you like (please) 如果你愿意，劳驾：

You can drop in on Saturday evening if you like. 如果你愿意，可以星期六晚上来。

If you please, sir, can you direct me to the station? 劳驾，先生，你可否指引我去车站的路？

266 illegal—illegitimate—unlawful

illegal 表示"不合法的"：

It's illegal to park your car here. 你在这里泊车不合法。

It is illegal to cycle without a light after dark. 天黑之后骑车不打开灯是不合法的。

❀ **illegitimate** 有两个意思，一是"非婚生的"：

She's illegitimate. 她是非婚生的。

an illegitimate child 私生子（女）

二是"非法的"：

illegitimate use of company property 非法使用公司财产

illegitimate use of public funds 非法使用公款

❀ **unlawful** 也有同样的意思：

unlawful possession of firearms 非法持有武器

All unlawful business activities came to a standstill. 一切非法的商业活动都中止了。

267 ill—illness—sickness—disease

ill 表示"生病的"：

She has been ill with influenza. 她患了流感。

His mother had been ill all through November. 他的母亲 11 月份一直生病。

illness 则表示"疾病"：

He was weak from a long illness. 由于长期生病，他身体很虚弱。

Tell me a little about your illness. 给我谈谈你的病。

❀ 美国人多用 sick 表示"生病的"：

I'm sick. 我生病了。

His wife was sick with a cold. 他的妻子患了感冒。

sick 还可用作定语，表示"生病的"（ ill 则不能这样用）：

Martin himself attended the sick man. 马丁自己来照顾这个病人。

She wrote a letter to her sick father. 她给她生病的父亲写了一封信。

sick 还可表示"恶心的""想呕吐的"：

The smell made him sick. 这气味使他恶心。

He has been sick several times today. 他今天有几次想吐。

因此 sickness 有两个意思，一是"病"：

Chicken pox is a common childhood sickness. 水痘是儿童的常见病。

Do you know what his sickness is? 你知道他得了什么病吗？

二是"呕吐""恶心"：

He's suffering from sickness and diarrhoea. 他上吐下泻。

He felt a wave of sickness come over him. 他感到一阵恶心。

❀ **disease 多指病菌引起的疾病：**

Disease is usually caused by germs. 疾病多由病菌引起。

Many antibiotic drugs are used to combat disease. 许多抗生素药品用来和疾病作斗争。

有时作可数名词，指某种疾病：

Arthritis is a chronic disease. 关节炎是一种慢性病。

Measles, mumps and influenza are common diseases. 麻疹、腮腺炎和流感是常见病。

268 illusion—delusion

illusion 表示"幻觉""幻象"：

A mirage is an illusion. 海市蜃楼是一种幻象。

The magician made us think he cut a woman in half, but it was an illusion. 魔术师使我们认为他把一个女人切成了两半，但这只是一种幻觉。

还可表示"幻想"和"不切实际的想法":

Perfect happiness is an <u>illusion</u>. 十足的幸福只是一种幻想。

He is under the <u>illusion</u> that he is always right. 他有一种错觉,认为自己总是对的。

❀ delusion 的意思接近后者,即表示"幻想""错觉":

He is suffering under the dangerous <u>delusion</u> that his policies are actually working. 他有一种危险的错觉,认为他的政策真在起作用。

I was still under the naive <u>delusion</u> that everyone was good at heart. 我还怀着天真的幻想,认为人人心地都是善良的。

②⑥⑨ imaginary—imaginative

这两个词都是从 imagine 派生出来的,但意思不同。

❀ imaginary 表示"幻想出来的":

Ghosts are <u>imaginary</u>. 鬼是幻想出来的。

This story is not real; it is only <u>imaginary</u>. 这个故事不是真实的,是虚构的。

❀ imaginative 主要表示"富有想象力的":

The <u>imaginative</u> child made up fairy stories. 这个富有想象力的孩子能编神话故事。

"The Rime of the Ancient Mariner" is a highly <u>imaginative</u> poem.《古舟子咏》是一首非常富有想象力的诗。

还可表示"表示出想象力的":

All <u>imaginative</u> creation is a reflection of the real world. 所有表现出想象力的创作都是现实世界的反映。

He was commended for fine <u>imaginative</u> power. 他因其卓越的想象力受到赞扬。

②⑦⓪ in- —im- —ir- —il-

这些是构成否定形式的词头,可构成形容词或名词。

❀ 以 in- 开始的这类词很多,常见的如:

inability 不能

inaccuracy 不精确

inaction 没有行动

inadequate 不充足的

inadvisable 不明智的

inanimate 没有生命的

inappropriate 不适当的

inaudible 听不见的

incapable 不可能（做出）的

incompatible 互不相容的

incomplete 不完整的

inconceivable 不可思议的

inconsequential 无关紧要的

inconsistent 前后矛盾的

incontrovertible 不可辩驳的

inconvenient 不方便的

incorrigible 不可救药的

incredible 难以置信的

indecent 不雅的，下流的

indigestion 消化不良

indiscretion 不慎重，行为不检点

indisputable 无可辩驳的

indistinguishable 无法区分的

inedible 不能吃的

inefficient 没有效率的

inept 不适当的，无能的

inequitable 不公平的

inescapable 无法逃避的

inevitable 无法避免的

inexcusable 不能原谅的

inexpensive 不昂贵的

inaccessible 无法接近的

inaccurate 不精确的

inadequacy 不充足

inadmissible 不允许的

inalienable 不能剥夺的

inapplicable 不能适用的

inattentive 不注意的

incalculable 无法估计的

incomparable 无比的

incompetent 不称职的

incomprehensible 无法理解的

inconclusive 非决定性的

inconsiderate 不为别人着想的

inconspicuous 不引人注意的

inconvenience 不便

incorrect 错误的

incorruptible 无法腐蚀的

incurable 无法可治的

indigestible 无法消化的

indirect 间接的

indispensable 必不可少的

indistinct 不清楚的

indivisible 无法分割的

ineffective 无效的

ineligible 没有资格的

inequality 不平等

ineradicable 无法改变的

inestimable 无法估量的

inexact 不精确的

inexhaustible 用不尽的

inexperienced 没有经验的

inexplicable 无法解释的   inexpressible 无法表达的

infallible 从不会错的   infidelity 不忠实

infinite 无限的   inflexible 没有灵活性的

informal 非正式的   inglorious 可耻的

ingratitude 忘恩负义的   inhuman 不人道的，残忍的

inhumane 极为残酷的   injustice 不公平

inoperable 无法切除的   inopportune 不合时宜的

inorganic 无机的   insanitary 不卫生的

insatiable 无法满足的   insecure 不安全的

insensitive 迟钝的，不敏感的   inseparable 无法分开的

insignificant 微不足道的   insincere 不诚恳的

insufferable 无法忍受的   insufficient 不充足的

intolerable 无法忍受的   invariable 不变的

invincible 不可战胜的   invisible 看不见的

再就是以 im- 开头的词，它们中间常见的有：

imbalance 不平衡   immature 不成熟的

immeasurable 无法衡量的   immobile 不动的

immodest 不谦虚的   immoral 不道德的

impartial 不偏不倚的   impassable 无法通过的

impatient 不耐烦的   impenetrable 无法穿过的

imperceptible 无法察觉的   imperfect 不完美的

impolite 不客气的   impossible 不可能的

impracticable 无法实行的   impractical 不现实的

imprecise 不精确的   improbable 可能性不大的

improper 不合适的   imprudent 不慎重的

impure 不纯净的

以 ir- 开始的词也有一些，常见的如：

irrational 没有道理的   irreconcilable 不可调和的

irredeemable 无法补救的   irrefutable 无法驳倒的

irregular 不规则的

irrelevant 无关的

irreparable 无法弥补的

irreplaceable 无法取代的

irreproachable 无法接近的

irresistible 不可抗拒的

irresolute 缺乏决断的

irresponsible 不负责任的

irretrievable 无法扭转的

irreversible 无法恢复的

irrevocable 无法改变的

以 **il-** 开始的词较少，常见的有：

illegal 非法的

illegible（字迹）认不清的

illegitimate 不合法的

illiterate 不识字的

illogical 不合逻辑的

271 in

in 是最常用的介词之一，可以表示：

在……里面（指空间）：

The telephone is in my study. 电话在我书房里。

I shall see you in London. 我将在伦敦和你见面。

常有较灵活的译法：

They went up in the lift. 他们乘电梯上去。

I shall be in Hong Kong tomorrow. 我明天到达香港。

This has always been in my mind. 这事我一直记在心上。

（放到）……里面（意思接近 into）（主要和 **put, jump, throw, push** 等动词连用）：

He put the papers in the briefcase. 他把文件放到公文包里。

I threw it in the wastepaper basket. 我把它扔进纸篓里。

在（某段时间）内：

I'm going there in July. 我 7 月份到那里去。

An hour in the morning is worth two in the evening. 早上一小时抵晚上两小时。

在（一段时间）之后：

The doctor will be with you in a few minutes. 医生几分钟后就来见你。

We'll be back in no time. 我们不久就回来。

（引起短语作表语）表示状态和特征：

He was in danger. 他处于危险之中。

He was obviously in good health. 他显然身体很好。

（引起短语作状语）表示行为方式等：

I stared at her in amazement. 我惊讶地凝视着她。

She spoke in grief rather than in anger. 她说话时很悲痛，而不是很气恼。

（引起短语作定语）表示特征：

A gentleman in black came forward. 一位穿黑衣裳的先生走向前来。

He was a Doctor of Philosophy in economics. 他是经济哲学博士。

此外还可用于许多短语，常用的有：

in a nut shell 总之

in a row 一连

in a sense 从某个意义上说

in accordance with 按照

in addition (to) 此外（除……外）

in advance 事前，提前

in all 总共

in any case 不管怎样

in case (of) 要是，以防

in conclusion （在发言末尾说）最后

in detail 详细地

in...fashion (manner) ……地（表示方式）

in front of 在……前面

in full 全部地，全文地

in general (particular) 一般来说

in itself 本身（特别是）

in one's opinion (view) 据……看

in order to (that) 以便，为了

in other words 换句话说

in part(s) 部分地

in person 亲自

in public (private) 公开地（私下地）

in regard (reference) to 关于（联系到）

in return 作为回报

in short (brief, a word) 总之

in so far as 就……来说

in spite of 尽管

in store for 等待着（某人）

in terms of 就……来说，以……衡量

in the course of 在……过程中

in the dark 不知情

in the day time 在白天

in the end 最后

in the event of 如果发生（某种情况）

in (the) face of 在……面前，尽管有

in the least 一点儿（也不）

in the long run 从长远来说，最后

in the main 一般（总地）说来

in the meantime 与此同时

in the middle (of) 在……中间

in the nick of time 恰好及时

in thousands 成千上万地

in time 及时，最后

in turn 轮流

in vain 白白地，无用

in view of 考虑

272 in case

in case 常引起一个状语从句，表示"以防（发生某种情况）"：

Take your raincoat <u>in case</u> it rains. 带着雨衣，以防下雨。

I shall sit up for a time, in case I am wanted. 我暂时不睡，以防需要我。

有时中间的谓语由 should 构成，强调偶然性，可译为"万一"：

I wrote down her address in case I should forget it. 我写下了她的地址，以防万一我忘记。

I've bought a chicken in case your mother should stay for lunch. 我买了一只鸡，以防万一你母亲会留下吃午饭。

美国有时用它引起条件从句，表示"如果""万一"：

In case he arrives before I get back, please ask him to wait. 如果他来时我还没回来，请你让他等一等。

In case I forget, please remind me about it. 万一我忘了，请提醒我。

有时后面从句省略，表示"以防有什么情况"：

Better take an umbrella in case. 最好带把伞，以防下雨。

The bus is usually on time, but start early, just in case. 公共汽车一般是准时的，但还是早一点儿走好，以防有什么情况。

in case 还可和 of 连用，后面跟名词，表示"在（发生……）时"：

Better keep a little for the night in case of need. 最好留点晚上用，以防有什么需要。

In case of need I can make a trip to Brussels. 如果需要，我可以去布鲁塞尔一趟。

273 indicate—show—signify

这三个词有近似之处，也有不同的意思。

在表示"表明""说明"时，indicate 和 show 都可以用：

Fever indicates illness. 发烧说明生病。

The black clouds indicate that it will rain soon. 乌云表明不久会下雨。

indicate 还可表示"以姿势、目光等表示"：

You can indicate the direction by pointing with your finger. 你可以用手指来表示方向。

The arrow on a sign indicates the way to go. 牌子上的箭头表示前进的方向。

还可表示"表示说"：

The senator indicated that he might resign. 参议员表示说他可能辞职。

They indicated that they were tired. 他们表示说他们很累。

show 还有一些别的意思，如"拿给……看""表露""展示""放映"等（这里都不能用 indicate）：

Show your tickets. 出示车票。

She showed no emotion. 她没表露什么情绪。

signify 也有"表示"的意思：

Her smile signified her happiness. 她的微笑表示她很高兴。

A nod signifies agreement. 点头表示同意。

但它也可指"用手势等表示"：

Please signify agreement by raising your hands. 请举手表示同意。

He signified his consent with a nod. 他点头表示同意。

274 industrial—industrious

industrial 表示"工业的"：

Italy was becoming an industrial nation. 意大利正在成为一个工业国。

Birmingham is the centre of an industrial area. 伯明翰是一个工业区的中心。

❀ **industrious** 表示"勤劳的"：

I knew that he was an industrious man. 我知道他是一个勤劳的人。

If you are industrious you can finish the job before dark. 如果你努力，你可以在天黑前完成这项工作。

275 inferior—superior

inferior 表示"质量较差的""地位较低的"：

Many sausage makers use inferior meat. 许多腊肠制造商使用劣质肉。

They thought it an inferior book. 他们认为这是一本质量较差的书。

常和 **to** 连用，表示"比……差（低）"：

This cloth is inferior to that one. 这块布比那块布差。

An assistant manager is inferior in position to a manager. 副经理比经理地位低。

❀ **superior** 是它的反义词，表示"优质的""高级的""优秀的""上级的"：

This is superior wool. 这是优质毛线。

This is a superior car. 这是一辆高级轿车。

有时表示"傲慢的""高傲的"：

Oh don't be so superior. 啊，不要这样高傲。

His superior manner makes people resent him. 他傲慢的态度使人们讨厌他。

它也可和 **to** 连用，表示"比……优越（强）"：

His knowledge of French literature is superior to mine. 他对法国文学的了解比我强。

This engine is superior to the other one. 这台发动机比那一台优越。

276 influence—effect

这两个词都可译作"影响"，但并不相同。

influence 多指人（包括团体）对人的影响：

He had great influence with the miners. 他在矿工中有很大影响。

Religion has a great influence on man's behaviour. 宗教对人的行为有很大影响。

也可指有影响的人或东西：

His friends were a bad influence on him. 他的朋友对他有不良影响。

Heredity and environment are influences on character. 遗传和环境影响性格。

❀ **effect** 多指物的影响：

It had an almost immediate effect on his thinking. 这对他的思想几乎立即产生了影响。

His satire had no effect on her. 他的讽刺对她没有影响。

有时指"效果""作用"：

Bitter pills may have wholesome effects. 良药苦口利于病。（谚语）

But I have never felt any ill effects. 但我从未感到有什么不良作用。

277 injure—wound—hurt

injure 表示"使受伤"：

The boy injured his leg. 这个男孩儿腿受了伤。

Three people were injured in the car accident. 车祸中三人受了伤。

injured 还可用作形容词：

Thousands of injured people still lay among the ruins. 成千上万受伤的人仍躺在废墟之中。

❀ wound 也有类似意思，多指刀、枪、子弹等造成的伤害：

He was wounded in the civil war. 他在内战中受了伤。

The bullet wounded the policeman in the left arm. 子弹打中了警察的左臂。

wounded 也可用作定语：

Wounded men lay on the carts. 受伤的人躺在大车上。

❀ hurt 可指重伤，也可指轻伤：

The driver hurt himself badly in the accident. 在车祸中，司机受了重伤。

The boy came home with a hurt knee. 男孩儿膝盖受了点儿伤，回到了家里。

278 in order to (that)—so as to—so that

in order to 可引起短语作状语，表示目的：

They arrived early in order to get a good seat. 他们到得早，以便有个好座位。

In order to raise our standard of living, we've got to step up production. 为了提高我们的生活水准，我们必须发展生产。

in order that 可以跟从句，起同样的作用。

In order that you may create such a picture, you have to possess certain artistic weapons. 为了画出这样一幅图画，你必须具备某些艺术"武器"。

❀ so as to 的意思和这差不多，也可引起短语，但不能用在句首：

We picked apples <u>so as to</u> make a pie. 我们摘了些苹果，以便做馅饼。

Go in quietly <u>so as not to</u> wake the baby. 进去时不要出声，以免把宝宝吵醒。

❀ **so that** 可引起从句，作表示目的的状语，也不能用在句首：

I hired a boat <u>so that</u> I could go fishing. 我租了一只小船，以便去钓鱼。

Speak clearly <u>so that</u> they may understand you. 说清楚些，以便他们能听明白。

279 **inquire—enquire**

这两个词意思相同，（inquire 用得稍多一些，特别是在美式英语中），都表示"询问""打听"。后面可以：

跟从句：

The doctor <u>inquired</u> what had occurred. 医生问发生了什么事。

We must <u>enquire</u> whether he really came. 我们必须打听下他是否真的来了。

跟名词：

I <u>inquired</u> his reason for coming. 我问他来的理由。

I <u>enquired</u> of him the way to Chicago. 我向他打听去芝加哥的路。

和 **about** 连用：

She <u>inquired</u> about my brother. 她打听我哥哥的情况。

Did he <u>enquire</u> about me? 他问了我的情况没有？

用在插入语中：

"Anything you need?" <u>inquired</u> the girl. 这个姑娘问道："你需要什么东西吗？"

"Who compiles these reports?" Philip <u>enquired</u>. "这些报告谁编写的？"菲利普问道。

还可用于一些短语中：

inquire (enquire) after 问候

inquire (enquire) for 找（某人）

inquire (enquire) into 调查，了解

inquire (enquire) of 向……问

这两个词在书面语中用得较多，在日常口语中人们多用 ask 表示同样的意思。

He asked me what I wanted. 他问我要什么。

She asked about his work. 她问到他的工作情况。

280 in spite of—despite

in spite of 表示"虽然""尽管"。

后面跟名词或代词：

In spite of the heavy rain, she went to the shop. 尽管雨很大，但她还是去商店了。

In spite of his efforts he failed. 他虽然做了努力，但还是失败了。

如果需要用从句，可用连词 (al)though：

They are generous (al)though they are poor. 他们虽然穷苦，却很大方。

✿ despite 的意思和 in spite of 完全一样：

He came to the meeting despite his illness. 他尽管生病，还是来开会了。

Despite (his) advanced years, he is learning to drive. 他虽然年纪大，仍在学开车。

 despite 后面不能跟 of。

281 instead—instead of

instead 是副词，表示"不……而……""作为替代"（常不译出）：

Last year I went to France. This year I'm going to Italy instead. 去年我去了法国，今年我不去法国而去意大利。

I don't like this one; give me that instead. 我不喜欢这个，给我那个好了。

✿ instead of 后面跟名词或动名词，表示"不……而……"：

We walked down the stairs instead of taking the lift. 我们没坐电梯，而是走下楼去。

I stayed in bed all day instead of going to work. 我没上班，而是在床上躺了一整天。

282 instinct—intuition

instinct 表示"本能":

An instinct leads birds to fly. 本能使鸟类飞翔。

Most animals have an instinct to protect their young. 多数动物都有保护幼兽的本能。

❀ intuition 表示"直觉":

My intuition turned out to be correct. 我的直觉证明是对的。

I had an intuition that something awful was about to happen. 我有一种直觉,一件可怕的事将要发生。

283 intelligent—intellectual

intelligent 表示"有头脑的""有智力的""聪明的":

He is an intelligent person. 他是一个有头脑的人。

All human beings are much more intelligent than animals. 所有人类的智力都比动物高得多。

The child made a very intelligent remark. 那个孩子说了一句非常聪明的话。

❀ intellectual 可作形容词,有时表示"有智力的""聪颖的":

An intellectual person is one who has good powers of thinking. 有智力的人就是有很好思维能力的人。

The intellectual girl won a research grant. 那个聪颖的姑娘获得了一笔研究补助金。

还可作名词,表示"知识分子":

These views were common among intellectuals. 知识分子中这种看法很普遍。

284 intend—intention—intent

intend 主要表示"打算(干某事)",后面可以跟各种结构:

跟不定式:

What do you intend to do today? 你今天打算干什么?

I intended to come to your house last night but it rained. 我本来打算昨晚到你家来的，但天下雨了。

跟动名词：

I intend coming (to come) back soon. 我打算不久就回来。

What do you intend doing (to do)? 你打算怎么办？

跟复合结构：

Where did you intend him to go? 你打算让他到哪里？

I intend you to come with me. 我打算让你和我一起去。

跟从句：

I intend that we shall arrive tomorrow. 我打算我们明天到。

We intended that you should be invited. 我们是打算邀请你的。

跟名词或代词：

We intended no harm. 我们没有恶意。

❀ intention 是名词，表示"意图""用心"：

Her intentions were good. 她的用心是好的。

I'm quite ignorant of their intentions. 我完全不了解他们的意图。

后面常跟由 of 引起的短语：

I have no intention of defending myself. 我无意为自己辩护。

They escaped to Paris with the intention of becoming painters. 他们逃到巴黎，希望成为画家。

❀ intent 为形容词。be intent on (upon) 表示"一心想（做某事）"：

He was intent on winning the race. 他一心想赢得这次比赛。

She was intent on going to Paris. 她一心想去巴黎。

也可用作名词，表示"意图"（这个词较文气，多指不良意图）：

The intent of the speech escaped no one. 讲话的意图谁都看得出。

He entered the house with intent to steal. 他进入这所房子，存心要偷东西。

285 interior—internal

interior 可作形容词，表示"内部的""室内的"：

The interior walls of the building were painted green. 大楼的内墙都漆

成绿色。

interior decorator 室内装修师

也可作名词，表示"（房子等的）内部"：

The interior of the house was spacious and bright. 房子的内部宽敞亮堂。

the lofty interior of the church 教堂巍峨的内部

也可指"内陆"及"国内事务"：

He was lost in the interior of Africa. 他迷失在了非洲内陆。

the Department of the Interior 内务部

❀ internal 多指"体内的""内服的"：

The bleeding must be coming from an internal injury. 流血一定来自内伤。

medicine for internal use 内服药（也称 internal medicine）

也可表示"内部的""国内的"：

internal combustion engine 内燃发动机

internal trade 国内贸易   internal affairs 国内事务

286 into—in

into 表示"进入"某处：

He crossed the border into Belgium. 他越过边境，进入比利时。

Come into town with me and hear a concert. 跟我进城去听一个音乐会。

但在 here 和 there 前不能用 into, 而需要用 in：

Come in here. 到这里来。

She went in there and looked out of the window. 她走进那里，往窗外望了望。

在 put, throw, drop, fall, go 这类动词后，用 into 或是 in 意思都一样：

He put the paper in (=into) his briefcase. 他把文件放进公文包里。

I threw it in (into) my wastepaper basket. 我把它扔进纸篓里。

He fell in (into) the water. 他掉进水里了。

into 还可表示状态的改变：

She made strawberries <u>into</u> jam. 她把草莓做成果酱。

Can you translate the letter <u>into</u> English? 你能把这封信译成英语吗？

还可表示进入某种状态：

I burst <u>into</u> laughter. 我笑了起来。

Their hydrangea were coming <u>into</u> flower. 他们的绣球花开花了。

287 intolerable—intolerant

intolerable 表示"无法忍受的"：

The pain was <u>intolerable</u>. 疼得无法忍受。

The noise of drilling was <u>intolerable</u>. 钻孔的声音令人无法忍受。

❀ intolerant 表示"不能容忍的"，有时表示"忍受不了的"：

Some pious church-goers are <u>intolerant</u> of other religions. 有些虔诚的信徒对别的宗教不能容忍。

He is <u>intolerant</u> of opposition. 他不能容忍别人反对。

288 invaluable—valuable

invaluable 表示"非常珍贵的"：

Thank you for your <u>invaluable</u> help. 谢谢你无价的帮助。

These manuscripts are <u>invaluable</u> to us. 这些手稿对我们来说是很珍贵的。

❀ valuable 并不是 invaluable 的反义词，valuable 也表示"宝贵的""有价值的"：

Her suggestions are always <u>valuable</u>. 她的建议总是很有价值。

We have already taken up too much of your <u>valuable</u> time. 我们已经占用了你过多的宝贵时间。

△若要表示"没有价值的"，可用 worthless：

The goods are often <u>worthless</u> by the time they arrive. 这些货物到达时常常已没有价值。

289 it

it 有很多用法：

作为人称代词，可代表具体的东西，多译为"它"：

You can't eat your cake and have it. 蛋糕吃掉就没有了。(谚语)

It's a gift from my sister. 它是我妹妹给我的礼物。

也可代表抽象的东西：

You've saved my life; I shall never forget it. 你救了我的命，我永远也不会忘记。

It's meningitis. 这是脑膜炎。

表示时间、天气、自然环境、距离等：

It's damp and cold. I think it is going to rain. 现在又潮湿又冷，我看要下雨了。

It's very quiet in the park. 公园里很静。

How far is it from your office to the bank? 从你办公室到银行有多远？

作为先行词，代表不定式表示的主语：

It takes two to make a quarrel. 两个人才吵得起架来。

It is against all my principles to work with them. 和他们一起工作违反了我所有的原则。

作为先行词，代表动名词表示的主语：

It's no use (good) waiting here. 在这里等，没有用。

It doesn't matter throwing it away. 把它扔掉没关系。

作为先行词，代表从句表示的主语：

It was clear enough what she meant. 她的意思是够清楚的。

It's a mystery to me how it all happened. 这一切是怎样发生的，对我是个谜。

用作先行词，代表不定式或从句构成的复合宾语：

I find it easy to get on with him. 我发现和他相处很容易。

He felt it his duty to mention the fact to Mr. Otis. 他感到有责任向奥蒂斯先生提及此事。

用来改变结构，使句子的某一部分得到强调：

It was he who had been wrong. 错的是他。(强调主语)

It was that President that Jean shot yesterday. 吉恩昨天枪击的是总统。（强调宾语）

It was on Monday night that all this happened. 这一切都是星期一夜间发生的。（强调状语）

It is then (that) I heard Phuong's steps. 就是那时，我听见了冯的脚步声。（用来表示是某人的动作）

❀ 用在某些词组中没有特殊意义：

The last train has gone. We'll have to foot it. 最后一班车已经开走了，我们得走回去了。

He escaped, and tramped it home, working at odd jobs. 他逃出之后，一路做零工，跋涉回到家里。

290 its—it's

its 是物主代词，表示"它的"：

What's its name? 它叫什么名字？

The dog has hurt its leg. 狗的腿部受了伤。

❀ it's 是 it is 的紧缩形式，它的读音和 its 相同，注意不要混淆：

It's impossible to get there in time. 不可能及时赶到那里。

It's quite warm here. 这儿很暖和。

291 -ize—-ise

-ize 这个词尾读作 /aɪz/，可加在形容词或名词后构成动词，表示：……化：

modernize 现代化	collectivize 集体化
industrialize 工业化	mechanize 机械化
nationalize 国有化	socialize 社会化
Anglicize 英国化	Americanize 美国化
magnetize 磁化	privatize 私有化
commercialize 商业化	

使成为，使具有某个特点：

materialize 实现

realize 实现，明白

crystalize 结晶

capitalize 大写，利用

civilize 使变得文明

fertilize 使肥沃，使受精

publicize 宣传，推广

chastize 惩罚，斥责

minimize 贬低，缩小

philosophize 思考，推理

organize 组织

hospitalize 使住院（治疗）

penalize 处罚

finalize 最后肯定

soliloquize 自言自语，独白

baptize 施洗礼

sterilize 消毒

televize 在电视上播送

在英国有不少人把它拼作 **-ise**。这两种拼法都是可以接受的。有些词以 **-ise** 结尾，但它不是上述词尾，只有一种拼法，如：

advise 劝告

surprise 使吃惊

despise 鄙视

exercise 练习

292 jewellery—jeweller's

❀ **jewellery** 指首饰珠宝，包括戒指、耳环、项链、手镯等，为不可数名词，在美国拼作 jewelry：

Some of her jewellery was missing. 她的一些首饰丢了。

Her jewelry was insured for one million dollars. 她的首饰投保一百万美元。

如指一件件的首饰，可用 jewels 表示：

She appeared at the reception wearing her finest jewels. 她出现在招待会上，戴着最漂亮的首饰。

❀ 珠宝商或首饰店称为 jeweller's 或 jeweller：

We buy jewellery from a jeweller's shop. 我们在首饰店买首饰。

It was a modern jeweller's. 这是一家现代化的首饰店。

这个词的美国拼法为 jeweler。

293 journal—magazine—bulletin

journal 表示学术性的刊物或机关刊物：

He is always writing articles for learned journals. 他经常给学术性刊物撰稿。

The study appeared in a leading medical journal. 这篇研究报告发表在一份一流的医学杂志上。

还可表示"日记""日志"：

She kept a journal for her activities. 她记日记，记录她的活动。

Do you keep a journal of the amount of work you do? 你对你做多少工作有没有日志？

❀ **magazine** 指一般的杂志、刊物：

He made some money from writing short stories for <u>magazines</u>. 他给杂志写短篇小说，挣了一些钱。

I like <u>magazines</u> full of illustrations. 我喜欢插图多的刊物。

❀ **bulletin** 指公告、公报：

Here is the latest <u>bulletin</u> about the President's health. 这是总统健康状况的最新公告。

Doctors issue <u>bulletins</u> on the progress of the sick person. 医生发布病人病情发展的公告。

也可指电视上的新闻公报：

The TV programme was interrupted by a news <u>bulletin</u>. 电视节目暂停来播放一份新闻公报。

294 journey—trip—travel

journey 可表示"旅行""旅程"：

I began to make preparations for this <u>journey</u>. 我开始为这次旅行作准备。

The <u>journey</u> was long and difficult. 这次旅程很长很艰苦。

"出去旅行"可有几种表达方法：

We <u>made a journey</u> from Paris to Berlin by car. 我们坐小汽车从巴黎到柏林。

She planned to <u>take a journey</u> to Europe. 她计划到欧洲去旅行。

❀ **trip** 也可表示旅行：

He's on a <u>trip</u> to India. 他正在去印度的路上。

Let's hear about your <u>trip</u> to the Yellowstone Park. 咱们听听你谈谈黄石公园之行。

"出去旅行"也有几种表示法：

She <u>made a trip</u> to the doctor's. 她到医生那里去了一趟。

I think I'll <u>take a trip</u> abroad. 我想我要到国外旅行一趟。

❀ **travel** 可作动词，也表示旅行，尤指长途旅行：

My uncle has <u>travelled</u> all over the world. 我叔叔曾在全世界旅行。

I have <u>travelled</u> all over Europe many times. 我曾多次在全欧洲旅行。

也可指"到（某处）""移动"：

Light travels faster than sound. 光比声音的速度快。

Bad news travels quickly. 坏消息传得很快。

travel 也可用作名词，表示"旅游""旅行"：

He's fond of travel. 他喜欢旅游。

He has returned from his travels. 他已旅游归来。

295 keep

keep 是常用动词之一，它主要有下面这些意思：

保留，保存：

I'll keep it for a souvenir. 我将把它留作纪念。

We keep food in a refrigerator. 我们把食物保存在冰箱里。

经营，管理，养活：

His mother would come and keep house for them. 他母亲会来帮他们管家。

He needs more money to keep his wife and children. 他需要更多钱来养活妻子儿女。

饲养，售卖：

The farmers here keep cattle. 这儿的农民养牛。

They keep hens on their farm. 他们在农场中养鸡。

遵守，庆祝（节日）：

Everyone must keep the law. 人人都要守法。

Most people keep Christmas at home. 多数人在家里庆祝圣诞。

（跟形容词等）保持，继续处于某种状态：

We'll keep in touch with you. 我们将和你保持联系。

They did their best to keep on their guard. 他们尽量保持警惕。

（跟带分词的复合结构）使继续处于某种状态：

She kept him waiting for twenty minutes. 她让他等了 20 分钟。

You must keep us informed of how things are going here. 你必须让我们了解这儿的情况。

（跟带一个形容词等的复合结构）使继续处于某种状态：

Good food keeps you healthy. 良好的饮食让你身体健康。

I'm sorry to keep you up so late. 抱歉，让你这么晚还不能睡觉。

（跟现在分词）不断做某事：

You shouldn't <u>keep</u> thinking about it. 你不应老想此事。

The young soldier <u>kept</u> dreaming of home. 这个年轻士兵不断梦到他的家。

△ **keep on doing something** 意思和这差不多：

Prices <u>keep</u> on increasing. 物价老是上涨。

He <u>kept</u> on blowing his horn. 他老是自吹自擂。

还可用于许多短语：

keep a close watch on 密切注意

keep an account (diary) 记账（日记）

keep an eye on 注视，照看

keep at 坚持干某事

keep at a distance 保持距离

keep away from 避开

keep back 隐瞒（不讲）

keep body and soul together 活命

keep... company 和……在一起

keep down 遏制，限制

keep faith 守信用

keep from 隐瞒，不做某事

keep going 能继续下去

keep in check 控制住

keep in mind 记住，放在心里

keep off 避开，不要踩（吃等）

keep on 继续（干，往前）

keep one's chin up 不泄气（灰心）

keep one's head 保持镇静

keep one's mind 把心思集中在

keep one's temper 忍住不发脾气

keep one's word 遵守诺言

keep out of 不牵扯进去

keep pace 跟上（不落后）

keep silence 保持安静（沉默）

keep the ball rolling 使不停顿

keep the wolf from the door 不至挨饿

keep time 守时

keep to 遵守，坚持（做某事）

keep to oneself 不告诉别人

keep to the minimum 控制到最低限度

keep under 控制，压制

keep under control 控制住

keep under observation 监督

keep up 保持，继续下去

keep up with 跟上，了解（最新情况）

296 lack—lacking—lack of

lack 可作动词，表示"缺乏""没有（所需的东西）"：

I lacked the courage to do it. 我缺乏这样做的勇气。

What you lack is perseverance. 你缺的是毅力。

可用于进行时态，表示"（某物）缺乏"：

Good food was lacking. 缺乏好的食物。

Money was lacking to complete the building. 没有足够的钱来建成这座大楼。

后面可跟 **in** 引起的短语，表示"（某人）缺乏（某样东西）"：

He seemed to be lacking in frankness. 他似乎不够坦率。

Her reception of us was lacking in warmth. 她对我们的接待缺乏热情。

有时和 **for** 连用（多用于否定句）表示"（不）缺"：

She does not lack for friends. 她不缺朋友。

You will not lack for money. 你不会缺钱。

lack 还可用作名词，常和 of 连用，表示"缺乏"（多作不可数名词）：

The plants died through lack of water. 由于缺水，那些植物枯死了。

Through lack of funds the scheme fell through. 由于缺乏资金，计划失败了。

有时前面可加不定冠词：

There has been a great lack of water this summer. 今年夏天很缺水。

The drought was caused by a lack of rain. 旱情是由于缺雨造成的。

297 lady—woman

lady 现在是对妇女的尊称：

This lady is my mother. 这位夫人是我母亲。

This shop sells ladies' hats. 这家商店出售女帽。

在过去它指贵族妇女：

Because she has a rich husband she lives like a lady. 因为她丈夫有钱，她过着贵妇人的生活。

Her bearing and appearance indicated she was a lady. 她的仪态外貌表明她是一位贵妇人。

在英国 ladies 表示"女厕所"（美国作 ladies' room）：

Is there a ladies near here? 这附近有女厕所吗?

❀ woman 指一般妇女（尤指成年妇女）：

Ask the women to come in, but not the girls or the men. 让妇女们进来，不要让姑娘们和男人们进来。

The women and children left the sinking ship first. 妇女和儿童先离开正在下沉的船。

当面不要称 woman，而要称 lady，这样显得客气一些：

This lady has come to help us. 这位女士是来帮助我们的。

woman 有时还可指"女佣人"：

A woman comes in twice a week to clean. 一位女工每周来两次打扫卫生。

表示性别时，名词前可加 woman 或 lady：

a woman doctor 女医生　　　　　a lady novelist 女小说家

在复数名词前，woman 要用复数形式，而 lady 仍用单数形式：

women workers 女工　　　　　lady guests 女宾

298　last—lastly

last 用作形容词主要表示"最后的"：

This is your last chance to do it. 这是你这样做的最后机会。

The accent falls on the last syllable. 重音落在最后那个音节上。

也可表示"上一个""去（年）""昨（晚）"等：

He left home last July. 他是去年 7 月离开家的。

We produced a new play last night. 我们昨晚演出了一个新剧。

还可和 the last few 连用：

My wife's been in Europe for the last ten months. 过去 10 个月，我妻子一直在欧洲。

He's lived here for the last few years. 过去几年，他都住在这里。

last 可用作副词，表示"最后"：

Mr. Green came in last. 格林先生最后一个进来。

He laughs best that laughs last. 谁笑在最后，谁笑得最好。（谚语）

也可表示"上次"：

When did you last go to the cinema? 你上次看电影是什么时候？

When I wrote last I was in bad spirits. 我上次写信时，情绪不好。

last 还可用作名词，表示"最后一个"（多和 the 连用）：

He was the last to take the floor. 他最后发言。

These are the last of our apples. 这是我们最后剩的几个苹果了。

也可指"最后一部分""最后一次"：

He has spent the last of his money. 他花完了最后一部分钱。

I hope we've seen the last of her. 我希望这是我们最后一次见她。

at last 表示"（经过一段等待、曲折）最后""终于"：

At last he knew the meaning of life. 最后，他懂得了生命的意义。

He felt himself at last absolutely free. 他感到自己最后自由了。

❀ lastly 可用作副词，表示"最后"（多指一些事中的最后一件）：

Lastly, let me mention the great support I've had from my wife. 最后，让我提一提我从我妻子那儿得到的巨大支持。

Lastly, George rang his aunt. 最后，乔治给他姑姑打了电话。（他先做别的事）（比较 George rang his aunt last. 乔治最后给他姑姑打了电话。）

299 legal—lawful—legitimate

legal 可表示"合法的"：

Gambling is legal in Nevada. 在内华达州，赌博是合法的。

Capital punishment is legal in many countries. 在许多国家，死刑是合法的。

❀ lawful 也表示同样意思：

It is not lawful to keep a child from school. 不让孩子上学是不合法的。

lawful marriage 合法婚姻　　　　lawful heir 合法继承人

❀ **legitimate** 也可表示"合法的":

Which prince is the legitimate heir to the throne? 哪个王子是王位的合法继承人?

The judge ruled that the claim was legitimate. 法官裁定这个要求是合法的。

legitimate child 指婚生子女,与之相对,**illegitimate child** 指私生子女。

△另外 **legal** 还有一个意义,表示"法律上的":

You'd better get a legal adviser. 你最好请一位法律顾问。

A lawyer is employed on legal matter. 在法律事务上要请律师。

legal action 法律行动　　　　legal formalities 法律手续

⑳ **legible—intelligible—readable**

legible 指字迹容易认出(因而易于阅读的):

The new edition is in larger, more legible type. 新版字体较大,较清晰,易读。

The inscription is still perfectly legible. 题词字迹还完全可以看清楚。

❀ **intelligible** 表示"可以理解的""能懂的":

An intelligible answer is one that can be understood. 能听懂的回答是能理解的回答。

His lecture was barely intelligible to most of the students. 他的讲课对多数学生来说只勉强能听懂。

❀ **readable** 指"内容可读的""易懂的":

A readable book is one that you enjoy reading. 一本可读的书是指你爱看的书。

a readable article on metal, without too many scientific words 一篇没有过多科学术语,有关金属的易懂文章

301 less—fewer

less 可用作形容词，是 little 的比较级，表示"较少""较小"，多用在不可数名词前：

They now do less work than they did before. 他们现在干的工作比过去少了。

More haste, less speed. 欲速则不达。（谚语）

修饰可数名词要用 fewer：

They buy less beer and fewer cigarettes now. 现在他们买的啤酒和香烟比过去少了。

She made fewer mistakes than before. 她现在的错误比过去少了。

△有时也有人在可数名词前用 less，如：

Less people are going to university than usual. 现在上大学的人比平时少。

有些人反对这种用法，认为在这里要用 fewer，但 fewer 显得有些文气，人们常用另外的说法，如：

There are not as many restaurants as there were. 现在餐馆没有过去多了。

There aren't so many trees there now. 现在那里的树没有那么多了。

less 还可用作名词，表示"更少一点儿"：

She gives them less to eat in summer. 夏天，她给它们吃的东西少一点儿。

Of the two evils, it is the less. 在这两样坏事中，这是程度较轻的一件事。

常可和 of 引起的短语连用：

He ate less of the food. 他东西吃得比较少了。

I'd like to spend less of my time answering letters. 我希望回信的时间花得少一点儿。

在可数名词前要用 fewer：

Fewer of us are interested in such games now. 现在对这个游戏有兴趣的人比较少了。

Fewer of the girls came than we anticipated. 来的女生比我们预期的少。

如果名词前没有限定词（如 **the**），则不宜用 **of** 结构，而直接用 **less** 或 **few**：

If you want to lose weight, eat <u>less</u> food. （不能说 less of food）如果要减肥，就少吃。

<u>Fewer</u> people make their own clothes these days. 现今自己做衣服的人少些了。

less 还可用作副词，表示"较不"，多用在形容词或副词前：

The movie was <u>less</u> funny than the book. 电影没有书那么滑稽有趣。

Would you mind speaking <u>less</u> quickly? 你可否讲得慢一点儿？

有时用在动词前：

He should speak <u>less</u> and listen more. 他应当少说多听。

Eat <u>less</u>, drink <u>less</u>, and sleep more. 少吃，少饮酒，多睡觉。

less than 可用作修饰语，表示"不到"（和 **more than** 相反）：

The population had decreased from about 8,300,000 to <u>less than</u> 6,600,000. 人口由 8 300 000 下降到不到 6 600 000。

By 1880, there were <u>no less than</u> fifty-six coal mines. 到 1880 年，煤矿总数不少于 56 座。

302 -less

-less 是一个常见的后缀（词尾），主要加在名词后构成形容词，表示"不""没有"：

artless	careless	cheerless	childless	cloudless
colourless	countless	doubtless	effortless	endless
fatherless	fearless	formless	fruitless	groundless
harmless	heartless	helpless	homeless	hopeless
lawless	meaningless	motherless	nameless	painless
powerless	priceless	rainless	remorseless	restless
senseless	shameless	speechless	starless	tasteless
thankless	thoughtless	useless	valueless	windless
wireless				

有时可加在动词后，构成形容词。

ceaseless   tireless

303 lest—for fear that

lest 可引起状语从句，表示"唯恐""以免"，从句谓语多由 should 构成，还可用动词原形：

He hurried on, lest she should meet him again. 他急匆匆往前走，唯恐她再次碰到他。

They trembled lest their father should hear of it. 他们发抖，唯恐父亲知道这件事。

在英式英语中这种结构现在用得比较少了，在美式英语中用得比较多一点儿。

❀ **for fear that** 的用法差不多：

He's working hard for fear (that) he should fail. 他在努力工作，唯恐他会失败。

Shut the window for fear (that) it may rain. 关上窗子，以防下雨。

这在现代英语中也用得比较少。

304 level—grade—standard

level 的基本意思是"水平（面）"：

Because of the heavy rain the level of the lake has risen 6 inches. 由于大雨，湖面上涨了 6 英寸。

The town is 2,000 feet above sea level. 这座城市海拔 2 000 英尺。

可以引申表示"水平""层""级"：

This problem is being considered at ministerial level. 部长们正在考虑这个问题。

Women must have a voice at all levels in the union. 妇女在各级工会都应有发言权。

❀ "等""级"也可由 **grade** 表示：

Only the highest grade of goods is sold here. 这里只出售最高级的商品。

Radio forecasts said a sixth-grade wind was on the way. 无线电预报说，将有 6 级大风。

grade 在美式英语中还可表示"年级"和"分数"：

An elementary school in America has eight grades. 美国的小学有 8 个年级。

The play was presented by the third grade. 这个剧由 3 年级演出。

❀ 水平也可由 **standard** 表示：

The people of the USA have a high standard of living. 美国人民有很高的生活水平。

His work this week hasn't been up to his usual standard. 他这星期的作业没达到他通常的水平。

standard 还可表示"标准"：

This food is below standard. 这种食物没达标。

Our teacher sets a very high standard of work in his class. 我们老师对班上的作业定了很高的标准。

305 licence—license

licence 表示"许可证""执照"：

Have you a driving licence? 你有驾驶执照吗？

He was given a marriage licence. 他拿到了结婚证书。

❀ 在美式英语中这个词拼作 **license**：

The restaurant applied for a license to sell wine. 这家餐馆申请了一份卖酒许可证。

在英式英语和美式英语中都可用 **license** 作动词，表示"发给执照""得到执照"：

A doctor is licensed to practise medicine. 一位医生获得了行医许可证。

This shop is licensed to sell tobacco. 这家商店有卖烟执照。

306 lift—elevator—escalator

lift（在英国）表示"电梯"：

He went up in the <u>lift</u>. 他坐电梯上去。

Is the <u>lift</u> going up or down? 电梯现在往上还是往下？

❀ 在美国，电梯由 elevator 表示：

We took the <u>elevator</u> to the tenth floor. 我们乘电梯到 10 楼。

❀ escalator 指"自动扶梯"：

Shall we take the lift or go up on the <u>escalator</u>? 我们乘直梯还是自动扶梯上去？

307 like—as

这两个词属于不同词类，却有某些相似之处。

❀ like 是介词，表示"像""和……一样"，后面可跟名词或代词：

She is <u>like</u> a narcissus trembling in the wind. 她像一支在风中颤动的水仙花。

We got on together <u>like</u> old friends. 我们相处得和老朋友一样。

前面还可用 very, quite 等副词修饰：

He's <u>very (much) like</u> his father. 他很像他父亲。

She looks <u>a bit like</u> Queen Victoria. 她的模样有点儿像维多利亚女王。

还可用来举例（可译为"如"）：

She is good at scientific subjects, <u>like</u> mathematics. 她长于科学学科，如数学。

There are several people interested, <u>like</u> Mrs. Brown. 有几个人有兴趣，例如布朗夫人。

❀ as 是连词，可引起从句，表示"像……一样"：

They often drink tea with the meal, <u>as</u> we do in China. 他们吃饭时也饮茶，像我们在中国那样。

When in Rome, do <u>as</u> the Romans do. 入乡随俗。（谚语）

有时跟介词短语：

On Friday, <u>as</u> on Tuesday, the meeting will be at 8:30. 星期五也和星期二一样，8 点半开会。

as 有时像介词，后面跟名词等，表示"作为"，常有较灵活译法：

They treated us <u>as</u> honoured guests. 他们把我们当座上宾对待。

She looked on him as a very great scholar. 她把他看作一位伟大的学者。

有时表示"充当""用作"等：

He wants me to go with him as his secretary. 他要我跟他去当他的秘书。

The letter served him as a bookmarker. 他把信用作书签。

有时还可表示"像"：

They talked as old friends. 他们谈起话来像老朋友。

They were united as one man and persisted in armed struggle. 他们团结得像一个人，坚持武装斗争。

有时还可跟形容词等，表示"是……样子"：

This plan struck her as very much worthwhile. 她感到这计划很有价值。

They agreed to regard the chapter as closed. 他们同意把这事当作已经结束。

△ like 在口语中也可用来引起一个从句，作用和 as 差不多，特别是在美国：

I love that boy like he was my son. 我爱那个男孩儿，就像他是我儿子一样。

He doesn't speak English like I speak it. 他讲英语的方式和我不一样。

在书面语中或正式场合不宜这样用。

308 likely—probable—possible

likely 主要作形容词，表示"可能的"，可用于下面结构中：

跟不定式：

We are not likely to veto our own proposal, are we? 我们不太会否决我们自己的提案，对吧？

She does not seem likely to get it from you. 她似乎不大可能从你这儿得到它。

跟从句（多以 it 作形式上的主语）：

It did not seem likely that he would continue long in that position. 他似乎不太可能长期留在这个职位上。

不跟特别结构：

That, I think, is hardly likely. 这个我想几乎不大可能。

That story of yours doesn't sound very likely. 你讲的那个情况听起来不太可能。

有时还可用作定语，表示"可能的""可信的""合适的"：

This is a likely place for him to stay. 这是他可能待的地方。

Is this a likely place to fish? 这是适合钓鱼的地方吗？

还可用作副词：

She'll very likely cry when you go. 你走时，她很可能会哭。

I shall very likely be here again next month. 我下个月很可能再来。

❀ 还有两个词也表示"可能"，那就是 **probable** 和 **possible**：

The weather forecast is for probable showers. 天气预报说，可能有阵雨。

He is the only possible man for the position. 他是唯一可能担任这个职务的人。

这两个词表示可能的程度是有差别的，**possible** 表示"有可能性的"，不管大小，而 **probable** 表示较大的可能性：

It's possible, but hardly probable. 这是可能的，但可能性很小。

likely 也表示较大可能。

309 literal—literary—literate

这三个词都是形容词，意思却不相同。

❀ literal 表示"本来的（意思）"：

In its literal sense "anti" means "against." 按本来意思，anti 等于 against。

It is to be understood in a poetic, not a literal sense. 应把它理解成在诗中的意思，而不是原来的意思。

还可表示"准确的""逐字逐句的"：

He wanted a literal account of their conversation. 他要求告诉他他们谈话的准确内容。

A literal translation is not always the closest to the original meaning. 逐字逐句的翻译并不一定总是最接近原来的意思。

❀ literary 表示"文学的"：

The <u>literary</u> club meets once a month. 这个文学俱乐部一个月开一次会。

The *Monthly* is the only <u>literary</u> magazine in Ireland.《月刊》是爱尔兰唯一的文艺刊物。

❀ literate 表示"能读能写的"或"受过教育的":

Only one half of the native population was <u>literate</u>. 只有一半的土著居民能识字。

A news commentator should be a highly <u>literate</u> man. 新闻评论员应当是受过良好教育的人。

310 little—a little

little 可用作形容词、代词或副词。

little 用作形容词时可表示"小小的""小的":

A <u>little</u> piano stood against the wall. 靠墙有一架小钢琴。

The <u>little</u> dog followed the boy everywhere. 小狗到处跟着那个男孩儿。

还可表示"很少的",带有否定意味,接近 no:

Arthur had <u>little</u> spare time. 阿瑟空闲的时间很少。

Cyril has very <u>little</u> affection for him. 西里尔对他没有什么感情。

a little 则有比较肯定的意思,表示"一点儿""一些"(接近 some):

Come in and have <u>a little</u> whisky. 进来喝点儿威士忌。

A little knowledge is a dangerous thing. 一知半解很危险。(谚语)

用作代词(有人称为限定词或名词)时,little 表示"很少"(有否定意味,接近 nothing):

He has done very <u>little</u> for us. 他给我们的帮助很少。

She had <u>little</u> to tell us. 她没有什么可告诉我们。

有时也有点儿肯定的意思,表示"一点点":

Every <u>little</u> helps. 集腋成裘。(谚语)

The <u>little</u> of his work that I have seen is excellent. 我看过他的一小点儿作品是非常精彩的。

而 a little 则有肯定意义,表示"一点儿""一些"(接近 some 或

something）:

Try and eat a little. 设法吃一点。

Tell me a little about your illness. 给我谈一谈你的病情。

用作副词时 little 表示"很少""非常少":

She slept very little last night. 昨晚她睡得很少。

I care very little for fame now. 我现在对名已很少感兴趣。

有时放在动词前面，可译为"一点儿没有":

He little thought that his wife was in danger. 他一点儿没想到他妻子病危。

She little imagined the consequences. 她一点儿也没想到后果。

a little 表示"有一点儿":

I'm a little deaf. 我有点儿耳聋。

She's a little over five. 她才五岁多一点儿。

△ (a) little 多和不可数名词连用，可数名词前要用 (a) few。

311 locality—location

locality 指"地区":

The two factories are in the same locality. 两家工厂都在同一个地区。

There are no hotels in this locality. 这个地区没宾馆。

❀ location 指"地点""位置":

The location of the house is near the highway. 房子的位置靠近公路。

A post office should be built in a central location. 邮局应盖在居中的位置。

312 long (for) —desire—yearn

long 可用作动词，表示"渴望"，后面可跟不定式:

She longed to be back in England. 她渴望回到英国。

Tavy is longing to see her. 塔维渴望见到她。

常和 for 连用，表示"渴望（迫切想）得到":

Her sister longed for children. 她姐姐迫切想有个孩子。

He longed for his wife's return. 他盼望妻子回来。

❀ desire 也可表示"渴望"或"期望"，可跟名词或不定式：

We all desire happiness and health. 我们都渴望得到幸福和健康。

We always desire to live in peace with our neighbours. 我们一向希望和邻居和睦相处。

❀ yearn 也表示"强烈希望"，可跟不定式：

They yearned to return home. 他们强烈盼望回家。

He yearned to ask her to marry him. 他迫切想请求她嫁给他。

也可和 for 连用，表示"特别想""盼望"：

The sailor yearned for home. 这个水手特别想家。

After such a long winter, she yearned for warm sunshine. 经过漫长的冬天，她盼望暖和的阳光。

313 lot—lots—plenty—a great deal—a large number (amount)

a lot of 表示"好些的""许多的"，可数名词和不可数名词都可修饰：

A lot of people have had the same experience. 许多人有过同样的经历。

We've wasted a lot of time. 我们浪费了好多时间。

a lot 还可用作状语：

She's feeling a lot better today. 今天她感到好多了。

You seem to have travelled a lot. 你似乎到过许多地方。

❀ **lots of** 表示"很多的"：

She bought lots of clothes in New York. 她在纽约买了很多衣服。

We need to have lots of patience. 我们需要有很大的耐心。

这两种结构中的 **of** 有时可以不用：

She has been through a lot. 她经历过许多艰难困苦。

She gave us lots to eat. 她给了我们好多东西吃。

❀ **plenty of** 也有类似的意思，可以修饰不可数名词，也可修饰可数名词：

There was plenty of work for us to do. 我们有很多工作可做。

There are plenty of men out of work. 大量的人失业。

有时可单独使用：

They had plenty in common. 他们有很多相同之处。

She gave us plenty to eat. 她给了我们好多东西吃。

❀ **a great (good) deal of** 意思也差不多，只修饰不可数名词：

He has given me a great deal of help. 他给了我很多帮助。

He seems to have a good deal of money. 他似乎很有钱。

也可不加 of，表示"很多东西"：

I've learned a great deal from you. 我跟你们学到了很多东西。

They had a good deal to talk about. 他们有很多东西可谈。

❀ **a (large) number of** 也表示"很多的"，只用来修饰可数名词：

We have lived here quite a number of years. 我们在这里住了很多年了。

There were a large number of people. 那儿有很多人。

(Great) Numbers of people came to the meeting. 许多人来参加了这次会议。

❀ **a (large) amount of** 意思相同，多用来修饰不可数名词：

A large amount of damage was done in a short time. 短期内造成了大量损害。

I had not expected such an amount of praise. 我没料想得到这么多的赞扬。

He must memorize large amounts of material. 他必须背熟大量材料。

③14 love—hate

love 表示"爱"：

Love all. 爱一切人。

Love me, love my dog. 爱屋及乌。（谚语）

He loved his country above all else. 他爱祖国胜过一切。

有时表示"喜欢"：

He loved music. 他喜欢音乐。

She loved nature. 她喜欢大自然。

人对于别人或事物的情感，从爱到恨有许多种，这里从爱到恨列出如下：

❀ **adore** 钟爱：

Her husband absolutely adored her. 她丈夫爱她之极。

❀ **love**（热）爱：

Oh, Amy, I love you. 啊，埃米，我爱你。

❀ **be crazy about** 爱得要命：

She was crazy about her baby. 她对宝宝爱得要命。

❀ **be mad about** 爱得要命：

I'm just mad about Harry. 我对哈利简直爱得要命。

❀ **like** 喜欢：

I always like her. She's so sensible. 我一向喜欢她。她很有头脑。

❀ **be fond of** 喜欢：

Is Dorian Gray fond of you? 多里安·格雷喜欢你吗?

❀ **be keen on** 喜欢：

She is very keen on art. 她很喜欢美术。

❀ **don't mind** 不介意：

You don't mind my being frank, do you? 你不介意我坦率，是吧?

❀ **dislike** 不喜欢，讨厌：

I dislike selfish people. 我讨厌自私的人。

❀ **hate** 讨厌，恨：

Most people hate him, but they don't dare to say so. 大部分人都恨他，但他们不敢说出来。

❀ **can't stand** 受不了：

I just can't stand this life any more. 我简直再也受不了这种生活。

❀ **can't bear** 受不了：

I can't bear the pain. 我受不了这种疼痛。

❀ **detest** 极其厌恶：

They detest all that shooting and killing. 他们极其厌恶这样打打杀杀。

❀ **loathe** 憎恶，憎恨：

We loathe the wicked villain. 我们憎恨那个狠毒的坏蛋。

315 machine—motor—engine—machinery

machine 是机器的通称：

I'll show you how to start the machine. 我做给你看，怎样开这台机器。

a sewing machine 缝纫机

a washing-machine 洗衣机

office machines 办公室机器（包括电脑等）

answering machine 电话回应机

❀ **motor** 是机器的一种，称为马达或电动机（把电能转变为动能的机器）：

This sewing machine is driven by an electric motor. 这台缝纫机由马达开动。

可用作定语，表示"机动的""汽车的"：

a motor mower 电动除草机　　　the motor industry 汽车工业

the motor trade 汽车贸易　　　motor racing 汽车赛

可构成合成词：

motor-vehicles 机动车辆　　　a motor-bike (motorcycle) 摩托车

motorboat 汽（机动）船　　　a motor-car 汽车

❀ **engine** 指汽车、飞机等的发动机：

He couldn't get his engine started. 他没能把发动机开动起来。

An electric spark ignites the petrol in a car engine. 电火点燃汽车发动机中的汽油。

❀ **machinery** 是机器的总称，为不可数名词：

How much new machinery has been installed? 安装了多少新机器？

I saw no big machinery at that factory. 在那家工厂，我没看见多少大机器。

316 mad—insane—crazy—mentally ill

mad 表示"疯癫的":

She went mad after the death of her son. 她儿子死后，她疯了。

Van Gogh had periods during which he was completely mad. 梵·高有几段时间完全疯了。

有时表示"生气的""气得要命的":

What is Henry so mad about? 亨利为什么那么生气？

be mad about 表示"特别（非常）喜欢":

I'm mad about tennis. 我非常喜欢打网球。

Some girls are mad about going to dances. 有些姑娘特别喜欢参加舞会。

❀ **insane** 也表示"疯癫的""精神错乱的":

Insane people are kept in asylums. 疯人都关在疯人院。

When people are insane, they are put in mental hospital to be cured. 人神经错乱时，就被送到精神病院治疗。

这个词还可表示"发疯的":

It's completely insane to fly in this weather. 这种天气出去飞行，简直是发疯。

an insane attempt 发疯的企图　　an insane action 发疯的举动

❀ **crazy** 也可以表示"疯的":

Not all the crazy people are in asylums. 并不是所有疯子都在疯人院。

Oh, my God, you will drive me crazy. 啊，我的天，你会把我逼疯的。

但更多用来表示"发疯的""发傻的":

You're crazy to go out in this stormy weather. 你真是发疯，这种暴风雨天气还出去。

To publish that poem was crazy. 发表那首诗发疯（傻）了。

be crazy about 也可表示"爱得要命":

She is crazy about her baby. 她爱宝宝爱得要命。

She is crazy about dancing. 她爱跳舞爱得要命。

❀ **mentally ill** 也表示"疯癫的""精神病的":

They were found mentally ill. 发现他们精神有毛病。

At least ninety percent of the men and women who kill themselves are <u>mentally ill</u>. 自杀的人至少 90% 精神有毛病。

如果情况并不那么严重，可以说 **mentally disturbed, unbalanced** 或 **have psychological problems**：

an institution for <u>mentally disturbed</u> children 精神不安儿童疗养院

This area of the jail is reserved for women with <u>psychological problems</u>. 监狱的这个区域是留给有心理障碍的妇女的。

> mad, insane, crazy, demented, deranged 以及 lunatic, maniac, madman 这些词现在在严肃的发言及文章中都避免使用，大家认为这些词令人反感。用 mentally ill 这种说法的更多一些。

317 madam—ma'am—madame

madam /'mædəm/ 是对妇女的尊称，可译为"夫人""女士"：

Can I help you, <u>madam</u>? 我能帮你做什么吗，夫人？

<u>Madam</u>, it is a pleasure to serve you. 女士，很荣幸为您服务。

❀ 在口语中常可紧缩为 **ma'am**，在英国读作 /mæm, mɑːm, məm/，在美国读作 /mæm/：

Can I help you, <u>ma'am</u>? 我能为你做点儿什么吗，夫人？

Yes, <u>ma'am</u>, I will. 是的，夫人，我会这样。

❀ **madame** 是法国对妇女的尊称，读作 /'mædɑːm, mə'dɑːm,（美）mə'dæm/：

<u>Madame</u> Fauré is Mr. Fauré's wife. 佛莱夫人是佛莱先生的妻子。

318 made of—made from—made out of

❀ **made of** 表示用什么原料做的：

Most things seem to be <u>made of</u> plastic these days. 现今，大部分东西似乎都是塑料做的。

A drink <u>made of</u> orange juice, sugar and water. 由橘汁、蔗糖和水制成的饮料。

❀ **made from** 表示"由（经过加工）……做成的"（形态往往发生变化）：

Nylon is <u>made from</u> air, coal and water. 尼龙是用空气、煤和水制成的。

The wine is <u>made from</u> grapes. 红酒是用葡萄做的。

Paper is <u>made from</u> wood. 纸是用木头制成的。（这里不能用 made of）

❀ **made out of** 多表示以特殊方式或材料做成：

He seemed as if he was <u>made out of</u> ivory and rose leaves. 他仿佛是用象牙和玫瑰叶做成的。

artificial meat <u>made out of</u> soya-bean protein　用大豆蛋白质做的人造肉

319 magic—magical

magic 可作名词，表示"魔法""魔术"：

Some Haitians still practise <u>magic</u>. 有些海地人仍能施展魔法。

The magician thrilled the audience with his feats of <u>magic</u>. 那位魔术师用他的魔术使观众兴奋不已。

也可用作形容词，表示"（像）有魔力的"：

He flew on his <u>magic</u> carpet to Arabia. 他坐在他的魔毯上飞到阿拉伯去了。

<u>magic</u> flute　魔笛　　　　　　　<u>magic</u> mushrooms　有魔力的蘑菇

<u>magic</u> lantern　幻灯　　　　　　<u>magic</u> hand　机械手

❀ **magical** 也是形容词，意思差不多：

<u>magical</u> garments　魔衣　　　　a <u>magical</u> food　一种有魔力的食物

<u>magical</u> power　魔力

有时有引申意义，表示"神奇的""绝妙的"：

the <u>magical</u> world of Disney　迪士尼的神奇世界

The whole experience was <u>magical</u>. 整个这段经历美妙至极。

320 majority—minority

majority 表示"多数"，常跟 **of** 引起的短语：

The <u>majority</u> of doctors believe smoking is harmful to health. 多数医生相信吸烟有害健康。

The <u>majority</u> of the union members voted to strike. 工会成员大部分投票赞成罢工。

有时不跟 **of** 引起的短语，表示"多数人"：

I disagree with the <u>majority</u> on both points. 在这两点上，我的意见都和多数人不同。

But the <u>majority</u> were on Ben's side. 但多数人都站在贝恩一边。

在指投票的"多数"时，前面可加不定冠词：

The bill was carried by a <u>majority</u> of 34 (301 to 267). 这项法案以 34 票多数通过（301 票赞成，267 票反对）。

The resolution was adopted by an overwhelming <u>majority</u>. 这项决议以压倒多数通过。

❀ **minority** 是其反义词，表示"少数（人）"：

The nation wants peace, only a <u>minority</u> want the war to continue. 全国希望和平，只有少数人希望战争继续下去。

A <u>minority</u> of the children wanted a dance, but the majority chose a picnic. 少数孩子想开舞会，而多数孩子都选择野餐。

有时表示投票时的少数（多和 **in** 连用）：

They found themselves <u>in the minority</u>. 他们发现自己处于少数。

还可表示"少数民族"：

The Mexican <u>minority</u> in the southwestern part in the United States numbers up to three million. 美国西南部的墨西哥少数民族人数达 300 万。

Members of 21 <u>minorities</u> live in this area. 21 个少数民族成员居住在这个地区。

可作定语，表示"少数派（党）的"：

a <u>minority</u> government 少数派政府

the <u>minority</u> leader of the Senate 参议院少数派领袖

321 make (vt.)

make 多用作动词，主要有下面用法：

做，造，做出某成品：

We're making a bed from scrap timber. 我们在用碎木料做一张床。

She made a skirt out of the material. 她用这块布做了一条裙子。

在不同情况下可有不同译法：

Make hay while the sun shines. 趁有太阳晒草垛。（谚语）

He made sketches of the dancing children. 他画了一些跳舞的孩子的素描。

Maria set about making tea. 玛丽亚张罗着沏茶。

和表示动作的名词连用，表示动作，可有各种译法：

Have you any suggestion to make? 你有什么建议要提吗？

I've made this decision of my own will. 我是自愿做出这个决定的。

I've made all my arrangements now to go to Germany. 我已做好去德国的一切安排。

能这样用的名词很多，常见的如：

allusion	answer	apology	appeal
appearance	appointment	arrangement	arrest
attack	attempt	change	choice
comment	comparison	concession	decision
demand	detour	distinction	enquiry
error	examination	excuse	explanation
fight	guess	headway	inspection
investigation	journey	mention	mockery
motion	noise	objection	observation
peace	plan	point	preparation
progress	promise	proposal	provision
purchase	reference	remark	reply
resolution	round	sacrifice	search
slip	sound	speech	statement
start	stay	stride	study
success	suggestion	tour	translation
trip	visit	war	

可跟一个复合结构（如名词或代词 + 一个不带 to 的不定式），表示

"让某人做某事"：

You have made me feel secure. 你使我感到安全。

What makes you tremble so? 什么使你这样发抖？

但在被动结构中不定式要带 to：

People who won't work should be made to work. 让不肯工作的人工作。

He was made to repeat it. 人们让他重说了这句话。

还可跟其他复合结构（可由形容词、名词、过去分词或介词短语构成）：

She asked us to make ourselves at home. 她让我们不要拘束。

He tried to make himself of more importance in the company. 他设法使自己在公司里有更重要的地位。

跟名词，表示"成为""成了"等：

She'll make a good wife. 她会成为一位好妻子。

Cold tea makes an excellent drink in summer. 凉茶在夏天是很好的饮料。

还可用于一些其他意义：

赚得： He makes a lot (of money) in his job. 他干这项工作能赚很多钱。

She is making $50, 000 a year. 她一年赚 50 000 美金。

估计： What time do you make it? 你估计现在是什么时候？

I make the distance seven miles. 我估计距离为 7 英里。

搭上（车，船）：They barely made the train. 他们勉强搭上火车。

If you hurry, you can make the next flight. 如果抓紧时间，你可赶上下班飞机。

赶到（某处）： We made the city in four hours. 我们用 4 个钟头赶到城里。

We at last made the party. 最后，我们赶上了晚会。

赶（多少路程）：We've made 80 miles since noon. 从中午起，我们已走了 80 英里。

We can make 300 miles before dark. 天黑前，我们能走 300 英里。

等于： Two and two make four. 2 加 2 等于 4。

A hundred pence makes one pound. 100 便士等于 1 英镑。

还可构成许多短语：

make a clean breast of 坦白交代

make a day of it 玩（干）了一整天

make a deal (with) 做成交易

make a difference 有关系，有影响

make a face 做鬼脸，做苦相

make a fool of 捉弄，使出洋相

make a friend of 和……搞好关系

make a fuss 大惊小怪

make a go of 使……成功

make a good job of 干得好

make a habit of 经常那样做

make a hit 很成功

make a mess 弄得乱七八糟

make a mountain of a molehill 小题大做

make a name for himself 成名

make a note of 注意，记下来

make a point 提出一个论点

make a point of 特别注意

make a scene 吵架

make a success of （使）成功

make an attempt on someone's life 企图暗杀

make an example of 惩罚（某人）以儆效尤

make an impression on 给……留下印象

make amends for 弥补（过失等）

make away with 偷走，抢走

make believe 假装

make do 凑合用

make ends meet 使入能敷出

make eyes at 向……抛媚眼

make for 向……走（冲）去

make free with 擅自使用

make friends with （和……）交朋友

make fun of 取笑，嘲笑

make good 实现（诺言），赔偿

make haste 赶快

make head or tail of 看懂

make into 把……做成，使变成

make it 到达某处，成功

make light of 显出不在乎

make love (with) 和……发生关系

make much of 对……大肆渲染

make nothing of 把……不当一回事

make off 逃跑

make one's bed and lie on it 自作自受

make one's living 维持生活

make one's way to 前往（某处）

make out 看清楚，理解

make over 移交，转给

make peace 讲和

make ready 准备好

make room 腾出地方

make sense 清楚，有道理

make shift 凑合用

make short work of 匆忙干完（吃掉）

make sure (certain) 一定做到，使有把握

make the most of 充分利用

make up 编造，和解，弥补，化装等

make up for 弥补

make up one's mind 打定主意，决定

make up to 拍马屁，讨好，报答

make use of 利用

make way 让路

322 make (*n.*)

make 还可用作名词，主要表示"牌子""型"：

I don't remember the <u>make</u>, but it was a good car. 我不记得是什么牌子，但是是一辆好车。

What <u>make</u> of car did you buy? 你买的是什么牌子的车?

a camera of Japanese <u>make</u> 日本造的照相机

还可表示"式样""体型"：

I like the <u>make</u> of that dress. 我喜欢那件衣服的式样。

A man of his <u>make</u> is rare. 他那样体型的男人是少的。

323 male—masculine—manly

male 指男人或雄性动物：

On the average, <u>male</u> babies weigh more at birth than female ones. 一般说来，男婴出生时比女婴重。

A bull is a <u>male</u> animal; a cow is not. 公牛是雄性，母牛不是。

还可用作名词，表示"雄性动物"：

<u>Males</u> are generally taller than females. 雄性动物一般比雌性动物高。

❀ **masculine** 表示"男性的""有男子气的"：

He likes to show off his <u>masculine</u> physique. 他喜欢显示他男性的体魄。

A <u>masculine</u> fellow is one who is particularly manly. 一个有男子气的人是特别像男子汉的人。

❀ **manly** 表示"男子汉的""有男子气的"：

A <u>manly</u> man would not have run away. 一个称得上男子汉的男人不会跑掉。

He was her ideal for all that was <u>manly</u>. 他是她理想的有男子气的男人。

Each soldier must do his duty in a <u>manly</u> fashion. 每个士兵执行任务都得像个男子汉。

324 man—mankind

man 有几种意思：

最主要的意思是"男人"：

He's a perfectly sensible <u>man</u>. 他是一个非常有头脑的（男）人。

<u>Men</u> are generally taller than women. 男人一般比女人高。

Two <u>men</u> asked to see you. 有两个男子要求见你。

有时指"人"（包括女人）：

All <u>men</u> must die. 所有的人都会死。

Every <u>man</u> must follow his own beliefs. 每个人都应按自己的信仰行事。

也可指"人类"（总称，多作单数，不加冠词）：

<u>Man</u> is a rational animal. 人是理性的动物。

<u>Man</u> must change in a changing world. 在变化着的世界中，人类也得改变。

有时指"男子汉""勇敢的人"：

Come, pull yourself together and be a <u>man</u>. 来，振作起来，做一个男子汉。

The army will make a <u>man</u> of you. 军队会使你成为一个勇敢的人。

He took his punishment like a <u>man</u>. 他勇敢地承受了处分。

有时可表示"士兵""工人"：

Our platoon lost two officers and twenty <u>men</u>. 我们排损失了 2 名军官和 20 名士兵。

He's in charge of a factory and has a hundred <u>men</u> under him. 他负责一家工厂，手下有一百个工人。

可构成许多合成词：

postman 邮差	businessman 商人
milkman 送牛奶的人	armyman 军人，士兵
newspaperman 报纸从业人员	boatman 船夫
workman 工人	airman 飞行员
doorman 看门的人	sportsman 运动员
fireman 消防队员	salesman 推销员

fisherman 渔夫	hangman 刽子手
oilman 石油工人	best man 男傧相
policeman 男警察	clergyman 教士
craftsman 手艺工人	gunman 杀手
footman 男仆	seaman 海员
serviceman 维修人员	weatherman 气象员

❀ **mankind** 是人类的总称：

Disease is an enemy of <u>mankind</u>. 疾病是人类的敌人。

Our chief purpose is to serve <u>mankind</u>. 我们的主要宗旨是为人类服务。

He has devoted his whole life to benefiting <u>mankind</u>. 他把自己一生都献给了造福人类的事业。

325 **mark—sign—symbol**

mark 可表示"印记""标记"等：

His feet left (dirty) <u>marks</u> all over the floor. 他的脚在地板上留下了大量印记。

That spilt coffee has left a <u>mark</u> on the carpet. 溅出的咖啡在地毯上留下了一块印记。

❀ **sign** 也可表示"标记"，但更多表示"符号"：

Written music uses lots of <u>signs</u>. 乐谱上有许多标记。

"+" is the <u>sign</u> for addition. "+"是加法的符号。

❀ **symbol** 也表示"符号"：

H_2O is the chemical <u>symbol</u> for water. H_2O 是水的化学符号。

marsh 指"沼泽地"：

When they tried to cross the <u>marsh</u>, their shoes sank into the soft ground. 当他们设法穿过沼泽地时，他们的鞋子陷进松软的土地中。

❀ **bog** 指"泥沼"，由腐烂的植物构成：

The meadow in Dolores Park had become a <u>bog</u>. 杜洛斯公园的草坪变成了泥沼。

❀ **swamp** 也指"沼泽地"，常有花草甚至树木生长其中：

They waded for hours in a cold <u>swamp</u>. 他们在冰冷的沼泽地跋涉了几小时。

326 mathematics—math(s)

mathematics 表示"数学"：

Mathematics is a subject studied in nearly every school. 数学是几乎每个学校都学的课程。

the laws of mathematics 数学定律

✿ 在作为学科时，常常缩写，在英国缩写为 maths, 在美国缩写为 math：

I enjoyed maths. 我喜欢数学课。

the method for teaching math 教数学的方法

maths 作单数看待：

Maths is my favourite subject. 数学是我最喜欢的课程。

327 may—might

may 和 might 主要用来谈可能性。在很多情况下，两者可以换用，意思差不多：

表示"可以"（用 may 比较直接，用 might 口气更委婉一些）：

May I come round in the morning? 我早上来可以吗？

Might I have a little brandy? 我可以喝点儿白兰地吗？

表示"可能性"，可译为"可能""或许"（用 might 时，可能性稍少）：

I may go to London tomorrow. 明天我可能去伦敦。（或许有 50% 的可能性）

Joe might come with me. 乔可能和我一道来。（或许有 30% 的可能性）

He may be engaged. 现在他可能有事。

She might not like the idea. 她或许会不赞成这个想法。

不定式可能用进行式、完成式，表示"或许正在（已经）"等：

I may be going back in the fall. 我可能秋天回去。

He might be waiting for you. 他可能在等你。

may (might) as well 可用来提出建议等，可译为"不妨"（用 might 时口气更委婉一些）：

Catherine, you may as well come too. 凯瑟琳，你不妨也去。

Since it's a fine day we might as well walk. 既然天气很好，我们不妨走着去。

may (might) as well 表示"很可能"：

You might as well be right. 你很可能是对的。

might 可用在虚拟条件句中（这时不能用 **may**）：

If you went to bed for an hour, you might feel better. 如果你去躺一个钟头，你可能会觉得好些。

If I had been less cautious, I might have been more wise. 要是我不那么谨慎，也许我更明智一些。

还可用于比较含蓄的条件句中或表示"本来可以""就仿佛""简直可以"等。

It was really very dangerous; you might have injured him seriously. 情况确实很危险，你有可能使他受到严重的伤害。

I still think I might have made a go of it. 我仍然认为我本来可能成功的。

How quickly time passed! It might have happened yesterday. 时间过得真快！这仿佛是昨天发生的事似的。

He was getting on for forty, but he might have passed for younger. 他已经快 40 了，他可以说还很年轻。

might 还可用来提出客气的建议和请求，或表示轻微的抱怨：

It might be a good idea to stop the recording now. 现在停止录音或许是个好主意。

If you hear of anything you might let us know. 如果你听到什么，可以告诉我们。

might 可用来表示过去情况，特别是用在从句中，这时它是 **may** 的过去形式：

He suggested a few books which she might buy. 他提出几本她可以买的书。

He thought it might be wise to try his luck there. 他想，在那里去碰碰运气可能是明智的。

在某些从句（特别是表目的、让步的从句）中，表示现在情况时用

may, 表示过去情况时用 might:

However much they <u>may</u> desire it, they cannot express their sympathetic feelings. 不管他们多么想这样做，他们却无法表达出他们的同情。

Try as he <u>might</u>, he could not persuade his friends to go. 不管他怎样努力，他都无法劝说好他的朋友去。

Come what <u>may</u>, he would never let her know what he was doing for her sake. 不管发生什么情况，他绝不会让她知道他为她做的一切。

may 可以用来表示祝愿（这时不能用 might）:

<u>May</u> you have a long and happy life! 祝你幸福长寿！

<u>May</u> all your dreams come true! 祝你一切梦想都实现！

328 maybe—perhaps—probably—possibly

maybe 和 perhaps 都是副词，都表示"或许"；

<u>Maybe</u> we'll see you tomorrow. 或许，明天我们会见到你。

<u>Perhaps</u> they wouldn't like our coming. 或许，他们不愿意我们来。

maybe 通常放在句中或从句开头，意思上没有差别:

<u>Maybe</u> you're right. 或许，你是对的。

I think <u>maybe</u> they don't want him. 我想或许他们不想要他。

❀ **perhaps 可用于其他位置:**

Julius Caesar is <u>perhaps</u> the greatest of Shakespeare's early plays. 《恺撒大帝》或许是莎士比亚早期剧作中最伟大的一部。

He was alone for <u>perhaps</u> half an hour. 他或许单独待了半个小时。

在英式英语中这两个词都很常用。perhaps 常被读作 /pəˈhæps/。在美式英语中 maybe 可能用得更多一些，perhaps 显得有些太正式。

❀ **probably 也表示同样意思，可以放在句中的各个位置:**

<u>Probably</u> Ted ought to come down. 或许，泰德应该来。

I <u>probably</u> didn't try hard enough. 或许，我不够努力。

❀ **possibly 也可有类似用法，也可放在不同位置:**

I'll see you today, or <u>possibly</u> tomorrow. 我今天也或许明天，会来看你。

<u>Possibly</u> we'll meet again soon. 或许，不久我们又能会面。

What he says is true, possibly. 或许，他说的是对的。

后两个词在英国和在美国都有人用。

329 media—medium

media 是 **medium** 的复数形式，常加定冠词，表示"传播媒介"或"媒体"：

Radio, television, newspapers and magazines are known as the mass media. 广播、电视、报纸、杂志都可称为大众传媒。

The media are covering the presidential election thoroughly. 媒体正细致地报道总统选举。

the media 后面虽说应用复数动词，但有些人愿用单数动词：

The media have generally refrained from comment. 传媒一般都未作评论。

The media is (are) to blame for starting the rumours. 引起这些谣言得怪媒体。

❀ **medium** 还可有一些别的意思，如"媒介物""介体"：

The atmosphere is a medium for sound waves. 大气是声波的媒介。

Most bacteria grow best in slightly acid medium. 多数细菌在略带酸性的介质中生长最好。

还可表示手段、方式、艺术形式：

Television can be an excellent medium for education. 电视可以是非常好的教育手段。

Oil paints and water colours are mediums for the creation of works of art. 油画和水彩都是创造画作的方式。

还可用作形容词，表示"中等的"：

The boy is of medium height. 这个小伙子是中等身材。

a medium-sized firm 中等规模的公司

330 meet—meet with

meet 主要表示"会见"，可指偶然见到，也可表示有意会见：

I <u>met</u> her at the end of Drunback Road. 我在德伦贝克路的尽头碰到了她。

I <u>met</u> him at Diana's in London. 我是在伦敦戴安娜家里见到他的。

也可用作及物动词，表示"见面"：

The last time we <u>met</u> was in New Zealand. 我们上次见面是在新西兰。

We chanced to <u>meet</u> in the park that morning. 那天早上，我们碰巧在公园见面了。

还可表示"接（人）""开会""应付""遭到"：

We'd better go to the station to <u>meet</u> your mother. 我们最好到火车站去接你母亲。

The committee <u>met</u> for two hours. 委员会开了两小时的会。

❀ **meet with** 更多表示"遇到""受到"等：

We <u>met with</u> rough weather. 我们遇到了恶劣天气。

Her suggestion <u>met with</u> opposition. 她的建议遭到了反对。

也可表示"遇见""碰到"：

I <u>met (with)</u> a friend on the steamer. 我在轮船上遇见了一个朋友。

In the woods, he <u>met with</u> two strangers. 在树林里，他碰到了两个陌生人。

331 metre—meter

在英式英语中，"米"由 metre 表示：

The blue whale grows to over 30 <u>metres</u> long. 蓝鲸可长到三十多米长。

❀ 在美式英语中，这个词拼作 **meter**：

A <u>meter</u> is equal to 39. 37 inches. 一米等于 39. 37 英寸。

meter 还有一个意思，即表示某些仪表（这在英式、美式英语中都如此）：

A gas <u>meter</u> measures the amount of gas you use; an electricity <u>meter</u> measures the amount of electricity. 煤气表测量你煤气的用量，电表则测量电的用量。

a parking <u>meter</u> 泊车计时表

332 middle—centre—midst

middle 通常指一个平面的中央（心）：

There is writing table in the <u>middle</u> of the room. 房间中央有一张办公桌。

In the <u>middle</u> of the lawn was a great cedar tree. 草坪中心有一棵大柏树。

也可指"中间"：

He came to a sudden halt in the <u>middle</u> of the road. 他在马路中间突然停了下来。

Come and sit in the <u>middle</u>. 来坐在中间。

也可表示时间等的中间：

He got here in the <u>middle</u> of the night. 他在半夜时来到这里。

We landed at Guangzhou in the <u>middle</u> of torrential storm. 我们在倾盆暴雨中在广州降落。

❀ **centre** 指更确切的"中心""中央"：

He placed the roses in the <u>centre</u> of the table. 他把玫瑰花放在了桌子中央。

After that I walked round the <u>centre</u> of the town. 之后，我在市中心一带走了走。

可用于引申意义：

She likes to be the <u>centre</u> of attention all the time. 她喜欢一直是大家关注的焦点。

Broadway is the theatrical <u>centre</u> of the United States. 百老汇是美国的戏剧中心。

cultural <u>centre</u> 文化中心   financial <u>centre</u> 金融中心

❀ **in the midst of** 也表示"在……中间（当中）"：

They wanted the picnic to be <u>in the midst of</u> the forest. 他们希望在森林中举行野餐。

She took ill <u>in the midst of</u> the ceremony. 在举行仪式的过程中，她生病了。

333 million—billion—trillion

million 指百万（后面一般不加 -s）：

The population of Scotland was nearly two <u>million</u>. 苏格兰的人口近 200 万。

She made two <u>million</u> dollars in one year. 她一年赚了 200 万美元。

在个别情况下可加 -s：

<u>Millions</u> of lives have been saved. 数以百万计的生命得救了。

His idea is worth <u>millions</u>. 他的主意值数百万。

❀ **billion** 现在都指"十亿"（通常不加 -s）：

A human adult has about 100 <u>billion</u> cells. 成人身体约有 1 000 亿个细胞。

3 <u>billion</u> dollars 30 亿美元   over 1. 3 <u>billion</u> people 13 多亿人

在个别情况下可加 -s：

Their light has taken <u>billions</u> of years to reach us. 它们的光线经过许多亿年才到达我们这里。

He thought that it must be worth <u>billions</u>. 他认为这准值几十亿。

过去在英国它曾表示 1 000 000 000 000，但现在已经过时。

❀ **trillion** 表示 1 000 000 000 000（1 万亿）：

The central bank printed over 2 <u>trillion</u> roubles. 中央银行印制了 2 万亿卢布。

334 mis-

mis- 是一个前缀（词头），可加在动词前，构成它的反义词，表示"错误地"：

misadvise	misapply	misapprehend	misappropriate
misbehave	miscalculate	miscall	miscarry
misconceive	miscount	misdeal	misdirect
misemploy	misgovern	mishandle	mishear
misinform	misinterpret	misjudge	mislay

mislead	mismanage	misplace	mispronounce
misquote	misread	misremember	misreport
misrepresent	mistrust	misspell	misunderstand
misspend	misuse	mistreat	

也可加名词前面，表示"不当的""错误的"：

misapplication	misapprehension	misbehaviour
miscalculation	miscarriage	misconception
misconduct	misdeed	misfortune
misinformation	misinterpretation	misjudg(e)ment
mismanagement	misprint	misrepresentation
misrule	misspelling	misuse
mistreatment	misunderstanding	

335 mistake—error—fault

mistake 可作名词，也可作动词。

mistake 作名词时表示"错误"：

You made three <u>mistakes</u> in grammar. 你犯了三个语法错误。

I made a <u>mistake</u> about the time. 我把时间弄错了。

by mistake 表示"错误地"：

I took your umbrella <u>by mistake</u>. 我错把你的雨伞拿走了。

He went into their office <u>by mistake</u>. 他错误地走进了他们的办公室。

in mistake for 表示"错当成"：

I took someone else's umbrella <u>in mistake for</u> my own. 我拿了别人的雨伞，错当成自己的了。

mistake 作动词时表示"误会""弄错"：

You must have <u>mistaken</u> my intention. 你一定是误会了我的意图。

He's <u>mistaken</u> the address, and has gone to the wrong house. 他弄错了地址，找错了房子。

mistake for 表示"把……错当成"：

She's often <u>mistaken for</u> her twin sister. 她常常被人（错）当成她的孪生姐妹了。

You may <u>mistake</u> an aircraft light <u>for</u> star. 你可能会把飞机灯当作星星。

mistaken 为形容词，表示"错的""弄错的"，多作表语：

I assure you you're <u>mistaken</u>. 我确定你错了。

If I'm not <u>mistaken</u>, there's the man we met on the train. 如果我没弄错，那就是我们在火车上碰到的那个人。

有时用作定语，表示"错误的"：

Bob has the <u>mistaken</u> idea that tomorrow is a holiday. 鲍勃错误地认为明天是一个假日。

A <u>mistaken</u> person should admit his <u>error</u>. 犯了错的人应当承认错误。

❀ **error** 也可表示"错误"（多作可数名词，偶尔作不可数名词）：

Their <u>error</u> was serious. 他们的错误是严重的。

There are three <u>errors</u> in your composition. 你的作文里有三个错误。

Haste may be productive of <u>error</u>. 忙中容易出错。

in error 可作表语，表示"错了"，也可作状语，表示"错误地"：

If you realise you are <u>in error</u>, you should admit it. 如果你认识到自己错了，你应当承认。

The letter was sent to you <u>in error</u>. 那封信错寄到你那里去了。

❀ **fault** 也可表示"错误"：

The <u>faults</u> in the manuscript have been corrected. 稿子里的错都改正了。

There are several <u>faults</u> in that page of figures. 在那页的数字中有好几个错误。

但它的意思较宽，还可表示"缺点""毛病""责任"等：

His only <u>fault</u> is that he lacks ambition. 他唯一的缺点是胸无大志。

Of his many <u>faults</u> the greatest is vanity. 在他的许多缺点中，最大的是虚荣心。

at fault 表示"有毛病""有责任"：

The boys are not <u>at fault</u> in this case. 在这个事件中，男孩子们没责任。

My memory is <u>at fault</u>. 我的记忆有毛病。

336 **moment—momentary—momentous—momentarily**

❀ **moment** 表示"一会儿""时刻"：

Do be quiet a <u>moment</u>. 请你安静一会儿。

Just a <u>moment</u>, she's coming. 稍等一会儿，她就来了。

the moment 可引起一个状语从句：

<u>The moment</u> he spoke we recognized his voice. 他一说话，我们就听出了他的声音。

He felt a thrill <u>the moment</u> he got into the theatre. 他一进剧场就感到非常兴奋。

❀ 由 **moment** 可派生出两个形容词，一是 **momentary**，一是 **momentous**。

momentary 表示"一时的""暂时的"：

His feeling of fear was only <u>momentary</u>; it soon passed. 他的恐惧情绪是一时的，很快就过去了。

There was a <u>momentary</u> lull in the storm. 暴雨暂时停了一下。

momentous 表示"（极为）重要的"：

Jack took a <u>momentous</u> decision—to run away from home. 杰克做出一个重要决定——离家出走。

We listened on the radio to the <u>momentous</u> news that war had begun. 我们从收音机上听到了一条极为重要的消息——战争爆发了。

❀ **momentarily** 表示"临时地""一时地"：

Our train was <u>momentarily</u> delayed. 我们的火车临时耽搁了。

He was so surprised that he was <u>momentarily</u> unable to speak. 他是那样吃惊，一时间说不出话来了。

在美式英语中，**momentarily** 还可表示"一会儿""不久"：

We'll be landing <u>momentarily</u>, so buckle your seat belts. 我们一会儿就要降落，请系好你们的安全带。

I'll be back in my office <u>momentarily</u>. Wait for me there. 我不久就回办公室，请在那里等我。

337 **moral—morality—morale—immoral**

moral 可用作形容词，也可用作名词。

作形容词时主要表示"道德上的""品格上的"：

The war had reduced moral standards. 战争降低了道德水准。

Our moral sense controls passion. 我们的道德观念控制我们的感情。

有时表示"（合乎）道德的""讲究品格的"：

He didn't lead a moral life before his marriage. 在他结婚前，他的生活是不太道德的。

It was not moral for a practicing attorney to offer a bribe. 执业律师贿赂人是不道德的。

有时还指"精神上的""道义上的"：

I've come to give you a little moral support. 我来是给你一点儿精神上的支持。

作名词时表示"寓意"：

Every story he tells has a moral. 他讲的故事每个都有寓意。

I am afraid you don't quite see the moral of the story. 恐怕你没完全看出故事的寓意。

它的复数形式 morals，表示"品格""道德"：

George Washington's morals were excellent. 华盛顿的人品是极好的。

In his business affairs he has no morals. 在商业活动中，他是不讲道德的。

❀ morality 表示"道德""品德"：

It had a high standard of morality. 它有很高的道德标准。

One sometimes wonders if there is any morality in politics. 人们有时纳闷政治里是否有道德。

❀ morale /məˈrɑːl,（美）məˈræl/ 是名词，指"士气"：

The army recovered its morale and fighting power. 军队恢复了士气和战斗力。

The team's morale is on the rise. 球队的士气正在提升。

❀ immoral 是 moral 的反义词，表示"不道德的"：

Selling drugs to children is immoral. 把毒品卖给儿童是不道德的。

The court banned two immoral films. 法院禁演了两部不道德的电影。

△另一形容词 amoral 表示"不讲道德的"：

a totally amoral person 一个完全不讲道德的人

338 most—the most

most 可修饰名词，表示"大多数的""大部分的"：

Most English nouns form their plural by adding "-s". 英语中大多数名词都以加 -s 的方法构成复数。

In most schools, sports are compulsory. 在大部分学校，体育都是必修课。

常可和 of 一道用：

The tree had shed most of its yellow blossoms. 树上大部分黄花都已谢落。

Most of them don't agree with his opinion. 他们大多数人都不同意他的意见。

most 可作 **many, much** 的最高级，表示"最多的"（多加 the）：

Least talk, most work. 话要说得最少，活要干得最多。（谚语）

Which of you have made (the) most mistakes? 你们谁的错最多？

还可用作主语、宾语或表语：

This is the most I can do. 我最多只能做这些。

It is said that those who eat the most are the least healthy. 据说，吃得最多的人身体最差。

most 还可和形容词或副词连用，构成最高级（也常加 **the**）：

You are most convincing. 你最有说服力。（作表语时不必加 the）

One of the persons whom I saw most frequently was George. 我见得最多的人之一是乔治。（修饰动词时有时不加 the）

most 还可修饰动词，表示"最"：

Of these sports, I like rowing most. 在这些运动中，我最喜欢划船。

I suffered most from lack of rest. 我最苦的是缺乏休息。

有时 **most** 可表示"非常"（这时都不加 **the**）：

It is a most joyful occasion. 这是一个非常欢快的时刻。

They have been most kind to me. 他们对我非常好。

339 mountain—mount—hill—hillock—mound

mountain 表示"高山"：

Everest is the highest <u>mountain</u> in the world. 珠穆朗玛峰是世界上最高的山。

❀ **mount** 也表示"山"，但只用于地名中，常缩写成 **Mt**，如：

the <u>Mount</u> of Olives 橄榄山   St Michael's <u>Mount</u> 圣迈克山

Mt Everest 珠穆朗玛峰

❀ **hill** 表示"小山"：

The park is on a <u>hill</u> overlooking the town. 公园在一座能俯瞰全城的小山上。

The truck went up the <u>hill</u> in first gear. 卡车挂到一挡，开上小山。

❀ **hillock** 指"小丘"。

❀ **mound** 可指"土丘"：

on a grassy <u>mound</u> 在一个长有草的土丘

340 must

must 是一个情态动词，主要表示"必须""一定要（得）"：

The play began at eight, so they <u>must</u> dine at seven. 戏 8 点开始，因此他们必须 7 点吃饭。

You <u>must</u> see the doctor. 你一定要去看病。

可用于进行式或被动结构：

I'm afraid I <u>must</u> be going. 恐怕我得走了。

The book <u>must</u> be finished by the end of the month. 这本书必须在月底前完成。

否定式多紧缩成 **mustn't** /ˈmʌsənt/，表示"一定不要"（可译为"别""不要""不能"等）：

Of course she <u>mustn't</u> leave us. 当然，她不能离开我们。

You <u>mustn't</u> forget to call her. 你别忘了给她打电话。

在回答带有 **must** 的问题时，若是否定意思要用 **needn't**：

<u>Must</u> I come at four o'clock?" "Oh no. You <u>needn't</u> come at four." "我一定要在 4 点钟来吗？" "啊不，你不必在 4 点钟来。"

表示过去情况时也可用 **must**：

It was too late to go back. We <u>must</u> (had to) go on. 回去已经太晚了，我们必须继续往前走。

I said I must leave, but I stayed. 我说我得走，但我还是留下了。

在这种情况下，用 **had to** 的时候更多一些，因为这样时间关系可表示得更清楚些。试比较：

I must leave at six. 我得 6 点钟走。

I had to leave at six yesterday. 昨天我得 6 点钟走。

must 可用来表示揣测，可译为"一定是""准是""想必"：

Judging by the smell, the food must be good. 从气味上看，这菜一定很好。

If you can eat all those apples you must have a good digestion. 如果你能把这些苹果全吃下去，你的消化想必很好。

有时后面可跟完成形式，表示已发生的情况：

He must have arrived by air. 他一定是坐飞机来的。

His watch must have stopped. 想必是他的表停了。

也可跟进行形式表示正在发生的情况：

You must be joking! 你一定是在开玩笑。

Rose must be looking forward to his return. 罗丝准是在盼望他回来。

341 mutual—reciprocal

mutual 有两个意思，一是表示"相互的"：

There had been a great measure of mutual respect. 他们相互间非常尊重。

They are in danger of mutual destruction. 他们有同归于尽的危险。

另一个意思是"共同的"：

The two friends had a mutual enthusiasm for music. 这两位朋友都很热爱音乐。

They met each other through a mutual friend. 他们是通过一个共同的朋友认识的。

❀ **reciprocal** 表示"互惠的""相互的"：

Canada and the U.S. made reciprocal trade agreements. 加拿大与美国缔结了互惠的贸易协定。

Our relationship's based on reciprocal respect. 我们的关系是建立在相互尊重的基础上的。

342　naive—naivety—naïveté—innocent

naive 也可拼作 **naïve**，读作 /naɪˈiːv，（美）nɑːˈiːv/，表示"天真的"：

It's <u>naive</u> to believe he'll do what he says. 要是相信他会照他说的做，就太天真了。

Their view was that he had been politically <u>naive</u>. 他们的看法是他在政治上太天真了。

❀ **naivety** 是它的名词形式，亦可拼作 **naïveté**，读作 /naɪˈiːvɪti，（美）nɑːˌiːvəˈteɪ/，表示"天真"：

His <u>naivety</u> was obvious from the way he told everyone his life story. 从他向任何人都谈他的身世看，很明显他很天真。

I cannot believe that such <u>naïveté</u> is unassumed in a person of her age and experience. 像她这个年龄和经历的人，我不能相信这样的天真不是装出来的。

❀ **innocent** 也可表示"天真的"：

Helen is an <u>innocent</u> girl. 海伦是一个天真的姑娘。

Don't be so <u>innocent</u> as to believe everything he says. 不要天真得他说什么都相信。

343　nation—national—nationalist—nationality—nationalized

nation 表示"民族"或"国家"：

A novelist must be able to use the cultural heritage of his <u>nation</u>. 一个小说家必须能利用本民族的文化遗产。

No agreement was reached between the two <u>nations</u>. 两国间未达成协议。

The United <u>Nations</u> 联合国　　　　most favoured <u>nations</u> 最惠国

nation 表示国家综合体，包括它的政治及社会结构。如果指的是地理上的国家，则应用 **country** 表示：

China is a very picturesque country. 中国是一个风景如画的国家。

He has travelled in many countries in Europe. 他游历了欧洲许多国家。

❀ **national** 可用作形容词，表示"国家的""国立的""国民的""国内的"：

This island would make a superb national park. 这个岛可以成为一座优美的国家公园。

On Saturday afternoon he went to the National Gallery. 星期六下午，他去参观了国家美术馆。

也可表示"民族的"：

That's the Swiss national character. 这是瑞士人的民族性。

But the national feeling was strong with Romanians. 但是罗马尼亚人的民族情绪很强。

还可用作名词，表示"某国人（公民）"：

One of a consul's duties is to help his own nationals. 领事的责任是帮助本国公民。

British nationals in Spain 西班牙境内的英国公民

❀ **nationalist** 表示"民族主义者"（尤指主张民族独立者）：

He was a great Indonesian nationalist. 他是印度尼西亚的一位伟大的民族主义者。

Scottish nationalists 苏格兰的民族主义者

还可用作形容词，表示"民族主义的"：

Nationalist leaders demanded the extension of democratic rights. 民族主义领袖要求扩大民主权利。

nationalistic 词义相近，但略带贬义，表示"强烈的民族主义的"：

nationalistic fervour during the Would Cup 在世界杯足球赛期间的强烈民族主义情绪

nationalism 表示"民族主义"：

a surge of nationalism 民族主义的高涨

❀ **nationality** 有两个意思，一是表示"国籍"：

What is your nationality? 你是哪国国籍？

She lives in France but has British nationality. 她住在法国，却是英国国籍。

二是表示"民族"：

Various nationalities were represented at the conference. 会议有各民族的代表参加。

the different nationalities of the country 这个国家的不同民族

✤ **nationalized** 指"国有化的"：

Thus Mexico nationalized its railroads. 就这样，墨西哥把铁路收归国有了。

the nationalized sector of the economy 国有经济

也可指"取得国籍的"，如：

nationalized Poles and Greeks in the U.S. 入了美国籍的波兰人和希腊人

但更多还是用 **naturalized** 表达这个意思：

He has naturalized after living in Britain for 10 years. 在英国居住10年之后，他取得了英国国籍。

He is a naturalized British citizen of Greek origin. 他是希腊裔的英国公民。

344 near—close

near 可作形容词，多用作表语，表示"近的"或"临近的"：

How near is the museum from here? 博物馆离这儿多近？

Christmas is near. 圣诞节已经临近。

也可用作定语：

We had twenty miles to walk to reach the nearest station. 我们到最近的车站要走20英里。

Can you tell us the nearest way to the station? 你可否告诉我们到火车站最近的路？

Near East 近东　　　　nearsighted 近视

还可用作副词，表示"近地""在附近地"：

There is no garage near. 附近没有车库。

Easter is drawing <u>near</u>. 复活节已经临近。

near 作定语时有时表示"几乎成为":

The absence of a chairman turned the meeting into a <u>near</u> riot. 主席不在，会议几乎一片混乱。

The Government faces a <u>near</u> impossible dilemma. 政府面临着一个令人难以置信的困境。

near 可以和 **by** 连用，或构成合成词 **nearby**，表示"近"或"在附近":

They lived <u>nearby</u>—less than a block from us. 他们住得很近，离我们不到一个街区。

We'll stop <u>nearby</u> for lunch. 我们将在附近停下来吃午饭。

near(-)by 可用作定语:

They often climbed a <u>near-by</u> hill. 他们常常爬附近的一座小山。

At a <u>nearby</u> table a man was complaining in a loud voice. 在附近一张桌子旁，一个人在大声发牢骚。

near 还可和 **to** 连用，表示"接近""靠近":

As we got <u>near to</u> London the traffic grew denser. 我们快到伦敦时，车辆密集了起来。

He called for us to sit <u>near to</u> him. 他叫我们坐得靠他近些。

也可表示"差点儿就""几乎":

We were <u>near to</u> being killed. 我们差点儿给打死了。

She found him again <u>near to</u> death. 她发现他又差点儿死掉了。

near 还可用作介词，表示"靠近""近":

Cork Street was <u>near</u> Bond Street. 柯克街临近邦德街。

Don't stand so <u>near</u> the train. 不要站得离火车这么近。

有时用于引申意义:

His opinion is very <u>near</u> my own. 他的看法很接近我的看法。

No one else comes <u>near</u> her in intellect. 没有别的人在智力上接近她。

❀ **close** 作形容词也可表示"靠近的""接近的"，但多和 **to** 连用:

His house was <u>close to</u> the Observatory. 他家靠近天文台。

There is a bus stop <u>close to</u> the school. 在学校附近有一个公共汽车站。

可用于引申意义:

She felt something close to despair. 她感到一种接近绝望的情绪。

Spanish is close to Italian. 西班牙语接近意大利语。

还可作定语，表示"亲密的""紧密的"：

We must maintain close ties with the masses. 我们必须和群众保持紧密联系。

There must be close relationship between us. 我们之间应有紧密联系。

还可表示"密切的""仔细的"：

He made a close study of the life of the peasants. 他仔细研究了农民的生活。

Please make a close translation. 请准确地翻译一遍。

close 还可用作副词，表示"靠近地""接近地"：

Come closer so that I can see you. 走近些，以便我能看清你。

They sat down, close together, hand in hand. 他们手拉手紧挨着坐下。

常可和 **to** 连用，表示"靠近"，意思和 **near** 差不多：

He came quite close to where I was hiding. 他走到非常靠近我藏身的地方。

Just one magnolia flower blossomed close to her window. 只有一朵木兰花在她窗前开花了。

还可表示"接近""约莫"：

He was close to fifty. 他接近五十岁了。

They have close to a thousand correspondents. 他们有近乎一千个通讯员。

⑤45 necessary—necessity—need

necessary 是形容词，表示"需要的"，多用作表语：

Oxygen is necessary for life. 氧气是生命所必需的。

Sleep is necessary to health. 睡眠是健康所必需的。

常用 **It is necessary** 这种结构表示"有必要的"：

It is necessary to fill in all these forms. 有必要填写这些表格。

Is it necessary that I should return it this morning? 有必要今早把它还回来吗？

也可用作定语：

He didn't have the <u>necessary</u> training. 他没有必要的训练。

I haven't got the <u>necessary</u> tools. 我没有必要的工具。

✿ **necessity** /nɪ(ə)'sesɪ(ə)ti/ 是名词，主要有两个意思。一是"必要（性）""需要"：

I went only out of <u>necessity</u>. 我去完全出于必要。

<u>Necessity</u> is the mother of invention. 需要是发明之母。（谚语）

二是"必要的东西""必需品"：

Food and clothing are <u>necessities</u> of life. 衣食是生活必需品。

Sleep is a <u>necessity</u>. 睡眠是必不可少的。

material <u>necessities</u> 物质需要　　　daily <u>necessities</u> 日用必需品

✿ **need** 也可用作名词，表示"需要""必要"（在日常生活中这个词比 **necessity** 用得更多）：

There is no <u>need</u> for alarm (fuss). 没有必要惊慌（大惊小怪）。

There is no <u>need</u> to worry at all. 完全没有必要发愁。

还可表示"需要的东西"：

What are your basic <u>needs</u>? 你有什么基本需要？

The government failed to meet the <u>needs</u> of the people. 政府没有能满足人民的需要。

还可用于 **in need of**，表示"需要"：

He was hurt, and <u>in need of</u> help. 他受了伤，需要帮助。

We are <u>in need of</u> different types of designs. 我们需要不同类型的设计。

346　need

need 可用作动词，表示"需要"，后面可跟各种结构：

跟名词或代词：

George <u>needed</u> a new pair of shoes. 乔治需要一双新鞋。

It <u>needs</u> no explanation. 这无需解释。

跟不定式：

I don't think you <u>need</u> to worry. 我认为你不必发愁。

The instruments <u>need</u> to be sterilized. 这些器具需要消毒。

跟动名词（这时动名词和主语有动宾关系）：

These shoes <u>need</u> repairing. 这双鞋需要补。

The pants do <u>need</u> pressing. 这条裤子确实需要熨烫。

跟复合结构：

I <u>need</u> you over to help me with the children. 我需要你过来帮我照顾孩子。

I <u>need</u> this tooth out. 这颗牙需要拔。

need 还可用作情态动词，主要用于否定句和疑问句：

否定句：

You <u>needn't</u> fuss. 你不必大惊小怪。

I think you <u>needn't</u> be impolite to him. 我想，你没有必要对他不客气。

疑问句：

<u>Need</u> they have done it yesterday? 这事他们需要昨天做吗？

I wonder if I <u>need</u> bring my mosquito-net. 不知我需不需要带蚊帐。

这两种用法在意义上差别不大，两种结构都可表示同样意思：

He <u>doesn't need</u> to go.

He <u>needn't</u> go. ⎫ 他不需要去。

You <u>don't need</u> to talk about it.

You <u>needn't</u> talk about it. ⎫ 你们不必讨论此事。

Do I <u>need</u> to fill in this form?

<u>Need</u> I fill in this form? ⎫ 我需要填这张表吗？

Do I <u>need</u> come in tonight?

<u>Need</u> I come in tonight? ⎫ 今晚我需要来吗？

但肯定句一般都用 **need** 作动词：

We'll <u>need</u> to repair the roof next year. 明年我们需修房顶。

③47 negligent—negligible

这两个词虽然同根，但意思却不相同。

❀ **negligent** 表示"疏忽的""不注意的"：

He was <u>negligent</u> of his duties. 他玩忽职守。

He was <u>negligent</u> of his personal appearance. 他对个人形象不注意。

❀ **negligible** 表示"微不足道的""很少（小）的"：

His contribution to the effort was <u>negligible</u>. 他对这一成就做出的贡献微不足道。

The damage to my car is <u>negligible</u>. 对我汽车造成的损害微不足道（很少）。

348 neither

neither 可以用作代词或副词。

neither 可用作代词，表示"（两者中）哪个也不"：

I tried on two dresses, but <u>neither</u> fitted me. 我试了两件连衣裙，但哪一件也不合身。

If you run after two hares, you will catch <u>neither</u>. 如果两只兔子都追，那就哪个也抓不着。（谚语）

若用作主语，后面动词多用单数形式：

<u>Neither</u> (of them) was satisfactory. 两个都不令人满意。

<u>Neither</u> of the books is of any use to me. 两本书哪一本对我也没用。

在口语中有时有人用复数动词，例如：

I quite agree that <u>neither</u> are suitable for a newspaper. 我完全同意，两者都不适宜在报纸上发表。

但在正式语言中还是用单数动词较好。

neither 可用作定语（有人称作限定词，有的字典标作形容词），表示"两……都不"：

<u>Neither</u> statement is true. 两种说法都不是事实。

In <u>neither</u> case can I agree. 在这两种情况下，我都不同意。

neither 还可用作副词，表示"也不"：

If you don't go, <u>neither</u> shall I. 如果你不去，我也不去。

He cannot speak, <u>neither</u> can he hear. 他不能讲话，也听不见。

有时用来接着别人的话讲：

"I don't like it." "<u>Neither</u> do I." "我不喜欢它。""我也不喜欢。"

"I can't swim." "<u>Neither</u> can I." "我不会游泳。""我也不会。"

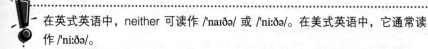

在英式英语中，neither 可读作 /ˈnaɪðə/ 或 /ˈniːðə/。在美式英语中，它通常读作 /ˈniːðə/。

349 neither... nor

neither... nor 可用作连词，连接两个词或短语，表示"和……都不"或"既不…… 又不"：

But neither Austria nor Germany would listen to this suggestion. 但是奥地利和德国都不听从这个建议。

They work neither for fame nor for personal gain. 他们工作既不为名，也不为利。

当连接两个主语时，动词和最近的主语一致：

Neither he nor they are wholly right. 他和他们都不全对。

Neither your aunt nor I have any other thought but what is best for you. 不管是你姑姑还是我都没有任何别的想法，只是想怎样对你最好。

350 no—nobody—no one—nothing

no 除了作否定词外，主要用作形容词（有人称作限定词），表示"没有……"（多和 have, there is 等连用）：

I've got no home. 我没有家。

There is no fire without some smoke. 有火就有烟，无风不起浪。（谚语）

和其他动词连用时，常表示"不（没有）……任何"：

It will do you no harm. 它不会给你造成任何损害。

Martin did no reading that night. 那天晚上，马丁没看任何书。

有时也表示"不是"（=not a）：

I'm in no mood for jokes. 我无心说笑话。

He is no financial expert. 他根本就不是金融专家。

有时表示"禁止""不许"：

No smoking. 禁止吸烟。　　　　　No spitting. 不准吐痰。

No entry. 不得进入。　　　　　No dogs. 不准带狗入内。

在作否定词时用在否定回答中：

"Is it raining?" "No, it's snowing." "在下雨吗?" "不，在下雪。"

注意在对否定疑问句作出回应时，表示"对"：

"Won't you come?" "No, I won't." "你不去吗?" "对，我不去。"

"Hasn't it stopped snowing?" "No, it hasn't." "雪还没停吗?" "对,还没停。"

"You are not from these parts?" "No, I come from Corsica." "你不是这一带的人吧?" "对,我是科西嘉人。"

❀ nobody 和 no one 都表示"没有人":

I saw nobody here. 在这里,我没看到任何人。

No one dared speak of it. 没有人敢谈及此事。

nobody 还可表示"小人物""无关紧要的人":

Mr. Povey was nobody. 波维先生是个无关紧要的人。

Don't marry a nobody like James. 不要嫁一个像詹姆斯这样的小人物。

❀ nothing 表示"没有什么(东西)":

There's really nothing to be said. 的确,没有什么可说的。

But nothing could make her alter her views. 没有什么能让她改变看法。

有时有较灵活译法:

Nothing is your fault. 不是你的错。

He knew absolutely nothing. 他什么也不知道。

有时表示"没有地位的人""没有价值的东西":

He rose from nothing to a position of power. 他从一个没有地位的人成为了一个有权有势的人。

His latest play is nothing. 他最近发表的剧本没有什么价值。

❀ no 还可用作副词,和形容词或副词的比较级连用,表示"并不……些":

She was no older than Diana. 她并不比戴安娜大。

His French is no better than my English. 他的法语并不比我的英语好。

还可和某些形容词连用,表示"不是":

He seemed no different from an ordinary worker. 他似乎和一个普通工人没有什么两样。

351 **no more—not any more—no longer—not any longer**

no more 和 not any more 意思是差不多的,表示"没有(更多)"或"不再":

There is no more bread. (There isn't any more bread.) 没有面包了。

We saw him no more. (We didn't see him any more.) 我们没再见到他了。

❀ **no longer** 和 **not any longer** 也一样，都表示"不再"：

She could no longer go to school. (She couldn't go to school any longer.) 她不再能上学了。

I can no longer stay here. (I can't stay here any longer.) 我不能在这里再待下去了。

352 non-

non- 是一个前缀（词头），可以：

加在名词前，构成反义词，如：

non-aggression 不侵略	non-alignment 不结盟
non-attendance 不出席	non-combatant 非战斗人员
non-conductor 非导体	non-confidence 不信任
non-cooperation 不合作	non-existence 不存在
non-fiction 非故事性读物	non-intervention 不干涉
non-member 非成员	non-payment 不交付
non-proliferation 不扩散	non-resident 非本地居民
non-resistance 不抵抗	non-smoker 不抽烟的人
non-violence 非暴力	non-white 非白种人

加在形容词前，构成反义词，如：

non-alcoholic 不含酒精的	non-aligned 不结盟的
non-antagonistic 非对抗性的	non-belligerent 非交战的
non-committed 不表态的	non-essential 非必不可少的
non-existent 不存在的	non-finite 非谓语的
non-human 非人类的	non-nuclear 非核子的
non-profit-making 非营利的	non-restrictive 非限制性的
non-sexual 无性的	non-smoking 非吸烟（区）
non-specific 不具体的	non-standard 不标准的
non-stop 中途不停的	non-union 非工会的
non-verbal 非言语（交际）的	non-violent 非暴力的

353 none

none 主要用作代词，可以指人，表示"没有人"：

None of them spoke English. 他们谁也不会讲英语。（他们没有人会讲英语。）

A friend to all is a friend to none. 和谁都是朋友，就和谁都不是真朋友。（谚语）

也可以指物或动物，表示"没有一个"：

I like none of the books. 这些书我全不喜欢。（这些书没有一本我喜欢。）

"How many fish do you catch?" "None." "你捕到多少鱼?" "一条也没捕到。"

在用作主语时，动词有时用复数形式，有时用单数形式。表示"所有……都不"时，动词多用复数形式：

None of us are perfect. 我们都不是完人。

None of the things he was saying were new to her. 他讲的所有情况，对她都并不新鲜。

若表示"其中一个也不"时，用单数形式更好：

None of them has any great ability. 他们中间没有一个有大本事。

None of his friends has ever been to Paris. 他的朋友谁也没去过巴黎。

在很多情况下界限并不清楚，因此常常单复两种形式都可以用：

None of the dogs was (were) there. 狗都不在那里。

None of the telephones is (are) working. 电话机都坏了。

有时 none 可以指不可数的东西，表示"一点儿都没有"：

"How much petrol is there in the car?" "None." "车里还有多少油?" "一点儿都没有了。"

He has none of his brother's selfishness. 他哥哥的自私他一点儿都没有。

I wanted some more coffee but there was none left. 我想再喝点咖啡，但一点儿都不剩了。

354 nor

nor 可引起并列成分，表示"也不（没有）"：

I have no mother, <u>nor</u> any relations. 我没有母亲，也没有任何亲戚。

For ten days he did not see Helen <u>nor</u> telephone to her. 在 10 天中他没去见海伦，也没给她打电话。

在引起分句时，后面部分要用倒装语序：

He never went again, <u>nor</u> did he write to apologize. 他再也没去，也没去信致歉。

I didn't see it, and <u>nor</u> did you. 我没见到它，你也没见到它。

在回应别人的话时也可以用它：

"I don't like him." "<u>Nor</u> do I." "我不喜欢他。" "我也不喜欢。"

355 nowadays—today—present day

nowadays 是副词，表示"现今"（常有和过去相比的意思）：

<u>Nowadays</u> children are much healthier. 现今，孩子们比过去健康。

Children are not so well-behaved <u>nowadays</u> as they used to be. 孩子们现在没有过去那样听话了。

也常常带有感慨的色彩：

No one cares about distant relatives <u>nowadays</u>. 现今，没有人关心远房亲戚了。

People <u>nowadays</u> are so superficial. 人现今都那样肤浅。

❀ today 也有类似意思，表示"现在""现今"：

Life is easier <u>today</u> than a hundred years ago. 现今，日子比一百年前好过了。

Children get a better education <u>today</u> than at any time in the past. 现今，孩子们受的教育比过去任何时候都好。

❀ present day 的意思也很相近，也表示"现在"：

To the <u>present day</u> I can't make out why I did so. 直到现在，我都不明白我为什么这样做。

The young men of <u>present day</u> are beyond my comprehension. 如今的年轻人，我不能理解。

356 observance—observation

observance 表示"遵守":

He insisted on the observance of training rules. 他坚持遵守训练规则。

Local councils should use their powers to ensure strict observance of laws. 地方政务委员会应当运用它们的权利保证人们严格遵守法律。

❀ observation 意思则不同,表示"观察":

His powers of observation were highly developed. 他的观察力得到很大提升。

This telescope is used for the observation of distant stars. 这台望远镜可用来观察远方的星星。

357 occur—happen—take place

occur 表示"发生"(多指事故、火灾等):

He related how the accident had occurred. 他讲述了这起事故是怎样发生的。

Several fires have occurred. 已发生了几次火灾了。

也可指其他的事:

She hoped that some kind of miracle would occur. 她希望能发生某种奇迹。

Great popular demonstration occurred in favour of the bill. 为支持这项法案,出现了大规模的群众性示威游行。

此外,occur 还可表示"(突然)想起""在脑中出现":

It occurred to her that she might adopt the child. 她突然想起她可以收养这个孩子。

That view of the case did not occur to me before. 对案情的这种看法,

过去没在我脑海中出现过。

❀ occur 是比较文气的词，在日常口语中多用 happen 来表示"发生"：

When did the explosion <u>happen</u>? 爆炸是什么时候发生的？

What <u>happened</u> next? 后来发生了什么事？

happen 还可和 to 连用，表示"某人发生某事"：

What has <u>happened to</u> her? 她发生了什么事？

I hope nothing has <u>happened</u> to my friend. 我希望我的朋友没发生什么事。

这里 happen 不能用其他词代替。

❀ 前两个词都表示无意发生的事。按计划发生的事都用 take place 表示：

The wedding will <u>take place</u> next week. 婚礼将在下星期举行。

The dance will <u>take place</u> after the graduation exercises. 舞会将在毕业典礼之后举行。

不过 take place 也可表示"发生"：

The accident <u>took place</u> only a block from his home. 车祸发生的地点离他家只有一个街区。

The action of the play <u>takes place</u> in ancient Rome. 剧情发生在古罗马。

358 of

of 是最常用的介词之一，它有很多用法：

表示所有关系，可译为"……的"：

He was a graduate <u>of</u> Harvard University. 他是哈佛大学毕业的。

可以和物主代词和名词所有格连用：

Have you seen those sonnets <u>of</u> Hawkshaw's? 你看过霍克肖的十四行诗吗？

表示人或物的特征，引起短语作表语：

They were both <u>of</u> middle height. 他们两人都是中等身材。

The director is <u>of</u> the same opinion. 主任也持同样看法。

表示人或物的特征，引起短语作定语：

She was a woman <u>of</u> even temper. 她是一个性情平和的人。

He was a man <u>of</u> progressive views. 他是一个有进步观点的人。

Birds of a feather flock together. 物以类聚。（谚语）

和某些动词连用，意思接近 about，常可译为 "……到"：

She began to talk of Paris. 她开始谈到巴黎。

He told her of what he had been doing. 他给她讲到了他近来做的事。

和某些形容词或过去分词连用，表示 "对于" "为" 等：

He was tired of doing things of this kind. 他对于做这种事已感到厌倦。

We are proud of our motherland. 我们为祖国感到骄傲。

和名词或数词连用，表示数量或种类：

Democracy is a form of government. 民主是政府的一种形式。

The examiner failed 25 of the candidates. 考官让 25 名考生没通过。

用在某些结构中，表示 "从" "向"，意思接近 from：

Of idleness comes no goodness. 懒惰没有好结果。（谚语）

We cannot do what you asked of us. 我们不能做你要求我们做的事。

和某些动词连用，表示 "使失掉" "使摆脱" 等：

No medicine can cure a man of discontent. 没有药能治好一个人的不满足。（谚语）

A dishonest solicitor had cheated him of part of his legacy. 一个不诚实的律师骗走了他的一部分遗产。

和一些表示动作的词连用，表示动宾关系：

It was sheer waste of money. 这完全是浪费金钱。

This war completed the unification of Germany. 这场战争实现了德国的统一。

和一名词连用，起同位语的作用：

She was a mere slip of a girl. Could she do that? 她只是一个小姑娘，能干得了这事吗？

In rushed a giant of a French officer. 冲进来一个大个子法国军官。

359 off

off 可以作介词，表示：

从……下来：

He jumped off the horse. 他从马上跳了下来。

It takes a load off my mind. 这去掉了我一件心事。

在离……不远处：

You will find the post office just off Bond Street. 你会在邦德街旁找到邮局。

The ship sank a mile off Langness. 船沉没在蓝内斯岸边一英里处。

不在……上面，偏离：

The ship was blown off her course. 船被风刮得偏离了航道。

Half of what he said was off the subject. 他一半的话都偏离了话题。

off 用作副词时更多一些。它可以表示：

（和某些动词连用）……开，……掉：

They went off together. 他们一块离开的。

She went to the station to see Philip off. 她到车站给菲利普送行。

（作表语）走掉，动身：

I must be off; I'm meeting Paul at six. 我得走了，我 6 点钟和保罗会面。

I'm off to Europe on Monday. 我礼拜一动身去欧洲。

（作表语）表示各种不同意思：

She is always off on Saturday and Sunday. 她一向星期六和星期天都不上班。

Is the gas (radio) off or on? 煤气（收音机）关着还是开着？

（和某些动词连用）……下来：

The handle came off. 把手掉下来了。

Mind you don't fall off. 小心你别掉下去了。

离……多远（可指空间，也可指时间）：

Christmas is a long way off still. 圣诞节还远着哩。

Summer is only a week off. 再过一星期就是夏天了。

不工作，休息（假）：

He tried to write poetry in his off hours. 他用休息时间试着写诗。

Tickets are cheaper during the off season. 淡季机票要便宜一些。

360 officer—official

officer 一般指"军官"：

His uncle was an <u>officer</u> in the army. 他叔叔是军队里的一位军官。

<u>officers</u> and men 官兵

也可指某些机关的负责人：

Suddenly the press <u>officer</u> came out and announced the result. 突然一位新闻发布官走了出来，宣布了结果。

a police <u>officer</u> 警官　　　　　　a health <u>officer</u> 卫生官员

a customs <u>officer</u> 海关关员　　　<u>officers</u> of state 国家官员

❀ **official** 主要指"政府官员"：

The President and the Secretary of State are government <u>officials</u>. 总统和国务卿都是政府官员。

He's an <u>official</u> in the War Office. 他是国防部的一位官员。

也可指某些"团体的负责人"：

They had the full support of the trade union <u>officials</u>. 他们得到工会负责人的全力支持。

the <u>officials</u> of a political party 一个政党的负责人员

361 on—onto

on 作介词，有很多用法，表示：

在（平面）上：

Her apartment is <u>on</u> the 14th floor. 她的公寓在 14 楼。

A mirror hung <u>on</u> the wall. 一面镜子挂在墙上。

在一条线上：

London stands <u>on</u> the Thames. 伦敦位于泰晤士河畔。

He sat down <u>on</u> the edge of the bed. 他在床边上坐下。

（用于引申意义）在……身上，在心上等：

My mind was still <u>on</u> this research. 我的心仍然在这项研究上。

Have you got any money <u>on</u> you? 你身上带钱了吗？

在某一段时间（如某天，某天晚上、早上等）：

A reception was held <u>on</u> New Year's Eve. 新年前夕开了一个招待会。

On this occasion he said nothing. 这一次他没讲话。

在……时（跟动名词或名词，表示前一动作一发生，后一动作立即发生）：

On reaching the city, he called up Lester. 到达城里时，他给莱斯特打了电话。

On his return from Europe, he set to work in earnest. 从欧洲回来后，他认真干了起来。

（表示原因）根据，由于，在……下：

He did it on the instructions of his superior. 他是根据上级指示这样做的。

She read the book on the recommendation of a friend. 由于一个朋友的推荐，她读了这本书。

（表示目的）去（做某事）：

She had come on a visit to England. 她来访问英国。

They had journeyed to Russia on a mission. 他们到俄罗斯去执行一项任务。

引起许多短语作状语：

That's very satisfactory on the whole. 总的说来，这很令人满意。

Don't give it up on any account. 不管有什么理由，都不要放弃。

引起各种短语作表语：

She was on night duty. 她值夜班。

Crimes are on the rise. 犯罪率正在上升。

关于（某个题目），在（某个问题上）：

Write a term paper on Shakespeare. 写一篇关于莎士比亚的学期论文。

I differ from you on that point. 在这一点上，我和你有不同看法。

靠……生活：

They lived mostly on vegetables from their garden. 他们主要靠他们园子里的蔬菜生活。

The prisoners could not exist on bread and water. 囚犯也不能单靠面包和水生活。

对于：

Don't be hard on the child. 不要对孩子太苛刻。

He was very strict on discipline. 他对纪律要求很严格。

on 可以构成许多短语, 如:

on account of 由于   on the average 平均

on board 在船(飞机)上   on fire 失火, 烧起来

on foot 步行   on hand 在手边

on the go 忙碌, 爱动   on the move 东跑西颠

on the other hand 另一方面   on the run 奔忙, 忙碌

on the spot 当场, 立即   on one's way 在(回家)路上

另外, **on** 还可以用作副词, 表示:

往前(走), 继续干:

She hurried on. 她匆忙往前走。

The two strolled on, arguing. 两人辩论着往前散步。

到……上面, 穿(戴)上:

Put on some warm clothes. 穿上些暖和衣服。

She was trying on a new hat. 她在试戴一顶新帽子。

(和 **be** 连用) 开着、上演等:

The war is still on. 战争还在进行。

What's on at the Capital Theatre? 首都剧场在演什么?

❀ onto 表示 "到……平面上去" (也可写成 **on to**):

When we came out on to the steps, a thin rain was falling. 我们出来走在台阶上时, 天正下着小雨。

She poured some shampoo onto my hair. 她在我头发上泼了一些洗发水。

on 也可表示同样意思, 在某些动词后, 用 onto 或 on 都可以:

Stuart put the reel of film onto the bench. 斯图尔特把一卷胶卷放在了长凳上。

I put a hand on his shoulder. 我把一只手放在了他肩上。

但在 **climb, step, lift, hoist** 等动词后, 应用 onto, 而不宜用 on:

The little boy was hoisted onto a piano stool. 小男孩被抱到了琴凳上。

Please lift the package onto the counter. 请把这包东西放到柜台上。

onto 有时表示 "抓住不放" (以免自己掉下去):

She had to hold onto the edge of the table. 她得抓住桌子边。

He held <u>on to</u> the rope. 他紧紧抓住绳子。

362 or

or 是连词，可连接平行的成分，表示"或（者）""还是"：

连接两个名词（或代词）：

Would you like coffee <u>or</u> tea? 你想喝咖啡还是茶？

One is grateful for a gift <u>or</u> a kind word. 人会为一份礼物或一句好话
而感激。

连接两个形容词或数词：

Is it green <u>or</u> blue? 它是绿色还是蓝色？

There's one <u>or</u> two things I'd like to know about. 有一两件事，我想知道。

连接两个动词：

She may do some work in the fields <u>or</u> help in the house. 她可以在地里
干活，也可以在屋里帮忙。

The egg should be hard-boiled, <u>or</u> cooked until the inside is firm. 鸡蛋
可以煮得很熟，也可煮到蛋黄刚成为固体。

连接两个副词：

Are you coming today <u>or</u> tomorrow? 你准备今天来还是明天来？

It's now <u>or</u> never. 要么现在干，要么永远别干。

连接两个介词短语：

Are you going to water the garden before <u>or</u> after supper? 你准备在晚
饭前还是晚饭后给花园浇水？

Would you like to sit in the front <u>or</u> at the back? 你想坐前面还是后面？

连接两个从句：

Do you want a bath at once, <u>or</u> shall I have mine first? 你想马上洗澡还
是我先洗？

有时可连接三样或更多东西：

The sea can be blue <u>or</u> green <u>or</u> grey. 海水可以是蓝色、绿色或是灰色。

Savings may come in useful for holidays, for expensive items of clothing,
<u>or</u> perhaps for buying a car. 存款可以用来度假、买昂贵的衣服或
买车。

在某些否定句中，要用 **or** 而不能用 **and** 连接两样（或更多）东西：

He never smokes <u>or</u> drinks. 他从不抽烟喝酒。

His chief trouble was that he did not know any editors <u>or</u> writers. 他的主要麻烦是他不认识什么编辑或作家。

or 还有一个意思，就是"否则"：

He had to have a job <u>or</u> go hungry. 他得有工作，否则就要挨饿。

Hurry <u>or</u> you won't make the train. 赶快，否则就赶不上火车了。

or else 也起同样作用：

Hurry up <u>or else</u> you'll be late. 赶快，否则你就要迟到了。

otherwise 也有同样意思：

Do it now. <u>Otherwise</u> it will be too late. 现在就干，否则就太晚了。

㊣ other—another

other 可用作形容词，表示"另外的""其他的""别的"：

I'm busy now; ask me about it some <u>other</u> time. 我现在很忙，另外找时间问我。

People fool themselves, and try to fool <u>other</u> people. 人们欺骗自己，还设法欺骗别人。

但更多用作代词，表示"另一个""其他的人""别人"：

One of them is named Richard, the <u>other</u> named Joseph. 他们一个叫理查德，另一个叫约瑟夫。

We got home by 6 o'clock, but the <u>others</u> didn't get back until about 8 o'clock. 我们6点到家，但其他的人8点左右才到家。

❀ 在表示"另一个"时，可用 **another** 作定语：

He opened <u>another</u> shop last month. 上个月，他开了另一家店。

Now she was in <u>another</u> difficulty. 现在，她又碰到另一个困难。

another 也可用作代词：

There was a rainbow in the sky, and <u>another</u> in his breast. 天上有一道彩虹，他心里有另一道彩虹。

Saying is one thing and doing <u>another</u>. 说是一回事，干是另一回事。（谚语）

364 out—out of

out 为副词，有许多用法：

表示"出来""到（在）外面"（可以和许多动词连用）：

Are you going out tonight? 你今晚出去吗？

You oughtn't to stay out so late. 你不应当在外面待到这样晚。

和各种动词连用，表示"……出""……掉"等意思：

We'll work out some solution. 我们将想出一些解决办法。

The doctor wrote out two prescriptions. 医生开了两个方子。

The stains will wash out. 这些污渍会洗掉的。

和 **be** 连用，表示许多不同的意思：

The truth is out at last. 终于真相大白了。

His new book is just out. 他的新书刚出版。

❀ **out of** 为介词，也有许多用法：

和许多动词连用，表示"从……出来"：

He came out of the library to welcome us. 他从图书室走出来欢迎我们。

My place is six miles out of town. 我家在城外，离城 6 英里。

和一些动词连用，意思接近 **from**（从……）：

I watched the country out of the window. 我从窗子里遥望田野。

He had torn a leaf out of his notebook. 他从笔记本上撕下了一页纸。

引起短语作状语，表示"出于""由于"：

She did it out of pity. 她这样做出于同情。

They were keeping her only out of kindness. 他们收留她只是出于好心。

引起短语作状语，表示"不在……里面""不要……"：

Out of sight, out of mind. 眼不见，心不烦。（谚语）

Get out of the way. 别挡道。

和 **be** 连用，表示各种不同意思：

She knew she was out of danger. 她知道她已脱离危险了。

The bell won't ring; it's out of order. 门铃不响，坏了。

The book is out of print. 这本书已不再印刷。

Rest was now out of the question. 休息现在已不可能。

365 outdoor—outdoors

outdoor 为形容词，表示"户外的""露天的"：

There's an <u>outdoor</u> concert in the park tonight. 今晚公园里有一个露天音乐会。

American football is the most scientific of all <u>outdoor</u> games. 美式足球是所有户外运动中最科学的运动。

❀ **outdoors** 为副词，表示"在户外""在外边"：

He spends much of his time <u>outdoors</u>. 他很多时间都在户外度过。

Some classes were held <u>outdoors</u>. 有些课在户外上。

366 over

over 可用作介词，也可用作副词：

用作介词时可表示多种意思：

在……上方：

A lamp was hanging <u>over</u> the table. 一盏灯悬挂在桌子上方。

The sky is <u>over</u> our heads. 天空在我们的头上方。

在……上面：

The lady wore a white shawl <u>over</u> her shoulders. 这女郎肩上披了一块白披肩。

He wore a thick coat <u>over</u> his ordinary coat. 他在普通大衣外面又穿了一件厚大衣。

从上面（越过、跳过）：

The dog jumped <u>over</u> the fence. 那条狗从栅栏上方跳了过去。

He escaped <u>over</u> the frontier. 他越过边界逃跑了。

用于各种引申意义：

She had already told me <u>over</u> the telephone about it. 她已在电话里把这事告诉了我。

The money will tide him <u>over</u> the difficulties. 这些钱可帮助他渡过困难。

在（某问题）上，为（某事）：

We quarrelled <u>over</u> the colour. 我们在颜色问题上发生争吵。

He is troubled over his health. 他为自己的健康烦恼。

（指时间）在……中，度过：

Over the years he's become more and more patient. 在这些年中，他变得越来越有耐心了。

Our region has made great advances over the past ten years. 在过去 10 年中，我们地区有了很大发展。

超过，……多：

Its population is over two million. 它的人口超过 200 万。

He stayed in London for over a month. 他在伦敦待了一个多月。

over 作副词时也有不少意思：

到某地来（去）：

Henry came over and examined the picture. 亨利走过来，查看了这张画。

I will go over to his office and have a talk with him. 我到他办公室去和他谈一谈。

（和某些动词连用）……一遍：

I stood for five minutes thinking the business over. 我站了 5 分钟，把这件事想了一遍。

He decided to talk all this over with his wife. 他决定把这一切和他妻子好好谈一谈。

（和某些动词连用）翻倒，翻转：

Don't knock the vase over. 别把花瓶碰倒了。

It's time I turned over a new leaf. 我该重新做人。（翻开新的一页）

布满，盖住，溢出：

It was clouding over outside. 外边浓云密布。

The milk boiled over. 牛奶开得溢了出来。

（和 be 连用）过去，结束：

Summer is over—it is autumn. 夏天已经过去，现在是秋天。

I mean to go there when the war is over. 我打算等战争结束后到那里去。

剩下，还多：

I've paid all my debts and have £15 over. 我把债都还了，还剩 15 镑。

I have all I need and a bit over. 我需要的都有了，还剩一点儿。

重复（一遍）：

He did the work over. 他把这工作又重做了一遍。

Do that three times over. 把这做三遍。

过于，太：

Perhaps he was over cautious. 或许他过于谨慎。

I think he's over excited. 我想他过于激动了。

367 **over-**

over- 是一个常用的前缀，可以构成大量合成词：

加在形容词前，表示"过于"：

overabundant	over-active	over-ambitious	over-bold
over-busy	over-careful	over-confident	over-critical
overdue	over-emotional	over-enthusiastic	over-excited
over-familiar	over-full	over-generous	over-greedy
over-hasty	over-jealous	over-proud	over-serious
over-suspicious	over-sensitive	over-zealous	

加在名词前，表示"过多的""超过的"：

over-abundance	overage	over-anxiety	over-confidence
over-dose	over-draft	over-indulgence	over-load
over-payment	over-population	over-production	over-strain
overtime	overweight	over-work	

有时有其他意思，表示"上面的""外面的"等：

overcoat	overhead	overland	overlord
overpower	overshadow	overshoe	oversight

加在动词前，表示"过分"：

overact	overbid	over-burden	over-cook
over-crowd	over-develop	over-do	over-emphasize
over-estimate	over-heat	over-indulge	over-praise
over-produce	overrate	over-simplify	overtax
overwork			

有时有其他意思：

overbear	overflow	overhand	overhear
overlap	override	overrule	overrun
overtake	overthrow	overturn	

368 overwork—overtime

overwork 作名词，表示"过度劳累"：

Overwork brought on insomnia. 过度劳累引起失眠。

Perhaps I was suffering a little from overwork. 或许，我有点儿过于劳累。

也可用作动词：

Don't overwork yourself. 不要过于劳累。

He was tired, overwork. 他很累，过于劳累。

❀ **overtime** 可作副词，表示"超时工作""加班"：

They're working overtime to finish the job. 他们正在加班来完成这项工作。

He never complained about working overtime. 他超时工作，从不抱怨。

也可用作名词：

They were paid extra for overtime. 他们因加班发了额外工资。

I don't do overtime straight after a full shift. 上完全班后，我不立即加班。

overtime pay 加时工资

369 pain—painful—in pain

pain 主要表示"疼痛":

She had pains in her back all the time. 她老是背疼。

Betty is crying because she has a pain in her stomach. 贝蒂在哭,因为她肚子疼。

也可表示"痛苦":

The pain in her heart was intolerable. 她内心的痛苦简直无法忍受。

❀ **painful** 为形容词,表示"疼的"(往往指身体某部分疼痛):

His legs are very painful. 他的腿很疼。

Is your tooth still painful? 你的牙还疼吗?

❀ 若表示某人疼痛,不能用 **painful** 这个词,而要说 **in pain**:

I'm wounded and in pain. 我受了伤,很疼。

That child looks as though it is in pain. 那孩子看起来像是很疼的样子。

370 pair—couple

a pair of 表示"一双""一幅""一把""一条"等:

a pair of chopsticks 一双筷子   a pair of glasses 一副眼镜

a pair of trousers 一条裤子   a pair of socks 一双袜子

pair 也可指"一对(夫妻或情人)":

The bride and groom are a good-looking pair. 新娘新郎是漂亮的一对。

He never heard of any misunderstanding between the pair. 他从未听说这对夫妻间有什么误会。

❀ 夫妻俩用 **couple** 表示时更多:

They were a model couple. 他们是一对模范夫妻。

There they were taken in by an aged couple. 在那里,一对老年夫妇收

留了他们。

a couple of 可表示"一两个""（少数）几个"：

She was expecting a baby in a couple of months. 一两个月后，她就要生孩子了。

There's a couple of vacant rooms behind the office. 办公室后面有一两间空房。

371 pants—shorts—briefs

在英式英语中，**pants** 指内裤。男人的内裤有时称作 underpants，女人的内裤有时称作 **panties** 或 **knickers**。

在美式英语中，**pants** 指一般的裤子，和 **trousers** 意思一样：

This sports jacket will match those pants nicely. 这件运动衫和那条裤子配得很好。

❀ 男人的内裤在美国称为 shorts 或 underpants，女人的内裤称为 panties。不管在英国还是美国，shorts 还可表示"短裤"：

Today he wore shorts instead of his long trousers. 今天他穿短裤，没穿长裤。

pants 和 **shorts** 都是复数名词，后面跟复数动词：

The pants were big in the waist. 裤腰很大。

His grey shorts were sticking to him with sweat. 他灰色的短裤被汗粘在了身上。

❀ 男女内裤也可称作 **briefs**：

He bought a new pair of briefs. 他买了一条新内裤。

372 paper—papers

paper 表示"纸"时，为不可数名词：

Parcels are wrapped in brown paper. 包裹是用棕色纸包的。

The plates were made of paper. 这些盘子是用纸做的。

一张纸可用 **a piece of paper** 或 **a sheet of paper** 表示：

I need a sheet of letter paper. 我需要一张信纸。

He picked up the <u>piece of paper</u> and gave it to her. 他捡起那张纸，递给了她。

paper 还可表示"报纸"，这时为可数名词：

Have you seen today's <u>paper</u>? 你看见今天的报纸了吗？

I asked her to fetch me an evening <u>paper</u>. 我让她帮我拿一份晚报来。

此外还可表示"文件""证件"，这时也作可数名词：

Important <u>papers</u> were stolen. 重要文件被偷了。

Where are my <u>papers</u>? 我的证件在哪里？

You will have to show your <u>papers</u> at the gate. 在大门口你得出示证件。

另外还可表示"论文""试题""考卷"（这时也是可数名词）：

Dr. Jones read a <u>paper</u> on American art. 琼斯博士宣读了一篇关于美国艺术的论文。

The teacher set us a history <u>paper</u>. 老师给我们出了一份历史试卷。

373 parcel—package—packet—pack

parcel 和 **package** 都可表示"一包（东西）"：

Among the <u>parcels</u> was a package for me. 包裹中有一个包是给我的。

How much is this <u>package</u> of detergent? 这包洗涤剂多少钱？

两者的意思差别不大。在美式英语中，**package** 用得比较多一些。

❀ **packet** 多指"一小包东西"：

I have a <u>packet</u> of sweets. 我有一小包糖果。

The postman brought a small <u>packet</u>. 邮递员送来一个小包裹。

❀ 在美式英语中，常可用 **package** 或 **pack** 表示"一小包"：

He took a <u>package</u> of cigarettes out of his pocket. 他从口袋里掏出一盒香烟。

The boy bought three <u>packs</u> of gum. 小男孩买了三包口香糖。

374 part—partial—partly

part 作名词时主要表示"一部分"：

The story is told in three <u>parts</u>. 这故事分三部分讲。

Parts of the book are interesting. 这本书有些部分很有意思。

在表示"一部分"时，冠词常不说出：

They talked part of the time in Italian. 他们一部分时间用意大利语交谈。

It's part of the tradition of our race. 这是我们种族传统的一部分。

如果 part 前有形容词修饰，前面可加 a 或 an：

A large part of the roof was missing. 一大部分房顶没有了。

I walked a good part of the way. 我步行了一大段路。

part 还可表示"地区""零件""角色"等：

Have you been in this part of the country before? 你过去到过这个地区吗？

I went through the workshops where the separate parts are made. 我在制造各个零件的车间转了一趟。

还可用于一些短语：

in part 部分地

The house is furnished in part. 房子里只有一部分家具。

part and parcel 不可少的一部分

Receptions are part and parcel of the mayor's job. 接待是市长工作不可少的部分。

play a part in 在……起作用

They played a big part in developing Latin American unionism. 在开展拉丁美洲的工会工作中，他们起了很大作用。

take part in 参与

Did you take part in the fighting? 你参加战斗了吗？

❀ **partial** 是它的形容词形式，表示"部分的"：

The play was only a partial success. 这个剧只部分地获得了成功。

This is only a partial list of the books needed. 这只是所需书的部分清单。

还可表示"有偏心的""偏爱的"等：

Our teacher sometimes seems partial to girls. 我们老师似乎偏爱女生。

The referee was accused of being partial to the home team. 裁判被控偏向主队。

partially 表示 "部分地"：

I am <u>partially</u> to blame for the accident. 出了这次事故，部分得怪我。

The work is only <u>partially</u> finished. 这项工作只是部分完成。

❀ **partly** 也表示 "部分地"：

Perhaps you're <u>partly</u> right. 或许你有些部分是对的。

It was made <u>partly</u> of wood and partly of metal. 它一部分是用木头做的，一部分是用金属做的。

part 还可作动词，表示 "和……分开"：

He <u>parted</u> with us at the end of the trip. 旅行结束时，他和我们分手了。

We <u>parted</u>, and we haven't met since. 我们分开了，之后再也没见面。

part with 还可表示 "出让" "卖掉" 等：

They were sorry to <u>part with</u> the old house. 他们出让旧房子，心里很难过。

He hated <u>parting with</u> his piano. 他很不愿意把钢琴卖掉。

375 pay—salary—wage—remuneration

pay 表示 "工资" 或 "薪水"：

The miners went on strike for higher <u>pay</u>. 矿工罢工要求增加工资。

His <u>pay</u> went up every year. 他每年都加薪。

 pay 是不可数名词，不能加 a，也没有复数形式。

❀ **salary** 表示 "薪水"，多作可数名词：

He earns a <u>salary</u> of £20,000 per annum. 他年薪两万英镑。

Their company pay good <u>salaries</u>. 他们公司薪酬很高。

也可用作不可数名词：

How much <u>salary</u> does the job pay? 这个工作薪酬多少？

❀ **wage** 表示 "工资"，多用复数形式，一般每周发一次：

What are your weekly <u>wages</u>? 你每周工资多少？

His <u>wages</u> were 4,000 pounds a year. 他一年的工资是 4 000 英镑。

有时作单数，特别是有定语修饰时：

He gets a weekly <u>wage</u> of £200. 他每周工资 200 英镑。

The average worker's <u>wage</u> is only \$180. 一个工人的平均工资为 180 美元。

❀ **remuneration** 也可表示"薪酬""酬金"：

\$31,000 is a generous <u>remuneration</u>. 31 000 美元是相当丰厚的酬金。

Our company offers a competitive <u>remuneration</u> package including a company car. 我们公司待遇是比较优厚的，还有一辆公司的汽车可用。

这个词比较文气，用得比较少些。

376 percentage—per cent

percentage 表示"百分比"，多和 of 一起用：

A great <u>percentage</u> of our pilots retire early. 我们很大百分比的飞行员都退休很早。

What <u>percentage</u> of babies die of this disease every year? 每年多少百分比的婴儿死于这种疾病？

可有比较灵活的译法：

What <u>percentage</u> of his income is paid in income tax? 他的收入有多大比例用来交所得税？

It's a tiny <u>percentage</u> of the total income. 它只是全部收入的一小部分。

如果连用的名词为复数，后面动词用复数形式，否则用单数形式：

A good percentage of the people <u>were</u> from India. 大部分人来自印度。

A high percentage of the population <u>has been</u> naturalized. 人口大部分都已归化入籍。

❀ **per cent**（也可连成一个词），表示"百分之……"：

Blacks constitute ten <u>per cent</u> of the population. 黑人占人口的百分之十。

About 90 <u>per cent</u> of most food is water. 大部分食物中约有百分之九十为水。

per cent 还可用作定语或状语：

I think it's ninety <u>per cent</u> probable. 我想这有百分之九十的可能性。

Prices have risen 5.5 <u>per cent</u> in the past year. 过去一年，物价上涨了 5.5%。

377 permissible—permissive

这两个词都是形容词，但意思不同。

❀ permissible 表示"可以允许的"：

It is not permissible for children to bring their pets to school. 孩子带宠物到学校是不允许的。

Is smoking permissible on this plane? 这架飞机上允许抽烟吗？

❀ permissive 表示"宽容""放纵"，尤指对儿童或两性关系的态度：

Should parents be strict or be permissive? 家长对子女应当严格还是放纵？

They grew up in a permissive society. 他们在宽容的社会中长大。

378 permission—permit

permission 是名词，表示"允许""准许"（不可数），可以和许多动词连用：

have	May I have permission to go home early? 能允许我早回家吗？
ask	He asked their permission to use the telephone. 他请求他们准许他使用电话。
give	The mayor gave them permission to meet in that city. 市长允许他们在那座城市开会。
get	We'll get permission to use some of the funds. 我们将获得批准使用部分基金。
obtain	He had obtained permission to extend his field of investigation. 他获得批准，扩大调查的范围。

还可和 with 或 without 连用：

With your permission we will fly to New York today. 经你同意，我们今天就飞往纽约。

You can't do it without permission. 未经同意，你不能这样做。

❀ permit / pɜ:mɪt/ 也是名词，但意思不同，它表示"许可证"（可数）：

Have you a permit to fish in this lake? 你有在这座湖里垂钓的许可证吗？

Do you have a driver's <u>permit</u>? 你有驾驶证吗？

She hasn't got a work <u>permit</u>. 她没有工作许可证。

379 persecute—prosecute

这两个词词形相近，意思却完全不同。

❀ **persecute** 表示"迫害"：

He set out to <u>persecute</u> Christians. 他开始迫害基督徒。

The puritans were <u>persecuted</u> for their religious beliefs. 清教徒因为他们的宗教信仰而受到迫害。

❀ **prosecute** 表示"对……起诉（提起公诉）"：

He was <u>prosecuted</u> for stealing. 他因偷窃被起诉。

The state is <u>prosecuting</u> him for murder. 国家对他的谋杀罪提起公诉。

380 personal—personnel

这两个词词形也近似，意思则不同。

❀ **personal** /ˈpɜːsənəl/ 为形容词，表示"个人的""私人的"：

In his <u>personal</u> life, he was a good-natured, kind man. 在私人生活中，他是一个天性善良、和蔼可亲的人。

I have my <u>personal</u> letters in this box. 我的私人信件都在这个盒子里。

❀ **personnel** /ˌpɜːsəˈnel/ 是名词，是"工作人员"的总称：

All <u>personnel</u> will receive an extra week's vacation. 所有工作人员将有一星期的额外假期。

The <u>personnel</u> are happy about these changes. 所有工作人员对这些变动都很高兴。

有时前面可加数词，表示"多少员工"：

Five airline <u>personnel</u> died in the plane crash. 在飞机坠毁时，航空公司有五名工作人员丧生。

The company transferred 50 of its <u>personnel</u> to the west coast office. 这家公司调派了 50 名工作人员到西海岸的办事处。

可用作定语，表示"管人事的"：

He's a personnel officer. 他是一名人事管理人员。

Please report to the personnel department tomorrow. 明天，请到人事处报到。

381 persuade—convince

persuade /pə'sweɪd/ 主要表示"说服（某人干某事）"：

The salesman persuaded us to buy his product. 推销员说服我们买了他的产品。

Who persuaded you to join the society? 谁说服你参加这个协会的？

在劝说而不一定说服时，可用 **try to persuade** 等表示：

He tried to persuade him to change his mind. 他设法劝说他改变主意。

I want to persuade her to go overseas with me. 我想劝说她跟我到海外去。

有时可表示"使相信"：

She persuaded him that she was telling the truth. 她让他相信她讲的是事实。

She would persuade them that she had done right. 她将让他们相信她做的是对的。

❀ convince 与 persuade 的后一种用法相同，表示"使相信"：

They convinced me Paul was innocent. 他们让我相信保罗是无辜的。

I couldn't convince him of my innocence. 我不能让他相信我是无辜的。

382 pitiful—pitiable

pitiful 主要表示"凄惨的""可怜的"：

What a pitiful sight! 多么凄惨的景象！

The pitiful sobs of the child softened our hearts. 孩子凄伤的哭泣使我们心软。

❀ pitiable 也表示"可怜的""值得同情的"：

The poor old man was a pitiable (=pitiful) sight. 那穷苦老头儿样子很可怜。

They were pitiable in their helplessness. 他们无依无靠，令人同情。

两个词中 pitiful 的意思稍强一点儿。

383　point of view—view—opinion

point of view 有两个意思。

一是表示"观点""角度"：

From your point of view this may be important, but from mine it is not. 从你的角度看，这可能很重要，但从我的角度看则并不如此。

It was an unsatisfactory meeting from every point of view. 从哪个观点看，这次会议都不令人满意。

二是表示"看法"：

Let's talk to Hillary. He'll have another point of view. 咱们去和希拉里谈谈，他会有另一种看法。

There was not much difference in their points of view. 他们的看法没有多大差别。

❀ view 主要表示"看法"：

I should like to hear others' view. 我想听听别人的看法。

She shared his rosy view about it. 她对此也有与他同样的乐观的看法。

有时也可译作"观点"：

Gradually he changed his political views. 慢慢地，他改变了他的政治观点。

in one's view 可表示"据……看来"：

In the mayor's view the town budget must be increased. 在市长看来，本市预算应当增加。

In the view of the magistrate, the offence was not a serious one. 在执法官看来，这项罪并不严重。

❀ opinion 也可表示"看法""意见"：

It's my opinion that the plan won't work. 我的看法是这个计划行不通。

He asked my opinion of the pictures. 他征求我对这些画的意见。

in one's opinion 也表示"据……看来"：

In his opinion, that House had become the great obstacle to progress. 在

他看来，下议院已成为妨碍进步的巨大障碍。

In the opinion of most people, the scheme is unsound. 在多数人看来，这个计划不行。

384 power—strength

power 有好几个意思：

力量，能力（不可数）：

Knowledge is power. 知识就是力量。

It is beyond my power to help you. 帮助你超出了我的能力。

imaginative power 想象力　　　　　will-power 意志力

creative power 创造力　　　　　　purchasing power 购买力

权力，权限（一般不可数，有时作复数表示各种权力）：

Congress has power to declare war. 国会有权宣战。

A judge has the power to send a person to prison. 法官有权送人进监狱。

Its powers are very extensive. 它的权力很广泛。

Are the powers of the Prime Minister defined by law? 首相的权限由法律规定吗？

势力（不可数），有影响的人或事物（可数）：

The cardinal was the real power behind the throne. 红衣主教是王位后面真正有影响的人物。

Is the press a great power in your country? 新闻界在你们国家影响大吗？

强国，大国：

The great powers held an international conference. 强国们举行了一个国际会议。

the superpower 超级大国

电力，功率：

power plant 发电厂　　　　　　　power failure 停电

a telescope of high power 大功率的望远镜

a 30 horse-power engine 一台 30 匹马力的发动机

❀ **strength** 主要指"气力""体力"：

Does he have enough strength to lift these weights? 他有足够的气力举起这些重物吗？

The athlete reserved his strength for the race. 运动员保持体力来参加赛跑。

I wish I had your strength. 但愿我有你这么大力气。

也可表示"力量"：

He underestimated the enemy's strength. 他低估了敌人的力量。

Her strength of will was extraordinary. 她的意志力是很突出的。

I admired his immense physical strength. 我很佩服他强大的体力。

385 practical—practicable

practical 主要表示"实际的""现实的"：

He was weak in practical matters. 他处理实际事务不行。

There is always a lot of practical work to be done. 总有许多实际工作要做。

We have to look at things in a practical way. 我们必须现实地看问题。

也可表示"讲求实际"：

We've got to be practical and buy what we can afford. 我们得实际点，只买我们买得起的东西。

He was a practical man and opposed to theory. 他是个讲求实际的人，反对理论。

还可表示"切实可行的""实用的"：

Your invention is clever, but not very practical. 你的发明很聪明，但不太实用。

We must adopt practical measures for settling problems. 我们必须采取切实可行的措施来解决问题。

❀ **practicable** 主要用来说明计划、办法等"可行的""行得通的"：

His plan, I feel certain, is practicable. 我肯定他的计划行得通。

The remedy is simple, easy and practicable. 这种疗法简单、容易、切实可行。

386 precaution—prevention

precaution 指"预防措施"（可数）：

The doctor would like you to be vaccinated as a precaution. 医生希望你打针作为预防。

Take every precaution so as not to catch cold. 采取一切预防措施以免感冒。

❀ **prevention** 表示"预防""防止"（不可数）：

Prevention is better than cure. 防病胜于治病。（谚语）

Prevention of disease is one of the duties of the government health officers. 预防疾病是政府卫生官员的职责之一。

387 prefer—preferable

prefer 是动词，表示"宁愿""更喜欢（愿意）"，可跟以下几种结构。
跟名词和代词：

I prefer the view taken by Balzac. 我更赞成巴尔扎克的意见。

Which do you prefer? 你更喜欢哪一个？

跟不定式：

She prefers to live among the working people. 她更喜欢生活在劳动人民中间。

At the moment, he preferred not to think about the future. 此刻，他宁愿不想未来。

跟动名词：

I prefer standing. 我宁愿站着。

Oh, I prefer being alone. 啊，我宁愿一个人待着。

跟带不定式的复合结构：

Cyril preferred her not to come. 西里尔宁愿她不来。

They preferred the matter to be discussed at the next meeting. 他们更愿意下次会上再讨论这件事。

跟从句：

She preferred that he should do it in the kitchen. 她更愿意他在厨房做这事。

Would you prefer that I come on Monday instead of on Tuesday? 你是否更愿意我星期一来，而不是星期二来？

△在表示"喜欢……而不喜欢（胜过）……"时可用 prefer... to 这个结构：

I prefer the town to the country. 我喜欢城市胜过乡村。

He preferred doing something to doing nothing. 他宁愿做事而不愿游手好闲。

同样意思也可用 prefer... rather than 表示：

I prefer to walk there rather than go by bus. 我宁愿走着去，也不愿坐公共汽车去。

He preferred to stay at home rather than go out with us. 他宁愿待在家里，也不愿和我们一道出去。

I should prefer beef rather than mutton. 我宁愿吃牛肉而不愿吃羊肉。

❀ preferable 是由 prefer 变来的形容词，表示"更好一些"，常和 to 连用：

A dark suit is preferable to a light one for evening wear. 晚上穿深色西服比浅色西服好。

In other uses "continue to" is preferable. 在其他用法中，continue to 更好一些。

388 principle—principal

principle 主要表示"原则"（可数，不可数）：

It's a matter of principle. 这是一个原则问题。

We agree in principle, but we dislike your methods. 我们原则上一致，但我们不喜欢你的方法。

还可表示"原理"：

These machines work on the same principle. 这些机器也遵循同样原理。

the principles of Archimedes 阿基米德原理

❀ principal 作为名词，表示"中小学校长"或"大学院长"：

The school principal announced the honour roll list. 校长宣布了光荣榜名单。

The principal of a college is the man or woman in charge of it.（大学）学院院长是负责这个学院的人。

也可指"本金"：

A principal of $500 earns 6% interest a year. 500 美元的本金每年的利率是 6%。

还可用作形容词，表示"主要的"：

The principal food of the Chinese is rice. 中国人的主要食物为大米。

The Nile is one of the principal rivers in Africa. 尼罗河是非洲主要河流之一。

389 proceed—precede

这两个词拼法相近，读音也相近，容易混淆。

❀ proceed 表示"向前走""继续前进"：

The train proceeded at the same speed as before. 火车继续按原来的速度前进。

She was glad that she had refused to proceed to Paris. 她很高兴，她拒绝了继续前往巴黎。

还可表示"接着做某事""开始……"：

As soon as he came in, he proceeded to tell us all his troubles. 他一进来就开始给我们讲述他的种种困难。

After drinking a cup of tea mother proceeded to cook the dinner. 喝了一杯茶后，妈妈开始做饭。

还可表示"进行"：

The experiment is proceeding as planned. 实验按计划进行。

The work is proceeding briskly. 工作进展迅速。

❀ precede 表示"在……之前"：

The Greek civilization preceded the Roman one. 希腊文明在罗马文明之前。

Twelve guards on motorcycles preceded the President's car. 在总统座车之前有 12 名骑摩托车的警卫人员开道。

390 produce—product

produce 作动词时读作 /prə'djuːs/，主要表示"生产""出产"：

Australia <u>produces</u> wool and meat. 澳大利亚出产羊毛和肉。

The factory <u>produces</u> 1,000 cars a week. 这家工厂每星期生产 1 000 辆汽车。

还可表示"产生""造成""引起"等：

It <u>produced</u> a false impression. 它造成了一个虚假印象。

Their efforts <u>produced</u> no results. 他们的努力没有结果。

它的名词形式，读作 /'prɒdjuːs/，表示"农产品"：

He has a small store where he sells groceries and <u>produce</u>. 他有一家小店，出售食品杂货和农产品。

The wine bottle was marked "<u>Produce</u> of Spain". 酒瓶上标有"西班牙出产"。

❀ 一般产品用 **product** /'prɒdəkt/ 表示：

Its principal <u>products</u> are cattle, sheep, wheat, corn and fruits. 它的主要产品为牛、羊、小麦、玉米和水果。

They must have new markets for their <u>products</u>. 他们必须有销售产品的新市场。

product 还可表示"产物"：

He saw man as a <u>product</u> of society. 他把人看作社会的产物。

391 programme—program

programme 为英式拼法，**program** 为美式拼法，主要表示以下三种意思：

计划：

The senate committee formulated a new crime prevention <u>program</u>. 参议院委员会制订了一个防止犯罪的新计划。

teaching <u>programme</u> 教学大纲

活动计划，日程：

This is his <u>programme</u> for a week. 这是他一周的活动计划。

Today's <u>program</u> includes a tour of the Statue of Liberty. 今天的日程包

括参观自由女神像一项。

节目单,(电视)节目:

Did you buy a programme? 你买节目单了吗?

New programs appear in the fall on television. 今秋电视上将出现新节目。

△在表示"电脑程序设计"时在两国都拼作 program:

I installed the new program in my computer. 我把新的程序设计安装在我的电脑中了。

A programmer is a person who prepares a computer program. 程序设计员是为电脑设计程序的人员。

392 progress—advance—advancement

progress 表示"进步""进展"(不可数):

His research made slow progress. 他的研究工作进展缓慢。

He gave her an account of his progress. 他向她谈了他的进展情况。

❀ **advance** 也可表示类似意思,它是可数名词:

Science has made great advances in the last fifty years. 最近 50 年,科学取得了巨大进步。

There have been great advances in space exploration in the last 40 years. 最近 40 年,太空探索有了很大进展。

❀ **advancement** 表示"促进(发展)":

The aim of a university should be the advancement of learning. 大学的目标应是促进学术的发展。

The Royal Society for the Advancement of Science 皇家科学促进协会

393 prohibit—ban—forbid

prohibit 主要表示"禁止":

Picking flowers in the park is prohibited. 公园内禁止攀摘花木。

Smoking in this railway carriage is prohibited. 本车厢内禁止吸烟。

还可用于 **prohibit somebody from doing something**:

The country has a law prohibiting employees from striking. 这个国家有

法律禁止雇员罢工。

Professor Brown was <u>prohibited</u> from speaking on campus. 布朗教授被禁止在校园内发表演说。

❀ ban 有类似意思，表示"禁止""禁演"等：

We will <u>ban</u> all smoking in our club. 在我们俱乐部，我们将完全禁止吸烟。

They threatened to <u>ban</u> the book. 他们威胁说要禁止出售这本书。

ban 还可用作名词，表示"禁止""禁令"：

The police lifted the <u>ban</u> against parking in this street. 警察解除了这条街不让泊车的禁令。

The principal announced a <u>ban</u> on guns at the school. 校长宣布在校内禁止携带枪支。

❀ forbid 也可表示"禁止"，可以跟好几种结构：

Their father <u>forbade</u> them to go. 他们的父亲禁止他们去。

The government decided to <u>forbid</u> the meeting. 政府决定禁止这一集会。

394 propaganda—publicity—promotion—advertisement—advertising—commercial

propaganda 指"宣传"（不可数）：

There has been a great deal of <u>propaganda</u> about the dangers of smoking. 有大量关于吸烟有危险的宣传。

The <u>propaganda</u> of a political party is planned to gain votes. 一个政党的宣传目的在于获得选票。

political <u>propaganda</u> 政治宣传

❀ publicity 也可指"宣传""报道"（不可数）：

The concert was a good one, but because of bad <u>publicity</u>, very few people came. 这个音乐会很好，但宣传工作没做好，来的人很少。

Bad <u>publicity</u> hurt the mayor's chances for reelection. 不良宣传损害了市长重新当选的机会。

也可表示"推广""促销""广告"：

Who's going to do the show's <u>publicity</u>? 谁负责这次演出的推广活动？

a <u>publicity</u> campaign 促销活动

❀ **promotion** 也有"推销（活动）"的意思（不可数）：

Heavy <u>promotion</u> helped to make that novel a best-seller within weeks. 大量的推销活动帮助这本小说在几周内成为畅销书。

The year's sales <u>promotions</u> hasn't been very successful. 今年的推销活动不太成功。

❀ **advertisement** 多指"一条广告"（可数），也可指"广告活动"（不可数）：

If you want to sell your piano, put an <u>advertisement</u> in the newspaper. 如果你想卖钢琴，可在报上登一条广告。

The store has an <u>advertisement</u> in the newspaper for a special sale. 这家商店为特别大减价在报上登了一则广告。

❀ **advertising** 是"广告"的总称（不可数）：

The zoo launched an <u>advertising</u> campaign to attract more people. 动物园发起了一次广告活动来吸引更多的人。

❀ 电视广播上的广告称为 **commercial**：

a soap powder <u>commercial</u> 一条肥皂粉的广告

I hate commercials on <u>television</u>. 我讨厌电视上的广告。

395 proud

proud 有正面的意思，表示"骄傲的""自豪的"：

She was <u>proud</u> to have brought up a daughter like her. 她为带大了这样一个女儿感到自豪。

I'm <u>proud</u> to be your friend. 做你的朋友，我感到骄傲。

常跟 **of** 引导的短语，表示"为……感到骄傲"：

She was very <u>proud of</u> her mother's confidence in her. 她妈对她有信心，她感到很骄傲。

I do admit I'm rather <u>proud of</u> this place. 我承认我对这个地方感到相当自豪。

也可有负面的意思，表示"高傲""骄傲自满"：

He's too <u>proud</u> to speak to poor people like us. 他高傲得不屑于和我们穷人讲话。

He was too <u>proud</u> to join our party. 他太骄傲，不愿参加我们的晚会。

Harold is a <u>proud</u>, vain man. 哈罗德是一个高傲虚荣的人。

△表示这类意思的还有一系列形容词（都带贬义）：

arrogant 骄傲自大的，傲慢无礼的：

John is so <u>arrogant</u> that he thinks he is better than everyone else. 约翰是那样高傲自大，自以为比谁都强。

The boss's son was <u>arrogant</u> to all the employees. 老板的儿子对所有雇员都很傲慢无礼。

conceited 骄傲自满的，高傲的：

All this made the girl <u>conceited</u> about herself. 这一切使得这位姑娘骄傲自满。

You mustn't think that I was a <u>conceited</u> man. 不要认为我是一个高傲的人。

haughty 高傲的，傲慢的：

The <u>haughty</u> woman did not respond when greeted by her servant. 这位高傲的女人，佣人向她问好都不理不睬。

Bill despised him because he had a <u>haughty</u> attitude. 比尔看不起他，因为他态度傲慢。

smug 沾沾自喜的，得意洋洋的：

Jim was <u>smug</u> because he had been right and I had been wrong. 吉姆得意洋洋，因为他对了，我错了。

The <u>smug</u> designer thought her designs were better than mine. 那个沾沾自喜的设计师认为她的设计比我的强。

supercilious 高傲的，自以为了不起的：

They were standing by themselves looking <u>supercilious</u>. 他们独自站在那里，显得很了不起的样子。

He is a <u>supercilious</u> man. 他是一个高傲的人。

vain 虚荣的，高傲的：

His wife was <u>vain</u> and extravagant. 他的妻子很虚荣、奢侈。

Ruth is very <u>vain</u> about her appearance. 露丝对自己的外貌感到骄傲。

self-satisfied 自满的，得意的：

"I knew I was right," Bill said with a self-satisfied laugh. 比尔得意地笑道：“我知道我是对的。”

He was too self-satisfied to pay attention to what they were saying. 他太自满，不注意他们说的话。

有的词则无贬义，甚至有称赞的意思，如 **self-respecting**, 表示“有自尊心的”：

They grew into responsible and self-respecting citizens. 他们成长为了有责任心、有自尊心的公民。

What self-respecting person would do such a horrible thing? 哪个有自尊心的人会做出这种可怕的事？

396 provide—provided—providing

provide 主要有两个用法：

表示“提供”：

The Red Cross provides food and shelter for disaster victims. 红十字会为灾民提供食物和住处。

On Sundays his landlord provided dinner as well as breakfast. 星期天，他的房东提供一顿早饭和晚饭。

表示“规定”：

The author's contract provided that he was to receive royalties. 这位作者的合约规定他将可以领取版税。

The law provides that valuable ancient buildings must be preserved by the government. 法律规定珍贵古建筑应由政府保护。

❀ **provided** 可用作连词（有时和 **that** 连用），表示“如果……”“只要……”：

They may swim provided an adult accompanies them. 只要有大人陪着，他们可以游泳。

Provided (that) there is no opposition, we shall hold the meeting here. 如果没人反对，我们将在这里开会。

❀ **providing** 也有同样作用：

You may go out providing you do your homework first. 只要你先把作业做好，你就可以出去。

We'll visit Europe next year, providing (provided) we have the money. 如果我们有这笔钱，明年我们将去欧洲。

Providing (that) there is no opposition, we shall hold the sports meet here. 如果没有人反对，我们将在这里开运动会。

397 pub—bar

pub 在英国通常指"小酒店"：

They've gone down to the pub for a drink. 他们到小酒店去喝酒去了。

The best pub around here is the King's Head. 这一带最好的小酒店是"王首小酒店"。

❀ 在美国通常用 **bar** 表示同样意思，常译为"酒吧间"：

We went to a bar after work and had a couple of beers. 我们下班后到酒吧间去喝了一两杯啤酒。

Let's have a drink in the bar before we go into the dining-room. 去餐厅前，咱们到酒吧去喝一杯。

398 purposely—purposefully

purposely 是副词，表示"故意地""有意地"：

She purposely ignored me at the party. 在晚会上，她故意冷落我。

He said it was an accident, but we all know he did it purposely. 他说这是偶然发生的，但我们都知道他是故意这样做的。

❀ **purposefully** 表示"有目的地""怀有某种目的"：

They should use the language purposefully. 他们应该有目的地使用语言。

The young woman stepped purposefully towards John Franklyn. 这青年女子怀着某种目的向约翰·富兰克林走过去。

399 put

put 的基本意思是 "放" "搁":

He put the paper in his pocket. 他把那张纸放进口袋里。

Where have you put my clothes? 你把我的衣服放哪儿啦?

可用于引申意义:

I can't put the blame on you. 我不能怪你。

Put as much expression as you can in it. 把它念得尽量有感情。

Put the idea out of your head. 打消这个念头吧。

还可表示 "使处于某种状态":

You put me in a very awkward position. 你让我处境尴尬。

He put the books in order. 他把书整理好了。

This put them on friendly terms with him. 这使得他们对他很友好。

It has put me a little out of breath. 这使得我有点气喘吁吁。

也可表示 "表达" "说" "写" 等:

He couldn't put the feeling into words. 他没法用言语把这种感情表达出来。

Can you put that in simpler words? 你能把这用简单点的话说出来吗?

I don't know how to put that into English. 我不知道该怎样把这译为英文。

还可用于许多短语中:

put a stop (an end) to 制止,使停止

put about 散布(谣言等)

put across 讲清楚

put aside 放在一边,存蓄

put at ease 使安心,使不拘束

put away 收起来

put back 放回原处,推迟

put behind bars 关进监牢

put by 存蓄

put down 放下,写下来

put forth 开(花),长出(叶子)

put forward 提出

put in 插嘴说，放进去

put in a nutshell 概括地说

put in a word for 替……说话

put in 提出（申请、要求等）

put in mind 使想起

put in touch 使和……接触

put into effect 执行，实现

put into power 使上台执政

put into practice 付诸实施

put into words 用语言说出来

put off 推迟，延期

put on 穿上（衣裳等），上演

put on airs 摆架子

put on one's guard 使警惕

put on weight 长胖，增加体重

put one's heart and soul into 全心全意（干某事）

put our heads together 集思广益

put out 扑灭，吹灭，出版，发表

put right 纠正

put to bed 安顿（孩子）睡觉

put to death 处死

put to flight 使逃走

put to music 谱成音乐

put to sea 开航，起航

put to shame 使感到羞惭

put to sleep 使睡着

put to the test 考验

put to use 加以利用

put together 装配在一起

put up 举（手），修建，住宿

put up a fight 进行战斗

put up with 忍受

400 **racialism—racism—racialist—racist—racial**

racialism 和 **racism** 都表示"种族主义":

Eurasians are constantly being hurt by the outside world's <u>racialism</u>. 亚裔欧洲人经常受到外界种族主义的伤害。

The journalist was disgusted by the candidate's <u>racism</u>. 这位新闻工作者对候选人的种族主义感到厌恶。

✤ 由它们派生的 **racialist** 和 **racist** 都可作名词,表示"种族主义者":

You <u>racialist</u>! 你这个种族主义者!

The <u>racists</u> threw stones at the immigrants in their neighbourhood. 那些种族主义分子向邻近的移民投石块。

也可用作形容词,表示"种族主义的":

That book is <u>racialist</u>. 那本书是种族主义的。

Some children's <u>racist</u> attitudes are instilled by their parents. 有些孩子的种族主义态度是他们的父母灌输的。

✤ **racial** 是中性词,表示"种族的":

Skin color, hair type, and eye shape are noticeable <u>racial</u> traits. 肤色、发型和眼睛的形状是显著的种族特征。

<u>racial</u> discrimination 种族歧视

<u>racial</u> conflict (hatred) 种族冲突(仇恨)

<u>racial</u> pride 种族优越感

<u>racial</u> customs 种族习俗

401 **raise—breed—bring up**

raise 可以表示"养大""培养":

We want to <u>raise</u> our children to be decent men and women. 我们希望把

孩子们培养成正派的人。

They <u>raised</u> a family in that village. 他们在那个村子里生儿育女。

❀ **breed** 也可表示"培养""使长大"：

Spartan youths were <u>bred</u> as warriors. 斯巴达青年都被培养成了战士。

a well-<u>bred</u> boy 一个有教养的男孩

❀ 前面两个词比较文气，通常多用 **bring up** 表示"带大""培养"：

I was <u>brought up</u> by my aunt. 我是我姑带大的。

The child was very badly <u>brought up</u>. 这孩子教养很差。

402 rather

rather 是副词，主要表示"相当""有些"：

They were <u>rather</u> old-fashioned people. 他们是相当老派的人。

I've been <u>rather</u> unwell this last fortnight. 这两个星期，我身子有些不舒服。

可修饰动词：

It <u>rather</u> surprised me. 这使我相当吃惊。

He was <u>rather</u> pleased when he won that prize. 他获奖后相当高兴。

也可修饰名词（常放在不定冠词前）：

£50 is <u>rather</u> a lot to pay for a dress. 50 英镑买一件衣服是够贵的。

She's <u>rather</u> a dear. 她是一个相当招人喜欢的姑娘。

△ **rather** 常和 **would** 连用，表示"宁愿"，后面多跟原形：

I'll never depend on anyone again. I'd <u>rather</u> starve. 我再也不依靠任何人，我宁愿饿死。

Which <u>would</u> you <u>rather</u> have, tea or coffee? 你愿意喝茶还是喝咖啡？

有时跟从句（中间谓语多用过去时，若谈过去情况，可用过去完成时态）：

I'd <u>rather</u> you came next Saturday. 我宁愿你下星期六来。

"Shall I open the window?" "I'd <u>rather</u> you didn't." "我要不要把窗子打开？""我看不要打开为好。"

I'd <u>rather</u> you hadn't done that. 我宁愿你没这样做。

△ **rather than** 可连接两个并列成分，表示"……而不是……"：

The colour seems green <u>rather than</u> blue. 这颜色似乎是绿色而不是蓝色。

It was what he meant <u>rather than</u> what he said. 这是他的原意，而不是他的原话。

有时把 **rather** 和 **than** 分开，表示"宁愿……而不愿"：

He would <u>rather</u> listen to others <u>than</u> talk himself. 他宁愿听别人谈，而不愿自己谈。

He would <u>rather</u> deal with a man <u>than</u> with a woman. 他宁愿和男人打交道，而不愿和女人打交道。

△ **or rather** 可用来改正前面的说法，可译为"或毋宁说""更确切地说"：

He's a psychologist—<u>or rather</u>, a psychoanalyst. 他是一位心理学家——或毋宁说是心理分析家。

We got home late last night, <u>or rather</u>, early this morning. 我们是昨天深夜回来的，更确切地说是今天清晨回来的。

有时只用 **rather** 一个词表示同样的意思：

He is not happy; <u>rather</u>, he is sad. 他不快乐，或毋宁说他很凄伤。

It's not generosity, <u>rather</u> self-interest. 这不大方，毋宁说是自私。

403 real—really—true—truly—genuine—genuinely

real 表示"真的""真正的"：

This story is not <u>real</u>; it is only imaginary. 这故事不是真的，是想象出来的。

Fairies are not <u>real</u> people. 仙女不是真人。

还可表示"不是假造的"：

Is it <u>real</u> leather, or plastic? 这是真皮还是塑料的？

This is <u>real</u> pearl (silk). 这是真珍珠（丝）。

Is it a <u>real</u> diamond? 这是真钻石吗？

real 在美国口语中有时被用在形容词或副词前：

He was <u>real</u> sorry. 他真的很难过。

She did <u>real</u> well. 她的确干得不错。

❀ 但许多人认为这不规范，应当用 **really** 作副词，表示"真的""的确"：

We <u>really</u> are very much obliged to you. 我们真的非常感激你。

I've nothing to complain of <u>really</u>. 我的确没有什么可抱怨的。

还可表示"确实""实际上"：

She is <u>really</u> a fine artist. 她确实是一位优秀的艺术家。

<u>Really</u>, that was a terrible mistake. 确实这是一个可怕的错误。

❀ **true** 也可表示"真的""真实的""真正的"：

Now we see this man in his <u>true</u> colours. 现在我们看到了这个人的真实面目。

He was a <u>true</u> humanitarian. 他是一个真正的人道主义者。

come true 表示"成为现实"：

His words have <u>come true</u>. 他的话成为现实了（应验了）。

Our dream has <u>come true</u>. 我们的梦想实现了。

❀ **truly** 也可表示"真的""确实"：

I am <u>truly</u> grateful for all your help. 对你的一切帮助我确实很感激。

Mozart was <u>truly</u> a brilliant composer. 莫扎特确实是一位出色的作曲家。

❀ **genuine** 主要表示"真正的"（非假造的）：

Is the bracelet <u>genuine</u> gold? 这只手镯是真金的吗？

The woman's coat is <u>genuine</u> mink. 这女子的大衣是真正的貂皮。

也可表示"真诚的""真实的"（尤指人的感情等）：

He had a <u>genuine</u> desire to serve his people. 他有为他的同胞服务的真诚愿望。

He showed <u>genuine</u> regret. 他表现出真诚的悔恨。

❀ **genuinely** 也可表示"真的""确实"：

She could see that he was <u>genuinely</u> shocked. 她可以看出他真的很震惊。

He was <u>genuinely</u> fond of Philip. 他真的很喜欢菲利普。

She was <u>genuinely</u> glad to see him. 她看到他确实很高兴。

404 reasonable—rational

reasonable 表示"讲道理的"：

After all, he's a reasonable man. 他毕竟是个讲道理的人。

Really, you must be reasonable. What have I done? 真的，你要讲道理。我做了什么事？

也可表示"合理的"：

Aren't these all reasonable demands? 难道这些不是合理的要求吗？

A reasonable price is a moderate one, not too expensive. 合理的价格是中等的、不太贵的价格。

❀ **rational** 也可表示"合理的""懂道理的"：

It was a rational plan and bound to succeed. 这是一个合理的计划，一定会成功。

As children grow older, they become more rational. 孩子们长大后，就更懂道理。

rational 还可表示"有理性的""理智的"：

Man is a rational animal. 人是有理性的动物。

When very angry, people seldom act in a rational way. 人生气时很少理智地行事。

405 receive—receipt—reception

receive 有几个主要意思：

收到，接到：

He has just received his fortnight's pay. 他刚收到了这两周的薪水。

得到，受到：

The patient received the best of care. 那位病人得到了最好的照顾。

The prisoners received harsh and unfair treatment. 犯人们受到了苛刻的、不公平的对待。

接见，接待：

The host received his guests at the door. 主人在门口接待客人。

得到（某种反应）：

My speech was very well received. 我的演讲收到了很好的反应。

The book was received with enthusiasm. 这本书引起了热烈的反应。

名词形式有两个：

❀ **receipt** /rɪ'siːt/ 表示"收到"或"收条"：

The receipt of your letter ended my anxiety. 收到了你的信，我就放心了。

This bill is payable upon receipt. 账单收到后即需付款。

❀ **reception** 表示"接待""招待会"等：

There was a reception after the wedding ceremony. 婚礼后有一个招待会。

His speech got a good reception. 他的演讲引起了良好的反应。

406 recently—lately—newly

recently 表示"最近"：

I ran into your sister in Harrods recently. 我最近在哈罗兹百货公司碰到了你的妹妹。

Our parents recently celebrated their golden wedding anniversary. 我的父母最近庆祝了他们的金婚纪念日（结婚五十周年纪念）。

❀ **lately** 表示同样的意思：

Here is a little song written lately. 这是最近写的一首小小的歌曲。

Lately I have read much of George Meredith's poetry. 近来，我看了许多乔治·梅雷迪思的诗。

❀ **newly** 表示"新近"（多和过去分词连用）：

They were a newly-married couple. 他们是一对新婚夫妇。

Don't sit on the newly painted chair. 别坐在新漆的椅子上。

407 recollect—recall—remember

recollect 表示"想起""记得"（可跟名词、从句或动名词）：

I can't recollect his name. 我想不起他的名字。

Do you recollect that Helen came to see us last year? 你记不记得海伦去年曾来看我们？

❀ **recall** 表示"（回）想起""记得"（也可跟名词、从句及动名词）：

I really can't recall your name at the moment. 此刻，我真的想不起你的名字。

I don't recall where I met him. 我不记得在哪里见到过他。

它还有其他一些意思，如"召回""收回"等：

The government has recalled its ambassador from Paris. 政府召回了驻巴黎的大使。

The car factory recalled all the cars which were supposed to be faulty. 汽车工厂收回了所有认为有毛病的汽车。

❀ **remember** 也表示"记得""记起"（可跟名词、动名词、复合结构、从句等）：

I remember the whole thing as if it happened yesterday. 我记得整个这件事就仿佛是昨天发生的。

还可用于其他结构：

This is a day to be remembered. 这是一个值得记住的日子。

Oh, yes, now I remember. 现在我想起来了。

此外还可用来表示"记住（做某事）"：

I will remember how to do this in future. 我将记住将来该怎样做这个工作。

Don't forget to post my letter. Please remember! 别忘了给我发信，请记住！

这个词日常用得最多，有些用法是 recollect 和 recall 所没有的。

408 referee—umpire

这两个词都表示裁判：

The referee sent two of the footballers off the field. 裁判罚了两名足球队员出场。

The umpire called the ball a foul. 裁判说这球犯规。

一般说来，篮球、足球、冰球、橄榄球、拳击、摔跤等的裁判称为 referee，而羽毛球、棒球、网球、乒乓球、排球等的裁判称为 umpire。

409 regard—regardless

regard 可用作动词也可用作名词。

△作动词时主要表示"认为"（经常和 **as** 连用）——可跟名词、形容词、介词短语等：

He seemed to regard it as a small triumph. 他似乎认为这是一个小小的胜利。

I regard him as stupid. 我认为他很愚蠢。

I regard myself as very much to blame. 我认为自己很有责任。

I regard the contract as having been broken. 我认为合约已经被破坏了。

还可以表示：

凝视： Dinny regarded her uncle with wide eyes. 丁妮睁大眼睛，凝视着她的叔叔。

看待： Ann regarded her sister with a new respect. 安怀着新的尊敬情绪看待她的姐姐。

尊重： She always regards her parents' wishes. 她一贯尊重父母的意愿。

和……有关： That does not regard me. 这与我无关。

可用于 **as regards** 关于，至于：

As regards money, what is to be done? 关于钱，怎么办？

As regards John, I will write to him at once. 至于约翰，我马上给他写信。

△用作名词时有几个意思：

关心：

He shows little regard for others. 他很少关心别人。

He had considerable regard for Betty. 他对贝蒂相当关心。

尊重，赞赏：

The teacher has high regard for John's ability. 老师很赞赏约翰的能力。

I have a very high regard for your parents. 我对你的父母十分尊重。

复数形式表示问候：

He sends his regards. 他表示问候。

Give my regards to Lucy. 请向露西问好。

还可用于一些短语：

hold in high regard 器重

I hold her in high regard. 我很器重她。

in one's regard 在……心目中

He stands high in their regard. 他在他们心目中地位很高。

in (with) regard to 关于，至于

I'll write you later in regard to this matter. 关于这件事，我以后再给你写信。

In regard to your problem, I should like to make a suggestion. 至于你的问题，我想提一个建议。

in this (that) regard 关于这一点

It's quite satisfactory in this regard. 关于这一点，它是令人满意的。

In that regard, we agree. 关于这一点，我们同意。

out of regard for 出于对……关怀，为了

I have done that out of regard for my sister. 我这样做是出于对我妹妹的关怀。

Out of regard for your father, I shall not dismiss you this time. 为了你的父亲，这次我不辞退你。

(with) kind regards（写在信末）请向……问好

With kind regards, yours sincerely. 向你问好，你诚挚的朋友……

Kind regards to your brother. 请向你哥哥问好。

without regard for (to) 不管，不考虑

He acts without any regard for other people. 他行事不考虑别人。

He is going to do it, without regard to consequences. 他准备这样做，不管后果如何。

❀ **regardless** 表示"不管怎样"：

We'll go regardless. 不管怎样，我们要去。

I must make the decision regardless. 不管怎样，我得做出决定。

常和 **of** 连用，表示"不管……如何""不顾"：

Some people act regardless of what will happen afterwards. 有些人行事，不管后果如何。

He went regardless of the risk. 他不顾风险地去了。

410 regret—regretful—regrettable

regret 可用作动词，也用作名词。

△ **regret** 用作动词时主要表示"懊悔""感到遗憾"，可跟几种宾语：

名词或代词：She did not regret her refusal. 她拒绝了，并不后悔。

You'll regret this later on. 将来你会为此后悔的。

动名词：We've always regretted selling the farm. 卖掉这座农场，我们一直后悔。

You'll regret having said these words. 说了这些话，你会感到遗憾的。

从句：I regret that I shall not be able to come. 我很遗憾，我不能来。

She bitterly regretted that she had no child. 她没有孩子，深感遗憾。

常用 **regret to say (tell, etc.)** 遗憾地说（告诉你……）：

We regret to inform you that your application hasn't been successful. 我们遗憾地通知你，你的申请不成功。

△ **regret** 作名词时主要表示"遗憾""懊悔"：

I left my home with some regret. 我有些遗憾地离开了家。

She expressed not the least regret for what she had done. 她对她的行为没表示丝毫的遗憾。

有时用于复数形式，表示"遗憾"或"歉意"：

Shelley had no regrets for his actions. 雪莱对他的行动并不感到遗憾。

Please accept my regrets. 请接受我的歉意。

❀ **regretful** 为形容词，表示"懊悔的""遗憾的"：

Father was regretful he could not send us to college. 父亲因没能送我们上大学，感到遗憾。

She shed regretful tears. 她流下了懊悔的眼泪。

❀ **regrettable** 也是形容词，意思是"值得遗憾的""令人遗憾的"：

Overpopulation has caused a regrettable situation. 人口过剩造成了令人遗憾的局面。

It is regrettable that such a great talent died so young. 这样一位伟大的天才死得这样早，真遗憾。

411 relation—relative—relationship

relation 有两个主要意思:

关系:

What is the relation(ship) between A and B? A 和 B 之间有什么关系?

Part of your answer has no relation to the question. 你的回答有些部分与问题没有关系。

复数形式可表示人与人或国与国的关系:

Their talks altered their relations. 他们的谈话改变了他们的关系。

Several South American states broke off diplomatic relations with Germany. 几个南美国家断绝了和德国的外交关系。

亲属,亲戚:

He's a near relation of mine. 他是我的一个近亲。

✿ **relative** 作名词时也表示"亲属""亲戚":

You see they are near relatives of mine. 你知道,他们是我的近亲。

Is he a relative (relation) of yours? 他是你的亲戚吗?

✿ **relationship** 也表示"关系":

I really don't know how to explain our relationship. 我真不知道,该怎样解释我们的关系。

Now a new relationship of sympathy and of understanding had been established. 现在一种新的相互同情、相互了解的关系建立了。

412 remain—stay

remain 主要有下面几个意思:

继续留在某处,待,留下(与 **stay** 的意思相近):

He remained there all through the year. 整个这一年,他都继续留在那里。

I did not remain long in that town. 我在那座城市没待太久。

保持,仍处于某种状态(与 **stay** 的意思相近):

She remained comparatively calm. 她保持相对平静。

Her face remained expressionless. 她的脸上仍然没有表情。

剩下，还有（**stay** 却没有这个意思）：

If you take away 3 from 8, 5 <u>remains</u>. 8 减去 3 还有 5。

All that <u>remains</u> of the city is ruin. 全城只剩下一片废墟。

❀ **stay** 有两个意思与 **remain** 相近：

待，留：

How much longer am I <u>staying</u>? 我还要待多久？

<u>Stay</u> where you are. 你仍留在原处。

保持（某种状态）：

The shop <u>stays</u> open till seven o'clock. 商店营业到七点钟。

Please <u>stay</u> seated. 请继续坐着。

它还可表示"暂时住在（某处）"（这和 **remain** 的意思是不同的）：

"Where are you <u>staying</u>?" "At the Grand (Hotel)." "你在哪里住？" "在格兰德（酒店）。"

How long can you <u>stay</u> in Brussels? 你能在布鲁塞尔住多久？

413 resolution—decision—determination—motion

resolution 主要表示"决心"：

He made a New Year's <u>resolution</u> to give up smoking. 他下了新年决心，要戒烟。

She made a strenuous attempt to carry out her <u>resolutions</u>. 她做了艰苦的努力来实现她的决心。

也可表示"决议"：

The committee has passed (adopted) a <u>resolution</u> to build a new library. 委员会通过了决议，修建一座新图书馆。

The <u>resolution</u> passed by two votes. 这项决议以两票之差通过。

❀ **decision** 主要表示"决定"：

You shouldn't come to such a <u>decision</u> hastily. 你不应匆忙做出这样的决定。

The umpire's <u>decision</u> is final. 裁判的决定是不能改变的。

还可表示"决断"：

That man lacks <u>decision</u>. 那人缺乏决断。

He acted with <u>decision</u> as soon as he heard the news. 他一听到这消息就果断地行动起来。

❀ **determination** 也可表示"决心""坚决":

It indicates want of foresight and lack of <u>determination</u>. 这说明没有远见和缺乏决心。

It took unusual courage and <u>determination</u> to make the break with his family. 和他的家庭决裂需要异乎寻常的勇气和决心。

❀ **motion** 可表示"动议":

Grey's <u>motion</u> was seconded by Thomas Paine. 格雷的动议得到托马斯·佩因的附议。

The <u>motion</u> was adopted (carried) by a majority of six. 这项动议以六票多数通过。

414 respectful—respectable—respective—respectively

❀ **respectful** 表示"尊敬的":

We must be <u>respectful</u> to our teachers. 我们应尊敬我们的老师。

I wish you would be more <u>respectful</u> to your father. 我希望你对你父亲更尊敬一些。

❀ **respectable** 表示"受人尊敬的""正派的":

My parents are <u>respectable</u> people. 我的父母是受人尊敬的人。

<u>Respectable</u> citizens obey the laws. 正派的公民都会遵纪守法。

还可表示"相当好的""可观的":

He had quite a <u>respectable</u> income. 他有相当可观的收入。

He is quite a <u>respectable</u> chess-player. 他是一个相当不错的棋手。

❀ **respective** 为形容词,表示"各自的":

They returned to their <u>respective</u> rooms. 他们回各自屋里去了。

They were given work according to their <u>respective</u> abilities. 他们都按各自的能力分配了工作。

❀ **respectively** 为副词,表示"分别为……":

Jones and Edwards are, <u>respectively</u>, the producer and director of the film. 琼斯和爱德华分别为该电影的制片人和导演。

The first, second and third prizes went to James, John and Tom <u>respectively</u>. 第一、第二和第三等奖分别授予詹姆斯、约翰和汤姆。

415 risk—danger—peril

risk 表示"风险""危险"：

Fishermen face a lot of <u>risks</u> in their daily lives. 渔民在日常生活中要面对很多危险。

If you skate on thin ice there is a <u>risk</u> of your falling through. 如果你在薄冰上溜冰，你就有掉下去的危险。

还可用作动词，表示"冒……的危险"：

They <u>risked</u> losing everything. 他们冒着失去一切的危险。

They <u>risked</u> defeat in fighting the larger army. 他们冒着失败的危险和更强的军队作战。

❀ **danger** 表示"危险"：

All <u>danger</u> was over. 一切危险都已过去。

A <u>danger</u> foreseen is half avoided. 预见到危险，危险就避免了一半。（谚语）

还可用于 **in danger** 和 **out of danger**，分别表示"有危险"和"脱离危险"：

He was <u>in danger</u> of losing his life. 他有丢掉性命的危险。

He has been very ill, but he is now <u>out of danger</u>. 他曾经病得很重，但现在已脱离危险。

❀ **peril** 也可表示"危险"：

The explorers knew they would face many <u>perils</u>. 探险家知道，他们会面临许多危险。

You are in great <u>peril</u>. 你处境十分危险。

416 rouse—arouse

rouse 主要表示"唤醒""惊醒"：

Her aunt <u>roused</u> her. 她姑姑把她唤醒了。

Sounds of gun fire roused us at daybreak. 黎明时炮火声把我们惊醒了。

可用于引申意义，表示"唤起""激起"等：

The speaker tried to rouse the masses. 演讲人设法唤起群众。

His conduct roused their suspicion. 他的行为引起了他们的怀疑。

❀ arouse 也有类似的意思：

We aroused him from his deep sleep. 我们把他从沉睡中唤醒了。

Aroused by the crash, he leaped his feet. 破碎声惊起了他，他一跃站了起来。

也可用于引申意义：

We must arouse them to fight for their own emancipation. 我们必须唤起他们为自己的解放而斗争。

Their terrible sufferings aroused our pity. 他们可怕的苦难引起了我们的同情。

417 **rude—impolite—impudent**

rude 表示"粗鲁无礼的"：

It's rude to stare at people. 瞪着眼瞧人是粗鲁无礼的举动。

Rude behavior will not be tolerated. 粗鲁无礼的行为不能容忍。

❀ impolite 表示"没有礼貌的"：

It would be impolite to refuse his offer. 拒不接受他的帮助会显得没有礼貌。

It is impolite to turn your back on someone who is speaking to you. 人家跟你说话，你把背朝人是不礼貌的。

❀ impudent 表示"无礼的""厚颜无耻的"：

That impudent boy put his tongue out at him. 那个无礼的男孩儿向他伸舌头。

What an impudent rascal he is! 他是一个多么厚颜无耻的坏蛋！

418 **run**

run 是常用的动词之一，有许多意思，最常用的用法有：

表示"跑"（ *vi.* ）：

She came <u>running</u> to meet us. 她跑过来迎接我们。

快速到某处（不一定跑）（ *vi.* ）：

I'll <u>run</u> and fetch the doctor. 我将赶紧去请医生。

He <u>ran</u> back to the town filled with joy. 他高兴地赶回到镇上。

走掉，跑掉（ *vi.* ）

Oh dear, I'm late. I've got to <u>run</u>. 啊，天呐，我晚了，我得走了。

The robbers took the money and <u>ran</u>. 强盗们抢了钱，跑掉了。

（车辆等）行驶：

The next train <u>runs</u> from London to Liverpool. 下一班火车从伦敦开往利物浦。

The express <u>runs</u> hourly between Boston and New York. 快车每小时在波士顿和纽约间开一次。

（机器）开动，（钟表）走动（ *vi.* ）：

The motor is still <u>running</u>. 发动机开动着。

This machine <u>runs</u> by electricity. 这台机器用电驱动。

The clock <u>runs</u> on batteries. 这座钟表靠电池走动。

（水等）流动：

Blood <u>runs</u> from a cut. 血从伤口中流出。

Tears were <u>running</u> down her face. 眼泪沿着她的面颊流着。

变为，变得（ *link v.* ）：

The well <u>ran</u> dry. 井干涸了。

My blood <u>ran</u> cold. 我的血凉了下来。

I have <u>run</u> short of money. 我的钱短缺起来。

管理，经营（ *vt.* ）：

Ruth <u>ran</u> the house extremely well. 鲁思把家管得很好。

They <u>run</u> most of the stores here. 这里大部分商店都是他们经营的。

还可用于许多短语：

run a race 赛跑

run a risk 冒风险

run a temperature 发高烧

run across 无意间碰到

run after 追，追求

run away 走掉，跑掉

run away with 偷掉，私奔

run back 倒（带）

run down 说人坏话，抓到

run for 竞选

run high（情绪）高涨

run into 碰见，撞上

run off 印出，复制，使流掉

run out 用完，过期

run over 辗过，匆匆看一遍

run short 快用完

run through 匆忙看一遍，简述

run up 升起，快速（盖起）

run up against 遇到（困难等）

run wild 放肆，狂妄不羁

419 sale—for sale—on sale

sale 表示"售卖""销售（量）"：

The sale of his old home made him sad. 售卖他的老屋令他感到凄伤。

Nigeria was prospering from its oil sales. 尼日利亚因出售石油而繁荣起来。

还可表示"贱卖""大减价"：

When a shop has a sale, things are sold at specially low prices. 当一个商店大减价时，商品都以特别低的价钱出售。

I bought my dress in sale. 我这件连衣裙是在大减价时买的。

❀ for sale 表示"供售卖"：

That car is for sale. 那辆车出售。

The sign on the house says, "For Sale." 房子上的牌子写着"本屋出售"。

❀ on sale 在英国表示"出售"：

There are some nice apples on sale in that shop. 那家商店有些好苹果出售。

The book won't be on sale till next week. 这本书要下礼拜才出售。

在美国却表示"削价出售"：

I got the hat on sale; it was very cheap. 这顶帽子我是在大减价时买的，很便宜。

420 same—similar

❀ same 主要用作形容词，表示"同样的""相同的"：

Men and women now get the same pay for doing the same job. 现在男女同工同酬。

We are all of the same opinion. 我们的看法都一样。

常可和 **as** 连用，表示"和……相同"：

He was about the <u>same</u> age <u>as</u> Philip. 他和菲利普的年龄大致相同。

Meet me at the <u>same</u> place <u>as</u> you did yesterday. 仍然在昨天见我的地方相见。

有时表示"同一个"：

The <u>same</u> knife cuts bread and fingers. 同一把刀可以切面包，也可切手。（谚语）

还可用定语从句修饰：

That is the <u>same</u> tune I heard yesterday. 那和我昨天听到的是同一个曲子。

You are still the <u>same</u> person I knew ten years ago. 你还是我十年前认识的同一个人。

也可用作代词，表示"同样的事"等：

People did the <u>same</u> for me when I first came. 我初来时，人们也为我做了同样的事。

❀ **similar** 表示"相似的""差不多的"：

They have <u>similar</u> political views. 他们有相似的政治看法。

The themes of the two novels are <u>similar</u>. 两部小说的主题相似。

常和 **to** 连用：

Wheat is <u>similar to</u> barley. 小麦和大麦很相似。

My problems are very <u>similar to</u> yours. 我的问题和你的问题很相似。

421 satisfy—satisfied—satisfactory—satisfying

satisfy 为动词，主要表示"使感到满意""满足"：

The team's performance didn't <u>satisfy</u> the coach. 球队的表现没能使教练满意。

Do you <u>satisfy</u> the entry requirements for that college? 你能达到那所大学的入学要求吗？

❀ **satisfied** 为形容词，表示"满意的"，多用作表语：

I'm not <u>satisfied</u> with the present situation. 我对目前的状况不满意。

Are you <u>satisfied</u> with your new house? 你对新房子满意吗？

也可用作定语：

He began to smoke a cigarette with a <u>satisfied</u> air. 他开始带着满意的神情抽烟。

I hated that conceited, self-<u>satisfied</u> creature. 我讨厌那个高傲自满的家伙。

❀ **satisfactory** 也是形容词，表示"令人满意的"：

The progress of the case isn't quite <u>satisfactory</u>. 案件进展情况不太令人满意。

I'm sure that's the only <u>satisfactory</u> way out. 我肯定这是唯一令人满意的出路。

❀ **satisfying** 也是形容词，表示"使人满意的""令人高兴的"：

The story had a <u>satisfying</u> ending. 这故事有一个令人满意的结局。

After a <u>satisfying</u> meal you no longer feel hungry. 痛快地吃一顿饭后，你就不感到饿了。

422　say—tell—speak—talk

say 多作及物动词，表示"说"，主要跟从句或引语：

She <u>said</u> he was a man of immense capacity. 她说他是一个有极大能量的人。

Whether this is true or not, I cannot <u>say</u>. 这是否属实，我说不上来。

有时跟名词或代词：

He <u>said</u> good night and went on. 他说了再见，接着往前走。

How dare you <u>say</u> such a thing to me? 你怎么敢对我说这样的话？

❀ **tell** 一般作及物动词，有比较多的意思：

告诉，讲给……听：

He <u>told</u> me of (about) his difficulties. 他给我谈了他的困难。

They <u>told</u> us where to shop cheaply. 他们告诉我们在哪里买东西便宜。

讲（故事等）：

Good children always <u>tell</u> the truth. 好孩子都讲真话。

He has one failing: He <u>tells</u> lies. 他有一个缺点：他撒谎。

让（某人做某事）：

She told me to be home by ten. 她要我 10 点前回家。

I told him not to climb trees. 我让他不要爬树。

说出：

He can't tell the difference. 他说不出（它们的）差别。

It's impossible to tell who'll win the next election. 不可能说出，谁会在下次选举中获胜。

❀ **speak** 作不及物动词时较多，可有几重意思：

讲，谈：

May I speak with you for a moment? 我能和你讲一会儿话吗？

We must not speak of it again. 我们再也不要谈这件事了。

演说，（向公众）讲话：

He spoke before the United Nations in New York. 他在纽约联合国大会发表了演说。

The chairman spoke for forty minutes. 主席讲了 40 分钟的话。

讲（某种语言等，作及物动词）：

He can speak several languages. 他能讲几种语言。

He spoke only a few words. 他只讲了几句话。

❀ **talk** 主要表示"谈（话）"（作不及物动词）：

We talked about it for hours. 这件事我们谈了几个钟头。

We often talked of you. 我们常常谈到你。

可以作及物动词，表示"谈某样东西（某种语言）"：

We talked music all night. 我们整夜谈音乐。

Don't talk nonsense! 不要胡说八道！

---

423 **scarce—scarcely**

这四个词有相同之处，也有不同之处，这从上面例句中可以看出。

❀ **scarce** 是形容词，表示"短缺的""稀少的"（不易找到）：

Food and fuel were scarce. 食物和燃料都很短缺。

❀ **scarcely** 是副词，主要表示"几乎不""简直不"：

We scarcely had time for breakfast. 我们几乎没有时间吃早饭。

All day long they had scarcely a free moment. 整天，他们几乎没有空

闲的时间。

有时可以和 when 连用，表示"还没有……就""刚……就"：

The noise had <u>scarcely</u> died away when someone started to laugh again. 声音还没有消失，就有人又开始笑了起来。

<u>Scarcely</u> had he gone out when it began to rain. 他刚刚出门，天就开始下雨了。

424 scene—scenery—sight—view—landscape

scene 有几个意思：

事故（情）发生的地方，现场：

A dark lane was the <u>scene</u> of the murder. 一条暗黑的巷子是谋杀案发生的现场。

Criminals are said to have returned to the <u>scene</u> of the crime. 据说，罪犯已回到了犯罪现场。

故事发生的地方：

The <u>scene</u> of the story is Victorian England. 故事发生在维多利亚时代的英格兰。

The <u>scene</u> of the opera is set in Switzerland. 歌剧的故事发生在瑞士。

剧中的场景（面）：

The parting of the lovers was a moving <u>scene</u>. 恋人的分手是一个动人的场面。

The king comes to the castle in Act I, <u>Scene</u> 2. 在第一幕第二场，国王来到城堡。

布景：

The <u>scenes</u> are changed during the intervals. 休息时换布景。

We had designed all the new <u>scenes</u> and costumes. 我们设计了所有新的布景和服装。

风景，景色：

The sunrise was a beautiful <u>scene</u>. 日出是美丽的景色。

He drank in the beauty of <u>scenes</u>. 他饱览美丽的风景。

景象：

Taxis and buses were part of the street scene. 出租车和公共汽车是街景的一部分。

As he entered the room he was confronted by a scene of disorder. 他走进屋里时，面前是一片混乱的景象。

❀ **scenery** 主要表示"风景":

The scenery at the lake is just breathtaking. 湖畔的风景简直使人陶醉。

She enjoys mountain scenery very much. 她很欣赏山里的风景。

还可表示"布景":

We're designing scenery for his play. 我们正在设计他剧中的布景。

The scenery pictures a garden in the moonlight. 那套布景表现一个月光下的花园。

❀ **sight** 也有几个意思:

景物，供参观的地方，游览胜地:

Niagara Fall is one of the sights in the world. 尼亚加拉大瀑布是世界游览胜地之一。

John enjoyed seeing the sights in New York. 约翰喜欢游览纽约的名胜。

情景，景象:

The sunset was a beautiful sight. 日落是一种美丽的景象。

The sight infuriated Andrew. 这情景使安德鲁大为震怒。

视力，视野:

He is going to have his sight tested. 他准备去验光。

Soon the train came into sight. 火车很快进入了视野。

❀ **view** 也可表示"风景""景色":

What a beautiful view! 多美的风景呀!

There's a fine view from here. 从这里可以看到一片美丽的景色。

还可表示"目光"、"视野"和"看法":

That hill blocks our view. 那座小山挡住了我们的目光。

He disappeared from view. 他从我们的视野中消失了。

❀ **landscape** 主要表示"风景":

From the hill he looked down on the peaceful landscape. 他从山顶俯瞰下面宁静的景色。

The two hills with the valley formed a beautiful landscape. 两座小山和

山谷构成一幅美丽的风景。

landscape 还可表示"风景画"：

She preferred a good landscape to a portrait. 她喜欢好的风景画胜过肖像画。

425 sceptic—sceptical

sceptic /ˈskeptɪk/，美式英语中拼作 **skeptic**，表示"持怀疑态度的人"：

He now has to convince sceptics that he has a serious plan. 现在他得让有怀疑的人相信他有认真的计划。

The sceptic may argue that there are no grounds for such optimism. 疑心的人会争辩说，这样的乐观看法是没有根据的。

❀ **sceptical**，美式英语中亦拼作 **skeptical**，为形容词，表示"怀疑的"：

I'm sceptical of (about) the team's chances of winning. 我怀疑这个队有获胜的机会。

He listened to me with a sceptical expression. 他带着怀疑的表情听我讲。

426 scheme—schedule—timetable—plan

scheme /skiːm/ 主要表示"计划""办法"：

He has a scheme for extracting gold from sea. 他有一个从海水里提取黄金的计划。

He suggested several schemes to increase sales. 他提出几个办法来增加销售量。

也可指"政府等实行的大计划"：

the state pension scheme 国家退休金计划

training schemes 培训计划

❀ **schedule** 在英式英语中读作 /ˈʃedjuːl/ 或 /ˈskedjuːl/，在美式英语中仅读作 /ˈskedjuːl/。主要表示"日程计划"：

We'll work out our schedule. 我们将制订日程计划。

What's on the <u>schedule</u> for today? 今天日程上有些什么活动？

还可表示"时刻表"：

I need a train <u>schedule</u>. 我需要一份火车时刻表。

a television <u>schedule</u> 电视节目表

可构成一些短语：

according to <u>schedule</u> 按日程表进行   ahead of <u>schedule</u> 提前

behind <u>schedule</u> 比规定时间晚   on <u>schedule</u> 准时

❀ **timetable** 可表示"时刻表""功课表"等：

You look at a railway <u>timetable</u> to find the times of the trains. 可查看铁路时刻表来了解火车的时刻。

The school <u>timetable</u> shows the time when we have the various lessons. 学校功课表表明我们什么时候上什么课。

❀ **plan** 表示一般的"计划"：

She formulated the <u>plan</u> in detail. 她制订了详细的计划。

I have a <u>plan</u> for overcoming the difficulties. 我有一个克服困难的计划。

还可表示"建筑物的图样"：

Show me the <u>plans</u> of the building. 把大楼的建筑图给我看看。

Here is a <u>plan</u> of the ground floor. 这是底层的图样。

427   seek—look for—try to find (get)

seek 主要表示"找寻""寻求"：

They were <u>seeking</u> employment. 他们在找工作。

Most men <u>seek</u> wealth; all men <u>seek</u> happiness. 多数人都寻求财富，所有的人都寻求幸福。

也可用于 **seek for** 表示类似的意思：

He <u>sought</u> vainly <u>for</u> an answer. 他寻求答案，却没找到。

They <u>sought for</u> the little boy for two days. 这个小男孩他们找了两天了。

❀ **seek** 主要用于书面语，在日常口语中常用 **look for** 表示：

They've been <u>looking for</u> the boy for two days. 他们找男孩已找了两

天了。

They were <u>looking for</u> work. 他们在找工作。

❀ 有时可用 **try to find** 或 **try to get** 表示：

We <u>tried to get</u> their support. 我们设法得到他们的支持。

They <u>tried to find</u> some work to do. 他们设法找工作做。

428 seem

seem 主要有两个用法：

表示"似乎""好像"，后面可跟几种形式的不定式：

（1）跟不定式的一般形式：

He <u>seemed</u> to have a high opinion of her. 他似乎对她的看法很好。

I don't <u>seem</u> to lack anything. 我好像什么都不缺。

（2）跟不定式的完成形式：

I <u>seem</u> to have caught a cold. 我好像感冒了。

He did not <u>seem</u> to have changed. 他似乎没有什么改变。

（3）跟不定式的进行形式：

They <u>seemed</u> to be doing alright. 他们似乎干得不错。

She <u>seems</u> to be sleeping. 她好像在睡觉。

（4）跟 **to be**：

He <u>seemed</u> to be a man without care. 他好像是一个无忧无虑的人。

You <u>seem</u> to be in a great hurry. 你好像很匆忙的样子。

表示"好像""似乎是"（作 *link v.*），可跟不同的表语：

（1）跟形容词：

He <u>seems</u> (to be) quite happy. 他好像很开心。

The doctor <u>seemed</u> very capable. 那医生似乎很能干。

（2）跟分词：

He <u>seemed</u> embarrassed by the question. 这问题似乎使他很尴尬。

She <u>seemed</u> lacking in enthusiasm. 她似乎缺乏热情。

（3）跟名词：

She <u>seemed</u> an unusually clever girl. 她似乎是一个聪明绝顶的姑娘。

That <u>seems</u> not a bad idea. 这主意好像不错。

（4）跟介词短语：

You seem in high spirits. 你的情绪似乎很好。

The driver seemed out of humour. 司机情绪好像不佳。

还可用于下面两个结构：

（1）**It seems (that)** 表示"好像""感觉"：

It seems that nobody knew what happened. 好像没人知道发生了什么事。

It seems to me that I have been neglecting my duty. 我感觉，最近我工作不认真。

（2）**There seems (to be)** 表示"好像有，似乎有"：

There seems no need to go now. 现在似乎没有必要去。

There seemed nothing wrong with his feet. 他的脚好像没有毛病。

429 seldom

seldom 表示"很少"，通常放在动词前面，或动词 **be** 后面：

She seldom showed her feelings. 她很少表现出她的情绪来。

Barking dogs seldom bite. 爱叫的狗很少咬人。（谚语）

如有助动词或情态动词，则放在它们后面：

I've seldom felt so happy. 我很少这样快活过。

We can seldom get a chance like that. 我们很少能有这样的机会。

有时可放在句首（后面要用倒装语序）：

Seldom have I seen such brutality. 我很少见过这样野蛮的行为。

430 semi-

semi- 是前缀（或称词头），加在形容词或名词前表示"半"：

semi-automatic 半自动的	semi-bankruptcy 半破产
semibarbarian 半野蛮的	semicircle 半圆
semicircular 半圆形的	semi-civilized 半开化的

semi-colonial 半殖民地的   semi-colony 半殖民地

semi-conductor 半导体   semidesert 半沙漠

semidiameter 半径   semifinal 半决赛

semi-feudal 半封建的   semi-finished 半成（品）

semifluid 半流体   semimetal 半金属

semiprecious 半宝贵（石头）   semi-professional 半职业的

semi-skilled 半熟练（工种）   semitransparent 半透明的

semivowel 半元音

431 sensible—sensitive

这两个词都是 sense 的派生形容词，但意思不同。

❀ sensible 主要表示"明智的""有头脑的"：

I wish you'd give her sensible advice. 我希望你能给她出些明智的主意。

You must pull yourself together and be sensible. 你必须振作起来，理智一些。

❀ sensitive 有两个主要意思：

一是"敏感的""容易生气的"：

Don't be so sensitive. I was only joking. 不要那么敏感，我只是在开玩笑。

He is very sensitive on the subject of religion. 在宗教问题上，他很敏感。

二是"敏锐的""灵敏的"：

An artist is sensitive to beauty. 艺术家对美是敏锐的。

His sensitive ear caught the slightest sound. 他灵敏的耳朵能听到最轻的声音。

432 sentiment—sentimentality—emotion—feeling

sentiment 主要表示"感情""情绪"：

Sentiment should be controlled by reason. 感情应由理智控制。

There is no place for <u>sentiment</u> in business. 做生意不能感情用事。

❀ **sentimentality** 表示"多愁善感""无病呻吟"：

When the author prolonged the heroine's death for two chapters, he is guilty of <u>sentimentality</u>. 当作者把女主人公的死描写了两章时，他就表露了多愁善感的弱点。

In this book there is no <u>sentimentality</u>. 这本书没有无病呻吟之处。

❀ **emotion** 也表示"感情""情绪"：

Joy, grief, fear, hate, rage and excitement are <u>emotions</u>. 喜、怒、哀、恨、恐惧、激动都是情绪。

His face showed nothing of his conflicting <u>emotions</u>. 他脸上没露出他矛盾的感情。

❀ **feeling** 可表示"感情""情绪"，也可表示"感觉"：

A <u>feeling</u> of shame came over Philip. 菲利普感到一阵羞愧。

This <u>feeling</u> seems to be natural. 这种感情似乎是很自然的。

有时表示"感觉""想法""看法"，后面常跟从句：

I have a <u>feeling</u> that you'd never let me down. 我感到你绝不会对不起我的。

He had the <u>feeling</u> that he would not see her again. 他觉得他再也不会见到她了。

还可表示"同情心""敏感""知觉"：

She has no <u>feeling</u> for the suffering of others. 对别人的痛苦，她没有同情。

He has no <u>feeling</u> in his left hand. 他左手没有知觉。

⑬ **serious—sober—solemn**

serious 主要表示：

严重的：

Their error was <u>serious</u>. 他们的错误是严重的。

There has been a <u>serious</u> accident on the highway. 高速公路上出了严重的车祸。

认真的，当真的：

I've made a serious study of this problem. 我认真研究了这个问题。

This proves that we are serious about overcoming the obstacles. 这证明，我们克服这些障碍是认真的。

严肃的，正经的：

Try to be serious for a moment. 设法正经一会儿。

Don't look so serious. 不要显得这样严肃。

❀ **sober** 有时也有"严肃的"的意思：

He was a sober man who seldom smiled. 他是一个不苟言笑的、严肃的人。

The Puritans led sober, hard-working lives. 清教徒过着严肃、勤劳的生活。

但主要表示"清醒的""头脑冷静的"：

Make a sober estimate of what is possible. 清醒地估计一下，什么是可能的。

The man was sober, honest and thrifty. 这人头脑冷静、诚实、节约。

❀ **solemn** 表示"庄严的""严肃的"：

You look very solemn; what's the matter? 你显得这样严肃，是怎么回事？

Frith wore a stiff solemn expression. 弗里思带着刻板、严肃的表情。

434 shadow—shade

shadow 表示"影子"：

No sunshine but hath some shadow. 有阳光就有影子。（谚语）

They watched the wavering shadows of the trees. 他们注视着摇曳的树影。

❀ **shade** 表示"阴凉处"：

It's cooler in the shade. 阴凉处凉快一些。

He slept in the shade of the trees. 他在树荫处睡觉。

435 shall—will

shall 和 **will** 都用来构成将来时态。过去认为 shall 用于第一人称，will 用于第二、三人称。现在在各人称后都用 will：

I will let you know tomorrow. 我明天通知你。

We will not be busy tonight. 我们今晚不忙。

在代词后 will, shall 都可紧缩为 'll：

I'll be waiting for you at the gate. 我在大门口等你。

They'll be back this afternoon. 他们今天下午回来。

shall not 和 will not 可分别紧缩为 shan't /ʃɑːnt/ 和 won't /wəʊnt/：

I shan't be late again. 我不会再迟到了。（用 won't 的人更多一些。）

They (We) won't be in tonight. 他们（我们）今晚不在家。

△只有在下面情况下需要用 **shall**：

用于问句，征求对方意见：

Shall we eat out tonight? 我们今晚要不要到外边吃？

Shall I get you something to drink? 要不要我给你弄点饮料喝？

用在 **let's** 引起的句子后：

Let's try and do it ourselves, shall we? 咱们设法自己干好吗？

△ **will** 也有几个特殊用法：

客气地提出请求：

Will you tell mother I won't be in tonight? 你可否告诉妈妈我今晚不回来了？

If you want anything, let me know, will you? 如果你需要什么，请告诉我，好吗？

用于否定问句，客气地提请求：

Won't you take off your coat? 你要不要把大衣脱下？

Won't you sit down? 请坐。

表示倾向或习惯：

Oil and water will not mix. 油和水不会混在一起。

She will sit there for hours, waiting for her son to come home. 她会一坐几个钟头，等她儿子回来。

表示猜测：

This will be the house you're looking for. 这想必是你要找的房子。

He will have gone back to England. 他想必回英国去了。

但注意在表示时间和条件的状语从句中，一般不能用 **shall, will**, 而用一般现在时：

I'll ring you when I get home. 我到家时，给你打电话。

Come and see us this Saturday if you have time. 星期六如果你有空，请到我们这儿来。

436 shop—store—stall

英国把一般商店称作 shop：

The shops in town close at 5:30. 城里的商店 5 点半关门。

而美国把商店一般称作 store：

He keeps a store in New York. 他在纽约开了一家商店。

在美国特小的只卖一种商品的店也有称 shop 的：

The local dress shop is having a sale. 当地那家服装店正在大减价。

在英国的大商店有时称为 store：

We can buy them cheaper at the stores. 我们在大商店买可以便宜一些。

The big London stores have the sales in summer. 伦敦的大的商店在夏天大减价。

在英美两国百货公司都称作 department store：

He visited some of the big department stores in London. 他参观了伦敦一些大的百货公司。

❀ stall 多指"售货摊"或"棚店"：

I bought some fruit from a stall in the market. 我在市场一家货摊上买了一些水果。

There is a book stall at the railway station. 火车站有一家书摊。

△商场有许多说法，一般称作 shopping centre，美国称为 shopping mall，亦作 mall。在美国小的商场也可称为 plaza。

437 should—would

❀ should 和 would 可用来构成过去将来时，在第一人称后 should，would 都可以用，意思上没有差别；第二、三人称后都用 would（在美国用 should 的人极少，在英国用它的人也越来越少）：

I knew you would agree. 我知道，你会同意的。

I said that I would arrange everything. 我说，我将安排一切。

I thought you would be sleeping. 我想，你会在睡觉的。

I thought Sophia would have told you something. 我想，索菲娅已告诉你一些情况。

He asked us if we would go in. 他问我们要不要进去。

也可用来谈现在情况或用在条件句中：

I should be very unhappy on the Continent. 在欧洲大陆，我会很不愉快的。

We would be glad to have money of our own. 我们愿意有自己的钱。

在表示愿望或提出请求时可用 **I should like** 或 **I would like**：

I should like to ask the minister a question. 我想向部长提一个问题。

I should like to live in a place like this. 我想住在这样一个地方。

I'd like to be able to help in some way. 我愿意能以某种方式帮忙。

也可用于否定结构，表示"不愿意"：

I shouldn't like to see so much money wasted. 我不愿看到这么多钱被浪费掉。

I wouldn't like to see that banned. 我不希望看到它被禁止。

I would rather 和 **I'd sooner** 也可用来表示"愿望"：

I would rather stay at home. 我宁愿待在家里。

I'd rather work in a supermarket. 我宁愿在超市工作。

I'd sooner go by bus than take a taxi. 我宁愿坐公共汽车去而不想坐出租车去。

❀ should 可作情态动词，用在各人称后，这时它的意思和 ought to 差不多，都可译作"应当"或"应该"：

I should (ought to) write some letters tonight. 我今晚应当写几封信。

You shouldn't come to such a decision hastily. 你不应匆忙做出这样的决定。

后面有时跟完成式或进行式：

I should have thought of it. 我应当想到这一点。

You shouldn't be reading a novel. You should be doing your homework. 你现在不应当看小说，你应当做作业。

在某些从句中（如 **propose, suggest** 等引起的从句）也常用 should：

He proposed that the Government should investigate the case. 他建议政府调查这起案件。

He wrote, suggesting that he should come to Paris. 他写信，建议他到巴黎来。

有时可不用 should，而直接用动词原形，特别是在美国：

Someone suggested that they break into small groups. 有人建议，他们分成小组（活动）。

It is necessary that he come to the office. 有必要让他到办公室来。

should 有时可用在条件从句中，可译为"万一"（有时还可用在句首，这时要用倒装语序）：

If you should be passing, do come and see us. 万一你从这儿经过，一定来看我们。

Should I be free tomorrow, I will come. 万一我明天有空，我会来。

有时还可表示惊异、不以为然等情绪（常可译作"竟然"）：

It is dreadful that anyone should be so miserable. 真可怕，有人竟会这样可怜。

It seems so unfair that this should happen to me. 这事竟然发生在我身上，太不公平了。

❀ would 常可用来提出请求或问题（比用 will 显得更委婉）：

Would you kindly send me the author's address? 你可否把作者的地址寄给我？

You'd like tea, wouldn't you? 你想喝点茶，对吧？

也可用来提出看法或表示自己的意愿：

Papa wouldn't allow it. 爸爸不会允许的。

Anyway, I wouldn't let any trouble come to you. 不管怎样我不会让你碰到麻烦。

还可用在虚拟条件句的主句中或含蓄条件句中：

I would do it if I could. 如可能，我是会这样做的。

She would have said more if he had not walked away. 要不是他走开了，她还会多说一些的。

还可谈过去情况，表示"（不）愿意"（可说是 will 的过去形式）：

No matter what happened, he would not say a word. 不管发生什么情况，

他一句话也不肯讲。

He felt Helen <u>would</u> never permit anything of the sort. 他感觉海伦绝不会允许发生这样的事。

有时可用来表示过去习惯性的动作或表示倾向：

Occasionally she <u>would</u> go out and paint little pictures. 偶尔，她会出去画点小画。

Now and then a bird <u>would</u> call. 不时会有鸟叫。

也可表示猜想，表示"想必……"：

That man <u>would</u> be her uncle. 那人想必是她叔叔。

I thought you <u>would</u> have finished by now. 我想，你现在一定已经干完了。

438 since

since 是介词，也是连词，表示"自从"，后面可以跟：

名词：She has loved Shakespeare <u>since</u> childhood. 她从小就热爱莎士比亚。

动名词：Charles has worked hard <u>since</u> leaving school. 从离开学校以来，查尔斯一直很努力。

when (then)：<u>Since</u> when have you been living in this country? 你是从什么时候起住在这个国家的？

介词短语：He had been there <u>since</u> before the war. 从战前起，他一直住在那儿。

从句：She has had another baby <u>since</u> I saw her last. 从上次我见到她以来，她又生了一个孩子。

在绝大多数情况下句子谓语都用完成时态（见上例）。

但在表示有多长时间时可以用一般时态：

It's a long time since I met you last. 上次见到你以来已经很久了。（好久不见了。）

How long <u>is</u> it since you were in London? 你到伦敦有多久了？

在 since 引导的从句中在多数情况下谓语都用一般过去时：

We've been friends ever since we <u>met</u> at school. 自从我们在学校遇见

以来一直是朋友。

Since I <u>was</u> a child I have lived in England. 我从小就住在英格兰。

有时从句中谓语可用完成时态：

I haven't seen you since I <u>have been</u> back. 我回来后一直未见到你。

It's a considerable time since I <u>have spoken</u> to you on these matters. 有相当长时间我没和你谈这些事了。

since 还可表示"因为""既然""由于"：

<u>Since</u> we've no money, we can't buy it. 因为我们没有钱，我们就买不了它了。

I'm on a diet, <u>since</u> I put on weight easily. 由于我很容易长胖，我现在在节食。

439 **skilful—skilled**

skilful 表示"技术很好的""熟练的"：

Only the most <u>skilful</u> pilots are employed by airlines. 只有技术很好的飞行员，航空公司才会聘用。

a <u>skilful</u> artist (driver/mechanic) 技艺高超的画家（司机/工匠）

美国人拼作 skillful：

Soon he became very <u>skillful</u> in doing this work. 后来，他做这种工作就很熟练了。

❀ **skilled 表示"有技能的""熟练的"：**

She was <u>skilled</u> enough in French to translate a novel. 她法语很好，翻译了一本小说。

He was a highly <u>skilled</u> flier now. 他现在是技术高超的飞行员了。

A <u>skilled</u> worker can perform the task easily. 熟练工人做这项工作很容易。

还可表示"需要技术的"：

Only two percent of them are qualified for <u>skilled</u> work. 他们只有百分之二的人有资格做这种技术性的工作。

This is a highly <u>skilled</u> job. 这是有高度技术性的工作。

440 small—little

small 表示"小的"（和 large 相对）：

Larger fish devour the smaller ones. 大鱼吃小鱼。

This bag is too small. Have you got a larger one? 这个包太小，你有大点儿的吗？

还可用来表示抽象的东西：

The business made only a small profit this year. 这家店今年只有小小的赢利。

This is only a small quarrel; it will soon be over. 这是一次小小的争吵，很快就会过去的。

常可用来表示"少量的"：

There is a small charge for mailing packages. 寄这些包裹只收少量费用。

Could I have a small brandy, please. 可否给我一些白兰地。

特别是和 quantity, amount, number 等词连用：

There is a small quantity of milk left in the cup. 杯子里还剩少量牛奶。

They come in small numbers. 他们只进来少数几个。

❀ little 也可表示"小的"，但常常带有一些感情色彩，可译为"小小的""小巧的"等：

That's a marvellous little hospital. 那是一座很好的、小巧的医院。

A little piano stood against the wall. 靠墙放着一台小小的钢琴。

还可表示"年纪小的"：

All the little children are in Class I. 所有年纪小的孩子都在一年级。

How are the little ones? 孩子们怎样？

还可用作表语，特别是在美国，表示"年纪小""小时候"：

She's too little to ride a bicycle. 她年纪太小，骑不了自行车。

Honey, you're too little to watch horror movies. 亲爱的，你还太小，不能看恐怖电影。

441 so

so 可用作副词，表示程度，可译为"这样""那样"等：

I wish I were not so busy. 但愿我不那样忙碌。

I had no idea that he was so ill. 我不知道他病得这样重。

常可用在感叹句及带感情色彩的句子中（可有灵活译法）：

I'm so glad to see you! 看到你真高兴！

You're so obstinate! 你真固执！

后面有时跟 as 引起的结构：

I'm not so young as you think. 我没有你想的那么年轻。

It did not take so long as he had feared. 它用的时间并不像他担心的那样长。

还可和一些动词连用，表示程度：

What makes you tremble so? 什么使你这样发抖？

Tell me what has upset you so. 告诉我什么使你这样不高兴。

❀ 和 **do** 连用，表示"这样做"，以避免重复前面的动词：

In doing so, she gave a little sigh. 在这样做时，她轻轻叹了一口气。

In so doing they only demonstrated their lack of good faith. 他们这样做，只能表现出他们缺乏信义。

还可和 **say, tell, think, suppose** 等动词连用，代表一个宾语从句：

It's all your doing. I told you so from the first. 这都是你干的事，我从一开始就对你这样说。

I know they enjoyed every minute of it. Don't you think so? 我知道他们非常欣赏这次演出，你不觉得吗？

也可用在 **if so** 中，表示"如果这样"：

If so, I had quite misjudged him. 如果是这样，我是错误地判断他了。

Do you enjoy romantic films? If so, you should watch the film on I TV. 你喜欢看浪漫的电影吗？如果这样，你可以看今晚独立电视频道上的电影。

还可和其他一些动词连用：

So the story goes. 故事内容是这样的。

While she was so employed, she heard a noise. 她这样做时，听到一个声音。

还可和动词 **be** 连用：

It isn't so with me. 我的情况却不如此。

<u>So</u> it was I became a sailor. 因此，我就成了海员。

❀ 可以用于 **so... that** 表示"那样……以致"：

My mother lives <u>so</u> far away <u>that</u> we hardly ever see her. 我母亲住得那么远，我们很少见到她。

It was <u>so</u> dark <u>that</u> he couldn't see the faces of his companions. 天是那样黑，他连同伴们的脸都看不清。

也可用于 **so that**，引导表示目的的从句：

I hired a boat <u>so that</u> I could go fishing. 我租了一条小船，以便我能去钓鱼。

Speak clearly <u>so that</u> they may understand you. 说得慢一些，以便他们能听懂你的话。

从句若为否定结构，谓语多由 **should** 构成：

He looked down <u>so that</u> she should not see his eyes. 他眼睛低着，以免她看到他的眼睛。

He wore a mask <u>so that</u> no one should recognize him. 他戴了一个面具，以便没人能认出他来。

有时只用 **so** 一个词引起这类从句：

Can't you fix it somehow <u>so</u> you could stay? 你不能安排安排以便你能留下？

Check carefully, <u>so</u> any mistakes will be caught. 仔细检查一遍，把所有错误都找出来。

这类从句还可表示结果，可译为"因此"：

One of her lungs is affected a little, <u>so that</u> she has to rest. 她有一叶肺受到一些影响，因此她得休息。

My pencil fell under my desk, <u>so that</u> I couldn't see it. 我的铅笔掉到了书桌下面，因此我看不见它了。

❀ **so** 有时用在句首，表示"也如此"（引起的短句在时态上要和前面句子一致）：

If Adam can do it, <u>so</u> can I. 如果亚当能办到，我也能。

"I've lost their address." "<u>So</u> have I." "我把他们的地址弄丢了。""我也是。"

I was tired, and <u>so</u> were the others. 我累了，其他人也累了。

so 也可用在下面这类句子的开头，表示"是这样……"：

It's going to be a cold winter, so the newspaper says. 今年冬天会很冷，报纸是这样说的。

"Mary is getting married." "Yes, so I heard." "玛丽要结婚了。" "是的，我听说了。"

so 还可以用作连词，表示"因此""所以"：

Nobody seemed about, so I went in. 似乎没有人在，因此我走了进去。

You aren't listening, so I'll shut up. 你不在听，因此我就不说了。

有时放在句首，表示惊异：

So you are going to get married this time. 原来，这次你要结婚了。

Oh! So that's what you think, is it? 啊，原来，你是这样想的，是吧？

❀ 还可用于某些词组：

or so 约摸，左右

I'll be back in a month or so. 我大约一个月后回来。

She had a little money, ten pounds or so. 她有一点钱，约十镑左右。

so-and-so 某某人，某某先生（夫人）

If I said I would meet so-and-so, I would do it. 如果我说了我要见某某人，我会这样做的。

Pick out furniture which you yourself like and forget what Mrs. so-and-so has in her parlor. 挑选你自己喜欢的家具，别去想某某夫人客厅里有什么。

so as to 以便

We picked apples so as to make a pie. 我们摘了些苹果，以便做果馅饼。

Go in quietly so as not to wake the baby. 悄悄地走进去，以免把孩子吵醒。

so far 到现在为止

So far he has done very well at school. 到目前为止，他在学校学得不错。

He says that is my best work so far. 他说这是到现在为止我最好的作品。

so long as 只要……

So long as you make Ruth happy I'm content. 只要你让鲁思幸福，我就满足了。

You may use the room so long as you keep it clean. 你可以使用这个房间，只要你能保持干净。

so much for... 就谈（讲）到这里

So much for that; let's talk about something else now. 这件事就谈到这里，现在咱们谈别的事。

So much for my past history. 我过去的情况就讲到这里。

so-so 马马虎虎，不怎么样，一般：

Marry liked the movie, but I thought it was just so-so. 玛丽喜欢这部电影，但我认为这部电影只是一般。

without (not) so much as 连……都没有

He departed without so much as a goodbye. 他连一句"再见"都没说就走了。

He didn't so much as say thank you, after all we've done for him. 我们帮了他这么多忙，他连一句"谢谢"都没说。

442 society—community

society 主要表示"社会"（通常不可数）：

We all have to learn how to behave ourselves in society. 我们都要学习在社会上怎样为人处世。

Women must have equal status in society. 女人在社会上应有平等地位。

有时可用作可数名词，表示某种社会：

We live in a multi-racial society. 我们生活在一个多民族的社会中。

the increasing complexity of industrial societies 工业社会中日益增长的复杂性

有时还可表示"协会""学会"：

She is the president of the literary society. 她是文艺协会的主席。

❀ **community** 表示一个国家和地区的公众，可译为"社会""社区"：

The job of a politician is to serve the community. 从政人士的任务是为公众服务。

The entire community is behind the appeal. 整个社区都支持这项呼吁。

the European Community 欧洲共同体

443 some—any

some 主要表示"几个"或"一些"，可以修饰可数名词复数或不可数名词（读作 /səm/）：

Ask some boys to help you. 找几个男孩子帮助你。

Now you can give me some advice. 现在你可以给我出点主意。

在疑问句、否定句和条件从句中通常用 any 代替 some（注意这类句子的翻译方法）：

Are there any boys in your group? 你们小组中有男生吗？

There aren't any boys in our group. 我们小组里没有男生。

在某些肯定句中也可能用 any（这类句子多少含有否定的意思）：

You never gave me any help. 你从不给我任何帮助。

We got there without any trouble. 我们毫无困难地到达那里。

但在表示请求的问句中或在否定问句中，可以用 some：

Will you like some more meat? 要不要再吃点肉？

Could you lend me some money? 你能借我点钱吗？

在条件从句中，用 some 也可以：

Do you mind if I put some music on? 我放点音乐你介意吗？

If we had some (any) money, we could buy it. 如果我们有钱，可以买。

some 还可表示"有些""有的"（这时读作 /sʌm/）：

Some children learn languages easily. 有些孩子学语言很容易。

Some French wine is quite sweet. 有些法国酒相当甜。

△ some 也可用作代词，多读作 /sʌm/，表示"一些"，可以单独使用：

I hadn't any cigarettes, so l went out to buy some. 我没有烟了，因此出去买了一些。

If you have no money, I will lend you some. 如果你没有钱，我可以借你一点。

也可指人：

Some are wise and some are otherwise. 有些人很明智,有些人则不然。（谚语）

Some still believe he was innocent. 有些人仍然相信,他是无辜的。

有时和 **of** 连用:

Won't you try some of this cake? 你要不要尝点这种蛋糕?

Some of us agree with that statement; some disagree. 我们有些人赞成这个说法,有些人不赞成。

❀ **any** 也可用作代词,用在疑问句、否定句及条件从句中代替 **some**:

I don't expect to see any of them there. 我预料不会在那里见到他们什么人。

I don't think any of my friends have seen them. 我想,我的朋友没有谁见到过他们。

any 还可表示"任何一个(几个)":

Any is good enough for me. 任何一个对我都是适用的。

They're all free: take any (of them) you like. 它们都是免费的,你可拿任何你想要的。

△ **any** 也可用作形容词,表示同样意思:

Any time you want me, just send for me. 任何时候你需要我,就派人来叫我。

We did the work without any difficulty. 我们做这工作没有任何困难。

444 somebody—someone—anybody—anyone

这四个词都表示"某人"。

❀ **somebody** 和 **someone** 意思完全相同,主要用于肯定句:

Somebody wants to see you. 有人要见你。

She wants someone to look after her. 她需要人照顾。

❀ **anybody** 和 **anyone** 主要用于疑问句、否定句及条件从句:

Did anyone call when I was out? 我出去时,有人找我了吗?

Whenever anyone was ill, he installed himself as sick nurse. 每当有人病了,他总是充当护士。

在提出请求或反问的句子中也可用 **somebody** 和 **someone**:

Will you ask <u>someone</u> to carry this bag for me? 你可否找人帮我提这件行李？

Why doesn't <u>somebody</u> clean up places like that? 为什么没有人像这样打扫房间？

anybody 和 **anyone** 还可表示"任何人"：

<u>Anybody</u> will tell you where the bus stop is. 任何人都可以告诉你公共汽车站在哪里。

Don't be dependent on <u>anyone</u>. 不要依赖任何人。

445 sometimes—sometime—some time

sometimes 表示"有时"：

<u>Sometimes</u> we're busy and <u>sometimes</u> we're not. 我们有时很忙，有时不忙。

Everyone is a fool <u>sometimes</u>, and none at all time. 每个人总有时会发傻，可没有人老是发傻。

❀ sometime 也是副词，表示"（将来）什么时候"：

I'll speak to him about it <u>sometime</u>. 我什么时候将和他谈谈这事。

We'll meet again <u>sometime</u> next week. 我们下星期找个时间再碰头。

也可表示"（过去）某个时候"：

I saw him <u>sometime</u> in May. 我是 5 月什么时候见到他的。

Our house was built <u>sometime</u> around 1950. 我们的房子是 1950 年前后盖的。

❀ sometime 有时写成 some time：

He died <u>some time</u> last year. 他是去年什么时候死的。

另外 some time（读作 /ˈsʌm ˈtaɪm/）还可表示"相当多时间"：

I'm afraid it'll take <u>some time</u> to repair your car. 恐怕修你的车要花相当多时间。

She's lived in Italy for <u>some time</u>, so she speaks Italian quite well. 她在意大利已经住了相当长时间，因此她意大利语讲得很好。

446 somewhat—somehow

somewhat 为副词，表示"有一些""在某种程度上"（可修饰动词、形容词、副词等）：

The idea <u>somewhat</u> alarmed his mother. 这个想法使他妈妈有些惊慌。

I was <u>somewhat</u> surprised (disappointed). 我有些吃惊（失望）。

❀ **somehow** 意思却完全不同，一是表示"以某种方式"：

She'll get me there <u>somehow</u>. 她将以某种方式把我送到那里。

We must celebrate the great occasion <u>somehow</u>. 我们必须以某种方式庆祝这个伟大的日子。

二是表示"不知怎么搞的"（什么原因）：

She never liked me, <u>somehow</u>. 不知什么原因，她从来不喜欢我。

<u>Somehow</u> the right chances never seemed to present itself. 不知怎么搞的，适当的机会似乎老是不来。

447 sort—kind—sort of—kind of

sort 表示"种""类"，多和 **of** 连用：

He had some <u>sort of</u> an English accent. 他有某种英国口音。

Pop music is the <u>sort</u> she likes most. 流行音乐是她最喜欢的一种音乐。

of 后面也可跟复数名词：

They sell all <u>sorts</u> of shoes. 他们卖各式各样的鞋。

There were five different <u>sorts</u> of biscuits. 这里有五种不同的饼干。

还可用在 **of... sort** 这种短语中：

I can't approve of things <u>of this sort</u>. 我不赞成这样的事。

Helen would never permit anything <u>of the sort</u>. 海伦绝不会允许发生这样的事。

Sarcastic remarks <u>of that sort</u> will only make him more angry. 那种讥讽的话只会使他更生气。

❀ **kind** 也表示"种""类"：

All <u>kinds</u> of difficulties have to be overcome. 各种困难都需要克服。

What (Which) <u>kind</u> do you prefer? 你愿意要哪一种的？

有时用 **kind of a** 这种结构：

You don't know what <u>kind of</u> a man he is. 你不知道他是怎样一种人。

What <u>kind of</u> a job are you going to take? 你准备干哪一种工作？

有人不赞成这种结构，认为不加 **a** 更好：

What <u>kind</u> (sort) of car is it? 这是哪种（牌子的）车？

of... kind 也是常用结构：

I don't like people <u>of that kind</u>. 我不喜欢那样的人。

Africa is rich in minerals <u>of many kinds</u>. 非洲盛产许多种矿物。

❀ **sort of** 和 **kind of** 都可用作状语，表示"有点儿……"：

The movie was <u>sort of</u> disappointing. 这部电影有点儿令人失望。

I <u>kind of</u> like an open car. 我有点儿喜欢敞篷汽车。

448 souvenir—keepsake—memento

souvenir 表示"纪念品"（读作 /ˌsuːvəˈnɪə, ˈsuːvənɪə/）：

The local shopkeepers sell <u>souvenirs</u> to the tourists. 当地商店给游客售卖纪念品。

My uncle left me his watch as a <u>souvenir</u>. 我叔叔给我留下了他的表作纪念。

❀ **keepsake** 也表示"纪念品"：

Mary's boyfriend gave her a bracelet as a <u>keepsake</u>. 玛丽的男朋友送给她一只手镯作纪念品。

She kept the partially torn photograph as a <u>keepsake</u> of her trip. 她保存了一张部分撕破的相片作为这次旅行的纪念品。

❀ **memento** /mɪˈmentəʊ/ 也表示"纪念品"：

My host gave me a small gift as a <u>memento</u> of my trip to France. 主人给了我一件小礼物作为我法国之行的纪念品。

I keep this small lock of hair as a <u>memento</u> of a dear friend. 我留下这一小绺头发，作为一个亲爱的朋友的纪念品。

449 speciality—specialty

speciality /ˌspeʃɪˈælɪti/ 有两个意思，一是"专业""专长"：

Embroidery is her speciality. 刺绣是她的专长。

His speciality (specialty) is heart surgery. 他的专业是心脏外科。

二是"特产""特有食品（特色菜）"：

Wood carvings are a speciality of the village. 木雕是这个村子里的特产。

Fish baked in pastry is the speciality of this restaurant. 软饼烤鱼是这家餐馆的名菜。

❀ **specialty** 意思和 **speciality** 差不多，美国人通常用它表示：

专业，专长：

My literature professor's specialty is German Literature. 我的文学教授主要研究德国文学。

The doctor's specialty was infectious diseases. 这位医生的专长是治疗传染病。

名菜，特产：

Roast lamb is this restaurant's specialty. 烤羊肉是这家餐馆的特色菜。

The brass work of Birmingham has long been one of its specialties. 伯明翰铜器长期以来都是它的特产之一。

450 **stand—bear—tolerate**

stand 主要表示"站着""站起来"等（*vi.*）：

Stand still! 站着别动！

He stood (up) politely when the lady entered the room. 那位女士走进屋时，他客气地站了起来。

可用于引申意义，表示"立在（某处）""在（某处）"等：

A little piano stood against the wall. 一台小钢琴靠墙立着。

A tall poplar tree once stood here. 以前这里曾有一棵高高的杨树。

还可表示"情况（如何）""处于（某种）状态"：

How do things stand at the moment? 目前情况如何？

They stand in danger of a lawsuit. 他们有卷入诉讼的危险。

也可用作 *vt.*，表示"使立在（某处）"：

Stand the bicycle against the wall. 把自行车靠墙放着。

Stand the table in the corner. 把桌子放在那个角落里。

还可表示"忍受""经受"：

This work won't stand close examination. 这项工作经不起仔细检查。

I just couldn't stand this life any more. 这种生活我再也忍受不了啦。

❀ **bear** 也可表示类似的意思：

I cannot bear the pain. 我忍受不了这种疼痛。

This evidence won't bear scrutiny. 这项证据经不起推敲。

这个词可跟不同结构，如不定式、动名词、复合结构等：

She can't bear being laughed at. 她受不了被人嘲笑。

She can't bear me to be unhappy. 她不忍心看我这样痛苦。

He could not bear that his friends should laugh at him. 他的朋友们笑他他受不了。

❀ **tolerate** 的意思有点接近，但不一样，主要表示"忍受""容忍"：

I can't tolerate that loud music. 我受不了这样嘈杂的音乐。

You should not tolerate such rudeness. 你不应当容忍这样的粗鲁无礼。

451 stationary—stationery—stationer

前两个词只差一个字母，意思却完全不同。

❀ **stationary** 为形容词，表示"静止的"：

Because of an accident, traffic was stationary for an hour. 由于出了车祸，车辆停滞不动达一小时之久。

The bus remained stationary. 那辆公交车仍然停在那里。

❀ **stationery** 表示"文具纸张"（总称，不可数）：

As a journalist you must spend a great deal of money on stationery. 作为一个新闻记者，你一定在文具纸张上花很多钱。

I bought some fancy stationery for my thank-you notes. 我买了一些花哨的信纸用来写感谢信。

❀ **stationer** 指"文具商（店）"：

Is there a stationer's (shop) near here? 这附近有文具店吗？

Can you buy stamps at a stationer's? 文具店里能买到邮票吗？

452 steal—pilfer—burgle—rob

steal 主要表示"偷窃"，过去式为 **stole**，过去分词为 **stolen**：

Someone <u>stole</u> a painting from the museum. 有人偷了博物馆的一张画。

He was accused of <u>stealing</u> a dog. 他被控偷了别人的狗。

❀ **pilfer** 表示"偷窃（少量东西）"：

The office worker who <u>pilfered</u> pens from the supply room was reprimanded. 办公室工人因为偷窃文具室里的钢笔而受到斥责。

Jimmy <u>pilfered</u> a few cookies when his mother wasn't looking. 吉米趁他母亲没瞧见偷了几块饼干。

❀ **burgle** 表示"进屋偷窃"：

Our house was <u>burgled</u> while we were away on holiday. 我们出去休假时，有人进入我们家行窃了。

We were <u>burgled</u> three times in a month. 一个月中我们家遭窃三次。

❀ **rob** 主要表示"抢劫"：

They <u>robbed</u> the jewellery store in broad daylight. 他们在大白天抢劫了一家珠宝店。

The thief <u>robbed</u> the tourists on a dark street. 窃贼在一条黑暗的街道上抢劫了旅游的人。

453 still—yet—already

still 作副词时主要表示"仍然""仍旧""还……"：

The moon is a moon <u>still</u>, whether it shines or not. 不管阴晴，月亮仍旧是月亮。（谚语）

My grandfather is <u>still</u> living at the age of 93. 我祖父 93 岁还活着。

❀ **yet** 作副词时表示"还（没有）"（多用于否定句）：

"Has he come yet?" "No, not <u>yet</u>." "他来了吗？""还没有来。"

I haven't enough data <u>yet</u>. 我还没有足够的数据。

有时也可用于肯定句，表示"还"：

It was too early <u>yet</u> to tell anything. 现在还太早，无法做出判断。

I have a few more pages to read <u>yet</u>. 我还有几页要看。

在用于疑问句时表示"已经"：

Have you finished yet? 你已经干完了吗？

I wonder if she's started yet. 不知她是否已经动身。

❀ **already** 表示"已经"（大多放在主要动词前面和动词 be 后面）：

I have already made a big start in this direction. 我已在这方面有了良好的开端。

The drawing-room lights were already on. 客厅的灯已经亮了。

有时放在句末或放在谓语或宾语后面，有时放在句首：

She had told me already how her sister longed for children. 她已经告诉我她姐姐多么想孩子。

Already the round sun was setting. 圆圆的太阳已经在落山了。

由此可以看出在肯定句中多用 **already** 表示"已经"，而在疑问句中要用 **yet**。**yet** 还可表示"还……"，而 **still** 表示"仍然"。三个词都表示某个时间的状态，或是已经发生，还在发生，或是仍然在发生。

454 stone—rock—pebble—boulder

stone 表示"一般的石头"（可数，不可数）：

Marble is an expensive stone. 大理石是一种贵重的石头。

The building is made of stone. 房子是石头盖的。

可用作定语：

a stone bridge 石头桥 a stone wall 石头墙

❀ **rock** 多指"岩石"（不可数）：

The men broke the rock with gunpowder. 工人们用炸药把岩石炸开。

He built his house on rock. 他把他的房子盖在山岩上。

也可指"一块岩石"或"礁石"（可数）：

Rocks fell down the hillside. 岩石顺着小山滚了下来。

The ship struck a rock and broke up. 船撞在礁上撞碎了。

还可指"（小）石块"（特别是在美国）：

The angry mob began to throw rocks at the speaker. 愤怒的群众朝演讲的人扔石块。

Rocks were thrown and police came running. 石块乱扔，警察跑着赶了过来。

❀ **pebble** 指 "鹅卵石"：

I bruised my feet on the pebbles in the bed of the stream. 我的脚被河底的鹅卵石磨紫了。

Pebbles are rounded and smooth, unlike rocks or sharp stones. 鹅卵石是圆形光滑的，不像岩石或锋利的石块。

❀ **boulder** 指 "圆形的巨石"：

Huge boulders chocked the stream bed. 巨大的石块堵塞了小溪。

455 storey—story—floor

storey 表示 "一层楼"：

My bedroom is on the second (third) storey. 我的卧室在二（三）楼。

A building with 100 storeys is a sky-scraper. 一百层的楼就是摩天大楼。

❀ 美国拼作 **story**：

The house is two stories high. 这房子有两层。

多少层的楼用 **-storeyed**（美作 **-storied**）表示：

A two-storied house is one with a ground floor and one floor above it. 两层楼的房子有底层和楼上一层。

a six-storeyed (storied) building 一座六层楼的建筑

❀ **floor** 也表示 "楼房的一层"：

You know my flat is on the top floor. 你知道我的寓所在顶层上。

This elevator stops at every floor. 这座电梯每一层都停。

在英国 **the ground floor** 指最下一层，**the first floor** 指二楼，以此类推。在美国最下一层称为 **the first floor**，以此类推。

floor 还可指 "地板" "地面"：

A Turkey carpet adorned the floor. 一张土耳其地毯装饰着地板。

The floor of this room is made of hardwood. 这个房间是硬木地板。

456　subconscious—unconscious

subconscious 可用作名词，也可用作形容词。

用作名词时表示"下（潜）意识"：

Something in his subconscious kept him from expressing his feelings. 他的潜意识中有某种东西阻止着他表达他的感情。

Much of Mary's anxiety was linked to fears in her subconscious. 玛丽的焦虑不安情绪很大部分和她潜意识中的恐惧是有联系的。

作形容词时表示"下意识的"：

The sleeping man's subconscious mind retained everything that was said around him. 这位酣睡的人的头脑中的潜意识能记住他周围的人说的话。

a subconscious cry for affection 下意识的对爱的呼唤

❀ unconscious 是形容词，表示"没有知觉的"：

The driver was unconscious for three days after the accident. 车祸之后，那个司机三天都没有知觉。

When he was hit on the head he became unconscious. 他头部受到重击时，失去了知觉。

还可表示"不自觉的"：

She had an unconscious hostility toward her sister. 她对她的姐姐有一种不自觉的敌意。

Her prejudice is quite unconscious. 她的偏见是相当不自觉的。

457　subway—underground—tube—metro

在美国地下铁道称为 subway：

Anne saves money by taking the subway to work instead of driving. 安为了省钱坐地铁上班而不开车去。

The New York city subway serves millions of passengers each year. 纽约市的地铁每年为千百万乘客服务。

❀ 在英国地铁称为 underground：

We went by underground. 我们坐地铁去。

She hates travelling by (on the) <u>underground</u>. 她讨厌坐地铁。

❀ 伦敦地铁也称作 tube：

I go to work on the <u>tube</u> (by <u>tube</u>). 我坐地铁上班。

❀ 巴黎的地铁称作 Metro：

travel on the <u>Metro</u> 坐地铁

a <u>Metro</u> station 地铁站

458 such

such 作形容词时表示"这样的"，可以修饰可数名词单数：

I had no idea you were <u>such</u> an orator. 我不知道你是这样一位演说家。

The news gave me <u>such</u> a shock. 那个消息使我如此震惊。

也可修饰可数名词复数：

We have been <u>such</u> friends! 我们是这样好的朋友！

I have met many <u>such</u> people. 我碰到过很多这样的人。

还可修饰不可数名词：

<u>Such</u> bad spelling is intolerable. 这样差的拼写是无法忍受的。

I didn't expect <u>such</u> cold weather. 我没料想到天气会这样冷。

有时 such 表示某种赞赏或鄙视的情绪（有时可译为"那样……"）：

You can have no idea what a girl she is. <u>Such</u> character! <u>Such</u> sense! 你不知道她是怎样一个姑娘。那样好的性格！那样有头脑！

She has <u>such</u> a marvellous voice! 她的声音是那样甜美！

它可用于一些特殊结构：

such-and-such 某某……（用来代替一个具体名称）

She told me to go to <u>such-and-such</u> street and turn right. 她让我去某某街，然后向右转。

He went to <u>such-and-such</u> a movie. 他去看了某某一部电影。

such... as 像……这样的

<u>Such</u> men <u>as</u> these are dangerous. 像这样的人是危险的。

<u>Such</u> things <u>as</u> family pride were out of date nowadays. 现在家庭尊严这类东西已经过时了。

such as 像……这样的，如，像

Boys such as John and James are very friendly. 像约翰和詹姆斯这样的男孩子是很友好的。

They export a lot of fruit, such as oranges, lemons, etc. 他们出口大量水果，如橘子、柠檬等。

such... as（as 作关系代词引导定语从句）像……这样的

I never heard such stories as he tells. 我从未听过他讲的这类故事。

We had such grapes as you never saw. 我们有你从未见过的那种葡萄。

such... that 这样……以致

It is such a small matter that I do not care to make any charge. 这是一件小事，我不想收费。

I gave him such a shock that his face turned white. 我使他这样震惊，他脸都白了。

459 suit—suite

这两个词只差一个字母，意思却不相同，读音也不同。

❀ suit 读作 /suːt/。作动词时主要表示"适合""合身"：

The arrangement suits them both. 这样安排对两人都合适。

I don't know what profession would suit me. 我不知道什么职业能适合我。

作名词时主要表示"一套（衣服）"：

George is wearing a new suit (of clothes). 乔治穿着一套新衣服。

可构成合成词：

a bathing suit 游泳衣（旧）　　　　　a sports suit 运动服

a space suit 宇航服　　　　　　　　a diving-suit 潜水衣

❀ suite 读作 /swiːt/，主要表示"一套（房间）"：

She has a suite of rooms in the hotel—a living-room, bedroom and bath. 她在宾馆有一套房间——一间客厅、一间卧室和一间浴室。

He has rented a suite of rooms on the ground floor. 他在底层租了一套房。

还可表示"组曲"或"一组家具"：

Tchaikovsky's "Nutcracker Suite" is my favorite piece of music. 柴可

夫斯基的《胡桃夹子组曲》是我最喜欢的乐曲。

That's a nice <u>suite</u> of furniture. 那是一套漂亮的家具。

460 suppose—supposing—what if

❀ **suppose** 可表示"假定""假设":

<u>Suppose</u> her father turned her out of doors! She did not care. 假定她爸爸把她从家里撵出来！那她也不在乎。

<u>Suppose</u> your father saw you, what would he say? 假设你父亲见到你了，他会怎么说？

也可用来提出建议:

<u>Suppose</u> we go for a swim. 咱们去游一会儿泳，如何？

<u>Suppose</u> you try now? 你现在就试试怎样？

❀ **supposing** 也可引起状语，表示"假定""假设"（美国人这样用时比较少）:

<u>Supposing</u> (that) she doesn't come, what shall we do? 她要是不来怎么办？

<u>Supposing</u> that he asks you, will you go? 假定她邀请你，你会去吗？

supposing 偶尔也可表示建议:

"Daddy, can I watch TV?" "<u>Supposing</u> you do your homework first." "爸，我能看电视吗？""你先把作业做了如何？"

❀ **what if** 也可用来表示"如果……怎么办？":

<u>What if</u> he comes back? 如果他回来了，怎么办？

<u>What if</u> she finds out that you've lost her book? 如果她发现你把她的书丢了，怎么办？

也可用来提出建议:

<u>What if</u> you go instead of me? 你替我去，如何？

<u>What if</u> we move the picture over there? 把那张画搬到那儿怎样？

461 take

take 是最常用的动词之一，主要有下面这些意思：

拿：

<u>Taking</u> a sheet of paper, he began to write a letter. 他拿了一张纸开始写信。

Mr. Smith <u>took</u> up the evening paper. 史密斯先生拿起晚报。

常可有较灵活译法：

The girl <u>took</u> in the washing as it began to rain. 开始下雨了，这个姑娘把衣服收了进去。

The old woman <u>took</u> off her spectacles. 老太婆取下了她的眼镜。

带（往某处）：

Are you going to <u>take</u> her to England? 你准备带她到英国去吗？

I've just <u>taken</u> him for a walk. 我刚带他去散了一会儿步。

有时有较灵活译法：

I <u>took</u> my things to a hotel in New Street. 我把我的东西搬到新街的一家宾馆里。

I must hurry and <u>take</u> Jim to school. 我得赶快送吉姆上学。

（和一名词连用）表示一个动作：

Let's <u>take a look</u> round the exhibition. 咱们看看展览会。

I want to <u>take a nap</u>. 我想去睡个午觉。

Later we went out to <u>take a walk</u>. 后来，我们出去散了一会儿步。

吃，喝，吸（入）：

<u>Take</u> some more bread. 再吃一点儿面包。

She was forever <u>taking</u> pills. 她老是在吃药。

I can't <u>take</u> alcohol. 我不能喝酒。

乘坐，搭乘，租用：

I'll <u>take</u> a taxi home. 我将坐出租车回家。

Then we <u>took</u> a bus into the town. 然后，我们坐公共汽车进城。

选修（学），选择，选购等：

I plan to <u>take</u> both French and Spanish this term. 这学期我打算选修法语和西班牙语。

I <u>took</u> a course in Geology last year. 去年，我选了一门地质学的课。

量，照（相），记下：

He <u>took</u> my temperature and pulse. 他量了我的体温和脉搏。

The doctor then <u>took</u> his blood pressure. 然后，医生量了他的血压。

需要（常有较灵活译法）：

The wound <u>took</u> a long time to heal. 那个伤口好久才愈合。

That night it <u>took</u> him a long time to sleep. 那天晚上他好久才睡着。

△还可用于许多短语：

be taken aback 吃惊

be taken ill 生病了

take a bet 打赌

take a bow 谢幕

take a chance 碰碰运气

take a fancy (liking) to 喜欢

take a firm stand 采取坚定立场

take a risk 冒风险

take a seat 坐下

take a step 采取某种措施

take a turn 发生某种变化

take a vote 投票表决

take an interest in 对……有兴趣

take advantage of 利用，占……的便宜

take after 长得像

take aim 瞄准

take apart 拆开

take... as 看作

take away 拿走，减去，使离开

take back 收回，送回

take by surprise 奇袭，使惊奇

take care 当心

take care of 照顾，处理

take control of 控制住

take credit of 说是……的功劳

take delight (pleasure) in 喜欢（做某事）

take down 拿下来，记下来

take effect 开始起作用，生效

take for (to be) （错）当作，以为是

take for granted 想当然地认为

take (for instance) 以……为例

take fright 突然害怕起来

take heart 受到鼓舞（安慰）

take hold of 抓住

take ill (sick) 生病

take in 接受……住，收留，订阅

take into account 把……考虑进去

take interest in 对……发生兴趣

take it easy 慢慢地，不过于紧张

take kindly to 喜欢，赞成

take leave of one's senses 发疯，神经错乱

take liberties with 对……随便，擅自使用

take note (of) 注意

take notice (of) 注意，理会

take notes 记笔记

take oath 发誓

take off 脱下，起飞，休假

take offence 生（某人的）气

take office 就职

take on 接受（工作），雇用，上车

take one's leave 告辞

take one's own life 自杀

take one's time 慢慢来，从容不迫

take over 接替，接管

take pains 下工夫

take part (in) 参加，参与

take pity on 可怜，怜悯

take place 发生，举行

take (a) pride in 对……感到自豪

take someone's place 代替（某人）

take stock (of) 估量，考虑

take the chair 担任主席

take the floor 在会上发言

take the initiative 采取主动

take the liberty of 冒昧，擅自

take the opportunity 利用这个机会

take (the) trouble 费事，下工夫

take to 喜欢，养成某种爱好

take to heart 牢记在心，介意

take to one's heels 逃之夭夭

take up 开始学习，从事某项活动

take up arms 拿起武器

462 **taste—tasteful—tasty—tasteless—distasteful**

taste 可作动词，也可用作名词。

△ taste 作动词时有下面几种情况：

有……味，吃起来……（作 *link v.*）：

The meat tastes good (awful). 肉味很好（糟极了）。

This medicine tastes horrible. 这药味道难吃极了。

尝（多作 *vt.*）：

Taste this coffee and see if you like it. 尝尝这咖啡，看你是否喜欢。

I'll taste and see if this soup needs more salt. 我来尝尝，看汤要不要加盐。

吃出某种味道（多作 *vt.*）：

I tasted almond in this cake. 这蛋糕里我吃出杏仁味。

Sometimes when you are ill, you can't taste properly. 有时，当你生病时，你吃不出味来。

吃，喝（某种饮料或食品）（*vt.*）：

I have never tasted alcohol in my life. 我一生从未沾过酒。

I haven't tasted such a beautiful curry for ages. 我好久没吃过这么好的咖喱。

领略，尝到……的味道（*vt.*）：

He had tasted the delights of country life. 他领略了田园生活的乐趣。

At last he tasted the joys of success. 最后，他尝到了成功的喜悦。

用于 **taste of**，有……的味道：

This pudding tastes of lemon. 这块布丁有柠檬味。

This soup tastes too much of salt. 这汤太咸。

△ **taste** 作名词时有下面几种意思：

味道：

This fruit has an unpleasant taste. 这水果有一股难吃的味道。

This medicine has a bitter taste. 这药有一种苦味。

尝一尝：

I'll take a taste of your cake. 我来尝尝你的蛋糕。

Have a taste of our soup. 尝一尝我们的汤。

领略，知道……的味道：

I've already had a taste of his temper. 我已领略了一下他的脾气。

This will give them a taste of success. 这会让他们知道一点儿成功的味道。

味觉：

Her taste is unusually keen. 她的味觉特灵敏。

I've got a cold so my taste's quite gone. 我感冒了，吃东西没味。

喜好，爱好：

He has no taste for sweet things. 他不喜欢吃甜东西。

He had a taste for music. 他爱好音乐。

鉴赏力，素养：

She had literary taste. 她有文学素养。

We all admire your taste in art. 我们都钦佩你的艺术鉴赏力。

格调：

His jokes showed poor taste. 他的笑话格调不高。

Her clothes are always in good taste. 她的衣服格调都很高雅。

△ taste 有一些派生形容词：

tasteful 格调很高的

The furniture in their house is very tasteful. 他们家的家具格调都很高。

Her jewellery is always very tasteful. 她的首饰格调总是很高的。

tasty 有味道的，有趣的

These sandwiches are tasty. 这些三明治味道很好。

She gave us a tasty piece of news. 她给我们讲了一条有趣的消息。

tasteless 没有味道的，缺乏修养的

It was tasteless of you to behave like that. 你这样做未免缺乏修养。

No one laughed at the tasteless joke. 对这个粗俗的笑话，没人发笑。

distasteful 令人不快（讨厌）的

I find his use of bad language extremely distasteful. 我觉得他使用的粗俗语言极其令人讨厌。

No one volunteered for the distasteful task. 没人自愿去干这令人厌恶的工作。

463　taxi—cab

这两个词都表示"出租（汽）车"，也可译成"计程车"。在英国和美国这两个词都可以用，不过，在英国用 taxi 时较多，在美国用 cab 时较多，也可称作 **taxicab**：

Mary hailed a taxicab (cab) from her office building. 玛丽从她的办公楼叫了一辆出租车。

464 technique—technology

technique 表示技术或技巧，作为总称时为不可数名词：

Writing poetry requires great <u>technique</u>. 写诗需要技巧。

He is learning the <u>technique</u> of painting. 他在学习绘画技术。

也可指具体的一种技术或方法，这时作可数名词：

Doctors are developing a new <u>technique</u> for treating diabetes. 医生们正在开发一种治疗糖尿病的新技术。

We should employ a variety of <u>techniques</u> in the test. 在化验中，我们应使用多种技术（方法）。

❀ **technology** 为科学技术的总称（尤指科学技术在工业上的应用）：

Modern <u>technology</u> has improved our standard of living. 现代科学技术提高了我们的生活水平。

Computer <u>technology</u> can be expected to change. 计算机科学可能会变化。

465 term—semester

term 和 **semester** 都可表示"学期"。英国一般分为三个 terms，即 **autumn term**、**spring term** 及 **summer term**。美国大学多分为两个 semesters，即 **the summer semester** 及 **winter semester**。

466 than

than 主要与形容词和副词的比较级一起用，表示"比……"，它后面可以跟各种结构：

跟名词：

His French was no better <u>than</u> Mr. Partier's English. 他的法语并不比巴蒂埃先生的英文强。

The profits are greater <u>than</u> the losses. 利润大于亏损。

跟代词（如为人称代词，在从句中作主语时用主格，作宾语时用宾格，在口语中一般都用宾格）：

He has more time <u>than</u> I.（其后代词在从句中作主语）他的时间比

我多。

I know you better than (I know) her. 我了解你胜过了解她（其后代词在从句中作宾语）。

跟从句（常有些部分会省略）：

It is easier than I thought. 这比我想象的容易。

Now she was happier than she had ever been. 这时她比过去任何时候都快乐。

跟一个充当状语的成分（如副词、介词短语或状语从句）：

Better late than never. 晚做总比不做好。（谚语）

You're a little fatter than when I saw you last. 你比我上次见你时胖一点儿了。

跟其他成分（如不定式、形容词或分词等）：

Better cut the shoe than pinch the foot. 宁愿把鞋剪开也不要夹脚。（谚语）

It is easier to do it yourself than (to) explain it to her. 自己干也比给她解释容易。

△此外 than 还可用于许多短语中：

less (fewer) than 不到

They earned less than twenty pounds a week. 他们每周的工资还不到20镑。

In 1960 there were fewer than one thousand students in our school. 1960年，我们学校的学生还不到一千人。

more than 表示"非常"或"超过"等：

They were more than glad to help. 他们非常愿意帮忙。

He was more than upset by the accident. 这次事故使他非常难过。

no (none) other than 不是别人而是……：

It was no other than my old friend Jones. 这不是别人而是我的老朋友琼斯。

It was none other than dear old Irving. 这不是别人而是亲爱的老欧文。

no sooner (hardly/ barely)… than 刚……就……

No sooner were the picnic baskets unpacked than it began to rain. 刚把野餐篮子里的东西拿出来，天就开始下雨了。

Hardly were the words uttered <u>than</u> he began to regret them. 话刚说出口，他就开始后悔了。

We <u>barely</u> arrived <u>than</u> it was time to leave. 我们刚一到，就又该走了。

(no) other... than 除了……别无其他的

There was <u>no other</u> way <u>than</u> the one by which we came. 除了我们来时走的这条路，没有其他的路。

She can't speak any <u>other</u> language <u>than</u> her own. 除了自己的语言，她不会讲别的语言。

rather than（宁愿）而不愿，是……而不

Life to him meant action, <u>rather than</u> thought. 对他来说，人生意味着行动而不是思考。

<u>Rather than</u> that you should go, I will go myself. 与其你去，不如我去。

467 the

the 是定冠词，通常读作 /ðə/，后面跟元音时读 /ði/，特别强调时读 /ðiː/：

Give me <u>the</u> /ðə/ book.

Look at <u>the</u> /ði/ old man.

She was <u>the</u> /ðiː/ greatest dancer of the time. 她是那时最伟大的舞蹈家。

the 的基本作用是表示后面的名词指一特定的人或东西，意思接近 **that** 或 **this** 等：

Who is <u>the</u> man at the door? 门口的那个人是谁？

<u>The</u> boys are playing in the garden. 男孩子们在花园里玩。

这种表示特定的人或东西的作用，可以称为特指，与之相对的称为泛指：

特指	泛指	泛指
单复数名词前都可加 the	可数名词单数	复数名词
This is (These are) the book(s) I bought. 这就是我买的那本（些）书。	I bought a book. 我买了一本书。	I bought a few books. 我买了几本书。
The park(s) is (are) very beautiful. 那座（些）公园很漂亮。	This is a park. 这是一座公园。	These are all parks. 这些都是公园。

定冠词的主要用法有：

△表示某个或某些特定的东西：

Where are the girls? 女孩子们在哪里？（彼此都知道指的是谁）

Let's turn on the light(s). 咱们把灯打开。（指这房间里的灯）

Mother is in the kitchen. 妈妈在厨房里。（指这个家里的厨房）

We've to wait for the next bus. 我们得等下一辆公共汽车。

有些定语可限制所修饰名词的意义，使指某一（些）特定的人或东西，这时就要加 the：

She knows little of the history of the country. 她对这个国家的历史知道得很少。

Here are the records you want. 这是你要的唱片。

How did you like the lecture given by Dr. Li? 李博士的报告，你觉得怎样？

△加在世上某些独一无二的东西的名称（如 sky, sun, moon, universe, earth, atmosphere, air 等）前：

The sun is down. 太阳已经落山。

The moon moves round the earth. 月亮围着地球转。

Don't build castles in the air. 不要想些空中楼阁了。

The universe exists in space. 宇宙存在于太空中。

△加在某些名词前表示一类东西或人：

The compass was invented in China. 指南针是在中国发明的。

The lion is found in Africa. 狮子在非洲。

△加在某些名词前表示一个民族、阶级或阶层：

The Spanish claimed that the money had not been paid. 西班牙人声称，这笔钱没有付。

△加在某些形容词前表示一类（些）人或某类事：

Only the rich could afford such luxuries. 只有有钱的人才买得起这种奢侈品。

Soon he would be among the unemployed. 不久，他将加入失业大军。

△用在某些专有名词前，如：

江河海洋：

the Yellow River, the Thames, the Suez Canal, the Red Sea, the Indian

Ocean, the Pacific

山脉、群岛：

the Alps, the Rocky Mountains, the Philippines, the Riukiu Islands, the Chou-shan Archipelago

海峡、海湾：

the English Channel, the Taiwan Straits, the Bay of Biscay, the Persian Gulf

某些国家名称：

the People's Republic of China, the United Kingdom, the United States, the Sudan

某些机构的名称：

the United Nations, the House of Commons, the State Department, the Ministry of Education

△用在下面各类情况中：

用在序数词前：

in the first year, on the 3rd floor, the 50th anniversary of the founding of the republic, on the 1st of July

用在形容词的最高级前（在副词最高级前常不加 the）：

the happiest man on earth, the hottest day in the year, the most difficult task of all, run the fastest of all, the language they know best

用在表示身体某部分的名词中代替一个物主代词：

take her by the hand, be wounded in the leg, hit him on the head, slap the boy on the face, to grab him by the arm

用在某些短语中：

in the morning, in the distance, on the whole, play the piano, listen to the radio, face the music（接受不愉快后果），at the moment, for the time being, get the upper hand

468 **there**

there 有两个主要用法。

一是用作状语，表示"在那里"：

It's cold out there. 外边儿很冷。

What's the green thing over there? 那边的那个绿东西是什么?

There's the book she sent me. 那儿就是她寄给我的那本书。

可用于引申意义，表示"在这一点上"等：

There I agree with you. 在这一点上，我同意你的意见。

There you are mistaken. 在这一点上，你错了。

还可和 come, go 等连用（通常用一般现在时）：

There they come! 瞧他们来了!

There goes the last bus. 最后一班公共汽车开走了。

第二个重要用法是引起一个句子，表示"有（发生）"，有下面几种情况：

（1）there＋is 或 are 构成谓语（be 可用于各种时态）：

Where bees are, there is honey. 有蜂就有蜜。（谚语）

There aren't many people in the streets now. 现在街上没有多少行人。

有时和 to be 一起用：

They wouldn't want there to be another war. 他们不希望发生另一次战争。

I expect there to be no argument about this. 我预料对此不会有什么争议。

主语后有时有一由分词等构成的定语：

Look out! There's a car coming. 当心，有辆车开过来了。

There's been a gentleman here asking for you. 刚才，有一位先生要求见你。

（2）there 可引起一个包含情态动词或不定式短语的结构：

He felt that there must be something wrong. 他感到一定出了问题。

There may be another demonstration tonight. 今晚可能再次发生示威游行。

There could be no doubt about that. 对此，不可能有什么怀疑。

（3）there 和其他某些动词连用：

There came a knock at the door. 有人敲门。

There remained just twenty-eight pounds. 只剩下 28 镑了。

There sprang from the audience a cry of indignation. 观众中发出一阵

愤怒的叫声。

There followed an uncomfortable silence. 接着是一段令人感到不舒服的沉默。

469 thin

表示"瘦"有许多说法：

bony	emaciated	lanky	lean
scrawny	skinny	slender	slight
slim	spare	thin	trim
underweight	willowy		

❀ thin 是中性的词，即不褒不贬，如：

Mrs. King was thin and tall. 金夫人是瘦高身材。

His face was thin and very tanned. 他的脸有些瘦，晒得黑黑的。

❀ 有些词是有称赞意味的，可译为"苗条的""瘦瘦的"等，如 lean, slender, slim, willowy, slight, trim 等：

She used to be pretty and slim. 她过去很俊俏，身材苗条。

The girl was pretty and slender. 这姑娘很漂亮，很苗条。

He is a lean, little runner with great stamina. 他是一个耐力极强、个子瘦小的径赛选手。

a tall spare figure 一个瘦高个儿

a willowy young actress 一个苗条的、有风韵的年轻女演员

She keeps herself trim. 她使身材保持苗条。

❀ 另一些词则有贬义，可译为"瘦削的""干瘦的"等：

She was rather ugly and skinny. 她相当丑陋，骨瘦如柴。

There stood at the door a tall bony man. 门口站着一个骨瘦如柴的高个子男人。

a scrawny kid in jeans and a T-shirt 一个穿牛仔裤、短袖衫的干瘦男孩

an emaciated child 一个瘦弱的孩子

an underweight baby 一个瘦小的婴儿

470 threat—threaten—menace

threat 主要有两个意思：

威胁，恐吓的话（可数）：

We did not take their threats seriously. 我们没把他们恐吓的话当一回事。

She never carried out her threats. 她从未把她的威胁付诸实施。

威胁，危险：

The flood was a threat to our homes. 水灾对我们家是一个威胁。

These murderers were a threat to society. 这些杀人犯对社会是一种威胁。

❀ **threaten** 为动词形式，主要有下面几个意思：

威胁说要（*vt.*，跟不定式）：

He threatened to inform the government of his radical activities. 他威胁说，要向政府报告他的激进活动。

威胁，恐吓（*vt.*，*vi.*）：

Don't threaten me! 不要威胁我！

Threatening won't do any good. 威胁不会有什么好处。

威胁，危害（*vt.*）：

Flood waters are threatening the town. 洪水威胁着这座城市。

This would threaten the peace of the Middle East. 这会危害中东的和平。

有……的危险（*vt.*）：

It threatens to rain. 有下雨的危险。

This rough life threatened to injure his health. 这种艰苦的生活有损害他健康的危险。

似要发生，可能来临（*vi.*）：

A storm was threatening. 暴风雨快来了。

While danger threatens, we must all take care. 当危机逼近时，我们都得注意。

用于 **threaten with** 威胁着要……

He threatened me with violence. 他威胁要用暴力对付我。

He was <u>threatened with</u> death if he refused. 如果他拒绝，他们就威胁要处死他。

❀ **menace** 有类似意思，可用作动词，表示"威胁""危害"：

The hoodlum <u>menaced</u> the local merchants. 那个流氓威胁当地的商人。

Hurricanes periodically <u>menace</u> the Gulf Coast. 飓风定期地威胁湾区海岸。

也可用作名词，表示"威胁""危险"：

Their policy of aggression is a great <u>menace</u> to world peace. 他们的侵略政策是对世界和平的巨大威胁。

Icebergs are a <u>menace</u> to ships in the North Atlantic. 在北大西洋，冰山对船只是一个威胁。

471 title—headline—caption—subtitle

title 指书、画及剧本、电影等的名称：

The <u>title</u> of the book is "Treasure Island". 书名是《金银岛》。

The <u>title</u> of the painting is "A Winter Evening". 画名是《冬日暮色》。

也可表示"称号""头衔"或"冠军称号"：

He was given the <u>title</u> of Duke. 他被授予了公爵的称号。

King, Duke, Lord, Countess, Captain, Doctor, Professor, Madame and Miss are all <u>titles</u>. 国王、公爵、勋爵、伯爵夫人、上尉、医生、教授、夫人、小姐都是称号。

❀ **headline** 指报纸的标题，标题也可用 **heading** 表示：

Here are the news <u>headlines</u>. 这些是新闻标题。

I only had time to read the <u>headlines</u>. 我只有时间看看标题。

❀ **caption** 可指文件或文章的标题：

I read no further than the <u>caption</u> because the subject of the article seemed uninteresting. 我只看了标题，因为文章题目似乎不引人兴趣。

也可指图片的说明或影片的字幕：

A short <u>caption</u> gave the names of the people in the picture. 一个简短的说明给出了图片中的人名。

The film was in French, but it had <u>captions</u> in English. 电影中讲的是法

语，但有英语字幕。

✿ subtitle 也可表示电影字幕：

I rented a French film with subtitles. 我租了一部有字幕的法国电影。

Hardly any of the television programs had English subtitles. 电视节目很少带英语字幕。

也可指书等的副标题：

The subtitle indicated that the book was based on a true story. 书的副标题表明，这书讲的是一个真实的故事。

472 **toilet—lavatory—WC—cloakroom—bathroom— washroom—public convenience—ladies—gents— rest room—the ladies' room—the men's room**

toilet 可指抽水马桶，也可指厕所。（I need to go to the toilet.）如果在一座房子里也可称作 lavatory 或 WC, 但这两个词也有些陈旧，也有人称之为 cloakroom, 这是比较含蓄的说法。

在美式英语中厕所可用 bathroom 表示，也可称为 washroom。

Jimmy has to go to the bathroom right now. 吉米现在得上厕所了。

When you've done in the washroom, turn out the light. 你上完厕所要关灯。

公共厕所在英国称为 (public) convenience, 也可称为 ladies（女厕所）和 gents（男厕所）：

There is a public convenience on the corner of the street. 街角上有一个公共厕所。

Is there a ladies (gents) near here? 附近有女（男）厕所吗？

在美国可称为 rest room 或 wash room, 也可称作 the ladies' room（女厕所）和 the men's room（男厕所）：

Excuse me, where is the nearest rest room? 对不起，最近的公共厕所在哪里？

473 touch—move—affect

touch 可表示"触碰""触摸"：

Don't touch these wires. 不要碰这些电线。

We touched glasses. 我们碰了碰杯。

Visitors are requested not to touch the exhibits. 参观的人请勿触摸展品。

I haven't touched the piano for months. 我有几个月没摸钢琴了。

还可表示"触动""感动"：

Her poverty touched his heart. 她的穷困触动了他的内心。

The story touched us all. 这故事感动了我们所有的人。

I was very touched by his kindness. 他的好心使我很感动。

He was deeply touched by what she said. 她的话深深触动了他。

❀ **move** 也可表示"感动""触动"：

Even Father was deeply moved. 连我父亲都深受感动。

They were much moved at the story. 听了这个故事，他们非常感动。

The news moved her profoundly. 这消息深深触动了她。

It moved me deeply. 它深深触动了我。

❀ **affect** 也可表示引起感情波动：

The speech deeply affected the audience. 这段讲话使观众深受感动。

The news did not affect her at all. 这条消息丝毫未触动她。

The incidents affected him for days. 这些事件使他好几天心情不能平静。

All the people in the room were affected to tears. 房里所有的人都感动得流下了眼泪。

474 transport—transportation

transport 作名词时有两个意思：

运送，交通（不可数）：

A car is a means of transport. 汽车是交通工具。

Moscow's public transport system is very good. 莫斯科的公共交通体

系非常好。

交通工具：

I'd like to go to the concert but I've no <u>transport</u>. 我想去听音乐会，但我没有交通工具。

I can take you in my car if you require <u>transport</u> to the meeting. 如果你去开会需要交通工具，我可以用我的车送你去。

△也可用作动词，表示"运送"：

A bus <u>transported</u> us from the airport to the city. 公共汽车把我们从机场送到城里。

The goods were <u>transported</u> by air. 这些货物是空运的。

❀ **transportation** 表示"交通""运送"：

The railroad gives free <u>transportation</u> for a certain amount of baggage. 一定量的行李铁路运送是免费的。

The <u>transportation</u> of lettuce requires refrigeration. 运送生菜需要（用）冷藏（车）。

475 trend—tendency—inclination

trend 和 **tendency** 都可表示"倾向""趋势"，但 **trend** 多指大众的行为：

The <u>trend</u> towards larger and faster airliners continues. 客机越来越大和越来越快的趋势还在继续。

They predicted a national <u>trend</u> toward conservatism. 他们预言了全国的保守主义倾向。

❀ **tendency** 可指集体、个人或某样物件的"倾向"或"趋势"：

Boys have a stronger <u>tendency</u> to fight than girls. 男孩子打架的倾向比女孩子大。

Stock market prices are showing an upward <u>tendency</u>. 股票市场的价格有上涨的趋势。

❀ **inclination** 也表示"倾向"或"趋势"：

My <u>inclination</u> is to agree. 我倾向于同意。

Prices have an <u>inclination</u> to go up. 物价有上涨的趋势。

476 true—real—truthful—genuine

true 表示"真的""真实的"：

Is it true that he has left London? 他离开了伦敦是真的吗？

It was a true story. 这是一个真实的故事。

还可表示"真正的"：

The table is a true antique. 这张桌子是一件真正的古董。

True love should last forever. 真正的爱情是永恒的。

❀ **real** 也表示"真的（不是假的）"：

This is a real pearl, not an imitation. 这是一颗真珍珠，不是人造珍珠。

Is it a real diamond or is it a fake? 这是真钻石还是赝品？

也可表示"真实的""真正的"：

The story is not real; it is only imaginary. 这故事不是真实的，只是想象出来的。

We need real help, not just promises. 我们需要真正的帮助，而不仅仅是诺言。

❀ **truthful** 可表示"真实的"：

The witness gave a truthful account of the incident. 那个证人真实地描绘了这个事件。

The letters give us a truthful picture of prison life. 这些信真实地描绘了监狱生活。

也可表示"说真话的""诚实的"：

You must always be truthful. 你必须经常说真话。

The truthful man returned the extra change to the cashier. 那个诚实的人把多找给他的钱还给了收银员。

❀ **genuine** 也可表示"真（正）的"（不是假造的或虚假的）：

Is the bracelet genuine gold? 这只手镯是真金的吗？

His illness is genuine. 他的病是真的。

还可表示"真心的""真诚的"：

She has a genuine passion for music. 她对音乐由衷的喜欢。

He had a genuine desire to serve his people. 他有真诚的为人民服务的愿望。

477 type—sort—kind—category

type 主要表示"类型""种类"：

He invented a new type of stethoscope. 他发明了一种新型的听诊器。

I would prefer a new type of education for my children. 我愿意我的孩子们接受新型教育。

它还可用在 **of** 后面：

I dislike men of that type. 我不喜欢那种类型的人。

Questions of this type compel the children to think. 这类问题迫使孩子们思考。

❀ **sort** 也表示"种""类"：

They'll never stomach that sort of attitude. 他们再也不能忍受这种态度了。

He wanted a job, any sort of a job. 他需要工作，哪类工作都行。

sort 也可用在 **of** 后：

Nothing of the sort! You're quite wrong. 没有的事！你完全错了。

❀ **kind** 也可表示"种""类"：

What kind of flower is this? 这是哪种花?

kind 也可用在 **of** 引起的短语中：

They have amusements of various kinds. 他们有各式各样的娱乐活动。

❀ **category** 也有"类（属）"的意思，主要指分类的人或东西：

Which literary category would this book go in? 这本书应属于哪类文学范畴?

Helen groups people into two categories: those she likes and those she dislikes. 海伦把人分成两类：她喜欢的人和她不喜欢的人。

U

478 un-

un- 是最常用的前缀之一。

可以用在某些形容词（或副词）前，构成反义词，表示"不"，如：

unacceptable	unaccountable	unaccountably
unadvisable	unapproachable	unavailable
unaware(s)	unavoidable	unbelievable
unbelievably	unceremonious	uncomfortable
uncommon	uncompromising	unconditional
unconquerable	unconscious(ly)	undesirable
undoubtedly	undue	uneconomic
unemotional	unendurable	unequal
unessential	uneven	uneventful
unfair	unfavourable	unfit
unforgettable	unforgivable	unfortunate(ly)
ungrammatical	ungrateful	unhappily
unimaginable	unimportant	unjust
unlawful	unlike	unlikely
unlucky	unnatural	unnecessary
unobtainable	unofficial	unpardonable
unpleasant	unprejudiced	unprofitable
unquestionable	unquestionably	unreadable
unreal	unrecognizable	unreliable
unsatisfactory	unscientific	unscrupulous
unselfish	unskilful	unspeakable
unsuccessful	unsystematic	unthinkable

untrue	untrustworthy	unusual
unwavering	unwelcome	unwell
unwilling(ly)	unwise	

或加在动词前，表示"解开""打开""拿开"等：

unbosom	unburden	unbutton	uncoil
uncover	undo	unhang	undress
unknit	unearth	unlace	unfasten
unleash	unfold	unload	unlock
unmask	unmoved	unpack	unpin
unquote	unscrew	unstring	untie
unwrap			

还可加在过去分词前，表示"不……""没有……"等，如：

unabridged	unaccompanied	unaccustomed
unaffected	unaided	unarmed
unbalanced	unconcerned	uncultivated
uncultured	undreamt-of	uneducated
unemployed	unexpected	unfinished
unforeseen	unfounded	unfulfilled
unfurnished	ungrounded	unheard-of
unidentified	uninvited	uninhabited
unknown	unmarried	unprecedented
unqualified	unreserved	unroll
unread	unrestrained	unsatisfied
unskilled	unseen	unstressed
untruth		

还可和个别名词构成反义词：

uncertainty	uneasiness	unemployment
unhappiness	unpleasantness	unrest
unwillingness		

479 under-

under- 也是一个常用前缀。

和名词构成合成词，表示"下面的""里面的"：

underbelly 下腹部

undercurrent 潜流

underclothes 内衣

undergarment 内衣

underground 地下的

underpants 内裤

undersea 海底（下）的

underside 下侧（面）

underwater 水下的

underworld 下层社会，黑社会

还可表示"下一级的"：

undergraduate 本科生（比研究生低的）

undersecretary 副部长

和动词构成合成词表示"……不足（太低）"，如：

underbid 出价偏低

undercharge 收费过低

underestimate 估计太低

underexpose 曝光不足

underpay 报酬过低

underplay 贬低，轻描淡写

undersell 低价出售

understate 少说，少报

undervalue 低估

和一过去分词构成合成词，表示"……不足的"：

underfed 营养不足的

undermanned 人未配足的

underestimated 估计不足的

undernourished 营养不足的

underprivileged 生活水平低下的

underrated 估计不足的

undersized 比较矮小的

understaffed 人员不足的

480 unless

unless 有下列两种意思。

除非……（否则就不），如果不（主句多用否定结构）：

Don't come unless I telephone. 除非我给你打电话，否则不要来。

I shouldn't dream of going unless you wanted me. 除非要我去，否则我不会想去。

除非（有下述情况），除非……（否则会）：

You will fail unless you work hard. 你会失败，除非你努力工作。

I shall return Thursday <u>unless</u> something unexpected happens. 我将在星期四回来，除非是发生意外情况。

△在两种情况下，**unless** 都等于 if... not, 引导的都是条件从句。因此在多种情况下里面动词都用一般现在时，在个别情况下用一般过去时。这从上面例句中可以看出。

481 **until—till**

这两个词的意思相同，只用来谈时间，都表示"到某时为止"或"到某时才（开始/发生）"。在口语中 till 用得较多，在书面语中通常都用 until。两者都可用作介词，后面跟名词。

在肯定句中表示"到某时为止"：

They talked on <u>until/till</u> one o'clock in the morning. 他们一直谈到深夜一点。

I shall go on working <u>until/till</u> next week. 我将一直工作到下星期。

在否定句中表示"到……才（开始/发生）"或"在……之前"：

They did not return home <u>till/until</u> nine o'clock. 他们到 9 点钟才回家。

I never <u>until</u> yesterday spoke of it to anybody. 昨天以前，我未向任何人谈起过此事。

它们后面还可跟一个副词或介词短语：

We never play bridge <u>until</u> after dinner. 我们要到晚饭后才打桥牌。

I hardly ever go to bed <u>till</u> past twelve. 我很少在 12 点以前睡觉。

这两个词还可用作连词：

Let's wait <u>until/till</u> the rain stops. 咱们等到雨停了再说。

I watched him <u>until</u> he disappeared in the distance. 我瞧着他直到他在远处消失。

在否定句中也可译为"到……才"：

He would not be back <u>till</u> Parliament sat. 他要到国会开会时才回来。

I didn't reach the station <u>until</u> after the train had left. 火车开了之后我才抵达车站。

有时表示"在……之前（不）"：

Don't promise him anything <u>till</u> we've had time to think about it. 在我

们有时间考虑之前，别答应他什么。

until 可用在句首，**till** 却只能用在句子中间：

<u>Until</u> then I had known nothing about it. 在那以前，我对此一无所知。

在下列句子中 **till** 不宜用 **until** 代替：

Up <u>till</u> now I've lived in the country. 到现在为止，我一直住在乡下。

482 unusual

下面的这些形容词都表示一个人的模样或性格与别人不同：

abnormal	anomalous	bizarre	curious	eccentric
extraordinary	funny	odd	peculiar	queer
strange	unusual	weird		

有些词汇表达正面意思，如 **outstanding, special, exclusive, exotic, exceptional**。其中有的有赞许的意思，如 **extraordinary** 表示"非凡的""不平常的""突出的"：

She is working with <u>extraordinary</u> energy. 她工作起来有非凡的精力。

Her strength of will was <u>extraordinary</u>. 她的意志力是不同平常的。

He has an <u>extraordinary</u> command of English. 他的英语特别好。

unusual 也有好的意思，表示"不寻常的""少见的"：

He married a girl of <u>unusual</u> beauty. 他娶了一个美丽非凡的姑娘。

He was an <u>unusual</u> man. 他是一个不寻常的人。

其他的词表示有趣或略有贬义：

He had a reputation for <u>bizarre</u> behavior. 他因行径古怪而出名。

She's an <u>odd</u> woman. 她是一个古怪的女人。

She has a <u>curious</u> way of talking. 她讲起话来很奇特。

He was <u>queer</u> in some ways. 他在某方面有些奇特。

She looks a bit <u>strange</u> today. 她今天显得有点儿奇怪。

She has some <u>weird</u> ideas. 她有些奇特的想法。

His behavior was rather <u>funny</u>. 他的行为很古怪。

Jennie is of a <u>peculiar</u> disposition. 珍妮有种奇特的性格。

483 up

up 可用作介词，也可用作副词。

作介词时主要表示：

（1）沿着……往上：

The cat climbed up the tree. 那只猫爬到树上去了。

The bus climbed slowly up the hill. 公共汽车沿着小山慢慢开上去。

（2）在某个较高的地方：

There was a workman up the ladder. 梯子上站着一个工人。

They saw him sitting somewhere up the hill. 他们看见他坐在山腰某个地方。

（3）沿……走去（来）：

They walked together up the garden path. 他们沿着花园小路一道走去。

Then he saw her coming up the street. 这时，他看见她沿着街道走来。

在用作副词时可以表示：

（1）……起来：

Hold your head up. 把头抬起来。

It gets hot quickly when the sun comes up. 太阳出来了，天很快热起来。

（2）到（较高处）去（来）：

Bring the things up to my room. 把东西送到我（楼上的）房间里来。

The boy climbed up to a higher branch on the tree. 那男孩爬到了较高的一根树枝上。

（3）在（高处）：

The office is up on the top floor. 办公室在上面顶层。

They're spending the summer up in the mountains. 他们在山里避暑。

（4）到（较大城市），到（远方某处）：

He has gone up to London. 他到伦敦去了。

He ran up to town for the day. 他今天进城去了。

（5）走来，向……走去：

Then a bus came up and everybody got on it. 这时一辆公共汽车开过来，大家都上车了。

He came up (to me) and asked the time. 他（向我）走过来问我时间。

（6）吃完，用完等：

Has the child eaten up all his food? 孩子把食物都吃完了吗？

I've used up the whole supply of paper. 我把存的纸全用完了。

Drink it up. 把它都喝完。

（7）和某些动词连用，表示完成某事：

She gathered up her things and left. 她收拾好她的东西就走了。

He buttoned up his jacket. 他把上衣扣好。

She hung the picture up. 她把画挂了起来。

Help me wash up the dishes. 帮我洗盘子。

（8）和 be 连用，表示许多不同的意思：

起床，没睡觉：

I was up early the next morning. 第二天一早，我就起床了。

He was up all night with a sick child. 他整夜没睡，陪着生病的孩子。

（时间）到了，到期，结束：

His leave is up tomorrow. 他的假期明天结束。

My holiday will be up in three days. 我的假期再过三天就结束了。

升起，上升，上涨：

The temperature is up 10 degrees today. 今天气温上升了 10 度。

The price of meat is up. 肉价上涨了。

……起：

The new house has not been up long. 房子盖起还没多久。

The wind was up again. 又起风了。

484 use—used to—be used to

use 可作动词，表示"用""使用""动用"等：

The president used his veto power. 总统动用了他的否决权。

Can you use your influence? 你能否运用你的影响？

Use your imagination. 发挥你的想象力。

❀ used to 表示"过去常常……"（现在已不如此），因此没有现在式，后面紧跟不定式：

It used to be a very prosperous town. 它过去是一个非常繁荣的城市。

I <u>used to</u> write poetry myself when I was your age. 我像你这么大时，常常写诗。

其否定句和疑问句有两种构成方法：

（1）借助 did（在口语中 did 后可用 use，在书面语中则多用 used）：

She <u>didn't use(d) to</u> do it. 她过去不常这样做的。

They <u>didn't use(d) to</u> mind what we said. 我们说什么，他们过去是不介意的。

（2）不借助 did：

You <u>usedn't to</u> make such mistakes. 你过去是不犯这种错误的。

<u>Used</u> you <u>to</u> play football? 你过去常踢足球吗？

❀ **be used to** 表示"习惯于（某事）"，后接名词或动名词：

<u>I'm used to</u> dealing with matters of this sort. 我已习惯于处理这类事。

<u>He's not used to</u> being treated like this. 他不习惯于受到这样的对待。

used to 还可和别的系动词（包括 get, become, grow, seem）一起用：

I've <u>become used to</u> a vegetarian diet. 我已习惯于素食。

He <u>seemed</u> a quiet man, <u>used to</u> practical work. 他似乎是一个安静的人，习惯于做实际工作。

485 victim—casualty

victim 表示"受害者"：

They were among the <u>victims</u> of Nazi persecution. 他们是纳粹迫害的受害者。

Several people fell ill, <u>victims</u> of blood poisoning. 几个人生病了，都是血中毒的受害者。

还可表示"灾民""遇难者"：

A fund was opened to help the <u>victims</u> of earthquakes. 成立了一个基金来帮助地震灾民。

Supplies are being sent to the <u>victims</u> of the disaster. 供应品正在运送给灾民。

❀ **casualty** 指在战争或事故中丧生或受伤的人：

There were heavy <u>casualties</u> on both sides. 双方的伤亡都很惨重。

The tornado took a fearful toll of <u>casualties</u>. 龙卷风造成的伤亡很惨重。

casualty 还可表示"事故急诊室"，也可称作 **casualty ward**：

They rushed her to <u>casualty</u> but she was dead on arrival. 他们赶紧把她送到急诊室，但刚到时就死了。

486 visual—visible

这两个词都与"看""视"有关。

❀ **visual** 表示"视力（觉）的"：

The animal's <u>visual</u> organs are different from ours. 这种动物的视觉器官和我们的视觉器官不同。

The effect is purely <u>visual</u>. 这完全是视觉上的效果。

还可表示"与视觉有关的""直观的"：

The visual arts include painting and dancing. 与视觉有关的艺术包括绘画与舞蹈。

Primary school teachers use a lot of visual aids. 小学教师大量使用直观教具。

还可构成动词 visualize，表示"想象（出）"：

Try to visualize sailing through the sky on a cloud. 设法想象你乘坐云彩在空中遨游。

Can you visualize how big this firm could be in ten years' time? 你能想象十年后这个公司会有多大吗？

❀ visible 表示"看得见（的）"：

The stars are visible on any cloudless night. 在任何无云的夜空中，都可看见星星。

Two ships were barely visible on the horizon. 在天边，有两艘船隐约可见。

可构成名词 visibility，表示"能见度"：

Visibility is poor tonight. 今晚，能见度很差。

Visibility is only a quarter of a mile today because of the fog. 因为有雾，今天的能见度只有四分之一英里。

487　viz

viz 为简写，原作拉丁文，表示"那就是""即"，通常读作 namely：

He had four sisters, viz Ella, Alice, Mary and Jane. 他有四个姐妹，那就是埃拉、艾丽斯、玛丽和简。

There are three very large rivers in Africa, viz the Congo, Niger and Nile. 非洲有三条很大的河流，它们是刚果河、尼日河和尼罗河。

488 want—should (would) like—wish—hope—desire

want 是常用的动词之一，主要表示"想要""愿意""希望"，后面可有不同宾语：

跟名词或代词：

She wants her mummy. 她要她的妈妈。

What do you want from me? 你想从我这里得到什么？

跟不定式：

She doesn't want to be separated from him. 她不想和他分开。

I've wanted to speak to you all these days. 这些天，我一直想和你谈一谈。

不定式有时可省略，只留下 **to**：

You can study any subject you want to. 你可以学习想学的任何学科。

I can finish the work tomorrow if I want to. 如果我愿意，明天就可完成这项工作。

跟带不定式的复合结构：

Don't you want someone to go along with you? 难道你不想有人和你一道去？

She wanted this meeting to be a successful one. 她希望这次会议成功。

跟带过去分词的复合结构：

We want the work finished by Saturday. 我们希望，这项工作星期六之前完成。

I don't want anything said about this. 我不愿意谁提到这事。

跟带现在分词的复合结构：

I don't want women meddling in my affairs. 我不希望女人干预我的事。

We don't want you getting into trouble. 我们不想你遇到麻烦。

有时表示"需要""缺乏"：

He seems to <u>want</u> nourishment. 他似乎缺乏营养。

He <u>wants</u> a good beating. 他欠打。

❀ **should (would) like** 常可用来代替 **want**, 使语气显得委婉一些，也可跟不同结构：

跟名词或代词：

I <u>should like</u> a little sunshine. 我想晒晒太阳。

I <u>should like</u> a word with you. 我想和你说一句话。

跟不定式：

The committee <u>would like</u> to see you again. 委员们愿意再和你会晤一次。

There are a lot of things I <u>should have liked</u> to ask you. 有好些事我本想问你的。

跟动名词（多用 **don't like**）：

I <u>don't like</u> discussing her behind her back. 我不想背着她议论她。

Perhaps they <u>wouldn't like</u> our coming. 或许，他们不希望我们来。

跟带不定式的复合结构：

I <u>would like</u> you to meet a friend of mine. 我想让你和我一位朋友见见。

I <u>should like</u> you to stay a bit if you have time. 如果你有时间，我希望你再待一会儿。

跟其他复合结构：

We <u>don't like</u> them coming late. 我们不愿他们晚来。

I <u>should like</u> this matter settled immediately. 我希望这事立即解决。

❀ **wish** 的意思也很相近，也可表示"愿意""希望"，还可表示"祝……"，后面可以跟：

名词或代词：

We <u>wish</u> you a safe journey. 希望你一路平安。

I certainly <u>wish</u> them victory. 我当然希望他们获胜。

不定式：

I don't <u>wish</u> to leave my mother. 我不愿离开我母亲。

I don't <u>wish</u> to be disturbed in my work. 我不希望工作时受到打扰。

跟带不定式的复合结构：

I <u>wish</u> him to remain. 我希望他留下。

I don't wish the subject to be raised again. 我不想谁再提这个问题。

跟带形容词等的复合结构：

I wish him safe at home. 我希望他在家平安无事。

He didn't wish it mentioned. 他不想人提到它。

跟从句（从句谓语多由 would, could 构成）：

I wish you wouldn't smoke any more. 我希望你不再抽烟了。

I wish you would be more respectful to your father. 我希望你对你父亲更尊敬些。

在表示不可能实现的愿望时，从句中的谓语要用虚拟语气：

I wish I were a bird! 但愿我是一只鸟！

I wish I knew more about it. 但愿我对此懂得更多。

不跟宾语：

I'll cancel the arrangement if you wish. 如果你愿意，我可以取消这个安排。

I can set to work now if you wish. 如果你愿意，我可以现在就干起来。

✿ hope 主要表示"希望"，后面只能跟两种宾语：

跟从句：

I hope that I have said nothing to pain you. 希望我没说什么话使你难过。

Let's hope you'll soon be feeling fit again. 希望你早日康复。

△可用于插入语中或跟 so 或 not：

Will it be fine tomorrow? I hope so. 明天天气会好吗？希望会好。

Will it rain tomorrow? I hope not. 明天会下雨吗？希望不会下。

跟不定式：

Jennie hoped to give her a good education. 珍妮希望给她良好教育。

I hope to find you in better spirits when we meet again. 希望下次见面时，你的情绪会好一些。

△有时可以和 for 连用，后面跟名词：

This time they really hoped for better results. 这一次，他们真希望获得更好的成绩。

After the dry weather everyone hopes for rain. 干旱天气之后，人人都希望下雨。

❀ desire 表示"期望""渴望""希望得到"，后面可跟下列宾语：

跟名词或代词：

Both nations desired peace. 两国都渴望和平。

We all desired happiness and health. 我们都希望得到幸福和健康。

跟不定式：

We always desire to live in peace with our neighbours. 我们一贯希望与我们的邻国和平相处。

She had never desired to do anything like that. 她从来没期望做这样的事。

跟从句：

The Queen desires that you (should) come at once. 女王期待你立即到这里来。

She desires that it shall not be mentioned for the present. 她希望这事暂时别提。

△偶跟复合结构：

What do you desire me to do? 你希望我怎么办？

489 **what**

what 有下列几种用法：

what 是一个疑问代词，在句中作宾语、表语或主语，表示"什么"：

What's your hobby? 你有什么爱好？

What happened next? 后来发生什么情况？

常有较活译法：

What's all this about? 这都是怎么回事？

What's the best way to get there? 怎样去最好？

也可用作定语：

What colour are your curtains? 你的窗帘是什么颜色的？

What time do we get into Pittsburgh? 我们什么时候到达匹兹堡？

还可用在某些结构中，如：

what... for 表示"作什么用""干什么"：

What's that button for? 那个按钮是作什么用的？

"I'm going to Shanghai." "What for?" "我到上海去。" "去干什么？"

what about 表示 "怎么样" "如何"：

What about sending him a copy? 送他一本怎么样？

Of course I'll come. What about Friday? 我当然要来。星期五怎么样？

what if 表示 "要是……怎么办"：

What if you go instead of me? 你要是代我去怎么样？

What if the weather is really bad? 要是天气真的不好怎么办？

what 还可引起一个惊叹句，表示 "多么" 等：

What a good heart you have! 你的心肠真好！

What nonsense you talk! 你说什么糊涂话！

这类句子有时有些词可以省略：

What lovely furs! 多漂亮的毛皮呀！

Oh, Charlie, what a cruel thing to say! 啊，查理，说这话真无情。

what 还可引导从句，意思相当于 **the thing which**，在语法上称为 "关系代词型的 **what**"（**relative what**），通常表示某样东西或事物。在句中可用作主语、表语、宾语或介词宾语：

What she saw (=The thing she saw) gave her a fright. 她看到的情况吓了她一跳。

That's what I hope. 这是我所希望的。

I want to tell you what I hear. 我想告诉你我听到的情况。

He gave a description of what he had seen. 他描述了他看到的情况。

在很多情况下可有较活译法：

They did what they could to console her. 他们尽量安慰她。

What will be, will be. 要发生的事总要发生的。（谚语）

what 在从句中可以作定语：

What little he said is full of wisdom. 他说的那点话充满智慧。

What education I have is fragmentary. 我受的那点教育是支离破碎的。

what 引导的从句还可构成插入语或让步从句：

He is an interesting speaker, and, what is more important, he knows the subject thoroughly. 他讲话很风趣，更重要的是，他对这个问题了解得很透彻。

Come what may, you'll always keep it a secret. 不管发生什么情况，你都要保密。

490 whatever

whatever 有下列几种用法。

引导从句，表示"……任何东西（一切事情）"，意思接近"**anything that...**"，可以在句中：

（1）作主语：

Whatever she did was right. 她做的一切都是对的。

Whatever I have is at your service. 我所有的一切都由你使用。

（2）作宾语：

I will do whatever you wish. 我可做任何你想我做的事。

I'll just say whatever comes into my head. 我想到什么就说什么。

（3）作介词宾语：

Talk to me about whatever is troubling you. 给我谈谈任何使你烦恼的事。

One should stick to whatever one has begun. 开始了的事就要坚持下去。

whatever 除了在从句中作主语、宾语等外（见上例），还可作定语：

She would tell him whatever news she got. 她得到的任何消息都会告诉他。

You can have whatever allowance you like. 你想要多少津贴就给你多少津贴。

whatever 可以说是关系代词型 what 的强调形式。

引导从句作状语（这种从句称为让步从句），表示"不管……什么（怎样）"：

Don't lose heart whatever difficulties you meet. 不管遇到什么困难，都不要灰心。

I'll post that letter whatever Wilson says. 不管威尔逊说什么，这封信我都要发出去。

这种从句中有些成分有时可以省略：

Whatever her faults, she's Arnold's mother. 不管她有什么毛病，她总是阿诺德的母亲。

The country is always beautiful <u>whatever the season</u>. 这一带田野总是那么美，不管是什么季节。

用来加强语气，意思和 **what** 差不多，可用来：

（1）代替 **what**：

<u>Whatever</u> are they afraid of? 他们怕什么？

<u>Whatever</u> are you going to do with it? 你准备把它怎么办？

（2）用于否定句或疑问句（意思接近 **at all**）：

I know nothing <u>whatever</u> about him. 我对他毫无了解。

And no pain <u>whatever</u> is felt. 不感到任何疼痛。

whatsoever 意思也一样，只是更文气一些：

They had no political rights <u>whatsoever</u>. 他们没有任何政治权利。

He has no talent <u>whatsoever</u> for this job. 他干这种工作没有任何天赋。

491 **when—whenever**

when 有下列几种用法。

when 可用作疑问副词，表示"什么时候"：

So you are going to get married. <u>When</u> is it? 这样说你们要结婚了，什么时候结？

<u>When</u> do you think it can be operated on? 你想什么时候可以给它动手术？

有时可用作介词宾语：

<u>Since when</u> have you been working here? 从什么时候开始你在这儿工作？

也可用作连接副词，表示同样意思：

<u>When</u> she'll be back depends much on the weather. 她什么时候回来在很大程度上取决于天气。

It all depends on <u>when</u> we can get the tickets. 这得看我们什么时候能拿到机票。

有时可引导一个不定式短语：

Ask him <u>when</u> to open it. 问他什么时候把它打开。

You'll learn <u>when</u> to use that construction. 你会知道什么时候使用这种结构。

when 可用作连词，表示"当……时"：

Don't get excited <u>when</u> you talk. 谈话时别激动。

I will discuss this with you <u>when</u> we meet. 我们见面时，再谈这事。

<u>When</u> he got up he felt dizzy. 他起床时，感到头晕。

从句中有些成分有时可以省略：

He got engaged to her <u>when</u> travelling last winter. 他去年冬天旅行时，和她订了婚。

Metals expand <u>when</u> heated and contract <u>when</u> cooled. 金属热则膨胀，冷则收缩。

Often she would weep <u>when</u> alone. 她一人待着时常常哭泣。

<u>When</u> in Rome do as the Romans do. 入乡随俗。（谚语）

在某些情况下可有特殊的译法：

I was just coming along to see you <u>when</u> I ran into Wilson. 我正要来看你时，碰到了威尔逊。

I had not been reading for half an hour <u>when</u> I heard steps outside. 我看书还不到半小时，就听见外面有脚步声。

when 还可用作关系代词引导定语从句：

There are moments <u>when</u> I forget all about it. 有的时候，这事我全忘了。

There are times <u>when</u> such things are necessary. 有时候，这样做是必要的。

Sunday is a holiday, <u>when</u> people do not go to work. 星期天是假日,（这天）人们不上班。

△有时和 **since** 连用，表示"从那时起"：

That was in 1929, <u>since when</u> things have been better. 那是 1929 年的事，从那时起情况就好些了。

They left on Monday, <u>since when</u> we have heard nothing. 他们是星期一走的，从那以后我们就没听到什么消息了。

有时用作表语：

That was <u>when</u> I was thirteen. 这是我 13 岁时的情形。

❀ **whenever** 可用作连词，表示"每当""每次"等：

<u>Whenever</u> we see him we speak to him. 我们每次见到他时都和他说几句。

I go to the theatre <u>whenever</u> I get the chance. 每当我有机会我都去看戏。

也可表示"在任何时候"：

You can have it <u>whenever</u> you like. 任何时候你愿意你都可以用。

Come and see me <u>whenever</u> you want to. 随便什么时候你想来看我你就来。

在上面两种情况下，从句中都可以省去某些成分：

Use the simple verb <u>whenever</u> possible. 在可能时，使用简单动词。

We arranged for him to come <u>whenever</u> needed. 我们安排好任何时候需要他，就让他来。

有时还可用来代替 when，表示强调：

<u>Whenever</u> will you grow up? 你什么时候才能长大？

492 where—wherever

where 有下列几种用法。

where 可作疑问副词，表示"在哪里"：

<u>Where</u> did the doctor study medicine? 这位医生是在哪里学医的？

<u>Where</u> have you put the newspaper? 你把报纸放在哪里了？

还可表示"到哪里"和"从哪里"：

<u>Where</u> shall we go (to)? 我们到哪里去呢？

<u>Where</u> do you want to fly to? 你想坐飞机到哪里？

where 还可用作连接副词，引导宾语从句等：

I shall use my own judgment as to <u>where</u> I aim that gun. 我得运用自己的判断力决定那只枪将对准哪里。

It's no business of yours <u>where</u> I spend my summer. 我在哪里度暑假不关你的事。

有时可引导不定式短语：

What I want to know is <u>where</u> to begin. 我想知道应该从哪里开始。

How did you know <u>where</u> to find me? 你怎么知道在哪里可以找到我？

where 可作关系副词，引导定语从句，意思接近 in (at) which：

This is the town <u>where</u> I was born. 这就是我出生的城市。

We'll find some big place where they'll appreciate your work. 我们去找一个大点的地方，那儿他们会欣赏你的作品。

有时可用于引申意义：

We have reached a point where a change is needed. 我们到了必须改一改的地步。

We are in a position where we may lose a large sum of money. 在我们的处境下，我们可能损失大量金钱。

也可引导一个非限定性定语从句，前面多有一逗号把从句和它修饰的词分开：

I am off to St. James Park, where I have to give a lecture on the theatre. 我现在去圣詹姆斯公园，在那里我将作一个关于戏剧的报告。

They went to the Royal Theatre, where they saw Ibsen's *Peer Gynt*. 他们去了皇家剧院，在那里他们看了易卜生的《皮尔·金特》。

有时可引导表语从句：

That's where the battle took place. 这就是那次战役发生的地方。

That's where we differ. 这就是我们分歧所在。

还有较活译法：

That's where the shoe pinches. 症结就在这里。

That's where we stand. 这就是我们的立场。

That's where you are wrong. 你就错在这里。

引导的从句有时作介词的宾语：

I can't see him from where I am. 从我在的地方我看不到他。

She was free to go to where she liked. 她想到哪里就可以到哪里。

where 可作连词，引导从句作状语：

Cross the stream where it is shallowest. 在水最浅的地方过（小）河。（谚语）

The thread breaks where it is weakest. 线从最薄弱的地方断。（谚语）

有时有较活译法：

He signed to her to stay where she was. 他打手势让她待在原处。

I'm quite comfortable where I am. 我这里挺舒服的。

✿ **wherever** 可用作连词，引导从句作状语，表示：

不管……在哪里：

Wherever I am I will be thinking of you. 不管我在哪里，我都会想着你。

I will find her wherever she may be. 不管她在哪里，我都要找到她。

在任何……的地方：

Sit wherever you like. 坐在任何你喜欢的地方。

Wherever the sea is, you will find seamen. 任何有海的地方就有海员。

只要……，凡属……：

Avoid structure of this kind wherever possible. 只要可能，都要避免这种结构。

They believed in the application of force wherever necessary. 凡属必要的地方，他们都主张使用武力。

△ **wherever** 还可用来代替 **where**，作为强调形式：

Wherever did you find him? 你在哪里找到他的？

Wherever are you taking me? 你究竟要把我带到哪儿去？

where 有时和 **ever** 分开写：

Where ever did you find it? 你在哪里找到它的？

有时表示"任何地方"：

at home, at school, or wherever 在家，在学校或在任何地方

493 whether

whether 有下列几种用法。

whether 表示"是不是""是否"，可引导从句作宾语：

I asked whether there are any letters for me. 我问是不是有我的信。

We discussed whether we should close the shop. 我们讨论是否应把商店关掉。

在口语中 **whether** 常可与 **if** 换用：

I wonder $\left\{ \begin{array}{c} \text{whether} \\ \text{if} \end{array} \right\}$ it's large enough. 不知它够不够大。

Ask him $\left\{ \begin{array}{c} \text{whether} \\ \text{if} \end{array} \right\}$ he can come. 问他是否能来。

He asked me $\left\{ \begin{array}{c} \text{whether} \\ \text{if} \end{array} \right\}$ I can show him the way. 他问我可否替他带路。

如从句提前，则只能用 **whether**, 不能用 **if**:

Whether it is a defect or not I don't know. 这是否是缺点，我可不知道。

whether 引导的从句还可以作介词的宾语，这时不能用 **if** 代替:

It all depends on whether we can get their cooperation. 这得看我们是否能得到他们的合作。

I worry about whether I hurt her feelings. 我担心我是否伤了她的感情。

whether 常可和 **or not (no)** 连用，这时也很少用 **if**:

Can you tell me whether or not the train has left? 你能不能告诉我，火车是否已经出发了?

I cannot recollect whether I told you or not about Allen Bennet. 我记不清我是否曾告诉你关于艾伦·本内特的事。

whether 有时后面也可跟不定式短语（这时也不能用 **if** 代替）:

I've been wondering whether to retire. 我一直在犹豫是否要退休。

He didn't know whether to feel glad or sorry at his dismissal. 他被辞退不知该高兴还是难过。

whether 还可引导从句作主语、表语或同位语等（在这种情况下一般不用 **if**）:

It was uncertain whether he would come (or not). 他来不来还不确定。

It's doubtful whether we shall be able to come. 我们能否来还是一个问题。

His first question was whether Holmes had arrived yet. 他的第一个问题是霍姆斯是否来了。

whether 还可引导状语从句，表示"不管……是否"或"不管是……还是":

Whether we go or whether we stay, the result is the same. 不管我们是走还是留，结果都一样。

Whether I lose my job through the strike, I stand firm by you. 不管我是否会因罢工失去工作，我坚定地站在你们一边。

494 *which—whichever*

which 有下列几种用法。

which 可以用作疑问代词，表示"哪个":

Which of you has got a computer? 你们谁有电脑？

Which do you prefer—fish or beef? 你愿意要鱼还是牛肉？

可用作定语：

At which station should I change trains? 我应在哪个站转车？

Which university did you go to, Oxford or Cambridge? 你上的是哪个大学，牛津还是剑桥？

which 也可用作连接代词，引导从句作宾语：

The twins are so much alike that I never know which is which. 那对孪生姐妹是那样像，我都分不清谁是谁了。

Let us know which train they'll be arriving on. 让我们知道他们坐哪班火车到达。

有时引导不定式短语作宾语：

I can't decide which to choose. 我不能决定选哪个好。

I don't know which to believe. 我不知道该相信谁。

此外还可引导主语从句、表语从句等：

Which side wins makes no difference to him. 哪边赢，他都无所谓。

She wasn't sure which is the best solution. 她不能肯定哪是最好的解决办法。

which 还可用作关系代词，引导定语从句，修饰一样东西或事物，在从句中 **which** 可以作：

（1）主语：

She wasn't in the train which arrived just now. 她不在刚到的火车上。

He lives in the house which is opposite ours. 他住在我家对面的那座房子里。

（2）宾语（常常可被省略）：

That is a factor which we mustn't neglect. 这是我们不能忽略的一个因素。

His mind was full of ideas which he wanted to discuss. 他脑子里有许多想法想讨论。

（3）作介词宾语（如不紧跟介词，也可以省略）：

This is a subject about which we might argue for a long while. 这是一个我们可以辩论很长时间的问题。

The documents for which they were searching have been recovered. 他

们找寻的文件已找到了。

如果引导的是非限定性定语从句，则 which 不能省略：

The London team, <u>which</u> played so well last season, has done badly this season. 伦敦队上个赛季打得很好，这个赛季却打得很差。

The current, <u>which</u> is very rapid, makes the river dangerous. 水流湍急使这条河变得很危险。

有时 which 不代表一个词，而代表前面整个句子或其中一部分：

This I did at nine o'clock, after <u>which</u> I sat reading the paper. 九点时我做这件事，之后我就坐在那里看报。

He has to work on Sundays, <u>which</u> he doesn't like. 他得在星期天工作，他是不喜欢这样的。

which 有时作定语：

I may have to go into hospital, in <u>which</u> case I won't be going on holiday. 我可能要住院，如果那样我就不去度假了。

Tom spent four years in college, during <u>which</u> time he learned French. 汤姆读了四年大学，在此期间他学了法语。

which 还可引导一个不定式短语作定语（作用和定语从句差不多）：

He had only the long nights in <u>which</u> to study. 他只有漫漫长夜可用来学习。

He had a couple of revolvers with <u>which</u> to defend himself. 他只有一两把手枪用来自卫。

✿ **whichever** 可用作代词，引导从句作主语或宾语，表示"无论哪个"：

<u>Whichever</u> (of you) comes in first will receive a prize. 无论（你们）谁先到都可以得奖。

<u>Whichever</u> you want is yours. 你要哪个哪个就是你的。

还可引导从句作状语，表示"不管哪（个）"：

<u>Whichever</u> side wins, I shall be satisfied. 不管哪边赢，我都会感到满意。

It has the same result <u>whichever</u> way you do it. 不管你怎么做结果都一样。

495 **while—whilst**

while 有以下几种用法。

while 是连词，引导从句作状语，表示"当……的时候"：

You must strike <u>while</u> the iron is hot. 你必须趁热打铁。

I'll be kind to him <u>while</u> you are away. 你不在时，我要好好待他。

while 引导的从句中有时有些词可以省略：

He had an accident <u>while</u> on his way here. 他在到这里的路上出了车祸。

Sophocles, <u>while</u> yet a youth gained a prize in poetic contest. 索福克勒斯还很年轻时，在诗歌比赛中就获了奖。

while 还可引导从句或分句，表示：

（1）对比关系（意思接近 **whereas**），可译为"而""当……却"，这两部分是并列关系：

<u>While</u> their country has plenty of oil, ours has none. 他们国家盛产石油，而我们不产石油。

Some people waste food <u>while</u> others haven't enough. 有些人浪费粮食，而另一些人却吃不饱。

（2）尽管，虽然（**while** 引导的从句多放在句首）：

<u>While</u> we don't agree we continue to be friends. 尽管我们意见不一致，我们仍然是朋友。

<u>While</u> I sympathize, I can't really do much to help. 尽管我很同情，我却不能真正帮多少忙。

（3）既然，如果，只要：

You'll never save any money <u>while</u> you're so extravagant. 如果你这样挥霍，你永远不会存下钱。

<u>While</u> there is life there is hope. 只要活着，就有希望。

while 还可用作名词，表示"一会儿"：

Just take a <u>while</u> to think; and then we'll see. 只要思考一会儿，然后我们就会明白。

After a <u>while</u> the train stopped at a station. 过了一会儿火车在一个车站停了下来。

还可用于一些短语：

Where have you been <u>all this while</u>? 这段时间你都在哪儿？

I have foreseen this moment <u>all the while</u>. 我一直预见到这一时刻。

I can only stay <u>a little while</u>. 我只能待一会儿。

❀ whilst 有时可用来代替 while：

Whilst she was at some distance, he turned and saw her. 当她还离他比较远时，他转身看见了她。

Wood is a natural material whilst glass is a manufactured material. 木头是自然材料，而玻璃是制造出来的材料。

whilst 主要用在书面语中，在口语中不宜使用。

496 who—whom—who(m)ever

who 可作疑问代词，主要用作主语或表语：

Who has borrowed my pen? 谁借了我的钢笔？

Who do you think is the best player this year? 你认为谁是今年最佳运动员？

作宾语时，在正式场合用 whom（它是 who 的宾格）：

Whom do you like best? 你最喜欢谁？

Whom are you writing to? 你在给谁写信？

但在日常口语中多用 who 代替：

Who did you give it to? 你把它给谁了？

Who did you go with? 你和谁一道去的？

在紧跟介词时只能用 whom：

With whom did you go? 你和谁一道去的？

To whom shall I speak? 我应找谁谈？

who 还可作连接代词，引导宾语从句、主语从句等：

I asked him who came into the room. 我问他谁进屋里来了。

Have you found out who Hegel is? 你弄清黑格尔是谁了吗？

在从句中作宾语时，可用 whom（在紧跟介词时，必须用 whom）：

I don't know who(m) you mean. 我不知道你指的是谁。

I wondered to whom he had addressed the letter. 我想知道这信他是寄给谁的。

但在口语中常可用 who 代替 whom（除非是紧跟在介词后面）：

I wonder who he's talking to. 不知他是在和谁谈话。

I don't know who he gave it to. 我不知道他把它给谁了。

who 和 whom 还可引导不定式短语（多用 whom, 但在口语中可用 who 代替，在介词后必须用 whom）：

I don't know to whom to give it (who to give it to). 我不知道该把它给谁。

I don't know who to ask advice from. 我不知道应向谁征求意见。

✿ who 和 whom 可作关系代词，引导定语从句，在从句中作主语时用 who：

He is a good physician who cures himself. 能给自己治病的是好医生。（谚语）

My sister who is a nurse lives in the hospital. 我当护士的姐姐住在医院里。

在从句中作宾语时用 whom：

Then I telephoned the doctor whom Charles recommended. 然后，我给查尔斯介绍的医生打了电话。

She was the person to whom Mrs. Burns looked for guidance. 她是一个伯恩斯夫人可以依靠作指导的人。

在口语中，如果不直接跟在介词后，常可用 who 代替 whom，或是省略掉：

The man who(m) I bought it from told me to oil it. 我从他手上买这东西的人让我给它上油。

The people (who) we are talking to are Swedes. 和我们谈话的人是瑞典人。

who 和 whom 都可引导非限定性定语从句，这时它们都不能省略，whom 也不能由 who 代替，同时从句要以逗号和句子其他部分分开：

My sister, who is a nurse, came home for a few days. 我姐姐是护士，她回来了几天。

That afternoon there was a search for Sophia, whom no one had seen since breakfast. 那天下午大家都去找寻索菲娅，从早饭后就没人看到她了。

在以 it 作主语的句子中，可使用 who 或 whom 对句子的某个成分加以强调：

That evening it was George who left first. 那天晚上是乔治先走的。

It was Jim whom Philip came to see that night. 那天晚上菲利普来找的

是吉姆。

❀ **who(m)ever** 可用作关系代词，表示"任何……的人"：

Whoever comes will be welcome. 谁来都欢迎。

Whoever wants the book may have it. 任何人想要这书都可以拿去。

在口语中可以 **whoever** 代替 **whomever**：

Whoever you invite will be welcome. 任何你邀请的人都欢迎。

whoever 还可用作连词，引导状语从句，表示"不管是谁"：

Whoever you are, you can't pass this way. 不管你是谁，都不能从这里过去。

Whoever rings, tell him I'm out. 不管谁来电话，都告诉他我不在家。

whoever 还可代替 **who**, 用在疑问句中，表示强调：

Whoever told you such a ridiculous story? 这个荒唐的故事是谁给你讲的？

Whoever can that be knocking at the door? 这会儿敲门的能是谁呢？

497 whose

whose 主要有下列几种用法。

whose 可作疑问代词，表示"谁的"：

Whose fault is it? 这是谁的错？

Whose painting won the first prize? 谁的画赢得了头奖？

还可用作连接代词，引导从句作宾语：

I asked her whose bag was stolen. 我问她谁的包被偷了。

It's hard to say whose fault it is. 很难说这是谁的错。

whose 还可作关系代词，引导定语从句，表示"他（她）的……"：

The girl whose work got the prize is the youngest in her class. 作品获奖的女孩子是她班上年纪最小的。

Those people whose houses were damaged will be compensated. 房子受到损坏的人将获得赔偿。

也可引导非限定性定语从句：

Chopin, whose works are world-famous, composed some of his music in this room. 肖邦的作品是全世界闻名的，他有些音乐就是在这个房间里谱写的。

The visitor, <u>whose</u> name was Samuel Box, professed to be well pleased with the apartment. 来客名字叫塞缪尔·博克斯，他声称很喜欢这套房。

whose 还可指动物或无生命的东西：

My dog, <u>whose</u> temper is very uncertain, often bites the judges at dog shows. 我的狗脾气不稳定，常常在比赛时咬裁判。

The factory, <u>whose</u> workers are all women, is closed during the holidays. 这家工厂工人都是妇女。在假期中工厂关门了。

498 why

why 主要有下列几种用法。

why 主要用作疑问副词，来构成问句，表示"为什么"：

<u>Why</u> should you be so interested in my affairs? 你为什么对我的事这么感兴趣？

<u>Why</u> haven't you been to see me all this time? 为什么这么久你没来看我？

有时可直接跟一个不带 **to** 的不定式，和 **not** 连用时最多，表示"干吗不""何不"：

<u>Why not</u> write from Lisbon? 干吗不从里斯本写信？

<u>Why not</u> give the £40 to Ezra Pound? 何不把这 40 镑给艾兹拉·庞德？

有时也可用于肯定结构：

<u>Why</u> go there? 干吗要去那儿？

<u>Why</u> run this risk? 何必冒这个风险？

why 还可用作连接副词，引导从句作表语、宾语、主语等：

I'll tell you <u>why</u> you have to study Shakespeare. 我要告诉你为什么你得研究莎士比亚。

<u>Why</u> he did it will remain a puzzle forever. 为什么他这样做将永远是个谜。

后面成分有时可省略：

He is very upset, none of us knows <u>why</u>. 他非常不高兴，我们谁也不知道是什么原因。

Even now I don't fully understand why. 甚至现在，我还不完全了解这是为什么。

why 可用作关系副词，引导定语从句，修饰 **the reason**：

The reason why he came is not very convincing. 他来的理由不太有说服力。

Give me one good reason why I should help you! 给我一个我应当帮助你的正当理由！

有时 **why** 可以省略：

That's one of the reasons I asked you to come. 这就是我请你来的原因之一。

That's the reason I'm checking it now. 这就是我现在检查它的原因。

why 还可用作感叹词，表示惊讶等：

Why, this is the very book I want. 嗨，这正是我要的那本书。

Why, what a bruise you've got! 唉，你伤得这么厉害！

Why! Why! The cage is empty! 糟糕！糟糕！笼子空了！

也可表示不耐烦、反驳等：

"When do you expect to be in?" "Why, I'm in every morning." "你什么时候可能在家？" "你难道不知道，我天天早上都在家。"

"What is twice two?" "Why, a child can answer that." "二加二等于多少？" "真是的，这连小孩都能回答。"

499 wide—broad

wide 和 **broad** 是同义词，表示街道、河流多宽时，两个词都可以用：

They came to a wide river. It might be a mile wide. 他们来到一条大河边，可能有一英里宽。

The river is 30 feet broad. 那条河有 30 英尺宽。

谈某样东西多宽时多用 **wide**，例如：

The door is three feet wide. 门有三英尺宽。

This material is three metres wide. 这种衣料有三米宽。

指胸部、肩部宽时多用 **broad** 表示：

He was tall, broad-shouldered, very handsome. 他高个子，肩很宽，很

英俊。

Their backs (chests) are broad. 他们的背部（前胸）很宽。

两者都可用于引申意义，**wide** 表示"广泛的""渊博的""丰富的"等：

He has a wide knowledge of French history. 他对法国历史有渊博的知识。

An executive should have wide business experience. 一个主管人员应有丰富的商业经验。

broad 可表示"宽阔的""广大的"等：

He has a broad mind. 他有广阔的胸怀。

Such struggle must have a broad people's basis. 这样的斗争需有广泛的群众基础。

⟨500⟩ **wish**

wish 主要有以下几种用法。

wish 作动词时，主要表示"愿意""希望"，后面可以跟不同结构：

（1）跟名词或代词：

I wish you a safe journey. 希望你一路平安。

That's what I have always wished. 这是我一向的愿望。

（2）跟不定式：

Maria is on the phone, wishing to speak to you. 玛丽亚来电话，想和你讲话。

I don't wish to be disturbed in my work. 我工作时不愿被打扰。

（3）跟带不定式的复合结构：

You know I wish you to be happy, don't you? 你知道我希望你快乐，是吧？

I don't wish the subject to be raised again. 我不希望这话题被重新提起。

（4）跟带形容词等的复合结构：

I wished him safe at home. 我希望他在家平安。

He didn't wish it mentioned. 他不希望提到此事。

（5）跟从句（从句谓语多由 **would, could** 构成）：

I wish you wouldn't smoke any more. 我希望你别再抽烟。

I <u>wish</u> you would be more respectful to your father. 我希望你对你父亲更尊敬一些。

（6）不跟特别结构：

I can set to work now if you <u>wish</u>. 如果你愿意我现在就可以开始工作。

I will if you <u>wish</u>. 如果你愿意我会这样做。

wish 还可表示"但愿""希望（有与事实相反的情况）"，多跟从句，从句谓语有下列几种情况：

（1）用过去时（如动词为 be, 多用 **were** 形式，第三人称后也可用 **was**）：

I <u>wish</u> I had a little lab of my own. 但愿我有自己的一间小实验室。（但我没有）

He <u>wished</u> Ruth was (were) there to share in his joy. 他希望鲁思在那里分享他的愉快。

（2）与过去完成时形式相同：

Monica <u>wished</u> she hadn't come. 莫妮卡希望她没来。（但她来了）

I <u>wish</u> that I had never met him. 但愿我从未见过他。

He <u>wished</u> he hadn't done that. 他希望他没这样做。（但他这样做了）

有时也可跟复合结构：

We <u>wished</u> the long journey over, but it wasn't. 我们希望这次长途跋涉已经结束，但仍未结束。

He began to <u>wish</u> himself out of the affair. 他开始希望自己没卷入此事。

wish 还可用于一些短语中：

wish for 希望得到，盼望

What more can we <u>wish for</u>? 我们还能期望什么呢？

Everybody <u>wishes for</u> happiness but few get it. 人人都希望得到幸福，但很少人能得到。

wish good night (morning, etc.) 道晚安（早上好等）

I <u>wished</u> her goodnight and went upstairs. 我和她道了晚安就上楼了。

When she saw me, she <u>wished</u> me good morning. 她见到我时向我说了早上好。

wish 还可用作名词，表示：

（1）愿望，意愿（可数）：

I have no <u>wish</u> for fame or position. 我并不想得到名誉和地位。

He tried to satisfy her every <u>wish</u>. 他设法满足她的每一个意愿。

（2）祝愿（多作复数）：

Please accept our sincere <u>wishes</u>. 请接受我们诚挚的祝愿。

Mary sends you best <u>wishes</u> for a Happy New Year. 玛丽祝你新年快乐。

501 with

with 是最活跃的介词之一，它有许多重要用法。

和：

（1）和（某人）一道（在一起）：

I'm happy <u>with</u> her. 和她在一起，我很高兴。

（2）和（某人进行某事）：

I want to make an appointment <u>with</u> the dentist. 我想和牙医约看病时间。

You'd better discuss the matter <u>with</u> your wife. 你最好和你妻子商量此事。

（3）和（某人关系如何）：

She wants to finish any connection <u>with</u> him. 她想断绝和他的关系。

He goes on well, too, <u>with</u> Doctor Milligan. 他和米利根医生也相处得很好。

（4）在身边，给某人：

Why don't you take your daughter <u>with</u> you? 你何不把你女儿带在身边？

She has left a number of her books <u>with</u> me. 她把她的一些书留给了我。

对……：

（1）指态度：

I have been obliged to be rather strict <u>with</u> him. 我不得不对他相当严格。

She was always good <u>with</u> the unfortunate. 她对不幸的人一向是很好的。

（2）指情绪：

I'm disappointed <u>with</u> you. 我对你很失望。

I'm very pleased <u>with</u> my small daughter. 我很喜欢我的小女儿。

用，以（表示工具和手段）：

She dried her eyes with a handkerchief. 她用一块手绢把眼睛擦干。

He tried to kill two birds with a stone. 他想一箭双雕。

常可和某些动词连用，有较活译法：

She filled my glass with lemonade. 她在我玻璃杯里斟满柠檬汁。

The tops of the mountains are covered with snow. 山顶白雪覆盖。

因，由于（表示原因，可有灵活译法）：

She was shivering with cold. 她冷得发抖。

She flushed with delight. 她高兴得容光焕发。

引导短语作定语，表示"有""带有"（常有较活译法）：

The lamp with the green shade was alight. 那盏带有绿色灯罩的灯还亮着。

Who is that girl with yellow hair and dark eyes? 那个黄头发黑眼睛的姑娘是谁？

引导短语作状语，表示状态、境况等：

（1）跟名词：

Lanny sat with knitted brows. 兰尼皱着眉头坐在那里。

He went home with a heavy heart. 他怀着沉重的心情回到家里。

常和一个表示情绪的名词连用，作用接近一个副词（常可译为"……地"）：

She spoke to him with tenderness. 她温和地和他谈话。

I stared at him with amazement. 我吃惊地凝视着他。

（2）跟各种复合结构：

We sat on the grass with our backs to the wall. 我们背朝着墙坐在草地上。

He was asleep with his head on his arms. 他头枕着手臂睡着了。

She sat with her head bent. 她低着头坐在那里。

引导短语作状语，表示"就……来说"（常有灵活译法，with 的宾语常可译成汉语句子的主语）：

It's the same with women. 女人也如此。

Everything was going well with me. 我一切都很好。

引导短语作状语，表示"随着……（情况发生某种变化）"：

With the battle of Waterloo, Napoleon's long rule in Europe was ended. 随着滑铁卢战役的失败，拿破仑在欧洲长时间的统治结束了。

His avarice increased <u>with</u> his wealth. 随着他财富的增加，他变得更加贪婪。

引导短语作状语，表示"尽管"：

<u>With</u> all your faults you are frank and honest. 尽管你有种种缺点，但是你是坦率诚实的。

<u>With</u> all his boasting, he has achieved very little. 尽管他那样吹嘘，成就却非常小。

引导短语作表语，表示：

（1）和……在一起：

He has been <u>with</u> us for ten years. 他和我们在一起已经十年了。

We shall be <u>with</u> you at Easter. 复活节时，我们将和你团聚。

（2）同意，赞成，支持：

I'm (not) <u>with</u> you there. 我（不）同意你的意见。

The whole country is <u>with</u> the Prime Minister. 全国都支持首相。

（3）在……一边，在……脑中：

His sympathies are completely <u>with</u> the workers. 他的同情完全在工人一边。

The question was always <u>with</u> him. 这个问题一直在他心中。

和一些副词连用，表示一个命令、口号等：

Away <u>with</u> him! 让他走开！

On <u>with</u> your clothes. 穿上你的衣裳。

Off <u>with</u> your shirt. 脱下你的衬衫。

502 work—job—occupation—employment—profession—task

work 可作动词和名词。作动词时主要表示"工作"：

Henry <u>works</u> in a bank. 亨利在一家银行工作。

Miss Diana has been <u>working</u> very well. 戴安娜小姐一直工作得很好。

作名词时也主要表示"工作"：

I cannot find <u>work</u> in this town. 我无法在这座城市找到工作。

When his <u>work</u> wasn't going right, he was restless. 工作进行不顺利时，

他感到不安。

还可表示具体的工作、职务、活计等：

I am taking some <u>work</u> home to do this evening. 我准备带些活回家去干。

也可表示"作品"（可数）：

Measure for Measure is a hard <u>work</u> to understand. 《一报还一报》是一部难懂的作品。

This painting is one of Matisse's greatest <u>works</u>. 这幅画是马蒂斯最伟大的作品之一。

复数形式可表示"工厂"：

He burnt his hands at the glass <u>works</u>. 他在玻璃厂把手烫伤了。

He works in the water <u>works</u>. 他在自来水厂工作。

❀ job 也可表示"工作"，指具体的一份工作，为可数名词：

He wanted a <u>job</u>, any sort of a <u>job</u>. 他想找工作，什么工作都行。

He had taken a <u>job</u> at a children's hospital. 他在儿童医院找到一份工作。

job 还可表示"任务""职务"：

"What's your <u>job</u>?" "I'm a schoolmaster." "你任什么职务？""我是校长。"

He knows his <u>job</u>. 他很内行。

❀ occupation 也表示"职业""工作"（作不可数名词）：

Teaching is her <u>occupation</u>. 她的职业是教师。

He's a carpenter by <u>occupation</u>. 他的职业是木匠。

在填写表格时，在 occupation 一栏，你可填入你的具体职业，如 **engineer, doctor, journalist** 等，如果没有工作，也可填入 **housewife, student, unemployed** 或 **retired**。

❀ employment 也可表示"职业""工作"，也是不可数名词：

All this year's graduates have found <u>employment</u>. 今年的毕业生全找到了工作。

If they had <u>employment</u>, it might prove the best plan. 如果他们有工作，这可能证明是最好的计划。

还可表示"就业机会""就业率"等：

Only 18 per cent thought <u>employment</u> would rise over the next year. 只有百分之十八的人认为就业率明年会上升。

The government is aiming at full <u>employment</u>. 政府的目标是全部就业。

还可用作定语：

employment office 就业办公室

employment exchange（政府）职业介绍所

employment agency（私人）职业介绍所

❀ **profession** 也可表示"职业""工作"，但多指应具有某些专业知识的工作：

She intends to make teaching her profession. 她打算以教书为职业。

I don't know what profession would suit me. 我不知道什么工作对我合适。

profession 也可指某一职业的全体人员：

The teaching profession claim(s) to be badly paid. 教师们声称他们的薪金太低。

The medical profession favors this law. 医务人员赞成这项法律。

❀ **task** 多指"任务""工作"，为可数名词：

That task had been fulfilled. 这项任务已经实现。

He knew that he bad set himself on impossible task. 他知道他给自己布置了一个不可能完成的任务。

503 worth—worthwhile—worthy

worth 可用作形容词，也可用作名词。

作形容词时由于后面经常跟名词，有些人认为它是介词。它的基本意思是"值（多少钱）"、"价钱为……"：

It was worth at least fifty francs. 它至少值 50 法郎。

Each of these stamps is worth 30 cents. 每张邮票的价钱是三角。

还可表示"值得……"，后面可跟名词或动名词：

The exhibition is well worth a visit. 这个展览会值得一看。

His suggestion is worth considering. 他的建议值得考虑。

worth 作名词时可表示"价钱"（不可数）：

I know the true worth of his friendship. 我知道他友谊的真正价值。

Compared with her affection, nothing else had any worth. 和她的爱相比，其他一切都没有价值。

有时表示"值（多少钱的）东西"（不可数）：

I've bought a shilling's <u>worth</u> of sweets. 我买了一先令钱的糖果。

I bought ten dollars' <u>worth</u> of postage stamps. 我买了十美金的邮票。

还可表示"价钱""价格"（可加不定冠词）：

The painting's <u>worth</u> was estimated at half a million dollars. 这张画的价钱估计为 50 万美元。

The appraiser put a <u>worth</u> of a thousand dollars on the ring. 估价师认为这只戒指值一千美元。

此外还可指一个人的财产、身价：

What would you estimate his <u>worth</u> at? 你估计他的财产有多少？

His <u>worth</u> is reckoned at over a million dollars. 他的身价估计为一百多万美元。

❀ **worthwhile** 为形容词，表示"值得（干）的"：

The visit to Paris was <u>worthwhile</u>. 巴黎之行是值得的。

The effort seemed <u>worthwhile</u> to them. 做这样的努力他们认为是值得的。

还可表示"有价值的"：

This is a <u>worthwhile</u> cause. 这是一个有价值的事业。

She has a very <u>worthwhile</u> job. 她有一个有价值的工作。

Here is some <u>worthwhile</u> advice to you. 这儿有一些对你们有价值的忠告。

❀ **worthy** 也可表示"有价值的""有意义的"：

He has lived a <u>worthy</u> life. 他度过了有价值的一生。

The school has graduated many <u>worthy</u> young people. 许多有出息的青年从这所学校毕业。

worthy 还可跟不定式或 of 引起的短语，表示"值得""配得上"：

He is <u>worthy</u> to take his place. 他值得担任这项职务。

She said she was not <u>worthy</u> to be his wife. 她说她不配做他的妻子。

504 would

would 是用得最多的助动词之一，在口语中可缩短为 'd，否定式多紧缩为 **wouldn't**，主要有下列用法。

构成过去将来时态，表示从过去观点看来要发生的事，各人称后都可以用：

From these outings he <u>would</u> return on Monday. 在这些短途出行后，他将在星期一返回。

He <u>would</u> go in spite of our warning. 尽管我们提出警告，他还是要去。

常可用于间接引语及某些宾语从句中：

She said she <u>would</u> be waiting for me in the lounge. 她说她将在大厅等我。

I asked if he <u>would</u> come and mend my television set. 我问他可否来修理我的电视机。

谈过去情况，表示"愿意""肯""会"（可说是 **will** 的过去形式）：

He felt Helen <u>would</u> never permit anything of the sort. 他感到海伦绝不会允许发生这样的事。

I had to obey whether I <u>would</u> or not. 不管我是否愿意，我都得服从。

这种 **would** 也可用在条件从句中：

I should be glad if you <u>would</u> give an account of it. 如果你愿给我讲讲这事，我会很高兴。

If Ann <u>would</u> admit this I shouldn't quarrel with her. 如果安肯承认这一点，我也不会和她争吵了。

用在虚拟条件句中，表示假想的情况：

If he were in town, he <u>would</u> help us. 如果他在城里，他会帮助我们的。（但他不在）

If they studied, they <u>would</u> learn. 如果他们学，也会学会。（但他们不学）

如果谈过去的情况，要用 **would have** 这种形式，从句中的谓语多为"**had + 过去分词**"：

She <u>would have</u> said more if he had not walked away. 如果他没走开，她还会多说几句的。

If she hadn't married, she <u>would</u> probably <u>have</u> achieved more. 如果她没结婚，成就或许会更大。

还常常用在含蓄条件句中：

Denial <u>would</u> have been useless. 否认是没有用的。

But for your help we <u>would</u> have been late. 若不是你帮忙，我们都会迟到了。

用在日常口语中代替 **will**，使语气显得更委婉：

Would you kindly send me his address? 你可否把他的地址寄给我？

Anyway, I wouldn't let any trouble come to you. 不管怎样，我不会让你遇到任何麻烦。

表示过去习惯性的动作：

He would sit there for hours sometimes, doing nothing. 有时，他会在那里坐几个钟头什么也不干。

也可表示某种倾向：

The window wouldn't open. 窗户打不开了。

They just would not believe what we told them. 他们就是不信我们给他们讲的话。

表示一种猜想：

The person you mentioned would be Uncle Li. 你提的这个人想必是李大叔。

I thought you would have finished this by now. 我以为你现在已经干完了。

505 **yet**

yet 可以作副词，也可以作连词。

作副词时表示"还"（多用于否定句）：

The moon had not yet risen. 月亮还没有升起。

I haven't enough data yet. 我还没有足够的数据。

还可用于疑问句，表示"已经"：

"Has he come yet?" "No, not yet." "他来了吗?" "还没来。"

I wonder if she's started yet. 不知她开始了没有。

肯定句中一般用 already 表示"已经"：

She's already started. 她已经开始了。

He's already left. 他已经走了。

在个别情况下在肯定句中也可用 yet：

It was too early yet to tell anything. 目前，要说什么还为时过早。

Go at once while there is yet (=still) time. 趁现在还有时间，立刻去。

还可表示将来还可能发生某事：

The plan may yet succeed. 这计划还可能成功。

It will be colder yet before spring comes. 春天来之前，还会更冷一些。

作连词时表示"但是""却"，语气比 but 弱：

The tongue is not steel yet it cuts. 舌头不是钢做的，却能刺伤人。（谚语）

Though the sore be healed, yet a scar may remain. 伤痛虽然好了，却可能留下伤疤。（谚语）

有时可连接两个形容词：

It is strange yet true. 这很奇怪，却是真的。

The judge was stern, yet completely fair. 法官很严峻，却完全公正。

也可和 **and** 连用：

She's vain and foolish, <u>and yet</u> people like her. 她很虚荣又愚蠢，但人们却喜欢她。

中国人民大学出版社外语出版分社读者信息反馈表

尊敬的读者：

感谢您购买和使用中国人民大学出版社外语出版分社的 ＿＿＿＿＿＿ 一书，我们希望通过这张小小的反馈卡来获得您更多的建议和意见，以改进我们的工作，加强我们双方的沟通和联系。我们期待着能为更多的读者提供更多的好书。

请您填妥下表后，寄回或传真回复我们，对您的支持我们不胜感激！

1. 您是从何种途径得知本书的：
   □书店　　　　□网上　　　　□报纸杂志　　　　　□朋友推荐
2. 您为什么决定购买本书：
   □工作需要　　□学习参考　　□对本书主题感兴趣　　□随便翻翻
3. 您对本书内容的评价是：
   □很好　　　　□好　　　　　□一般　　　　　□差　　　　□很差
4. 您在阅读本书的过程中有没有发现明显的专业及编校错误，如果有，它们是：

   ＿＿＿＿＿＿＿＿＿＿＿＿＿＿＿＿＿＿＿＿＿＿＿＿＿＿＿＿＿＿＿＿＿＿＿＿＿

   ＿＿＿＿＿＿＿＿＿＿＿＿＿＿＿＿＿＿＿＿＿＿＿＿＿＿＿＿＿＿＿＿＿＿＿＿＿

   ＿＿＿＿＿＿＿＿＿＿＿＿＿＿＿＿＿＿＿＿＿＿＿＿＿＿＿＿＿＿＿＿＿＿＿＿＿

5. 您对哪些专业的图书信息比较感兴趣：

   ＿＿＿＿＿＿＿＿＿＿＿＿＿＿＿＿＿＿＿＿＿＿＿＿＿＿＿＿＿＿＿＿＿＿＿＿＿

   ＿＿＿＿＿＿＿＿＿＿＿＿＿＿＿＿＿＿＿＿＿＿＿＿＿＿＿＿＿＿＿＿＿＿＿＿＿

6. 如果方便，请提供您的个人信息，以便于我们和您联系（您的个人资料我们将严格保密）：

   您供职的单位：＿＿＿＿＿＿＿＿＿＿＿＿＿＿＿＿＿＿＿＿＿＿＿＿＿＿＿＿

   您教授的课程（教师填写）：＿＿＿＿＿＿＿＿＿＿＿＿＿＿＿＿＿＿＿＿＿

   您的通信地址：＿＿＿＿＿＿＿＿＿＿＿＿＿＿＿＿＿＿＿＿＿＿＿＿＿＿＿＿

   您的电子邮箱：＿＿＿＿＿＿＿＿＿＿＿＿＿＿＿＿＿＿＿＿＿＿＿＿＿＿＿＿

请联系我们：黄婷　程子殊　吴振良　王琼　鞠方安

电话：010-62512737，62513265，62515538，62515573，62515576

传真：010-62514961

E-mail：huangt@crup.com.cn　　chengzsh@crup.com.cn　　wuzl@crup.com.cn
　　　　crup_wy@163.com　　jufa@crup.com.cn

通信地址：北京市海淀区中关村大街甲 59 号文化大厦 15 层　　邮编：100872

中国人民大学出版社外语出版分社